THE CYCLE OF GROWTH SUMMARY DIAGRAM

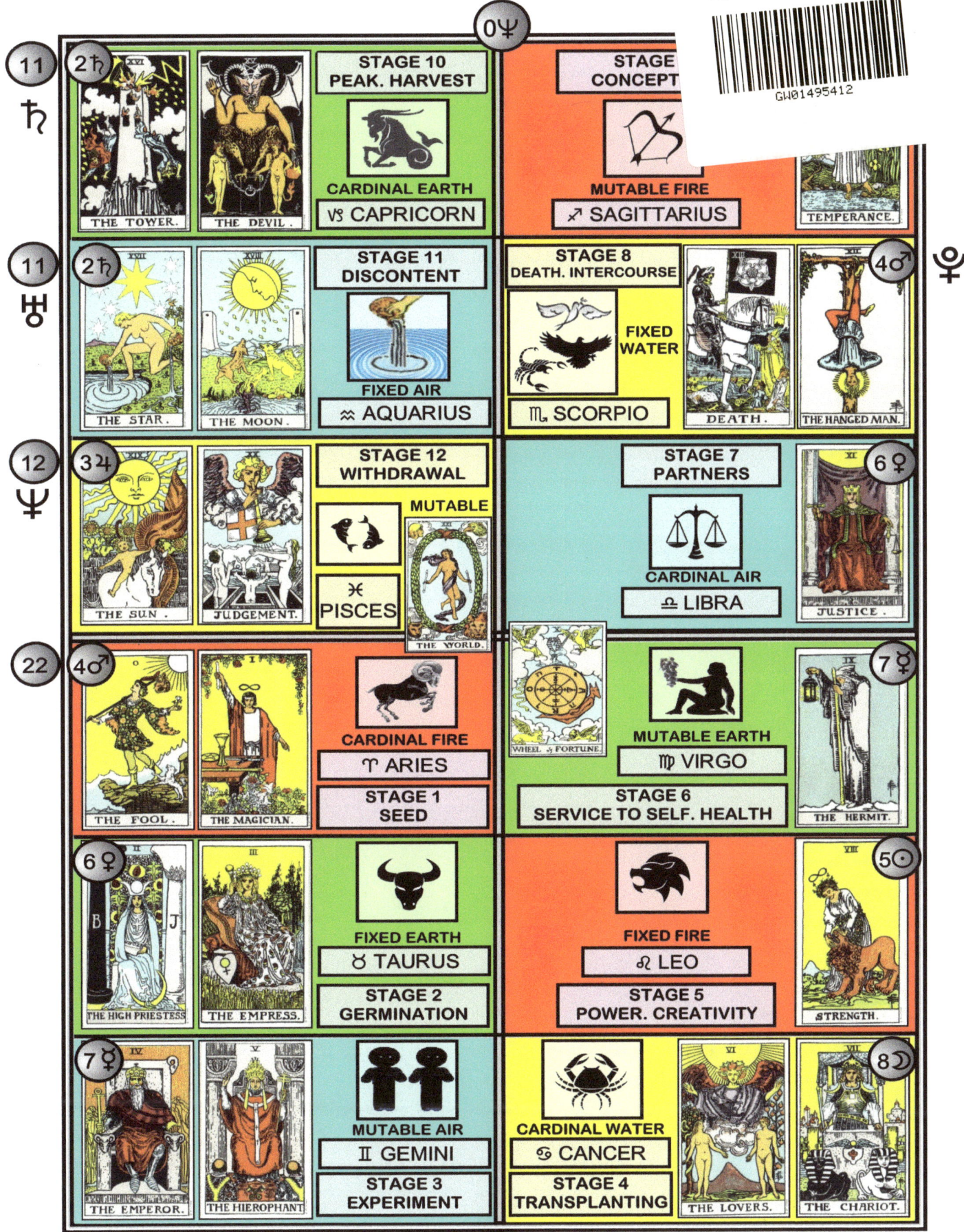

THE CYCLE OF GROWTH

12 STAGES IN THE PROCESS OF EVOLUTION AND GROWTH OF ALL THINGS (INCLUDING YOU AND ME)

By Brian. T. Baulsom M.N.F.S.H

CONTAINS CONCEPTS NOT FOUND ANYWHERE ELSE

© Brian Baulsom 2015. All rights reserved.
ISBN 978-0-9930926-3-3

Brief quotations are allowed providing reference is made to this book as source.
For example - *Source : "The Cycle of Growth" by Brian Baulsom*

NEW AND UNIQUE INFORMATION

This book covers nearly 40 years of research and contains original concepts not found anywhere else.

It compares and harmonises traditional philosophic and esoteric teachings with some of the latest discoveries in Psychology and Science - the most important being the discovery of the Transcendent Planets Uranus, Neptune, and Pluto, the now accepted story of Evolution beginning with The Big Bang, the modern scientific use of Number Zero - which was not recognised in earlier history, and C.G.Jung's concept of Individuation. It also considers insights given by the trance medium Edgar Cayce - who also gave verifiable information about people he never met. This also reconciles differences when authorities on a subject disagree.

The main principle of The Cycle of Growth is that all cyclic processes, no matter how many stages we split them into, are manifestations of the same Whole. In each cycle the positive and negative forces balance one another to return to the original Zero State. When we compare the Cycle of Growth with seeming different areas of study there is remarkable correspondence.

ASTROLOGY AND PSYCHOLOGY

- Ancient philosophy did not include knowledge of the psychological concepts that are available to everyone today, although it was present in symbolic form. We also recognise that, as with the Hunter Gatherer, the mental psychology was different to that of today because the Jungian Thinking Function has developed from the general public access to Reading, Writing, and Mathematics - which are also relatively new subjects.
- It is becoming recognised that our experiences in the womb affect our later life. When we compare the Astrological Logarithmic Timescale of a human lifetime from Conception to Death with The "Development of Personality" stages of Freud, Erikson, and Piaget there is exact correspondence.
- The Logarithmic Timescale also adds a "Transcendent Octave" which gives rise to evolutionary development.
- The planet Uranus clearly relates to the Jungian psychological concept of The Individuation Process.
- Now in The Age of Aquarius, we can use recent historical discoveries to understand the other Zodiac Ages.

THE TAROT

- The 22 symbols of the Major Arcana match the 12 Cycle of Growth Stages in sequence.

NUMEROLOGY

- Traditional philosophical systems and Numerology do not include Number Zero because it is a relatively new discovery – only becoming a number in its own right in the Computer Age.
- The sequence of Numbers corresponds with the process of Evolution – and therefore The Cycle of Growth - from The Big Bang onwards, as demonstrated by the development of all Chemical Elements from basic Hydrogen.
- Karma is a process to return us to the Original State of Zero where everything is in balance – but now with self-awareness.

THE KABBALAH TREE OF LIFE

- This symbolic system gets closer to the archetypal universal principles than the others and therefore associates with all other areas of study to the enrichment of them all.
- The Astrological symbol of Neptune is a basic depiction of the 3 Pillars of The Tree of Life.
- With the discovery of Number Zero, we are now able to associate Numbers Zero to 9 with the 10 Sephiroth of The Tree – which was not previously possible.
- With the discovery of the Transcendent Planets we are able to add them to The Tree of Life where there were traditionally no planetary associations.
- "The Lightning Flash" of Kabbalist involution and related Astrological planets exactly matches those of the sequence of stages in The Cycle of Growth. We can now add a transcendent function to The Tree which was not apparent before.

THE BIBLE

- The Life of Jesus relates to our life from Conception to Birth, and Transcendence.
- The First 3 chapters of Genesis describe the 3 Octaves of The Astrological Logarithmic Timescale.
- The Tree of Life mentioned in Genesis and Revelation (and The Kabbalah) refers to the human Chakra System of energy centres in the human body, and the related hormone-producing endocrine glands.

* * * * * * * * * * * * * * * *

THIS BOOK IS DEDICATED TO THOSE WHOSE LIFE WORK HAS ENABLED ME TO PRODUCE IT

* * * * * * * * * * * * * * * *

VERIFICATION

From my studies over nearly 40 years I have come to accept the fact that authorities on practically every subject can disagree. However, apart from my own practical experiments, I have discovered that many differences can be resolved by comparing material from different areas of knowledge and noting the similarities.

The method is even more useful when we consider that usually the different factions ignore, or are even somewhat antagonistic to, one another - as noted in the experiences of [MY STORY]. Another example is where historically and presently the various religions of the world war with one another whilst still purporting to worship the same God.

To aid the process, this book uses deliberate repetition of subject matter in the various chapters. This also aids understanding by being able to see things from different viewpoints.

Despite this, there are still areas where we need to apply Ockham's Razor to the material.

OCKHAM'S RAZOR

William of Ockham (1285-1347) was an English scholar and theologian. Although other authorities are said to precede him in its formation, the "Razor" principle is attributed to him and used in solving complicated logic problems, and states :-

*entities are not to be multiplied without necessity. [Ockhams Razor]

What this means is that when there are competing theories we should use the simplest one, even though it may not be the most accurate. It can then form a basis for later experiment.

THE GORDIAN KNOT

Nowadays the term refers to any very complicated problem – and its possible solution.

The Gordian Knot is part of Greek Mythology. It was a complicated knot, made to be undoable which was tied by Gordius, king of Phrygia and father of Minos to join the pole of a wagon to its yoke. In 333 BC Alexander the Great solved the problem by cutting the knot away with his sword [EB]. This is an example of an Aries/Mars decisive method of problem solving by "brute force". There is the simplicity of Ockham's Razor - with added method.

** SUMMARY TABLE OF CHAPTERS **

(Full Table Of Contents follows)

NEW AND UNIQUE INFORMATION	i
** SUMMARY TABLE OF CHAPTERS **	iii
** TABLE OF CONTENTS **	iv
** TABLE OF FIGURES **	xvii
APHORISMS	xx
ABBREVIATIONS	xxii
INTRODUCTIONS	xxiv
THE PURPOSE OF LIFE	1
THE PURPOSELESS LIFE	15
PSYCHOLOGY:DEVELOPMENT MODELS	23
THE 4 ELEMENTS	41
THE 4 FUNCTIONS OF C. G. JUNG	49
ASTROLOGY : ORIGINS AND OVERVIEW	57
ASTROLOGY : HOUSES	65
ASTROLOGY : LOGARITHMIC TIMESCALE	73
*1- FIRST OCTAVE : 0 TO 10 LM	79
*2 - SECOND OCTAVE : 10 TO 100 LM	85
*3 - THIRD OCTAVE : 100 TO 1000 LM	91
*4 - "FOURTH OCTAVE"	104
ASTROLOGY : SIGNS OF THE ZODIAC	109
THE ZODIAC SIGNS	113
ASTROLOGY : THE ZODIAC AGES	125
ASTROLOGY : PLANETS	149
ASTROLOGY : PLANETARY ASPECTS	173
ASTROLOGY : PLANET TRANSITS	179
ASTROLOGY : THE LIFE DIARY	199
ASTROLOGY : CHARTS EXAMPLES	203
ASTROLOGY : SYNASTRY	217
GENESIS AND THE CYCLE OF GROWTH	221
THE CALENDAR	251
THE TAROT	265
THE KABBALAH TREE OF LIFE	321
THE CHAKRAS	339
NUMEROLOGY	353
THE NUMBERS	359
MY STORY	409
BIBLIOGRAPHY	415
ASTROLOGY SOFTWARE	421
APPENDIX 1. ALCHEMY	423
APPENDIX 2. HUMAN EVOLUTION	435
APPENDIX 3. CRITICAL MASS	443
APPENDIX 4. EDGAR CAYCE (1877 – 1945)	445
APPENDIX 5. MEDITATION	446
APPENDIX 6. THE NITROGEN CYCLE	450
APPENDIX 7. THE MIDDLE PATH	454
INDEX	459

** TABLE OF CONTENTS **

NEW AND UNIQUE INFORMATION — i
- VERIFICATION — ii
- OCKHAM'S RAZOR — ii
- THE GORDIAN KNOT — ii

** SUMMARY TABLE OF CHAPTERS ** — iii

** TABLE OF CONTENTS ** — iv

** TABLE OF FIGURES ** — xvii

APHORISMS — xx

ABBREVIATIONS — xxii
- FREE ADDITIONAL CONTENT from www.CycleOfGrowth.com — xxiii
- NOTES — xxiii
- THE "MAYBE SHELF" – FAITH IS NOT BLIND — xxiii
  - BEYOND "TRUE OR FALSE", "RIGHT AND WRONG", "BLACK AND WHITE" — xxiii

INTRODUCTIONS — xxiv
- INTRODUCING MYSELF — xxiv
- INTRODUCING THIS BOOK — xxiv
- INTRODUCING THE CYCLE OF GROWTH — xxvi
- THE ARCHETYPES — xxvi
- THE COVER PICTURE COMPONENTS — xxvii
  - Part 1 : THE CHRYSOPOEIA OF CLEOPATRA — xxvii
  - Part 2 : TAROT CARD X.THE WHEEL OF FORTUNE — xxvii
  - Part 3 : THE TRANSCENDENT FUNCTION OF THE CYCLE OF GROWTH — xxvii

THE PURPOSE OF LIFE — 1
- OVERVIEW — 1
- THE BIBLE — 1
- C.G.JUNG – INDIVIDUATION AS A GOAL — 4
- REINCARNATION — 4
  - EDGAR CAYCE : THE INCARNATIONS OF JESUS — 4
  - EDGAR CAYCE : MIND AND WILL — 5
- DISCOVERING YOUR SOUL'S PURPOSE (Mark Thurston) — 5
  - HOW WE BEGAN — 5
  - CONSCIOUSNESS VERSUS WILL - AND "THE PATH" — 6
  - THE PLAN — 7
  - THE FALL — 7
  - STAGES OF WILL — 7
  - RETURNING TO THE PATH — 9
- YOUR LIFE PURPOSE – AN EXERCISE — 10
  - METHOD — 10
  - DIANA SPENCER'S LIFE PURPOSE — 11
  - YOUR LIFE PURPOSE TABLE — 12
- LADY DIANA SPENCER LIFE PURPOSE — 13
- SIGMUND FREUD LIFE PURPOSE *Father of Psychoanalysis* — 13
- C. G. JUNG LIFE PURPOSE "Discoverer of Individuation" — 13

THE PURPOSELESS LIFE — 15

- THE 'UNIVERSAL COMPUTER' AND CYCLES 15
- BASIC 'PROCESS MODELS' 15
- ARIADNE'S THREAD AND TRIAL AND ERROR 17
- ALGORITHMS 17
- A COMPUTER ALGORITHM "EVOLUTION" 17
  - THE RULES 17
- THE CYCLE OF GROWTH ALGORITHM 19
- FRACTALS AND NATURE – WHEELS WITHIN WHEELS 19
- EVOLUTION AND DNA 20
- DNA 20
- DNA MUTATION and DIVERSITY 21

PSYCHOLOGY:DEVELOPMENT MODELS   23

- INDIVIDUAL GROWTH CRADLE TO GRAVE (and before) 23
  - CONCEPTION AND LIFE IN THE WOMB 23
  - GENERAL DEVELOPMENT FROM BIRTH 23
  - MID LIFE CRISIS AGE 42 24
  - LIFE BEYOND 40 25
  - LIFE AFTER DEATH AND REINCARNATION 25
- THE FREUDIAN MODEL OF THE PSYCHE 26
  - CONSCIOUS, PRECONSCIOUS, AND UNCONSCIOUS 27
  - THE ID 27
  - THE EGO 27
  - THE SUPER EGO 28
- FREUD'S MODEL OF PERSONALITY DEVELOPMENT 28
  - ORAL STAGE : 0-2 YEARS OF AGE 28
  - ANAL STAGE : 2-3 YEARS OF AGE 29
  - PHALLIC STAGE : 3-7 YEARS OF AGE 29
  - LATENCY : 7-11 YEARS OF AGE 29
  - GENITAL STAGE : 11 YEARS OF AGE TO ADULT (AND DEATH) 30
  - MASLOW'S HIERARCHY OF NEEDS 30
- GROWTH OF PERSONALITY 31
  - THE [ASTROLOGY : LOGARITHMIC TIMESCALE] 31
- THE JUNGIAN INDIVIDUATION MODEL 33
  - 2 PATHS OF INDIVIDUATION 33
  - INDIVIDUATION (TRANSCENDENCE) AND ASTROLOGY 34
- THE TRANSACTIONAL ANALYSIS MODEL 34
  - SIMILARITY TO OTHER MODELS 35
  - TRANSACTIONAL ANALYSIS OVERVIEW 35
  - TA PSYCHOLOGICAL DEVELOPMENT 35
  - TA EGO STATES 37
  - TA GAMES 38
  - TA STAGES OF GROWTH 38
  - 4 POSSIBLE BASIC LIFE POSITIONS – DECIDED AT AGE 2 39

THE 4 ELEMENTS   41

- OVERVIEW 42
- HISTORY 43
- THE CLASSICAL 4 ELEMENTS 43
- THE 4 ELEMENTS OF ASTROLOGY 44
- THE 4 ELEMENTS OF THE TAROT 45
- THE 4 BEASTS OF REVELATION AND THE CHAKRAS 45
- MORE ELEMENTAL MANIFESTATIONS 45
  - 4 FUNCTIONS OF JUNGIAN PSYCHOLOGY 45
  - THE 5 SENSES 46

    4 FUNDAMENTAL NUCLEAR FORCES 46
    4 STATES OF MATTER 47

THE 4 FUNCTIONS OF C. G. JUNG   49

  RATIONAL AND IRRATIONAL FUNCTIONS 50
  INTUITION (FIRE. INSTINCT) – THE LOST ART ? 50
    SAVANTISM (Autism Spectrum Disorder) 51
    MEDITATION 52
    MARTIAL ARTS AND SPORT 52
    SPIRITUAL DEVELOPMENT. BECOMING AS CHILDREN 52
    PARADOX 53
  THINKING (AIR) 53
  FEELING (WATER) 53
  SENSATION (EARTH) 53
    SIGHT (Fire of Earth) 53
    HEARING (Air of Earth) 54
    TASTE AND SMELL (Water of Earth) 54
    TOUCH (Earth of Earth) 54
  JUNGIAN PSYCHOLOGY FUNCTION TYPES 54
    THE INTUITION TYPE 54
    THE SENSATION TYPE 55
    THE THINKING TYPE 55
    THE FEELING TYPE 55
    PERSONAL EXPERIENCE 55
    EXTRAVERSION AND INTROVERSION 56
    MID LIFE CRISIS 56

ASTROLOGY : ORIGINS AND OVERVIEW   57

  ARRANGEMENT OF CHAPTERS 57
  ORIGINS AND OVERVIEW 57
  ZODIAC SIGNS AND THE CALENDAR 58
  PLANETS 58
  BIRTH CHARTS (NATAL ASTROLOGY) 59
  SCIENTIFIC VALIDATION 59
    STATISTICAL ANALYSES 60
    HOW DOES IT WORK ? 60
    PSYCHOLOGY : C.G.JUNG (1875-1961) 60
    BBC NEWS STORY : MOON PHASES PROVED TO AFFECT CRIME 61
  HOW A BIRTH CHART IS CONSTRUCTED 62
  CIRCLE 1 : THE CENTRE CIRCLE 62
  CIRCLE 2 : THE CIRCLE OF HOUSES 63
  CIRCLE 3 : ZODIAC SIGNS – THE "CIRCLE OF ANIMALS" 63
    THE ASCENDANT SIGN 64
  PLANETS 64
  CONCLUSION 64

ASTROLOGY : HOUSES   65

  HOUSES OVERVIEW – PERSONAL AND GENERIC 65
  BIRTH CHART : PERSONAL HOUSES 66
    THE ORIENTATION OF PERSONAL HOUSES 66
    PERSONAL HOUSES AND PLANETS 67
    THE PATTERN OR STRUCTURE OF PERSONAL HOUSES 68
    HOUSES AND NUMBER 4 68
    BIRTH CHART QUADRANTS : division by 4 sets of 3 Houses 70
  BIRTH CHART : GENERIC HOUSES 71

| JUPITER GENERIC HOUSES EXAMPLE DIAGRAM | 72 |

ASTROLOGY : LOGARITHMIC TIMESCALE — 73

- 3 OCTAVES INTRODUCTION ... 74
- MONTHLY 3 OCTAVES – AND SIGN DECANS ... 75
- LOGARITHMIC TIMESCALE DIAGRAM OVERVIEW ... 76
- "THE ROUND ART" ASTROLOGY TIMESCALE ... 77
- THE LOGARITHMIC TIMESCALE MODEL ... 77
  - 3 + 1 "OCTAVES" OF DEVELOPMENT ... 77
- THE "SHELL" SUN SYMBOL ... 78
- BEFORE CONCEPTION : THE ZERO STATE ... 79

*1- FIRST OCTAVE : 0 TO 10 LM — 79

- CONCEPTION TO BIRTH ... 79
- STAGE 9 - CONCEPTION (Conception to 7 weeks) ... 80
- STAGE 10 - SOCIAL PEAK. HARVEST (7 to 12 weeks) ... 81
- STAGE 11 - DISSATISFACTION. REBELLION (12 to 22 weeks) ... 82
- STAGE 12 – WITHDRAWAL. CONFINEMENT (22 weeks to Birth) ... 83
- PSYCHOLOGY : GROWTH OF PERSONALITY ... 84

*2 - SECOND OCTAVE : 10 TO 100 LM — 85

- CYCLE OF GROWTH STAGE 1 (Seed) – 0 to 7 months ... 86
- CYCLE OF GROWTH STAGE 2 (Germination) ... 87
- CYCLE OF GROWTH STAGE 3 (Experiment) ... 88
- CYCLE OF GROWTH STAGE 4 (Transplanting. Roots) ... 89

*3 - THIRD OCTAVE : 100 TO 1000 LM — 91

- CYCLE OF GROWTH STAGE 5 (Power. Creativity) ... 91
- CYCLE OF GROWTH STAGE 6 (Service to Self) ... 95
- CYCLE OF GROWTH STAGE 7 (Partners) ... 98
- CYCLE OF GROWTH STAGE 8 (Sex. Death) ... 100
- SCORPIO PREPARATION FOR TRANSCENDENCE ... 103

*4 - "FOURTH OCTAVE" — 104

- TRANSCENDENT STAGE 9 – CONCEPTION ... 105
- TRANSCENDENT STAGE 10 – SOCIAL PEAK ... 105
- TRANSCENDENT STAGE 11 – DISCONTENT ... 106
- TRANSCENDENT STAGE 12 – WITHDRAWAL, CONFINEMENT ... 107
  - THE BUTTERFLY EFFECT ... 108

ASTROLOGY : SIGNS OF THE ZODIAC — 109

- OVERVIEW ... 109
  - BIRTH CHART HOUSE & SIGN RELATIONSHIPS ... 110
  - 4 ELEMENTS – FIRE, EARTH, AIR, WATER ... 110
  - POLARITIES – POSITIVE OR NEGATIVE ... 110
  - THE 3 OCTAVES ... 110
  - 3 QUALITIES – CARDINAL, FIXED, MUTABLE ... 110
- THE 4 ELEMENTS IN A CHART ... 111
  - SUN AND MOON SIGNS ... 111
  - THE ANNUAL CYCLE OF SIGNS ... 112
- ZODIAC SIGNS AND HEALTH ... 112

THE ZODIAC SIGNS — 113

- ARIES AND LIBRA ... 113
  - ARIES (Cardinal Fire. The Ram. Personal Projection of Energy) ... 113

- LIBRA (Cardinal Air. The Scales. Social Projection of energy) 114
- **TAURUS AND SCORPIO** 115
  - TAURUS (Fixed Earth. The Bull. Personal Collection of Energy) 115
- **GEMINI AND SAGITTARIUS** 116
  - GEMINI (Mutable Air. The Twins. Personal Mental Concepts) 116
  - SAGITTARIUS (Mutable Fire. The Archer. Social Mental Concepts) 117
- **CANCER AND CAPRICORN** 118
  - CANCER (Cardinal Water. The Crab. Personal Security. Shell. Roots) 118
  - CAPRICORN (Cardinal Earth. The Mountain Goat. Social Security) 119
- **LEO AND AQUARIUS** 120
  - LEO (Fixed Fire. The Lion. Personal Control of Energy) 120
  - AQUARIUS (Fixed Air. The Water Carrier. Social Control of Energy) 121
- **VIRGO AND PISCES** 122
  - VIRGO (Mutable Earth. The Virgin. Personal Service. Health) 122
  - PISCES (Mutable Water. The Fishes. The Collective Unconscious) 122

ASTROLOGY : THE ZODIAC AGES — 125

- **PRECESSION OF THE EQUINOXES** 126
- **OVERVIEW : FIXING THE WHEEL IN TIME** 126
- **PSYCHOLOGY OF THE AGES** 128
  - INTUITION 128
  - GENESIS 128
- **AGE OF LEO 11,720-9,550 BC** 128
  - Cycle of Growth Stage 5 (Power. Creativity) 128
- **AGE OF CANCER 9,550-7,380 BC** 129
  - Cycle of Growth Stage 4 (Transplanting. Roots) 129
  - THE SYMBOLISM OF CANCER – CARDINAL WATER 129
  - THE MESOLITHIC AGE. HUNTER GATHERER TO FARMER 129
- **AGE OF GEMINI 7380-5210 BC** 130
  - Cycle of Growth Stage 3 (Experiment. Communication) 130
  - THE SYMBOLISM OF GEMINI – MUTABLE AIR 130
- **AGE OF TAURUS 5210-3040 BC** 131
  - Cycle of Growth Stage 2 – GERMINATION 131
  - THE SYMBOLISM OF TAURUS – FIXED EARTH 132
  - PHYSICAL DEVELOPMENT AND GROWTH 132
- **AGE OF ARIES 3040 - 870 BC** 133
  - Cycle of Growth Stage 1 (Seed) 133
  - PSYCHOLOGICAL INFLATION 133
  - SYMBOLISM OF ARIES – CARDINAL FIRE 134
  - EVENTS OF THE AGE OF ARIES 134
  - MONUMENTS : PHALLIC POWER SYMBOLS UNITING EARTH AND HEAVEN 135
- **AGE OF PISCES 870 BC-1300 AD** 138
  - Cycle of Growth Stage 12 – (Withdrawal. Confinement) 138
  - SYMBOLISM OF PISCES – MUTABLE WATER 138
  - EVENTS OF THE PISCEAN AGE 139
  - CHRISTIANITY. THE BIRTH OF JESUS. COUNTING YEARS 141
  - PHILOSOPHY 143
- **AGE OF AQUARIUS 1300-3470 AD** 143
  - Cycle of Growth Stage 11 – Discontent 143
  - SYMBOLISM OF AQUARIUS – FIXED AIR 143
  - THE MIDDLE AGES 144
  - EVENTS OF THE AQUARIAN AGE 146

AGE OF CAPRICORN 3470-5640 AD 148

ASTROLOGY : PLANETS   149

PLANET RULERS OF ZODIAC SIGNS AND HOUSES 149
OVERVIEW 150
[THE KABBALAH TREE OF LIFE] SUMMARY 150
    PLANETS IN BIRTH CHARTS 151
    PLANET ASPECTS 151
    PLANET TRANSITS 151
    PLANETARY EFFECTS 151
MYTHOLOGY 151
PLANETARY RULERSHIPS 152
THE TRANSCENDENT PLANETS 153
    NEPTUNE 153
    PLUTO 155
    URANUS 158
THE OUTER PLANETS 160
    SATURN 160
    JUPITER 162
    MARS 163
THE INNER (PERSONAL) PLANETS 165
    THE SUN 165
    THE MOON 166
    VENUS 167
    MERCURY 168
EARTH 170
PLANET DESCRIPTIONS – TABLE 171

ASTROLOGY : PLANETARY ASPECTS   173

ASPECT EXAMPLES DIAGRAM 173
    CONJUNCTIONS (Zero degrees) 174
    TRINES (120 degrees) 174
    OPPOSITIONS (180 degrees) 174
    SQUARES (90 degrees) 175
THE CYCLIC INTER-RELATIONSHIPS 176
THE MOON AND THE CYCLE OF GROWTH 177

ASTROLOGY : PLANET TRANSITS   179

BIRTH CHART 179
HOUSES 179
PLANETS 179
TRANSITS 179
TWO TYPES OF TRANSIT CYCLES 180
    PERSONAL PLANET CYCLES 180
    GENERIC PLANET CYCLES 180
4 QUARTERS : THE MAIN TRANSIT 'CRISIS' POINTS 180
HOUSE & PERIOD MEANINGS 181
    1ST. QUARTER : SPRING 181
    2ND. QUARTER - SUMMER 182
    3RD. QUARTER - AUTUMN 184
    4TH. QUARTER : WINTER 186
THE GENERIC CYCLES OF JUPITER 188
THE GENERIC CYCLES OF SATURN 189
    SATURN'S FUNCTION 189

- THE FAMILY STRUCTURE 190
- SOCIAL STRUCTURE 190
- SATURN STRUCTURE OF A LIFETIME 190
- THE INNER PERSONAL SATURN – SELF DISCIPLINE 190
- SATURN'S OPPOSITION TO OUR LIFE PURPOSE. NECESSARY EVIL 191
- SATURN TRANSITS : 30 YEAR CYCLES 191
- SATURN AND JUPITER.. 191
- SATURN AND URANUS 192

GENERIC SATURN CYCLE 193
GENERIC SATURN CYCLE : 1st. QUARTER. SPRING. 193
- SEED PERIOD. REBIRTH. NEW IDEAS AND OPPORTUNITIES. 193
GENERIC SATURN CYCLE : 2nd. QUARTER. SUMMER. 194
- ACTION. BREAKING FROM THE PAST TO MAKE NEW FOUNDATIONS 194
GENERIC SATURN CYCLE : 3rd. QUARTER. AUTUMN. 195
- SUPPORT. JOINT ACTIVITY TO A WIDER VIEWPOINT 195
GENERIC SATURN CYCLE : 4th. QUARTER. WINTER 196
- HARVEST. PEAK OF DEVELOPMENT TO TEMPORARY RETIREMENT..... 196
PERSONAL SATURN CYCLE... 197
- 1st. HOUSE (Ascendant) TRANSIT – NEW SEED. REBIRTH 197
- SATURN TRANSIT OF HOUSES 2 TO 12 198

ASTROLOGY : THE LIFE DIARY   199
- MAIN GENERIC PLANET STRESS POINTS SUMMARY........................ 199
LIFE DIARY FORM showing planet cycle Quadrants 200
- TIMING OF MAIN PLANETARY EVENTS THROUGH A LIFETIME 201

ASTROLOGY : CHARTS EXAMPLES   203
BIRTH CHART EXAMPLE : COMMENTARY... 204
- THE PAST : MOON IN AQUARIUS (Fixed Air)...................................... 204
- MOON IN 2nd. HOUSE – PERSONAL POSSESSIONS 204
- THE FUTURE : SUN IN CANCER... 204
- SUN IN 7th. HOUSE – PARTNERSHIPS. FRIENDS AND ENEMIES 205
- 8Th. HOUSE EMPHASIS – INTERCOURSE. DEATH 205
- ASCENDANT (1st. House cusp). SELF PROJECTION......................... 206
- SATURN IN 1st. HOUSE – SELF PROJECTION 207
- SATURN IN CAPRICORN - Cardinal Earth 208
- NEPTUNE ("God of the Sea". The Unconscious) 208
- 10TH. HOUSE CUSP : LIBRA 208
GENERIC TRANSIT CHART EXAMPLE 209
- GENERIC TRANSIT CHART DESCRIPTION.. 209
DIANA'S LIFE DIARY.. 211
- 1ST. GENERIC JUPITER CYCLE 1961 – 1972...................................... 212
- 2ND. GENERIC JUPITER CYCLE 1973 - 1984 212
- 3ND. GENERIC JUPITER CYCLE 1985 - 1996 213
- 4TH. GENERIC JUPITER CYCLE 1997 213
- LADY DIANA SPENCER : NEPTUNE PERSONAL HOUSE TRANSITS..... 214
- A SIMILAR STORY – MICHAEL HUTCHENCE (22nd. Jan. 1960 – Sept. 1997)............ 216

ASTROLOGY : SYNASTRY   217
FREUD : JUNG - THEIR GENERAL RELATIONSHIP 217
- MOON'S NODES 218
SIGMUND FREUD "Father of Psychoanalysis" 218
G.G.JUNG "Discoverer of Individuation" 219

GENESIS AND THE CYCLE OF GROWTH — 221

- ROBERT YOUNG'S LITERAL BIBLE TRANSLATION AND CONCORDANCE — 222
- NUMBERS — 222
- GENESIS OVERVIEW — 223
  - GENESIS CHAPTER 1 – LOGARITHMIC TIMESCALE 1ST. OCTAVE — 224
  - GENESIS CHAPTER 2 – LOGARITHMIC TIMESCALE 2ND. OCTAVE — 225
  - GENESIS CHAPTER 3 – LOGARITHMIC TIMESCALE 3RD. OCTAVE — 225
  - GENESIS CHAPTER 4 — 226
- FURTHER CONSIDERATIONS — 226
- THE CYCLE OF GROWTH STAGES — 227
- CYCLE OF GROWTH STAGE ZERO — 228
- DAY 1. CYCLE OF GROWTH STAGE 9 (CONCEPTION) — 228
- DAY 1. CYCLE OF GROWTH STAGE 10 (PEAK. AMBITION) — 230
  - CREATION DAY 1 – DAY AND NIGHT — 231
- CYCLE OF GROWTH STAGE 11 (DISSATISFACTION) — 231
  - CREATION DAY 2 – SEPARATION OF THE WATERS. HEAVEN — 231
  - CREATION DAY 3 – EARTH AND SEA. VEGETATION — 233
  - CREATION DAY 4 – STARS – SUN – MOON — 233
  - CREATION DAY 5 – FISH AND BIRDS — 234
  - CREATION DAY 6 – LAND CREATURES. THE MAN. MALE AND FEMALE — 234
- CYCLE OF GROWTH STAGE 12 (WITHDRAWAL. CONFINEMENT) — 235
  - GENESIS CHAPTER 2 – RESTING FOLLOWED BY THE GARDEN OF EDEN — 235
  - CREATION DAY 7 – RESTING (ANOTHER EVEN-ING) — 235
- CYCLE OF GROWTH STAGE 1 (SEED) — 236
  - GENESIS : FORMATION OF "THE MAN" — 236
- CYCLE OF GROWTH STAGE 2 (GERMINATION) — 237
  - GENESIS : FORMATION OF THE GARDEN OF EDEN — 237
  - GENESIS CONTINUED — 238
- CYCLE OF GROWTH STAGE 3 (EXPERIMENT.COMMUNICATION) — 239
  - GENESIS : TREE OF KNOWLEDGE. NAMING OF ANIMALS. CREATION OF EVE — 239
  - GENESIS : THE CREATION OF EVE – WOMAN — 240
- CYCLE OF GROWTH STAGE 4 (TRANSPLANTING. ROOTS) — 241
  - GENESIS CHAPTER 3 – "THE FALL" — 241
  - GENESIS : DISCOVERY AND BANISHMENT. EVE IS NAMED — 244
- CYCLE OF GROWTH STAGE 5 (POWER. CREATIVITY) — 246
  - GENESIS CHAPTER 4 – CAIN AND ABEL — 246
- CYCLE OF GROWTH STAGE 6 (SERVICE TO SELF. HEALTH) — 247
  - GENESIS : CAIN KILLS ABEL — 247
- CYCLE OF GROWTH STAGE 7 (PARTNERS) — 248
  - GENESIS : CAIN STARTS A NEW GENERATION — 248
- CYCLE OF GROWTH STAGE 8 (SEX. DEATH) — 249

THE CALENDAR — 251

- THE FIRST OCTAVE OF THE CYCLE OF GROWTH — 255
  - CYCLE OF GROWTH STAGE 9 (CONCEPTION) — 256
  - CYCLE OF GROWTH STAGE 10 (SOCIAL PEAK. HARVEST) — 256
  - CYCLE OF GROWTH STAGE 11 (DISCONTENT) — 257
  - CYCLE OF GROWTH STAGE 12 (WITHDRAWAL. CONFINEMENT) — 258
- THE SECOND OCTAVE OF THE CYCLE OF GROWTH — 259
  - CYCLE OF GROWTH STAGE 1 (SEED) — 259
  - CYCLE OF GROWTH STAGE 2 (GERMINATION) — 260
  - CYCLE OF GROWTH STAGE 3 (EXPERIMENT. COMMUNICATION) — 260

- CYCLE OF GROWTH STAGE 4 (TRANSPLANTING) 262
- THE THIRD OCTAVE OF THE CYCLE OF GROWTH 262
  - CYCLE OF GROWTH STAGE 5 (POWER. LOVE) 262
  - CYCLE OF GROWTH STAGE 6 (SERVICE TO SELF. HEALTH) 262
  - CYCLE OF GROWTH STAGE 7 (PARTNERS) 263
  - CYCLE OF GROWTH STAGE 8 (DEATH. INTERCOURSE) 263
  - MONTH MEANINGS 263

THE TAROT   265

- TAROT READINGS 265
- HISORY OF TAROT CARDS 266
- HOW TAROT CARDS WORK : SYNCHRONICITY 266
  - COINCIDENCE 266
  - SYNCHRONICITY AND DIVINATION 266
  - THE I CHING AND OTHER ORACLES 267
  - ARCHETYPES 267
- THE MINOR ARCANA 268
- THE TAROT MAJOR ARCANA AND THE CYCLE OF GROWTH 270
- CARD XIV : TEMPERANCE 272
- CARD XV : THE DEVIL 274
- CARD XVI : THE TOWER 277
- CARD XVII : THE STAR 279
- CARD XVIII : THE MOON 281
- CARD XIX : THE SUN 283
- CARD XX : JUDGEMENT 285
- CARD XXI : THE WORLD 287
- CARD ZERO : THE FOOL 289
- CARD I : THE MAGICIAN 291
- CARD II : THE PRIESTESS 293
- CARD III : THE EMPRESS 296
- CARD IV : THE EMPEROR 299
- CARD V : THE HIEROPHANT OR HIGH PRIEST 301
- CARD VI : THE LOVERS 303
- CARD VII : THE CHARIOT 306
- CARD VIII : STRENGTH 308
- CARD IX : THE HERMIT 310
- CARD X : THE WHEEL OF FORTUNE 312
- CARD XI : JUSTICE 314
- CARD XII : THE HANGED MAN 316
- CARD XIII : DEATH 319

THE KABBALAH TREE OF LIFE   321

- THE TREE OF LIFE PARTIAL DESCRIPTION 322
- THE TREE OF LIFE AND NUMBERS 326
- THE TREE OF LIFE AND THE PLANETS 326
- THE TREE OF LIFE AND THE TAROT 327
  - THE TAROT MINOR ARCANA 327
- THE TREE OF LIFE AND THE CHAKRAS 327
  - THE CHAKRAS AND ENDOCRINE GLANDS 327
- THE PLANETS AND SEPHIROTH 330
  - DAATH, URANUS, AND THE MIDDLE PILLAR 331
- THE TREE OF LIFE AND THE CYCLE OF GROWTH 332
- THE OCTAVES OF THE LOGARITHMIC TIMESCALE 333
  - THE 1ST. AND 2ND. OCTAVES – GESTATION AND CHILDHOOD 333
  - THE 3RD. OCTAVE – SCHOOL & ADULT - INDIVIDUALITY 334

- THE TRANSCENDENT OCTAVE ... 335
- KABBALAH, NUMBERS, PLANETS AND TAROT ... 338

THE CHAKRAS — 339

- THE 4 ELEMENTS ... 340
- OVERVIEW ... 340
- REGENERATION ... 341
- THE BOOK OF REVELATION ... 341
- THE CHAKRA STRUCTURE ... 342
- PLANET RELATIONSHIPS ... 342
- THE 4 LOWER CHAKRAS ... 342
- THE HIGHER CHAKRAS ... 347
- GENESIS AND REVELATION ... 349
- "OPENING CHAKRAS" ... 350
- THE CHAKRAS - TABLE OF CORRESPONDENCES ... 351

NUMEROLOGY — 353

- INTRODUCTION ... 354
- HISTORY OF NUMBERS AND NUMEROLOGY ... 354
- PLANETS ... 355
- THE KABBALAH TREE OF LIFE ... 355
- NUMBER ZERO ... 356
- THE EVOLUTION OF NUMBERS ... 356
- THE BINARY NUMBER SYSTEM ... 357
- THE FIRST PRINCIPLES OF NUMBERS 1 TO 9 ... 358

THE NUMBERS — 359

- NUMBER 0 (ZERO) – BINARY 0 – NEPTUNE ... 359
  - THERMODYNAMICS AND ENTROPY ... 361
  - PLASMA ... 361
  - QUANTUM PHYSICS ... 362
  - QUANTUM COMPUTERS – USING "INTUITION" INSTEAD OF "THINKING" ... 362
  - CYCLE OF GROWTH STAGE ZERO AND STAGE 12 (WITHDRAWAL) ... 362
- NUMBER 1 – BINARY 1 - PLUTO ... 363
  - CYCLE OF GROWTH STAGE 9 (CONCEPTION) ... 364
  - NUMEROLOGY ... 364
  - OTHER ASSOCIATIONS ... 364
- NUMBER 2 – BINARY 10 – SATURN ... 366
  - CYCLE OF GROWTH STAGE 10 (PEAK. HARVEST) ... 367
  - CYCLE OF GROWTH STAGE 11 (DISCONTENT. INDIVIDUATION) ... 368
  - NUMEROLOGY ... 368
  - OTHER ASSOCIATIONS ... 368
  - EVOLUTION ... 370
- NUMBER 3 – BINARY 11 - JUPITER ... 371
  - CYCLE OF GROWTH STAGE 9 (CONCEPTION. PLUTO/JUPITER) ... 372
  - CYCLE OF GROWTH STAGE 12 (WITHDRAWAL. JUPITER/NEPTUNE) ... 372
  - NUMEROLOGY ... 373
  - 3 - OTHER ASSOCIATIONS ... 373
  - WAVE INTERFERENCE PATTERNS – 2 BECOMES 3 ... 375
- NUMBER 4 – BINARY 100 - MARS ... 376
  - CYCLE OF GROWTH STAGE 1 (SEED) ... 377
  - CYCLE OF GROWTH STAGE 8 (SEX. DEATH. INTERCOURSE. MARS/PLUTO) ... 377
  - NUMEROLOGY ... 378
  - 4 - OTHER ASSOCIATIONS ... 378
- NUMBER 5 – BINARY 101 – THE SUN ... 380

- CYCLE OF GROWTH STAGE 5 (POWER. CREATIVITY. CONSCIOUSNESS) 381
- NUMEROLOGY 381
  - 5 - OTHER ASSOCIATIONS 382
- **NUMBER 6 – BINARY 110 – VENUS** 383
  - CYCLE OF GROWTH STAGE 2 (GERMINATION) 384
  - CYCLE OF GROWTH STAGE 7 (PARTNERS) 384
  - NUMEROLOGY 385
  - 6 - OTHER ASSOCIATIONS 385
- **NUMBER 7 – BINARY 111 – MERCURY** 387
  - CYCLE OF GROWTH STAGE 3 (EXPERIMENT. COMMUNICATION) 388
  - CYCLE OF GROWTH STAGE 6 (SERVICE TO SELF. HEALTH) 388
  - NUMEROLOGY 389
  - 7 - OTHER ASSOCIATIONS 389
- **NUMBER 8 – BINARY 1000 – THE MOON** 393
  - CYCLE OF GROWTH STAGE 4 (TRANSPLANTING. ROOTS) 393
  - NUMEROLOGY 393
  - 8 - OTHER ASSOCIATIONS 394
- **NUMBER 9 – BINARY 1001 – THE EARTH** 395
  - NUMEROLOGY 397
  - 9 - OTHER ASSOCIATIONS 397
  - THE CYCLE OF GROWTH 398
- **NUMBER 10 – BINARY 1010** 398
  - CYCLE OF GROWTH STAGE 10 (PEAK. HARVEST) 398
- **NUMBER 11 – BINARY 1011 – URANUS** 399
  - CYCLE OF GROWTH STAGE 11 (DISCONTENT. WILL) 399
  - NUMEROLOGY 399
  - 11 - OTHER ASSOCIATIONS 400
- **NUMBER 12 – BINARY 1100 – JUPITER/NEPTUNE** 400
  - NUMEROLOGY 400
  - CYCLE OF GROWTH STAGE 12 (WITHDRAWAL. CONFINEMENT) 400
  - OTHER ASSOCIATIONS 400
- **NUMBER 13 – BINARY 1101** 401
- **NUMBER 22 – BINARY 10110** 401
  - CYCLE OF GROWTH STAGE 1 (SEED) 401
  - NUMEROLOGY 402
  - 22 - OTHER ASSOCIATIONS 402
- **EVOLUTION OF CHEMICAL ELEMENTS** 402
- **NUMEROLOGY PRACTICE** 405
  - NUMEROLOGY METHOD AND EXAMPLES 405

MY STORY — 409

- SPIRITUALISM 409
- KUNDALINI 410
- HEALING AND MEDIUMSHIP 410
  - MEDIUMSHIP TYPES 411
- TAROT 411
- ASTROLOGY 412
- ASTROLOGY 'LIFE DIARY' TRANSITS 412
- PSYCHOLOGY – MID LIFE CRISIS 412
- DREAMS 414
  - LUCID OR WAKING DREAMS 414
  - DREAMS PREDICTING THE FUTURE 414
  - MEDITATION 414

BIBLIOGRAPHY 415

BIBLIOGRAPHY : ASTROLOGY ... 415

- THE HOROSCOPE, THE ROAD AND ITS TRAVELLERS ... 415
- THE ASTROLOGY FILE ... 415
- THE TRUTH ABOUT ASTROLOGY ... 415
- THE THEORY OF CELESTIAL INFLUENCE : ... 415
- [TRA] THE ROUND ART - A. T. Mann ... 415
- [IHA] AN INTRODUCTION TO THE HISTORY OF ASTROLOGY ... 416
- [COB] CYCLES OF BECOMING ... 416

BIBLIOGRAPHY : PSYCHOLOGY ... 416

- [IOD] THE INTERPRETATION OF DREAMS ... 416
- [FYL]THE FREUD/JUNG LETTERS ... 416
- THE PORTABLE JUNG ... 417
- [P & A] PSYCHOLOGY AND ALCHEMY ... 417
- JUNG AND THE TAROT - AN ARCHETYPAL JOURNEY ... 417
- MAN AND HIS SYMBOLS ... 417
- [ACU] THE ARCHETYPES AND THE COLLECTIVE UNCONSCIOUS ... 417
- BECOMING ... 417
- [SLUC] THE SECRET LIFE OF THE UNBORN CHILD ... 418
- [GOP] THE GROWTH OF PERSONALITY ... 418
- EGO AND ARCHETYPE ... 418
- JUNG – MAN AND MYTH ... 418
- [TA] TRANSACTIONAL ANALYSIS BOOKS ... 418
- THE GAMES PEOPLE PLAY -Eric Berne M.D. ... 418
- I'M OK YOU'RE OK - Thomas A. Harris MD ... 418
- STAYING OK - Amy and Thomas Harris ... 418

BIBLIOGRAPHY : EDGAR CAYCE ... 418

- THE EDGAR CAYCE PRIMER ... 418
- [Edgar Cayce Reading] EDGAR CAYCE READINGS ... 419
- [ECOT] EDGAR CAYCE'S STORY OF THE OLD TESTAMENT ... 419
- [TBOTR] THE BOOK OF THE REVELATION ... 419

BIBLIOGRAPHY : OTHER SUBJECTS ... 419

- [BAB] BABYLON – MESOPOTAMIA AND THE BIRTH OF CIVILISATION ... 419
- [BF] HUMAN MIGRATION FROM AFRICAN ROOTS ... 419
- [DFCD] THE COSMIC DOCTRINE ... 419
- [DFMQ] THE MYSTICAL QABALAH ... 419
- [DHTS] DIANA - HER TRUE STORY ... 420
- [DNA] DEEP ANCESTRY INSIDE THE GENOGRAPHIC PROJECT ... 420
- [DNA] THE JOURNEY OF MAN ... 420
- [DSP] DISCOVERING YOUR SOUL'S PURPOSE ... 420
- [EB] THE ENCYCLOPAEDIA BRITANNICA (SOFTWARE) ... 420
- [EWM] EYEWITNESS TO MESOPOTAMIA ... 420
- [GEB] THE WORKS OF GEBER (721-815 AD) ... 420
- [HLC] Origin, Development and Regulation of Human Leydig Cells ... 421
- [IC] I CHING (or "BOOK OF CHANGES") – English version ... 421
- [KJ] THE WAY TO WISDOM : AN INTRODUCTION TO PHILOSOPHY ... 421
- [MERL] THE MICROSOFT ENCARTA REFERENCE LIBRARY ... 421
- [YLT] YOUNG'S LITERAL BIBLE TRANSLATION" ... 421
- [YAC] YOUNG'S ANALYTICAL CONCORDANCE TO THE BIBLE ... 421

ASTROLOGY SOFTWARE 421

- WIN*STAR STANDARD VERSION 4 (MATRIX SOFTWARE) ... 422
- WORLD OF WISDOM HOROSCOPE INTERPRETER ... 422

APPENDIX 1. ALCHEMY 423

- THE STATED PRINCIPLE OF ALCHEMY ... 425

THE SEVEN ALCHEMY STAGES	428
HISTORY OF GOLD	433
A PRACTICAL GOLD EXTRACTION METHOD	434

APPENDIX 2. HUMAN EVOLUTION — 435

- ADAM AND EVE ... 436
- EVOLUTION PATTERNS ... 436
- CORRESPONDENCES WITH GENESIS AND EXODUS ... 437
- EARLY HOMO ... 437
- HOMO HABILIS ("Handy Man") ... 437
- HOMO ERGASTER ("Workman") ... 437
- HOMO ERECTUS ("Upright Man") ... 437
- HOMO HEIDELBERGENSIS ... 437
- HOMO NEANDERTHALIS ... 438
- HOMO SAPIENS ("Wise Man") ... 438
- FIRST MIGRATION ... 438
- SECOND MIGRATION ... 438
- TABLE : HUMAN EVOLUTION FROM SINGLE CELLS ... 439
- MAP : MIGRATIONS OF HOMO SAPIENS FROM AFRICA ... 439

APPENDIX 3. CRITICAL MASS — 443

- CHAIN REACTION IN PHYSICS ... 443
- CRITICAL MASS ... 444
- CHAIN REACTION IN HUMAN AFFAIRS AND PSYCHOLOGY ... 444

APPENDIX 4. EDGAR CAYCE (1877 – 1945) — 445

- REINCARNATION AND KARMA ... 445
- GENERAL MEDIUMSHIP ... 445

APPENDIX 5. MEDITATION — 446

- THE AIMS OF MEDITATION ... 446
- "LETTING GO" ... 446
- STAGE 1 : EARTH. SENSATION ... 446
- STAGE 2 : WATER. EMOTIONS AND FEELINGS ... 447
- STAGE 3 : AIR. THINKING ... 447
- STAGE 4 : INTUITION. INSTINCT. CONTEMPLATION. ... 448
- THE IN-TUITION DIMENSION and CYCLE OF GROWTH ... 449
- PARADOX ... 449

APPENDIX 6. THE NITROGEN CYCLE — 450

- NITROGEN AND EVOLUTION OF MAN ... 451
- EVOLUTION OF THE NITROGEN CYCLE ... 451
- THE RETURN PROCESS ... 453

APPENDIX 7. THE MIDDLE PATH — 454

THE BIBLE TEMPLE ... 454
- THE BOOK OF REVELATION ... 455
- THE ABYSS ... 456

KUNDALINI YOGA ... 456
THE KABBALAH TREE OF LIFE ... 457
FREEMASONRY ... 457
THE HUMAN BRAIN ... 458

INDEX — 459

** TABLE OF FIGURES **

Figure 1 : Cover Picture Components	xxvii
Figure 2 : Graph of Consciousness versus Will	6
Figure 3 : Diana's Personal Life Purpose Table	11
Figure 4 : Life Purpose Table	12
Figure 5 : Basic process models	16
Figure 6 : Astrology process model	16
Figure 7 : Computer algorithm first 8 steps	18
Figure 8 : Computer algorithm result	18
Figure 9 : Fern Leaf dissection. An example of results of a fractal rule	19
Figure 10 : DNA Strand Reproduction	21
Figure 11 : Freud Psyche Model & Maslow's "Hierarchy of Needs"	26
Figure 12 : Growth of Personality Table	32
Figure 13 : Psychology Development Model - Jungian Individuation	33
Figure 14 : Psychology Development model - Transactional Analysis	34
Figure 15 : The 4 Elements and some associations	41
Figure 16 : The 4 Functions of C.G. Jung	49
Figure 17 : BBC News - Crime and the New Moon	61
Figure 18 : Birth Chart Houses and Zodiac Signs in relationship to Earth	62
Figure 19 : House basis of an astrological chart	65
Figure 20: Aries Sun House positions for sunrise & noon March 21st	67
Figure 21 : The 4 Quadrants of a chart	69
Figure 22: Astrology – pattern of 12 Personal Houses	69
Figure 23: Generic Houses of Jupiter	72
Figure 24 : 3 Octaves of Logarithmic Timescale and Zodiac Year	74
Figure 25 : The 3 Octaves of each Zodiac Sign	75
Figure 26 : Astrology - Logarithmic Timescale and Psychology stages	76
Figure 27 : Sun Symbol	78
Figure 28 : Transactional Analysis Development Model	94
Figure 29 : Astrology - Zodiac Signs	109
Figure 30 : Astrology : Zodiac Signs and parts of the body	112
Figure 31 : Zodiac Ages Summary	125
Figure 32 : The Solar System	149
Figure 33 : Planet Rulers of Zodiac Signs and Transcendence	149
Figure 34 : Neptune and The Tree of Life	153
Figure 35 : Table - Planet Descriptions	171
Figure 36 : Astrology Aspects - Examples of Planet Aspects	173
Figure 37 : Astrology Aspects - The Monthly Moon Cycle	176

Figure 38 : LIFE DIARY FORM	200
Figure 39 : Birth Chart of Lady Diana Spencer	203
Figure 40 : Transit Chart of Lady Diana Spencer	209
Figure 41 : Diana Spencer's Life Diary	211
Figure 42 : Freud and Jung Birth Charts	217
Figure 43 : Genesis and Evolution Summary Table	221
Figure 44 : The Pagan Cycle and Number 8	254
Figure 45 : Tarot Minor Arcana	268
Figure 46 : TAROT XIV - TEMPERANCE	272
Figure 47 : TAROT XV - THE DEVIL	274
Figure 48 : TAROT XVI - THE TOWER	277
Figure 49 : TAROT XVII - THE STAR	279
Figure 50 : TAROT XVIII - THE MOON	281
Figure 51 : TAROT XIX - THE SUN	283
Figure 52 : TAROT XX - JUDGEMENT	285
Figure 53 : TAROT XXI - THE WORLD	287
Figure 54 : TAROT 0 - THE FOOL	289
Figure 55 : TAROT I - THE MAGICIAN and MENSA	291
Figure 56 : TAROT II - THE HIGH PRIESTESS	293
Figure 57 : TAROT III - THE EMPRESS	296
Figure 58 : TAROT IV - THE EMPEROR	299
Figure 59 : TAROT V - THE HIGH PRIEST	301
Figure 60 : TAROT VI - THE LOVERS	303
Figure 61 : TAROT VII - THE CHARIOT	306
Figure 62 : TAROT VIII - STRENGTH	308
Figure 63 : TAROT IX - THE HERMIT	310
Figure 64 : TAROT X - THE WHEEL OF FORTUNE	312
Figure 65 : TAROT XI - JUSTICE	314
Figure 66 : TAROT XII - THE HANGED MAN	316
Figure 67 : TAROT XIII - DEATH	319
Figure 68 : TREE OF LIFE - NUMBERS, PLANETS, AND CHAKRAS	321
Figure 69 : Tree of Life and The Cycle of Growth 3 Octaves	333
Figure 70 : Tree of Life and Transcendent Octave	336
Figure 71 : Table - Kabbalah, Numbers, Planets, and Tarot	338
Figure 72 : The Chakras and Kabbalah planet relationships	339
Figure 73 : Chakras - Correspondences Summary Table	351
Figure 74 : Numbers - Binary System	358
Figure 75 : Numbers - Number Zero	359
Figure 76 : Numbers - Number 1	363

Figure 77	Numbers - Number 2	366
Figure 78	Numbers - Number 3	372
Figure 79	- Number 3 and The Cycle of Growth	373
Figure 80	Number 3 - Interference Pattern	375
Figure 81	Number 4 and The Cycle of Growth	378
Figure 82	Numbers - Number 4 = 2 x 2	379
Figure 83	Number 5 and The Cycle of Growth	382
Figure 84	Numerology - Number 6	385
Figure 85	Numbers - Number 7 and 12 Uranus 7 Year Sub-Cycles [COB]	387
Figure 86	Numerology - Number 8	394
Figure 87	The Cycle of Number 9	396
Figure 88	Table - Numerology : 18 Chemical Elements	403
Figure 89	Atomic Number 9 – Fluorine	403
Figure 90	Numerology - Numbers and Letters Relationship	406
Figure 91	Arbour Philosophica	424
Figure 92	Works of Geber - Sol (gold)	427
Figure 93	The 7 Alchemy Stages	428
Figure 94	Practical Gold Extraction	434
Figure 95	Main Species in Human Evolution	435
Figure 96	Table - Human Evolution Part 1	440
Figure 97	Table - Human Evolution Part 2	441
Figure 98	Map - Homo Sapiens Migration out of Africa	442
Figure 99	Nuclear Fission – chain reaction	443
Figure 100	The Nitrogen Cycle	450
Figure 101	Solomon's Temple	455
Figure 102	The Temple Pillars	458

APHORISMS

* * * * * * * * * * * * * * * * * *

FAITH

IS CONTINUING TO DISCARD THE ABSURD

EVEN IN THE FACE OF THE UNKNOWN
[Anon]

* * * * * * * * * * * * * * * * * *

When you have eliminated the impossible,

whatever remains, however improbable,

must be the truth.

[Sir Arthur Conan Doyle- Sherlock Holmes]

* * * * * * * * * * * * * * * * * *

SUCH IS THE SUBJECT OF RE-INCARNATION

And God said, Let there be lights in the firmament of the heaven to divide the day from the night; and let them be for signs, and for seasons, and for days, and years:

[Genesis Chapter 1 Verse 14] and Astrology

* *

And he shewed me a pure river of water of life, bright as crystal, going forth out of the throne of God and of the Lamb:In the midst of its broad place, and of the river on this side and on that, [is] a tree of life, yielding twelve fruits, in each several month rendering its fruits, and the leaves of the tree [are] for the service of the nations;

[Revelation 22 Verses 1-2] and The Cycle of Growth

* *

There are 3 ways of getting something done :-
1.Do it yourself. : 2.Get someone else to do it. : 3.Tell your children not to do it.
[Ref. Genesis and the "Fall"]

* *

AS ABOVE, SO BELOW.   AS BELOW, SO ABOVE

* *

To see a world in a grain of sand,
And a heaven in a wild flower,
Hold infinity in the palm of your hand,
And eternity in an hour.

[William Blake – "Auguries of Innocence"] and The Cycle of Growth

* *

And when he was demanded of the Pharisees, when the kingdom of God should come, he answered them and said, The kingdom of God cometh not with observation Neither shall they say, Lo here! or, lo there! for, behold, the kingdom of God is within you. *[Luke Chapter 17 Verses 20 & 21]*

* *

And God said, Let us make man in our image, after our likeness:
[Genesis Chapter 1 Verse 26] and The Cycle of Growth

* *

Man made God in his own image
[Eckhart Tolle "A New Earth: Awakening to Your Life's Purpose"]

* *

The religions of the world continue to fix our attention on knowledge of 'Good and Evil' rather than 'Life' – so perpetuating the Original Sin. [BTB]

* *

CHANGE IS STABILITY. STABILITY CHANGE.

* *

IGNORANCE IS BLISS

* *

ABBREVIATIONS

Reference to quotations from books in the bibliography

[ACU]	- "The Archetypes And The Collective Unconscious" (C.G.Jung 1959)
[AEW]	- A.E. Waite (re Rider-Waite Tarot)
[BAB]	- "Babylon-Mesopotamia and The birth of Civilisation (Kriwaczek 2010)
[BTB]	- Brian Baulsom (to distinguish author's notes where necessary)
[BF]	- Human migration from Africa http://www.bradshawfoundation.com/journey/
[COB]	- "Cycles of Becoming" (Alexander Ruperti 1978)
[COG]	- "The Cycle Of Growth" (abbreviation of)
[DFMQ]	-"The Mystical Qabalah" (Dion Fortune 1935).
[DFCD]	- "The Cosmic Doctrine" (Dion Fortune 1924).
[DHTS]	- "Diana, Her True Story" (Andrew Morton 1993)
[DNA]	- "Deep Ancestry" (2007) & "The Journey of Man" (2003) (Spencer Wells)
[DSP]	- "Discovering Your Soul's Purpose" (Mark Thurston 1984)
[E&A]	- "Ego And Archetype" (C.G.Jung Foundation)
[EB]	- Encyclopædia Britannica. 2011 Encyclopædia Britannica Ultimate Reference Suite. Chicago:
[EC]	- Edgar Cayce
[ECOT]	- Edgar Cayce's Story of The Old Testament
[EWM]	- "Eyewitness to Mesopotamia" (Dorling Kindersley 2007)
[GEB]	- "The Works of Geber" (Alchemy 1545)
[GOP]	- "The Growth of Personality" (Gordon R. Lowe 1972)
[HLC]	- "Origin, Development and Regulation of Human Leydig Cells" (Paper 2009)
[IC]	- "I Ching - The Book of Changes" (Richard Wilhelm 1969)
[IHA]	- "Introduction To The History of Astrology" (Nicholas Campion)
[IOD]	- "The Interpretation of Dreams" (Sigmund Freud 1953)
[KJ]	- "The Way to Wisdom" (Karl Jaspers 2003)
[KJV]	- The Bible: King James Version
[LT]	- Logarithmic Timescale (from "The Round Art" by A.T.Mann)
[MAHS]	- "Man and His Symbols" (C.G.Jung)
[MSE]	- Microsoft ® Encarta ® 2006. © 1993-2005 Microsoft Corporation
[P&A]	- "Psychology and Alchemy" (C.G.Jung 1953)
[SLUC]	- "The Secret Life of the Unborn Child" (Dr. Thomas Verny and John Kelly 1981)
[TA]	- Transactional Analysis (various books)
[TBOTR]	"The Book of the Revelation" (ref. Edgar Cayce 1971)
[YAC]	- Young's "Analytical Concordance to the Bible"
[TRA]	- "The Round Art" (A.T.Mann 1979)
[YLT]	- Young's "Literal Bible Translation" (1862)

FREE ADDITIONAL CONTENT from www.CycleOfGrowth.com

"The Cycle of Growth Picture Book" free download PDF file

Contains all the "Cycle of Growth" artwork in a free 80 page A4 PDF download. It was mainly intended as a companion to the eBook – but makes a good summary version of this book.

"Your Personal Life Diary" – free 2 page PDF and Excel spreadsheet forms.
Ref. chapter [ASTROLOGY : PLANET TRANSITS].
Download the Life Diary forms if you do not want to write in this book.

_____

"Your Personal Life Diary" is a separate book available in printed and ebook formats and contains a simplified summary of how a birth chart is set up and how to use the Life Diary.

_____

NOTES

- Cross-references to chapters are bracketed e.g. [INTRODUCTION]
- *Quotations are indicated with their sources like this. [BTB]*
- Please note that time periods and ages are all approximate. Although we divide cycles into convenient segments there is rarely such sharp delimitation in real life.
- If I use the word "opposite" anywhere in this book I mean "opposite by position". For example, "opposite" Houses or Signs are COMPLEMENTARY in effect. They BALANCE one another through time. There are no opposites in Nature. Everything has its proper function. The sum total of everything is Zero.
- Throughout this book "man" also includes "woman". This is correct in the sense of Genesis 1 Verse 27 :-
  And God prepareth the man in His image; in the image of God He prepared him, a male and a female He prepared them. [YLT]. Man, as Adam, did not appear until afterwards.

THE "MAYBE SHELF" – FAITH IS NOT BLIND

BEYOND "TRUE OR FALSE", "RIGHT AND WRONG", "BLACK AND WHITE"

FAITH IS CONTINUING TO DISCARD THE ABSURD EVEN IN THE FACE OF THE UNKNOWN

When you have eliminated the impossible, whatever remains, however improbable, must be the truth. [Sir Arthur Conan Doyle - Sherlock Holmes]

In Scottish Law, apart from an "innocent" or "guilty" verdict there is the possibility of a "not proven" verdict. There is much in the Occult field (which includes areas like Psychology) that comes under this heading. Early on I found it a useful principle to make a "May-Be shelf" in my mind where I could store such information. I have found that from time to time I get the opportunity to test out some of these theories. To experiment. If we look closely, this is, in fact, the Scientific Principle which has given rise to all scientific discoveries which have brought the Unknown to becoming Known. Translating Theory into Practice.

INTRODUCTIONS

INTRODUCTIONS

INTRODUCING MYSELF

My middle name is Thomas. The reason I state that is because, in relation to this book, it seems to be as important as my first. In the Bible "Doubting Thomas" was the disciple of Jesus who refused to believe the resurrection had occurred until he had seen Jesus for himself, and touched his wounds. He did get the evidence he wanted. I too tend to disbelieve what people tell me and look for empiric proof, or tangible evidence, when considering important matters.

I had a fairly normal life without any knowledge or interest in "occult" subjects (occult, really, just means "hidden") until age 34 when I had some unusual experiences which led me, via Spiritualism, to discover an ability for healing and realise that there is more to life than what we perceive with our normal 5 senses. I have met people who, when I mention occult subjects, accuse me of "dabbling". I realise that I never dabble. Once I am interested in a subject I pursue it in some depth. This book covers over 30 years of study and practical experience and experiment with several disciplines.

Although I eventually qualified as a full member of *The National Federation of Spiritual Healers* in the United Kingdom (now under the umbrella of *The Healing Trust*) and achieved probationer certificates with *The Institute of Spiritualist Mediums* as Spirit Communicator and Speaker I decided that these areas did not hold enough information about how things "worked", or, if there is a purpose to life, what it is. The same can be said about The Tarot. Having given hundreds of readings for people unknown to me, and being amazed at the accuracy, it was more interesting to put the cards back in order to see their overall story better.

My main interest is Astrology because not only does it have a scientific basis but is open to more scientific experimentation. It also gives a broader overview on life than the other disciplines which tend to be limited to more mundane activities. This is mainly because of the requirements of the client at the time. I am more interested in events in the context of a whole lifetime than day to day events. It is for this reason that, even though I had the opportunity to pursue the subjects on a professional basis, I decided to return to a "normal" job so that I could approach them in my own way, at my own speed.

The traditional methods, even though valid in their own terms, did not entirely relate to modern day thinking or experience, however, by taking new scientific discoveries into account they make more sense. In addition I studied numerous other related subjects such as Kabbalah, Numerology, Palmistry, and the I Ching – all of which I found worked, but, once again, did not give any sequential overview. In the process I have also learned some Psychology and have come to believe that everything works because we, and everything else, are linked by the Collective Unconscious.

Although having a 2 year group study in the past, during the writing of this book I have discovered that The Kabbalah Tree of Life gives a deeper, more basic, archetypal understanding of the other subjects.

(For more information about me and my experiences please see the [MY STORY] chapter).

INTRODUCING THIS BOOK

Because Astrology is based on cycles, and is well researched, I have used its 12 Development Stages for comparison. Despite our "Decimal Age" all humans are still forced to base measurement of Time on Number 12. We do not know the exact "reason" why, but we can understand that it is the same "reason" that our clocks are divided into 12 rather than any other number. Together, the 12 Stages make up the repetitive Cycle of Growth. We always need to keep the full cycle in mind when analysing data to see how the parts combine to make the whole – otherwise we get bogged down by too much detail. This is the "Holistic Method".

The book includes and compares principles of a wide variety of areas of study and assumes the reader has no knowledge of any of them. It excludes much of the practical detail – for example, there is no need to know how to set up a Birth Chart or know techniques of psychoanalysis.

ASTROLOGY

Includes the birth and life of Lady Diana Spencer as a practical example.

- **YOUR PERSONAL "LIFE DIARY"** : There is a form for you to fill in your own life changing experiences to see how you relate to the Astrological Generic Cycles. [ASTROLOGY : PLANET TRANSITS]
- Also find **YOUR PERSONAL LIFE PURPOSE** [THE PURPOSE OF LIFE] in basic form.

INTRODUCTIONS

- 12 Birth Chart Generic and Personal Houses
- The Cycle of 12 Zodiac Signs
- The Zodiac Ages from 10,000 BC to 5920 AD related to Historical events.
- Personal Transit Planet Cycles through the 12 Houses of a Birth Chart.
- 12 stages of the Generic Transit Planet Cycles that influence each of us in the same way through a lifetime.
- The Astrological Logarithmic Timescale of a human lifetime from Conception to Death.
- The 3 + 1 Birth Chart "Octaves" that make 4 main stages of human development

THE TAROT
- The 22 symbols of the Major Arcana match the 12 Cycle of Growth Stages in sequence.

THE KABBALAH TREE OF LIFE
- This symbolic system gets closer to the archetypal universal principles than the (traditional) others and therefore associates with all other areas of study to the enrichment of them all – including the understanding of Kabbalism itself.

PSYCHOLOGY
- A human lifetime from Conception to Death.
- Our life in the womb (ref. Dr. Thomas Verney and John Kelly) [SLUC]
- Jungian Psychology (The Collective Unconscious. Individuation. Functions)
- The "Development of Personality" model of Erikson, Piaget, and Gordon Lowe.[DOP]
- The Transactional Analysis lifetime development model and Jungian Individuation model.

EVOLUTION PATTERNS OF THE UNIVERSE AND MANKIND
- The now accepted story of human evolution from The Big Bang onwards corresponds with The Cycle of Growth

THE BIBLE
- The Life of Jesus.
- The Genesis Story of Creation corresponds with The Cycle of Growth.

THE CALENDAR
- The history of The Calendar we all use today.
- The annual cycle of Christian festivals.
- The annual cycle of Pagan festivals.

NUMEROLOGY
- Although Numerology shows us something about Numbers, the traditional associations with planets do not reach the Archetypal level. By comparing Numbers with The Cycle of Growth – especially with its relationships to The Kabbalah - and evolution of Chemical Elements from The Big Bang we get closer to the truth.
- Astrological Aspects give an idea of how Numbers relate to The Whole

OTHER AREAS MENTIONED
- Edgar Cayce – "The Sleeping Prophet"
- The Soul's Purpose (Mark Thurston)
- The "Purposeless Life" – [BTB] - my concept.

INTRODUCTIONS

- Human Evolution from "The Big Bang"
- DNA, Mutation, and Darwin's Diversity (perhaps there are no "mistakes")
- The development of an Idea in the mind, and its physical manifestation.

BIBLIOGRAPHY

- There is a Bibliography at the end.

INTRODUCING THE CYCLE OF GROWTH

The Cycle of Growth at base level is an examination of the Archetypes involved in Evolution. The same pattern exists in the growth and development of all animals and plants. Everything alive today has evolved from the same blobs of jelly (bacteria) millions of years ago. 50% of our DNA is the same as that in a banana, 99% the same as a chimpanzee. We see the same pattern in the cycle of a year in Nature, the growth of a child in the womb before birth, and our development over a lifetime after birth. Scientists now recognise that the stages of development during our life in the womb follows the same sequence as that in evolution - beginning with "blobs of jelly" and progressing through fish stage (with visible gills), reptile stage, and ape stage (with rudimentary tail and bodily hair, which disappear before birth). Psychologists also recognise that the same stages are repeated after birth, when Mind and Body develop together. The pattern is the same, the only difference is the form of expression.

This book is not meant to be a text book, or "how to" book but to update, and clarify older ideas. My aim is to distil information and extract basic principles so that readers can then relate them to their own understanding, and compare the theories with practical reality. For example, we now know what the Age of Aquarius means because we are living it now, so we can discard the ridiculous notions that exist. We can get a better idea of why Pyramids and Stonehenge were built because it occurred (and ended) during the Age of Aries – although similar and smaller, monuments with the same purpose are still being built in the present day.

Having said that, there is a rough test for your birth Sun position in the chapter [THE PURPOSE OF LIFE], and the chapter [LIFE DIARY] will help you test the validity of Astrological Transits for yourself.

This is also different from other books on similar subjects because it brings together in one place, and compares, different and often widely separated areas of knowledge – finding surprising similarities. Also it is new – incorporating recent scientific discoveries and research to update ancient teachings - such as in recent DNA evidence of evolution, the latest archaeological discoveries, and modern psychological experience and concepts that were only perceived intuitively in the past. It not only deals with Astrological Transits on a Personal basis but also a Generic one which is the same for everyone, and brings to light evidence of repeating cycles in a normal human lifetime and is an indication of why we all develop according to the same pattern throughout a lifetime. It also gives a new insight to the Jungian "Process of Individuation" with its "Mid Life Crisis" at age 42, and its relationship with the 84 year cycle of Uranus.

Because it combines several different areas of knowledge, it is written on the assumption that each subject is unknown to the reader, with chapters containing basic introductions. The benefit is that we do not have to study the whole subject. We can select information relating to growth cycles and leave the rest to the experts. For example, we can use psychological studies of human development, but do not need to know anything about psychoanalysis. When we focus on information related to The Cycle of Growth we find that different areas of knowledge are using different languages to describe the same thing. It is rather like the religions of the world worshipping one God, but in different ways.

THE ARCHETYPES

The Cycle of Growth is at base level the study of a set of 12 archetypes that exist in the Collective Unconscious and manifest themselves at physical and psychological forms at our level of consciousness. There are many others. Because of the limitation of our consciousness to a material world we are not able to fully perceive them, but we can get some indication of their activity by the use of symbolism. For example, at one level we can consider how the basic energy of the Sun is modified by the 12 Zodiac Signs in the course of a year to produce life on Earth. These same forces have been active in evolution over millions of years.

INTRODUCTIONS

THE COVER PICTURE COMPONENTS

The Cycle of Growth image is that of Evolution rather than mere repetition. The tail of MY Serpent ends at Cycle of Growth Stage 8 related to Scorpio/Pluto (Death and Regeneration. Elimination). The mouth no longer endlessly (is that a pun ?) swallows its own tail. The whole is a composite picture of the following parts :-

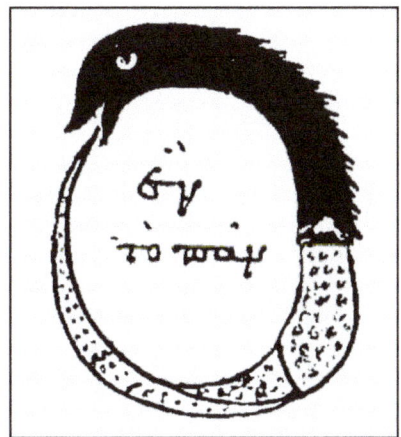  

Figure 1 : Cover Picture Components

Part 1 : THE CHRYSOPOEIA OF CLEOPATRA

The original "serpent" shows an endlessly repeating cycle - without development or evolution.

*The Ancient Greek words enclosed within the image of the 'Ouroboros' (Greek letters, ουροβόρος όφις meaning "tail-devouring snake") from "The Chrysopoeia of Cleopatra" ("Gold manufacture/'Gold-Making of Cleopatra, the alchemist) dating to ca. 2nd. century AD mean literally : "The one the all-seeing/ including", i.e. "One is All". ("hen to panops "in Latin transliteration; "έν τό πάνοψ" in Greek letters).

[Ref <http://en.allexperts.com/q/Greek-2004/2008/12/Ouroboros.htm>]

Part 2 : TAROT CARD X.THE WHEEL OF FORTUNE

- The picture is of a wheel endlessly turning.

It has, among other things, relationships with :-

- The Earth
- All cycles of Nature and other Wheels as contained in The Cycle of Growth.
- The Vision of Ezekiel and The Book of Revelation.
- The board game "Snakes and Ladders" (up the ladders, back down the snakes)
- Number 10 in numerology means beginning at a new level. 1 + 0 = 1. Here, entering a new area of Society half way through the Tarot cycle.

Part 3 : THE TRANSCENDENT FUNCTION OF THE CYCLE OF GROWTH

Please see the chapter [ASTROLOGY : LOGARITHMIC TIMESCALE]

INTRODUCTIONS

THE PURPOSE OF LIFE

OVERVIEW

This chapter examines the possibility of a Life Purpose from the perspective of The Bible, Reincarnation, Psychology, and Astrology.

YOUR LIFE PURPOSE *: There is an exercise for you to discover your basic spiritual Life Purpose as described by Astrology.*

My basic philosophy is that we have come to this Earth in order to learn spiritual lessons, and our Sun Sign is a good way of approaching the subject on a personal basis. At the end of the chapter is a practical method of ascertaining one's basic Life Purpose which goes beyond the usual "Star Sign" interpretation, but is simple enough to form the basis for further analysis.

Before starting the main narrative it is a good idea to consider if there is a purpose to human life, and, if so, what it is. In any sort of project it is necessary to keep the final goal in mind, which gives some sort of direction even if the exact path is not known.

The next chapter [THE PURPOSELESS LIFE] suggests an alternative scenario. My suggestion there is that there is no "rule". We can follow either or both paths during the course of a lifetime.

The problem here is that there are numerous philosophies, and they tend to rely on belief or faith rather than empirical evidence. In my case, however, I do have personal experiences that started me searching for answers to this question, and led me to continue. This is described in more detail in the [MY STORY] chapter; the point being that it did prove to me that there is more to this life than what we can perceive using the 5 senses. Since then I have found Astrology a useful basis of self-analysis.

In none of the philosophies does there seem to be much focus on why God bothered to create us in the first place. If we knew that, we might be able to co-operate better. A strong contender is that He got lonely and wanted another God to play with, and, in the absence of anything else, has had to start from scratch. Now having the Jungian concept of a Shadow, my suggestion is that he too was tempted by his Shadow (Satan) to "eat of the Tree of Knowledge of good and evil". As Above, So Below, As Below, So Above. There does seem to be a strong focus of God's attention on material manifestation (Cycle of Growth Stage 10. Peak. Career) rather than spiritual development. This also addresses the philosophical problem of where Satan comes from. If everything comes from God, then Satan must have too, so why not God's unconscious? In particular, if, as according to Jung, we each have a Shadow, we would expect God to have one too. We are "made in his image". This also makes sense when we consider natural laws and the Jungian concept that the Collective Unconscious acts as a complement to consciousness. An example of how this works is when we make a decision for action. If we observe ourselves carefully we note all kinds of ideas immediately come to mind to contradict it. There is always an inner and outer tendency to maintain, or return to, the initial universal state of inertia prior to The Number Zero Big Bang.

The Kabbalah Tree of Life shows that Kether (Sephirah 1. Crown) existed as primeval chaos, where everything is in balance, and Chockmah (Sephirah 2. Wisdom. Force. Creative Energy, God) was the first manifestation. To maintain universal balance Binah (Sephirah 3. Understanding. Form. Inertia. Satan) manifested afterwards as a complementary force. So we see that there is another Kingdom above the "Opposites" of God and The Devil. This gives credence to the statement that "Man made God in his own image", rather than in accordance with reality.

The Bible tells the same story. The beginning of Genesis show that "The Word" as an abstract concept preceded God. From there, the Bible avoids any speculation as to where Satan came from.

As we get deeper into the study of The Cycle of Growth we see it appears in all kinds of disguises of "wheels within wheels" cycles. Just look at a clock and consider the meanings of Spring, Summer, Autumn, Winter that can be applied – second, minute, hour, day, month, year, life time. The relationship between Time and Space. So God too must be subject to his own Laws, and more like us than we would originally guess.

THE BIBLE

The Bible does not give us much of a clue regarding any purpose or aim. In the book of Genesis the story of Creation seems to be just a record of events, and when it comes to Adam and Eve, rather than any positive advice, all they get is the command not to eat of the fruit of the Tree of Knowledge of Good and Evil. No help there. Apart from that, after naming the animals, they seem to not have much else to occupy their time, except

THE PURPOSE OF LIFE

perhaps a bit of gardening. The only discovery there was something that every parent knows today. If you want children to do something tell them not to do it. . "The Devil makes work for idle hands". However, there is agreement between the Creation story and The Cycle of Growth which is explored in detail in my chapter [THE GENESIS STORY].

In the New Testament of the Bible, John Chapter 1 we read :-

Verses 1 & 2 : In the beginning was the Word, and the Word was with God, and the Word was God. The same was in the beginning with God.

Again, there is not much help, but it does suggest that God evolved from somewhere (in line with my earlier observation from The Kabbalah), and that there is some sort of pattern. This again fits it with the Cycle of Growth. We also note that the God of the New Testament seems very different to that of the Old Testament - with The Ten Commandments and its floods, famine and diseases, and especially His treatment of Job with God's irrational bet with Satan that Job could not be made to curse Him even if he gave Job all types of suffering. Job was, in fact, a devout man and Satan suggested that Job only obeyed God because he had an easy life – not because he loved God. So Job was tested.

[There is a much more detailed analysis in the writings of C.G.Jung under the title "The Answer To Job" I have used that from [The Portable Jung].

Throughout The Bible there are several covenants (agreements) between God and man, with God promising to look after those who worship him. I don't think we can count The Garden of Eden as a covenant because there is no evidence of any negotiation, just instructions. At times man broke the covenant and was punished – such as by the flood from which Noah was saved. Another time, as soon as Moses turned his back to get the Ten Commandments on a mountain top, the Israelites made a golden calf to worship. When Moses came down with the stone tablets he smashed them in a fit of rage and had to make another set (is this "breaking the covenant" ? – sorry !). In modern law the "contracts" all seems a bit one-sided. At no time did anyone get a signed copy of what God agreed to do in return – especially as all the negotiations were in secret. Poor Job, as subject of a bet between God and The Devil, did not have a leg to stand on in his own defence. We note in this world there also seems to be a habit among powerful people to "forget" the early promises they make.

With Jesus and the New Testament we have a total change of focus and a seeming end to God's rather irrational behaviour. There is a statement by Edgar Cayce that many of the people in The Bible who had direct contact with God, such as Adam, Moses and Jesus (among others) were all a long line of reincarnations of the same being, so perhaps they were having "on the job training" for making negotiations. As I sit here today, Jesus seems to have done a fair job on my behalf.

As we reach this stage in the chapter I have to confess that what I have learned from The Bible does not seem to have solved the question of what is the purpose of life in general, or my life in particular. We do have some clues, perhaps, in the overall theme right from the beginning of creation of God giving commands and humans not taking a lot of notice. Probably because God does not seem to have lived up to his side of the bargain (whatever that was). One clear fact is that his priests, even the righteous ones, seem to suffer in life just as much as we normal people.

Another continual theme is the idea that somehow we started with God, and, although God did not really mean it to happen, we did not follow the lifestyle he had in mind for us. (Hands up those reading this who always did what their parents wanted ! .. I don't see a single hand).

However, there is something in the Bible that does seem to relate to life as I know it having had children of my own. That is the idea of children needing to leave parents to make their own life. This relates to the teachings of Jesus :-

In *Matthew Chapter 10* Jesus says he comes to PUT ("send" [KJV]) a sword. So he does not actually use it himself, just supply one.

To me a Sword (and Tarot Minor Arcana Swords suit) is symbolic of the Jungian Thinking function related to the Element Air – especially to the Zodiac Air Sign of Libra which, apart from The Scales, includes the symbol of 'The Sword of Justice'. Thus we have differences of opinion and communication. The early knight Crusaders equated the symbol of The Cross with that of The Sword. The symbol of The Cross, and Crucifixion, relating to Easter, and therefore Cycle of Growth Stage 1 (Seed) is more suggestive of the birth of a human child and the "crucifixion" of Spirit in Matter. There is also the suggestion of a Life Purpose, or duty which often requires that we take up a new role in society based upon personal talents and skills rather than the wishes of one's parents.

THE PURPOSE OF LIFE

The conflict, for example, between an individual and his/her mother in law is a standing joke in this country, and has become part of our mythology .

Verse 34 Ye may not suppose that I came to put peace on the earth; I did not come to put peace, but a sword;

Verse 35 for I came to set a man at variance against his father, and a daughter against her mother, and a daughter-in-law against her mother-in-law,

Verse 36 and the enemies of a man are those of his household.

Verse 37 He who is loving father or mother above me, is not worthy of me, and he who is loving son or daughter above me, is not worthy of me,

Verse 38 and whoever doth not receive his cross and follow after me, is not worthy of me.

Verse 39 He who found his life shall lose it, and he who lost his life for my sake shall find it.

My [GENESIS AND THE CYCLE OF GROWTH] chapter notes the rather tongue-in-cheek, 'Hide and Seek' approach of God on discovering their disobedience. I can easily relate to repetition of very similar exchanges between children and their parents, including mine.

Also, in Luke we have 3 parables from Jesus with the message of "loss and return". The first is of a lost sheep, the second a lost piece of silver, and the third is this one of the Prodigal Son. We note that the other son that did as he was told, and stayed home, does not get exactly what he expected :-

Luke Chapter 15 – Parable of 'The Prodigal Son'

Verse 13: And not many days after the younger son gathered all together, and took his journey into a far country, and there wasted his substance with riotous living.

Verse 17: And when he came to himself, he said, How many hired servants of my father's have bread enough and to spare, and I perish with hunger!

Verse 21: And the son said unto him, Father, I have sinned against heaven, and in thy sight, and am no more worthy to be called thy son.

Verse 22: But the father said to his servants, Bring forth the best robe, and put it on him; and put a ring on his hand, and shoes on his feet:

Verse 25: Now his elder son was in the field: and as he came and drew nigh to the house, he heard musick and dancing.

Verse 28: And he was angry, and would not go in: therefore came his father out, and intreated him.

Verse 32: It was meet that we should make merry, and be glad: for this thy brother was dead, and is alive again; and was lost, and is found.

Considering all of the above, it seems a necessary stage of evolution to depart from God too. Or, more correctly in psychological terms, identify one's self with God. i.e. to "become" or act godlike. By disobeying his rules we act as equals. This is borne out by Jung's process of Individuation and the seeming need for times of "inflated acts" or identification of the ego with God (as portrayed by Adam and Eve in Genesis). (There is more information about Individuation in my chapter [PSYCHOLOGICAL GROWTH].

I believe that there are no explicit instructions in the Bible because there are not meant to be any. Rather like me with my children, God gives us some basic training early in life with the hope that we will eventually find our own way. A way that suits us as individuals.

Life seems to be more like a "process" rather than a pathway to some fixed goal. It is interesting that, in Darwin's theory, over long periods of time evolution favours Diversity , that is mutations or changes in species, rather than clones, or exact copies of organisms. Even though the main task of DNA is to reproduce exact copies of itself, it is the "mistakes" that actually enable it to survive. Inbreeding in humans and animals (the mating of close relatives) tends to produce children that eventually sicken and die. At this level, God seems to have the role of a scientist experimenting with different life forms.

C.G. JUNG – INDIVIDUATION AS A GOAL

C.G. Jung coined the phrase "Individuation" :-

> *Individuation means becoming an 'in-dividual,' and, insofar as 'individuality' embraces our innermost, last, and incomparable uniqueness, it also implies becoming one's own self." – [C. G. Jung, Two Essays on Analytical Psychology, par. 266]

I mention it here because it is often suggested to be a goal in life, with a linear process beginning to end. This is clearly not the case. Rather, it is a CYCLIC process more fitted to our Cycle of Growth model. Once we reach a certain level of development we progress to the next. So I leave any further discussion until my [PSYCHOLOGICAL DEVELOPMENT] chapter.

REINCARNATION

Another philosophy suggests that there is a plan which takes numerous life times to carry out. It does, once again, suggest some process of trial and error. There is also a suggestion that each life time contains specific lessons to learn. This tends to be borne out by my astrological studies where the Sun Sign gives the main focus.

> *For, each soul enters with a mission. And even as Jesus, the great missionary, we all have a mission to perform. Are we working with Him, or just now and then ? [EC Reading reference 3003-1]

EDGAR CAYCE : THE INCARNATIONS OF JESUS

This is contained in a reading by Edgar Cayce (reference 262-36) on 22nd. January 1933. It is suggested that we all follow a similar pattern to that indicated here.

> *First, as Amilius, He led - or projected - souls into the earth as thought forms.

> *Then He came as Adam, the first physical man, who "fell" in the flesh and thus it became necessary for him to eventually come as the last Adam to show us the way.

> *Thirdly He came as Enoch, who walked with God and was not because God took him.

> *Then He came as Melchizedek, the prince of Salem, without father, without mother, without days; he was not born and he did not die. Abraham paid tithes to Melchizedek. Many parallels can be found here with the life of Jesus. According to the readings Melchizedek, as I understand it, had attained the state of mastership such as we find in the so-called Eastern masters. In order to save the souls who had become involved in the earth because of his example, he then realized he would have to start all over in the earth and really go through all the trials and tribulations just as every other soul. (As Melchizedek he wrote the Book of Job.)

> *He came then as Joseph. We see many parallels here with Jesus.

> *Then He came as Joshua, the medium through which Moses obtained the laws on the mount.

> *Next He came as Jeshua, the scribe, who compiled and rewrote the Biblical record as we have it to that date.

> *Then He came into the earth as Zend [San - Zan?], father of the first Zoroaster, who wrote - the readings say - the Zend Avesta, sacred writings of the Persians.

> *Finally He came as Jesus, the last Adam, in whom we all may be made alive - or at one with our Creator.

> *Until He started over again as Joseph, he had not actually taken on the trials and tribulations of man. He chose, as Melchizedek, to come down into the depths of materiality, and He moved step by step back to the father. Having chosen to do this, it was not possible then for him to get out of the flesh without perfecting himself in the flesh.

THE PURPOSE OF LIFE

The suggestion is that the Prodigal Son parable (please see above) refers to Jesus :-

Nothing is said in the story of the prodigal son about how long it took him to return to his father after he had decided he would return.

Gradually, life after life, here a little, there a little, the soul perfected itself in the earth and, as Jesus, took his spiritualized body back to God, becoming the Christ. [EC Reading reference 262-36]

According to the Edgar Cayce readings each of us must do the same.

EDGAR CAYCE : MIND AND WILL

WILL is described by Edgar Cayce as the prime motivational force, with MIND as " the builder". Mind should be the servant of Will, but, in this life, Mind has taken control. Among other things, the Mind has created habit patterns of acting and thinking that block information coming from higher levels of consciousness. Meditation and prayer are ways of allowing the information through. Dreams can be useful too.

At present the Mind is "first". Will "last". Eventually the "first" becomes "last". Mark Thurston encapsulates this in his philosophy as described in the next section.

DISCOVERING YOUR SOUL'S PURPOSE (Mark Thurston)

I include a description of Mark Thurston's [DSP] philosophy at length because it combines and distils many of the ideas mentioned here into a homogeneous whole, with a more practical focus. Although his book is comparatively small it contains a lot of "meat" so I can only briefly touch on aspects that are appropriate here. His book has the benefit of being understandable in the face of his original sources that are often difficult to understand.

There is a difference between his philosophy and my Cycle of Growth in that he (and others) tend to emphasise the suggestion that the growth process is linear with each stage neatly following one after the other. There is a suggestion that the habits of the "Personality Wheel" are something to escape from as soon as possible. I suggest it is more practical to work with the Cycles of life. For example, my experience is that I can be at a different level of consciousness at any time of day or night. I still need to feed myself and mow the lawn occasionally. Some psychologists seem to suggest that we can only develop by having some years of psychoanalysis. I do not deny the usefulness of such people - although I have been keeping my eyes open for one, I have not found one yet. Others suggest we need some other sort of teacher or guru. Mark does at least give a "self-help" option. Astrology and The Cycle of Growth does suggest a more automatic, natural, but unconscious process. Perhaps by making the process more conscious we can learn to use it more effectively (as in Farming, for which Astrology was originally developed). My attitude is, for now, that I just need to carry out the tasks that God puts in front of me each day. I have an infinity of time at my disposal. If the process does not exist, and there is no reincarnation (another process?), there would not seem to be any purpose to this lifetime at all.

HOW WE BEGAN

Some of Edgar Cayce's work and philosophy is used, and Mark also draws information from other sources including C.G Jung and P.D Ouspensky. One of his main premises is that our individual soul or spirit was created with infinite or divine consciousness. To begin with there is no Will, which needs to be developed by entry into realms of reduced consciousness. In the process we also awaken our sense of identity as individual beings, so we can return to our original state of consciousness and become co-creators with God.

This fits perfectly with what we observe in the development of an infant. Psychologists are beginning to suggest that whilst in the womb, or at least just after birth, a child is at some other level of consciousness with no awareness of things outside itself. It is born in a psychologically "inflated" state (identified with God). It gradually becomes more aware of its own body, and the people and objects in its surroundings, and, later on, of itself as an individual able to say "me" and "I". Around 2 years of age there is demonstration of an almost "God-like" omnipotence, trying to tell those around what to do, which usually disappears in the face of the reality of its physical inferiority and dependence.

It is well to note here that Edgar Cayce stated that the soul or spirit does not enter the body until the first breath or even slightly later.

THE PURPOSE OF LIFE

(Q) Does a soul ever enter a body before it is born? (A) It enters either at the first breath physically drawn, or during the first twenty-four hours of cycle activity in a material plane. Not always at the first breath; sometimes there are hours, and there are changes even of personalities as to the seeking to enter. [EC Reading 2390-25 December 1940]

He also states that the incoming soul has no control over the physical body produced in the womb, or the attitudes of the parents.

At present we are at the level of 3 Dimensional consciousness and have somehow "lost the way" back because we have become diverted from the pathway by the images produced by our minds. In terms of levels of consciousness we are "asleep" and "dreaming", living life more like automatons with very little use of Will. I equate this with the Astrological "wheel" of a Birth Chart – which can be called the "Personality Wheel" – that which is seen (and to some extent, controlled) by others.

It includes the idea that increasing consciousness artificially, such as by the use of drugs or mediumistic development, is detrimental because there can be a corresponding loss of Will in the process. It also suggests this returns to an earlier state of existence where we had such abilities but no Will. Will is basically the development and use of self-discipline.

CONSCIOUSNESS VERSUS WILL - AND "THE PATH"

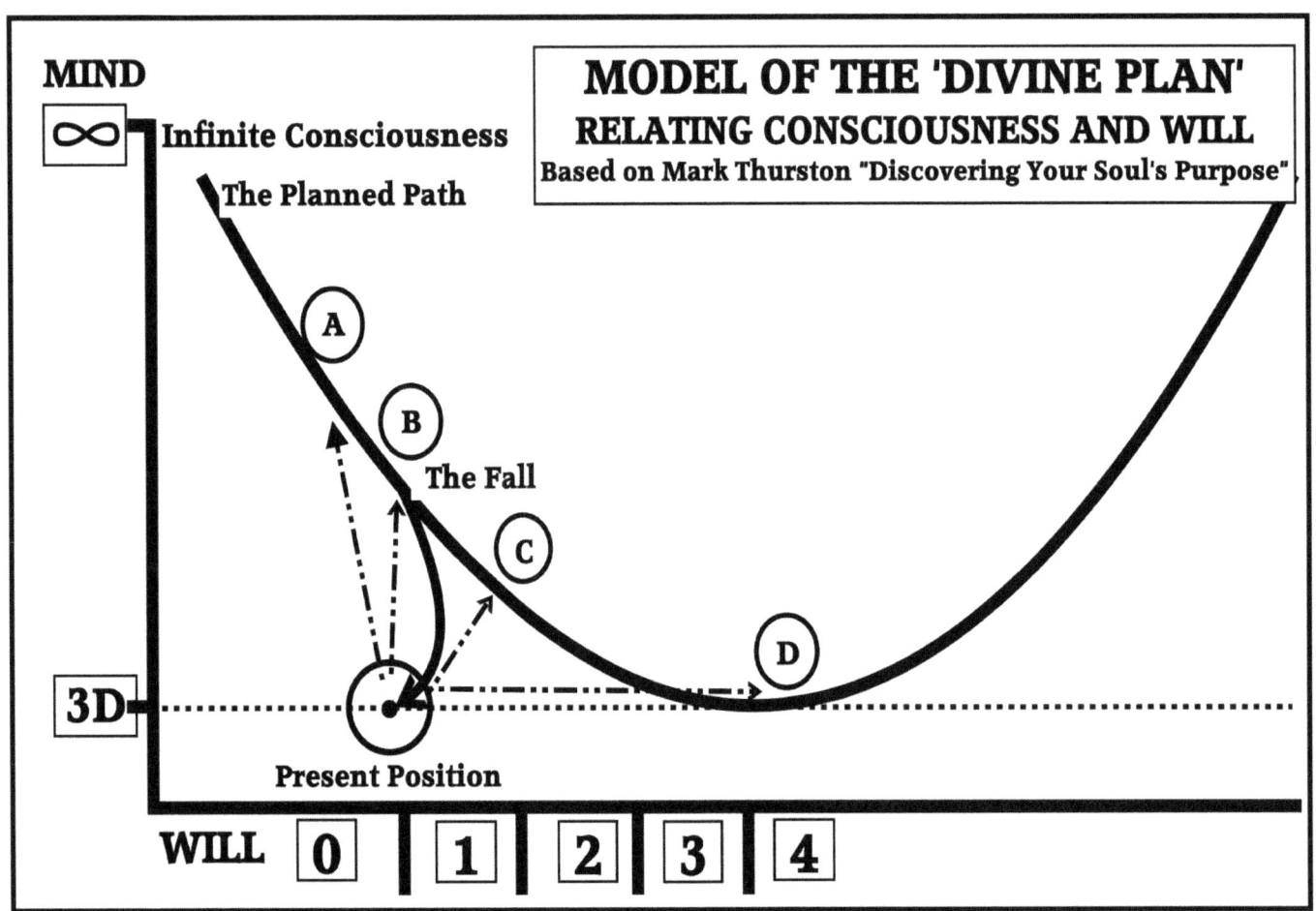

Figure 2 : Graph of Consciousness versus Will

THE PURPOSE OF LIFE

THE PLAN

The basis of Mark's hypothesis is outlined in the diagram which I have amended slightly. The left axis of the chart indicates Mind, or level of Consciousness from zero to infinity. The level of 3 dimensional, physical, consciousness is indicated as being where we are now. The lower, horizontal axis shows the development of Will over time, which has 4 stages of development. The main curved line of the graph left to right shows the path of the "Divine Plan" where we begin at a level of infinite consciousness and no Will, and gradually descend into lower states of consciousness but with increasing Will. The line reaches 3 dimensional consciousness at Stage 4 Will. Having achieved that state it continues to show that we were expected to advance again into increasing levels of consciousness, now with Will fully developed.

THE FALL

The graph shows that, at some time in the past, from Zero Will we almost achieved Will Level 1. At that stage, instead of developing further, we "fell" into 3 dimensional consciousness, also, at the same time, losing our consciousness of the Plan. On the chart that event is indicated by the arrow descending to the "Present Position" at 3D consciousness and some Will. Not quite level 1 on the Path, but better than Zero.

I have added a circle to the chart at that stage indicating what is termed the "Personality Wheel". The description of the Personality Wheel is remarkably similar to that of a Birth Chart. The situation we are in is not static. The circle is not wholly accurate in dimensions because, at times during the day or night, we might briefly reach higher or lower levels of consciousness, or even Stage 4 Will. I have come across people in life who clearly have a higher development of Will but whose consciousness is firmly at the 3D level. The point and the circle in the chart indicate our normal state based upon our HABIT PATTERNS. One of Edgar Cayce's fundamental principles is that our repetitive mental habit patterns prevent us moving forward on the path. This is clearly correct. Indian sages give the picture of life as a Wheel turning (Tarot Wheel of Fortune). Habit. Routine. Occasionally the wheel hits a "bump in the road", a problem to solve, where we are temporarily forced to expand our realm of consciousness and/or use a higher level of will. The normal reaction is to either try to ignore it, or sort the problem out as quickly as possible and return to our former routine.

STAGES OF WILL

Will Stage 1 – ZERO WILL

It is difficult to define exactly what Will is. In my case I can simply relate it to Self-Discipline - it is, however, related to some form of task, such as we perform on behalf of the whole, or in self-development. Zero Will is probable best described in terms of comparison with the other stages. There is the tendency in spiritual writings to condemn us humans for the state we are in - as if God is omnipotent and is unable to make mistakes. Such an attitude is displayed by human representations of "godlike" figures in history, such as the Caesars, and Adolph Hitler, who identified themselves as "gods" (psychological inflation) - who we cannot entirely blame because the people they controlled reinforced their illusion. On the other hand, it does seem that they were not entirely wrong in that we are all supposed to be "gods in the making". From our model it is clear that Mind and Will are inseparable. Can we be blamed if being forced to more limited levels of consciousness (when, by definition, we had no Will and therefore no choice in the matter) that we lost sight of The Path?

Suffice to say that at our "Zero Will Plus" level we generally are "asleep" to the higher levels of consciousness and live according to the "illusions" and habit patterns created by our minds. This seems to equate with my position when I am asleep, when the scenarios in my dreams are often so unusual that when I wake up I wonder why I had not noticed this fact at the time. On rare occasions when asleep I do notice, and realise that I am dreaming – which causes me to wake up to our conscious world.

Will Stage 2 – SKILFUL WILL – Inner and Outer Negotiation

At this stage we are more aware, and critical, of the ideas which come to mind. There is more introspection. Rather than simply living life as routine, or copying others, one is more aware of one's own inner needs (Cycle of Growth Stage 6 (Service to Self. Health). A problem then arises that, not only are those needs often outside the "box" of normal routine, by may very likely affect the "boxes" of others around. So the first reaction is to ignore them. Having noticed a need, we then have to decide if it is real, and, if so, when and how it can be satisfied. We see straight away that, to begin with, we are involved in a great mental effort (Tarot Card : Temperance which takes us to a level "above the opposites" so we can see both sides). Next, if we decide to proceed, we

THE PURPOSE OF LIFE

have to take it outside ourselves into the world. So I call this the stage of Inner and Outer Negotiation. Apart from listening to "Inner and Outer Voices" we need to negotiate in order to achieve our aim. So this does not happen all at once - at any stage we may decide the aim is not possible or not realistic. Interestingly, if we do give up, the desire or wish may be repeated until eventually "the crying baby gets attention". I add the warning here that if we do not negotiate properly with our inner self(s) we are likely to be prone to accidents or illness.

The important thing is that we need to at least be listening to our inner voices. It is only when they are ignored or suppressed that they begin to turn nasty – forcing attention, and mediation with hospitalisation or the help of a psychiatrist. I remember at the time I was beginning to explore Spiritualism in greater depth beginning to feel very apprehensive. I found myself explaining to myself (?), as to a child, that I would be taking things very slowly, and was not going to do anything rash – as I did so, the negative feeling disappeared.

Will Stage 3 – EMPOWERING WILL – Making decisions and actions based on real data

Until now the Mind has been the controlling force. We have taken the "line of least resistance" and "gone with the flow". However, our consciousness has increased to include awareness of our own, personal, inner world as well as beginning to notice inconsistencies in both it and the outer world. We also begin to recognise a growing sense of power to make decisions for our self. The inner voices are not always "right", the outer voices are not always right – for me. None of this is achieved overnight. We can see that not only is a lot of mental effort required, but we also need a great deal of practical, worldly, experience. To this end Success and failure are the same. To some degree we are helped by the increased rate of change in the world nowadays. We are continually forced to re-evaluate our lives and ideas in the light of new information and experience. That which stops growing simply dies. It is very much like exercising a muscle. For example, there is no such thing now as "a job for life".

Somewhere in all this is the willingness to make mistakes. However, the Scientific Method came to my aid here, when I became my own "experimenter" and my own "guinea pig". With this scientific, experimental, attitude THERE ARE NO MISTAKES – only steps toward greater knowledge and understanding. I have to say that as, time has gone by, the word "vindication" has figured more in my vocabulary, when I have made more and more decisions against seeming inner or outer opposition with satisfactory, often unexpected, results – for me.

I am learning to trust myself (ego ?) – and so are my inner "selves". I am "Captain of my Ship". Well, at least most of the time. This relates to the Transactional Analysis concept of becoming "jerk free". [PSYCHOLGY : DEVELOPMENT MODELS]

Will Stage 4 – REAL WILL – The Power of God

The next stage requires surrender of will to transpersonal forces, or God. Early in life (as in the book of Genesis) we are led to believe that this is all we need to do. The attitude seems to be held by all forms of religion on the planet – usually with the priest or guru as the intermediary saying what that is. However, **we first need to have a Will or ego to be able give it up**. WE CANNOT BYPASS EARLIER STAGES OF DEVELOPMENT. The aim, then, is to ALIGN one's developed will with that of God – or, in Jungian terms, The Self – or The Cycle of Growth.

I have not reached this stage yet, however there have been brief moments when some sort of "magic" seems to be working. Like when I walked away from a car crash with just a bruised arm. The car overturned and was written off. We need to fully realise that we can be working at all the levels of Will at the same time. 4th. Level will means, simply, that we accept the leadership of God and whatever duty is imposed, as did Jesus. I realise that throughout my life I have always carried out such Duty to the best of my ability– although God has had "deputies" disguised as my bosses at work. I have had some strange experiences here. For example, at one time after a takeover, I did not yet have a "proper job" and was given investigative tasks to do. At one time I had to interview several people at an external site and could not make appointments because the time involved with each would be small. To my surprise as I finished with one, another became available until I was left at lunch time with one more to see. Even more surprise when that person was delayed going to lunch and willing to see me for the few minutes it took.

I have always held the belief that if God wanted me to do something he would materialise the task for me to perform. Just as any other "employer" he would want to see a good Curriculum Vitae.

In my experience, a key factor is the need to "test the spirits".

> *1 John:4:1: Beloved, believe not every spirit, but try the spirits whether they are of God: because many false prophets are gone out into the world. [KJV]

THE PURPOSE OF LIFE

In reading the biblical records of Jesus' healings we note that, at one stage, he was asked about healing and his reply suggested that a man blind from birth was in that state so that Jesus could eventually heal him. John Chapter 9 [KJV] says :-

Verse 1: And as Jesus passed by, he saw a man which was blind from his birth.

Verse 2: And his disciples asked him, saying, Master, who did sin, this man, or his parents, that he was born blind?

Verse 3: Jesus answered, Neither hath this man sinned, nor his parents: but that the works of God should be made manifest in him.

Verse 4: I must work the works of him that sent me, while it is day: the night cometh, when no man can work.

Verse 5: As long as I am in the world, I am the light of the world.

We note the esoteric meaning where "light" and "blind" relate to Consciousness.

Jesus was also being given evidence of his good relationship with "the spirits".

Edgar Cayce was in a similar position. He was very troubled when he began giving information about Reincarnation, having been brought up as a traditional Christian. He decided to continue in the light of the accuracy of the other information he was given.

We now return to The Cycle of Growth. No matter how omnipotent God is, he is still apparently subject to the laws of time and space. Here is a verse about the time when Jesus was reluctantly persuaded to turn water into wine (well, we all have to do what mum says. Even God must know that.) :-

John Chapter 2: Verse4: Jesus saith unto her, Woman, what have I to do with thee? mine hour is not yet come.[KJV]

RETURNING TO THE PATH

Looking at the model of the planned path there is a suggestion of 4 ways of returning to the plan.

A. Psychic Development by use of drugs. Although there would be heightened consciousness the method would require returning to an earlier stage of one's evolution with zero will development, so there would be no possibility of control. Although no drugs were involved, this seems to relate to my brief "peak experience". A problem with drug users is loss of Will. They lose control of the habit.

B. Mental development with no change in Will– such as by taking some form of "mind development" or psychic development training. Although it seems possible to return to the path, and the exercise would allow some development of will, it is still a backward step – perhaps to that of a state might be hundreds of years in the past. A suggestion is to Atlantean or early Egyptian times. Another problem is that it is likely to reinforce the existing Mind set, making it harder to release from it at the appropriate time. Again, this seems to relate to my 'peak experience' mentioned in the [MY STORY] chapter where the contact, or 'spirit guide', was Chinese.

C. Development of Will and higher states of mind together using dream analysis, meditation, self-study and physical attunement (etc.). The problem with this method is that one continues the path on the 3D level and loses the sense of contact and guidance from an enhanced level of consciousness. This seems to relate to my experience. My peak experience led me to explore a whole new area of life – especially with Meditation, Psychology, Astrology and The Tarot. If I had not had not had that I may have given up and returned to "normal life". I guess that Psychoanalysis would fit into this category too.

D. Development of Will with no development of consciousness. This, would seem the most difficult method from having no sense of guidance, and seems to relate to Eastern methods requiring a guru or teacher.

Now seems to be a good time to mention that Eastern spiritual methods are usually (not always) not good for Westerners. In my early development years I got to know an English couple who were both Yoga teachers – in fact, I attended one of their residential courses. The husband went to India with the intention of spending some time being taught by a guru. In the event he contracted dysentery and spent the whole time in hospital (Cycle of Growth Stage 12. Withdrawal. Meditation. Waiting rebirth). When he returned he said that the experience taught him that such travel is not necessary. He was in the right place.

THE PURPOSE OF LIFE

At that time I was exploring the various areas of study mentioned in the [MY STORY] chapter and it amused me that, while I was living in London with everything I needed close by, at various places I went to there were people who had travelled from all over the world just to be there.

In my philosophy, we are exactly where we are supposed to be at any time. Life will bring to us the experiences we need for our growth. It does require that we remain alert to such opportunities.

YOUR LIFE PURPOSE – AN EXERCISE

Although this fits into this chapter, you may prefer to leave the exercise until you have read the Astrology chapters.

Here is the opportunity to do a very basic Birth Chart Analysis for yourself and friends. Because it is simplicity and focus it could be more valuable than a complete interpretation. It does, however, require a bit more information. Now, with the Internet, it is possible to get a more accurate Birth Chart. You will need to find out your Moon Sign and House position, your Sun Sign and House position, and the position of the ruling planet of your Sun Sign by Sign and House.

1. The basic principle is that we have come to this Earth level to learn one of 12 lessons which are concerned with handling different forms of energy as symbolised by our Sun Sign and position. Earth is a "school".
2. The Moon position shows what we have already developed from the past – contained in our subconscious.
3. It is possible to go a step further than the usual simple Star Sign descriptions by examining the placing of the Sun in our Birth Chart by Sign and House, and also the placing of the natural planet ruler of that Sign by Sign and House.
4. The position of the ruling planet may be helpful or challenging to the Sun lesson. Our life task may include the need to find an area of life where both can work harmoniously. Where there is dual rulership of a Sign you will need to decide which is more appropriate – probably either one at different times.
5. In the case of a Leo Sun position, as The Sun rules Leo we can only observe its position by House at this level of interpretation.
6. Our Birth Chart does not control our life. It is an indicator of our position at the time of birth. Everything is subject to Will.

METHOD

1. Obtain a personal Birth Chart. There are various sources of obtaining a chart on the Internet. You will need to supply the Date, Time, and Place of birth. The more accurate the time is known, the better. It would need to be correct within 1 to 2 hours to get accurate House positions due to the 24 hour rotation of the Earth – otherwise use Sunrise or Noon and ignore House positions.
2. There are 2 software recommendations in [BIBLIOGRAPHY].
3. Timing is a bit complicated because it needs conversion to Greenwich Mean Time and there may need to be an additional allowance for Daylight Saving Time (British Summer Time). The software should have facility to enter Place of Birth to enable this. As a rough check, the Sun Position will be at 1st. House cusp at sunrise, 10th. House cusp at Noon, 7th. House cusp around Sunset ("Evening"), and 4th. House Cusp around Midnight.
4. Take a sheet of paper and divide it into sections as the sample for Lady Diana.
5. Add the Moon and Sun Sign & House details from your Birth Chart.
6. Refer to the table below and add appropriate information to your sheet.
7. Make up 3 sentences as the samples, using your data.
8. Do not expect immediate results. We often have to give time for our subconscious to process the information, especially for a new subject. You may be prompted to look up information in this or other books. "Sleep on it". Keep picking up your sheet and read it at odd times.
9. Expect to get some help from the Unconscious.
10. There is no need to go into too much detail. This would require an analysis of the other planet positions and their aspects.

THE PURPOSE OF LIFE

DIANA SPENCER'S LIFE PURPOSE

MOON POSITION (THE PAST)

	MOON SIGN	
	Moon Trait	Moon Sign
☾	Original and Unconventional	Aquarius

	MOON HOUSE	
House	Area	Lesson
2	Personal Resources and Possessions	Practical Management, Organisation and Routine

I am a [Moon Trait] [Moon Sign] with ability to handle [House Area] by using [House Lesson] - and am learning lessons about [Sun Lesson] in the area of [Sun House Area].

SUN POSITION (THE FUTURE)

	SUN SIGN			
	Sign	Lesson	Life Task	Negative
☉	Cancer	Motherhood	Building a secure 'shell' for Myself and Family	Fear of Society, Secret worries and over sympathy.

	SUN HOUSE		
House	Area	Lesson	
7	Close Partnerships	Finding Inner Balance and Peace	

My Life Task is [Sun Lesson] by [Sun Life Task] in the area of [Sun House Area] and [Sun House Lesson] - whilst avoiding [Sun Negative]

RULING PLANET OF SUN SIGN

	RULING PLANET SIGN			
	Planet Sign	Lesson	Life Task	Negative
☾ Moon	Aquarius	Becoming an Individual	Inventing New Ways and Methods	Destructiveness Without Creativeness.

	RULING PLANET HOUSE		
House	Area	Lesson	
2	Personal Resources and Possessions	Practical Management, Organisation and Routine	

My Life Task will be affected by the need for [Planet Lesson] and [Planet Life Task] in the area of [Planet Area] and [Planet Lesson] - whilst avoiding [Planet Sign Negative].

☾	I am a [Original and Unconventional][Aquarius] with ability to handle [Personal Resources and Possessions] in the area of [Practical Management, Organisation and Routine] and am learning lessons about [Building a secure 'shell' for Myself and Family]- in the area of [Close Partnerships].
☉	My Life Task is to learn about [Motherhood] by [building a secure 'shell' for Myself and Family] - in the area of [Close Partnerships] and [Finding Inner Balance and Peace] - whilst avoiding [Fear of Society, Secret worries and over sympathy].
Sun Sign Ruler	My Life Task will be affected by learning about [Becoming an Individual] and [Inventing New Ways and Methods] - in the area of [Close Partnerships] and [Finding Inner Balance and Peace] - whilst avoiding [Destructiveness Without Creativeness].

Figure 3 : Diana's Personal Life Purpose Table

THE PURPOSE OF LIFE

YOUR LIFE PURPOSE TABLE

DISCOVERING ONE'S LIFE PURPOSE THROUGH ASTROLOGY

Octave	COG Stage and House	Zodiac Sign	Ruling Planet	Moon Sign (The Past)	Sun Sign Lesson (The Future)	Sun Lesson Activity	Negative Tendency	HOUSE (Area of Life)	Cycle of Growth Stage	Element and Jungian Function
1 Gestation (Transcendence)	12	Pisces	♆ Neptune	Compassionate and Understanding	withdrawal and meditation	Freeing from the Past by Forgiving Self and Others	Unrealistic Fantasy and 'Drugs². Over-sympathy.	Social Service and Karma	Withdrawal. Confinement. Karma	Water (Feeling)
	11	Aquarius	♅ Uranus	Original and Unconventional	Becoming an Individual	Inventing New Ways and Methods	Destructiveness Without Creativeness.	Unconventional Friends and Science	Discontent. Individuation	Air (Thinking)
	10	Capricorn	♄ Saturn	Ambitious	Perseverance and Focus	Making and achieving long range plans	Ruthless Ambition.	Social Status	Peak. Harvest	Earth (Sensation)
	9	Sagittarius	♃ Jupiter	Inspiring, Freedom Loving	Mind Broadening Experiences	Searching for truth and Asking "Why?"	Restless search without a foundation and lack of focus.	Social Mental Concepts and Academic Study	Conception	Fire (Intuition)
2 Abstract	1	Aries	♂ Mars	Pioneering and Independant	Leadership by example	Exploring new areas of life	Aggression and Impatience.	Self Projection and Leadership	Seed	Fire (Intuition)
	2	Taurus	♀ Venus	Versatile, Controlled	Practical Management, Organisation and Routine	Patience and Self Control	Fear of Change and Obstructiveness.	Personal Resources and Possessions	Germination	Earth (Sensation)
	3 Personality	Gemini	☿ Mercury	Versatile, Thinking	Experiment and Communication	Cross-pollination of ideas and Mental Concentration	Lack of Practical Mental Focus and Inconsistency.	Personal Mental Concepts and Ideas	Experiment. Communication	Air (Thinking)
	4 Childhood	Cancer	☽ Moon	Sensitive, Caring	Motherhood	Building a secure 'shell' for Myself and Family	Fear of Society, Secret worries and over sympathy.	Personal Security	Transplanting. Persona	Water (Feeling)
3 Psychological	5	Leo	☉ Sun	Confident and Powerful	Fatherhood (Parental control of the weak)	the Wise use of Power and ability to share it	Dictatorship and Fixed Opinions.	Personal Creativity and Children	Power. Creativity	Fire (Intuition)
	6 Individuality	Virgo	☿ Mercury	Analytical and Thorough	Craftsmanship and Self Development	Maintaining a Healthy Mind and Body	Worry Over Trifles. Intolerance. Hypercriticism.	Personal Service and Health	Service to Self. Personal Identity	Earth (Sensation)
	7 Adulthood	Libra	♀ Venus	Balanced, Diplomatic	Finding Inner Balance and Peace	Diplomacy, "Resolution of Opposites"	Being Untrue to Myself and Indecisiveness.	Close Partnerships	Partnerships	Air (Thinking)
	8 Practical	Scorpio	♇ Pluto	Resourceful and Secretive	Death and Rebirth (Metamorphosis)	Exploring the Secrets of Life	Secret Manipulation.	The Secrets of Life	Death. Intercourse	Water (Feeling)

Figure 4 : Life Purpose Table

THE PURPOSE OF LIFE

LADY DIANA SPENCER LIFE PURPOSE

Please see a different form of analysis of Diana's Birth Chart in the chapter [ASTROLOGY : BIRTH CHART EXAMPLES].

We note that this method gives a slightly different viewpoint to what we might expect – bearing in mind that we are never fully aware of what happens in the private lives of other people.

We see an extra emphasis on Diana's Moon as ruler of her Sun Sign. We note her much publicised relationships, and that at the end of her life she was involved in helping children- especially those injured by bombs in Bosnia, and associated with Mother Theresa who encouraged her to support family planning there – thus expanding the concept of Motherhood.

THE PAST : MOON SIGN (Aquarius) – MOON HOUSE (2ND.)

I am an **Original and Unconventional Aquarius** with ability to handle **Personal Resources and Possessions** by **Practical Management, Organisation and Routine** and am learning lessons about **Motherhood** in the area of **Close Partnerships**.

THE FUTURE : SUN SIGN (Cancer) – SUN HOUSE (7TH.)

My Life Task is **Motherhood** by **Building a secure 'shell' for Myself and Family** in the area of **Close Partnerships** and **Finding Inner Balance and Peace** - whilst avoiding **Fear of Society, Secret worries and over sympathy**.

PLANET RULER of Cancer (The Moon) – SIGN (Aquarius). HOUSE (2ND.)

You will note the slightly different interpretation of the same planet position as a result of the duplication.

My Life Task will be affected by the need to **Become an Individual** and **Inventing New Ways and Methods** in the area of **Personal Resources and Possessions** and **Practical Management, Organisation and Routine** - whilst avoiding **Destructiveness Without Creativeness**.

SIGMUND FREUD LIFE PURPOSE *"Father of Psychoanalysis"*

This example, and that of C.G.Jung refer to Birth Charts in [ASTROLOGY : SYNASTRY] where there is more detail. We see their focus on Close Partnerships – which is what Psychoanalysis basically involves. Both had a strong Uranus conjunction with their Sun which relates to Original and Unconventional Aquarius – which shows a limitation of this method, and how it could be extended.

THE PAST : MOON SIGN (Gemini). MOON HOUSE (7TH.)

I am a Versatile, Thinking, Gemini with ability to handle Close Partnerships by Finding Inner Balance and Peace and am learning lessons about Practical Management, Organisation and Routine in the area of Close Partnerships.

THE FUTURE : SUN SIGN (Taurus) – SUN HOUSE (7TH.)

My Life Task is Practical Management, Organisation and Routine by Patience and Self Control in the area of Close Partnerships and Finding Inner Balance and Peace - whilst avoiding Fear of Change and Obstructiveness.

PLANET RULER of Taurus (Venus) – SIGN (Cancer). HOUSE (6th.)

My Life Task will be affected by the need for Motherhood and Building a secure 'shell' for Myself and Family in the area of Personal Support and Health and Craftsmanship and Self Development - whilst avoiding Fear of Society, Secret worries and over sympathy.

Although his title includes "Father" we could perhaps see him in the role of "Nurturing Parent" which has more feminine connotations.

C. G. JUNG LIFE PURPOSE *"Discoverer of Individuation"*

We see a similar chart to Freud with Sun in 7th. House and focus on Gemini.

THE PURPOSE OF LIFE

THE PAST : MOON SIGN (Taurus). MOON HOUSE (3RD.)

I am an Organising and Controlled Taurus with ability to handle Personal Mental Concepts and Ideas by Experiment and Communication and am learning lessons about Fatherhood in the area of Close Partnerships.

Jung had a difficult early life with little close relationship with his parents. He had to take over the handling of family affairs at age 21 due to the death of his father, and incapability of his mother. His strong Saturn position is an indication of an "Absent Father", which usually means the individual has a poor role model, and has to therefore 'construct' their own version. There is a tendency to seek it outside one's self rather than inwardly. He treated Freud, 19 years older, as a "Father Figure" – and Freud regarded him as a son – until their acrimonious split due to disagreements about the basis of Psychology. Perhaps it was then that Jung finally "became of age".

THE FUTURE : SUN SIGN (Leo) – SUN HOUSE (7TH.)

As with Freud, the 7th. House is a weak position for the Sun. A strong Leo influence (with related planets in difficult aspect) often brings a focus on children – or those who allow themselves to be treated as such . Jung had 5 children. With difficult aspects they can be denied altogether, or bring other problems.

My Life Task is Fatherhood by Wise use of Power, and ability to share Power in the area of Close Partnerships and Finding Inner Balance and Peace - whilst avoiding Dictatorship and Fixed Opinions.

PLANET RULER (Sun – SIGN (Leo). HOUSE (7TH.)

As with Lady Diana, you will note the slightly different interpretation of the same planet position as a result of the duplication.

My Life Task will be affected by the need for Fatherhood and Wise use of Power and ability to share Power in the area of Close Partnerships and Finding Inner Balance and Peace - whilst avoiding Dictatorship and Fixed Opinions

THE PURPOSELESS LIFE

After considering [THE PURPOSE OF LIFE] we consider matters more related to The Cycle of Growth. Evolution depends on endless repetition of the same processes as well as requiring "mistakes" are made to ensure adaptation and development. It is not suggested that this is an alternative to "The Purpose of Life" in the sense of "Either – Or" of opposites. This is an additional process.

THE 'UNIVERSAL COMPUTER' AND CYCLES

Many years ago on television I saw part of a programme ("*Hitch Hiker's Guide to the Galaxy* "?) that had a scene where there were some "super-beings" that had explored the universe in its entirety and evolved to a state where they knew everything about it and had eliminated all diseases and crime, and lived a long life time with all their physical needs met by machines, but had still not answered the question "Why ?". So they decided to build a super computer to find the answer. (They would need to find something to do with all that spare time). As they did not know the answer they had to build in some kind of randomness. They had developed biological components that, although they eventually wore out, could replicate and even improve on the original design. The answer would take a long time to discover, so it would need some sort of long lived nuclear reactor to power it. They called this computer "Earth", the nuclear reactor "Sun". This is not all impossible science fiction. Research is already under way using biological components in computers, and also "Nanites" which are microscopic "machines" expected, among other things, to be injected into the human body to fight disease.

More realistically for now, my study of The Cycle of Growth has led me to consider it as a similar "computer model" of the way our universe operates. So let's take it a step further. In this chapter we look at the on-going life process in the light of some problem solving methods.

BASIC 'PROCESS MODELS'

We here have 3 process models.

1. The first shows a simple process that changes inputs to outputs. We could apply this to a factory that takes in raw materials and produces products for sale, or an animal feeding and producing waste products (and energy). In the case of the factory the internal process is visible. In many cases the actual process is hidden - we can only observe the inputs and outputs. The workings of the Brain and The Unconscious are an example. The tendency is to provide varied inputs and see what comes out at the other end.

2. The second model adds a Feedback Loop where some of the outputs are converted into inputs for the system. So the factory may begin to record production data or install quality control, and adjust the inputs to the process accordingly. A feeding animal decides when it has had enough to eat, or needs more. Our 5 senses and people around us provide feedback for our actions.

3. The astrological third example is more complicated. Not only is there processing of inputs to produce outputs at a personal level, as in the simple process, but the outputs (and actions) produce external reactions from the environment, which consists of such things as people and objects.

A further complication with The Cycle of Growth is that the period of time between an input and output (sowing and reaping) varies depending on what we are referring to. i.e. the length of the cycle. For example, the natural cycle of a year, or that of a whole lifetime. It does, however, divide the process into stages.

1. BASIC MODEL OF ANY PROCESS

2. SOME OF THE OUTPUTS USED AS INPUTS

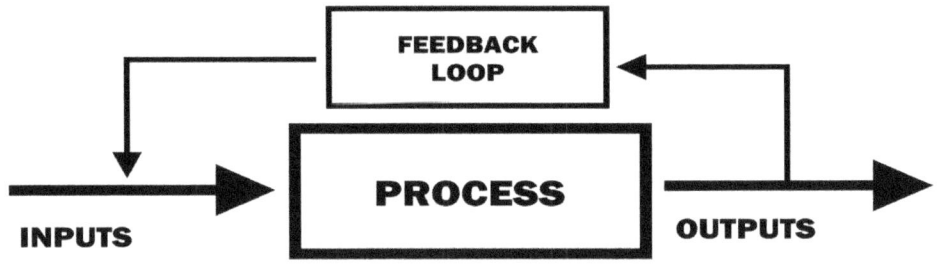

Figure 5 : Basic process models

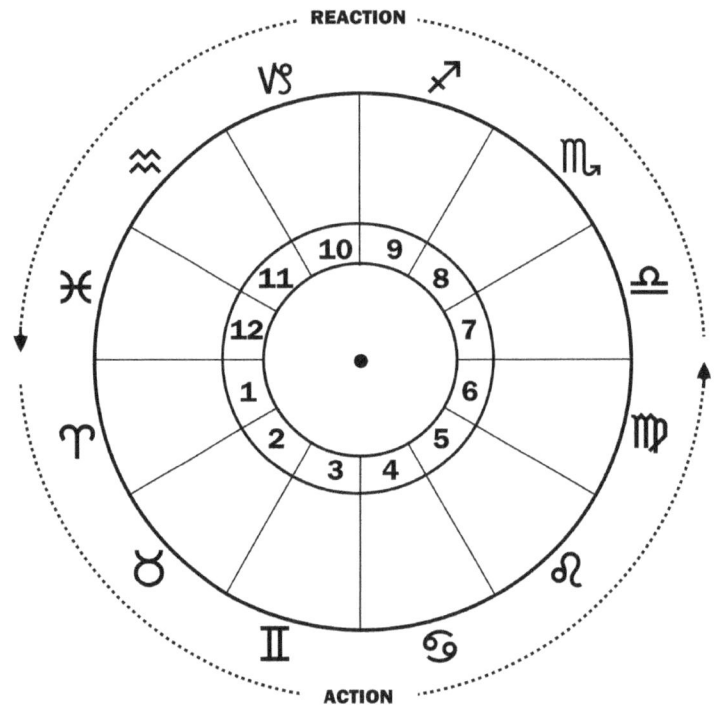

Figure 6 : Astrology process model

ARIADNE'S THREAD AND TRIAL AND ERROR

In Greek mythology Ariadne fell in love with Theseus and decided to help him with his mission to enter a labyrinth, or maze, to destroy the Minotaur, a creature with the body of a man and head of a bull, that lived there. He wanted to stop the sacrifice of young men and maidens that were regularly required. To navigate the maze she gave him a thread to unwind as he explored. If his progress was blocked he could rewind the thread to go back to a suitable place and try another passage. He was able to kill the Minotaur and escape the maze.

The myth is applied to methods of problem solving. For example, I wrote a computer programme to solve Sudoku puzzles, part of which tries possible numbers until it reaches one that gives an error, when it goes back to the last correct position to try another number. The method includes Trial and Error because it has a known solution. The method can also be used on problems where it is not known if there is a possible solution.

*"When you have eliminated the impossible, whatever remains, however improbable, must be the truth". [Sir Arthur Conan Doyle- Sherlock Holmes]

*Faith is continuing to discard the absurd, even in the face of the unknown.[Anon]

ALGORITHMS

In Mathematics an algorithm is a method of using a series of simple steps to solve a complex problem. The Arithmetic long division method is an example. This is also applied to computer programmes that do a similar job. A computer is very good at doing things that require repetition of clearly defined rules. Although we can include Ariadne under this heading, the term 'algorithm' tends to apply to a process where the steps and goal are more clearly defined so there is no need to "go backwards". It works in straight lines rather than cycles, unless it involves repetition of the same task.

A COMPUTER ALGORITHM "EVOLUTION"

Because computers are good at carrying out repetitive processes very fast there is a large number of programmes that combine algorithm rules and graphics. This example is an oddity because it starts out in a seemingly random fashion but after 10,500 steps begins to progress in an entirely orderly manner ad infinitum. Until it does so, it does not go outside a self-limited boundary. We see a few simple rules producing a very complex structure.

THE RULES

We begin with a "limitless" grid of White squares and fill it by using the following rules :-
1. The first move is on to any square.
2. If the square is White (which, to begin with, it must be) colour the square Black and move to the square on the right.
3. If the square is Black, colour the square White and move to the square on the left.
4. Continue from 2.

Here is a diagram showing the first 8 moves. The first 4 moves are to White squares so the movement continues to the right. On move 5 it arrives back at the original Black square, which now becomes White, and forces a left turn. It is then on White squares again, so the movement continues to the right.

THE PURPOSELESS LIFE

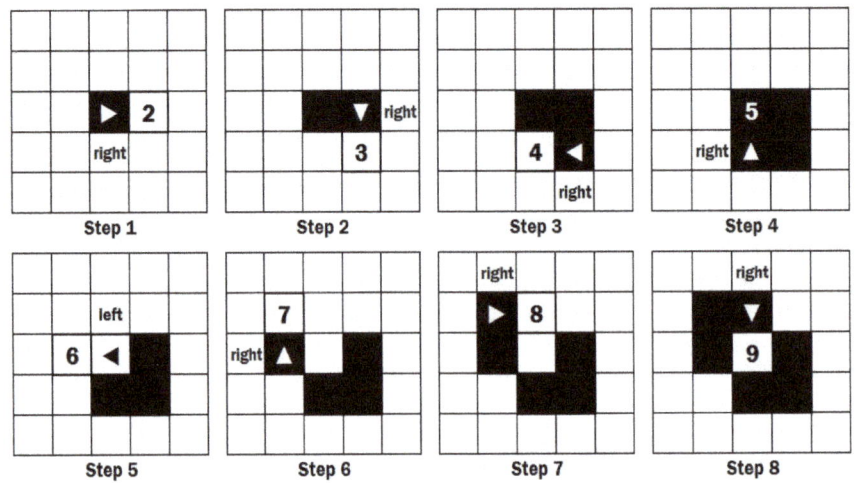

Figure 7 : Computer algorithm first 8 steps

Below is the result after 11,700 steps. The extension continues in the direction of the arrow ad infinitum. The yellow squares are to show the original starting square at the centre. We can see that the progress is outward from the original square as a "centre". It actually returns to that square and 2 others nearby 28 times. The maximum number of "visits" are 33 times to the single Step 2 square on its right, and 32 times to the 3rd. square above that.

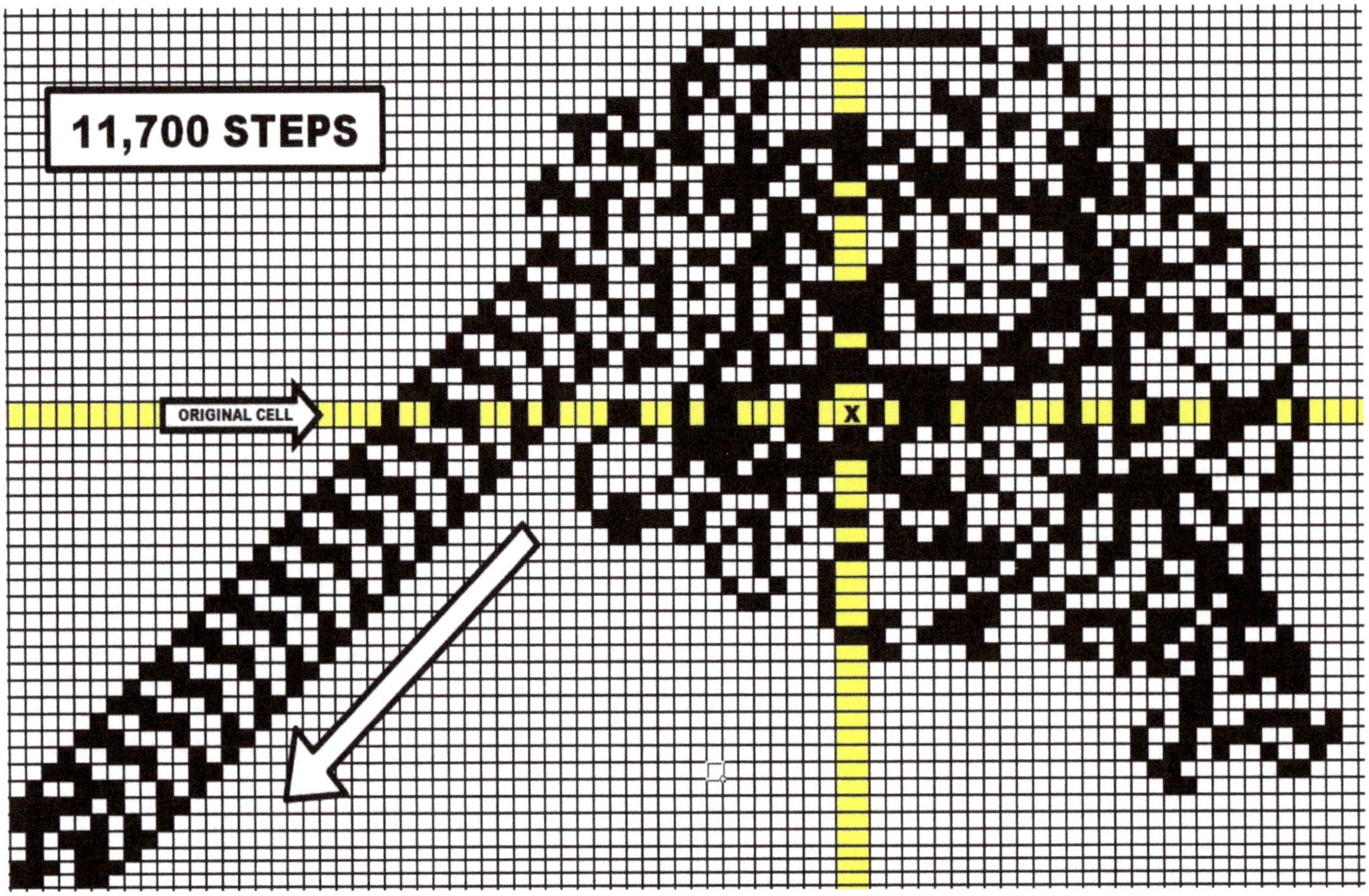

Figure 8 : Computer algorithm result

THE CYCLE OF GROWTH ALGORITHM

With The Cycle of Growth we have a basic process that applies to life as a whole. We can observe its effects in the internal and external worlds. The repetition of a few simple rules. The problem is that it is mainly unconscious. For example, a daily cycle starts when we get up in the morning and ends when we go to sleep at night. A return to our unconscious source. A life cycle starts with birth and ends at death – a return to our unconscious source. It is also a fractal because each small part of the "picture" (day) is an image of the year, as well as the whole lifetime. Wheels within wheels.

To summarise, it seems to me that the Purpose of Life, rather than having some set goal, is to experiment and learn. We all seem to be part of some great computer game, and have an infinity of time.

FRACTALS AND NATURE – WHEELS WITHIN WHEELS

The Fractal is based on the repetition of some simple "rule". When we observe Nature closely we can see that it is extremely efficient. It uses processes that repeat over and over again. A fractal is a complex geometric shape that, when magnified, will show the same shape or structure as the whole. Fractals can appear in nature, such as in the formation of a tree or snowflake (although no tree or snowflake is exactly the same as another), or from a repeated mathematical formula producing a computer graphic. Another example is how living things on this planet have evolved from the repetitive copying of DNA.

The picture below is of a leaf in which the same pattern is repeated in the parts that make the whole, as well as the whole itself.

Figure 9 : Fern Leaf dissection. An example of results of a fractal rule

THE PURPOSELESS LIFE

EVOLUTION AND DNA

Around 3,700 million years ago microscopic life evolved in the form of simple single-celled bacteria with no nucleus. This corresponded with the formation of the first super-continent or "island" on earth which was otherwise covered in water.

> *At around the same time about 27 percent of all gene families that exist today were born between 3.3 and 2.8 billion years ago .*
>
> [Science News. http://www.wired.com/wiredscience/2010/12/dna-life-fossils/]

Its prime objective was to reproduce itself. It learned to do this by cell division. It split into two identical parts, which grew and in turn split again, and so the process continued. It could have continued unchecked to completely cover the Earth but was limited by the availability of food and adverse environmental conditions. Bacteria are still doing a similar job to what it did then. We would not be able to live without them. For example, they are still turning nitrogen in the atmosphere into nitrates in the soil [APPENDIX : NITROGEN CYCLE], which in turn drives photosynthesis in plants and the Carbon Cycle and Oxygen Cycle involved in the production of the oxygen we breathe. When living things die, other bacteria convert them back to nitrates for the plants to feed on. Our human body is host to various forms of bacteria called "normal flora" that perform various functions. There are also Denitrifying Bacteria that further break down some of the nitrates into simpler chemicals and nitrogen gas, which is returned to the atmosphere. Wheels within wheels.

At around 600 million years ago some of the cells learned to stick together and by so doing were able to exploit alternative environments and food sources where there would, for a time, be less competition. They formed colonies for protection. From there cells began to differentiate to be able to perform different functions on behalf of the whole organism. As time went on more complex organisms evolved, until 2 million years ago a more human species arrived which finally evolved into the Homo Sapiens species (the genetic family root of you and me) a mere 200,000 years ago in Africa. Being on the equator living conditions were more suitable for human life, most of the rest of the world being covered in desert or ice.

We have to note the archetypal similarity between the early formation of cell communities, which allowed later differentiation of function on behalf of the whole, to that of the formation of human communities and civilisations starting with Hunter Gatherers settling down in suitable places.

DNA

DeoxyriboNucleic Acid is a chemical carrying coded instructions that is contained in, and controls the activities of, living cells. Its function is like that of a repeating computer programme or algorithm. It exists in long strands called genes, in turn the genes make up chromosomes. The main function of DNA in life is to replicate – that is, reproduce by making copies of itself. It does this by splitting the strand into 2 parts each of which forms a matrix to regenerate the "missing" half of the strand. The process can be likened to hundreds of typists all copying the same document over and over again.

The diagram below shows how a strand of DNA reproduces itself. In reality it is much longer than shown. The ability to form long strands enables a greater number of variations in sequences of its components, and therefore greater diversity of function.

The DNA process then enables single cells to divide into two identical replicas of the original cell each with its own set of chromosomes. Those cells then grow and divide, and so on. For example, at the time of conception a single cell is formed which begins to divide, so there are, in turn, 2, 4, 8, 16, 32, 64 cells – and so on.

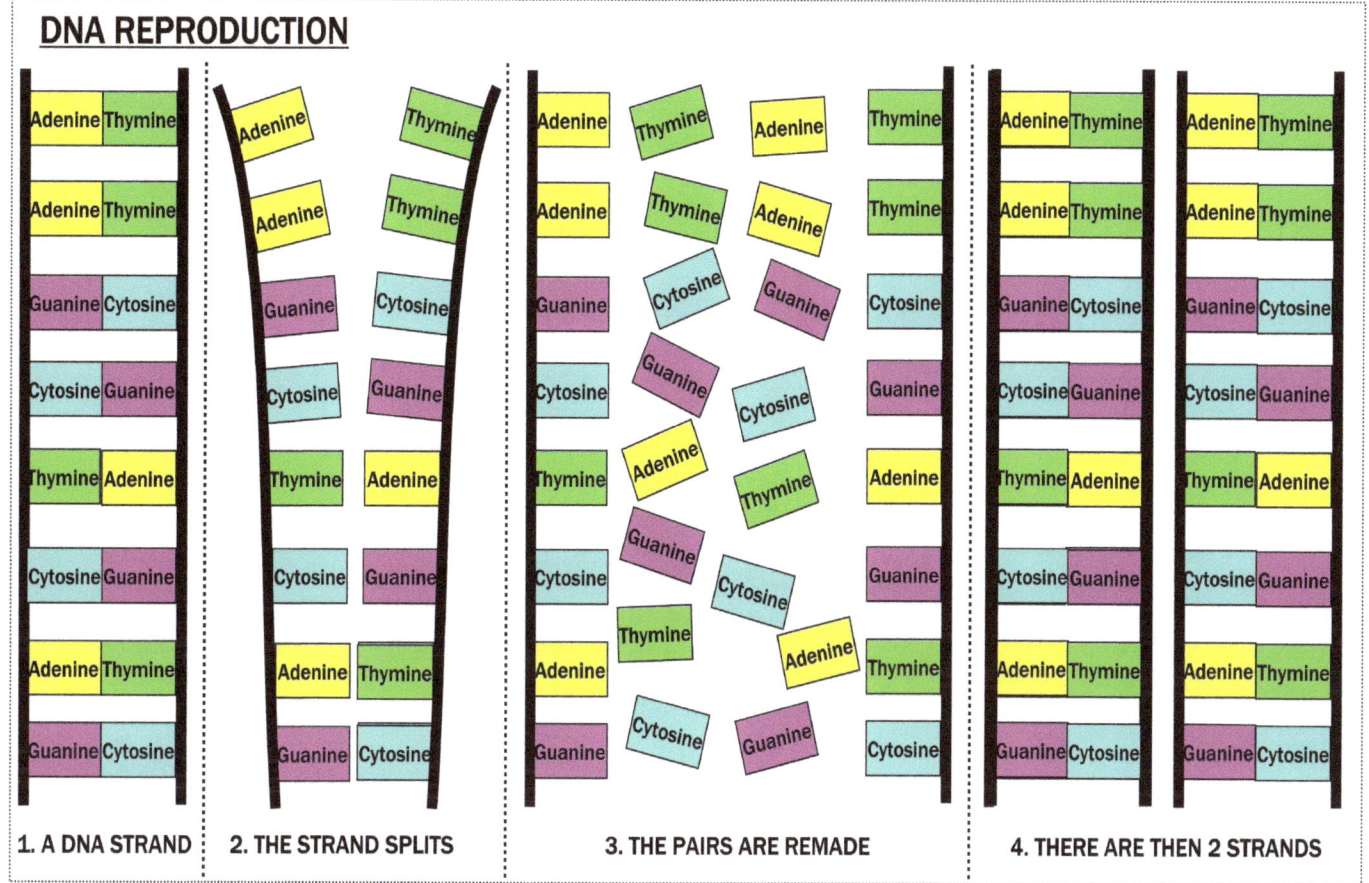

Figure 10 : DNA Strand Reproduction

DNA MUTATION and DIVERSITY

The story of the evolution of every living thing is the story of DNA. Human DNA is about 50% the same as a banana, and 99% the same as a chimpanzee. That leaves about 1% to make us human and .001% that makes us different humans. It means that something must have happened to DNA since it first appeared in bacteria – which was the first life form to evolve, and still exists today, somewhere, in almost the same form.

Originally all DNA was the same, existing in some kind of single cell organism such as algae or bacteria that lived in water. It is stated that sometimes something goes wrong with the DNA copying process and a 'mistake' is made. A copy differs from the original in some small way. A "word" in the "document" is "spelled" wrongly. We must, however, note that these "mistakes" occur on a fairly regular timescale – around every 10,000 years – and regularly enough that scientists can confidently calculate when the changes occurred in our history. This suggests that there are natural laws that are not yet fully understood.

The cells containing the different DNA grow differently to the original cells because the instructions are different, and continue to replicate the different DNA. This is called a Mutation. Sometimes the difference is helpful to the survival of the organism, so the changed DNA lives on, sometimes it is not, when the changed DNA dies with its host organism. This is what Charles Darwin called "natural selection of species". Some call it "survival of the fittest".

There is a tendency to suggest that evolutionary developments came about with some purpose. For example, we could say that crabs developed shells to protect themselves. According to Charles Darwin this is not the case. He would say that at some stage in evolution there was a mutation whereby some creatures developed shells, and this gave them a better chance of survival than their ancestors without shells.

Despite DNA's seeming resistance to change in relying on reproducing the same material over and over again, Nature, which ultimately controls whether an organism lives or dies, seems to **favour** mutation, or changes in organisms. If this were not the case all living organisms would still be just microscopic blobs of jelly. Instead, over millions of years, millions of different species have evolved, many of which are now extinct. This is called Diversity. Over this period of time the climate and structure of Earth has changed dramatically numerous times.

THE PURPOSELESS LIFE

There have been huge events affecting the whole planet, such as meteorite explosions, volcanic eruptions and earthquakes. There has also been numerous ice ages. Those species unable to adapt have died out. At another level we have mutations such as those that allow an organism to live in different habitats or "eat" different foods to others, which means that there is less competition for space and food - until the organism has reproduced to a stage where it uses up the available resources, and, in effect limits itself. One example is the gradual mutations that enabled some sea creatures to eventually live on dry land for the first time. In some cases the competition eventually became so intense that they returned to the sea again.

MANKIND

Mankind may appear an exception to this rule, but there is growing evidence that we will multiply to such an extent that someday we will use up all of the resources of Earth. However, we do have something else that sets us apart from other animals, and that is "brain power". We seem to have the ability to "mutate" at a mental level with inventions, tools, and ideas. In fact, ideas, once conceived, seem to have a life of their own, spreading to all parts of the globe. This has led to another kind of evolution – that at a mental level, which operates at a faster speed than normal evolution– so the actual RATE of change is increasing. For example, 100 years ago many people could expect to be doing the same job for their whole lifetime. This is no longer the case. In my lifetime I have faced redundancy at work on numerous occasions – sometimes at around 6 monthly intervals. Sometimes having to re-apply for my own job. Apart from wilful job changes and promotions, 3 times I have had to find other employers, other times I was able to "mutate" and adapt my skills to new tasks, and learn new skills such as computer programming, or even change to a new "habitat" by moving house when the company I worked for was taken over and relocated ("follow the food supply"). Those people and animals nowadays that are unable to adapt ("mutate") and learn new things will find survival very difficult indeed – going the way of the dinosaur.

An important feature of DNA is that, as it has evolved, it has also developed a structure whereby different parts of the strand give rise to the different parts of the body – all appearing in the relative place. Scientists have done experiments with the DNA of fruit flies by moving parts of the DNA strand to another position in the strand which eventually produces abnormal flies that, for example, have parts of eyes growing on legs and wings.

ASTROLOGY

Apart from other things, the 12 sections of the wheel of an astrological chart also have correspondences with various parts of the body. The placing of planets in the wheel give indication of what health problems are likely. For example, I have 5 planets in the Sign of Gemini (Mutable Air) which, among other things, relates to breathing and lungs. At around the age of 5, for several years, I had breathing problems, including a collapsed lung. I have Mars in the Sign of Cancer which, among other things, is related to the stomach. I had a stomach ulcer around the age of 35. I do not think that the planet positions actually cause illness but rather define the "line of least resistance" for physical symptoms to manifest at times of stress. Since my mid-life crisis around 30 years ago I have not had to visit a doctor. Interestingly, I had a friend who was a researcher at a big London hospital who had no interest in occult subjects. He said several times that he was amazed by their receptionist who was able to state what was wrong with a patient by looking at their birth date on the entry forms.

My belief is that the overall structure itself did not evolve, and has always existed in a non-material form. An archetype in the Collective Unconscious that I am calling The Cycle of Growth. Another algorithm.

PSYCHOLOGY:DEVELOPMENT MODELS

I was drawn to study Psychology because I became aware of "odd things" about myself that seemed outside my control – such as dreaming and forgetting things and not being able to recall them. We also have "The Freudian Slip" when we say something we do not really mean. An example given is a church minister who by "mistake" began reading the funeral service instead of the marriage service. The suggestion being that he was revealing his true opinion of the match.

This chapter brings together development models of some areas of psychology for comparison.
It includes :-

1. *Freud's original ideas – with Maslow's development.*
2. *The Jungian model (Based on Individuation, which deliberately avoids stages)*
3. *Transactional Analysis – which uses different terminology, but looks very similar.*
4. *"The Growth of Personality" - a more modern concept based on the work of Erik Erikson combining the work of several psychologists, including Freud. This model divides personality development into stages related to the age ranges at which they occur. Because there is correspondence with the Astrological Logarithmic Timescale I just give an outline here, and consider the detail in the chapter [ASTROLOGY : LOGARITHMIC TIMESCALE].*

We also note the similarity between the Transactional Analysis development and Jungian Individuation model diagrams below with that of the Middle Pillar development of [THE KABBALAH TREE OF LIFE] which, in turn, refers to [THE LOGARITHMIC TIMESCALE].

There is more information about Freud and Jung, and their relationship with one another, in [ASTROLOGY : SYNASTRY] which compares their Birth Charts.

INDIVIDUAL GROWTH CRADLE TO GRAVE (and before)

CONCEPTION AND LIFE IN THE WOMB

In their book "The Secret Life of the Unborn Child" [SLUC] Dr. Thomas Verny and John Kelly give strong evidence that our life experiences begin at conception, and those in the womb are as important as those after physical birth. In some respects they can be considered more important because we are not consciously aware of them. Indeed, Nature seems to deliberately "erase" them from our then limited consciousness. At the time of birth the mother releases large quantities of the hormone Oxytocin which controls labour. This hormone has been found to produce amnesia in laboratory animals, so it clearly affects babies in a similar way. Indeed, some mothers have amnesia at this time as well. This occurs at the end of the 1st. Octave of The Logarithmic Timescale. There is suggestion that a similar wiping of childhood memories occurs at the end of the 2nd. Octave at Age 3.

GENERAL DEVELOPMENT FROM BIRTH

From birth onwards we tend towards a gradually widening viewpoint as our consciousness expands from mother, to family, and later a widening experience of society outside the home. At the beginning of life we develop according to the requirements of our parents and other authority figures. Certain energies we have are developed, and others are suppressed depending on what kind of behaviour is deemed appropriate. For example, the competitive nature of Mars is generally deemed appropriate, and encouraged, in men but not women, even though the planet has the same effect in any birth chart. Boys and girls are handled differently from birth ("Pink or Blue "). This is often described as the reaction between (inner) Nature and (outer) Nurture. However, a man and woman born at the same time and place will have identical Birth Charts and it is not possible to tell which is which.

Gradually life, and time, takes us away from our parents towards a more individual lifestyle. However, the basic pattern still tends to mimic theirs. Not too long ago it was usual for children to "follow in the footsteps" of their parents – even continuing the same daily occupations later on. Family surnames often emphasise this – for example Smith and Baker. Things have changed a lot nowadays, and there is now no such thing as "a job for life". People who rebel against their upbringing are not always as free from this effect as they think. By deliberately following a different lifestyle they are still governed by its influence because it determines what to rebel against. At another level it is very difficult to change our basic psychological nature - which psychologists tell us is well established by 6 years of age as a result of the relationship between personal traits (Birth Chart/Nature) and environmental influences (Planet Transits/Nurture).

MID LIFE CRISIS AGE 42

It is nowadays recognized that, for many people, a "Mid Life Crisis" occurs. The possible age range seems very variable with a focus on ages 35 to 50. I relate this to the mid "crisis" point of the Generic Uranus Cycle which occurs at age 42 (Uranus has a cycle of 84 years) and which I believe is connected with the Jungian process of Individuation. I can personally testify to having such an experience [MY STORY]. This relates to Cycle of Growth Stage 8 (Sex. Death), which includes symbolism of the "Death" card of the Tarot Major Arcana, and "Scorpio" in the Zodiac cycle. Many older people deny it occurred in their life. This could mean, of course, that this was not an issue for them. However, it generally means that they did not recognise it, or may have missed out a necessary stage in personal development. Although prompted to change they are still acting according to the programming of their early life experience.

This crisis is an intensely personal experience when the individual begins to feel an inner discontent despite the fact that, to all intents and purposes, the exterior life may be going well and receiving social approval. Actual changes to the lifestyle may not occur until triggered by some external event. Such events are - death of a parent, breakdown of a relationship (or, more specifically, an attraction to another partner), growth of children beyond the need for parental care, or other forms of 'redundancy', especially that of facing the now closer reality of one's own death. A physical or mental illness is another common trigger that forces attention to one's personal needs. If existing partnerships cannot adapt to the new goals, one way or another they are severed.

The Mid Life Crisis is generally a modern event. Until recently people did not live much beyond the age of 40. Even today the effects of 'old age' are felt at this time. Physical decline is more apparent, especially in such areas as sport - where athletes become unable to compete with those younger than themselves, and women come to the end of childbearing years. This can result in attempts to recover past youth by seeking new partnerships, have more children ("last chance"), moving house - or "making a comeback" – starting again rather than face the uncertainty of an unknown future. If this is the case it is futile because it merely postpones the event to a later stage of life. At such a time one may be less able to cope with it. Indeed, as in my case, it can lead to symptoms of ill health which, if the true cause is not realised, can result in physical death. Another factor to be taken into account is that of society in general which has still not come to terms with "life beyond 40" - the daily publicity which we are faced with tending to glorify youth over old age - such as a huge cosmetic industry geared to making us look younger (and "more attractive"). Some go so far as to have plastic surgery.

Although it is not fully clear what is happening at this time, it seems that, psychologically, the previously suppressed or ignored parts of our individual character are now coming forward to be recognized and put to use. With the decline in our physical state we need to be able to have full use of all our resources – not just the ones that have enabled our survival so far - especially the ones that involve development of the Mind. Previously held attitudes and beliefs are challenged with the need to consider opposing arguments. The firmer these beliefs, the more difficult the process. This is a time requiring a reappraisal of all one has experienced in the past so that one can go forward using all one's faculties rather than having to waste energy fighting one's true self. As we get older it becomes more apparent that each one of us is ultimately alone. The psychologist C. G. Jung called this process, which lasts whole lifetime, "Individuation". It contains the strange paradox that as we become more of an individual we grow into a wider perspective and experience of life.

A main area of study of this process is Psychology. A difficulty with Psychology is that there is a tendency to spend time considering problems rather than healthy solutions. The symptoms are seen as a disruption to life with an attempt to return to an earlier state, rather than a step forward in growth. This attitude is largely supported by the advertising and drug industries, who fund the research which supports their products. With society in general, there is little consideration of the future and what goals might be in later life, beyond retirement. This attitude is being forced to change as a result of people living longer. We are also having to overcome our natural ignorance. Thanks to the work of C.G. Jung and other psychologists we are beginning to think of Life Goals in terms of Birth to Death - which might be in terms of personal or social achievement, but also related to some sort of personal development. Natal Astrology has held this viewpoint for some years, although nowadays its users are beginning to consider possible achievements beyond those of physical survival and reproduction – a result of, for example, not having to grow our own food. Most minds nowadays are capable of perceiving time spans beyond 12 months, even to the length of a lifetime. Gradually we are even becoming forced to look beyond that.

PSYCHOLOGY : DEVELOPMENT MODELS

LIFE BEYOND 40

After mid-life, physical decline continues. However, the rate that this occurs varies enormously depending on the individual. Much depends upon one's attitude and practical observance of proper diet and exercise. Part of this is the attitude of younger people who are naturally more attracted to those of their own age. I was extremely surprised in my early thirties when our children, who were about 10 years old, seriously stated the opinion that my wife and I were too old to do much now. I wonder if their attitude changed when they reached that age. (we could call this a form of Karma). Another problem is the general social attitude that work is just a necessary evil to be given up as soon as possible in favour of a life of ease and pleasure. My observations over many years show that such a goal is rarely achieved. I have had several working colleagues retire, to hear that they have died around a year later – which gave them just enough time to get their home decorating and gardening done, with nothing much else to look forward to – despite having reasonable pensions. As a healer I visited the homes of people who spent the day watching television and seemed surprised that their legs and other parts of the body were not working properly. At another level I have my mother who was a sewing machinist working at home doing piece-work well into her eighties with father helping. It was clear that this was keeping them both alive mentally and physically.

It is a simple observable fact that whatever stops growing dies – even in the human world. As we get older, what we actually reap becomes more a matter of Personal Responsibility. We are less able to blame our parents or upbringing – or Society. This brings a different slant to general concepts of Karma. As we reach the end of a lifetime on this Earth we reap exactly according to what we have sown, which includes our physical and mental health as well as our general life situation. What of beyond that ?

LIFE AFTER DEATH AND REINCARNATION

History shows us that over the years much evil has been done in the name of religion. Even as I write this there are indiscriminate bombings of the general public by religious fanatics. This is activity at a childish level of "mine is better than yours" – which, in fact, is the sign of a deep inner sense of insecurity.

The Christian religion does not seem to have come to terms with the possibility of life continuing after physical death, other than suggesting that we enter some form of Heaven or Hell, let alone the possibility of reincarnation – which means the soul, or spirit, returning to this earthy level of existence on numerous occasions. In Eastern countries there are millions of people who accept reincarnation as fact. Spiritualism is an area of practical study of the subject of life after death - although many spiritualists have difficulty accepting the possibility of reincarnation.

In the absence of empirical evidence, and having a normal Christian upbringing, I also find it hard to accept reincarnation as a fact. I can empathise with Edgar Cayce's discomfort when he began giving information about past lives. However, I am gradually learning to accept it for two reasons. Firstly, Edgar Cayce gave so much other factual, verifiable, information, and secondly, after years of study, it is one thing that shows a real purpose to our existence.

I also have to mention the area of Occultism. The word "occult" merely means "hidden". So Sex, Astrology and Psychology are occult subjects, as are any other areas where humans are investigating matters so far unknown, feared, taboo, or ignored by "the general public" – and especially established religions. Its "opposite" seems to be "general knowledge" - which was occult until enough people came to know more about it. Much of accepted knowledge today – especially in the areas of Science and Medicine - was the province of "witches and wizards" not too long ago - and condemned by the pillars of society – and especially the Church.

One of the failings of most forms of knowledge is that they find it difficult to relate generalities to an individual person. Not only that, they tend to end up with yet another set of rules and regulations that may or may not be appropriate. In my researches over the years I have studied various "occult" subjects in some depth. One thing that surprised me was the antagonism between (or fear of ?) people involved in the various areas of knowledge – such as Astrologers, Spiritualists, and Healers, simply because it was clear that each was entirely ignorant of the concepts and practices of the other. I had some strange reactions from people in one group when I mentioned one of the others' subjects.

The main problem is ignorance coupled with a fear of exploring the unknown. I recognised this in myself during my time of "awakening" [MY STORY]. Another problem is that, to become an expert in any of the various fields of knowledge, people have to spend a lifetime in study, so have no time to explore elsewhere. There is also the tendency to give attention to the DIFFERENCES in areas of knowledge rather than the AGREEMENTS. Hopefully, this book will help to rectify that. For example, most modern religions believe in the principle of one God, it is the outer form that differs. There does seem to be a degree of infantile penis envy involved ("mine is bigger/better than yours") which, although present in modern times, refers back to the age of the pyramids, and the rulership of groups by kings. In later history, with their loss of power, religions seems to have taken over the role – although their power is gradually waning too . Part of the reason is that they seem unable to apply their philosophy to a practical lifestyle, whereas things like Astrology can. As you see, this book is an attempt to reconcile some of these differences by viewing life in a more practical rather than theological context. Studying the agreements.

THE FREUDIAN MODEL OF THE PSYCHE
(UPDATED BY ME)

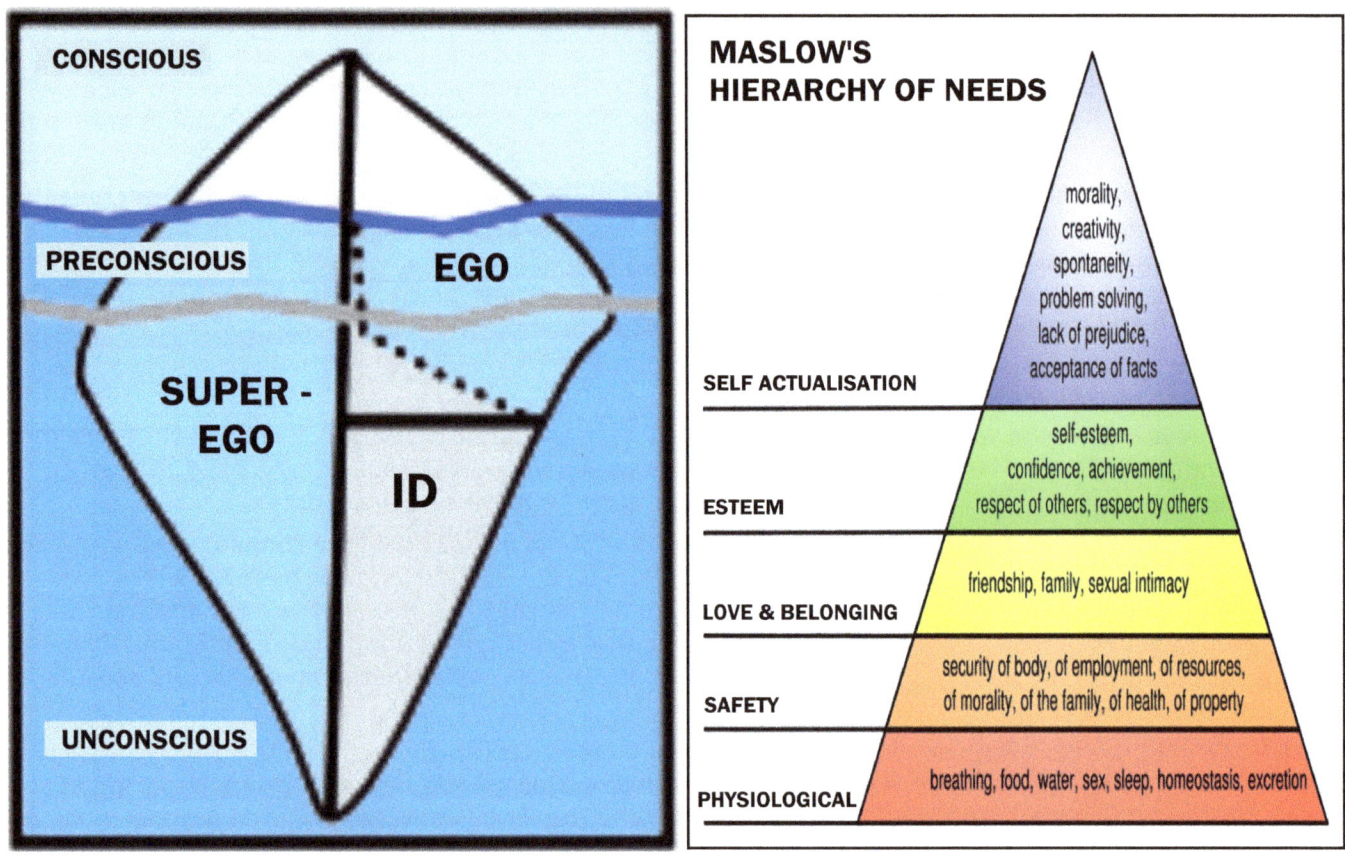

Figure 11 : Freud Psyche Model & Maslow's "Hierarchy of Needs"

Sigmund Freud (1856-1939) is said to be "The Father (or Founder) of Psychoanalysis" in that he pioneered the "Talking Method" of treating mental disorders. He was among the first to use hypnotism and dream interpretation in his work. Although his concepts are now considered rather outdated, we have to note that he considered psychological affects in terms of a single basic form of sexual energy – in a similar way that we consider the Sun as the prime source in Astrology. Perhaps if he had called it something other than "sexual" he might have been more widely accepted. This is another example of how human language is often found inadequate in the face of new discoveries. His protégé Carl Jung used the term "Psychic Energy" in his (different) model when he split from Freud and developed his own theories and methods under the term "Analytical Psychology" to differentiate from Psychoanalysis. With their brain scanners, psychologists nowadays seem to be more interested in the "firing" of physical neurons in the brain and treatment with drugs – a more physical approach than behaviour, which takes more time, effort, and skill, to examine. Probably because drug companies supply the money for research.

There is more information about the relationship between Freud and Jung , with comparison of their Birth Charts and Transits, in the chapter [ASTROLOGY : SYNASTRY]. Synastry is the comparison of 2 Astrological charts to examine the relationship between the subjects.

PSYCHOLOGY : DEVELOPMENT MODELS

CONSCIOUS, PRECONSCIOUS, AND UNCONSCIOUS

Before continuing we need to note that in reality there is no physical division between the parts mentioned. Everything co-exists in the same space.

Although the "iceberg" model above is attributed to Freud it seems to borrow more from Jung's later concepts. Freud was mainly interested in individual minds, whereas the diagram fits in more with Jung's concept of The Collective Unconscious as the "Sea" surrounding the individual mind. Nothing in the model relates to the physical brain. We are rather dealing with forms of energy.

He first divided the mind into 3 parts :-

1. <u>CONSCIOUS MIND</u> consists of everything which we are aware of. We can see that this is very limited and shifts dynamically. You are currently aware of the words in this book, but not your surroundings. If you look away the focus of consciousness changes away from the book.
2. <u>PRECONSCIOUS MIND</u> which consists of thoughts, memories and experiences that, although not currently conscious, can be remembered (also called "Subconscious". Jung's "Personal Unconscious")
3. <u>UNCONSCIOUS MIND</u> which consists of thoughts, memories and experiences that we can no longer remember, or bring to consciousness. The Unconscious Mind also contains material that is "repressed" – which is an unconscious method of preventing us from becoming aware (conscious) of desires and impulses that might upset our pleasurable mental state or sense of well-being. This is different to normal forgetting. As we see, our unconscious usually regulates our lives in a positive way – we learn things, like riding a bicycle, or driving a car, and no longer need to think about it, we just do it. The contents become negative when past experiences interfere with our "reality processing" at the present time. In Freud's philosophy the Unconscious Mind is entirely personal.

Freud's model represents the mind of an individual person. Jung added a 4th. component, the surrounding "Collective Unconscious" which contains psychological patterns which are shared by everyone of all races and creeds. It seems to be like a "DNA" of the mind. So we can add other "icebergs" to our model which would represent other people.

Freud further postulated that The Mind consisted of 3 parts, Id, Ego, and Super Ego - which share the conscious and unconscious to varying degrees. In describing Id, Ego, and Super Ego in objective terms we recognise (become conscious of) 3 different forms of energy within us that are more or less independent of conscious control.

THE ID

The Id consists of pure, basic, primitive human (and animal) instincts that are required for survival – mainly sex drive and aggression. It is basically raw energy with neither logic nor reason. This is similar, but not the same as, the Transactional Analysis concept of "Child" (below). It operates in simple response to pleasure (approach) or pain (avoidance). Or "Fight or Flight". The mind of a new born child consists mainly of the Id. Ego and Superego develop later. Freud said that the Id remains unconscious throughout the whole of our lives.

We can relate the Id to the instinctive Fire energy of the planet Mars, God of War, that enables our basic survival. In humans, the balanced energy can be described as Assertiveness – that is, self-confident action without violence or submissiveness.

I have taken the liberty of amending the model to indicate that, as a result of his work, and self-observation, we are now partially conscious of our Id. We can see it in a new born child, as well as in our own lives if we act totally without reason – such as when in a rage or running in fear ("Fight or Flight"). The other parts of the mind and Will can modify this polarity of behaviour.

THE EGO

The Ego is that part of the mind that is self-aware so we can recognise that "I am". It provides a central point of reference for past, present, and future experiences (anticipation and imagination). We can see this as being similar to the TA concept of "Adult" (below). The Ego has a conscious and unconscious component.

The Ego is only present in "embryo" form at birth. Although, as with all growth processes, development is continuous, does not really begin to develop until Cycle of Growth Stage 5 (Power. Creativity) at Erikson's "School Age". At Age 7 the child is less under parental control, and beginning to make its own decisions. This is the beginning of the 3rd.Octave of The Logarithmic Timescale that ends in physical death.

PSYCHOLOGY : DEVELOPMENT MODELS

THE SUPER EGO

The Superego also has conscious and unconscious components and develops after the Ego. It consists of moral standards by which the Ego operates and develops during the first 5 years of life as a result of parental inhibitions or approval. It is the seat of Conscience – that is, the internal sense of moral conduct, or "right and wrong". Later in life the standards of a wider society are incorporated. In the model, the Superego is shown as becoming partially conscious as we develop in life. We can relate this to the TA concept of "Parent" (below) – which has some negative connotations.

FREUD'S MODEL OF PERSONALITY DEVELOPMENT

I have deliberately kept Freud's original model separate from the more modern one "Growth of Personality" because it contains a certain basic simplicity.

The latter is covered in the chapter [ASTROLOGY : LOGARITHMIC TIMESCALE] which includes Freud's concepts, but also combines ideas from several later psychologists. An important principle from Freud's, and the later work of others, is based the necessity of solving the appropriate "problem" at the appropriate age. We only have a certain amount of energy, so it is better to have all of it available to be solving problems in the present day rather than be dealing with matters that existed in the past and remain unresolved, or using it to unconsciously repress unpleasant memories (which leads to tiredness or depression). This principle is the same as that of Astrology which is based on performing the right actions at the appropriate time.

Freud considered our psychological development as a series of "Psychosexual" stages where the pleasure seeking energy of the Id, "Libido", becomes focused on specific erogenous areas of the body. The Erogenous Zones are parts of the physical body that have particularly large numbers of sensory nerves close to the surface of the skin. Development problems arise when either one becomes fixated in a particular stage, and does not go on to the next, or in later life we regress to an earlier stage of coping with life's problems – perhaps as a form of denial of a current problem. He equated Libido with sexual energy, and stated that mental disorders were the result of repressed sexual energy. The repressed energy resulted in depression (the mind fighting itself) or the energy would be released in inappropriate, but more socially acceptable, ways - perhaps producing physical symptoms. He was highly criticised for this simplistic approach, but we need to recognise that many of his patients' problems at the time were based on the fact that sex was a socially taboo ("evil") subject, not to be discussed or even mentioned. A lot of people got married with no idea of the physiology of the opposite sex. This could lead, for example, to feelings of sexual arousal being consciously suppressed or unconsciously repressed.

His model suggests that repression can occur at any of his stages from things like parental or social disapproval, or physical illness or dysfunction leading to lack of development in the area concerned.

When we develop it does not mean that the effects of earlier stages disappear – they are merely "forgotten" (go unconscious). As we shall see, many of the public advertisements use material designed to unconsciously re-stimulate the earlier, more basic, urges to sell their products ("arousing needs").

We have to note that, especially during the early years of total dependency on others, one's parents are considered to be almost "godlike" figures with the power of life and death. Their reaction to each stage of development is extremely important – and recorded in our mind.

We note that Freud's concept of Libido energy is very similar to the Astrological one which considers the basic energy of the Sun being modified by the Zodiac Signs and Planets – and also forms the basis of The Cycle of Growth. This suggests that both models are manifestations of the same archetypes.

ORAL STAGE : 0-2 YEARS OF AGE

Freud only recognised a single Stage covering this age range. [ASTROLOGY : THE LOGARITHMIC TIMESCALE] shows 2.

Cycle of Growth Stage 1 (Seed. Aries. Cardinal Fire) and

Cycle of Growth Stage 2 (Germination. Taurus. Fixed Earth)

At the beginning of the Stage the psychology of the infant consists of pure, instinctive, Id and drive for survival. There is not much difference between a human infant and an animal.

The "parasitic" infant is expelled from the comfortable "Garden of Eden" world of the womb where there is no discomfort, no desire, and all needs are satisfied instantly. From day 1 of birth there is a delay between a need arising and its gratification. As life goes on, the time delay gets ever longer – even, eventually, to our needing to

PSYCHOLOGY : DEVELOPMENT MODELS

consciously balance our own desires and needs, and their gratification. Later, we also learn to balance our needs with those of others.

The lips and mouth contain an extremely high concentration of sensory nerves. The infant is stimulated by sucking and putting objects to the mouth. Feeding at the breast is usually the first pleasure. There is suggestion that bottle feeding too soon brings problems later on. Depending on how its needs are gratified the infant gains its first sense of trust, or otherwise, of the world outside. Memories of this first impression, and those of the following stages, remain with us unconsciously throughout life. Included in this stage is weaning. I have always had a sense of surprise that Nature, normally so efficient with resources, produces teeth that are eventually discarded. It would seem that they form an important part in the process of separating from the breast at the appropriate age (biting) [BTB].

Advertisements appealing to this stage focus on physical comfort, eating, drinking, biting and chewing, and smoking (with close-ups of mouths), and raising concerns about whether there will be enough to eat. Kissing is included in this scenario – often a beginning to all kinds of activities.

Negative regressions to this stage consist of over attention to oral needs. We all have to eat, but the need can be over emphasised. So things like over eating and drug addiction can come under this heading. The personality may be over-dependant and clinging, or somewhat "parasitic" in its demands for attention from others. Crying to get attention is included.

ANAL STAGE : 2-3 YEARS OF AGE

Cycle of Growth Stage 3 (Experiment. Communication. Gemini. Mutable Air)

Here pleasure is obtained from controlling bladder and bowels. How "potty training" is handled is important. Self-esteem develops from praise or criticism of how one "delivers the goods". Psychologists suggest that later in life this is connected with abilities for self-control, cleanliness and organisation. Negative regression results in a personality that is either too rigid ("solid") or too disordered ("loose" or "messy"). Anal people have a tendency to try to control every aspect of one's life – an impossible task. Some mothers compete to demonstrate that their child is "clean" at an early age – even though psychologists suggest that it is entirely dependent on muscular development. The young child can use this stage to gain some control of people around. ("If I am forced to sit here, I will sit – and sit – and sit …"). The anal, controlling, adult will develop this into always demanding perfection – so nothing ever gets done. The idea that mistakes are deadly sins.

In terms of people "stuck" in this age, there seems to be a strong connection with the "anal" type of character and the negative TA "Parent" (below) where life tends to be run according to strict rules ("should", "must", etc.)

Advertisements focused on this age refer to our ability for control of others, our self-worth (being "the best"), and "keeping clean". Anything that makes us competitively "better" than everyone else, with the minimum of effort. Some newspapers capitalise by arousing feelings under the guise of crusading against sexual deviation and vice.

PHALLIC STAGE : 3-7 YEARS OF AGE

Cycle of Growth Stage 4 (Transplanting. Cancer. Shell. Roots. Cardinal Water. Persona)

This is the Play Age of modern psychology, age 4 to 7 years, when the child is mainly relating to the close family.

Attention at this time is focused on one's own genital organs. We become aware of our own sexuality and the difference between sexes. Included here is the male Oedipal and female Electra complexes when children flirt with the parent of the other sex. We note that in Freud's time, due to social taboos, it was not unusual for couples to marry without any knowledge of the physiology of the other sex. Negative regression is over concern with sexual arousal, such as an addiction to sex or pornography – although actual intercourse may not be included. This is the realm of the "Tease". Advertisements are based on "easy" sexual, or other, conquest if you buy the product. This might be more subtle with daughter/father or son/mother oedipal coupling.

LATENCY : 7-11 YEARS OF AGE

Cycle of Growth Stage 5 (Power. Creativity. Leo. Fixed Fire. Sun. Ego. Consciousness).

This is the beginning of the 3rd. and last Octave of The Logarithmic Timescale.

During this period physical development continues, but sexual energy is relatively quiet. We see relationship with the concept of Leo being the FIXED (controlled) Fire Sign. The focus is generally on further development of

PSYCHOLOGY : DEVELOPMENT MODELS

physical and mental skills. Hobbies and other interests develop. Relatively free of parental control, the child develops its own Ego Consciousness.

Modern psychologists call this the "School Age" which is PART OF The Growth of Personality below, and covered in more detail in [ASTROLOGY : LOGARITHMIC TIMESCALE]. At this age work is put before pleasure, and children are judged in terms of what they produce or create.

GENITAL STAGE : 11 YEARS OF AGE TO ADULT (AND DEATH)

Covers the rest of life and 3rd. Octave of the Logarithmic Timescale.

This begins with Puberty when sex hormones start pumping. Sexual interest is transferred from one's self to the other sex. This is coupled with a more external social interest in general. We are all aware of the use of "beautiful people" in advertising to associate a product with feelings of sexual arousal. This is where Freud's model ends, and therefore indicates the kind of problems that came to his attention at the time, which he mainly based on unconscious sexual repression. Some control is necessary, however, over-control of life energy, leads to things like deep depression ("lack of energy"). His work was largely concerned with uncovering (bringing to consciousness) how it had occurred in childhood and "updating" the patient's attitude to the realities of present day circumstances. This is similar to the education of the Adult in Transactional Analysis (below).

MASLOW'S HIERARCHY OF NEEDS

I have included his model here because it tends to follow Freud's into adulthood. Maslow (1908-1970) suggested that we have basic Physiological needs in support of a physical body, and once we have achieved one we seek satisfaction at the next highest level. If the needs of an earlier level are threatened we have to give it priority. His model does not explicitly include Individuation. We can see how it includes and develops Freud's ideas further.

His stages are :-
1. PHYSIOLOGICAL – simple survival. Being physically healthy and getting enough food and drink.
2. SAFETY– stability in home and surroundings.
3. LOVE & BELONGING – relationships with others.
4. SELF ESTEEM - respect of self and being respected by others.
5. SELF-ACTUALISATION – Creativity and problem solving.

GROWTH OF PERSONALITY
THE COMBINED MODEL OF ERIKSON, FREUD AND PIAGET
This is just a brief overview.
The stages of the subject are dealt with in more detail in the [ASTROLOGY : LOGARITHMIC TIMESCALE] .

Since Freud there has been a lot of work done by psychologists and others observing people through their lifetimes to see how people develop mentally and physically, and they have arrived at a series of stages that relate to various age ranges. We note that they seem to have the attitude that personal growth ends when we reach adult age, and after that there is only a decline ending in death. This is probably based on their experience and those of the majority of their patients. In the Cycle of Growth we have a Transcendent Octave which includes Jung's concept of Individuation. This is not surprising, because Individuation does not occur in everyone. We can expect that this might change some-time soon as, at the time of writing , it is expected that life expectancy for many young people today will be 100 years or even more. So, the "Adult" and "Old Age" Stages, said to begin at age 42, will last longer than that of the whole previous lifetime.

THE [ASTROLOGY : LOGARITHMIC TIMESCALE]
The remarkable point is that the ages related to the Erikson stages match with the ages of Houses 1 to 8 of the Astrological Logarithmic Timescale which is based on the number of Lunar Months following Conception (Cycle of Growth Stage 9).

The model devised by Erik Erikson (1902-1994) is the basis of what is agreed by psychologists today. Freud's original stages mentioned above are included in the model. Erikson departed from the simple idea of sexual development to add more detail. We note that social attitudes have changed greatly since Freud's time. Although the stages are fixed, there are differences of opinion about which age ranges they cover, and some overlap. There will be variations of personal experience. This is obviously because people differ in speed of development. I have used those of The Logarithmic Timescale.

1. The 1st. Octave starts at Cycle of Growth Stage 9 (Conception. Sagittarius. Mutable fire)
2. The 2nd. Octave starts at 10 Lunar Months – Cycle of Growth Stage 1 (Seed. Birth. Aries. Cardinal fire)
3. The 3rd. Octave starts at 100 Lunar Months - Cycle of Growth Stage 5 (Power. Creativity. Leo. Fixed Fire)
4. The return to Cycle of Growth Stage 9 is at 1000 Lunar Months – which is also the "Death" position at the end.
5. However, 1000 Lunar Months is almost an 84 year cycle of Uranus, which refers to Individuation – so we can have a repetition of the 1st. Octave, which becomes a 4th. "Transcendent" Octave.

PSYCHOLOGY : DEVELOPMENT MODELS

PSYCHOLOGY : GROWTH OF PERSONALITY - Erikson, Freud, & Piaget [GOP]

CYCLE OF GROWTH	LOG TIME SCALE	ERIKSON [GOP]	(Freud Stages) PHYSICAL	ANXIETY	DILEMMA	SOLUTION ACHIEVES	SOCIAL RELATIONSHIPS	NOTES
1. SEED	0 to 7 months	0-2 years INFANCY	(Oral) Sucking. Biting. Weaning	Fear of starvation	Trust vs. Mistrust	Hope	Individual Persons Sensory stimuli	Increasing time between physical needs and their satisfaction. Incorporation. Dependency. Aggression. Seeks physical stimulus -> seeks people stimulus
2. GERMINATION	7m to 1yr. 8m							
3. EXPERIMENT	1y.8m to 3y.6m	2-4 years EARLY CHILDHOOD	(Anal) Muscular control Retention & Expulsion	Fear of and doubts about impending disgrace (conscience)	Autonomy vs. Shame/Doubt	Will	Parental Persons	Physical Control. Mastering the self (body control) Self esteem (depending on parental encouragement)
4. TRANSPLANTING	3y.6m to 7 years	4 - 7 Years PLAY AGE	(Phallic) Infantile-genital Locomotive	Fear of punishment for intrusiveness, seductiveness, or rivalry	Initiative vs. Guilt	Purpose	Basic Family	Mastering the world around. Oedipal Identification with parents. Acceptability of age & sex roles. Intrusive/Exclusive. Setting limits.
5. POWER	7 to 13 years	6 - 12 years SCHOOL AGE	(Latency) No major physical changes	Fear of not knowing how	Industry vs. Inferiority	Competence	Neighbourhood School	Compares self with others. Completes tasks. Puts work before pleasure.
6. SERVICE TO SELF	13 to 23 years	13-19 years ADOLESCENCE	(Genital) Puberty	Fear of failing to master new and conflicting inner drives	Identity vs. Identity Diffusion	Fidelity	Peer Groups & Models	Recapitulation. Finding one's own sexual/social role. Emancipation from parents wishes. Concerned with how we appear to others.
7. PARTNERSHIPS SOCIAL ROLE	23 to 42 years	20-30 years YOUNG ADULTHOOD	(Genital) No major physical changes	Fear of spontaneity and mutual responsiveness	Intimacy vs. Isolation	Love	Partnerships	Intimate relationships. Work Competition & Co-operation
8. INTERCOURSE. DEATH	42 years to Death	30-65 years ADULTHOOD	(Genital) Gradual senescence	Fear of the responsibilities of leadership	Generativity vs. Stagnation	Caring	Parenting. Social involvement	MID LIFE CRISIS (NOT RECOGNISED) Producing something of value. Helping the next generation.
		65+ OLD AGE	(Genital) Senescence	Fear of death	Ego Integrity vs. Despair (disappointment)	Wisdom	Mankind. My kind	Retirement ("disengagement") Recapitulation. Facing death

This chart is based on one contained in "The Growth of Personality" by Gordon R.Lowe with my additions

Figure 12 : Growth of Personality Table

PSYCHOLOGY : DEVELOPMENT MODELS

THE JUNGIAN INDIVIDUATION MODEL

Although the model is similar to others it is different in (stated) meaning.

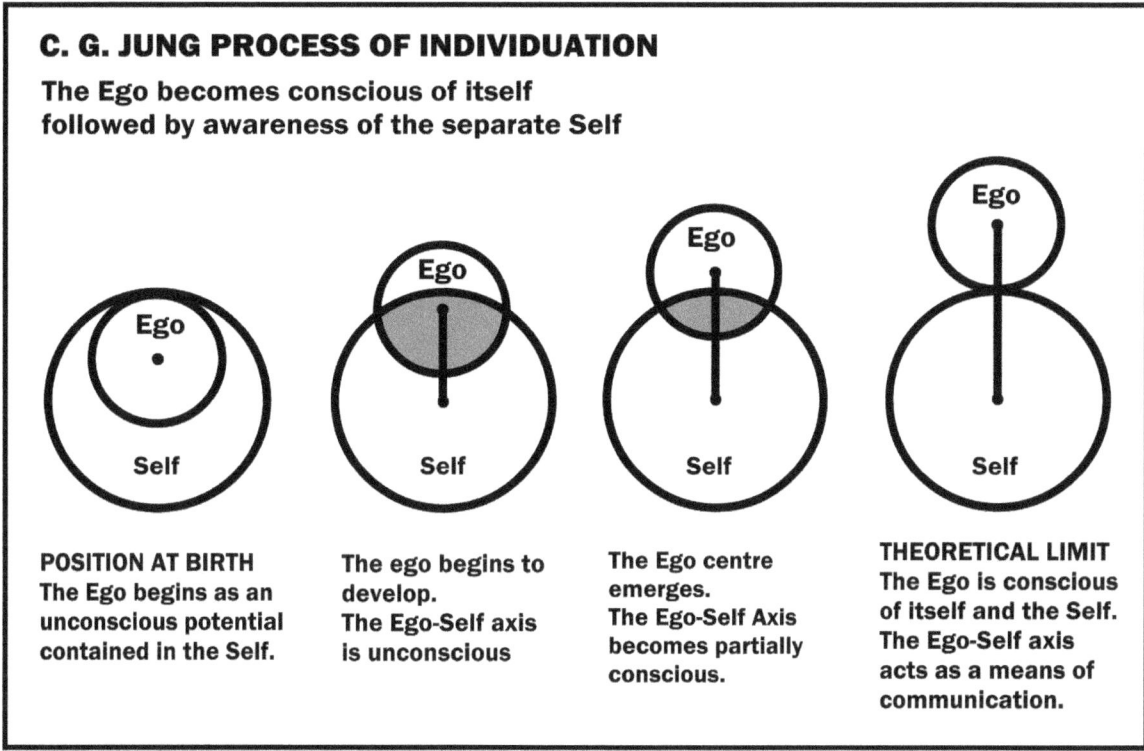

Figure 13 : Psychology Development Model - Jungian Individuation

The individual Ego develops from an undifferentiated unconscious. First becoming a human being, then becoming different to other human beings. The Ego is the centre of conscious identity and recognises itself as "I am".

The Self is the centre of the total personality–including consciousness, the unconscious, and Ego (the diagram does not show this exactly).

The Ego-Self Axis is the connection between the Ego and Self. As the separation occurs the Ego becomes more aware of the separate Self, and later, the Ego-Self Axis itself as a link of communication. The Ego-Self Axis can become damaged, and the connection lost.

Jung deliberately refrained from suggesting any methodology in approaching his patients, or even in the process of Individuation, stating that he wished to avoid "recipes".

[THE KABBALAH TREE OF LIFE]

We see in the model a similarity with the concepts that :-
1. There is development of a "Middle Pillar".
2. The "Lightning Flash" of Evolution does not connect with The Middle Pillar until it reaches Sephirah 9 (Yesod. Foundation. Moon. Unconscious) and (10. Malkuth. Earth. Physical Body).
3. Sephirah 6 (Tiphareth. Sun. Consciousness. Cycle of Growth Stage 5) at the centre of The Middle Pillar does not begin development until later on (Age 7. Erikson's School Age).
4. The previously un-numbered Sephirah Daath near the top of The Middle Pillar, which I now associate with Cycle of Growth Stage 11 (Discontent. Uranus – not Jupiter) at the Transcendent Octave Stage, is also undeveloped until this Stage

2 PATHS OF INDIVIDUATION

There are basically 2 paths to individuation.

PSYCHOLOGY : DEVELOPMENT MODELS

1. UNCONSCIOUS – which is where we develop a certain independence but are still ruled by group attitudes and ideals. Development depends on solving life problems as they arise. This is similar to my chapter [THE PURPOSELESS LIFE]. In essence, this is the unconscious Way of The Cycle of Growth.

2. CONSCIOUS – a deliberate attempt to develop in ways corresponding to my chapter [THE PURPOSE OF LIFE]. Jungian Analysts say that this can only be achieved with the help of a Jungian Analyst. Do we assume that they themselves have individuated and know what they are talking about?

3. THE MIDDLE PATH - At present, for me, in the absence of a teacher who I respect, I am content with the "Middle Path" in that I follow my normal life - but with greater awareness and attention to the problems that are put before me. Perhaps trying to face rather than ignore them – without becoming a "revolutionary". My experience so far has been that if I need to attend to a task, it will be put in front of me – that is, I will be conscious of it. [MY STORY].

INDIVIDUATION (TRANSCENDENCE) AND ASTROLOGY

Erikson's model makes no mention of Individuation, tending to treat old age as merely a time of decline in preparation for death. Comparing Jung's concepts with The Cycle of Growth Stage 8 (Death. Intercourse), however, does imply the possibility of continued growth. Stage 8 of The Logarithmic Timescale begins at age 42 – the time of the Mid Life Crisis, which is half way through the 84 year Generic Cycle of Uranus [ASTROLOGY : PLANET TRANSITS]. Jung stated that Individuation is a task for the latter part of life.

However, there is an overall similarity because Erikson's stages recognise a changing awareness of, and (usually) participation in ever widening external social relationships – starting with Mother, Family, School, and Society outside the family. Jung's Individuation takes development a step further by finally separating from the wider Society ("The Human Collective") to individualise. This, in fact, completes the "wheel" of a lifetime in that we enter into this world alone, and eventually depart from it alone.

If we look again at the Logarithmic Timescale and Maslow's Hierarchy of Needs "Self Actualisation", one of the keys to Transcendence seems to be the individual investigating, or taking some interest in, worldly or spiritual matters beyond the need for survival, sex, family, job, and pursuit of pleasure (etc.).

THE TRANSACTIONAL ANALYSIS MODEL

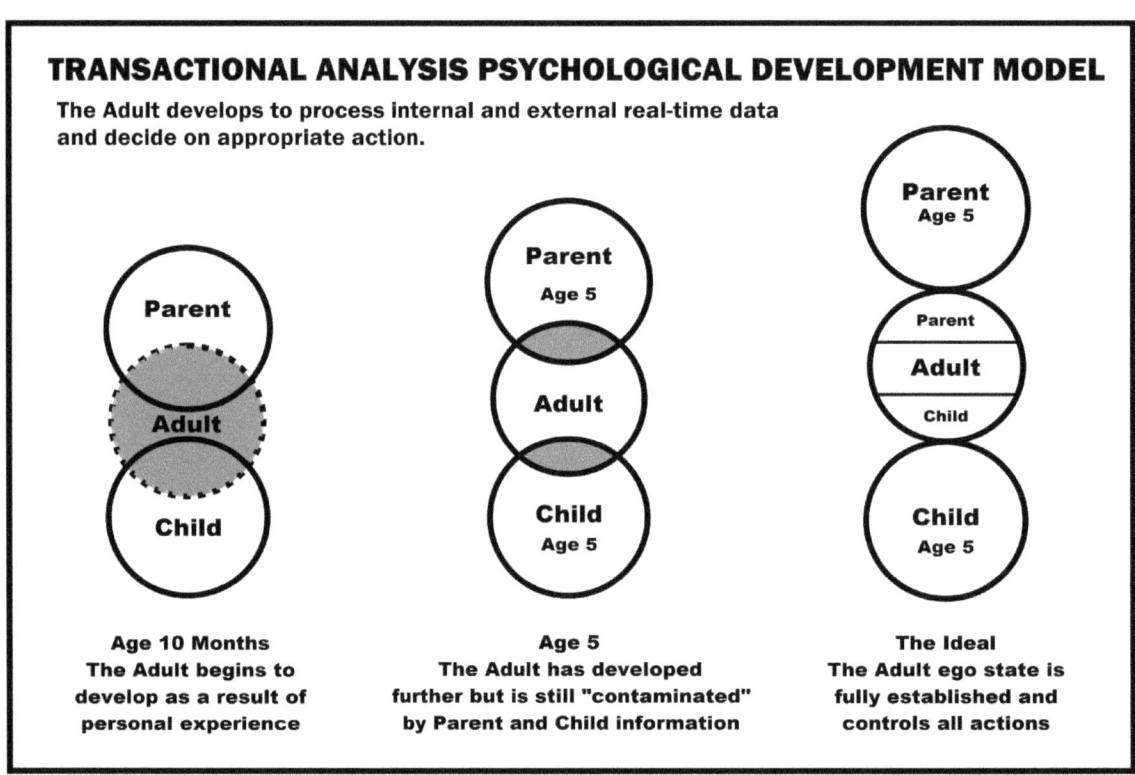

Figure 14 : Psychology Development model - Transactional Analysis

PSYCHOLOGY : DEVELOPMENT MODELS

We see a remarkable similarity with Jung's model above and the concept of the development of The Middle Pillar of The Kabbalist Tree of Life.

An important point to note is that Transactional Analysis uses many terms and words which we would normally use elsewhere, but here take on a different meaning. For example "Parent", "Adult" and "Child" are capitalised to indicate that they are specialised terms. Some other terms are defined below.

The picture above shows stages in the TA model of psychological development, which is based on the development of the Adult ego state – which I have mentioned as beginning development at Cycle of Growth Stage 5 (Power. Creativity. The Sun. Ego Consciousness) at around age 7. The Adult also equates with Sephirah 6 (Tiphareth. Beauty. The Sun) at the centre of [THE KABBALAH TREE OF LIFE].

When a child is born there is no Adult ego state which develops later on as a result of processing data in real time, which, in turn, is a result of life experience. To begin with, the Adult is more or less "contaminated" by the Parent and Child as indicated by the overlaps in the circles. This is kind of "blurring" between inner thoughts and feelings based on the past, and outer present reality. A tendency to pre-judge present experiences as the same as past ones and act accordingly (prejudice). Expectations tend to be reinforced by the same behaviour obtaining the same positive or negative result. To change the result, some kind of conscious behavioural change is usually necessary – which first requires becoming aware of one's behaviour. When I was young I had the unconscious habit of biting my fingernails. I "cured" myself by simply taking my hand away from my mouth when I realised that I was doing it. It took a while to finally stop.

The final "ideal" state shows a fully developed, separate, Adult which is aware of and able to mediate between the original Parent and Child states. The Adult has accepted some Parent and Child data as useful and real, which forms the "Parent in the Adult", and the "Child in the Adult".

SIMILARITY TO OTHER MODELS

1. There is similarity with the Jungian model of the development of an "Ego-Self Axis". The concepts are not identical, so there must be room for adjustment in both cases.
2. There is similarity with the Numerology concept of Number 1 being "Thesis", Number 2 being "Antithesis" and number 3 being "Synthesis". That is like two people meeting (1 & 2) with Number 3 being the resulting relationship, or "child", that is formed. The pattern also applies to any other grouping of 3, such as "Father, Son, and Holy Ghost" (Parent, Child, Adult ?) (Ego. Self. Ego-Self Axis ?).

TRANSACTIONAL ANALYSIS OVERVIEW

A Transaction consists of a stimulus ("stroke") from one person to another which is expected to produce a response. We can see a similarity with Freud's concept of Psychosexual energy and pleasure seeking. If there is no response, or the response is an unexpected one, problems can arise. We tend to relate to people who are programmed with similar expectations.

The model is based on 3 psychological states called Parent, Adult, and Child (capitalised to show that the words are used as psychological terms). The Parent and Child probably begin developing before birth and are fully formed by the age of 5, after which they do not develop further. Whether this is physiological or due to development of the Adult is not clear. The Child is our internal response to external events. The Parent is externally derived as a recording of actions of parental people. The Adult, which should continue developing throughout the lifetime, is internally derived from the individual's actual experience is basically concerned with the processing of real life data. It is the mediator between the Parent, Child, and the outside world as well as being the conscious "decision maker". Early in life it is "contaminated" by not being fully separated from the Parent and Child, and therefore is unable to make entirely objective decisions based on the reality of the present time.

TA PSYCHOLOGICAL DEVELOPMENT

1. The brain functions as a high fidelity tape-recorder of the events of our lives. These recordings begin before birth and are in sequence and continuous.

2. The feelings which were associated with past experiences also are recorded and are inextricably locked to those experiences.

3. Persons can exist in two psychological states at the same time.

PSYCHOLOGY : DEVELOPMENT MODELS

4. The recorded experiences and feelings associated with them are available for replay today in as vivid form is when they happened and provide much of the data which determines the nature of today's transactions. Evidence of this, apart from hypnosis, is from a Canadian neurosurgeon Wilder Penfold who applied weak electric currents directly to the brains of patients (the brain has no nerves, so there is no need for a general anaesthetic). Past experiences were not just recalled but "relived" in detail of sights, sounds, and feelings.

5. Infants - and even adults in a lesser sense (such as in solitary confinement) - deprived of handing ("Stroking") over a long period will tend to sink into an irreversible decline and are more prone to disease - perhaps even death.

STROKING
All people need "Stroking" which means getting some kind of stimulus from other people. It can be subdivided into (1) "Stimulus Hunger" (2) "Recognition Hunger" and (3)"Structure Hunger". For the purposes of survival it does not matter whether the Stroking is pleasurable or painful. Perhaps this explains Sado-Masochism. Without Stroking we wither and die.

There is also similarity with Maslow's "Hierarchy of Needs", with a similar hierarchy of development. [BTB].

STIMULUS HUNGER
Psychologist Rene Spitz (1887-1974) found that infants deprived of physical handling over a long period will tend to sink into an irreversible decline and to be more prone to disease - perhaps even death. Similar effects are discovered in people subjected to long terms of solitary confinement. This gave rise to the concept of "Stimulus Hunger". A conclusion was reached that any social intercourse whatever has a biological advantage over no intercourse at all. Experiments with animals shows that gentle handling and painful electric shocks, both being forms of Stroking, are equally effective in promoting their health. The health of animals and people declines if they are not stroked. The ultimate stimulus would seem to be sexual intercourse (or torture ?).

I am reminded of "Number 5", the anthropomorphic robot in the 1986 film "Short Circuit". A lightning strike causes a power surge that wipes out some of its programming, and it wanders erratically - continually craving "input". A child later explains to it about death, after which he experiences fear of "disassembly". At the end of the film, after a self-built facsimile is destroyed in his place, the robot becomes "Johnny 5". There is a strange similarity in this scenario and what is described by The Cycle of Growth.

RECOGNITION HUNGER
As time goes on we learn to do without as much physical stimulation as we need in childhood. Stroking then becomes more symbolic when it is enough for one person to recognise the presence of another. Some people may require many strokes a day, others just a few a year. A stroke can consist of merely raising an eyebrow, or a nod, in recognition.

STRUCTURE HUNGER
After stimulus hunger and recognition hunger comes Structure Hunger. This is the need to structure the waking hours. While the purpose of stimulus hunger and recognition hunger is to avoid sensory and emotional starvation, the purpose of structure hunger is to avoid boredom. The structuring of time is one of the functions of social life. Transactional Analysts call this "programming" and recognise 'Material Programming' and 'Social Programming '- both of which are opportunities for mutual stroking. Material programming is basically data-processing and dealing with external reality. Social programming relates to traditional ritualistic behaviour depending on the culture to which one belongs and is taught as "how to behave". This would include such activities as parties, weddings, and funerals.

There are several ways of structuring time. Examples are "Rituals"," Pastimes", and "Games ".

RITUALS
In Rituals the stroking is based on social programming and depends on the familiarity between the two parties and social customs. At base level it can be just the recognition of the other by a nod or "Hi". Closer relationships demand a longer series of transactions. Rituals mainly come from the Parent (ego state mentioned next).

PSYCHOLOGY : DEVELOPMENT MODELS

PASTIMES

Pastimes are similar to Rituals except that there is no defined structure other than taking it in turns to give and receive strokes. An example of a Pastime in the UK is discussion of the weather. This usually occurs between people who do not know one another very well and serves as a safe topic of conversation on which most people can agree. It is a form of mild stroking while looking for opportunities of continuing the exchanges further.

TA EGO STATES

A person has three possible psychological "ego states" - Parent, Adult, and Child (capitalised to show they are psychological terms rather than people) and can be in any one or two of these states at any time, and can change to another at any moment. With Parent and Child it is much like viewing, and taking part in, an old movie at the same time. There is a tendency in transactions for one party to take on a parental role, when the other takes a complementary child role. The ideal is for both to be in Adult state.

We have to be aware that each of the ego states is autonomous – that is, exists separately from the other. This is similar to the concept of Sub-personalities.

I disagree with the TA assertion that we can be in 2 ego states at the same time. My observations are that we can switch from one to another in a split second, which would give that appearance. I particularly remember a train journey hearing a long conversation where the changes were continuous – almost from transaction to transaction. [BTB].

THE CHILD

is internally derived as permanent recordings of the feeling response to external events during the first 5 years of life, especially the interactions with parents. The Child includes our instincts and biological urges, genetic recordings, physical selves, curiosity, and intuition. It also includes our desires. The Child can also be a problem part of our personality if it is fearful, intimidated, or selfish. The Child has 2 basic states. For example, it may have been programmed by parents to be embarrassed, guilty, or fearful in some situations – even though the feeling might not be appropriate at that time. On the other hand the Child may not care what anyone might think.

We also need to be aware that a young child is likely to make incorrect assumptions about what was happening at the time. I myself was born during the Second World War and do not (consciously) remember any of it - even though I was evacuated from London to the countryside as a toddler. As an "outsider", it seems to me that a lot of psychologists' work consists of helping people remember things that happened in the past so they can re-evaluate them (Adult) in the present. [BTB]

Apart from anger or rage (tantrums) our internal Child can be manipulative rather than using direct action - undermining and misdirecting us when we really need to be clear minded or assertive. The Child controls much of our main life energy and can "run away and hide". Some affects are mental depression, tiredness, and forgetting [BTB].

THE PARENT

is externally derived as a recording of the actions of parents and parental people during the first 5 years of life. At this time the Parent is "fixed" in the sense that what our parents think and do today may not be the same as what is recorded in our head. The Parent has a god-like quality in the sense that whatever has been recorded is unquestioned. Not only did we not have the mental capacity or power to do so, but we depended totally on our parents (or substitutes) for our existence. The Parent is filled with negative criticism, demands, directions, and dogma. Its aim seems to be to enable us to feel superior in the face of our inadequacies.

The Parent uses words like "should", "ought", "must", "always", "never". The Parent confuses us because it demands "perfection" in everything we do. It takes a while before we realise that firstly the standards are impossible to meet, and, secondly, if we try to learn new things we will make mistakes as part of the process. Some companies spend millions of pounds making mistakes. It is called "Research". [BTB]

We need to recognise that at a certain age we do need simple instructions to ensure our survival. Apart from the "Critical Parent" there is another version which is termed the "Nurturing Parent". Their traditional and moral values are not all wrong. They can also supply a lot of "know how". They take care of us and other people.

PSYCHOLOGY : DEVELOPMENT MODELS

Unfortunately, they can overdo their concern, and become more of a "smothering mother" (men too) by insisting that we need taking care of, and to let them take over ("tying us to their apron strings").

In "Staying OK" Thomas Harris cites an example where a hospital put all "depressed" patients in the same ward and asked for volunteers to care for them. The attendants and therapist volunteers were mainly Nurturing Parent types. After 6 months they closed the unit because nobody got better. Patients were transferred to normal wards where they soon got better and left. The average stay thereafter was 3 weeks.

I was around 35 years of age when my mother finally stopped telling me what I should and ought to do (although, by then, I was well away from her daily control).

In the past there was mention of "The Jewish Mother" syndrome. There is a certain subtlety with the "nagging" that occurs because it is always "right", and always "for our own good". The reality of this was made evident to me when I worked some years with a Jewish owned company. I have seen grown men in their 30s and 40s disoriented and reduced to seeming despair after a telephone conversation with their mother.

THE ADULT

is internally derived and formed from the individual's actual experience. It is able to process physical, mental, and feeling information and make decisions as a result - even including future possibilities and likely repercussions. The Adult can update the Parent (perhaps defending the Child) - but may not be aware of the possibility or necessity. Although there is suggestion that there is some beginnings of consciousness in the womb, the Adult does not really start developing until the infant is able to leave full parental control and begin exploring the world around on its own volition. This starts at around 10 months of age , and corresponds with the time that, not only does the infant have some control of its physical body, but mental faculties have developed enough to make this possible, as well as to begin communicating using words.

I have mentioned Cycle of Growth Stage 5 (Power. Creativity. School Age) as being the beginning of freedom to practise. This is the beginning of The 3rd. and final Octave of The Cycle of Growth that leads to Individuality.

Mental development seems to begin with the infant learning to connect a person or object with its name. [BTB]

TA GAMES

Although examination and analysis of "Games" is a major part of Transactional Analysis, here we just need to record their existence.

1. A "Game" consists of a repetitive sequence of Transactions which progress to a predictable outcome ("pay-off").
2. On the surface the Transactions are plausible and might seem to be Adult to Adult, but in Games the pay-off is not what it seems. There is a dishonest quality. Most games have their origin in the childhood game of "Mine Is Better Than Yours" designed to bring a little relief from the burden of the central "Not OK" emotional position (Life Positions described later).
3. There is a tendency for Games to be based on the Parent of one party talking to the Child of the other. This is a "complementary" transaction in that it is likely to continue until one or the other changes ego state. Other complementary transactions can be Parent to Parent, Adult to Adult, and Child to Child – assuming they agree with one another - although only Adult to Adult is likely to be based on reality in the present time. "Crossed" transactions tend to terminate the exchange of strokes – such as when the Adult questions the validity of Parent or Child information from the other. Crossed transactions give rise to inner discomfort.

TA STAGES OF GROWTH

We note that, once again, the Cycle of Growth ages match the psychological ones.

1. CONCEPTION to BIRTH

Cellular Birth starts the growth process, after which physical needs are instantly gratified, from continual close symbiosis with the mother. In essence, this is a "parasitic" stage.

PSYCHOLOGY : DEVELOPMENT MODELS

2. 9 MONTHS LATER : PHYSICAL BIRTH – Cycle of Growth Stage 1 (Seed)

A catastrophic event. The baby is suddenly subjected to light, noise, and cold, and separation from the mother.

3. IMMEDIATELY AFTER BIRTH : ABANDONMENT

The child is totally alone for a short period until it is picked up for the first time.

4. "RESCUE"

The baby is picked up and "stroked" by another human being. In early foundling homes (for unwanted babies) babies were found to be prone to Marasmus – a body-wasting condition considered to be a result of malnutrition - where they lost up to 80% of body weight. Results here suggest that the main cause would be lack of human contact (stroking).

5. 10 MONTHS OLD : Faster development of the Adult -Cycle of Growth Stage 2 (Germination)

Depends on the actual experiences of the child. Although there is suggestion of some initial development in the womb, the infant is now able to explore on its own and begin to think and reason for himself to construct his own understandings. Developing "know how".

5. FIRST 2 YEARS - Cycle of Growth Stage 3 (Experiment. Communication)

With an undeveloped Thinking Function (words) , the baby is still mainly recording Feelings related to stroking/non stroking. Incoming data starts to form in some semblance of patterns (Piaget).

(Jung likened the growth of consciousness to the formation of "islands" which grew and joined to become "continents")

6. 3rd. YEAR DECISION : BASIC LIFE POSITION – Cycle of Growth Stage 4 (Transplanting)

The Adult of the infant has sufficiently developed to form its first conclusion about himself and others. "What can I do to make you be good to me?" (Piaget called this a "State of Equilibrium"). The Adult in the little person has achieved its first mastery in "making sense of life", in solving what Adler called a "life-central-problem" our attitude towards others.

> *"it is possible to make one certain deduction: namely, that early in life, sometimes within the earliest months and sometimes later, a central emotional position is frequently established. The clinical fact which is already evident is that once a central emotional position is established early in life it becomes the effective position to which the individual would tend to return automatically for the rest of his days" .... "whenever the central emotional position is painful the individual may spend his whole life defending himself against it, again using conscious, pre-conscious, and unconscious devices whose aim it is to avoid this pain filled central position." [Lawrence Kubie]*

Inner, emotional "Pain" can often be likened to the inner Parent "beating" the inner Child. It can only be prevented by intervention by the Adult [BTB].

7. AGE 5 YEARS AND ONWARD : "RE-DECIDING" – Cycle of Growth Stage 5 (Power. Creativity)

This is the beginning of the 3rd.Octave of The Cycle of Growth. Erikson's School Age. The rest of life appears to be related to further development of the Adult, when Ego Consciousness begins to develop away from parental control. There is more opportunity to process internal and external data in real time and decide on appropriate action. The Adult needs to separate and stand alone to be able to mediate between the inner Child and Parent.

4 POSSIBLE BASIC LIFE POSITIONS – DECIDED AT AGE 2

There are 4 basic subjective life positions depending on one's inner feelings and perception of one's position in the outside world. Around the age of 2 years an internal unconscious "decision" is made.

1. I'm Not OK - You're OK'

This is the more usual position. If stroking was present, by the end of the second year this original position may be confirmed. The infant is still a small person with no real freedom of action.

PSYCHOLOGY : DEVELOPMENT MODELS

2. I'm Not OK - You're not OK'

Now the infant is walking the parent decides that it has no need to be picked up, so there is no more stroking. The baby days are over.

3. I'm OK - You're Not OK'.

The criminal position. Brutalised by parents (or sometimes from not being "rescued" soon enough after birth). OK comes from the comfort of being alone. "I'm OK on my own". Survival.

4. I'm OK - You're OK'

An Adult decision. What was once decided can be re-decided in favour of 'I'm OK, You're OK' - but this takes experience and conscious effort together with further development of the Adult. It is helpful to recognise which of the ego states we are involved with at any time.

Our childhood central emotional position was based on feelings about how life seemed to us then - and at that time is always wrong to varying degrees. It requires a conscious decision to reject our childhood assumption and to assert that "I am no longer a helpless, dependent, child - and nor are you".

Which sounds very much like "Love thy neighbour AS thyself". We cannot love our neighbour if we do not love our self. We cannot love our self if we cannot love our neighbour. At present, in my case, I can live with the word "respect" in place of "love" – "love" in our society covers a multitude of meanings. [BB].

THE 4 ELEMENTS

The diagram shows some manifestations of the 4 archetypal Principles.

		FIRE	**AIR**	**WATER**	**EARTH**
4 Nuclear Forces	Atomic Level	Weak (atomic) [Fire of Earth]?	Electromagnetic [Air of Earth]?	Strong (atomic) [Water of Earth]?	Gravity [Earth of Earth]
4 States of Matter	Molecular Level	Plasma [Fire of Earth]	Gas [Air of Earth]	Liquid [Water of Earth]	Solid [Earth of Earth]
5 Senses	Perception via nerves	Sight [Fire of Air]	Hearing [Air of Air]	Taste/Smell [Water of Air]	Touch [Earth of Air]
4 Functions (C.G.Jung)	Mind/Brain	Intuition [Fire of Water]	Thinking [Air of Water]	Feeling [Water of Water]	Sensation [Earth of Water]
	Triplicity	POSITIVE	POSITIVE	NEGATIVE	NEGATIVE
4 Zodiac Elements (4 Triplicities)	Cardinal	Aries	Libra	Cancer	Capricorn
	Fixed	Leo	Aquarius	Scorpio	Taurus
	Mutable	Sagittarius	Gemini	Pisces	Virgo

Figure 15 : The 4 Elements and some associations

This chapter describes the original Classical 4 Elements and their associations. We have to distinguish The 4 Elements (capitalised in this book) from the numerous physical Chemical Elements(lower case "elements") mentioned in the chapter [NUMEROLOGY] and elsewhere.

We first note that The 4 Elements are a sub-archetype of Number 4 which concerns "sets of 4" related manifestations –and which, at that level, have no separate identity.

The 4 Elements are each given 3 "Qualities" – Cardinal (Initiating), Fixed (Concentration. Bringing Form), and Mutable (Changing. Communicating) which gives rise to [ASTROLOGY : ZODIAC SIGNS].

The archetypal 4 Elements are fundamental to our understanding of almost all occult subjects as well as The Cycle of Growth. In their "pure" form they are non-material forms of energy. In one sense they are like academic Ideals, or Principles. We only get to recognise them by observing the various psychological and material manifestations that they produce – and using Philosophy and Meditation rather than Science, and the Jungian Function of Intuition. A problem is that the early, philosophical, intuitive, Principles have become "contaminated" by the development of the rational Thinking Function, and science. They are also disguised, by appearing in a wide multiplicity of forms. This chapter gives some examples of the various forms.

Having said that, we must continually bear in mind that The 4 Elements as different forms of the same basic energy are themselves merely partial representations of a single Whole. This is the Whole that existed before "The Big Bang" when there was No-thing. Since that simple beginning evolution has gradually produced an uncountable number of physical manifestations – first of material planets, and, later on, carbon based life forms. The evolution of life on this planet has followed the same "rule" of development from simplicity to more and more complexity. This chapter tries to return to that simplicity.

Here we are concerned with the classical set of 4 Elements – Fire, Earth, Air, and Water - which are active in all areas covered by this book. THE CLASSICAL 4 ELEMENTS ARE THE ORIGINAL ONES which came into being before the discovery of the Chemical Elements. In the diagram above they are in order of their "temperature", or state of activity (frequency of vibration) – Fire is the hottest and most active, Earth is the coldest and relatively inert. It is not possible to give an exact description of each, so we observe their activity in various contexts. By observing how ice is converted to water and then steam by supplying more energy we get an idea of how they are related.

Until now it has been unclear how The 4 Elements affect our human lives, however, with C.G.Jung's discovery and description of the psychological 4 Functions we now have the tools for greater self-awareness.

To get a more tangible grasp of The 4 Elements we can compare them with other "sets" of 4. Here I mention the Classical 4 Elements, The 4 Fundamental Nuclear forces inside an atom, and The 4 States of Matter. Apart from The Cycle of Growth in general, there is more detailed information in these chapters, where they are considered in more "practical" terms. Here they remain in a more academic level.

OVERVIEW

The 4 Elements are basic to our understanding of life. A problem is that the original meanings of the terms have been lost because "the elements" have been taken over by Chemistry and Physics, and the material world in general, during the ensuing period. The 4 Elements are much more basic than that, and are clearly not material at all. In fact, from the more recent work by C.G.Jung we can see that they are Archetypes that live in the Collective Unconscious and can (among other things) be shown to relate to his 4 Functions.

It is a fact of life that there are less words available than there are meanings to words, so we have to continually observe the context in which they are used. Many conflicts occur in life from misunderstandings caused by misinterpreting (the same) words. Unfortunately for us here, the word "Element" is one of them. Here, I capitalise and use the term "The 4 Elements" to distinguish them from the physical "elements" of the scientific atomic Periodic Table. We can only understand The 4 Elements by contemplating their physical manifestations and looking for the "common denominator" . The Chemical Elements, being composed of matter, are all basically related to "The Element Earth". Our human bodies are also related to Earth, being made up of Chemical Elements – however we, and chemical atoms, are also motivated by other forces to give us life. Some call the basic force "Spirit" related to The Element Fire.

We can consider that chemical atoms possess a very basic form of consciousness.

1. Electrons perform repetitive cycles around a central point in a similar way to the planets around The Sun. This is a form of "memory". There does not seem to be any explanation where the energy comes from to keep these activities going. Perhaps scientists should take something from Astrology and spend more time observing WHOLE atoms instead of just smashing them to pieces. Nowadays, Naturalists prefer to observe animals in the wild rather than killing and dissecting them as in earlier times.

2. The Chemical Elements show a form of Evolution. Each has evolved in an orderly fashion from the simplest one, Hydrogen - which has a single negatively charged Electron orbiting a single positively charged Proton – to Helium with 2 Protons and 2 electrons, and so on. There are complications later on in the series when atoms contain neutrally charged Neutrons. This is similar to the beginning of all life forms on earth that come from a single celled organisms consisting of a blob of jelly with a nucleus. It is unclear how the nucleus evolved, just as it is unclear how the first protons and electrons evolved.

There is more about this in the chapter [NUMEROLOGY] (COUNTING NUMBERS IN NATURE – ATOMS).

When we examine the history of use of the term "Elements", we see that it has come to mean something entirely different to that originally intended. Evidence of this is in the fact that the chemical "elements" as we know them today did not exist (in human consciousness) in those early days. Science as we know it today did not exist at the time, and the word "element" was used by philosophers, so it was originally a philosophical term – and, specifically, a Greek philosophical term. It comes from a Latin translation of a Greek word that means "rudiments", or "first step" [YLT]. There are so many physical "elements" today that I fail to see how they can be considered elemental – especially in the light of the discovery that they consist of even more numerous smaller ("elemental") atomic particles which seem to grow in number by the day. Scientists need to ignore particles and pay more attention to the Number Zero "space" between.

We have to realise that the basic psychology of those early days would have been completely different to that of today. In fact, study of The 4 Elements as applied to Psychology [PSYCHOLOGY : THE 4 FUNCTIONS] enables us to consider what changes have taken place. The early philosophers were much more mystical in their approach, which suggests more use of the Jungian Function of Intuition, which, in turn, relates to the Fire Element. With the growth of Science and the use of the written word since then, the Jungian Thinking Function has developed and become more valued by society. This is also a feature of the progression from the Age of Pisces (Water. Feeling) to the present Age of Aquarius (Air. Thinking) [ASTROLOGY : THE ZODIAC AGES].

THE 4 ELEMENTS

The 4 Elements have survived the millennia as a basic part of Astrology, so by comparing them with modern Psychology we can gain a better understanding of them, and how they operate. We note Jung's statement that contents of the Collective Unconscious cannot, and should not, be fully brought into consciousness. The fact that there are 4 Elements seems to make them self-regulating. Like the classical "Gods" they tend to "waste" energy by "squabbling" among themselves rather than combining forces. Despite their obvious power, more so from being unconscious, we also note that they exist as a manifestation of the One. As a complete set of 4 they are together a manifestation of the archetypal Number 4. Their sum total is Zero- which is the ultimate single Element where everything is in balance.

HISTORY

The concept of the 4 Elements arose in ancient Greece where the philosophers Thales (625-546 BC), Anaximenes (570-500 BC), and Heraclitus (540-480 BC) suggested that all matter is composed of one essential principle – the problem being that they could not agree whether it was Water or Fire. Empedocles (492-432 BC), expressed a different belief—that all substances are composed of four elements: Air, Earth, Fire, and Water – an example of the growing complexity in life.

(In this book we consider that the one essential principle is Zero, or No-thing).

Aristotle (384-322 BC) agreed, and the concept has survived more than 2,000 years – during which time the study of chemistry, via the Alchemists [APPENDIX : ALCHEMY], became more sophisticated. A feature of The 4 Elements is that they are separate and cannot combine with one another, and cannot be extracted from other substances. This fact was used in 1661 by the chemist Robert Boyle (ref. Boyle's Law), said to be a founder of modern chemistry [EB], to "disprove" the ancient thesis. This is a good example of how the rational Thinking Function can conflict with the Intuition Function (ref. Jung's 4 Functions below). Later discoveries have shown that the Chemical Elements are not really "elemental" in they are made up of smaller parts. The focus of attention on the atom firstly came up with the idea that they were composed of a positive nucleus and negatively charged electrons, then, from anomalies in measuring atomic weights, extra positive Protons and neutral Neutrons were discovered in the heavier elements. Nowadays there are even smaller Constituents in String Theory.

As science developed, a separate field of study, Physics, evolved in the 19th. century - concerned more with the physical world and structure of atoms rather than the interaction between them (Chemistry), and still smaller particles were discovered. Nowadays there are around 200 known types of sub atomic particles some of which exist for less than one hundred-millionth of a second [EB]. So much for "elements". There are around 118 known Chemical Elements today, some of which only exist in the laboratory.

THE CLASSICAL 4 ELEMENTS

1. The first thing to note is that The 4 Elements are not just physical entities. They are also Archetypal Principles, or forms of a single, basic, energy – more related to The Laws of Nature, such as those of Physics, Chemistry, and Psychology.

2. The Kabbalah, Astrology, and Numbers, show us that the non-material, indivisible, set of 4 Elements is itself manifestation of a single force which comes from another level or dimension. The 4 Elements define various levels of their own, which eventually give rise to physical manifestation. One example is how our theoretical ideas become material actions, or objects. The common denominator in the Zodiac is the power of the Sun which contains all electromagnetic frequencies, and which is modified by each of the Signs in turn (a product of the relationship between Sun and Earth). The Sun source energy does not change, but how it manifests on Earth does. We can also consider the spectrum of light in the same context. (White light contains all the other colours).

3. This concept brings another problem with our terminology, because The 4 Elements are not really "elemental" – the basic raw energy (Spirit. Fire) is the true root.

4. On their own, The 4 Elements are easy to describe. It is only when we begin to consider how they are expressed in life that things begin to get complicated. Open any book on Astrology and for each Zodiac Sign you will see a huge list of Correspondences for each one – such as Planet, Animal, Tarot Card,

THE 4 ELEMENTS

Perfume, Roman God, Greek God, Gemstone, Colour, Weapon, Health Correspondence and Body Part. There are some correspondences in this book, but I have tried to keep them to a minimum and consider their ACTIVITY (wave ?) rather than physical manifestations (particle ?).

5. The 4 Elements – in decreasing vibration frequency - Fire, Air, Water, and Earth each has a manifestation as its physical counterpart (Earth) – that is, perceived by the physical 5 Senses. When considering their relationship with the physical elements we can see correspondences - Earth is the most stable form (Solid. Earth of Earth), Water is a low temperature fluid state (Liquid. Water of Earth), Air is a high activity fluid state (Vapour. Gas. Air of Earth), Fire is the least physical but most active (Fire of Earth).

6. To become aware of each of The 4 Elements separately we have to observe their material correspondences and consider what is the abstract common denominator, or Intuitive link, between them.

7. The discovery of the Chemical Elements is an example of how human consciousness grows by "discovering" what is already there.

8. We can consider the Fire Element to be a more tangible representation of the basic Spiritual energy, but it cannot be the basic energy itself because it is balanced with the other 3 Elements.

9. In space, black holes return matter to the "Zero" state - No Thing - to complete the Cycle. Perhaps creating new universes elsewhere. Our study here suggests that scientists will learn more by studying "Zero" instead of multiplicity. It is clear that is what they are attempting to do, and where they will eventually succeed.

10. Zero, No-Thing, has everything is in Balance, Still and Silent. Creation requires Imbalance and Noise – especially of (human and non-human) Words.

11. As Above, So Below. As Below, So Above.

*In the beginning was the Word, and the Word was with God, and the Word was God. [John 1 : 1 KJV]

THE 4 ELEMENTS OF ASTROLOGY

The Elements of Astrology are perceived intuitively, and a major interest is in seeing how they react with one another. This is the conflicting , competitive, natures of the Classical "Gods" of which modern man has lost consciousness from ignore-ance, and is therefore more subject to their influence.

The 12 Signs of the Zodiac are representations of the 4 Elements – which, in order of decreasing frequency of vibration , are Fire (Spirit. Basic Energy), Air (Mind, Mental Realm), Water (Feeling, Emotional Realm) , Earth (Physical, Material Realm), each of which has 3 forms :-

1. Cardinal – initiating, impulsive (destructive, wasteful)
2. Fixed – controlled, stable (unmoving, inert)
3. Mutable – changing, evolving (uncontrolled, disorganised)

When observing the Zodiac Signs in their natural order we note that each of the 3 Octaves of the Logarithmic Timescale begins with a Fire Sign, then Earth, Air, and Water. The 4 Quarters each contain Signs in order Cardinal, Fixed, Mutable. The year begins at the Spring Equinox with the entry of The Sun into the Sign of Aries – Cardinal Fire.

They give rise to physical manifestation on Earth on an annual basis, and the development of a human on a lifetime basis from conception. The 12 Archetypal Stages of The Cycle of Growth, which includes the Signs, gives rise to Evolution. The 12 is a manifestation of the 4 combined with 3. Everything manifests with first an Idea (conception), and then a Word (vibration) – but not always in the mind of man.

A main principle of Astrology is that over many reincarnations we learn to master the basic Creative Life Force via The 4 Elements as symbolised by the 12 "Sun Sign Lessons" and the tasks required at the various stages of the Agricultural year. So one's Sun Sign is a basic indicator of the current Life Purpose at an elemental level.

Astrology states that Fire and Air are Positive (outward-going), and Water and Earth are of Negative polarity (inward-drawing). When observing the Zodiac Signs in their normal order as depicted in a chart we have the surprising fact that the complementary pairings of the Elements on opposite sides of a chart are of the same polarity. For example Aries (Cardinal Fire) is complementary to Libra (Cardinal Air). This differs from the pairings of the Jungian 4 Functions (below) where Irrational Intuition (Positive Fire) is paired with Irrational Sensation (Negative Earth), and Rational Thinking (Positive Air) paired with Rational Feeling (Negative Water).

THE 4 ELEMENTS

THE 4 ELEMENTS OF THE TAROT

There is more description in the [THE TAROT] chapter.

The 4 Elements of The Tarot are depicted in the 4 suits of the Minor Arcana. Wands (Fire), Swords (Air), Cups (Water), and Pentacles, or Coins (Earth). In readings the Minor Arcana is acted upon by the Major Arcana of 22 "Trumps", which I refer to stages in The Cycle of Growth. The Minor Arcana depicts activities of our normal outer life.

Each suit of the Minor Arcana consists of 10 cards, Ace to 10, plus 4 additional Court Cards – Page, Knight, Queen and King. The Court cards depict 16 different types of people. In the A.E. Waite pack used in this book the images of the cards in order show an escalation of power of each Element. The Ace of each suit is the primal Principle of each Element as a "seed" or beginning, which gradually increases as the number increases. The "balance point" is card number 6 of each suit. As the number/power increases beyond that an imbalance is produced which produces conflict until the force reaches maximum with Number 10, when it is finally spent and begins again at the Ace. The dynamics are better demonstrated when compared with The Kabbalah Tree of Life. [THE KABBALAH]. Waite was a Freemason and Kabbalist.

THE 4 BEASTS OF REVELATION AND THE CHAKRAS

The Chakra/Endocrine System [THE CHAKRAS] are 7 "energy centres" of the human body with bases on the spine. They each exist at 4 energy levels related to The 4 Elements. At the Fire level – which is the least material – there is greater connection with the external universal forces. Some psychics are able to see the Chakras as differently coloured vortexes of energy.

We have, in increasing order of frequency :-

1. EARTH LEVEL – the physical endocrine gland.
2. WATER LEVEL – the hormone production and effect on the body via the blood stream.
3. AIR LEVEL – the "intelligence" of the Chakras in communication with one another via the nervous system. Imbalance between them causes physical and/or mental disharmony.
4. FIRE LEVEL – the "electrical" energy of the Chakras which extends beyond the physical to produce the human aura. We see something like this in pictures from modern thermal imaging cameras which pick up the lower Infra-Red heat frequencies of the electromagnetic spectrum. The Chakras themselves each have a different frequency of vibration related to 7 colours.

In addition, we have association between The 4 Elements and the 4 lower Chakras.

According to Edgar Cayce [EC Reading 281 – 29], when giving readings concerning The Book of Revelation, the 4 lower Chakras/Endocrine Glands are associated with The 4 Elements, and Beasts and Horsemen of Revelation, thus :-

1. EARTH   - ROOT (Gonads)   Calf   – White Horse   – Red Chakra
2. WATER   - LYDEN (Cells of Leydig) Man   – Black Horse   - Orange Chakra
3. FIRE   - SOLAR PLEXUS (Adrenal) Lion – Red Horse   - Yellow Chakra
4. AIR   - HEART (Thymus)   Eagle – Pale Horse   - Green Chakra

The colours are indications of different frequency rates of vibration – as of light.

> *As given, the four destructive influences that make the greater desire for the carnal forces, that rise as the beasts within self to destroy. [EC 281 - 16]*

(Sounds a bit Freudian [BTB])

MORE ELEMENTAL MANIFESTATIONS

4 FUNCTIONS OF JUNGIAN PSYCHOLOGY

Covered in detail in the chapter [PSYCHOLOGY : THE 4 FUNCTIONS]

I associate these psychological Functions with Water because they are concerned more directly with the "Sea" of The Collective Unconscious. We can see that they are similar to The 5 Senses but are related more to our inner mind.

1. INTUITION (Fire of Water)

THE 4 ELEMENTS

2. THINKING (Air of Water)
3. FEELING (Water of Water)
4. SENSATION (Earth of Water) – related to the realm of the physical 5 Senses.

THE 5 SENSES

I associate these with the Element Air because they are forms of Communication - ways we receive information from our environment and transmit it, via nerves, to the brain. The physical organs relate to the Earth Element..

Although we say we have 5 Senses, there are really only 4 in terms of their methods of perception - which relate to different frequency ranges of electromagnetic vibration – and psychological cognition. For example, we see a flash of lighting before we hear the thunder that was generated at the same time. Because sensory information travels to us from large or small distances away we can say that it relates to the Air Element, which is concerned, among other things, with Communication at all levels. Here, Air not only refers to the air that we breathe, but includes the electromagnetic nerve impulses that are conveyed from our physical bodily "receivers" to our brain :-

1. SIGHT (Fire of Air) : Visible light frequencies. (Eyes)
2. HEARING (Air of Air) : Sound Waves (and thoughts induced by reading and writing).
3. SMELL and TASTE (Water of Air) : Chemical receptors of nose and mouth. Memory.
4. TOUCH (Earth of Air) : Physical sensory organs and nerves.

4 FUNDAMENTAL NUCLEAR FORCES

There is still a long way to go in our understanding particles at sub atomic level because it has been found that, like light, they can seem to act like particles or waves – and it depends on the experimental method used which of those states they demonstrate at any time. Also, atomic particles can appear, and disappear, and appear somewhere else – and appear to be in 2 places at the same time. Because the governing laws are not known, scientists can only calculate the PROBABILITY of a particle's activity and position in the atom at any one time.

We have the 4 fundamental Nuclear Forces of Physics, the Earth science, that operate at sub-atomic and universal levels. Please note that, as I do not fully understand the forces, I could be in error. However, the aim is to understand the principles – so feel free to work out your own associations. There is an additional factor to take into account in that I have ascribed the Weak and Strong Nuclear forces to Fire and Water – which seem to be more basic and precede Air and Earth as mentioned above. When speaking of "Forces" we are concerned with the hidden, non-material, relationships between material particles (Earth), and therefore the Traditional Element, Fire.

The Nuclear Fire forces are very considerable as demonstrated when they are released in a nuclear explosion. $E=Mc^2$.

1. WEAK NUCLEAR (Fire of Fire) : The Weak Force is concerned with causing particle energy decay in a nucleus to keep it stable by adjusting the Proton/Neutron ratio. It seems that a Proton can lose its electrical charge and become a neutrally charged Neutron, and vice versa. It only acts at atomic level. Fire because it seems to have only 2 states – neutral Zero, or 1 (i.e. "on, or off"). (This is not Positive or Negative).
2. ELECTROMAGNETIC (Air of Fire) : The Electromagnetic Force is concerned with attraction and repulsion of electrically charged particles. For example, positive Protons and negative Electrons. It acts at infinite distances. Related to Air here because of its positive/negative changeability and electrical connotations.
3. STRONG NUCLEAR (Water of Fire) : The Strong Force holds a nucleus together (normally, similarly charged particles repel one another). It acts only on particles that are in close proximity at atomic level. I have ascribed it to Water because it is basically a force of negative, inward-drawing, polarity (in Astrological context. Water is considered negative).
4. GRAVITY (Earth of Fire). : The Gravitational Force is that which attracts physical bodies together. It keeps us attached to the Earth, and holds our solar system together. It also acts at bigger distances throughout the universe.

THE 4 ELEMENTS

4 STATES OF MATTER

Also in Physics we have the 4 States of Matter which relate to The 4 Elements in terms of decreasing temperature/frequency, which are concerned with molecular activity. We are dealing with the behaviour of Earthy chemical molecules here, in theory any element or compound can exist in any of these states, so we relate the States of Matter to the classical 4 Elements thus :-

1. PLASMA (Fire of Earth) : This is the stuff that stars are made of, and accounts for 99% of the mass in the universe. It consists of superheated gas – mainly hydrogen and helium - at such extremely high temperature that the molecules move around in entirely random fashion – without form.
2. GAS (Air of Earth) : Molecules are more attracted to one another.
3. LIQUID (Water of Earth) : Molecules "stick together" more.
4. SOLID (Earth of Earth) : The most stable state of matter. A state of <u>relative</u> molecular Inertia (atoms are never entirely still, and there is actually much more space present than matter). The form is fixed and requires external energy to change or move. We note from Nuclear Physics that solids, such as exemplified by Uranium and other fissionable materials, contain an enormous amount of locked-in energy. $E=MC^2$.

THE 4 ELEMENTS

PSYCHOLOGY : THE 4 FUNCTIONS

THE 4 FUNCTIONS OF C. G. JUNG

Following a general description of The 4 Elements, we now consider a specialised example. This chapter describes The 4 Functions of Psychology as conceptualised by C.G.Jung. The 4 Functions relate directly to The 4 Elements in that, in both cases, each member acts entirely in its own realm and does not combine with any of the others.

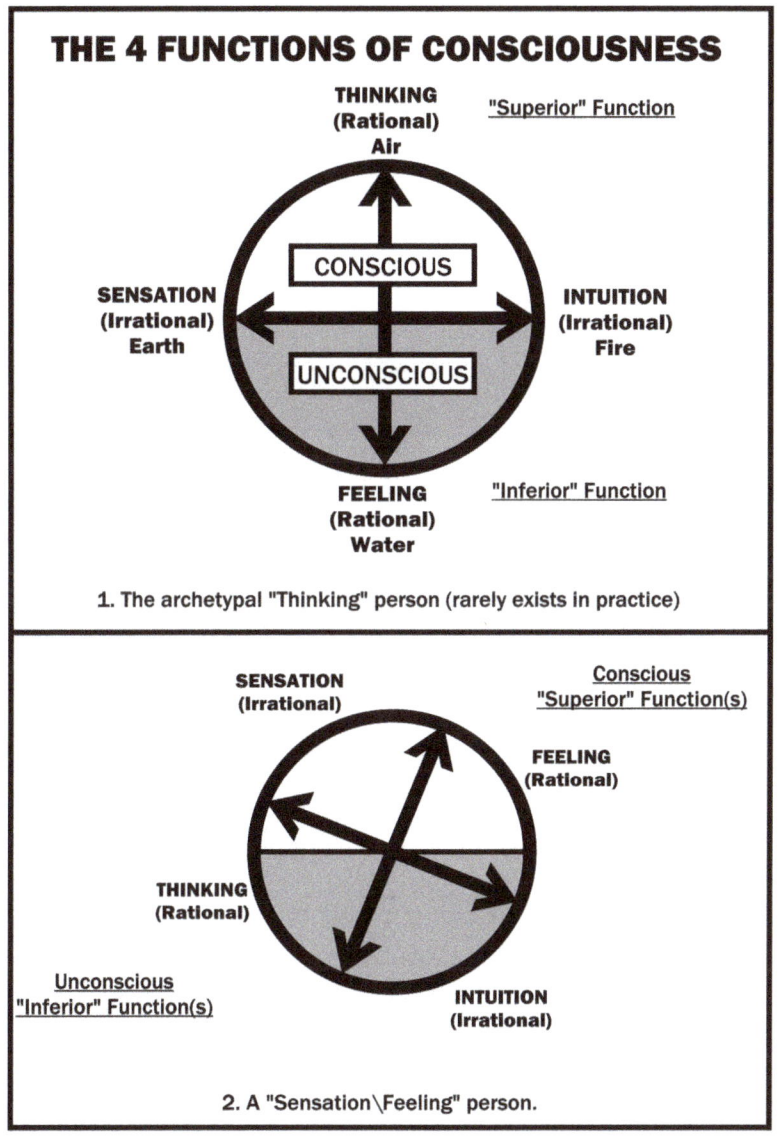

Figure 16 : The 4 Functions of C.G. Jung

The Magician of The Tarot suggests a single higher energy being directed downwards to be used in conjunction with the 4 "tools" on the table at the time of birth. The "tools" are those of the Tarot and the mind – Wands (Fire), Cup (Water), Sword (Air), Coin (Earth).

The 4 Functions can be considered as offering 4 completely different viewpoints, or ways of perceiving the world. It is this concept that enables us to bridge the gap between Psychology and Astrology because The 4 Functions Intuition, Sensation, Thinking and Feeling - relate to the classical 4 Elements. At the end of this chapter there is mention of "Function Types" in people, and Introversion and Extraversion that Jung applied to The 4 Functions . By comparing the 4 Functions with their Astrological counterparts and The Cycle of Growth we can get a better idea of their activity.

The 4 Functions can be considered to be skills or abilities in use of the mind. In childhood, depending on our inner nature and life circumstances, we develop, and therefore tend to rely on, one or two more than the others. The undeveloped Functions remain mainly unconscious. It seems that part of the Mid Life Crisis is the requirement for recognition of the undeveloped Function(s), and requires an attempt to take up activities that use, and therefore develop, them. There is usually a problem with this because the conscious attitude to the undeveloped Functions (and their activities, or people that use them) is usually negative. Also, because the functions are not developed, we will be clumsy when trying to use them. Apart from our natural tendency or personal preferences, society tends to favour those who have developed certain functions. Nowadays the Thinking Function is favoured. We note that not too long ago in history with a more agricultural environment for the masses the Thinking Function was not so complex. The Hunter Gatherer had no real need for it at all. As a result of The Age of Aquarius and its development of Communication via Education, Science, Reading, Writing, Mathematics, and the computer, Thinking is developing at an increasing rate. Society also decides which of the 4 Functions are more appropriate to men or women – although this is changing too.

We need to take note of the fact that The 4 Functions have a historical, or evolutionary, development. The psychology of our ancestors would have been quite different to that of today – more based on Intuition - which would help understand some of their "strange behaviour" when considered from a modern viewpoint. We see repetitions of our evolutionary development in the stages of development of a child in the womb, and, later on, in the stages of physical and psychological development during childhood.

RATIONAL AND IRRATIONAL FUNCTIONS

The 4 Functions of Psychology are divided into 2 sets of 2. The 2 Functions of each set are complementary in that there seems to be a conflict between them. They cannot be used (conscious) at one and the same time. Each pair consists of a positive\masculine and negative\feminine Function – which has nothing to do with male and female persons. All 4 Functions appear in men and women – although, as Astrology shows, not in the same personal or individual balance.

Thinking and Feeling are "Rational" functions. The word "rational" has its root in "ratio" and "ration" which suggests that it is possible to divide them into parts and compare the parts. They enable things and experiences to be evaluated. So we have rational Feeling as well as rational Thinking. An example of problems caused by misunderstanding this pair is when a logical Thinking Person tries to obtain a verbal explanation for a Feeling Person's decision –which they are unable to give. ("It just feels right").

Intuition and Sensation are termed "Irrational" because they deal with perceptions as a whole and entirely objectively – that is, without any evaluation.

A problem is that we are here attempting to understand Intuition, Sensation, and Feeling through the written word – which is a tool of the Thinking Function. The only real way to understand The 4 Functions is by way of our own personal perceptions and experience. A guide to this for yourself would be to observe your reactions, positive, negative, or neutral, to what follows.

INTUITION (FIRE. INSTINCT) – THE LOST ART ?

I deal with Intuition first because a new born child exists solely in this state. We can also see that Intuition would also have been the main psychological state of Homo Sapiens, and our early evolutionary ancestors - the Hunter Gatherers. It seems that human evolution has required that we lose some of its abilities in favour of the other Functions as we become more "civilised". There is, however, a movement to recover our Intuitive abilities such as through techniques of Meditation and via the Eastern Martial Arts.

Intuition is probably the least understandable of all the Functions. It is often confused with "feminine intuition" which, depending on the individual may or may not apply, and (from my contact with mediumship) which may refer to a developed Feeling ability. Intuition is a masculine energy related to Instinct. It is better understood by comparing it with Sensation– its complementary, feminine, Irrational Function - the concept of which we are more familiar. Intuition is even feared by some – to such an extent that those who have a natural intuitive ability are locked away, or it is treated as a "mental illness". The problem is that such individuals often have low abilities in the other Functions (especially that of relating to Sensation and the material world and physical body) which makes them unable to care for themselves – at least in the modern world. They might, however, survive better than most in a Hunter Gatherer lifestyle. The "psychology" of animals seems to be more related to Intuition.

We can observe Intuition in the modern world by looking where there is a bias towards instinct with greater or lesser development of the other Functions. At base level, Homo Sapiens evolved with the apes, so chimpanzees are pure forms. The next stage of human development was the Hunter Gatherer, and there are still forms of life today that are based on small groups surviving in basic natural surroundings. For example, we have the Bushmen of Africa, the Swamp Men of America who survive by hunting alligators, and the Aborigines of Australia who seem to be finally dying out by becoming "civilised", as were the American Indians. At another level we have the modern Savants who demonstrate unusual mental abilities, and it is, perhaps, from them we learn most about the Function.

SAVANTISM (Autism Spectrum Disorder)

As seems usual, we learn most about various human conditions when things seem to go wrong. There are numerous different levels of Savantism, and I am only taking a broad view here. Savant comes from the French, and means "knowing".

The 1988 film "Rain Man" starred Tom Cruise and Dustin Hoffman who takes the part of Raymond (which he pronounces "Rain Man"), who is a savant. The film is based on real-life savant Kim Peek (1951-2009). In the film, among other things, someone drops a box of matches which empties on the floor, and Raymond immediately states the exact number there. Kim Peek was able to do the same. He was also able to keep track of playing cards gambling in a casino. Kim Peek was a lot more complicated than the character portrayed in the film. He died of a heart attack.

[*YouTube Video of Kim Peek : http://www.youtube.com/watch?v=AfDEAIszuQI]

[*Kim Peek Obituary Article : The Telegraph 22 December 2009
http://www.telegraph.co.uk/news/obituaries/medicine-obituaries/6867567/Kim-Peek.html]

I remember reading that this same ability was present in Australian Aborigines who kept very large flocks of sheep and were instantly aware if any were missing.

Savantism brings some mental abilities that amaze us with skills related to such areas as music (being able to replay long pieces of music only heard once), mathematics (being able to do computations using huge numbers), and art. The downside is that there is some difficulties with handling, what, to us, is normal life – that is, an under-developed complementary Sensation Function. In fact, not too long ago savants were considered mentally retarded or psychologically abnormal and institutionalised. Perhaps some still are. The encyclopaedias describe savants as being of "subnormal intelligence". Nowadays psychologists are beginning to recognise that there are other forms of intelligence apart from the Thinking Function. They are not the same as prodigies, who are otherwise normal in development.

There is a similarity to Autism that tends to appear at the age of 3, which seems to be mainly related to language skills which do not develop normally (Thinking. Air), and difficulties in relating to other people.

One of the main abilities is that savants have is that they remember everything, and recall memories at will. In the chapter [PSYCHOLOGY : TRANSACTIONAL ANALYSIS] there is mention of the discovery that we all "record" every experience we have, and if a weak electric current is directly applied to various places in our brain they are recalled in vivid detail – with sights, sounds, and smell. The only difference, then, is that we do not all have the power of total recall at will. Kim Peek had, among numerous other things, memorised The Bible by the age of 7.

In the chapter [MY STORY] you will see that I had contact with various forms of mediumship, and have a slight experience myself. Although not the same as savantism, some forms of mediumship are similar. In particular there is one type where the medium has no foreknowledge of what they are about to say. They have to start talking, and keep going. One, I remember, had to keep moving physically, pacing up and down the platform. I know someone who had trouble at school because she was able to give answers to mathematical problems, but unable to say how she "worked then out" (which, of course, she had not in the normal sense, which requires Thinking). She was accused of cheating, and learned not to mention it in future. Many people with the ability for mediumship never develop it for the same reason.

We all recognise that Sensation is perception by means of the 5 senses - Hearing, Seeing, Touch, Taste and Smell. It brings practical abilities. With Intuition, perception seems to bypass the 5 senses and become an instant "photograph" in the mind. As we will see below with the Function Types, a bias toward a particular Function leads to problems with its complementary Function. Savants generally have physical problems (Earth. Sensation), and some famous savants were born blind. In Kim Peek's case the left hemisphere of his brain was damaged at birth impairing his language (Air. Thinking) and motor skills (Earth. Sensation).

In Astrology we relate Intuition to the Element Fire, which is the Element which vibrates at the fastest rate. Light speed. Kim Peek has 3 planets in the Fire Element in his Birth Chart which include Mercury (mental abilities) in Sagittarius and Jupiter, "Expansion/Inflation" (ruler of Sagittarius) in the instinctive Sign of Aries. Without an accurate birth time, that is all we can say, and I have not been able to find birth dates for other known savants. At another level this is pure Instinct. Intuitive people are not very practical (normal life is "too boring") and often do not look after their physical body very well – such as by eating regularly.

PSYCHOLOGY : THE 4 FUNCTIONS

Although Kim Peek had problems earlier in life, and needed a "minder", he was trained to walk (Earth. Sensation) and lead a more "normal" life. His bias toward Intuition was naturally strong, so it was not fully "programmed out" as it has been with most of us. I have read about other young people who have shown unusual abilities which disappear as they learn to communicate in words (Thinking Function). In my case there is a family story that at around 2 years of age I was able to "read" a fairy story from a book word for word, turning the pages at the right times. My father had read the story to me. I cannot recall any memory of this. I was not actually able to read until 4 or 5. I distinctly remember the occasion when I realised I could.

We can see why intuitive people generally keep themselves in the background of life. At one time in my exploration of the "occult" world I met a young man who had no fixed home and travelled the world where he was led to help certain people. He said that, when it came time to move on, money and other means always became available to enable him to do so.

MEDITATION

The act of meditation is clearly designed to achieve a state where we are in touch with our Intuition by reducing attention to the other Functions. There is a more practical coverage in the Appendix. We reduce Sensation by finding a comfortable seat in a quiet place. We reduce Feeling by putting attention to pleasant thoughts or playing calming music. We reduce Thinking by putting attention to our breathing.

MARTIAL ARTS AND SPORT

A similar state of mind is required in the Martial Arts and Sport. We see that one of the aims of martial arts is to be able to act solely on Intuition – even to the extent of the master being blindfolded (or is this a myth ?). Sport is similar in that, during a match, there is not time to pay conscious attention to Sensation, Feeling, or Thinking. Both, however, require training of the physical body (Sensation) to be able to act and react quickly. We note that the Birth Charts of sports persons often show some focus on the Fire Element as well as a strong Mars.

SPIRITUAL DEVELOPMENT. BECOMING AS CHILDREN

In The Bible there is reference for the need to "become as a child", which seems to relate to Intuition. In-tuition can be defined as a way of obtaining information or knowledge without recourse to reason or experience (i.e. child like). I summarise the foregoing :-

- We have seen that forms of spiritual development such as meditation and martial arts require focus on the Intuition Function.
- We have seen its relationship to instinct. Animals appear to act at this level and survive without the other Functions.
- We have seen the evolution of man has involved developing from an animal state by developing the other 3 Functions – Thinking being the last.
- We see that a new born baby (Cycle of Growth Stage 1. Fire) is close to an animal state by not yet having developed the other 3 Functions, and that its later development focuses on the undeveloped Functions. Cycle of Growth Stage 2 (Earth. Sensation) focuses on development and control of a physical body. Cycle of Growth Stage 3 (Air. Thinking) focuses on mental development and communication. Cycle of Growth Stage 4 (Water. Feeling) focuses on emotional development from entry into a wider society.
- We note that in the cycle of a human lifetime we begin as a child and seem to return to a "second childhood" at the end.

And said, Verily I say unto you, Except ye be converted, and become as little children, ye shall not enter into the kingdom of heaven. [KJV Matthew:18:3:]

In December 1945 in Nag Hammadi, Egypt, a buried jar was uncovered containing 52 books among which is "The Gospel of Thomas" containing sayings attributable to Jesus speaking to his disciple Thomas.

Jesus said: The man aged in his days will not hesitate to ask a little child of seven days about the place of life, and he shall live. For there are many first who shall be last, and they shall become a single one. [Gospel of Thomas # 4]

Jesus saw some infants at the breast. He said to his disciples: These little ones at the breast are like those who enter into the kingdom. They said to him: If we then be children, shall we enter the kingdom?

PSYCHOLOGY : THE 4 FUNCTIONS

Jesus said to them: When you make the two one, and when you make the inside as the outside, and the outside as the inside, and the upper as the lower; and when you make the male and the female into a single one, that the male be not male and the female; when you make eyes in the place of an eye, and a hand in place of a hand, and a foot in place of a foot, an image in place of an image, then shall you enter [the kingdom]. [Gospel of Thomas # 22]

*His disciples said: On what day wilt thou be revealed to us, and on what day shall we see thee? Jesus said: When you unclothe yourselves and are not ashamed, and take your garments and lay them beneath your feet like little children, and tread upon them, then [shall ye see] the Son of the living One, and ye shall not fear. [Gospel of Thomas # 37]

PARADOX

The Intuition Dimension is that of Paradox. We are wasting time trying to describe what Paradox is because we are using the non-compatible Thinking Function - so here are some examples :-

1. MEDITATION IS DOING NOTHING.
2. DESCRIBING THE INDESCRIBABLE
3. "THIS SENTENCE IS FALSE."
4. "THE SOUND OF ONE HAND CLAPPING" (from Zen Buddhism)
5. "Less is more."
6. "All animals are equal, but some are more equal than others" *("Animal Farm". George Orwell)*
7. We also have from Zen the question "If a tree falls in a forest and there is no-one there, does it make a sound ?"

We can see that, to the realm of Thinking and Logic the statements are nonsense. However, what is your inner reaction to them ?

THINKING (AIR)

Thinking is a Rational Function paired with Feeling. Thinking evaluates and classifies perception by means of thought or cognition, and is a set of metal abilities which includes such things as memory and understanding language. Thinking tends to evaluate according to "True or False", "Right or Wrong". If animals have a Thinking function it would be at the most rudimentary level. Human communication is transmitted by Air, which includes the "air waves" of radio, television, and mobile telephones. The vibration frequency level of Air, or gases, comes between that of Fire and Water. Gases act like fluids.

FEELING (WATER)

Feeling is a Rational function paired with Thinking. At this level evaluation is made on a scale between Pleasant and Unpleasant. It is closely allied to the sense of smell and taste. For example, things may not "smell right", or someone may "have good taste" – neither of which evaluations can be related to the Thinking Function, which is more concerned with logical analysis.

SENSATION (EARTH)

Sensation is, perhaps, the most easy Function for us to comprehend because it is the realm of our 5 Senses. It is an Irrational Function paired with Intuition in that it deals with perception rather than evaluation. Each Sense requires a physical bodily organ to convert the stimulus to electrical energy and transmit information to the brain via special nerves. Despite the overall 5 Senses being related to the Earth Element, we can relate them individually to each of The 4 Elements. We note that each of the Senses is concerned with perception of a different range of frequencies. The physical receptors also act as filters – so we do not perceive every frequency. Animals have a greater range of sensory perception than humans.

SIGHT (Fire of Earth)

Sight deals with high frequencies of vibration in the middle levels of the Electro-magnetic Spectrum. At the top end of the Spectrum we have Gamma Rays, X-rays and Ultra Violet – then the Spectrum of Visible Light. As the frequencies decrease further we have Infra-Red (heat) followed by Radio and Television frequencies.

PSYCHOLOGY : THE 4 FUNCTIONS

HEARING (Air of Earth)

Hearing depends upon vibrations of air physically vibrating our ear drums. Manufacturers of high fidelity sound reproducing equipment have established that to achieve the most realistic effect their equipment must be capable of reproducing sound in the range 10 hertz (cycles per second) for low notes and 20,000 hertz for high notes. At the lower end of the scale, low notes are not so much perceived by the ear as felt by the body and require more energy to vibrate the air. Not only does our hearing mechanism filter the input by only being receptive to certain frequencies, but it is most sensitive to the range of the human voice. There is therefore a connection to the Thinking Function.

I remember reading about someone in the past who was considered a genius in school because he was able to read without moving his lips.

TASTE AND SMELL (Water of Earth)

Taste and Smell can be considered a pair because they both depend upon chemical receptors to perceive stimuli. We are now at the vibration frequency of liquids. At an Astrology course I attended "Water people" came to the common agreement that smell was one of their most important perceptions. We note that smells often evoke past memories.

TOUCH (Earth of Earth)

Here we perceive at the lower end of frequency. It is notable that we can sense heat – which is in the Infra-red electromagnetic range, just below that of visible light.

JUNGIAN PSYCHOLOGY FUNCTION TYPES

The descriptions here relate closely to those of the Sun Signs and their Elements.

To further understand The 4 Functions, psychologists describe 4 Function Types. We note that the "pure" type is not met frequently in normal life, and it seems that, when they are, the people concerned have psychological problems – as in the case of Kim Peek, above. There is lack of balance, and it seems that a lot of the work of C.G.Jung was in attempting to restore a balance. In dreams the undeveloped ("Inferior") Function might appear in images such as animals, children, or crippled figures – or in even more frightening guises if neglected too long.

In normal life we maintain balance by being involved in a variety of activities that require the use of different functions. We might, for example, have hobbies that different functions from those we use to earn our daily bread. The latter tends to rely on our main developed function.

The Collective Unconscious often tends to attract us to relationships with people of our Inferior Function Type. I remember meeting a lady with 5 planets in Fire Signs in her Birth Chart who was married to a bank manager – so we see she supplied the creative Fire and he the stability of Earth.

The diagrams at the beginning of the chapter are attempts to show the psychology. The top diagram is that of an archetypal Thinking Type - which tends to be more highly valued in society today. We see that FOR THE INDIVIDUAL DEPICTED Thinking is fully conscious, and is therefore the "Superior Function", which means that complementary Feeling is the "Inferior Function" and rarely used, it is therefore undeveloped, unconscious and unrecognised. In the diagram, the Irrational Functions Sensation and Intuition are only partially developed.

The lower diagram is more "true to life" having imbalance in the Inferior Functions. The individual is a Sensation Type with Inferior Function Intuition – and would be more concerned with practical "reality" than abstract theories or beliefs. However, in this case, Feeling is somewhat developed, and more conscious, so it is called the "Auxiliary Function". The Thinking Function, being antithetical to the Auxiliary Function, is largely unconscious – however, Jung suggests that this function would be considered a way of reaching the totally unconscious Inferior Function.

THE INTUITION TYPE

We have seen above that Savantism is an extreme example of an Intuition Type, as is a new born baby. I also suggest that some forms of mediumship are related. Having had experience in this field, I can say that mediumship training is mainly concerned with being able to "switch on" and "switch off" (or "close down") so one can handle a normal life. I also refer to my experience in the [MY STORY] chapter. It does seem that Intuition is an Inferior Function in most of us. Because it is Unconscious, our Inferior Function is the one that gives us connection to The Collective Unconscious. It seems that Intuition gives rise to "hunches" or other forms of premonition. Nowadays we tend to be taught to ignore our hunches in favour of more rational methods. Intuition is Irrational (as is Sensation, remember). Because of this the Function is undeveloped and does not give reliable results – which, in turn, leads to further ignore-ance.

I have known several psychics and mediums who had their abilities suppressed early in life because their parents did not understand, or became afraid.

The Intuition Type (Fire) has to learn to check their hunches with external facts (Earth). To "earth" the energy. Fire Signs tend to neglect care of their physical body.

Many artists seem to be of this Type. They attempt to express inner perceptions through material objects such as paint and stone. Typically, they do not look after themselves very well in physical terms. The better they are able to represent the archetypes of the Collective Unconscious, the more they are valued. They have an unconscious "hook". Many people try to rationalise the creations of artists. The Irrational cannot be rationalised. Others are able to channel the creativity through the Thinking Function in words, such as Poetry, and/or the Feeling Function in Music and Dance.

THE SENSATION TYPE

Whereas Intuition is an inner perception, Sensation is more related to external circumstances, and so is considered to be Reality as we know it. Sensation types are more concerned with practical, material, details and "facts of life" as perceived by the 5 Senses. They pay attention to care of their physical bodies. Although many may seem to be over concerned with money, this is often more related to physical security and comfort. As we have seen above, they can be attracted to Intuition Types, or, fearfully reject people that do not fit in with their "norm". Irrational functions are "black or white" with no shades of grey.

THE THINKING TYPE

The Thinking Type is concerned with thought, which is mainly communicated in written or spoken words. We take an idea and "chop it up into bits" which are delivered piecemeal. It is left to the "receiver" to put it all back together again. In our scientific age, society nowadays seems to value this Function more than others nowadays – as is evidenced by our education system. Reading, 'Riting, and 'Rithmatic. We note that it is probably due to its virtual non-existence in past history. The Type tends to ignore whether things are pleasant or unpleasant, being concerned with "Right and Wrong" and moral principles – obeying the letter, rather than the spirit of, the law. In past society, Thinking was the province of men, and Feeling of women. We can see in this how social expectations and early training in childhood could lead to reinforcement of this belief in actual life.

THE FEELING TYPE

The Feeling Type is more concerned with inner reaction to outer circumstances (emotions), and whether they are pleasant or unpleasant. In the Feeling Type, the emotions are more conscious than unconscious (as they would be in the Thinking Type). Perhaps more than other Types, the Feeling person can empathise more with others. We must note that, being a Rational Function, the Feeling Type is aware of a greater range of feeling affects than the Thinking Type and is able to make judgements based on them. The problem comes that, having an undeveloped Thinking Function, they are unable to communicate their "reasons" for decisions, resulting in frustrating conversations. Some Feeling people prefer to arouse unpleasant feelings rather than experience no emotions at all.

It could be that the tendency for society today to value the Thinking Function above the others has brought a lack of emotional empathy.

PERSONAL EXPERIENCE

I find that my personal experience is somewhat different to that suggested by Jung who states that the Inferior Function always remains unconscious. I am predominantly a Thinking Type, my daily work for the last 22 years being concerned with financial data analysis and computer programming – which makes my Inferior Function Feeling. However, among my hobbies is Ballroom Dancing with which I currently have an agreement with my partner that, at practice we concentrate on learning the routines – which I write down in detail (Sensation/Thinking), when we dance normally we go solely to enjoy the movement and music – which exercises Intuition and Feeling. The Intuition comes from having to adapt our routines to avoid other couples on the dance floor, when there is no time to think. I am able to avoid bumping into other couples even when dancing backwards. We can see that I might further exercise Intuition by taking up some form of competitive sport (which I dislike).

EXTRAVERSION AND INTROVERSION

In addition to the Function Types, Jung also identified "Attitude Types". The attitude of Extraversion or Introversion modifies the main Function, and therefore the Inferior Function. So a person's main Function could be Extraverted Thinking, when the Inferior Function would be Introverted Feeling. An introverted thinker would have extraverted feeling.

The Attitude determines the main focus of one's attention in experiences. An Extrovert has a positive relationship with the objective outside world in that actions are determined by what is happening there. An Introvert is more concerned with inner subjective activity, and the first reaction to external changes will be to withdraw.

Where one's Superior Function is introverted, one's Inferior Function is extroverted, and this is what people around will see. We may therefore tend to act somewhat clumsily in social gatherings – and therefore tend to avoid them.

MID LIFE CRISIS

When the Mid Life Crisis occurs at around age 40 it is characterised by the Inferior Function beginning to become to consciousness. It is as if there is psychological movement towards wholeness and a more balanced personality where each and every Function plays a part. I suggest that this is related to the 84 year cycle of Uranus, which seems to have some involvement in the Jungian Individuation process. At 42 years of age it has completed the outward half of its cycle and is returning to the position it occupied at the time of birth – as indicated in one's Birth Chart. We have to remember that the Inferior Function is only "inferior" because it has remained unconscious so far, and has therefore not been developed at all. The problem is that, because of its still child-like state, it begins to reveal itself in inappropriate or childish ways. At mid-life one has usually achieved a state where one has become established and has some control over circumstances. One now starts to become clumsy. The first reaction is an attempt to exert more control in the habitual direction, but this is thwarted because one does not seem to have the energy any more, or one is not equipped to deal with the problems. There is a certain boredom as psychic energy is channelled into the unconscious. Accidents or ill health can occur.

The first half of life is a drive to establish one's self in the outer world. The second half of life seems to be a movement towards achieving the state of wholeness one was in at the time of birth by giving attention to one's inner world. It is clear that the mainly extroverted personality finds the first half of life relatively easy, and the second half more difficult - whereas the introvert is the opposite. For example, people involved in extroverted physical activities, such as sport, recognise that they will become less able to compete as they approach mid-life.

ASTROLOGY : ORIGINS AND OVERVIEW

ARRANGEMENT OF CHAPTERS

Because Astrology is a major part of this book the subject is subdivided into several chapters . Please note that this is not an extensive study and is only meant to give a basic understanding of the various factors that affect The Cycle Of Growth.

ASTROLOGY : ORIGINS AND OVERVIEW (this chapter)

The beginnings and how Astrology developed. Birth Charts. Scientific validation. Psychology. BBC News story – New Moon affecting crime rate and police activity.

ASTROLOGY : PLANETS

ASTROLOGY : SIGNS

ASTROLOGY : HOUSES

ASTROLOGY : BIRTH CHART (Natal Astrology)

Includes an example Birth Chart and brief Interpretation : Lady Diana Spencer

ASTROLOGY : TRANSITS

Includes an example Transit Chart and brief Interpretation : Lady Diana Spencer

ASTROLOGY : ZODIAC AGES (eg. Age of Aquarius)

ASTROLOGY : SYNASTRY

The comparison of 2 Birth Charts to examine the relationship between the people concerned. Sigmund Freud and C.C.Jung.

ORIGINS AND OVERVIEW

In The Bible there is mention of The Tree of Life and The Tree of Knowledge of good and Evil. In fact there is only a single Tree, which basically refers to the human Chakra system [THE CHAKRAS] which are the energy centres of the body and related endocrine glands. The choice of Adam and Eve put "seals" on the Chakras of The Tree of Life, which transformed it into The Tree of Knowledge. At the end of The Bible, in Revelation, we have a description of one man's experience of opening the Chakras. The point here is that despite there traditionally being 7 Chakras recognised, we see a relationship with Astrology in that they bear 12 fruits.

> *And he shewed me a pure river of water of life, bright as crystal, going forth out of the throne of God and of the Lamb:in the midst of its broad place, and of the river on this side and on that, [is] a tree of life, yielding twelve fruits, in each several month rendering its fruits, and the leaves of the tree [are] for the service of the nations; [Revelation 22 Verses 1-2 YLT]*

The original main use of Astrology was to define an annual Calendar to co-ordinate human (and heavenly) activities.

> *And God said, Let there be lights in the firmament of the heaven to divide the day from the night; and let them be for signs, and for seasons, and for days, and years: [Genesis Chapter 1 Verse 14]*

> *"There shall be signs in the sun, the moon, and the stars." [Luke 21:25]*

> *"There is a time for everything, and a season for every activity under heaven: a time to be born and a time to die, a time to plant and a time to uproot, a time to kill and a time to heal, a time to tear down and a time to build, a time to weep and a time to laugh, a time to mourn and a time to dance, a time to scatter stones and a time to gather them, a time to embrace and a time to refrain, a time to search and a time to give up, a time to keep and a time to throw away, a time to tear and a time to mend, a time to be silent and a time to speak, a time to love and a time to hate, a time for war and a time for peace." [Eccl. 3:1-8]*

> *Astrology originated in Mesopotamia, perhaps in the 3rd millennium BC [EB]*

> *Evidence of the recording of lunar phases has been revealed by notches carved on animal bones dating back to 15,000 BC during the old Stone Age, and before the development of agriculture. Such recording would have become far more important as a result of the development of agriculture between 10,000 BC*

ASTROLOGY : OVERVIEW

and 5000 BC, and evidence from many early cultures shows that the heliacal rising (= seeming rising and setting on the horizon) of the stars was used by 2000 BC to give a more precise timing to the agricultural year." [IHA]

Astrology has grown in relationship to the evolution of mankind, and our expansion of consciousness. It started from men observing the heavens at different times of the year and keeping records of what they saw on whatever materials were to hand - such as bark, bone, or clay tablets. Some of these still exist today. From these early times it has been clear that there is a connection between what is happening in the heavens and what is happening on Earth. To begin with, the short term changes in climate, then the phases of the Moon, and later the greater annual cycle of the Seasons became apparent. From this evolved a more cyclic notion of Time, and the development of a Calendar which could be used to plan agriculture and events. Mankind is still learning how to work with Nature and Time. Consciousness was expanding beyond a mere recognition of Day and Night to encompass longer time periods.

The pattern of more distant stars was seen as unchanging. Nowadays we know that, due to the "Precession of the Equinoxes" [THE ZODIAC AGES : AGE OF AQUARIUS] the Sun no longer rises at 0 degrees of Aries on the day of the Spring Equinox, but the symbolism related to the Signs is valid in that it refers to the calendar and months of Spring, Summer, Autumn, and Winter <u>as we see them on Earth</u> - which have not changed. The principle is the same as that of using imaginary lines of Latitude and Longitude. Using this information we can date the naming of the constellation back to the time when this was the case. Each Age lasts around 2000 years, so omitting the recent 2,000 year Age of Pisces takes us to The Age of Aries around 2,000 to 4,000 years ago.

ZODIAC SIGNS AND THE CALENDAR

It was noticed that at sunrise, when stars and the Sun are visible at the same time, there is a slightly different view each day. It was later found that this repeated depending on the time of year, so the pattern of distant stars was seen as a fixed circular path along which the Sun travelled once a year. This was related to the phases of the Moon with its 29 day cycle, which enabled the year to be roughly divided into "moons" later to be called "months". To identify the "moons" the clusters of stars visible at the time were given names, and the circular frame of reference was divided into 12 equal "Signs" of 30 degrees. As the names are mainly those of animals, the Signs together comprise "The Zodiac " (="circle of animals"). Please note that the division of the circle into equal Signs came first, and they were given names relative to the star patterns at that time. This fixed the Calendar for the first time. The fixed frame of reference enabled the discovery of other bodies that also seemed to follow this path, but at a much slower rate. They are the visible planets, the furthest being Saturn. The discovery of the planets beyond Saturn required further expansion of consciousness and the use of technology.

To begin with, the attitude to this study was rather superstitious. The Sun does have an earthly affect depending on its annual position, and the Moon phase affects the sea tides and women's menstruation (and crime – please see the figure below). The planets were thought to "rule" the Earth. As they cannot be controlled, and seem to control us, they were viewed as "Gods" that had to be appeased by worship and sacrifice.

Further development over the centuries has involved a wider division between Astrologers and Astronomers. Astronomy is now more concerned with such things as the observation, measurement and mapping of heavenly bodies. With modern tools such as the visual and radio telescopes, and computers, they are probing further into the Universe that surrounds us. This study has enabled the discovery of the planets beyond Saturn - Uranus (1781), Neptune (1846), and Pluto (1930) which, invisible to the unaided eye, also orbit our Sun at great distances away.

PLANETS

Astrologers are still more concerned with the closer environment of our Solar System consisting of Sun and orbiting Planets Earth, Moon, Mercury, Venus, Mars, Jupiter, Saturn, Neptune and Pluto - all included in the term "Planets". We make use of Astronomy from having a better picture of the true layout of our Solar System, as well as having accurate figures to be able to plot the position of the planets at any moment in time - past, present, or future.

Astrology too has developed in many ways. It is still concerned with the study of energy relationships between the Planets, but no longer just related to agriculture. It also includes other human affairs, and with cycles of change lasting much longer than a single year, or even a human lifetime. Especially from the work of the psychologist C.G.Jung, there has been found a relationship between Astrology and Psychology.

ASTROLOGY : OVERVIEW

BIRTH CHARTS (NATAL ASTROLOGY)

Here we are mainly concerned with Natal Astrology, which relates the moment of birth of an individual to the positions of the Planets at the same time, and deals with the development of the Individual person. There are other areas of study such as Mundane Astrology that deals with the chart of a country or town. The Birth Chart can be considered a "snapshot" picture of the of the solar system at that time. We no longer believe the planets control us. Rather, they are indicators of the "climate" existing at that time. An indicator of the Universal forces which both we and they are subject to. I am expecting to see an eventual connection with the study of Genetics and DNA . We use a chart that puts the Earth at the centre, rather than the Sun. The reason for this is that this is the VIEW-POINT from which we see life, and from which all our observations are made. Everything seems to revolve around us as an individual "centre". This fits in with Einstein's concept of Relativity which relates a moving object and its observer. For example, even though we know that it is the rotation of the Earth that determines the position of the Sun in the sky, it does not change the relative position (angle) between it and the horizon from the viewpoint of an observer, which can be used for navigation.

We can see that Astrology has developed alongside human and scientific growth over the years. We are no longer tied to agriculture, and a rural life. As we have escaped from bondage to the Sun and soil Astrology has grown too. However, the main principles still remain. It is still a study of Nature. Just like a farmer has to learn to work with natural forces to grow crops, so we do too. Our personal "crops" may not nowadays be such things as wheat or beef, but the principles of achieving growth in life are the same. It still surprises me that I never physically made or grew anything to sell in order to make a living. Neither "sowing or reaping". We can do things against Nature - human or otherwise – but, like farmers, it is far easier to use the "time" to work with natural forces. Astrology also takes into account new knowledge from other areas of life, such as Psychology. In Natal Astrology the type of "vehicle" of Body and Mind our Spirit has to work through is part of our "climate". Part of our personal Nature. Such concepts now familiar to us were not available to early Astrologers, who therefore had to use symbols to communicate them. There is still need for symbols - which are basically mnemonic (="memory") systems - even though most of us can now read and write.

In modern Astrology there are no "Good" or "Evil" influences, although there are certainly "Easy" and "Difficult". If life was all easy, how else would we grow? Unfortunately the mind and ego do not wish to acknowledge this fact. Or tries to ignore the matter completely until things get out of hand, or ill health arises. It is much easier to deny responsibility for our actions by blaming life, other people, the Devil, or planets. Unfortunately, many contemporary astrologers have not grown with the times either, and, to remain popular, continue to foster the belief of "evil influences" and maintain the simplistic viewpoint that we are all completely governed by the Sun (Sign). Nowadays life and Astrology are much more complicated. This comes from our having a greater variety of choice. Greater freedom brings greater responsibility. However, it is still better to know whether the current "time" is better for "sowing", "reaping" or "resting", for example.

The principle on which my analysis is based is that the main purpose of life is the development of Individuality, which includes development of Will and Consciousness. At a practical level this involves finding our true "life purpose" or vocation, which might be a goal rather than an actual job. This personal growth is a lifetime task, as demonstrated by the movements of planets in relation to our Birth Chart. When we travel our true path we fulfil our destiny. We know when we have found it because there is in inner sense of joy and happiness - despite possible difficult external circumstances, or needing to work behind the scenes in self-development. Also a balance between doing something that gives us pleasure, for Love rather than gain, and at the same time being of service to others.

SCIENTIFIC VALIDATION

Before examining Astrology in any depth it is worthwhile to consider if the exercise is worthwhile. Is Astrology valid?

There are many people who assert that Astrology is "rubbish". When we ask for further clarification of that statement we discover that none of them have bothered to explore the subject in any depth - possibly from fear, or as a result of some negative religious belief, or just laziness. However, they are more likely to know their "Sun Sign" than the name of their local member of parliament. We note that one of the biggest antagonists is Western religion, which, among other religions, has been one of the biggest obstructions to the growth of human scientific knowledge through the ages. In the East, for millions of people, Astrology is part of normal life. There is a hint of this influence in the Tarot card "The Hierophant" and the Transactional Analysis concept of the "Parent". In the Eastern world Astrology is part of the lives of millions of people, as is Reincarnation.

ASTROLOGY : OVERVIEW

STATISTICAL ANALYSES

There are two books mentioned in the bibliography - "*THE ASTROLOGY FILE*" -by Gunter Sachs 1998 and "*THE TRUTH ABOUT ASTROLOGY*" -by Michael Gauquelin 1983 - who gathered birth records and subjected them to statistical analysis. In the case of Gunter Sachs there were millions, Michael Gauquelin processed hundreds of thousands. In both cases they conclude that Astrology has some basis in factual reality. In statistical terms the correlation of data showed more than a random distribution. Shuffling the data to ignore Astrology altogether did show random distribution.

HOW DOES IT WORK ?

A big problem with Astrology is that no one can explain how it works. My suggestion is that it is a function of the Collective Unconscious. The symbols used are pictorial representations of Archetypes – especially those of [THE 4 ELEMENTS]. In this quandary is contained the age old problems concerning "Nature and Nurture". How much of our lives are a result of our genes, and how much one's upbringing and life circumstances ? It is obvious that BOTH affect us. In Astrology, Nature is the subject of a Birth Chart, and Nurture is represented by the later Transits of planets relative to the Birth Chart. My later explanation and examples of Birth Charts and planetary Transits show something about how Astrology approaches the question.

At a personal level we have a connection between the planets and the endocrine gland system of our body. [THE CHAKRAS] These glands control all body functions by releasing hormones directly into the blood stream. The connection is made via the Chakra system. There are 7 main chakras and numerous minor ones. The 7 Chakras each vibrate at a different frequency which corresponds to that of a planetary energy. The Chakras operate at several levels. We have the physical endocrine glands (Earth), each of which has a form of intelligence to perform its function, as well as nerve connections to the brain (Air), there is a psychological and emotional component (Water), and finally a non-material basic energy (Fire). Some psychics can see the Chakras as swirling vortexes of energy, each of which has a different colour which relates to those of the visible spectrum frequency of vibration. The colours of the Chakras vary depending on the energy level and state of physical and emotional health of the individual.

PSYCHOLOGY : C.G.JUNG (1875-1961)

C.G. Jung actually made his own investigations into Astrology by setting up Birth Charts. In fact his "discovery" of the Collective Unconscious gives us the best model of how these things work.

> *Although the psychological interpretation of horoscopes is still very uncertain matter, there is nevertheless some prospect today of a causal explanation in conformity with natural law.*
>
> *Consequently, we are no longer justified in describing astrology as a mantic method, Astrology is in the process of becoming a science………………………*
>
> *But as there are still large areas of uncertainty, I decided some time ago to make a test and find out how far and accepted astrological tradition would stand up to statistical investigation will…………………………*
>
> *Although I was obliged to express doubt earlier about the magic character of astrology I'm now forced as a result of my astrological experiment to recognise it again.*
>
> *[THE PORTABLE JUNG (chapter : "On Sychronicity")]*

"Mantic" means pertaining to divination or prophecy.

This eminent psychologist, C.G.Jung, among others, actually used Astrology in his work. If we look for answers in the external world we will never find them. We need to look within.

In "*THE FREUD/JUNG LETTERS*" we find this :

In a letter written to Hindu astrologer, B.V. Raman, September 6th 1947 - Dr. Jung wrote:-

> *"Since you want to know my opinion about astrology I can tell you that I've been interested in this particular activity of the human mind since more than 30 years. As I am a psychologist, I am chiefly interested in the particular light the horoscope sheds on certain complications in the character. In cases of difficult psychological diagnosis I usually get a horoscope in order to have a further point of view from an*

entirely different angle. I must say that I very often found that the astrological data elucidated certain points which I otherwise would have been unable to understand. From such experiences I formed the opinion that Astrology is of particular interest to the psychologist, since it contains a sort of psychological experience which we call 'projected' - this means that we find the psychological facts as it were in the constellations.

BBC NEWS STORY : MOON PHASES PROVED TO AFFECT CRIME

Crackdown on lunar-fuelled crime

Extra police officers are to patrol the streets of Brighton on nights when there is a full moon.

It follows research by the Sussex force which concluded there was a rise in violent incidents when the moon was full - and also on paydays. Inspector Andy Parr said he compared crime statistics for Brighton and Hove with lunar graphs to discover the trend. The legend that people can become violent, or even turn into wolves, can be traced back to ancient times.

" Research carried out by us has shown a correlation "

Sussex Police spokeswoman. But nobody has been able to explain a link between lunar cycles and human behaviour. A spokeswoman for Sussex Police said: "Research carried out by us has shown a correlation between violent incidents and full moons." More officers will be out on Brighton's streets during full moons over the summer months, she added.

"Strange behaviour"

Mr Parr has said he would be interested in contacting universities who may be interested in examining the link further. He told the BBC: "From my experience, over 19 years of being a police officer, undoubtedly on full moons, we do seem to get people with, sort of, stranger behaviour - more fractious, argumentative. "And I think that's something that's been borne out by police officers up and down the country for years." Past research into the phenomenon includes a study by Professor Michal Zimecki, of the Polish Academy of Sciences, who argued that a full moon could affect criminal activity and health. In 1998, a three-month psychological study of 1,200 inmates at Armley jail in Leeds discovered a rise in violent incidents during the days either side of a full moon. Meanwhile in 1994, Jack Nicholson starred in a film called Wolf, in which a publisher becomes infected by a creature and turns into a wolf at full moon.

Story from BBC NEWS:
http://news.bbc.co.uk/go/pr/fr/-/1/hi/england/southern_counties/6723911.stm

Published: 2007/06/05 15:51:16 GMT

Figure 17 : BBC News - Crime and the New Moon

ASTROLOGY : OVERVIEW

HOW A BIRTH CHART IS CONSTRUCTED

Here we consider Birth Chart Houses and their relationship to Zodiac Signs separately. There is a later chapter [ASTROLOGY : CHART EXAMPLES] which shows them in practical combination. There are separate chapters [ASTROLOGY : HOUSES] and [ASTROLOGY : SIGNS] which go into more detail.

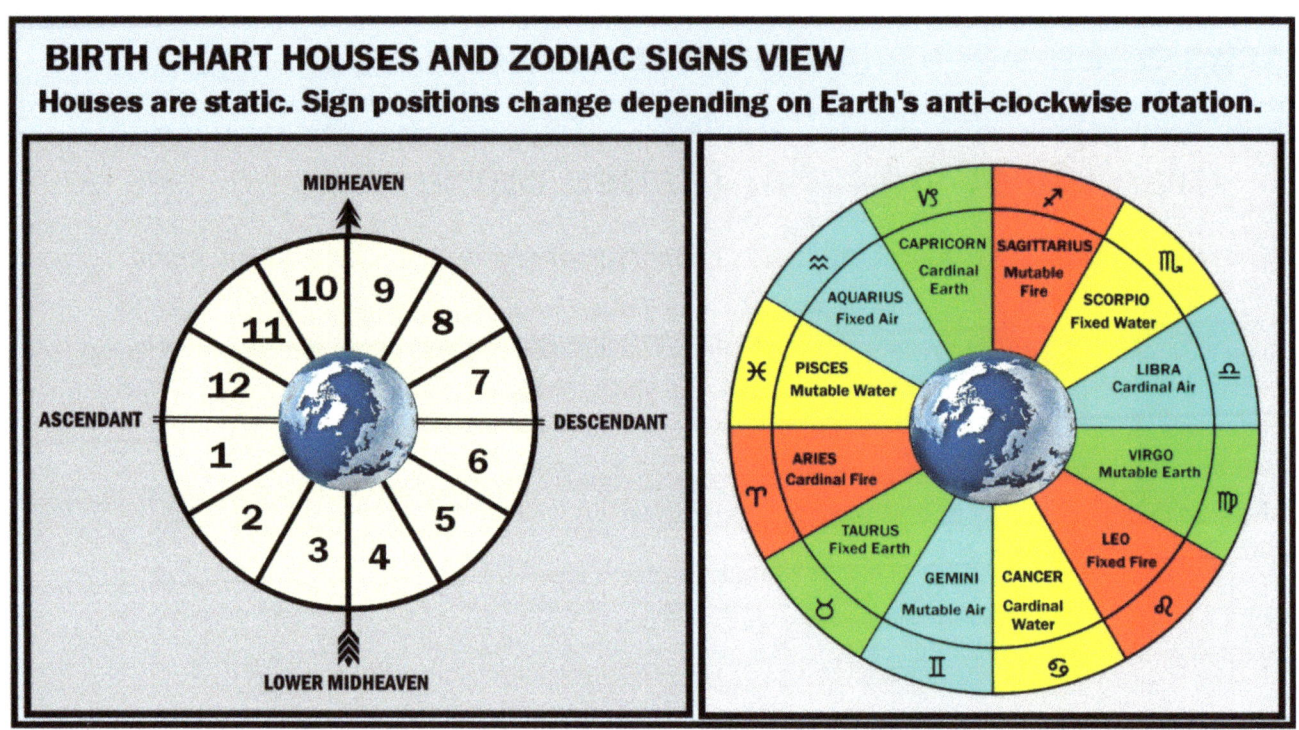

Figure 18 : Birth Chart Houses and Zodiac Signs in relationship to Earth

A Birth Chart is a snapshot picture of the solar system at the time of birth, so it aligns the Event with universal energies at the time. The circles depict the position of the Earth as seen from above the North Pole rather like a map. It is surrounded by the planets of our solar system, and, further outwards, the patterns formed by the other stars of the universe which include the Zodiac Signs which, apart from their own affect, enable us to place the planet positions. Although the diagram is 2 dimensional it represents a 3 dimensional sphere like a view of the segments of an orange cut in half. Each part of a segment is representative of the whole segment.

The overall Birth Chart is mainly an indicator of the earthly body and life of an individual as a "vehicle" for the soul, or spirit, in relation to the internal and external universe – which are as mirror images of one another. We are told by Edgar Cayce that the soul enters the body at the time of birth and has no control of it beforehand. We can recognise that the first task of a baby is that of learning to control its physical "vehicle" (Houses).

As we analyse the Birth Chart further we need to keep in mind that it is just a beginning of a life. However, as a child develops it will come into contact with external influences – firstly under control by parents, and later with more freedom to make personal decisions. The planets continue to move in their orbits, and we can examine their later positions – called "Transits" - related to the fixed positions of those in the Birth Chart.

We examine the Birth Chart as a series of 3 concentric circles beginning at the centre of the whole. We need to note that in reality the 3 circles combine as 1. They are each part of a single real and symbolic whole.

CIRCLE 1 : THE CENTRE CIRCLE

This is the part with no dividing lines. Most Astrologers do not explicitly mention this important area. However, it is a depiction of our central Inner, partially unconscious, Self which is the inner focus of, or reaction to, all

ASTROLOGY : OVERVIEW

external activity. As an indicator of this, Astrologers use the space in the chart to draw the aspects between the planets. That is, the angles that planets make with one another at the single, central, point of the Birth Chart that is the focus of all activity. This is the Number Zero of our self [NUMEROLOGY].

CIRCLE 2 : THE CIRCLE OF HOUSES

This part of any Astrological chart never varies. The Houses divide the Earth and the surrounding area of space containing our solar system into 12 parts. Each segment is numbered. The 1st. House is always the one that is "rising" on the Eastern Horizon (on the left) at the time of birth. The dividing lines between Houses are called "cusps". The cusp of the 1st. House, which forms half the horizon line, is given special importance and called The Ascendant.

There is a horizontal dividing line which indicates the natural Earth horizon at the time. The East of a Birth Chart is on the left. The Earth is turning anti-clockwise, and as it turns, the Sun, Moon, and other planets <u>seem</u> to rise on the Eastern Horizon, travel to midheaven, and set in the West. Because all measurements are taken from our perspective on Earth they are valid. For example, in Einstein's Relativity Theory the RELATIVE motion between a train travelling at 100 miles an hour and a station it passes through is the same. From the perspective of someone on the train, it can be considered as unmoving with the station passing by.

The Houses of a Birth Chart depict the physical level at which we humans are all the same. There are several levels of interpretation.

1. One example is the structure of a human body, where the 1st. House is at the head, and the 12th, House at the feet, with the intervening houses concerned with other specific areas between, going downwards.
2. Another example is the structure of a human lifetime – which we can recognise as having a Spring, Summer, Autumn, and Winter. [ASTROLOGY : LOGARITHMIC TIMESCALE]
3. At yet another level, the "1ST. Octave" of the 4 Houses from 9 to 12 cover life in the womb from Conception to Birth, the Houses 1 to 4 cover childhood in the home, and 5 to 8 cover life outside the birth home from School Age to Death. There is a gradual expansion of life experience in a widening social sphere – and widening consciousness.

This area of the Birth Chart is used to show the positions of the planets of our solar system around the Earth at the time of birth. We can therefore see in which House each planet is located, and therefore which part of the physical life it affects.

CIRCLE 3 : ZODIAC SIGNS – THE "CIRCLE OF ANIMALS"

Moving still further from the Earth, the Zodiac Signs are some of the patterns of bright stars we see as the universe outside the orbit of the Earth. Because they are so far away – millions of miles – they do not appear to move in relationship to one another or the Earth, even though we now know that the universe is expanding at the rate of thousands of miles an hour. The stars are moving apart from one another, and will eventually not be visible from Earth. The star patterns have been used for navigation since early times. They are also used to reset the annual Astrological calendar each year. The important day of the year for this is that of the Spring Equinox. This is the first day of Spring when day and night are both equal - 12 hours each. Because of the way the Calendar is devised, this is nowadays March 21st.

In 2000 BC when the Zodiac Signs were first used there was no writing, and no set calendar – although they recognised the monthly Moon cycles. We can see this as an expansion of consciousness of mankind. Having earlier recognised a time cycle beyond a single day, then that of a monthly Moon Cycle, they could now consider the Annual Cycle of the Sun. It was not until the birth of Jesus that numbers of years could be accurately counted. We note that despite several other mono-theistic (one God) religions being "born" at around the same time, this is of unchangeable global effect.

They looked at the heavens and noticed that at the time of the Spring Equinox there was a certain pattern of stars seeming to rise on the Eastern Horizon (Ascendant) at the same time as the Sun. They observed what was happening in Nature at the same time and matched the two images – and called it the beginning of the time of Aries The Ram. Likewise they compared the agricultural activities with star positions at other times to divide the rest of the year.

ASTROLOGY : OVERVIEW

Due to the Precession of the Equinoxes caused by the Earth wobbling on its axis on a 26,000 year cycle, the Sun no longer rises with the star constellation Aries in the background at the time of the Spring Equinox. Nowadays Aquarius does – hence "The Age of Aquarius". However, on the Earth it is still the beginning of Spring and therefore the time of Aries. It is rather like the use of imaginary lines of Latitude and Longitude for navigation.

THE ASCENDANT SIGN

Returning to our Birth Chart, this means that someone born at sunrise on March 21st. would have Aries rising (an "Aries Ascendant") on the Eastern Horizon – with the rest of the Signs spread evenly around the outer circumference. Because the Earth rotates once every 24 hours there is a new Zodiac Sign rising every 2 ½ hours. This is why it is important to have an accurate birth time as possible. In our example, someone born 2½ hours after sunrise on March 21st. would have a Taurus Ascendant.

Having defined the Ascendant of a Birth Chart, we can define the other Houses as being at 30 degree intervals apart. This is the Equal House System. I use another system defined by Placidus which is defined by Time rather than Space as described here. There are numerous other Astrological House Systems. The difference is that some planets close to House Cusps can appear in different Houses. The choice of House system is related to the experience of the Astrologer depending on feedback from subjects of charts. The interpretation is always the same.

The Sign of Aries will be rising at sunrise for around 1 month until Taurus takes over on April 20th. Someone born at sunrise at the beginning of, and during, the time of Taurus would have a Taurus Ascendant – and so on.

PLANETS

Having oriented our Birth Chart to the Zodiac Signs we can now put the planets – which include Sun and Moon – into position using their positions relative to the outer Zodiac Signs. Luckily we now have books of tables and computers to help us do the calculations. Each of the 12 Zodiac Signs has 30 degrees which makes a whole circle of 360 degrees, and it is known exactly where each planet will be located at any particular date and time by Sign and Degree. Taking our example above for someone born at sunrise on March 21st. we know that the Sun will be located at 0 (zero) degrees of Aries – and exactly on their Ascendant (cusp of 1st. House).

CONCLUSION

Just as the beginnings of Astrology were concerned with the planting of crops. In effect, "telling the Time", it is the same today. We are given a certain amount of free will to "sow seeds" and "reap harvests" in our lives. We can do this in obedience to, and working with, the Laws of Nature and the changing of the seasons. We can also try to sow and reap at the wrong time, when things can go wrong.

At another level, in common with millions of people in the Eastern world, I have had to recognise the existence of Reincarnation. This is largely as a result of the Edgar Cayce [APPENDIX : EDGAR CAYCE] readings where he gave a huge amount of checkable, empirical, factual, information, and included information about reincarnation almost against his will. It seems that a Birth Chart is an indicator of what we have come to learn about in our present lifetime, with the Sun position as the prime factor and the Moon position indicating past experience.

ASTROLOGY : HOUSES

This chapter introduces the structure of Houses in a Birth Chart as a prelude to the next chapter which shows how they affect us before, during, and after a lifetime. [ASTROLOGY : LOGARITHMIC TIMESCALE].

The overall construction of a Birth Chart, which includes the Houses, is described in [ASTROLOGY : OVERVIEW].

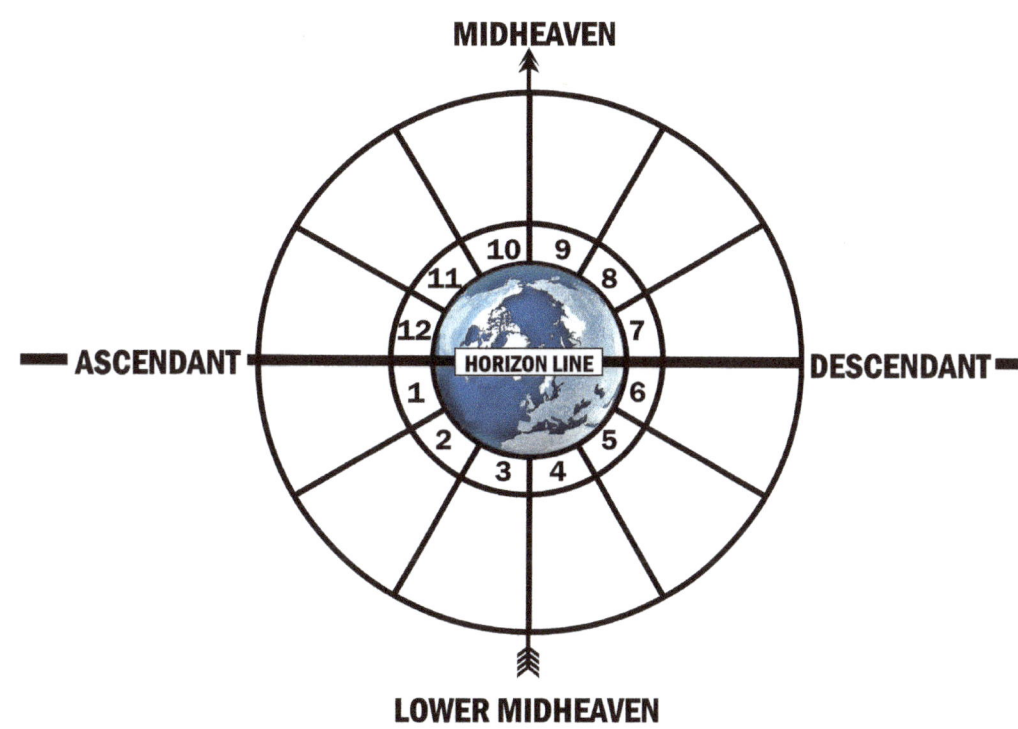

Figure 19 : House basis of an astrological chart

HOUSES OVERVIEW – PERSONAL AND GENERIC

Here we deal with how the Houses are set up to form the basis of an astrological chart, and how they relate to one another. The meanings of each separate House are dealt with in the Stages in the Cycle of Growth.

In this book I refer to 2 types of House – Personal Houses which are related to Birth Charts, and are fixed in time and space, and Generic Houses which relate to Transits [ASTROLOGY : PLANET TRANSITS] of individual planets as they continue to move over time. There are working examples of both House types for Lady Diana Spencer in the chapter [ASTROLOGY : CHARTS EXAMPLES].

The basis of an astrological chart is a circle with the Earth at its centre. The circle is theoretically infinite in size, reaching far out into space beyond the Earth, and divided into 12 Houses like slices of a pie. Although the size of each House can be considered as infinite, each part carries the effects and experiences of the whole – just like a normal domestic house. The Houses of a Birth Chart also refer to different parts of a human, including body, conscious mind, subconscious mind, and unconscious mind. Because concepts concerning the mind are new, they only existed in ancient Astrology in the form of vague symbols. Mankind has still a lot more work to do in this area of knowledge. The point at the centre of the circle represents the individual subject of the chart as the focus of all activity. This centre is where the various energies are controlled and combined. If combined successfully FOR THAT INDIVIDUAL (Birth Chart) there is a state of inner harmony resulting in physical and mental health.

There are several possible uses for an astrological chart where a clear beginning or "birth" can be identified – such as a new business or partnership. There is a separate branch of Astrology called "Mundane Astrology" that deals with countries and nations. Not having a clear "birth" date or time, the Ascendant for a country has been arrived at by observation over time. In this book we are only concerned with a Birth Chart (or "Natal Chart") of an individual person.

We use this basic chart structure for setting up the Personal Houses of a Birth Chart, as well as considering the Generic Houses of a single planet, or considering the relationship between any 2 planets.

BIRTH CHART : PERSONAL HOUSES

Personal Houses refer to the Houses of a Birth Chart. We note here that a Birth Chart can be interpreted at several different levels. You will see something of this from the different pictures and diagrams of this book. At another level, using the [LOGARITHMIC TIMESCALE], the Houses indicate the physical and psychological development of an individual from Conception to Death as well as the ability to transcend physical reality. There are others. By removing consideration of Signs and Planets from this chapter we portray an individual as the "raw clay" which will be worked on and moulded by life experiences on Earth. At this level we are all identical humans.

A Birth Chart is a map of the heavens showing the positions of planets at the time of birth of an individual person – more specifically that of the "first breath" - who is then the subject of the chart. The focus of activity is at the centre of a chart – which can be considered the axle of the "wheel" around which movement takes place. It is still - does not rotate itself - but nevertheless converts the energy into evolutionary motion or progress. The centre of a Birth Chart is the "Still Centre" of an individual.

Without adding any more information to the basic Birth Chart than is shown above it indicates where we are all the same. This is the basic structure, or template, of a Birth Chart and a human being. This is the 99.9% of DNA that makes us human and determines not only the structure of our human bodies and minds but how they develop over a lifetime. As we align the Birth Chart with the rest of the universe by determining the Rising Sign, and show the planet positions, it becomes more unique.

The figure above shows the basis of a Birth Chart with Earth at the centre and the surrounding space divided into Houses. The dividing lines between the Houses are called "Cusps". The single horizontal line is called " The Horizon " which defines the cusps of the 1st. and 7th. Houses – which are also the East and West points of the chart. You will see from this book that the House cusps at the 4 quarters of the chart have special significance, so they are given names. The 1st.House cusp is "The Ascendant", the 7th. Is "The Descendant", the 4th. House cusp is the "Lower Midheaven" (Immum Coeli)" and the 10th. is "The Midheaven (Medium Coeli)". We are beginning to see that, to understand the Houses fully, we need to treat them as complementary pairs (not opposites !). If I use the word "opposite" anywhere in this book I mean "opposite by position".

THE ORIENTATION OF PERSONAL HOUSES

"Orient" means East, so orienting the chart means aligning its East-West Horizon with that seen on Earth at the time and place of birth.

The first task in setting up a Birth Chart is determining the Ascendant, or Rising Sign, which symbolically aligns the event with those occurring in the rest of the universe at that same moment in time. This is the degree of the Zodiac Sign "rising" on the Eastern horizon (of the Earth location) at the time of the event. The Earth makes a complete rotation every 24 hours, and the Planets and Signs rise and set in the same way as the Sun. With 12 Signs, each one is in the Ascendant for only 2 ½ hours a day. It is a problem that we often do not have an accurate birth time. In this case we set up a chart as accurately as possible – often using Noon or Sunrise. We can still examine the chart in terms of the planetary positions in the Zodiac, but are unable to make any observations concerning physical events. Despite this, by examining physical evidence we are often able to "correct" (the birth time of) a chart to a greater or lesser degree.

In short, the Houses of an astrological chart, as a method of dividing or mapping space, and, referring to Earth, are always fixed in the same position, as shown in my diagram at the beginning of the chapter. We add the other details to that template. Through time we see the Sun continually rising in the Eastern Horizon (the Orient) and continuing until it sets. The chart therefore has similarities with the face of a clock. The Earth rotates anti-clockwise, so the Sun appears to rotate clockwise. It is exactly the same situation with the planets and Zodiac Signs which also seem to rise in the geographic East and set in the West. The East is symbolic as the position of the "rebirth" of the Sun, Moon, and planets each day. The Eastern point of a Birth Chart is the same as the geographic East at the time of birth, and defines the cusp of the 1st. House, which is also called the Ascendant as well as those of the other Houses. Having positioned our grid map we can now put the Sun, Moon, and other planets in the places they occupied at that time. The birth of an individual person is now oriented as an event in time and space, which is also related to the rest of the universe. A "rising star". A "star is born".

As an example, by setting up our chart for a particular time we know where the Sun is positioned. If we want to know approximately which direction is North on Earth we can point the hour hand of a clock at the Sun, when North is midway between it and 12 o'clock position (1 o'clock if the clock is set for Daylight Saving or Summer Time). We still need to do more accurate calculations, but this will serve to show how the Houses are oriented.

To begin with, we recognise Sunrise and Sunset, and, by definition, Noon, the 12 o'clock position, is the time when the Sun reaches its highest point in the sky. Having said that, to be perfectly accurate I should have said "seems to reach its highest point". We all know nowadays that the Sun is not actually moving, and its position in our sky is relative to the rotation of the Earth. This does not make our observations invalid, however (even the ancient ones). In Astrology we are always considering the RELATIVE POSITIONS of planets and the Earth. So it does not matter if we make our measurements from the Sun or the Earth. This is embodied in Einstein's Relativity Theory when it considers the relative positions of two moving bodies – such as moving trains, planets, or space ships.

In the figure below the Sun positions are shown for sunrise (Sun in the 1st.House) and noon (Sun in the 10th.House). This is true for any one day.

If we use the date of March 21st. when we know the Sun is in the Sign of Aries, the sunrise position gives an Aries Ascendant and Capricorn Midheaven, the noon position on the same day gives a Cancer Ascendant and Aries Midheaven.

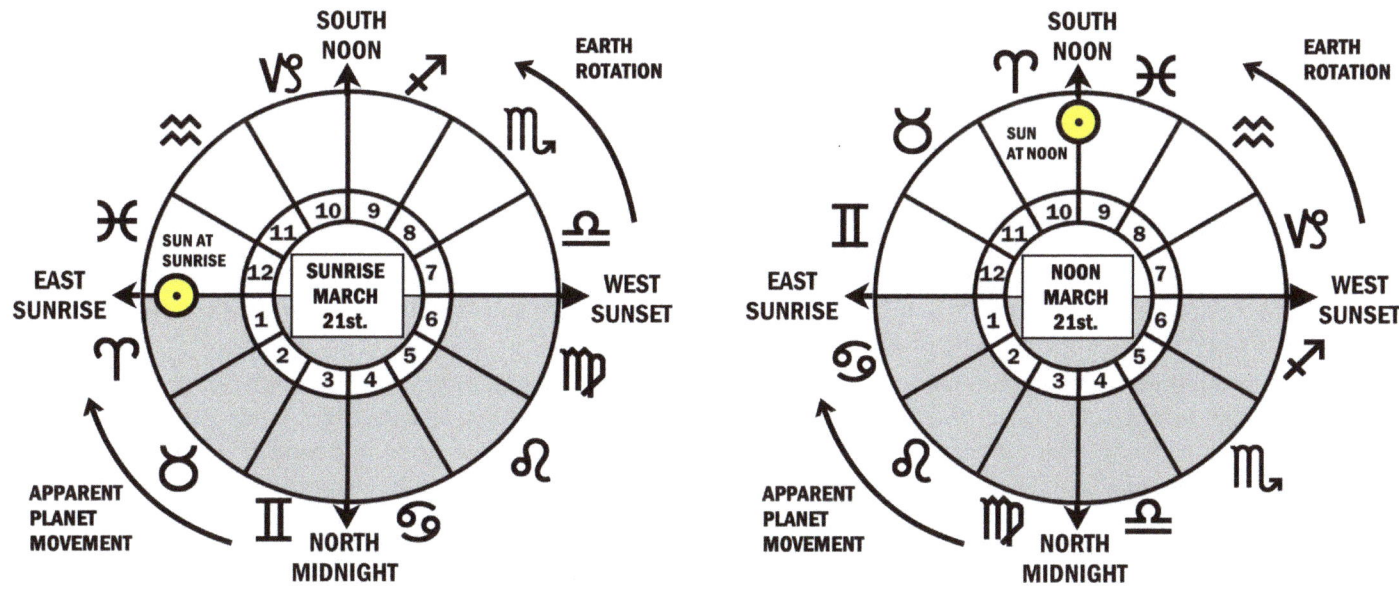

Figure 20: Aries Sun House positions for sunrise & noon March 21st.

PERSONAL HOUSES AND PLANETS

Interestingly, as noted in my chapter [ASTROLOGY : PLANETS], the orbits of the planets and the Earth are all concentric, with the Sun as central point, within very close limits. The orbits are actually elliptical rather than circular, so the planets do not travel at exactly the same speed through the Zodiac all the time, but the calculations take this into account. This means that the astrological "map" is a good representation of what would actually be seen from a view point above the North Pole of the Earth. It is not accurate when considering the relative distances in space between the planets, but, again for practical purposes, this can be ignored. We are only interested in the position of a planet by House and Sign.

The next step in setting up our chart is to insert the planets in their positions relative to that of the Earth at that moment in time. For that we need to make a lot of complicated calculations, which a computer nowadays does

ASTROLOGY : HOUSES

in a second. In the past it might have taken me an hour using various tables, with the ever present possibility of making errors. I am leaving that to the chapter [ASTROLOGY : PLANETS]. We also need to have a knowledge of the astrological Zodiac Signs. I am leaving that stage until the chapter [ASTROLOGY : SIGNS].

THE PATTERN OR STRUCTURE OF PERSONAL HOUSES

Here we deal with Birth Charts and the overall pattern of their Personal Houses. By comparing the Houses with one another we gain a better understanding of their separate functions. They are similar to, but not the same as, the meanings of the Signs. Clearly, both sets are influenced by the same 12 archetypes, but Houses refer to manifestation in *physical forms in space* (Earth. Physical Body. Mind), whereas Signs refer to different *energy forms through time*. Bearing in mind Einstein's statement that physical forms are also energy.

Taken as a set of 12, we can see that the Houses are numbered consecutively starting at the Ascendant, which is the cusp of the 1st. House, and continuing anti-clockwise. The Houses at opposite sides of the chart complement and balance one another. Later on, when we add Planets to the chart there is a state of imbalance produced which focuses energy on one House rather than its complementary one.

HOUSES AND NUMBER 4

Although for all practical purposes we can ignore it, I have to mention that this is a 2-dimensional representation of 3- dimensional space. The Earth and its surrounding space is actually spherical. What we are seeing is like an orange that has been cut in half and viewed from above. Because of this, as well as the tilt of the (also imaginary) Earth's axis in relation to the Sun, there are various astrological house systems that vary the sizes of the 12 Houses. They still make a set of 12, but the slices of the "pie" are different sizes. "Opposite" (by position) Houses are the same size. We are using the "Equal House System" here. In my example charts chapter [ASTROLOGY : CHARTS EXAMPLES] I use the Placidean House System.

The overall principle is very similar to that of the imaginary lines of latitude and longitude used for navigating the Earth. An added similarity is that the House divisions are symbolically based on the Number 4, as are the points of a compass. Number 4 is the most stable of numbers, and relates to such symbols as the Square and the Cross - which refer to physical matter as energy in its most stable or fixed form. The 12 Houses become 4 sets of 3 Triplicities, compared with the 12 Signs which are 3 sets of 4 Elements. The astrological symbol of Earth is a cross within a circle, looking like the British "Hot Cross Bun" at Eastertime, which marks the beginning of Spring and the crucifixion of the Christ Spirit on the Cross of Matter. (All this mention of oranges, pies and buns is making me feel quite hungry).

Although, for convenience, I tend to match the cusps of Houses and Signs in this book - this is rarely true in practice. For this to occur the cusp of a House must coincide with zero degrees of a Sign. I also put Aries as the Ascendant because its form of energy is similar to that of the 1st. House. An Aries Ascendant to a Birth Chart would give an easier general progress in life because the Houses and Signs would combine their energies in the most harmonious way. The individual would naturally work in harmony with the Time. The planet positions add another dimension of interpretation that might correspond with, or challenge, this activity.

Having set the chart up, we can begin to analyse it by ascribing meanings to the various areas. The first is a simple observation of the 4 Quadrants – which are each subdivided into 3 parts later on.

ASTROLOGY : HOUSES

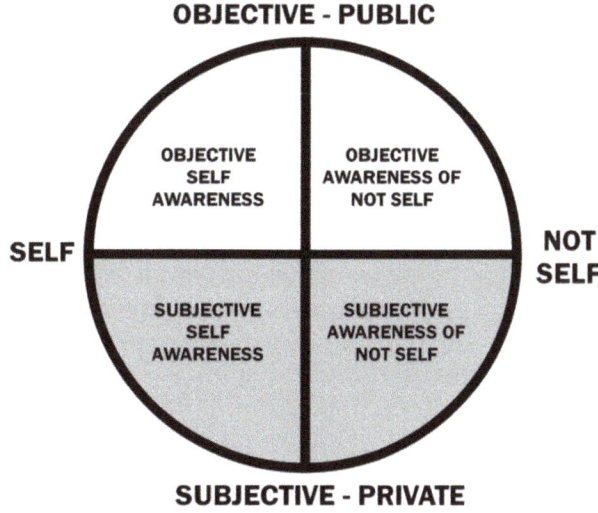

Figure 21 : The 4 Quadrants of a chart

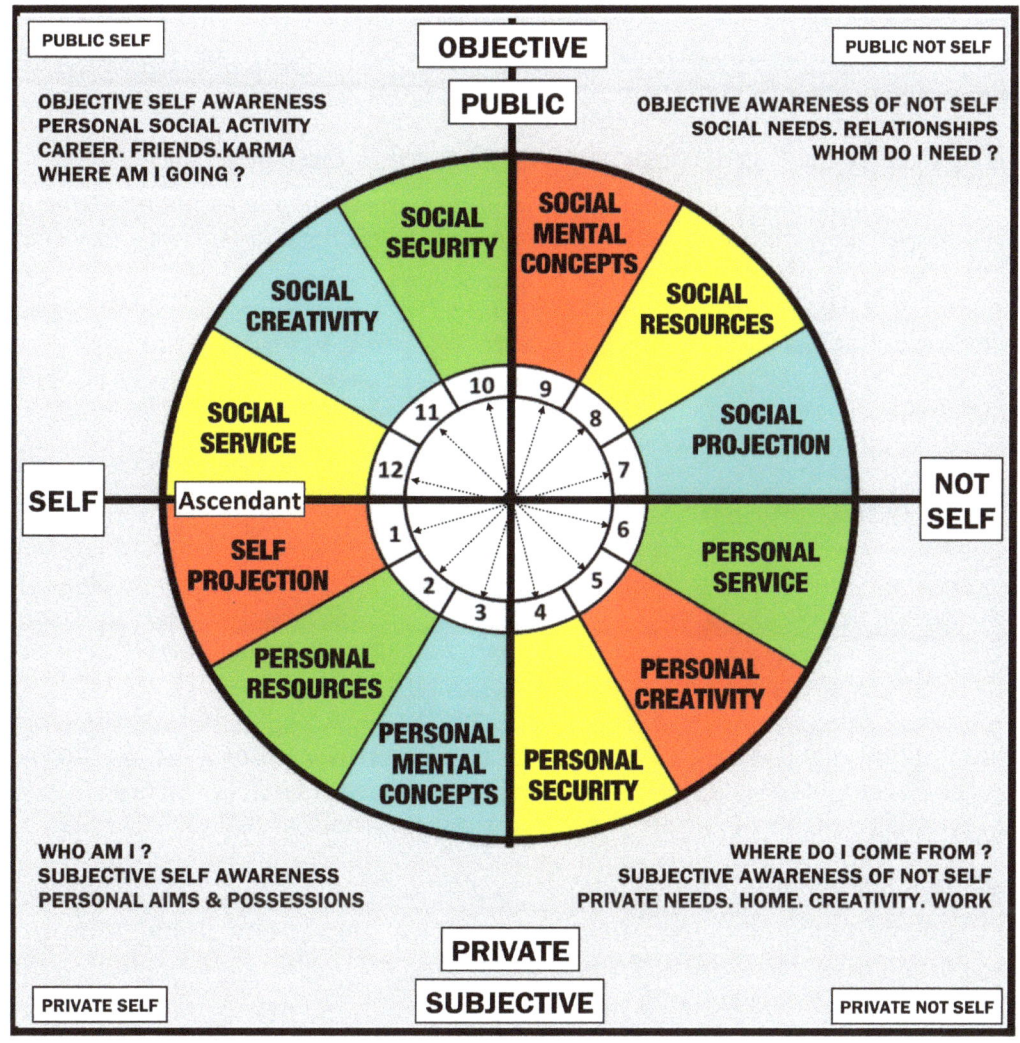

Figure 22: Astrology – pattern of 12 Personal Houses

ASTROLOGY : HOUSES

BIRTH CHART HEMISPHERES : divisions by 2

There are 2 ways of dividing the chart circle (sphere) into hemispheres. We can see that each complements the other.

THE HORIZON

Dividing line EAST : WEST (SELF : NOT SELF)

Gives rise to hemispheres   DAY : NIGHT. (OBJECTIVE : SUBJECTIVE) (PUBLIC : PRIVATE)

The East – West horizontal Horizon line which forms the cusps of the 1st. and 7th. Houses is a representation of the Earth's horizon which separates the earth below and sky above. It represents the unique personal outlook, or world view, of the subject of the chart. What is near and what is at a distance. Our Private Life and Public Life. Above the Horizon is day time, where the journey of the Sun consciousness from sunrise to sunset brings us awareness of the external world. Below the horizon is night time when Sun/Moon consciousness brings attention to our inner world.

THE LOWER MIDHEAVEN - MIDHEAVEN LINE

Dividing line NORTH : SOUTH. (SUBJECTIVE : OBJECTIVE) (PRIVATE : PUBLIC)

Gives rise to hemispheres SELF : NOT SELF.

The line divides the chart into left and right hemispheres. The main focus of the left hemisphere is on the Ascendant and the 1st.House. This indicates how the individual projects his or herself into life, as at birth. It indicates the natural way for that person to "plant seeds" of new projects and experiences. The activities of the Houses in that hemisphere are more or less under one's personal control.

The Houses in the right hemisphere are those which require co-operation with other people and the environment.

BIRTH CHART QUADRANTS : division by 4 sets of 3 Houses

Each Quadrant contains a Triplicity of Houses which have similar properties to Cardinal, Fixed, and Mutable Signs. They are Angular (Active. Initiating "Creator"), Succedent (Resisting. "Preserver"), and Cadent (Changing. Adapting. "Destroyer").

Applying both hemisphere divisions together divides the chart into 4 quadrants, each containing 3 Houses. I have deliberately not described each House in the narrative. My aim is to describe the basic House structure in as simple terms as possible. You will probably note some seeming anomalies which will hopefully be clarified and explained in the chapters about the separate Cycle of Growth stages. There is more detail in [ASTROLOGY : LOGARITHMIC TIMESCALE] and [ASTROLOGY : TRANSITS].

QUADRANT 1 : SUBJECTIVE SELF AWARENESS (Houses 1 to 3)

The Quadrant is concerned with development from physical birth to 3 years 6 months of age when a child is weaned from its mother, develops body and mind, and learns to control them. It is indicative of the inbuilt abilities and talents waiting to develop.

QUADRANT 2 : SUBJECTIVE AWARENESS OF NOT SELF (Houses 4 to 6)

The Quadrant is concerned with development during ages 3 to 23 years beginning with growing awareness of the world outside that of home and family, which enables the awareness of one's self as a separate individual – and which requires the development of a Persona, or "mask" to become an actor on the stage of life, where it is not appropriate to reveal all of one's inner self. There is the development of an Ego which can say "I am".

QUADRANT 3: OBJECTIVE AWARENESS OF NOT SELF (Houses 7 to 9)

The 7th. House cusp is opposite that of the 1st. House cusp of Birth. It is the end of the "outward journey" into life and the beginning of preparation for death and return to our Source. The 7th. House is that of Partners.

The Quadrant includes the time of life from 23 years of age to death. To develop further, and to reproduce so that our genes survive our physical death, we need the co-operation of others outside our self.

ASTROLOGY : HOUSES

QUADRANT 4 : OBJECTIVE SELF AWARENESS (Houses 10 to 12)

This Quadrant takes us out of the realms of personal growth and into that of a wider society, and mankind as a whole. In terms of the Logarithmic Timescale it has 2 functions. Firstly, as applied to the time of Gestation, it includes the time of life from conception to birth and the development of the human body as a vehicle which is determined by past human evolution. At another level, as following after the previous Quadrant that includes Death, it covers our Transcendence of earthly concerns. This is always relative to the individual concerned. For example, it may relate to the individual gaining a social overview by running a business, becoming active in politics, or studying science or religion.

In traditional terms, at the beginning of the Quadrant we have the 10th. House as an indicator of the power we have to control others. It is the House of Career as well as being the place where we come into full public view. In the Cycle of Growth, and the Birth Chart, this is "The Peak" position. The position of the Sun at the height of its power at mid-day. The point is that, in life, such times are transitory. There is always a decline afterwards. The decline is indicated by the activities of the 11th. And 12th. Houses – which return us to the 1st. House Birth position.

For me, this is the most difficult Quadrant to understand – especially in view of its dual nature. Another factor to consider is that the traditional meaning needs to be updated. You will see in the chapter [ASTROLOGY : PLANETS] that each planet has a compatible energy with certain Signs and Houses which tend to reinforce and support its activity. With others its expression is limited or restricted.

Traditional Astrology gives "Rulership" of the 10th. and 11th. Houses to Saturn as being the most compatible planet with its concern for bringing order and structure to life. It gives rulership of the 12th. House to Jupiter – with its principle of bringing Expansion and Growth to whatever it comes into contact.

Since then we have the discovery of planets beyond Saturn which are invisible to the (physical) naked eye, and which required advanced technology to discover. These are Uranus, Neptune, and Pluto. Saturn still rules the 10th. House, but Uranus and Neptune have been given rulership of the 11th. and 12th. Houses respectively. When we apply this to our Transcendent Quadrant this makes sense. To begin with, the attitude of modern Astrologers is that the discovery of these planets is a sign that modern humans have reached a stage in evolution where we can, if desired, respond to the energies that they express.

I do not wish to go into more detail in this chapter, but, to me, the difference is that modern humans are no longer tied to an agricultural life. Once people began gathering together in cities and forming "civilisations" there was a greater specialisation of activity to include those that rely use of the mind. Very few people nowadays have to grow food or make any physical object to live. In terms of the planets mentioned, whereas Saturn and Jupiter tied individuals to a practical life, where the expansion or growth was related to what they managed to produce, we now have the growth of a "Virtual World" of mind and imagination. There was also a long period of time when children had little choice but to follow the occupations of their parents. Nowadays, through education and technology, there is more time for leisure pursuits and education.

BIRTH CHART : GENERIC HOUSES

Generic Houses refer to Planet Orbits and are not the same as Birth Chart Houses unless the planet is located in the 1st. House of a Birth Chart. The Cycle of Growth meanings of Personal and Generic Houses are identical.

Each Planet has its own set of Generic Houses depending on its position in a Birth Chart – which is the starting place of its Generic Cycle for the person concerned.

Here we deal with the Transits of planets as they move after birth and compare their positions with the Birth Chart. They refer to external experiences and influences throughout life. The Personal Houses give us similar physical bodies, The Generic Transit cycles of each planet are what makes human development the same. Even though the planets in our Birth Chart may be in different places to those of other people, they are in the same Generic House position at the same ages and we tend to have similar experiences and growth stages at around the same age. During its transit cycle a planet will make every possible aspect (angular relationship) - harmonious or otherwise - with every other planet in the birth chart as well as the other transiting planets – so the sum total is Zero for each cycle.

The Moon orbiting the Earth has a Transit Cycle of 28 days. The Sun, Mercury and Venus, being inside the orbit of the Earth, can be considered as having a 1 year Transit Cycle. These transits tend to "fire off" events set up by the slower planets. Their transits make every possible aspect with Birth Chart planets and other transit planets every 12 months.

ASTROLOGY : HOUSES

Mars has a 2 year cycle, Jupiter 12 years, Saturn 30 years, Uranus 84 years, Neptune 165 years, Pluto 247 years. Neptune and Pluto, because of their slow movement, are in the same Sign for several years and therefore affect whole generations of people in the same way. The Uranus cycle matches what we are beginning to expect as a whole life term of 84 years and seems to me to be connected with the Jungian concept of Individuation. My main interests in this book are the cycles of Jupiter and Saturn. Because they repeat during a lifetime we can compare actual life events at times when their positions are the same.

You can test this for yourself by adding your main life experiences to the "Life Diary" form at the end of [ASTROLOGY : PLANET TRANSITS].

The separate Generic Houses are dealt with in the individual chapters for the Cycle of Growth Stages.

JUPITER GENERIC HOUSES EXAMPLE DIAGRAM

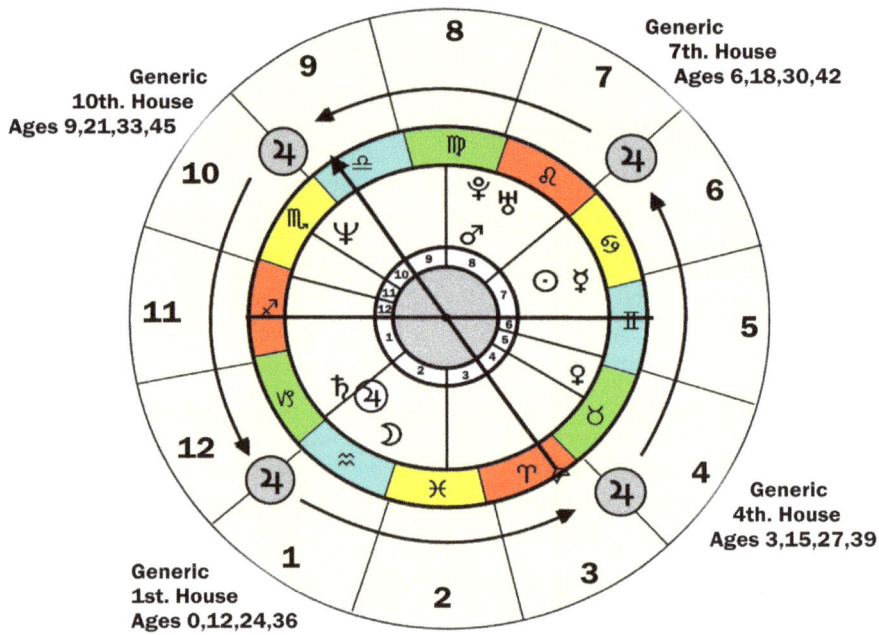

Figure 23: Generic Houses of Jupiter

1. The inner Birth Chart is that of Lady Diana Spencer as in the chapter [ASTROLOGY : CHARTS EXAMPLES]. The inner numbers are of her Personal Houses. Jupiter is in the 2nd. (Personal) House of her Birth Chart. The outer numbers are Generic Transit Houses.
2. The Birth Chart uses the Placidus unequal house system. The outer one has Equal Houses.
3. The outermost circle represents that of the area of space surrounding the Earth. This is where the planets continue to move after birth. It is divided into 12 Generic Houses of 30 degrees each. Each Generic House is the same size because of the regular planet cycles. Each planet has its own Generic House cycle.
4. The cusp of the 1st. Generic House of any planet coincides with its position at birth – so each one has a separate set of Generic Houses.
5. Jupiter has a 12 year cycle so it is in each Generic House for approximately 1 year. The time varies because Jupiter sometimes goes retrograde (seems to go backwards through the Signs).
6. The chart above shows 4 positions of Jupiter in its orbit when it reaches the beginning of each Quadrant at the cusps of its 1st.,4th.,7th.,and 10th. Houses together with the ages of the subject when it does so. These are the "crisis points" of its cycle.
7. With Saturn, which has a 30 year cycle, it is in each Generic House for approximately 2 ½ years. As it is close to Jupiter in this Birth Chart, its 12 Generic Houses will be in almost the same positions.

ASTROLOGY : LOGARITHMIC TIMESCALE

We now extend our study of the Personal Houses of a Birth Chart.

This chapter can be considered a main one in the book because it brings together information dealt with under different subject titles and is a practical demonstration of The Cycle of Growth. There is a summary of information dealt with in more detail in other chapters.

The Logarithmic Timescale is another way of looking at the Personal Houses of a Birth Chart. Despite the different viewpoint, the meaning of the Houses is the same as described in [ASTROLOGY : HOUSES].

An important feature of The Logarithmic Timescale - which refers to human development over a lifetime - is that the Stages are not of equal length of time. This is different to consideration of Planetary Transits [ASTROLOGY : PLANET TRANSITS] where the cycles of planets are regular. That chapter has a more detailed analysis of the activities of the 12 Houses.

For those not familiar with the concept of Astrological Houses it will probably help understanding to first read the chapters [ASTROLOGY : OVERVIEW] and [ASTROLOGY : HOUSES].

There is a detailed study of The Octaves in relationship with The Kabbalah in [THE KABBALAH TREE OF LIFE]

1. The Logarithmic Timescale of a human lifetime begins with Cycle of Growth Stage 9 (Conception) and ends with Death at the end of Cycle of Growth Stage 8 (Sex. Death).

2. The Timescale consists of 3 "Octaves" which cover different periods of the lifetime. Each Octave consists of 4 House Stages, making 12 Stages altogether. In addition, the 1st.Octave, apart from covering the time of Gestation in the womb, also becomes the "Transcendent Octave" when an individual begins to seek for a meaning to life beyond the physical world of normal human existence. In effect, it becomes a symbolic "rebirth" in terms of expanded consciousness. Readers of this book will be somewhere along that pathway.

3. The 3 Octaves also form a "Triplicity" based on Number 3 [NUMEROLOGY] which has the basic dynamics Action – Reaction – Final Result. Father – Mother _ Child.

4. The Octaves become more understandable when compared with the "Growth of Personality" model of Psychology which is concerned with human development from Birth to Death. Although each Stage is of a different length, there is almost exact correlation between the timescales of Astrology and Psychology.

5. There is comparison table comparing Logarithmic Timescale Stages with Erikson's GROWTH OF PERSONALITY stages in [PSYCHOLOGY : DEVELOPMENT MODELS].

3 OCTAVES INTRODUCTION

We first consider the 3 Octaves as a whole, where they form a Triplicity corresponding with the meaning of Number 3 [NUMEROLOGY]. As with all cycles in this book, the sequence is anti-clockwise.

We first consider 3 examples of the activity of Triplicities.

1. The human life cycle from Conception to Death. The main subject of this chapter.
2. The cycle of a Calendar Year which is "conceived" in Sagittarius in November, and "reborn" at the Winter Solstice. It has its "physical birth" when it brings life to Earth in Aries at the Spring Equinox.
3. The equivalent development of each Calendar Month each of which is "conceived" around the 21st. of each month and is "born" on the 1st. day of the following month.

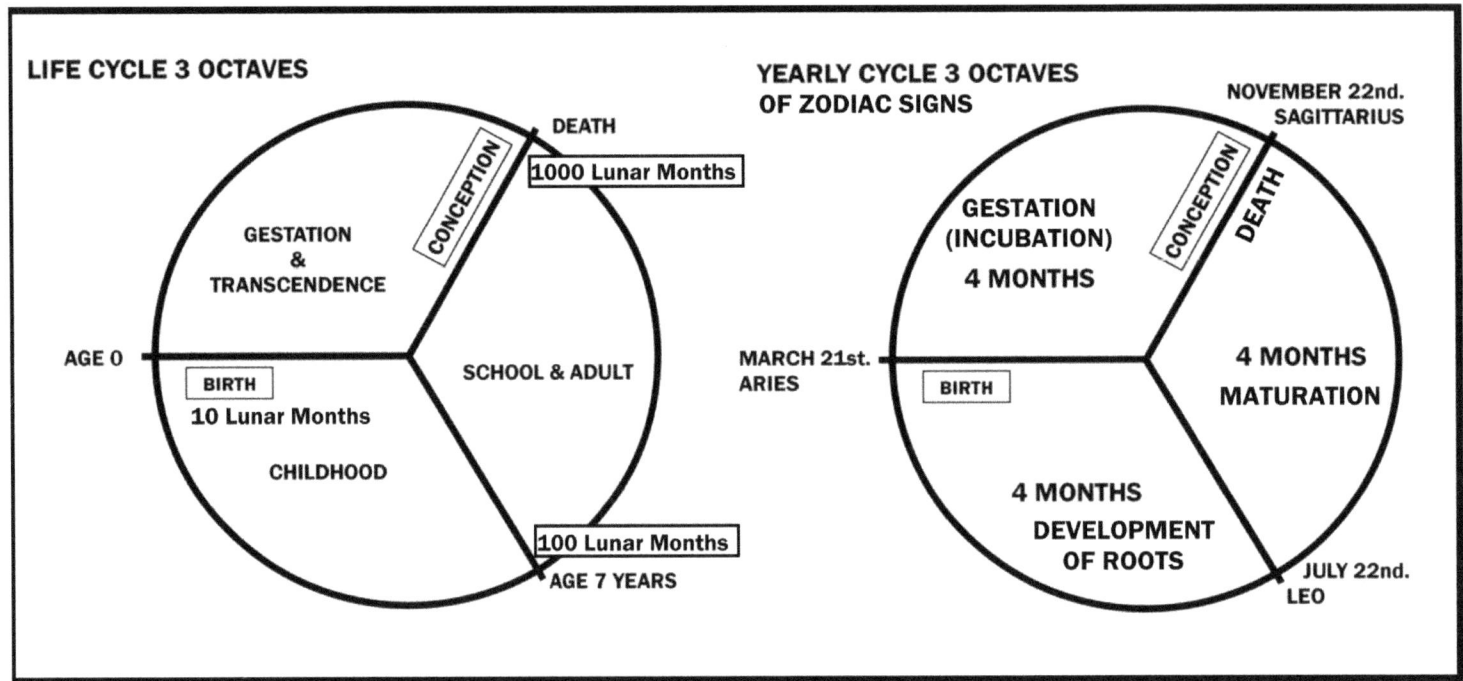

Figure 24 : 3 Octaves of Logarithmic Timescale and Zodiac Year

Before looking at 12 Stages detail we gain an overview of the Astrological Logarithmic Timescale by observing that it is divided into 3 Octaves of 4 Stages each. The division is of Time. Each Octave of the Logarithmic Timescale covers a different length of time. When we divide the Annual Cycle into 3 Octaves, each of them is the same length of 4 months. Despite this, in both systems the Octaves comply with the standard meaning of and Triplicity (a "set" consisting of 3 parts – and therefore based on Number 3) :

1. Number 1 – Action (eg. Father. Thesis) – Conception to 10 Lunar Months.
2. Number 2 - Reaction (to the action. eg. Mother. Antithesis) – Physical Birth to 100 Lunar months.
3. Number 3 - Synthesis of the Action and Reaction (eg. Child. Synthesis) – Social Birth to 1000 Lunar Months.

MONTHLY 3 OCTAVES – AND SIGN DECANS

We can also consider the development of each Calendar Month as a Triplicity relating to Number 3.

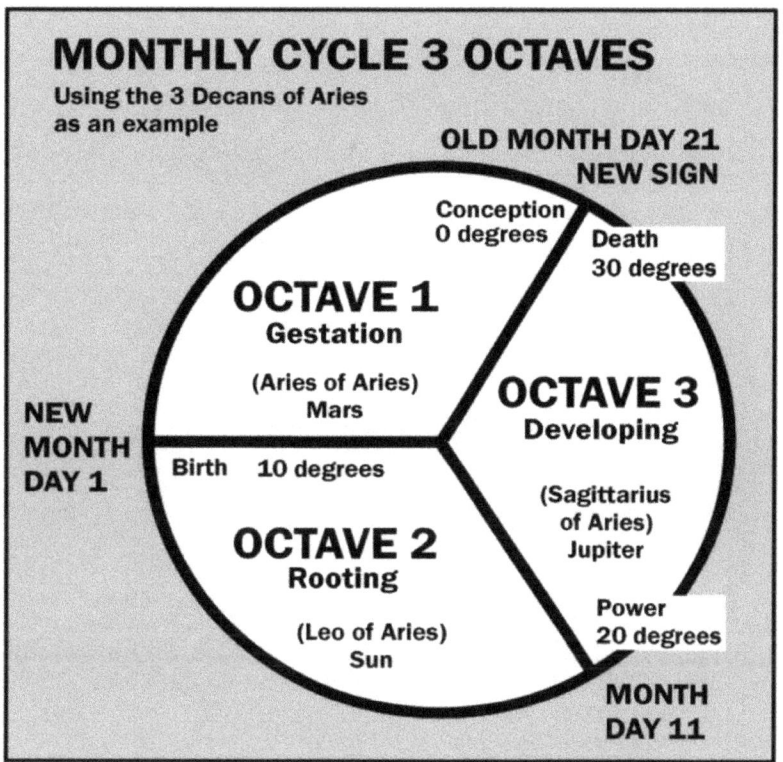

Figure 25 : The 3 Octaves of each Zodiac Sign

1. We note that the 3 Octaves of a Calendar Month conform to The Cycle of Growth. The CONCEPTION of the "physical" month occurs at around the 21st. Day of the PREVIOUS month when The Sun enters the new Zodiac Sign at Zero Degrees. This is equivalent to Cycle of Growth Stage 9 (Conception).
2. The actual "BIRTH" of the month occurs on its first day – as of a child.
3. The 30 degrees of a Sign roughly relate to the 30 days of a month.
4. Each Zodiac Sign can be divided into 12 stages by the following method :-
5. Astrologers divide the 30 degrees of each Sign into 3 Decans of 10 degrees each. The 3 Decans each takes on the rulership of a Sign of the same Element and its related Planet. The 3 Decans are the same as the 3 Octaves.
6. The 1st. Decan is ruled by the actual Sign itself. In the diagram this is Aries, itself ruled by Mars. I have called this "Aries of Aries".
7. The 2nd. Decan starts at 10 degrees of the Sign, and is ruled by the next Sign of the same Element. Our next Fire Element Sign is Leo ruled by the Sun. I have called this "Leo of Aries".
8. The 3rd. Decan is ruled by the remaining Sign of the Element – in this case Sagittarius which is ruled by Jupiter. I have called this "Sagittarius of Aries".
9. The new month is 'born' on its first day, which begins the 2nd. Decan.
10. The 3rd. Decan begins around the 10th. day of a month.
11. Given other Birth Chart differences, this is another reason why everyone of a particular Sun Sign is not the same. The energy of the Sun is modified by the Decan.

ASTROLOGY : LOGARITHMIC TIMESCALE

LOGARITHMIC TIMESCALE DIAGRAM OVERVIEW

We enter into more detailed analysis and divide the 3 Octaves into 12 Stages.

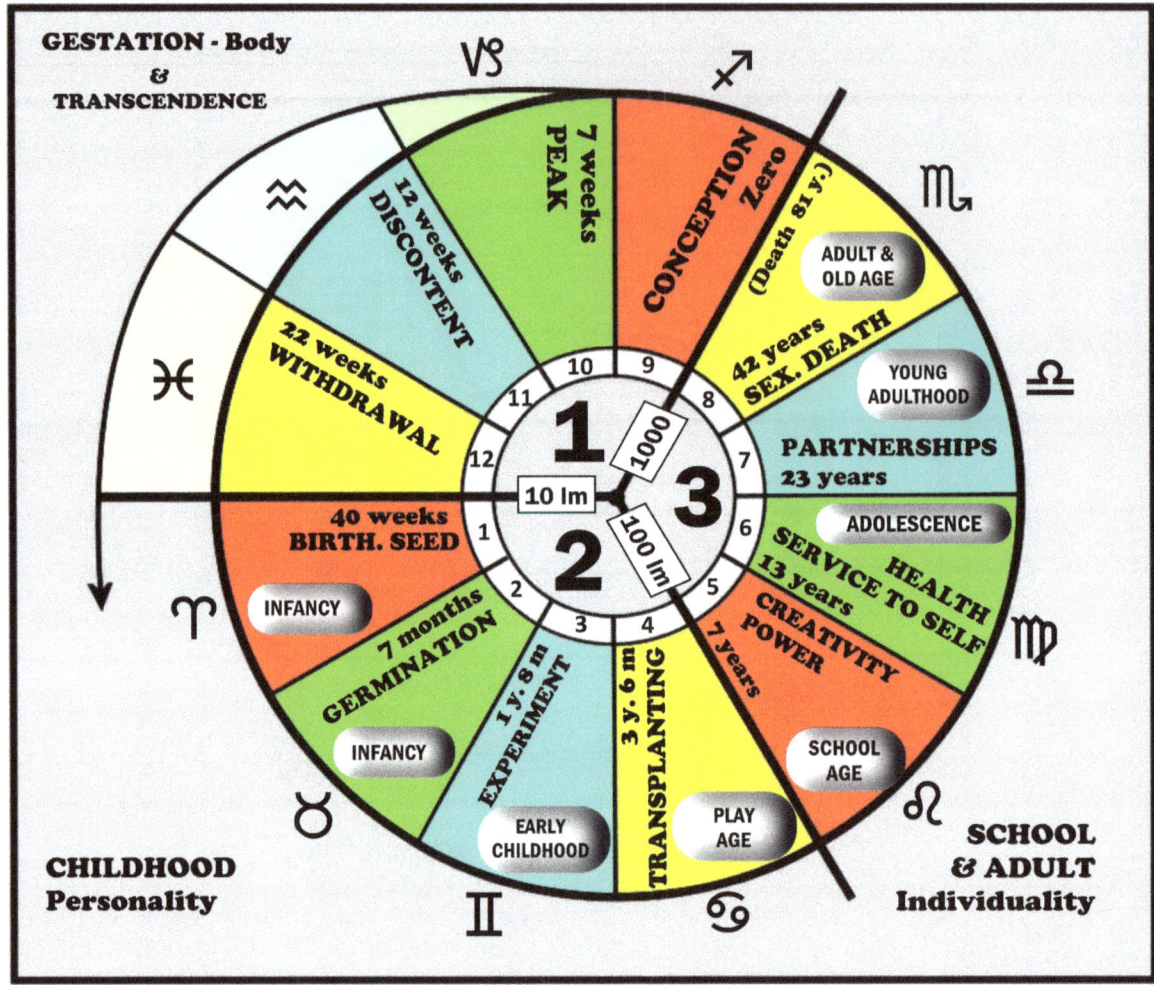

Figure 26 : Astrology - Logarithmic Timescale and Psychology stages

1. The picture shows the 12 Personal Houses of a Birth Chart. The Personal Houses are always fixed in position, as numbered. Each House has an archetypal relationship with a Zodiac Sign as shown in the diagram – although, in a chart, they may actually be ruled by another Sign, depending on the time of Birth. The 12 Houses match the 12 Stages of The Cycle of Growth.

2. Although the Houses may be ruled by other Zodiac Signs in a Birth Chart their meanings do not change.

3. This is a depiction of the fixed pattern of a lifetime from Conception to Death.

4. Conception occurs in the 9th. House, which refers to Cycle of Growth Stage 9 (Conception). The physical birth occurs at the 1st. House, Cycle of Growth Stage 1 (Seed).

5. The Logarithmic Timescale divides the Houses into 3 "Octaves" of 4 Houses each. Although we show the Houses as equal in the diagram, the 12 Stages are not of equal length of time. Each Stage is nearly twice the length of the preceding one. The overall cycle is based on 3 "Octaves" of time. The principal being the same as that of the cycle of musical scales which repeat the same note at regular intervals, each repetition of a higher note being double the frequency of vibration ("an octave higher").

6. The Octaves are based on the number of Lunar Months from Conception. The 1st. Octave covers the 10 Lunar months from Conception to Birth, the 2nd. Octave ends at 100 Lunar Months and the 3rd. Octave ends at 1,000 Lunar Months.

7. The ages related to House cusps 1 to 8 of the Logarithmic Timescale correspond almost exactly with that of Erik Erikson's "Growth of Personality" ages of psychological development from Birth to Death. There is a comparison table at the end of the chapter.

8. The 1st. Octave is also the Transcendent Octave which is concerned with Individuation later in life. Its stages have exactly the same meaning – in this case, of development, or growth, at another dimension of existence. The suggestion of "rebirth".

"THE ROUND ART" ASTROLOGY TIMESCALE

In A.T.Mann's book *"The Round Art"* There are references to *"The Theory of Celestial Influence"* by Rodney Collin. As an Astrologer, Mann's version is a lot simpler to understand - and practical rather than theoretical.

Apart from being an excellent astrological textbook covering all aspects of the Art, this is the only one I have found which answers the fundamental question which puzzled me for several years. The symbolism of Birth Chart Houses 1 to 8 are concerned with the period of one's life between Birth and Death. The question then arises : What is the lifetime function of the other Houses 9 to 12 ? The answer is, they cover the DUAL FUNCTION of life time in the womb from conception to Birth AND the more traditionally recognised function of man's Transcendence of the material world – which has relationship with Jungian Individuation.

> *"The ability to reach the transcendent state is equivalent to making supreme use of the constitution as a whole". [TRA]

On its own this offers a powerful insight, however, when one compares The Logarithmic Timescale with the psychologists' stages of psychological development developed from ideas formulated by Erik H. Erikson (1902-1994) and their related ages, there is a remarkable agreement. (Please see GROWTH OF PERSONALITY in [PSYCHOLOGY : DEVELOPMENT MODELS]).

This also establishes another fact - that THE LIFE OF AN INDIVIDUAL BEGINS AT CONCEPTION. Scientists have only recently discovered that our experiences while in the womb have a profound effect on our later life. More so from being unconscious.

The Logarithmic Timescale also suggests a reason/measurement method for the growing scientific awareness that, as our body metabolism slows down throughout life, our *perception* of Time slows down too - so Time seems to be passing faster. Young children become bored very easily because things seem to be happening slowly. This is because old experiences are continually being re-evaluated in the light of new ones (or should be). Each day, and year, is a smaller proportion of the overall life experience. So the process takes longer as we get older. It seems like a filing job where the database keeps getting bigger, requiring that indexing be revised, with an ever increasing numbers of sub categories.

THE LOGARITHMIC TIMESCALE MODEL

3 + 1 "OCTAVES" OF DEVELOPMENT

The first thing to note is that, although the model shows the same 12 Houses of a Birth Chart, there is a fundamental difference in that the structure here is a division into 3 sets of 4 Houses rather than the 4 sets of 3 of the Personal House structure. You will see in the [ASTROLOGY : TRANSITS] chapter that the cusps of the Houses 1,4,7 and 10 (Spring, Summer, Autumn, Winter) at the beginnings of the 4 quarters are "Square Aspect", or "crisis" positions, where major changes occur in a lifetime. The division of the circle into 3 x 120 degree (Trine Aspect) parts produces more harmonious changes. Secondly, we begin our life story at the 9th. House point of Conception, rather than the 1st. House of physical birth.

Although we are dealing solely with Birth Chart HOUSES in our diagram, I have coloured them with the archetypal arrangement of Zodiac Signs and Elements in order – Fire, Earth, Air, Water. This is to convey the fact that the MEANING and activity of each House is equivalent to those of the matching Zodiac Sign – apart from where Planets and Signs may be positioned at the time of birth.

In effect, the sequence of units in any "set" of 12 will conform to this pattern – being based on the archetype of Number 12. There is more detail in the chapter [NUMEROLOGY].

We note that, in life, each Octave begins with a step forward into a different level of life experience. Each requires a protective "shell". The First Octave begins with the development of a single cell in a protected environment (womb/shell). The Second Octave begins with the birth of a child into a new, less safe, environment (family home/shell). The Third Octave once again takes the child from a relatively safe, secure, home environment to enter a broader experience of life outside the home (society). It refers to another type of "shell" – the psychological Persona. The Transcendent Octave takes the individual away from normal society to individualise. In fact, approaching a wider collective of Mankind.

ASTROLOGY : LOGARITHMIC TIMESCALE

THE "SHELL" SUN SYMBOL

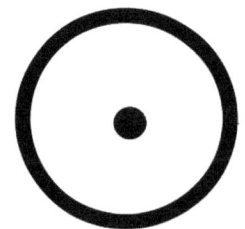

Figure 27 : Sun Symbol

We now bring to mind the "Sun Symbol" and note that it appears in several different contexts. Please also see Number 1 [NUMEROLOGY]. This is an important symbol to keep in mind because :-

1. THE MAIN MEANING OF THE "SHELL" IS THAT IT ENABLES THE SEPARATION OF AN INDIVIDUAL LIFE FORM FROM THE COLLECTIVE ENVIRONMENT.
2. The principle focus of Evolution is THE DEVELOPMENT OF CONSCIOUSNESS as symbolised by The Sun. We can consider even a Hydrogen atom as having a basic form of consciousness.
3. In the beginning was No-Thing – Number Zero has no centre, it is, however a "container". It is the First Shell. The first stage of life on earth was the evolution of a living cell without a nucleus. We will see that the basic purpose is to separate the contents from its surroundings and so allow separate, individual, development to take place.
4. Each Octave of development begins with the Fire Element, and is followed by Earth, Air, and Water.
5. The Sun Symbol appears at the beginning of each Octave as representing the Fire – energy producing, initiating – Element which is modified in later stages.
6. We note that each Octave actually begins with Zero – No-Thing - which is invisible. Here we describe it as a "Shell" which has several forms depending on the stage of evolution.
7. The basic representation is of a central nucleus and surrounding "shell".
8. At the beginning of Evolution of the universe this is the Singularity of The Big Bang. Hydrogen was produced together with a great deal of energy.
9. It is a depiction of an atom of Hydrogen with a Proton with a single Electron in orbit. This has Atomic Number 1, and is the basis of all Chemical Elements.
10. It is also a depiction of the first single cell organism with a nucleus (eg. Bacterium) surrounded by a membrane.
11. It is a depiction of the single cell of a fertilised egg, human or otherwise.
12. In this chapter the symbol represents The Sun of our Solar System, as depicted in a Birth Chart. The Sun – like other suns in the universe - is a nuclear reactor converting Hydrogen (Atomic Number 1) to Helium (Atomic Number 2) and, eventually, smaller amounts of other heavier elements and giving off energy – such as heat and light, which are basically the same thing with different frequencies - as part of the process. The reaction is occurring at the centre of The Sun, as a nucleus of a cell.
13. It is a symbol of the Ego of Psychology. That is, the Centre of Individual Human Consciousness which begins at Cycle of Growth Stage 5 (Power. Creativity)
14. We can also consider the orbits of the planets of our Solar system as Shells similar to those of a Chemical Element (please see Cycle of Growth Stage 4 below and [NUMEROLOGY]).
15. Chemical Elements develop from Hydrogen by the addition of Electron Shells.
16. The Tarot Card association are dealt with in more detail in the chapter [THE TAROT].

ASTROLOGY : LOGARITHMIC TIMESCALE

BEFORE CONCEPTION : THE ZERO STATE

1. This is the state before The Big Bang when everything was in balance. There was no-thing but "empty" space. Everything was still. In effect, the universe was dead.
2. This refers to Sephiroth 1 (Kether. Crown) of the Kabbalah Tree of Life and Number Zero. Everything and anything is possible – but not yet.
3. The related planet is Neptune – which is a symbolic representation of the 3 pillars of the Kabbalah Tree of Life, with Malkuth (Earth) at the bottom. An idea is beginning to take form. It becomes a Singularity containing all the matter of the universe, and releases an unimaginable amount of energy. Expansion begins.
4. In the beginning was The Word. A mental concept. A New Year's Resolution.
5. The egg is prepared to eventually accept the sperm.

*1- FIRST OCTAVE : 0 TO 10 LM

In human terms the First Octave covers our time in the womb – which is the formation of the human body as a "shell" or "vehicle" for the soul.

Practical scientific information concerning this stage of life is very limited so it is not possible to make detailed associations.

There is more detailed information concerning this Octave in the chapters [NUMEROLOGY] and [THE KABBALAH TREE OF LIFE].

The Octave relates to the first 6 stages (days) of the Biblical story of Creation in the first chapter of Genesis [GENESIS AND THE CYCLE OF GROWTH], which follows the now scientific accepted story of Evolution from The Big Bang. We note that Adam does not appear in physical form until Chapter 2 as a baby does not "appear" until it is born at Cycle of Growth Stage 1 (Seed).

The seed shell Sun Symbol here relates to the Singularity of The Big Bang, The Hydrogen Atom, and the first living cell with a nucleus, the fertilised egg. It next refers to the "Shell" of the female womb which contains the developing life form ("seed. nucleus").

CONCEPTION TO BIRTH

The Octave covers the period of Conception and the 10 Lunar Months, or 40 weeks in the womb from Conception to Birth and refers to the time of development of a physical human body.

Full term is reached at the end of the tenth lunar month of pregnancy. [MSERL]

1. Gestation is a repetition of 3,500 million years of evolution which started with a single cell organism - later evolving via fish, reptile, bird, and ape stages into Homo Sapiens 200,000 years ago.
2. During the 9 months gestation period a human foetus goes through the same stages of development in the same order as human evolution including the development of gills, a tail, and a type of body hair (lanugo) which subsequently disappear. I had a friend who worked in a maternity hospital and he saw evidence of this in aborted foetuses.

Indeed, in the months from conception to birth he is recapitulating the whole of mankind's evolution. He starts as a small blob of protoplasm, changes into a kind of fish (his gills are observable), then into a near reptile, and finally into the monkey-like creature which foreshadows its ultimately human form. Of course the infant's condensation of centuries of ancestral evolution into nine months of pre-natal development does not imply intention on his part. Recapitulation is not something he initiates; it is merely something that happens to him because he is a member of the human species. [GOP]

3. Gestation is not just about the development of an egg to a baby. We also need to take into account the mother's attitude and condition as a result of the pregnancy. At Conception she is unconscious of the pregnancy. During gestation she first becomes <u>consciously</u> aware of the possibility of new life – followed by an

increasing physical awareness of its actuality. There seems to be a relationship between hers and the foetus's expanding consciousness. What does she imagine the baby will be like?

4. Modern science is beginning to recognise that Gestation is not just a period of passive physical growth. In 1981 Thomas Verney published his book *"The Secret Life of the Unborn Child"* [SLUC] which showed the results of 20 years of research. Basically, he has proved that experiences in the womb have just as much effect upon us as those of later life. An important factor, apart from the possibility of physical injury, or the mother's state of physical health, is <u>how the mother reacts to the circumstances of her outer life</u>. Her emotional reactions are passed on to the foetus. This, incidentally, solves an Astrological problem concerning the 10th. House of a Birth Chart. Until now it has not been clear whether it refers to Father or Mother. The answer is both. How the Father reacts to the coming birth has an effect on the Mother – whose feelings are transmitted to the baby.

Edgar Cayce states that the incarnating soul has no control of its destination (physical body).

Cycle of Growth Stages 9 to 12

The symbolism of the First Octave of The Cycle of Growth relates to :-

1. That of the time of year between the Winter Solstice and the first day of Spring, when The Sun enters the Sign of Aries. We have the "rebirth" of the SUN at the time of the Winter solstice in December, with the gradual increase in light (consciousness) as days lengthen.
2. The birth of the SON, Jesus, at Christmas time, and his subsequent life until his crucifixion on the Cross (of Matter) at Easter time in Spring (Rebirth) –Stage 1 (Seed).
3. The story of the 6 "days" of Creation followed by a "day" of rest in Genesis.
4. The Gestation of a child in the womb. The preparation of a human body and its gradual increase in consciousness (light).
5. Evolution of the universe beginning with "Conception" at "The Big Bang". [NUMEROLOGY]

STAGE 9 - CONCEPTION (Conception to 7 weeks)

The Sperm fertilises the Egg which starts a nuclear "chain reaction". The first form of human life is an Embryo. In our evolution the earliest life forms were single cells that reproduce by division – as do those in an embryo.

We note that, at this stage, each cell is an identical clone with all the information required to make a complete human body. The cells are called "Stem Cells" which Medicine is beginning to use to repair human tissue by using their property to grow into any of its various forms.

The mechanism for this is in the strands of DNA contained in the cells. Although research is still in its early days, it seems that each strand of DNA is a miniature "replica" of the human body in terms of where information is stored on a "head to toe" basis. Perhaps scientists should consider the DNA strand in this light.

1. *An important point of note here is that the principle is the same as the House structure of a Birth Chart, where each House in order refers to a different part of the body from head (1. Aries) to toe (12. Pisces).*
2. *Another point is that we see a physical example of the Principle of The Number Zero Collective State at the beginning of evolution, before The Big Bang" where everything existed- albeit in an undifferentiated state.*
3. *From this stage, the same Archetypes are at work producing cells with different functions (on behalf of the whole) in a body, as well as people with different functions in Society. For example, 1st. House/Aries/Mars "at the Head" are our pioneers and leaders, 12th. House/Pisces/Jupiter-Neptune at the feet are concerned with our "under-standings".*

SAGITTARIUS – UNFOCUSED ENERGY

Mutable/Changeable Fire is indicative of pure energy in a chaotic, unfocused state. This is the state of 99% of the matter in the universe which exists as Plasma in stars such as our Sun – it consists of superheated gas which is mainly Hydrogen being converted to Helium – which, in turn, converts to the heavier Chemical Elements. The nuclear reaction releases a great deal of energy. Plasma is the state of matter which precedes Gas, Liquid, and Solid.

1. This is the Orgasm of The Big Bang.

2. The traditionally related Planet to Sagittarius is Jupiter. The principle is "Expansion" which basically means increasing what is already in existence – such as knowledge or property. In a chart it also refers to Human Society as a collective.
3. We now have to consider the influence of Pluto. This is new life rather than just a continuation of the past. Although traditionally related to Scorpio, we can see it as a link between Stage 8 and Stage 9 of The Cycle of Growth. It contains the process of Elimination.
4. Since the discovery of Pluto – related to the discovery of Nuclear Energy – we now have a more basic interpretation. It is concerned with the equivalence of Energy and Matter. $E=MC^2$.
5. Sagittarius/Jupiter relates to academic, theoretical, activity in schools and colleges rather than the practical application of knowledge of its complementary Gemini/Mercury.
6. The Calendar time of year is the beginning of a new academic year. The pupils move into a higher class. Parliament reforms after the holidays.

THE TAROT : XIV. TEMPERANCE

Temperance shows a figure with one foot on earth and the other in water pouring liquid from one cup to another. This can be considered as a depiction of the formation/separation of a Singularity from the Number Zero state of the universe ("waters" below) which produced the energy release of The Big Bang –and which continues at a slower rate in stars today.

At a Biblical level this is Creation Day Zero before any manifestation. The separation of No-Thing and Matter has not yet fully occurred.

> *In the beginning of God's preparing the heavens and the earth – the earth hath existed waste and void, and darkness [is] on the face of the deep, and the Spirit of God fluttering on the face of the waters [Genesis Chapter 1 Verses 1 & 2 YLT]*

THE KABBALAH TREE OF LIFE SEPHIRAH 2 (Chockmah, Wisdom, Force. Pluto)

Chockmah provides the motivational energy for the whole of The Tree of Life, and controls The Pillar of Mercy (Force) from its position at the top. This was the original Big Bang .

STAGE 10 - SOCIAL PEAK. HARVEST (7 to 12 weeks).

The embryo becomes a foetus.

The mother has missed 2 Lunar, 29 day, monthly menstruations and is certain of the pregnancy. Her social standing changes as those around (especially the father) are made aware. Her reactions to their reactions are passed on to the foetus.

The next important stage in Evolution is the beginning of the Digestive System. Worms were one of the earliest forms of "organised" life. They consist of not much more than a mouth, gut, and anus. The spine begins to develop - which eventually will form a structure for the whole body. The spine is probably a physical form of the DNA strand which contains cells appearing to have no function. We see a Capricorn Principle of "Organisation and Structure" which, among other things, gives rise to the hierarchies of "large organisations".

CAPRICORN

Capricorn is the Cardinal , initiating, Earth Sign ruled by Saturn/Satan. Its traditional association is the concentration of energy over a long period of time to achieve some goal ("long range plans". Career). We can see how this relates to this stage in the formation of the material universe (and human body) and Sephirah 3 (Binah, Understanding, The Principle of Form).

1. In the Annual Calendar we celebrate Christmas as the birth of the Christian SON, and the Winter Solstice as the rebirth of the SUN – each with its promise of new life to come.
2. This is the basic challenge of Force and Form, Light and Dark, Good and Evil.
3. In Genesis this relates to Creation Day 1 which saw the creation of Light and Day (from the original Zero Darkness) which then gave rise to Night to maintain universal balance.
4. From this we get a basic idea of how the universe operates. By generating Cycles each form of complementary ("opposite") energy is separated and "takes turns" through Time - which prevents the

positive and negative energies from recombining and annihilating one another in a return to the Zero State.

5. This Stage of the Cycle of Growth is that of Winter - reaping the benefits of the activities of the whole of the previous cycle and beginning to consider the new beginning not yet come.
6. This is the focus of the purpose of the building of ancient stone circles like Stonehenge which are aligned with the sunrise at the Winter Solstice. They often include human burial remains. This is a time of looking back to the past and forward to the future.
7. We see this as a time of family social gatherings.
8. A function of Saturn is that of "Lord of Karma". Reaping what has been sown.

THE TAROT : XV. THE DEVIL AND XVI. THE TOWER

The related Tarot cards are the 2 faces of The Devil – Satan as a negative force seeming to oppose the creative energy of God (Chockmah), and Lucifer "Bringer of Light" (consciousness).

The creative force needs material to work with.

THE KABBALAH TREE OF LIFE SEPHIRAH 3 (Binah, Understanding, Principle of Form. Saturn)

We see the first appearance of the Kabbalist "Lightning Flash" in the depiction of XVI.The Tower. The pure energy of Sephirah 1 (Chockmah, Force) is released to eventually connect Heaven and Earth at Sephiroth 10 (Kingdom).

With Number 2 we have 2 points making a straight line which can be considered a "string" – which modern String Theory suggests is the basis of all matter in the universe.

In The Kabbalah this equates with Sephirah 3 (Binah. Form. Mother. Saturn/Satan. Negative Polarity). Here the "Irresistible Force" of Chockmah meets the "Immovable Object". Form (consolidating, negative energy) develops as a result of the universal imbalance caused by the creation of positive energy. Each Stage (Day) of Creation requires an "Even-ing" to maintain the original universal balance of Zero. Force and Form, Light and Dark, Positive and Negative, are the basic requirements of Creation.

Binah controls The Pillar of Severity (Form) from her position at the top.

STAGE 11 - DISSATISFACTION. REBELLION (12 to 22 weeks).

The foetus becomes human.

*At 16 weeks the unborn child shies away from light [SLUC]

*At 20 weeks there is response to speech patterns [SLUC].

The rulership of Aquarius, the Fixed Air Sign (Discontent, Independence), suggests mental development and individualisation (separation) from the mother, albeit at a basic level.

Aquarius has 2 planet rulers. The traditional Saturn where the message of the possibility of new life is stifled by Tradition (Capricorn), and Uranus where one separates from the Collective to Individualise. Although the unborn child is separating from the mother, Saturn (DNA) rules. We see the depiction of this dilemma in the life of Jesus when he was tempted by Saturn/Satan to use his powers to escape his later crucifixion and gain personal social status (Capricorn) as The Messiah. In the event, he was rejected by the crowd (who at first received him with rejoicing as the New Messiah on Palm Sunday) in favour of Barabbas who was a more traditional type of rebel –an anti-Roman reactionary.

He spent 40 days and nights alone in the "wilderness", which equates to the 40 weeks of "isolation" in the womb. The Winter Time of Aquarius has "wilderness" conditions.

Here the Individualisation process creates a separate human being – albeit in accordance with natural evolution. There is no Free Will.

THE CREATION STORY

This Cycle of Growth Stage includes the Genesis Creation Days 2 to 6 which cover the creation of Heaven and Earth, Stars, Sun and Moon, the separation of the Sea and Dry Land, the creation of vegetation, animals and birds, "male and female" - and finally "man" (but not Adam yet).

ASTROLOGY : LOGARITHMIC TIMESCALE

This is totally in line with the accepted scientific "timetable" of the development of the universe and the consolidation of planets, including Earth, and the final appearance of vegetable and animal life. We note again that our foetus in the womb relives those stages.

THE TAROT : XVII. THE STAR. XVIII. THE MOON.

At one level we can see these cards as a vague depiction of the Creation Story. XVII. The Star shows the separation of sea and dry land, The Moon is a depiction of the evolutionary stage of creatures coming out of the sea on to dry land. We have the creation of planetary bodies as matter cools and solidifies.

In human terms the cards seem to be mainly concerned with unconscious development. We know the autonomic nervous system that controls things like breathing and heartbeat are developing now.

THE KABBALAH TREE OF LIFE – DAATH AND URANUS

Daath is the previously un-numbered Sephiroth which we can now equate to Number 11 and Uranus. At this Stage in a human life it is unformed. Daath, and Uranus relate to the use of Will and this cannot exist without consciousness. If the Transcendent Path is chosen later on in life it becomes the path across The Abyss on the Middle Pillar. At this stage of life it has no direct effect.

STAGE 12 – WITHDRAWAL. CONFINEMENT (22 weeks to Birth).

In the Genesis Story of Creation this refers to Day 7 – a day of rest.

The Time is of preparation and waiting for the actual birth. We note that this Stage begins around half way through pregnancy. After the "Individualisation Stage" the foetus has now become a sentient being able to survive apart from its mother. In effect, the baby "decides" when to be born.

After 24 weeks (in the UK) the pregnancy can only be legally terminated under exceptional circumstances – as the foetus is now considered a sentient being, able to survive outside the womb.

*At 25 weeks the baby can kick in time to music [SLUC].

*At 6 months the unborn child can understand the subtle shift of its mother's emotions.[SLUC]

The rulership of Pisces, the Mutable Water Sign (ref. the Sea of The Collective Unconscious, Feelings, Emotions) is clearly representative of the watery surroundings of the womb at this time. The other associations with places of confinement such as hospitals, prisons, and other places of retreat, mirror the state of the mother. We have the mythical association of being "swallowed by a whale".

The traditional rulership if Pisces by Jupiter (Expansion) relates to the process of growth in accordance with "Tradition", or Nature.

Later on in life, when we are dealing with the Transcendent function of this Octave, if the Uranus drive to Individuation has succeeded this Stage is subject to Neptune whose action is to dissolve the past in preparation for a new future. This relates to Winter time breaking down the old growth structures to fertilise the new ones in Spring, and at psychological levels where one can be released from Karma by forgiveness or atonement. We can do better next time.

The activity of Neptune can also be applied to the process of "Forgetting" – the "dissolution" of memories. We do not generally remember our past experiences in the womb.

THE KABBLAH TREE OF LIFE SEPHIROTH 4 (Chesed. Mercy. Jupiter. Number 3)

This Sephiroth is related to Jupiter on the Pillar of Mercy (Force) its function being already mentioned at Stage 9 (Conception). Its symbol also applies to social concepts, so we can see it acting in that capacity at this Stage (differentiation of cells to perform specific functions on behalf of the whole).

The next Cycle of Growth Stage 1 (Seed) ruled by Aries/Mars is concerned with our leaving the "collective" womb to become a separate human being, beginning a new life on Earth. This is the province of Sephiroth 5 (Geburah, Severity) on the opposite side of the Middle Pillar – on the Pillar of Form. This relates to Number 4 which includes relationship to what is described in the chapter [THE 4 ELEMENTS] - and the Tarot Cards 0.The Fool and I.The Magician.

THE TAROT – XIX. THE SUN. XX. JUDGEMENT,   AND XXI. THE WORLD

THE SUN. The first signs of consciousness. The card shows a child riding on a horse. Jesus entered Jerusalem riding on a donkey just before his crucifixion. At the end of the 1st. Octave we have the symbolism of a child (as yet undeveloped) coming into control of its physical/animal nature by use of the mind – which is what is now happening in the womb. There is a similar symbol at Cycle of Growth Stage 4 with Tarot card VII. The Chariot – which is the end of the 2nd. Octave – which refers to Cancer (Crab. Shell), another Water Sign.

JUDGEMENT - is symbolic of hearing "the call" to another state of existence. It shows human figures rising from the grave in answer to the call of the trumpet, which has a banner depicting a cross. We note that trumpets were used in Revelation as an aid to opening the Chakras. In the Biblical story this is the Crucifixion of Jesus on the Cross of Matter, his burial in a cave/womb, and his subsequent resurrection. The symbol of a soul imprisoned in a human body. The Cave and The Womb are both symbols of Transition from one state to another. This is now celebrated at the beginning of Spring at Easter time as the time of actual appearance of new life on Earth. Here it is still just a potential.

"The Call" could be connected to the 12th. Stage association with Neptune – which, in turn, is associated with Sephiroth 1 (Kether. Crown. Number Zero). Here we have a remembrance of "The Original Plan" or "Ideal" which, as in Jesus' case, is also a prediction of the future. This memory is wiped by subsequent events of the birth.

In the normal world XX.Judgment refers to Vocation, a higher calling, or promotion.

THE WORLD - with a hermaphrodite figure enclosed in an elliptical wreath can be considered as the child leaving the womb and/or its enclosure in the "body shell". Entry into a new stage of life. At this stage, although the child has physical sex organs it has not developed the psychological sexual traits. The next card is 0. The Fool.

PSYCHOLOGY : GROWTH OF PERSONALITY

The 2nd. and 3rd. Octaves refer to the Logarithmic Timescale stages which cover a normal human lifetime from Birth to Death. We have more detailed Stages by being able to compare the Cycle of Growth symbols with the growth stages of Psychology.

We recall from above that each of the Octaves consists of the same order of stages – Fire, Earth, Air, Water – albeit at different levels, and taking proportionally longer amounts of time. An example given is the physical development of the 1st. Octave which occurs in the womb is <u>repeated</u> by the 2nd. Octave psychological development of early childhood.

In the chapter [PSYCHOLOGY : DEVELOPMENT MODELS] there is comparison of some structures used by different areas of Psychology to enable consideration of human growth and development from cradle to grave – including, among others, Freud's (1856-1939), and later Jung's (1875-1961), pioneering concepts. These were later developed by Erik Erikson (1902-1994), and, later, others, into a more detailed picture which divided a lifetime into various stages, each related to a specific age range. Erikson's stages and age ranges compare almost exactly with Stages 1 to 8 of The Astrological Logarithmic Timescale. <u>There is a summary comparison table included in that chapter.</u>

From his observations, Erikson conceived 8 Stages of psychological development, each of which is related to an ever widening consciousness of our surroundings and participation in relationships with an increasing number of people – that is also a widening experience and view of society. As we enter each stage we are faced with a dilemma, or problem to solve, from coming into conflict with the people there. In simplest terms, we do not know how to handle the situation and have to learn by experience. *It seems that we have to solve the problem "Me and/or You" each time [BTB].* If we consider it in terms of "Nature versus Nurture", the "Nurture" part is related to other people. Each Stage therefore consists of :-

1. A new area of social relationship.
2. A dilemma of seeming opposing courses of action – perhaps what Jung meant by the need to "reconcile opposites".
3. An inner anxiety, or fear.
4. A "Reward" for arriving at a solution, and progression to the next stage. (Rather like a modern computer game).

Although a linear process of stages is implied, in reality we can be working at several levels at the same time. At times of stress we can psychologically revert back to an earlier stage – such as by crying when feeling overwhelmed by life circumstances, which is more appropriate to the Infancy stage.

ASTROLOGY : LOGARITHMIC TIMESCALE

The ages used here are those of the Astrological Logarithmic Timescale. The only difference is that The Cycle of Growth has 2 stages covering Erikson's single one of Infancy, and Erikson has two stages at the end - Adulthood from 30-65 and Old Age from 65 years upwards. The Cycle of Growth Stage 8 (Intercourse. Death) lasts from 42 years to death. This suggests Jung's concept of Individuation at Age 42 – which is ignored in Psychoanalysis.

N.B. Where necessary, to differentiate my comments from the accepted concepts of Psychology they are italicised[BTB].

*2 - SECOND OCTAVE : 10 TO 100 LM

In this Octave the aim is to find one's place in a small family.

Jung describes the state of consciousness of this Octave as a series of "islands" that gradually grow and combine to form a "continent" in keeping with his image of "the sea" of the Collective Unconscious.

Where before we had a fertilised egg, or single cell with nucleus, the seed Sun Symbol here relates to the "Shell" of a human body into which the living soul incarnates as its "nucleus".

In the Biblical story of Creation we are now at Genesis Chapter 2 with the stages of the actual physical creation of Adam "from dust" and later on, Eve - who could also be considered as the psychological, unconscious, Anima("counterpart" [YLT]) of Adam. The Bible states that Eve came from Adam's "rib" while he was asleep (unconscious). Scholars interpret this as being from Adam's "side" or "bias" which is in accordance with the psychological concept of the development a man's <u>unconscious</u> Anima (and a woman's Animus) as a "counterpart" to one's conscious attitude. Psychologically, at birth both sexes are identical - as is confirmed by a Birth Chart ("Nature"). The difference is in the "Nurture" of subsequent relationships. The Bible does not explicitly state that Adam returned to consciousness. [GENESIS AND THE CYCLE OF GROWTH].

BIRTH TO 7 YEARS OF AGE : Cycle of Growth Stages 1 (Seed) to 4 (Transplanting)

Having developed from a single cell to a multi-cellular organism, the Octave covers the evolutionary period of human development from animal-like existence - moving about on all fours on the ground to finally "standing on his own two feet". This covers Infancy and Early Childhood development within the family home.

The child enters the physical world. The Octave covers the life time from Birth at 10 lunar months to 100 Lunar months (7 years) - referring to the time of Childhood and psychological development of a separate Personality. This period repeats the same sequence of development as in the womb, albeit at a different level. So the Second Octave is a repetition of the cycle of the First Octave. As the Sperm "seed" was implanted into the Egg, the "Seed" child is planted in the Earth.

> ** Now there is a marked similarity between the growth of the embryo and subsequent psychological development, that is, between the stages of physical development before birth and the stages of bio-psychological development after birth. The postnatal development of human beings, without exception,*

centres successively on certain zones of the body: first the mouth, then the anal system, then the genitals - the order is invariable. As the growth of the embryo recapitulates evolution, so psychological development recapitulates that of the embryo. [GOP]

Edgar Cayce states that the individual soul enters the physical body at birth. This suggests that, in order to live, the physical body has a basic consciousness of its own (the autonomic nervous system). It certainly has developed a brain which would have recorded experiences so far, and an autonomic nervous system that takes care of such unconscious things as heartbeat, breathing, and digestion. It gives us an idea of the difference between Soul, and Body and Mind. At this stage the baby is solely the product of the mother's experiences during her pregnancy.

*(Question) Does a soul ever enter a body before it is born? (Answer) It enters either at the first breath physically drawn, or during the first twenty-four hours of cycle activity in a material plane. Not always at the first breath; sometimes there are hours, and there are changes even of personalities as to the seeking to enter. [EC reading 2390-2]

CYCLE OF GROWTH STAGE 1 (Seed) – 0 to 7 months

THE NEW BORN

Erikson does not recognise this as a separate stage. We see this as the newly born child completely uncoordinated and unaware of its surroundings, and spending much of its time in a state of unconsciousness.

Focus of consciousness is mainly on the mouth. The psychology is mainly "animal" Instinct and Intuition. Feeling, Thinking, and Sensation are in their undifferentiated embryo stage.

In the annual calendar this is the time of Easter with the crucifixion of Jesus on The Cross of Matter, and his subsequent resurrection. We can see an association with the Soul or Spirit becoming "crucified" in a material, physical body. We also have "The April Fool" in line with The Tarot.

THE TAROT – 0.THE FOOL AND I.THE MAGICIAN

The Tarot Fool with his "unconscious" dog is a state of innocence where animal instinct is the motivator – he does not recognise the danger ahead. "The Magician" shows the potential development of Mind and Will to control The 4 Elements on the table before him – that also refer to the 4 Jungian Psychological Functions.

In the Tarot the Suit of Wands represents the Fire Element – Clubs in a modern pack. They are rather tame versions of the energy depicted here - although to stone age man the principle is the same. This is life on its simplest terms – the individual will to survive.

ARIES – IMPULSIVE ENERGY

1. The principle aim at this stage is Survival (of the fittest).
2. Here we are at the traditional beginning of a lifetime and Calendar Year. Spring. The Rutting Season. The energy of Aries is that of pure instinctive impulse. This is demonstrated by the symbol of The Ram, although we are more familiar with the similar rutting of male deer where, at this time, they fight one another by locking their antlers. At this stage they are not really interested in the females. The biological aim is in selective breeding to ensure that only the strongest males pass their genes on to the females. In the bird – and other – world this is called "establishing a pecking order". This is the phallic erect penis status symbol of the pyramids and ziggurats – full of potential not yet realised.
3. Aries is ruled by planet Mars "God of War".
4. The Kabbalah Sephiroth Geburah (Severity. Mars) is associated with Number 4.
5. Whereas at Stage 9 (Conception) the Fire energy was unfocused, it is now directed towards a particular object. In engineering terms, edged and pointed weapons and tools (ruled by Aries/Mars) focus energy.
6. Aries people are independent and prefer occupations that give them a task to perform and they are left alone to complete it. They are the Pioneers and Competitors of the world. The main goal is to "make a name for themselves".
7. The complementary Sign is Libra (Partnerships), but at this time there is no conscious recognition of others, except the mother, at this stage – although there is a clear form of dependence.

ASTROLOGY : LOGARITHMIC TIMESCALE

THE KABBALAH TREE OF LIFE SEPHIRAH 5 (Geburah, Severity, Mars)

The 2nd. Octave again begins with the Fire Element. We see how the purely nuclear energy of Sephirah 2 (Chockmah, Force) at the top of the Pillar of Force now has some-thing to focus on lower down The Tree at Sephirah 5 (Geburah, Severity) on the Pillar of Form.

CYCLE OF GROWTH STAGE 2 (Germination)

7 months to 1 year 8 months.

INFANCY   (Freud Oral Stage)

Trust versus Mistrust. "Who can I trust ?". Fear of starvation. The rewards is "Hope."

Erikson's first Stage focuses on Oral Sucking, Biting, and Weaning. The Infant begins to experience Hunger for the first time - its needs are not met instantly, as they were in the womb. The first anxiety is said to be "Fear of Starvation" – although this really means the cycle of Comfort versus Discomfort. His dilemma is "Trust versus Mistrust" (of the environment) depending on how those needs are met. We note the Transactional Analysis concept [PSYCHOLOGY : DEVELOPMENT MODELS] that the most important requirement from now until the end of our life is "Stroking" – that is, basically, some form of external stimulus. The Goal for this Stage is "Hope".

The Seed first meets Earth in the form of a physical human body over which it has no initial control. It has to learn how to take in the sustenance it needs. The "blank sheet" of the brain begins to record new experiences.

THE TAROT – II.THE PRIESTESS AND III.THE EMPRESS

We can associate the meaning of this time with "The Child" of Transactional Analysis mentioned below in Stage 5. This refers to our early emotional responses to life circumstances which are recorded in the Personal Unconscious – and the reaction of the outside world to them.

At this age we are subject to the Feminine Power of The Mother.

At this psychological level "The Priestess" "blank sheet" becomes the pregnant "Empress" as pictures take "form" in the mind. We become aware of our physical body. The outer physical world begins to become conscious – and is recorded.

TAURUS – CONTROLLED ENERGY AND POSSESSIONS

1. Taurus, Fixed Earth, embodies the principle of Kabbalism's Sephirah 3 (Binah. Form. Inertia) which resists the creative Sephirah 2 (Chockmah. Force). We can see its activity of this time of early Spring where the earth containing the seed must become warm and moist in order for germination to take place. There is seeming resistance by the earth because this takes a long time.
2. The Seed from Stage 1 is now planted in the Earth from which it gains sustenance and is enabled to grow and put down "roots". Its impulsive energy is now modified to produce physical results. The child is beginning to develop physically, and control muscles that it did not need before.
3. Taurus and the 2nd. House are concerned with personal possessions, which includes the human body as well as our physical/mental abilities.
4. Although Taurus people are said to be materially minded and concerned about having enough money, their main goal is physical comfort. Although they are labelled elsewhere as "Stubborn", "Patient", or "Peaceful" it is merely that they are slow to absorb new information, and, quite rightly, do not like being rushed. Like the Earth in Spring, they are "slow to warm". Their main ability is in management of practical or domestic affairs, and tasks that have a fixed routine. In Nature this is the cycle of Seasons. Taurus people often feel cold from having slow blood circulation.
5. Venus co-rules Taurus and Libra. In the Earth Sign desires are focused on the body and other physical objects. "Beauty is Comfort". He need for "stroking".
6. The complementary Sign to Taurus is Scorpio. At base level Taurus is concerned with personal possessions and building the human body, Scorpio is concerned with "other people's possessions" and the decline of the human body. The balance is in sex and other forms of intercourse, such as buying and selling – which demand some form of interchange. We can see a relationship between "holding on and letting go".

ASTROLOGY : LOGARITHMIC TIMESCALE

THE KABBALAH TREE OF LIFE SEPHIRAH 7 (Netzach, Victory, Venus. Number 6)

The energy of "The Lightning Flash" crosses Sephirah 6 (Tiphareth, Beauty, The Sun) without hindrance because at this stage there is little consciousness, and no personal Ego Development or control - which does not begin until Cycle of Growth Stage 5 (Power, Creativity) when the child begins to experience the world outside the family home, and develop its own conscious self-control independent of parental control.

We are now at Sephiroth 7 (Netzach, Victory) on the Pillar of Force. The active Mars energy of Sephiroth 5 is now more passive Desire lower down The Tree. The physical body has its own needs. The Sephirah below Sephiroth 6 (The Sun) relate to the Personal, Inner, Planets with orbits between the Sun and Earth. Venus is concerned with inner feelings.

CYCLE OF GROWTH STAGE 3 (Experiment)

1year. 8 months to 3 years 6 months.

EARLY CHILDHOOD (Freud Anal Stage)

Autonomy versus Shame/Doubt. "When do I hold on ? When do I let go ?". Fear of impending disgrace. The reward is "Will".

In this Stage awareness expands beyond the Feminine World of The Mother to incorporate new relationships. Whereas the previous goal was that of simple survival we now have the recognition of the need to keep on good terms with those who are able to keep us comfortable – or alive. The issue is now that of Control – Who is in charge ? You or Me ? Erikson's dilemma "Autonomy versus Shame and Doubt". The "fear of impending disgrace". This is the beginning of a developing Conscience which is the ability to predict possible results of our actions.

The Goal for this Stage is Will – the ability to get what one wants. Symbolically and actually learning when to "Hold On", and when to "Let Go". At a physical level we have the development of muscular control – principally those of the bladder and bowels.

Potty training is a big issue at this age and how it is carried out can have a psychological effect on later life. Doctors state that many parents try to get their children "clean" before the necessary muscles are fully developed – which varies from child to child. It also varies depending on which part of the world we live in – although it is not clear whether this is due to early muscular development or not. In undeveloped countries infants are often in control before they walk, whilst others are not able until age 3. Much seems to depend on whether diapers/nappies are available – an indicator of how much control parents have.

THE TAROT – IV.THE EMPEROR AND V.THE HIEROPHANT

We can associate these images with "The Parent" of Transactional Analysis mentioned below in Stage 5.

Erikson's social relationships expand to include "Parental Persons", which now include the masculine father as well as the feminine mother. We have the appearance of 'The Emperor' who rules by established power, and 'The Hierophant' who rules by stating "The Law" (of "Right or Wrong", "Yes and No") in our Cycle of Growth. These were the first main roles established in the development of new civilisations. Powers beyond pure feminine nurture, or the need to gather one's own food. We see an underlying focus that "clean is right".

> *.. at the age of two he has a much firmer and stronger sense of his own identity. The development of Ego in a child goes hand in hand with the development of intellectual powers. According to Piaget the child has passed through the stage of 'sensori-motor intelligence' and beginning to develop 'conceptual intelligence'. [GOP]*

GEMINI – MENTAL DEVELOPMENT AND COMMUNICATION

1. Air Signs refer to mental development and use. Gemini is Air in its Mutable, or most unstable state. The Mind is continually "changing". At this Stage it is a benefit to be told what to do to avoid the worry of making decisions.
2. The Sign of Gemini is concerned with mental development – especially the Thinking Function – something not usually mentioned by psychologists at this stage. If we observe ourselves closely we can see that it is the Rational Functions, Thinking (Air. Mercury) and Feeling (Water. Venus), that are involved in recognition of dilemmas, which usually consist of 2 alternatives ("The Twins") until a creative resolution is conceived. The Irrational ones, Intuition and Sensation, are not divided. At this age there

may be few actual dilemmas because we are told what to do, and experiences are not fully conscious. Some people prefer this scenario throughout their lives. Dilemmas are uncomfortable until a decision is made – and risk is involved.

3. From The Bible, we have to especially note that "naming things" is an important part of this stage – a mental concept, or structure, being formed to symbolically represent an object. To me, this seems an important stage that leads to the discovery that "I have a name, so I AM (an object)". We see in [GENESIS AND THE CYCLE OF GROWTH] :-

*Genesis 2 - Verse19: And Jehovah God formeth from the ground every beast of the field, and every fowl of the heavens, and bringeth in unto the man, to see what he doth call it; and whatever the man calleth a living creature, that [is] its name. [YLT]

4. We note that "the man" did not yet have a name of his own. Psychologists say that, to a child of this age, parents are symbolically God-like figures with the power of life and death.
5. The complementary Sign to Gemini (Personal, Practical, Mental Concepts) perhaps related to The Emperor at this stage, is Sagittarius (Social, Abstract, Mental Concepts - which include religion) perhaps related to The Hierophant.
6. "The Twins" can also refer to the separation of masculine and feminine traits according to social pressures. This is when Adam falls unconscious and Eve is formed from his "rib" (side, or conscious bias).

THE KABBALAH TREE OF LIFE SEPHIRAH 8 (Hod, Glory, Mercury. Number 7)

Balancing Venus (Desire, Feelings, Emotions) on the Pillar of Force we now have Mercury (Rational, Logical Mind) on The Pillar of Form. We can see the conflict between these 2 forces exemplified at this stage of life. The child learns to voice its needs, and argue if necessary. Crying and emotional tantrums of earlier stages are not now deemed appropriate.

CYCLE OF GROWTH STAGE 4 (Transplanting. Roots)

3 years. 6 months to 7 years.

This is the last Stage of the 2nd. Octave. As with the end of the 1st. Octave, Stage 12 (Withdrawal. Confinement) it is ruled by the (psychological) Water Element, and is a preparation for a new phase of life. Whereas development of the physical body was the focus, we now have the development of a psychological "body" or "shell" – the Persona, or mask of The Actor.

Traditional Astrology includes "Roots" as part of the list of associations - here concerned with the Mother and childhood family.

It is interesting to note that Birth occurs about 42 weeks after Conception (1st. Octave), this Stage begins at 42 months (ending the 2nd. Octave), and Individuation begins at 42 years of age (the last stage of the 3rd. Octave)

In the Biblical story of Creation Eve was tempted by The Serpent, and Adam was tempted by Eve, to eat from The Tree of (carnal) Knowledge – thus choosing regeneration by physical reproduction and death of the body - rather than Resurrection (cell regeneration by use of Will) as demonstrated by Jesus at his Resurrection. They were "transplanted" away from The Garden of Eden and Tree of Life where all their needs were met. The Tree of Life refers to the body energy system of The Chakras which are, as a result closed down. The Serpent could be considered as the "Serpent Fire" of Kundalini which activates the Chakras, which are rooted on the spinal column.

We see a clear relationship between this story and the Oedipal "temptation" of children, and subsequent exclusion from the father/mother relationship.

PLAY AGE. (Freud Phallic Stage)

Initiative versus Guilt. "How much initiative is appropriate ?" Fear of punishment for intrusiveness or seductiveness. The reward is "Purpose".

The child is now mobile. Walking and other muscular control is more or less an unconscious act. One is now "Transplanted" – able to explore a wider world on a more individual basis.

Here, Erikson says the stage is concerned with "Initiative versus Guilt". The child's parents have become "internalised" so they "exist" even when not actually present – in the form of Conscience – so there is a modifier

ASTROLOGY : LOGARITHMIC TIMESCALE

to self-expression. The fear is that of Punishment (or lack of Stroking from rejection or isolation). There is now interest in the genitals, and comparing them with others. Boys are now different to Girls. We see the Tarot card 'The Lovers' applies. Play is an important method of learning – in modern days psychologists say that this is true even for adults. This is the age of Oedipal relationships with the child flirting with the parent of the opposite sex.

There is the tendency for girls and boys to take on a role suitable for their sex based on the example of the parents. Boys are generally encouraged to be "exclusive" - assertive and competitive - while girls become "inclusive" to become more "attractive" to others. Nowadays the difference tends to be more blurred – which is correct in that, in Astrology, there is no difference between charts of males or females, but which may lead to increased anxiety in not knowing how to behave. This could give rise to a child having too much freedom of expression which it is not yet equipped to handle. If someone else makes the decision we do not have to suffer the anxiety of a dilemma. The goal for this stage is of having a Purpose (perhaps to be like Mum or Dad ? Or perhaps not, according to the experience).

We note that there is pressure for a child to have a room of its own at this age. Indeed, the family may move house (transplant) to enable it. The child tends to fiercely defend its territory – especially excluding adults.

We note a recent increase in child suicide perhaps due to lack of parental guidelines or control at this stage resulting in increased anxiety from the responsibility of making decisions that they are not equipped to handle.

THE TAROT – VI.THE LOVERS AND VII.THE CHARIOT

We see The Lovers as development of sexual identity, and The Oedipal Complex, and The Chariot as development of a Persona to enable advance to the next Octave. The Tarot Card 'The Chariot' shows the mobile person using mind control of opposing forces to progress, within a shielded environment. We can equate this in the modern world to, later on, learning to drive a car (Chariot)

CANCER – THE DEVELOPMENT OF A SHELL. INNER SECURITY. ROOTS

1. Cancer is a Water Sign concerned with unconscious development and is concerned with Personal Security.
2. At the time of Cancer the Seed has developed Roots and is ready to be moved from the greenhouse pot to the outside world where the roots can spread further. The plant will become hardened by changes in climate, and more able to survive later changes.
3. Cancer is a Cardinal (initiating) Sign. However, unlike Positive Aries The Ram who uses direct attack, The Negative Crab retreats or makes progress sideways – indirectly, cautiously.
4. The importance of Cancer, The Crab, is the external shell which can symbolise the human body.
5. The home is also a shell (Erikson's Social Relating at this stage is concerned with close family)
6. Another form of "shell" is the psychological Persona – the "mask" we all wear as defence against the external world. We learn to act a part and keep much of our inner thoughts and feelings to ourselves.
7. Another form of "shell" is required in the development of Mediumship which requires the ability to extend the aura to connect with spirit entities coupled with the ability to "close the door" afterward. This is "Psychic Self Defence".
8. Cancer is ruled by The Moon which principally refers to The Mother as a symbol of care and protection. The concept can be developed further at this stage where the development of a "shell" can be considered as a new egg, or a new womb. What develops in the next Stage is the solar Ego Consciousness of the individual, albeit now restricted by The 5 Senses– as distinct from the original birth state of undifferentiated "cosmic consciousness".
9. The Moon is also related to the physical brain and Personal Unconscious.

THE KABBALAH TREE OF LIFE SEPHIRAH 9 (Yesod, Foundation, Moon. Number 8)

The Sephirah is located on The Middle Pillar between those related to The Earth and The Sun, as we might expect. We are at the end of the 2nd. Octave in the 4th. House of a Birth Chart, which is the lowest point. The following Stage – beginning the 3rd. Octave - is the first step on the "upward" "return journey".

Sephirah on the Middle Pillar of Equilibrium and Balance have a more direct link with the ideals of Sephirah 1 (Kether, Crown). Lower down The Tree, there is less free will.

ASTROLOGY : LOGARITHMIC TIMESCALE

From the above we get a better idea of the function of The Moon. In modern terms this is the Personal Unconscious. There are further observations concerning Yesod in the following Stage.

CHEMICAL ELEMENTS AND SHELLS

In our study of [NUMEROLOGY] we examine how all the Chemical Elements evolve from the basic element Hydrogen which consists of a single positive Proton nucleus and single negative Electron in orbit around the nucleus.

1. Electrons exist in non-physical Shells which restrict their orbits around the nucleus.
2. Elements develop into heavier ones by adding positive Protons to the nucleus with matching negative Electrons (and Neutrons).
3. A shell can contain only 2 Electrons. If the outer shell contains 2 Electrons, and other Electrons are added, a new Shell is created.
4. This seems to be how Nature prevents positive and negative charged particles from coming together and neutralising one another. In Nature there is a continual attempt to achieve the original Zero State which occurred before the Big Bang (entropy).
5. We can see that the behaviour of electrons is similar to the Oedipus Complex where a child flirts with the parent of the opposite sex, and is rejected (there can only be 2 to a shell), which forces the child/electron to seek "completion" outside the family shell. The traditional Tarot card VI.The Lovers shows a man having to choose between 2 women. This "Eternal Triangle" can be repeated throughout life until he begins to seek for the "perfect partner" within.
6. The orbit of The Moon around The Earth can be considered as being similar to the orbit of an electron around a nucleus – as can the orbits of the planets around The Sun.
7. The Moon's orbit gives the illusion that Earth is the centre of the universe.
8. We note that The Persona can be considered a Shell, or womb, inside which the next stage of development can take place – that of Ego Consciousness.

---

*3 - THIRD OCTAVE : 100 TO 1000 LM

7 YEARS OF AGE TO DEATH – THE OCTAVE COVERING THE LONGEST TIME PERIOD

Cycle of Growth Stages 5 (Power. Creativity) to 8 (Intercourse. Death)

With the previous development of a Persona "shell", the seed/egg Sun Symbol here refers to the development of inner Ego Consciousness and the development of Individuality.

There is now an entry into a wider experience of life outside the family home and experience of Peer Groups.

We see a close relationship between this Stage and the Transactional Analysis Development model.

We note that this includes the time of Mid Life Crisis at Age 42 which C.G.Jung states as the natural age for the beginning of Individuation. That is, after an individual has become fully established outside the parental home and reproduced. The Logarithmic Timescale puts the 8th. House (Intercourse. Death) as beginning at Age 42 – which is also when Uranus reaches its half-way opposition point in its Generic Cycle at the end of Cycle of Growth Stage 7 (Partners. New Social Role). It could mean that the "new partner" is a man's inner Anima or a woman's Animus, which until then, being unconscious, is projected on those of the opposite sex.

CYCLE OF GROWTH STAGE 5 (Power. Creativity)

7 to 11 years of age.

As with the others, The 3rd. Octave again begins with a Fire Sign.

Consciousness is now continuous for around 16 hours a day (8 hours sleep, unconscious). It cannot grow any more in terms of time usage, so needs to become more selective and focused. This means the Unconscious

ASTROLOGY : LOGARITHMIC TIMESCALE

Mind (Moon – which "goes through phases") "filters" consciousness in terms of what it considers important for attention at any moment in time.

Having developed a Persona mask it is necessary that this should not become too rigid. There is the need to be able to perform numerous roles in life – some as "follower" and some as "leader" depending on the social environment.

Because it is clearly related to the concept of this Stage, especially that of The Kabbalah Tree of Life, I once again reproduce the diagram of the Transactional Analysis Development model [PSYCHOLOGY : DEVELOPMENT MODELS] below.

SCHOOL AGE (Freud Latency Stage)

Industry versus Inferiority. "What practical and social skills do I have ?". Fear of not knowing how. The reward is "Competence".

This is Freud's Latency Stage of development which has no major physical or psychological changes in favour of gaining social and practical skills. Instincts lie fallow (ref. Leo FIXED Fire). The ability for initiative from the last stage is directed towards achievement in the external physical world. When we enter school we, and others, compare our activities with those of our peers. There is pressure for group conformity and co-operation. Erikson says that the dilemma of this stage is "Industry versus Inferiority" based on the fear of "not knowing how". The goal is being able to achieve Competence in the use of physical and mental skills. Work is put before pleasure. The School Age can be extended by continuing to further education and university.

School age is a time of segregation of the sexes. More so in my youth than now. But there is still the tendency for boys to associate with boys, and girls with girls at this age – with a sense of rivalry between the groups (gangs). This would seem to be related to the shared interests (including that of the opposite sex, albeit at a distance). Perhaps, despite, or because of, sexual latency we might call this the Homosexual Age. There is certainly comparison of the differences in performances of boys and girls in school. Nowadays, in contrast to past experience, girls seem to be doing better than boys in passing examinations, perhaps from a tendency to conform more to social expectation (as in the past). In the past women were considered inferior to men, now they are expected to be equal, or more than equal – whether or not they want to, or are able to.

TAROT – V.STRENGTH

The Tarot card 'Strength' shows The Lion being gently controlled by a feminine force. She is not trying to kill it – in fact some say she is actually opening its mouth. When dealing with Leo people a little flattery goes a long way. The feminine, Lunar, force could be interpreted as the Persona development of the previous Stage. At another level this is control of personal energy by group/social energy.

In the Pagan Year the time of Leo is that of the Lammas (="Loaf Mass") Festival of "First Harvest" when the first corn crop can be used to make bread. It is the first festival of the year. In Wicca they even make the figure of a god in bread and symbolically sacrifice it by eating it. In essence, having taken on god-like creative powers, consuming the fruits of their labour. We can see the Leo Lion, "king", association.

We can see a connection with the Erikson Stage in the focus on PRACTICAL creativity and achievement.

LEO – DEVELOPMENT OF EGO AND CONSCIOUSNESS

1. We note that Cycle of Growth Stage 5, as a Fire Sign (Leo), is the beginning of the 3rd. Octave of development. Stage 9 (Sagittarius. Conception) began the development of a human body contained in the womb. The 2nd. Octave was concerned with the control of the physical body and mental development. The 3rd. Octave continues the process – moving out of the "womb" of the family home into the outer material world of Society.

2. Leo is the Sign of Fixed Fire – which means that the Fire of instinct is structured or controlled by the need to manipulate and shape Matter . Schools focus on Arts and Crafts at this Stage – rather than more academic subjects, which come next.

3. Leo, generally, is concerned with Personal Creativity, especially related to hobbies and other interests - things we do for love rather than money. It is also related to our contact with younger children (or those who we can control, or treat as such).

ASTROLOGY : LOGARITHMIC TIMESCALE

4. The rulership of Leo by The Sun indicates that this is a time of development of Consciousness and Ego beyond that of parental control. In Astrological terms, it is only now that the Sun Sign nature can begin to develop as the child becomes in control of its own "solar system" (Tree of Life).
5. The main trait of Leo people is the sense of inner self confidence. A desire and ability to be at the centre of any social activity. They have difficulty with more mental pursuits. For example, many form their own business when they often need to hire an accountant. Salesmen are not too keen on doing their paperwork.

AGE 7 - GENERIC SATURN WAXING SQUARE TO BIRTH POSITION

At age 7 to 8 the first Generic Waxing (growing) Square aspect of transiting Saturn occurs when the planet position forms an angle of 90 degrees to its position in the Birth Chart. This is equivalent to its own Cycle of Growth Stage 4 (Transplanting) in its 30 year cycle. The crisis is an opportunity to break away from the traditions and structure of one's past to find a more individual pathway. We can see how this relates to the beginning of the 3rd. Octave.

THE KABBALAH TREE OF LIFE SEPHIRAH 6 (Tiphareth, Beauty, The Sun. Number 5)

By applying The Cycle of Growth to The Tree of Life we can do something not previously possible using traditional methodology. We can follow the "return journey" back to The Source – Sephirah 1 (Kether, Crown). This is the first step.

Stage 4 (Transplanting) is placed at the lowest point of the Astrological House diagram. The only way forward is upwards.

We note that the trend is similar to that described in [THE PURPOSE OF LIFE] which is stated to be an incarnation into matter to develop Will, and then return to The Source.

Sephirah 6 (Tiphareth. Beauty. The Sun) is at the centre of The Middle Pillar and refers to the Heart Chakra. It has direct connections to all other Sephiroth except Malkuth, Earth where its energy is mediated by Sephirah 9 (Yesod, Foundation, The Moon, The Personal Unconscious). Nowadays psychologists recognise that the unconscious mind "filters out" information that it deems unimportant.

1. The first thing to note is that Sephirah 6 (The Sun. Ego Consciousness) is not active on the involutionary journey of energy via "The Lightning Flash". This is understandable in view of its (potential) multiple connections which might interfere with physical development.
2. On the involutionary journey Sephirah 9 (Yesod, Moon) is the first contact The Lightning Flash has with The Middle Pillar since the energy was envisioned in Sephirah 1 (Kether, Crown) and created in Sephirah 2 (Chockmah, Force) which was complemented by the creation of Sephirah 3 (Binah, Gravity, Matter). By "going through phases" it modifies the energy in a similar way to an electrical transformer. This is similar to Direct Current being converted to the Alternating Current used in domestic conditions.
3. The Yesod energy is "earthed" in Sephiroth 10 (Malkuth, Kingdom, Earth, Physical Body) which maintains a stable state and provides the basic Life Rhythms. This also refers to the physical body.
4. This is similar to the un-numbered Sephirah Daath which refers to Individuality at a higher level, and develops later on.
5. In terms of human evolution this is a similar stage to that of the diversity of species enabled by the development of sexual reproduction - as distinct from cloning by cell division, which merely makes duplicate organisms. This is "Diversity of Consciousness" beyond that of simple survival, leading to the possibility of humans gathering together into large civilisations, with individuals performing specific functions on behalf of the whole – being released from the need to supply their own food and shelter.
6. .... albeit, as yet, all in an embryonic state at the beginning of The 3rd. Octave.
7. We see the Solar force as the integrating Centre of Ego Consciousness, where it is a symbol of Jung's The Self. Being connected by pathways to all other Sephiroth other than Malkuth (Kingdom, Earth), Tiphareth is often described as a spider at the centre of its web. Until now there has been no Ego.

*What is particularly noteworthy here is the consistent development of the central symbol. We can hardly escape the feeling that the unconscious process moves spiral - wise round the centre, gradually getting closer, while the characteristics of the centre grow more and more distinct, or perhaps we could put it the other way round and say that the centre itself virtually unknowable acts like a magnet in the disparate

materials and processes of the unconscious and gradually captures them as in a crystal lattice. For this reason the centre is ……. often pictured as a spider in its web, especially when the conscious attitude is still dominated by fear of unconscious processes. But if the process is allowed to take its course ………… then the central symbol, constantly renewing itself, will steadily and consistently force its way through the apparent chaos of the personal psyche and its dramatic entanglements. ["The Portable Jung" page 450]

PSYCHOLOGY : THE TRANSACTIONAL ANALYSIS DEVELOPMENT MODEL

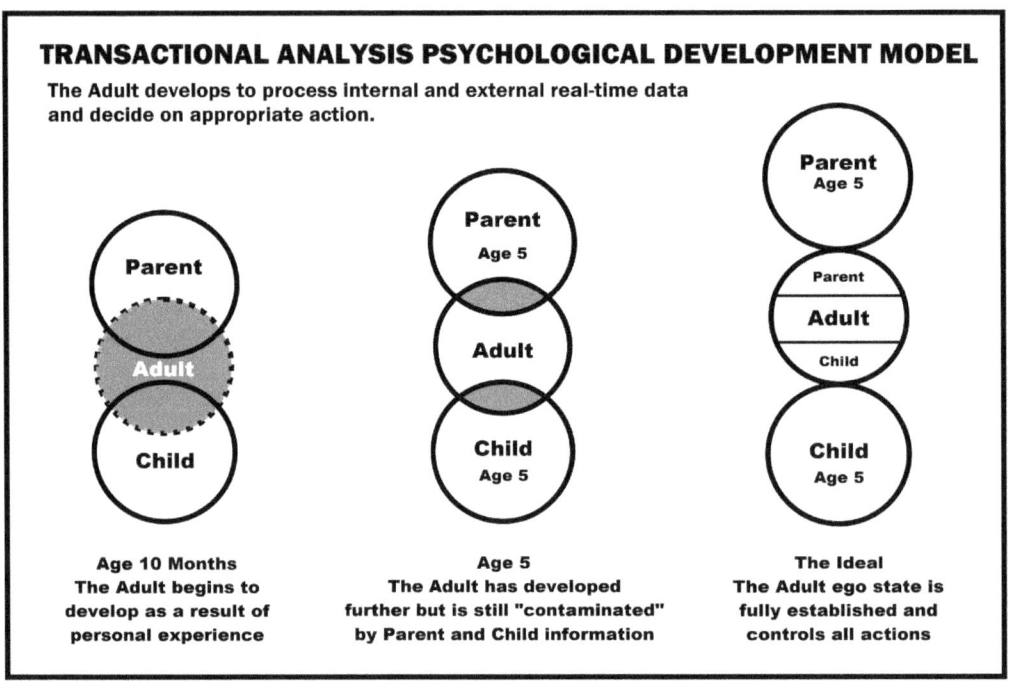

Figure 28 : Transactional Analysis Development Model

The Transactional Analysis Development model reproduced here in reduced form clearly applies to 3rd. Octave development. It is concerned with the development of "The Adult" which is basically a "real time data processor" as distinct from "The Parent" and "The Child" [PSYCHOLOGY : DEVELOPMENT MODELS] which are mainly unconscious and related to the past.

1. Development of The Adult is a lifetime task. Although there is some development early in life, it does not begin to grow until the child is moving away from parental influence, where it has more freedom and more social comparisons available – from Age 5 [TA].
2. We can see the Transactional Analysis Model as a simplified version of The Kabbalah Tree of Life Centre Pillar with Tiphareth in embryo form until it develops later on.
3. The described function of the psychological Adult is identical with the description and function of Tiphareth and its relationship with The Sun in a Birth Chart.
4. We note that the "final" depiction of The Adult includes "layers" similar to The 4 Sephiroth layers related to The 4 Elements.
5. The top layer is "The Parent in The Adult" (Air) where previously unconscious parental "rules and regulations" have been consciously re-assessed and found to be useful.
6. The central layer is that of The Adult (Fire. The Sun) conscious data processor.
7. The bottom layer is "The Child in The Adult" (Water) which is concerned with the child-like emotional response to The Parent. Here, the CHILD-ISH (eg. Fighting, crying, tantrums, secret manipulation) responses to life have been modified to be appropriate to a more mature way of adjustment – yet the individual can still express the more positive CHILD-LIKE qualities (eg. curiosity, playing).
8. We note that Psychology has omitted a level related to Earth. We can assume that The Adult learns new practical skills throughout life, which can come under the heading "Know-How".

CYCLE OF GROWTH STAGE 6 (Service to Self)

13 to 23 years of age.

ADOLESCENCE (Freud Genital Stage)

Identity versus Identity Diffusion. "Who am I ?". Fear of failure to master new and conflicting inner drives. The reward is "Fidelity".

*Teenagers as a separate group did not emerge until the 1940's. [GOP]

*"Just an in between. Too old for toys. Too young for boys". [Judy Garland "In Between" by Roger Edens]

According to Erikson a successful resolution to the adolescent stage is the achievement of **Fidelity**. According to the Concise Oxford Dictionary, Fidelity means "faithfulness, loyalty, strict conformity to truth or fact" (which clearly relates to the previous Stage 5 with "The Adult" and "The Sun"). It seems that Erikson had a slightly different interpretation. He states: -

*Fidelity when fully matured, is the strength of disciplined devotion. It is gained in the involvement of use in such experiences as revealed the essence of the era they are to join as the beneficiaries of its tradition as the practitioners and innovators of its technology, as readers of its ethical strength, as rebels bent on the destruction of the outlived, and as deviants with deviant commitments. [Erikson]

We also have ....

*.... here again diversity and fidelity are polarised: they make each other significant and keep each other alive. Fidelity without a sense of diversity can become an obsession and a bore: Diversity without a sense of fidelity an empty relativism.

[Daedalus - Vol. 117, No. 3, "Three Decades of Dædalus" ("Proceedings of the American Academy of Arts and Sciences" Summer, 1988) Contains: Youth: Fidelity and Diversity]

This is the age of Puberty when inner drives begin to arise once again. Freud said that the psychosexual energy is transferred outwards to the opposite sex (*as Desire [BTB]*). Hormones start pumping - stimulating new inner drives. Having found one's place among one's peers, there is what Erikson called an "Identity Crisis" with the dilemma "Identity versus Identity Diffusion". In some ways this is not surprising because Stage 5 was concerned with separating from parents and becoming part of a social group. Now, having found similar people outside the home, we now have to find how we are different to the others in the group.

Energy directed outward must now be re-focused inwardly. Looking ahead, we see that the final resolution usually comes when one finds a partner of the opposite sex and separates from past association with those of the same sex. In effect, entering yet another new world. The past associations die away as new, shared, interests arise. This is the time of formation of teenage Gangs that act as a kind of external family group.

An important factor seems to be the type of music of the time – meaning that produced by those of around the same age. Looking at the lyrics of the new songs (if we can hear them) they tend to express the inner feelings and dilemmas of those involved. We note that the style of music changes considerably over time, and it seems especially necessary for it to conflict with the tastes of the parents. Apart from the music, teenagers are also looking for role models outside their normal sphere (especially when seeming to be different to the social norm of their parents), whom they identify with and try to emulate. We all want to be "A Star" (ref. The Sun Cycle of Growth Stage 5).

An early example, said to be one of the first, was Frank Sinatra (1915-1998) who embodied a challenging attitude to "The Establishment" (Saturn). His career started in 1935 at the age of 20. Although a solo singer and actor he was part of a group of associates called "The Rat Pack". The more modern, younger, style of musical group seems to have begun with The Beatles (1960) and The Rolling Stones (1962) who were in their late teens, and who really pioneered the concept that anybody could make music. We note that the names of the groups were an important statement of group identity, albeit shared. We also note that these groups tended to split up as the individuals involved found their own personal ways as, timore or less, solo performers. In the case of The Beatles the split between them occurred in 1970. John and George were 27 years of age, Paul 28, and Ringo right on the Generic Saturn Return age of 30 years. The task encouraged by the Generic Saturn Return is to find a more individual pathway distinct from that of the past traditions of our upbringing. The beginning of

ASTROLOGY : LOGARITHMIC TIMESCALE

any new cycle is that of Cycle of Growth Stage 1 (Seed). A form of rebirth. There is a sense that they were "late developers" in that they were still part of a peer group after the "normal" age of finding a mate. We see that they tended to develop more lasting partnerships afterwards.

AGE 12 – FIRST GENERIC JUPITER RETURN TO ITS BIRTH POSITION

One is about to become "A Teenager".

Jupiter has made its first orbit of the Birth Chart and returned to where it began at the moment of birth. In essence, it is repeating that same "birth state" – now as "rebirth". This is its Cycle of Growth Stage 1 (Seed). At this time, with the new Persona, the "body/vehicle" is at a more psychological level.

The earlier Stages of The Cycle of Growth have once again developed us to a state where we are ready to step forward like Tarot 0.The Fool into an unknown future life. Jupiter (Expansion) is mainly concerned with our Social relationships – so we once again enter into a wider social experience – at this time away from the close family. We note the new inner "Spring" influx of energy which forces us forward.

In outer life the time is that of leaving Primary School, where the emphasis on practical Play and creativity from manipulating materials (Stage 5. Leo. Sun) to that of Secondary School – and more academic Mental activity. Discovering more about the world around in a more theoretical way than actual experience. Jupiter also rules Academic Study, Schools, and Universities..

At this time we have the polarisation of 2 mental energies. The Stage of Life is related to Virgo/Mercury (Rational Mind) and the focus on practical down-to-earth matters such as Work and Health, whilst Jupiter's (ruler of Gemini's complement, Sagittarius) orbit is bringing Academic, Theoretical Mind into activity.

Together the dilemma between the 2 planets defines such things as the need to find evidence or practical expression for theories, or ensure that advanced philosophies can be applied to life as we know it. The dilemma will present itself in different forms at each subsequent 12 year Jupiter Return.

AGE 15 - GENERIC SATURN OPPOSITION TO ITS BIRTH POSITION

This is one of Saturn's crisis points.

At age 15 the Generic Transit of Saturn has reached the half-way stage in its 30 year cycle, when it forms an Opposition Aspect with its position in the Birth Chart. This is equivalent to Cycle of Growth Stage 7 (Partnerships). The partnerships at this age tend to be of the same sex. As with other challenging aspects of Generic Saturn, the aim is another step to our finding a more individual pathway away from past traditions and controls and accepting a more social role. We note that this crisis is more intense than that of age 7 – probably because at this age we seem more able to challenge the authority of those older than ourselves, and we have the support of our peers. There is also the inner pressure of hormones. This is the time of necessary "teenage rebellion".

At this time we learn more about the conflicting energies of Jupiter (Expansion) and Saturn (Consolidation. Tradition).

The earlier Jupiter Return has begun to widen our perception of the world, and, in some cases, we may know more about some modern subjects than our parents. At age 16 Jupiter reaches its Stage 4 (Transplanting) period where some action is required which takes us to a new area of society. For the first time there is opportunity to question parents' previously unchallenged concepts and beliefs. This is inwardly at first (Tarot IX.The Hermit) - we keep things to our self – they perhaps might not seem important. Later on Cycle of Growth Stage 7 (Partners. Social Responsibility) will focus on more specific issues that arise. Jupiter reaches a Cycle of Growth Stage 7 (Partners) Opposition in its orbit at Age 18 (when Society now confers "adult status") – and, later, Logarithmic Timescale Age 23/24 is the end of the 2nd. Generic Jupiter Cycle, preparing for the next).

VIRGO – SUPPORTING A HUMAN BODY. HEALTH

1. Virgo is Mutable Earth. Although related to Mercury, it is not so unstable as other Mutable Signs from the slower frequency of vibration. Here, the Mercury Mind is applied to more practical matters.
2. Virgo, The Virgin, is a difficult Sign to understand. We can see the connotation of a potential for sexual consummation not yet realised. In Nature's Year this is the time of fruitfulness, which, apart from feeding us, provides the seeds for new growth later on. In terms of sexual development in humans we have the separate sexes containing the sperm (seed) and unfertilised ovum ("earth"). Mutable (changeable) Earth suggests the wide range of physical changes taking place at this time, especially

those that separate male from female – animals have separate bodies, plants have both sets of organs. This seems to be a time when Identity "falls apart" too, and needs to be re-integrated. The symbolic Chariot of Stage 4 (Transplanting) later becomes a motor car.

3. Virgo people learn Discrimination as a result of having highly critical abilities, able to see minute details. There is therefore a tendency to worry about insignificant details rather than see the bigger picture. Health is often a big worry.
4. Virgo is, among other things, the Sign of 'The Craftsman', which relates to our needs to find a practical job to support ourselves when we reach adulthood, and develop skills accordingly.
5. Virgo also relates to our state of Health. This underlines the Cycle of Growth title "Service to Self" – because this and our work force us to focus on our own personal needs, rather than those of others.
6. We note that the complementary Sign to that of Virgo is Pisces (The Collective), which is traditionally titled "Service To Others". Society and religion quite naturally prefer the latter. This stage of development requires we find our own balance between the two. To retain Individuality without becoming re-absorbed into The Collective. The task seems to be related to discovering and developing our personal skills.
7. We can never truly be an individual until we become self-supporting practically and financially.

TAROT CARD : IX. THE HERMIT

The Tarot Hermit depicts a lone individual, traditionally one who leads a solitary life. He is following a path dimly lit by his own inner light. He has no peer group or mate. If he was among others he might not see the light – or it might be extinguished altogether. Indeed, as a "Virgin" he might be celibate. He could be someone whose daily work involves no close personal relationships.

The Hermit is "Isolation by a Secret". At this Stage there is the beginning of recognition of our own Personal Unconscious and listening to the "voices" it contains.

Isolation by a secret results, as a rule, in an animation of the psychic atmosphere, as a substitute of loss of contact with other people. It causes an activation of the unconscious, and this produces something similar to the illusions and hallucinations that beset lonely wanderers in the desert, seafarers, and saints. [C.G.Jung "Memories, Dreams, Reflections"]

The first stage of Individuation requires that we meet, and come to terms with, our "Shadow". This is "the dweller on the threshold" and consists of all the parts of our –self that we might consider Evil or "Bad". It also includes the recognition of our Personal Unconscious (which might be considered in the same light). More commonly, they are parts of ourselves that have been repressed – that is, not expressed in life because of parental or social disapproval – realistic or otherwise. Rather than being "Evil" they are merely undeveloped from not being used.

This is another step on the road to Consciousness. The Light of The Sun (Stage 5) always casts A Shadow.

In our dreams they may appear as children, or deformed people. At this stage in life they need to be recognised, and some use made of them, which might make us clumsy to begin with – something we might not like others to see. Not only do they contain life energy, but the psychic energy used to repress them could be put to better use. All this, however, is in the unconscious - and requires careful attention to bring to light. We need to consider that, in life, much Evil is done in the name of Good, and that Good can come from Evil methods.

Consider, for one, the Commandment "Thou shalt not kill". Consider the killing done by many religions throughout history.

THE KABBALAH TREE OF LIFE SEPHIRAH 8 (Hod, Glory, Mercury. Number 7)

1. The Sign of Virgo and The 6th. House are ruled by Mercury. Each Sephirah exists at 4 levels relating to The 4 Elements. By maintaining the sequence of Elements (Fire, Earth, Air, Water) – as in The Zodiac - we now "turn the corner" and begin to retrace the pathways back up The Tree.
2. Hod is at the bottom of The Pillar of Form and is concerned with formation of mental ideas. That is, an intermediate stage between an abstract concept and physical manifestation. A Word is a mental form of an object which can be manipulated in imagination and communication.
3. In The Tree of Life Mercury relates to Sephirah 8 which was first crossed by The Lightning Flash at Cycle of Growth Stage 3 (Experiment. Communication) which is also ruled by Gemini – the Mutable

(changeable) Air Sign - when the principle of Form is applied to mental concepts – principally relating Names to Objects and development of the Thinking Function.

4. With the Stage 3 associations with The Tarot Emperor and Hierophant we can relate this to "The Parent" of Transactional Analysis – whose "laws" are now being re-assessed at a practical, evidential, level.
5. Virgo is an Earth Sign where the mental faculties are focused on practical matters of the physical world and human body.
6. The difference between the descent of The Tree and the climb now begun is that Sephirah 6 (Tiphareth, Beauty, The Sun) is now more active than it was before. There is opportunity to apply Consciousness and Will to control our actions. This is not an automatic process. To control something we must first become consciously aware of it. At the early stages of Cycle of Growth Stage 5 much of day to day life is still at an unconscious, automatic level.

THE TAROT : X.THE WHEEL OF FORTUNE

Animal – like visions arise.

I put this card "between stages" because it is at one of the 2 main "turning points" of the whole Cycle of Growth. Here it is at the boundary between the past life of home and family, and entry into a wider social sphere of more public relationships. The other card being 'XXI. The World' at the beginning (and end) – which shares the partial meaning of individual rebirth into a "new world". The 2 cards form an Opposition Aspect with one another, and are therefore complementary.

Erikson states that this age is a time of "Recapitulation" and indecision - which could be an interpretation of the repetitive turning wheel of the image. (there is a sense that all stages involve recapitulation – which can also refer to the "Even-ings" of each day of Biblical Creation [GENESIS AND THE CYCLE OF GROWTH]).

Until the sword is used decisively there can be no further progress. 'The Wheel of Fortune' carries the additional sense of needing to gamble, or take a chance, faced with an uncertain future – similar to 'The Fool', which follows 'The World' at birth, but now with responsibility for actually making conscious decisions and choices, rather than following the instinctive lifestyle of The Hunter Gatherer.

CYCLE OF GROWTH STAGE 7 (Partners)

23 to 42 years of age.

YOUNG ADULTHOOD (Freud's Genital Stage is his final one, ending at death)

Intimacy versus Isolation. "Who are my friends ?" Fear of spontaneity and mutual responsiveness. The reward is Love.

Young Adulthood has no major physical changes. In keeping with Astrological concepts the main events at this time are :-

1. Finding a mate.
2. Finding work to earn a living
3. Entering a new social sphere away from the original family home. Traditional Astrology tended to emphasise that the social area occupied by one's mate had a bearing – almost like entering a foreign country – but the world was a much smaller place then, with no radio, television, Facebook, or Twitter..
4. At the time of writing this in 2014 there is news of a decline in population in China. The suggested reason is that young people are becoming "computer nerds" and engaging in relationships via the Internet rather than in person. This seems an interesting development in this Age of Aquarius – another Air Sign. {ASTROLOGY : THE ZODIAC AGES}

As with the other stages, this one is a challenge to the previous one - in this case, that part of one's hard-won Identity must be surrendered to achieve Intimacy. Erikson suggests that Identity must be temporarily surrendered altogether during sexual intercourse, because his definition required an orgasm. His social area of relationships is stated as that of Partnerships. That contains an interesting plural because, strangely, what happens is that when in a close one to one partnership we suddenly realise that all of our previous peer group friends have disappeared and we have joined a society consisting of other couples. There seems to be an avoidance of odd numbers (ref. shells of atoms [NUMEROLOGY]). In fact the world of entertainment makes much of its income from depicting various types of "triangular" relationships, which serve to disturb the equilibrium. Erikson's achievement in this Stage is 'Love' (without defining what that means). In a strange way this not a conscious act. Anyone who has "fallen in love" will recognise that it does not involve an act of Will. It is rather something that happens to us – perhaps even against our Will. Love takes us beyond just sexual intercourse. In fact, at this stage, although we give up part of our Individuality, as a couple we gain more. In occult terms, when a male and female come together the relationship between them becomes an almost tangible reality – if they have a child, it is a tangible manifestation of that relationship. A manifestation of Number 3.

We have to note that there is a big difference between pure Love (which comes from Chockmah at the top of the Pillar of Force) and the Desire of Netzach at the bottom of that pillar of The Tree of Life. The latter is related to Venus, Ruler of Libra (and Taurus). True Desire is that of obtaining the balanced "completion" – the Whole that was the Original State before Creation began the process of separation and division. Until it is sought within, it is projected on to the people and objects of the external world.

It is a fact that the best business partnerships (for example) are those where the abilities of both participants are complementary rather than being the same. For example, I have noticed that it takes a certain kind of person to start up a business (Leo). Those people are usually not too good at paperwork, so, as the business grows they need to employ an accountant (Virgo).

1. ASTROLOGY suggests a broader scenario which includes any form of Partnership at this Stage – not just that between a man and woman – but also such as those in business. There is a form of Astrology called "Synastry" which, among other things, compares 2 Birth Charts, where important indicators are comparison of the Mars position of one with the Venus position of the other to see how Mars satisfies the needs and desires of Venus in the other. There is a brief example in the chapter [ASTROLOGY : SYNASTRY] comparing the Birth Charts of Freud and Jung which focuses more on Sun and Moon positions. The Chapter mentions other types of Astrological pairings.
2. An important point to remember is that there is no difference between a Birth Chart of a man or woman born at the same time and place. The suggestion is that, although there are biological differences, the essential psyche is the same. It is a fact that male and female babies are handled differently from birth ("Pink or Blue ?"). As life continues, some character traits are encouraged, others suppressed depending on the biases of the parents. The suggestion is that we unconsciously attempt to discover our "missing" traits by forming close relationships with others. The process of Individuation requires that we begin to seek inwards rather than outwards.
3. ANALYTICAL PSYCHOLOGY– which contains the concepts of C.G.Jung – so named to distinguish it from Psychiatry – when considering relationships, focuses on the Anima (the female constituent of a man's psyche) and the Animus (the male constituent of a female's psyche). There is a distinct similarity with the parent of the opposite sex – so there is a wide variation possible. Both are <u>unconscious</u> components of the psyche. Basically, Jung stated that men and women seek this "missing" part of themselves in the external world and are attracted to people who seem to have the qualities they are unconsciously seeking. "The Other" is projected into the outside world. Problems arise when a close relationship forms and the partner does not match with earlier (unconscious) expectations.

AGES 21 AND 22 GENERIC TRANSITS
We have 3 major Generic Transits at this time. Jupiter and Saturn both enter their 4th. Quarter - Waning Square, Cycle of Growth Stage 10 (Peak, Harvest), and Uranus enters its Generic 2nd. Quarter – Waxing Square, Cycle of Growth Stage 4 (Transplanting).

THE TAROT : XI. JUSTICE
As with the Zodiac Sign of Libra, this is the beginning of the "return" half of an earthly lifetime. As such it requires reconsideration and re-appraisal of the whole of the previous life. Its activity is clearly not as peaceful as the traditional Libra association suggests. It is stated that at the time of Death the whole of one's past life passes before one's eyes. This Stage suggests an earlier preparation for that time.
1. The Decision suggested by THE WHEEL OF FORTUNE is yet to be made. But it is now conscious.
2. In psychological terms, the balance to be found is that between Conscious and Unconscious energies.
3. The Hermit, having become objectively aware of inner conflict has to make a decision.

ASTROLOGY : LOGARITHMIC TIMESCALE

LIBRA – BALANCE AND HARMONY

Libra refers to INNER balance and harmony, which may or may not be mirrored externally.

The Zodiac Sign of Libra, The Scales, and the Tarot card XI. Justice are clearly of equivalent meaning, that is, based upon the same Archetype. It is a point to note that, despite the high emotional, psychological, content of this Stage (Water), Libra is an Air Sign, concerned with the Jungian Rational Thinking Function. "rational" comes from "ratio" which suggests a form of analysis – such as enabling us to make the punishment fit the crime, rather than punish any infringement of The Law with death, as they did in the past. It also suggests that the process of achieving balance is more that of mixing black and white to get grey - which, as we see from The Kabbalah and Science, was the original Zero State of the universe before The Big Bang.

The point here is, that although the Archetype is always attempting to achieve Balance, we may not always achieve it – in fact, growth, and we, require "controlled imbalance" to keep moving. Walking is "controlled falling". The Tarot card shows a state of Inertia which continues with XII.The Hanged Man. With Libra we are on the first step of the "return journey" of the Zodiac – moving/returning toward the beginning of a new cycle. It is the "Full Moon" position in Opposition Aspect to the Aries Ascendant, or Birth, at Cycle of Growth Stage 1 (Seed). We note throughout this book that every cycle constitutes a Whole in that all the forces released in the first half have to be balanced in the second half – to finally total Zero ready for the new cycle to begin with a fresh input of energy. It's a bit like a 4-stroke engine. Induction. Ignition. Power. Exhaust.

THE KABBALAH TREE OF LIFE SEPHIRAH 7 (Netzach, Victory, Venus)

1. Netzach is on the Pillar of Mercy (Force) albeit at the bottom close to Yesod (9. Moon) and Malkuth (10. Earth). With Venus it is concerned with emotional responses to life events and Desire. It is balanced on The Pillar of Form by Hod (8. Mercury, Rational Mind).

2. Our first connection with Venus was in the Fixed Earth Sign of Taurus at Cycle of Growth Stage 2 (Germination) at Age 7 months to 1 year 8 months, when undifferentiated emotional response was our only means of self-expression, based on physical body needs – and our desires for physical internal and external comfort were fulfilled almost immediately.

3. The position of Venus on the Pillar of Force is a depiction of how emotional Desire becomes a motivator. Its relationship with Mars on The Pillar of Form indicates how a desire can be focused on an external object. The path between now includes Tiphareth (The Sun) on The Middle Pillar indicating the possibility of conscious control that was not available on the downward journey.

4. In planetary orbits the Personal Planet Venus is inside (closer to the Sun) than that of the Earth, Mars is on the outside.

5. We now have Venus in the Cardinal (active) Air Sign of Libra where our actions are more under the conscious control of the mind. With increased consciousness life has become more complicated, and we learn to balance one Desire with another. We can no longer have our desires automatically fulfilled, and often have to give up one satisfaction in favour of another – especially the ones concerned with sex.

6. With the Libra Scales and Tarot Justice we have a clearer depiction of Jung's "Resolution of Opposites" – the need to solve dilemmas – which results in expansion of consciousness. We note that the mind needs to first become aware of a Dilemma. Having done that, we have to reach a state of consciousness <u>above</u> the dilemma from which we can clearly see both sides (Stage 9. Conception. XV.Temperance). The resolution then comes from finding a 3rd. "child" Principle which enables action. Dilemmas are 2 ends of the same scale.

7. This is a description of Diplomacy in action, and is an example of Number 3 [NUMEROLOGY] creativity (Father, Mother, Child).

8. The Tarot Cards V.The Hierophant and XV.The Devil show similar depictions of Dilemmas, as well as being involved in dilemmas between themselves.

CYCLE OF GROWTH STAGE 8 (Sex. Death)

42 years of age until death

Here we include 2 of Erikson's Stages – "Adult" and "Old Age"

AGE 35 – 65. ADULTHOOD. (Freud – Genital Stage)

Generativity versus Stagnation. Fear of the responsibility of leadership. Caring.

ASTROLOGY : LOGARITHMIC TIMESCALE

AGE 65 - DEATH. OLD AGE (Freud – Genital Stage)

Ego Integrity versus Despair. Fear of death. Wisdom.

The problem for psychologists when attempting to examine this age group is that, by this time, our lives are a lot more complicated than those of younger years. We note that Erikson's period includes over 30 years, during which time a lot can happen. Adults generally, by this time, have "served their apprenticeship" and are expected to be in charge – that is, reproduced and being in a position of responsibility for controlling other people. The period covers what are usually the most fruitful working years until retirement. So the adult is still looking forward to some change in lifestyle later on. The Stage is said to be that of Consolidating what one has achieved so far. One's children are usually getting to a stage where they have their own interests outside the family – and, indeed, may make a point of not wanting adults around. So, apart from work, there is more time for leisure and more personal interest – and, perhaps, spare money to do it.

Erikson's dilemma of "Generativity versus Stagnation" would seem to relate to how that spare time is used. A wide area of society prefers to do nothing in a creative sense when not actually working. It may be that work does not leave such free time.

Stagnation is doing nothing. Inertia. There is a tendency for adults to get a bit lazy. We have to realise that without some form of mental, physical, or social exercise our "muscles" will eventually stop working. That which stops growing dies. We can see this in a negative aspect of Scorpio which rules this Stage when FIXED Water can become a stagnant pool.

Erikson suggests that this is a time of Caring for younger people in various ways – such as from support or training.

AGE 30 – GENERIC SATURN RETURN

Age 30 is the time of our first Generic Saturn Return – that is, it has come to the end of its first cycle and returned to its position in our Birth Chart. This relates to its Cycle of Growth Stage 1 (Seed) – new beginnings. Astrologically speaking, in the time from birth until now we have tended to live a life based on the past traditions of our father and mother, and position of our early family roots. The opportunity now is to consider new horizons and a new pathway based on what we have discovered about our self in the intervening period. In common with the general Cycle of Growth, there is no need for sudden changes of direction – unless they are forced by circumstances, or one feels a slave to "the rat race".

By this time we would expect that ideas would have arisen concerning what one might "like" to do – and not found the time for. These are our "seeds". At this early stage they just need to be recognised rather than dismissed. Seeds first develop underground. Later on one may pick a few to investigate further. A new life path may develop to occupy some of the next 30 years. One of the principles of Saturn is Self-Discipline, which suggests that the exercise may not necessarily be easy. We have to combat Erikson's "Stagnation" - not giving up as physical death becomes more of a reality. Whatever "seeds" are sown now will develop according to how they are cultivated, to produce results later on.

We have to bear in mind that our early ancestors did not tend to live longer than 30 years. In fact, even nowadays, age 35 is that when those involved in physical activities, such as sport, are now forced to consider some other occupation as they are now no longer able to compete (Mars) with those younger than themselves. Age 37-38 is the time of the first Waxing Square crisis point of Generic Saturn - Cycle of Growth Stage 4 (Transplanting) – which brings an opportunity to change direction. Life opens doors to us, but does not always push us through. This is the time of Menopause in women. The sense of a "last chance" of having another child.

Age 30 – GENERIC JUPITER OPPOSITION TO ITS BIRTH POSITION

This is Cycle of Growth Stage 7 (Partners) suggesting new relationships and emphasising the possibility of a new form of public self-expression.

AGE 36 – GENERIC JUPITER RETURN AND SATURN WAXING SQUARE

If the earlier Jupiter Cycle of Growth Stage 7 (Partners) was productive, there is opportunity to begin a new phase of life. This is aided by Saturn entering its Cycle of Growth Stage 4 (Transplanting).

AGE 42 – GENERIC URANUS OPPOSITION TO ITS BIRTH POSITION

This the age that Jung suggests is that of the Mid Life Crisis and beginning of the Individuation process. There is more detail in the chapter [PSYCHOLOGY : DEVELOPMENT MODELS].

ASTROLOGY : LOGARITHMIC TIMESCALE

Astrologically speaking the beginning was at the time of birth. Age 42 is the time of the Opposition Aspect of Generic Uranus to its position in the Birth Chart. It is half way through its 84 year cycle – at its Cycle of Growth Stage 7 (Partnerships). By observing the Cycle of Growth in various areas of life we can get an idea of the whole process.

AGE 45 – GENERIC SATURN CYCLE OF GROWTH STAGE 10 (PEAK. HARVEST)

Astrologically this is the Peak of the whole cycle which precedes a decline in preparation for the beginning of a new one. We receive the social results of everything we have done since the beginning of the cycle at Age 30 – for good or ill. We are within the Mid Life Crisis period of life which typically evokes inner feelings of discontent despite the outer life, perhaps, being perceived as successful.

The time is probably symbolised by the consideration of what one will do at the beginning of the next cycle at age 60 – which is typically concerned with retirement from work. The Harvest may include the amount of pension one may be entitled to. The Uranus opposition at Age 42 may now be taking a more tangible form.

AGE 60 – SECOND GENERIC SATURN RETURN TO ITS BIRTH POSITION

Age 60 is the beginning of our second Generic Saturn Cycle – Cycle of Growth Stage 1 (Seed). The previous Stage 12 (Confinement. Withdrawal) also includes the concept of Karma. In this case described by the phrase "As you sow, so shall you reap" – which can refer to Agriculture or human activity. We now harvest the fruits of our working life, such as a pension, in preparation for old age. Whereas during the first Saturn Cycle the results were largely a product of our early home conditions and parental upbringing, as adults any success or failure is entirely of our own making. We have built our own condition. As that before "childbirth", Stage 12 is a time of consideration of the past and preparation for a new future. The Sign Pisces is ruler of such places of confinement as hospitals, prisons, and monasteries. Stage 1 is the opportunity to sow new "seeds" for the future.

In terms of Personal Responsibility during a lifetime, we have to recognise that we enter this life alone, and leave it alone.

OLD AGE : over 65 years (Freud – continued Genital Stage)

Ego Integrity versus Despair.

Nowadays experts are predicting that we are coming to a time when life expectancy will be 100 years or more. So this Stage from retirement to death could last as much as one-third of a whole lifetime. Most of the experiences of this time will depend upon what physical state we find our self in.

The individual situation at this time could be considered as a result of Karma resulting from the activities of the Stage. Having discovered Independence, we can no longer blame our parents.

THE TAROT – THE HANGED MAN AND DEATH

1. This is Stalemate.
2. Having recognised the need to make a decision at card XI.Justice, The Hanged Man is unable to take action. This is symbolic of the Jungian task of the second (return) half of life to "reconcile the opposites". During the first half the aim was to establish one's-self in the material world. Now, to achieve further development, something must be sacrificed. To achieve a new dimension, or level, of life we must die to the old one.
3. This is a symbol of the need for the individual to modify personal desires in order to achieve social co-operation – such as in the give-and-take Intercourse of everyday life, and the Intercourse to enable survival of genes. Some problems are beyond the possibility of an individual solution.
4. Progress requires a state of imbalance. Walking is controlled falling. Taking a chance.
5. By solving this dilemma The Hunter Gatherer was eventually enabled to form large cities and civilisations.
6. In the face of Death all men and women are equal.

THE KABBALAH TREE OF LIFE SEPHIRAH 5 (Geburah, Severity, Mars)

1. We first experienced Mars at Cycle of Growth Stage 1 (Seed) when the only consideration was simple survival.

2. Mars is the first planet outside Earth in their orbits of the Sun, symbolically taking us into a wider social sphere.
3. We are now above The Sun at Sephirah 6 (Tiphareth, Beauty) outside Earth's orbit on the return journey. This is the realm of Higher Mind. At the stage of the Lightning Flash of Involution this was unconscious – and Tiphareth Conscious control was not yet developed. Now one is conscious of seeming opposing forces.
4. Here, Geburah on The Pillar of Form (Mars, Personal Self Expression and competition), is balanced with Sephirah 4 Chesed(Mercy, Jupiter, Social Activity) which brings the seeming conflict between Personal and Social aims.

SCORPIO – SEX AND DEATH
1. Mars (God of War) and Pluto (Death and Regeneration) both rule Scorpio.
2. Scorpio is the Fixed Water Sign of control of inner emotional desires.
3. Among other things, Scorpio and the 8th.House has concern for "Other People's Possessions" in the give-and-take of life, as well as what will be passed on to later generations – such as children (as survival of one's genes) and wills and bequests (as survival of one's property).
4. There is concern about what we will leave behind when we die. "Life After Death".
5. In Scorpio we transcend personal desires to co-operate with others.
6. The complementary Sign is Taurus which built the body which will eventually be discarded.

SCORPIO PREPARATION FOR TRANSCENDENCE

Scorpio is perhaps the most complex of the Zodiac Signs. It even has 3 symbols – something that is missed by most astrologers. This is probably because most people do not get beyond The Serpent/Scorpion. As the Fixed Water Sign its principle is that of emotional control. The earthly form of fixed water is ice, and Scorpio people demonstrate an icy nature – "cool" and emotionally detached. They are best described by the phrase "still waters run deep". They tend to maintain Silence, so they learn more from you than you do from them. In Astrology we need to be careful of how we use Sun Sign models. It is easy to over simplify. Here we compare it in relation to its place in the Logarithmic Timescale of a lifetime and Cycle of Growth Stage 8.

The 3 symbols are "The Scorpion" or "Serpent", "The Eagle" and "The Dove". To give further insight, we must first note that, since the discovery of Pluto in 1930, Scorpio has 2 ruling planets. The suggestion is that mankind has reached a stage where we can begin to respond to a different vibration, distinct from that of Mars, the original ruler. Mars, remember, is also the ruler of Aries (Cardinal, Initiating, Fire) that operates in Cycle of Growth Stage 1 (Seed) which lasts 7 months and enables our survival after birth. If we did not have the drive of "the Selfish Gene" we would probably not survive. At this Stage of life the same form of energy is used in sexual intercourse - Stage 8 (Sex. Intercourse. Death) - to reproduce, and carry the "gene" into the next generation. We can see that its one purpose at the beginning and end of life is that of Survival. We can also see that it has been active throughout the millions of years of evolution, and is summarised by Herbert Spencer's term "Survival of the Fittest" which he used to replace his original term "persistent force" and complement that of Charles Darwin's "Natural Selection" in 1864. In many ways, Spencer's work pre-dated that of Darwin.

The traditional relationship between wills and inheritances, and Scorpio/8th. House, is a representation of the concern about what we will leave behind for future generations, and what is left to us.

TRANSCENDENCE : PLUTO – RULER OF SCORPIO

The 3 symbols are representative of the energy of Pluto, which is co-ruler of the Sign. Its principle is Regeneration, which at base level is concerned with the renewal of body cells. Throughout our life cells die and are replaced.

The activity of the symbols is best exemplified by the development of a butterfly which requires Metamorphosis - complete breakdown and re-arrangement of its body structure. So we have 3 stages which are based on the control of the reproductive sexual energy by use of the Will :-

1. **SCORPION/SERPENT** – Caterpillar. Feeding, earthy, stage. In human terms, we are ruled by our material emotions and desires. Here we use the traditional energy of Mars.

2. **EAGLE** – Pupa. Transition stage – which can be likened to some forms of meditation. In human terms we are able to control our desires by use of Will. This brings the power of objective observation and ability to manipulate our environment. From Libra balancing one to one relationships man learns co-operation with those in society around. It takes less energy and resources to negotiate peaceful settlement than to engage in competition and war. This level also has relationship with in-depth research into the secrets of Life, and Nature. The usual example is the production of the Atom Bomb which occurred around the time of Pluto's discovery – which was itself a product of "secret" research. This stage begins to convert Mars energy to Pluto energy. The principle of Pluto is Regeneration. Pluto relates to Sephirah 2 (Chockmah. Force. Wisdom) at the top of The Pillar of Force on The Tree of Life. The Eagle has long been associated symbolically with Wisdom and keen vision. From his experience with dream interpretation Jung equates it with "The Wise Old Man" symbol which comes as part of Individuation. As such it is the source of all creative energy. Its activity is that of nuclear reaction, first from The Big Bang, and now manifest in the internal activity of the Suns of the universe, which are still converting Hydrogen to heavier elements. At this level Scorpio still expects personal recompense for its activity.
3. **DOVE** – Butterfly. Reproductive stage. (Stage 9. Conception) In human terms the previous selfish, defensive, attitude is transformed to spiritual development. We make Peace, not War. At a higher level there is the ability for healing, and to regenerate the cells of the body by use of Will. The main example is the Resurrection of Jesus after his crucifixion – Pluto (Regeneration) energy under conscious control.

We have to note that, although linear development is implied, as humans we are more likely to experience the stages at various times during our lives. Whilst here considering the overall cycle of a lifetime, we recognise that the shorter cycles of the other planets follow the same sequence of Stages. Wheels within Wheels.

The principle is based on how we choose to use the basic spiritual Fire energy. We can see how this also applies to the Biblical "Tree of Knowledge", which, among other things, refers to The physical Chakras, and how we can choose the cyclic need for Death (Reincarnation) rather than "The Tree of Life" (Regeneration by use of Will) – which also refers to the Chakra system of energy centres and endocrine glands of the human body.

*4 - "FOURTH OCTAVE"

THIS REMINDS US THAT, SO FAR, WE HAVE BASICALLY CONSIDERED THE CYCLE OF GROWTH AS A 2-DIMENSIONAL CIRCLE, WHEREAS IT ACTUALLY TAKES THE FORM OF A 3-DIMENSIONAL SPIRAL – AS DEPICTED IN THE SHAPE OF A DNA STRAND.
SIMILARLY, WHEN WE CONSIDER THAT THE SOLAR SYSTEM IS MOVING THROUGH SPACE, THE ORBITS OF THE PLANETS ARE ACTUALLY SPIRAL IN FORM. THEY NEVER ACTUALLY RETURN TO THE SAME POSITION THEY PREVIOUSLY OCCUPIED.

A repetition of the First Octave at another level. (Cycle of Growth Stages 9 to 12).
1. The 1st. Octave covered the time of the formation of a human body in the womb which follows the sequence of stages of Human Evolution. We note from Astrology and Psychology that exactly the same sequence of development occurs in early childhood (2nd Octave) - and a similar sequence occurs at the 3rd. Octave (age 7 onward). We can safely assume that the "4th. Octave" is similar.
2. In this Octave is also the concept of "becoming as a child".
3. The meanings of the Cycle of Growth Stages do not change.
4. This Octave coincides, among other things, with C.G. Jung's concept of Individuation. It takes us beyond the collective ideals, attitudes and traditions of society to an individual path. Part of the process is the

necessity to consciously become aware of the contents of our Personal Unconscious and, where appropriate, bring them to expression in everyday life.

5. The process is not automatic. There is a choice between submission to the earthly routine existence, or accepting Change and entering into a wider experience of life to find a personal meaning. Everything is subject to one's individual Will. Doors to other experiences may be opened, but one is usually not forced through. Such opportunities often require that we come to a "bump on the road of life" which wakes us up" to new possibilities. Our usual tendency is to "solve the problem" and return to our normal unconscious routine. We often need to wait for such "bumps" in our outside lives to be able to make use of the opportunity of temporary instability in the resistance of others.

TRANSCENDENT PLANETS

Apart from the Houses of a Birth Chart another factor to be taken into account is the relatively newly-discovered planets beyond Saturn – Uranus, Neptune, and Pluto – which together have been termed "Transcendent Planets". Saturn is the furthest planet that is visible to the naked eye - the others needed some form of modern technology to discover (become conscious of). Uranus has correspondence with the energies of Aquarius and the 11th.House – originally assigned to Saturn - and Neptune relates to Pisces and the 12th.House – originally assigned to Jupiter. It seems that the "new" planets are concerned with the process of Individuation. Most people today are still "earth-bound" with the traditional Saturn and Jupiter controlling Cycle of Growth Stages 11 and 12 respectively. It takes a fundamental change in attitude to one's life to relate to the "newer" planets (becoming interested in books like this is a beginning). At our current stage of evolution the full meaning of this Octave is not clear. At a personal level it is clearly related to C.G. Jung's concept of Individuation. A sense of "life after death".

TRANSCENDENT STAGE 9 – CONCEPTION

(Sagittarius. XIV. Temperance)

Related to the rebirth principle of the Winter Solstice (SUN) and birth of Jesus (SON) - at a human level we have another experience of "virgin birth" with the Conception of ideas in the mind – which are often called "brain children".

At another level it could mean "the second coming of The Messiah" which is an inner, psychological event.

It is stated that Creation of the universe began with an abstract Idea beginning to take form (Word) in the mind of God.

Scientists call it the creation of a Singularity out of "nothing" followed by a Big Bang.

THE KABBALAH SEPHIRAH 2 (Chockmah, Force. Pluto. Number 1)

1. With the return to Chockmah we once again come into contact with The 3 Supernals on The Pillar of Life.
2. At the top of The Pillar of Mercy (Force) the Sephirah is related to the planet Pluto, which is a symbol of Nuclear Reaction. We have pure Force or Energy. Electricity. At the more mundane level of Astrology, Sagittarius and the 9th. House are ruled by Jupiter – which is related to Sephirah 4 (Chesed, Mercy) just below Chockmah on The Pillar of Force – and on the other side of The Abyss.
3. It is not possible for humans to reach this level, but we make contact by indirect means - such as visions or mental conceptions of the Ideals and Principles of Kether (Crown) at the top of The Tree.
4. Because Chockmah is activated, Binah (Form, Understanding) at the top of The Pillar of Form is active too – otherwise the concept would have no form, and therefore there would be no perception – albeit at this abstract level. So we have a "thought form", or Inspiration.
5. However, the inherent inertia of Binah may mean that the energy does not travel further than mere perception of Light.

TRANSCENDENT STAGE 10 – SOCIAL PEAK

(Capricorn. XV.The Devil. XVI.The Tower)

Stage 10 is related to Capricorn and Saturn/Satan. The realm of earthly ambitions. Even God had such ambitions – otherwise we would not be here. We see innumerable occasions in past history where ruling authorities and the Church have stopped progress in such areas as Science and Medicine. The paradox is that, in the end, any changes must be practical, and tend to give rise to their own "devils". There is strong resistance to new ideas from those in authority – as well as our own inner "devil" - as Jesus was tempted.

In the story of Jesus his birth came to the attention of authority and narrowly escaped being killed along with many other babies. Our "brain children" may never develop into practical, earthy, use. He reached his "social peak" at around the age of 12 years (just before his Generic Jupiter Return. Puberty) when he was found questioning the elders of the temple. After that he retired into obscurity until his ministry at around age 30 (the Generic Saturn Return when we begin to find our own life path distinct from that of our parents).

This time of year is that of New Year Resolutions, which are "brain children" – many of which do not survive.

Even God wanted to create and rule his own world. Please see the chapter [THE GENESIS STORY] where we see further evidence of this Octave of The Cycle of Growth.

*[Give back the things of Caesar to Caesar, and the things of God to God." [Mark 12 : 17 YLBT]

THE KABBALAH SEPHIRAH 3 (Binah, Understanding, Form. Saturn. Number 3)

1. The conflict between Chockmah and Binah can be considered as that between God and The Devil.
2. The Struggle is contained in the story of the temptation of Jesus in the wilderness - where he was tempted to use his higher knowledge to achieve a "Stage 10 Peak" of social recognition and power. (He was later welcomed by the people as The Messiah, come to solve all their problems for them, and rejected when he did not fulfil their expectations of him).
3. This is in keeping with Cycle of Growth Stage 10 onwards.

THE TAROT : XV. THE DEVIL AND XVI. THE TOWER

1. We note the related Tarot cards The Devil (Saturn/Satan) and The Tower (Lucifer/Bringer of Light).
2. The Tower shows the destruction of a long established structure of the past. The Tower of Babel was built with man-made bricks rather than The Stone of Nature and gave rise to meaningless "babble".

TRANSCENDENT STAGE 11 – DISCONTENT

(Aquarius. XVII.The Star. XVIII.The Moon)

This stage can be controlled by the old ruler of Aquarius, Saturn, or Uranus.

With Saturn, the inner and outer resistance of social traditions and methods, and one's own inner rigidity, override the impulse to take on something new. An example of this is New Year resolutions that do not develop.

The energy of Uranus is required to overcome inner and outer resistance to Change. It still requires the Self Discipline of Saturn. Making new structures and habits to replace the old. Revolution to destroy the old structures merely brings chaos.

The symbolism of the 11th.House/ Aquarius has been related to Invention, Revolution, and Change from ancient times. Challenging authority and traditional structures. Jesus was a rebel who challenged authority and paid the ultimate price. Although originally welcoming Jesus into Jerusalem as their saviour, the people of the time eventually preferred a more "traditional rebel", or active revolutionary against the Romans, by choosing to release Barabbas instead.

The evolutionary development (change) of all life on this planet has occurred because of "mistakes" in copying DNA. Some mutations have enabled survival, others have not. Quite often in life "accidents" are not quite what they seem. They can occur as a result of ignored prompting from the inner self. They force attention to one's personal needs for Self Development. At least we are made aware of areas of life we would not otherwise explore. DNA mutations are quite regular in their occurrence at around 10,000 year intervals – so there must be some kind of Natural Law involved which is as yet unknown.

This also relates to our capacity to Individualise, which requires that we re-assess traditional methods and concepts to decide which are appropriate to our lives. This is often interpreted as a need to challenge any or all social authorities, ignoring the fact that the Rule of Law is very useful in maintaining social stability.
[PSYCHOLOGY : DEVELOPMENT MODELS – Transactional Analysis Model]

Individuation is replacing external Discipline with Self Discipline.

ASTROLOGY : LOGARITHMIC TIMESCALE

THE KABBALAH SEPHIRAH "DAATH" (AND THE MIDDLE PILLAR)

1. Although traditionally without a number, we can refer Daath to Cycle of Growth Stage 11 (Discontent). Uranus is related to the Throat Chakra, which, in turn, is related to Will.
2. Daath does not exist in the downward path of Evolution – that is our time in our mother's womb and The 1st. Octave of The Cycle of Growth.
3. We have noted that it is not possible for humans to reach the level of The Supernals, except indirectly – especially as they are located above The Abyss.
4. Daath provides the possibility of bypassing the natural dilemma between Chockmah and Binah by building a "bridge" across The Abyss to make contact with Kether (Crown).
5. Kether and Daath are together at the top of The Middle Pillar of Balance and Equilibrium.
6. As with the triads lower down The Tree, with the Sephiroth on The Middle Pillar mediating 2 others, so Daath can mediate between Chockmah and Binah.
7. Both Daath and Tiphareth are mediators. Both have some contact with Kether at the top of the tree. Kether is the ultimate "mediator" – but everything there is in a Zero state.
8. Both Daath and Sephirah 6 (Tiphareth. The Sun. Consciousness. Ego) on The middle Pillar are undeveloped on the involutionary path of The Lightning Flash.
9. When Daath and Kether are in contact, the path of a new Lightning Flash from Kether to Malkuth is activated. This is the vision of Saul (= Number 8. Moon) on the road to Damascus which converted him to become Paul (= Number 5. Sun).
10. Both Daath and Tiphareth are states of Will and Consciousness.
11. Sephirah 6 (Tiphareth, Beauty, The Sun, Consciousness) is lower down on The Middle Pillar, below Daath. We can therefore understand Daath better from this lower level. Like Daath, Tiphareth (Beauty, The Sun, Consciousness. Ego) is only in embryo form at the time of our birth. Until this time we are wholly subject to the Laws of Evolution that form the human body. Tiphareth begins its development at Cycle of Growth Stage 5 (Power, Creativity, School Age).
12. Sephirah 9 (Yesod, Foundation, The Moon) and 10 (Malkuth, Kingdom, Earth) are at the bottom of The Middle Pillar. Their equilibrium is forced by obedience to natural cycles which automatically balance to the Zero of Kether. There is no Free Will.
13. Without Daath, Cycle of Growth Stage 12 is ruled by Jupiter (Chesed) rather than Kether (Neptune).

THE TAROT : XVII. THE STAR.   XVIII. THE MOON.

At this level we are concerned with the inner re-adjustment required to the destruction of the previous order. Conflicting, complementary, light and dark images arise from the Unconscious. No progress can be made until "even-ing".

TRANSCENDENT STAGE 12 – WITHDRAWAL, CONFINEMENT

(Pisces, The Collective Unconscious, "Even-ing")

Again, with dual planetary rulership of this stage there are 2 scenarios. If Saturn, The Past, is stronger in Stage 11 we have the traditional rulership of Jupiter merely expanding what is there already, and the same "seeds" will be sown in the following Cycle of Growth Stage 1, so the new cycle will be a repetition of the old one.

If the need for Change has been accepted, the new ruler Neptune will act to "dissolve" past structures that have outlived their usefulness – such as old habits and life routines. Pisces rules areas of life where one is put into isolation – such as hospitals, prisons, and spiritual retreats. Also, holidays. By separating from our habits we are helped to discard them.

This is also the province of Karma, when we may need to atone for past "sins" before going forward. A simple example is when we actually have to forgive ourselves, and atone by promising to "do better next time" – or spend time in prison or hospital.

In the life of Jesus we are told that, before he publicly entered Jerusalem to eventually face his crucifixion, he spent 40 days (perhaps relating to 40 weeks of Gestation ?) and nights alone - being tempted in the wilderness. He had the opportunity to use his powers for self-aggrandisement and to escape his coming fate.

ASTROLOGY : LOGARITHMIC TIMESCALE

THE KABBALAH SEPHIRAH 1 (Kether, Crown, Number Zero, No-Thing)

1. In trying to describe Kether we are trying to explain the unexplainable.
2. Kether is the beginning and end of the Tree of Life and Cycle of Growth.
3. We contact Kether by considering the relationship between our actions and the abstract Ideals of life.
4. It seems that we begin life full of ideals ("New Resolutions") which become untenable in the face of the realities of material life.
5. Unfortunately, our Ideals are forced to adapt in the face of earthly reality (Binah. Saturn. Satan).

THE TAROT – XIX. THE SUN. XX. JUDGEMENT, AND XXI. THE WORLD

Here we have the birth of a new consciousness. Hope. Having overcome the destruction of past routines and habits there is a seed of new practical possibilities for the future. However, the theory will still need to be developed in practice. The next step is "rebirth" into an area where we have no previous knowledge. We "become as a child" – Zero, The Fool.

In adult life many people will not face new learning possibilities because it means becoming a "Fool".

Negatively, the seed will not be recognised or given opportunity to grow. Or one may not wish to give up the earlier sense of power and control (Stage 10 Peak - Capricorn, Saturn). Sometimes in life we have to "start at the bottom" again.

THE BUTTERFLY EFFECT

In our examination of [NUMEROLOGY] we realise that any creative act requires that the rest of the universe has to rebalance to maintain the sum total of Number Zero. Each day of Creation in Genesis required an "even-ing" and God rested on Creation Day 7 (as we do at night). To dispute this is to ignore "The Butterfly Effect" of Chaos Theory that states a small change, such as the movement of a butterfly wing, can be included in a larger change at a later stage – such as changing the course of a hurricane.

In their study of the atom, scientists are beginning to suggest that local activity at this level can have an immediate effect on the other side of the universe – overcoming the current suggestion of limitations by the speed of light.

An example is that weather forecasting has improved by the introduction of more accurate computers able to handle more decimal places. Edward Lorenz discovered that very small differences in their data caused big differences in the results, and realised that the amount of energy involved in the addition of each decimal place was decreasing to the extent of being almost "negligible".

*For want of a nail the shoe was lost,
for want of a shoe the horse was lost,
for want of a horse the knight was lost,
for want of a knight the battle was lost,
for want of a battle the kingdom was lost.
So a kingdom was lost—all for want of a horseshoe nail [Ancient Proverb]

ASTROLOGY : SIGNS OF THE ZODIAC

The Signs of the Zodiac are different forms of expression of the basic Solar source of energy which contains them all. White light contains all possible colours. This chapter outlines the principles of The Zodiac Signs which are covered in more detail in other chapters.

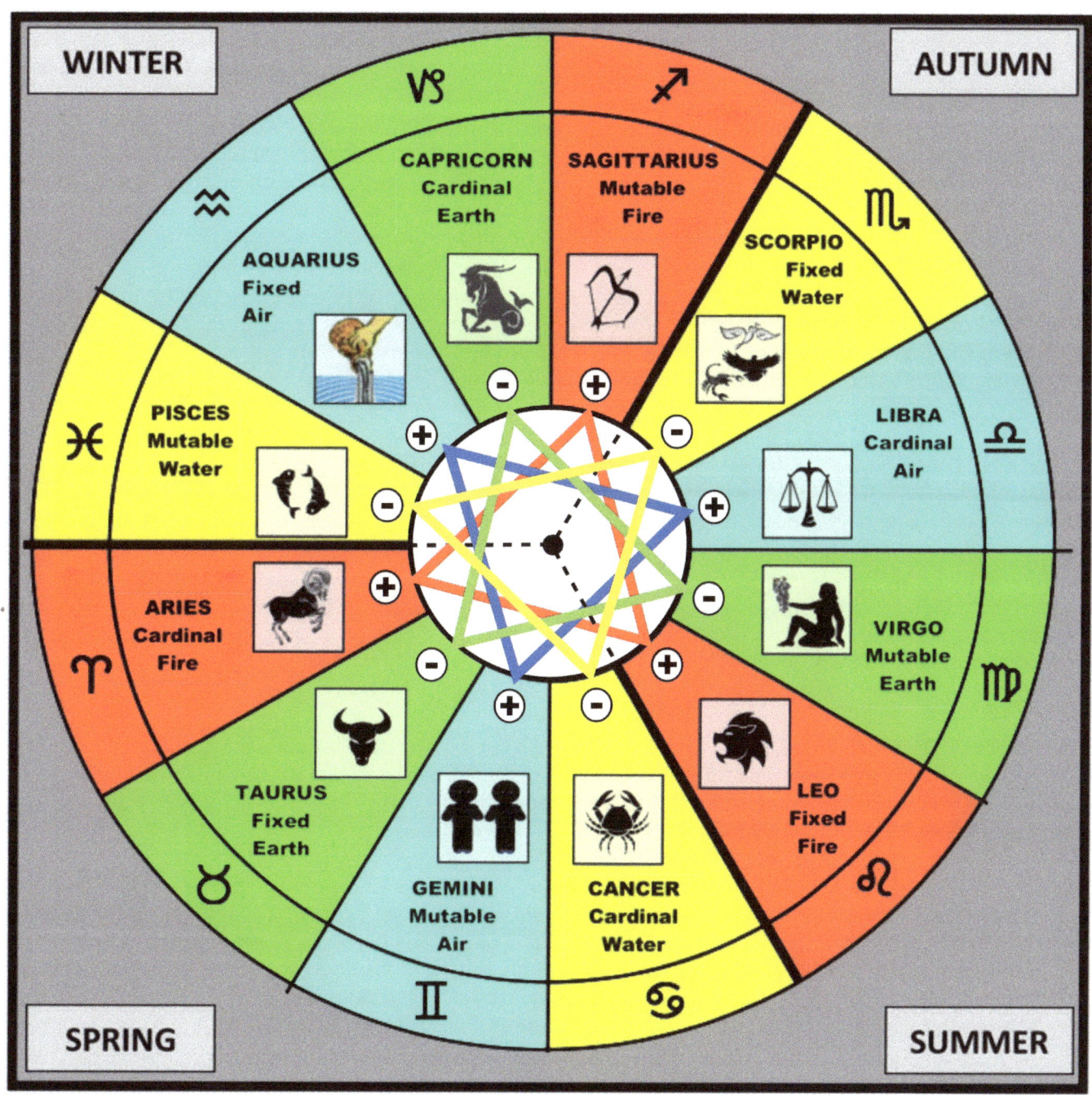

Figure 29 : Astrology - Zodiac Signs

OVERVIEW

This chapter is an overview of the "set" of 12 Zodiac Signs which are dealt with individually in the chapter [ASTROLOGY : THE LOGARITHMIC TIMESCALE], and elsewhere. In keeping with the main principle of this book, the aim is to show them as Archetypes in their most simple form, and their inter-relationship as a "set of 12". We note that this task is not fully possible using the Jungian Thinking Function alone - which includes reading and writing. It requires much inner thought, and/or meditation, to gain understanding – which is a very personal thing.

ASTROLOGY : SIGNS

BIRTH CHART HOUSE & SIGN RELATIONSHIPS

The 24 hour rotation of The Earth gives a new Zodiac Sign rising on the Eastern Horizon (The Ascendant) every 2 hours. The 1st. House of a Birth Chart is always on the Eastern Horizon, and its relationship with a Sign is fixed at the time of birth, they are mainly concerned with [ASTROLOGY : THE LOGARITHMIC TIMESCALE].

The 12 Zodiac Signs relate to Time and various forms of energy, whereas the 12 Houses of a chart relate to Space, and the physical manifestation on Earth –No Sign is more or less "spiritual" than another. To become a whole individual we eventually have to master the abilities and problems brought by each one – perhaps over several lifetimes. A Birth Chart – with the Sun Sign as a main focus - is an indicator of what we have come to learn in the current lifetime. The Signs are related to the annual cycle of 12 months.

The diagram above is similar to an Astrological chart but has the outer Zodiac Signs extended to show more detail. In effect, the outer Zodiac circle extends to infinity. The white circle at the centre represents Earth and would normally show the 12 Houses of the chart. The central Earth circle defines the orientation of the chart around which the Signs (appear to) rotate clockwise, or rise and set, like the Sun, with time – so defining the months of the year. The Signs are here shown in their positions as at sunrise at the Spring Equinox each year.

It is important to note that nowadays the Zodiac Signs bear no relationship with the star patterns of the heavens. They were set at around 3000 BC when Astrology as we know it today was born. Due to the Precession of the Equinoxes caused by the Earth wobbling on its axis we now have Aquarius rising at the Spring Equinox instead of Aries. The Signs are divisions of EARTH which are set by Time rather than space. This is similar to the imaginary divisions of Earth by lines of Latitude and Longitude which define Space. [ASTROLOGY : THE ZODIAC AGES]

4 ELEMENTS – FIRE, EARTH, AIR, WATER

The 4 inner triangles indicate the relative positions of the 3 Signs which relate to each of the 4 Elements. Fire (Red. Positive), Earth (Green. Negative), Air (Blue. Positive), and Water (Yellow. Negative). [THE 4 ELEMENTS]

POLARITIES – POSITIVE OR NEGATIVE

The mathematical Plus and Minus signs in the diagram indicate the Polarity of the Zodiac Signs. Fire and Air are Positive, Earth and Water are Negative. We note that complementary Signs on the opposite sides of the chart are of the same polarity. There is some conflict there because like polarity repels – opposite attracts.

THE 3 OCTAVES

The white centre circle is also divided into 3 parts with dotted lines. Each part contains a Sign of each Element in the same order. This is an indication of how the Signs' archetypes relate to the 3 Octaves of the Logarithmic Timescale of the (fixed position) Houses of a Birth Chart. They will only coincide with the Signs as here once a year at sunrise of the day of the Spring Equinox.

3 QUALITIES – CARDINAL, FIXED, MUTABLE

Whereas Houses are mainly treated as 4 sets of the Signs are arranged as 3 sets of 4 Elements in the order Fire, Earth, Air, Water. Each Element has 3 Qualities, or modes of action - Cardinal, Fixed, and Mutable. The diagram shows that a Cardinal Sign is followed by a Fixed Sign, then a Mutable Sign (of different Elements). In this arrangement, based on (sets of) Number 3, the 3 Quality types of Elements (Cardinal, Fixed, Mutable) are similar in activity to the 3 Triplicity types of the Houses (Angular, Succedent, Cadent).

The Number 3 is a discrete "set". It consists of 3 modes which exist (repetitively) in turn in such triplicities as Action, Reaction, Result - Creator, Preserver, Destroyer – Thesis, Antithesis, Synthesis - (etc.). These are examples of how an Archetype (in this case Number 3) can manifest in numerous "forms".

Although the House positions in an astrological chart are fixed, the set of Sign positions varies depending on the time and place the chart is set up for. If you refer to the Birth Chart of Lady Diana Spencer [ASTROLOGY : CHARTS EXAMPLES] you will see that she has the Mutable Fire Sign Sagittarius rising on the cusp of her 1st. House (Ascendant) instead of the archetypal Cardinal Fire Sign Aries in the diagram above. The departure from the archetypal arrangement (which is common to most of us) brings difficulties in life from the need to consciously control and rebalance the energies involved when undertaking personal projects or activities. Having a Fire Sign rising is useful in promoting one's personal activities, but Mutable (Changeable) Sagittarius makes it difficult to focus the energy, whereas archetypal Cardinal (Initiating) Aries has complete focus and is not too bothered with side issues (Me-Me). The art of chart analysis consists of taking such things into account for each House\Sign\Planet position.

THE 4 ELEMENTS IN A CHART

The 4 Elements refer to Number 4 which are another set of archetypes affecting more than the Zodiac Signs, so I have discussed them as a "set" in overall terms in a separate chapter [THE 4 ELEMENTS]. Every astrological chart has the 12 Signs in the same order. The difference depends on which planets appear in which Signs, and which Houses are ruled by the Signs. Angular, Creative, Houses 1, 4, 7, and 10 at the 4 Quarters of a chart have more influence over the whole, especially if one or more planets are contained in the House.

In the case of a Birth Chart we can gain an overall idea of the energy balance in the subject by counting the number of planets in each element. Some astrologers also include the Ascendant and Midheaven. We also take note of the fact that Fire and Air are of Positive, and Water and Earth Negative polarity.

In the sample Birth Chart for Lady Diana Spencer we see :-

Earth   (Negative) – 4 planets

Water (Negative) - 3 planets including Sun

Air   (Positive-) - 2 planets including Moon plus Air Midheaven

Fire   (Positive)   - 1 planet plus Fire Ascendant

With the 7 out of 10 emphasis on Negative Signs, and only 1 planet in Fire (basic energy), Diana would not find it easy to express herself or initiate activities – and we have seen that Sagittarius has difficulty of focus, so she would try to do too much at once. She would need help to control her activities. We note her planet emphasis on Earth which will moderate the negative effects mentioned by enabling her to maintain a practical basis.

We remember that any aspect of a Birth Chart can be overcome by the use of individual Will – the difference is in the amount of personal effort that would be required, and the ability to get other people to co-operate.

SUN AND MOON SIGNS

The most important Signs of a Birth Chart are the ones in which the Sun and Moon are located at the time of birth. The Sun Sign is easy to define because it relates to an Annual Cycle of the Sun– so we just need to know the date of birth. The Moon position is harder to define because of its 29 day Cycle. The difference in their activity is that, very basically, the Moon position shows what abilities we have inherited from the past, especially from our mother but also from past incarnations. With benefit of modern psychological concepts not available to the early astrologers we can say that The Moon relates to our Personal Unconscious, or Subconscious Mind. The Sun position indicates what we have come to learn in this lifetime, and can be an indicator of the influence of our father. We usually do not begin to realise our Sun potential until later in life away from parental control – which begins at Cycle of Growth Stage 5 (Power. Creativity. The Sun. Number 5) at the "School Age" of Psychology. [THE LOGARITHMIC TIMESCALE]. The Sun position is also an indicator of our basic Elemental energy source and relates to our Conscious Mind.

LADY DIANA SPENCER

In the case of Lady Diana we can see something of what was behind the public image she presented. At a very fundamental level, we have an independent Aquarian (Moon) trying to become more like a Cancerian (Sun) - "Mother"/"Shell Provider". Without wishing to increase the detail too much, we note that her 2nd. House Moon is in the "Private" area of her chart, below the Horizon line, and her Sun is in the more public 7th. House of "Partnerships" – which is a weak House position because it brings the need to seek support from someone else, or work in partnership. We note how Prince Charles brought her out of obscurity into public view. In the [ASTROLOGY : SYNASTRY] chapter there are Birth Charts for Freud and Jung, both of whom also had Sun in 7th. House (Cycle of Growth Stage 7 (Partnership) giving rise to a slightly different interpretation of "Partnerships". As you will see below, the Sign of Libra has a close archetypal relationship with the 7th. House. In her chart Libra is ruling her 10th. House (Peak. Public View. Career) which was clearly affected by her marriage. "Partnerships" refer to friends and enemies.

Diana's 7th. House is ruled by the Sign of Gemini – the Mutable (changeable) Air Sign which complements her Mutable Fire Sagittarian 1st. House/Ascendant so she would need a lot of variety and change among her close relationships to maintain her interest.

ASTROLOGY : SIGNS

THE ANNUAL CYCLE OF SIGNS

The Signs show different forms of Solar energy. The Sun Sign of a Birth Chart shows the basic form of energy (consciousness) available to its subject, and which gives life to the rest of the Chart.

From this, and the foregoing, you can see something of the factors involved in analysing an Astrological Chart. There are further details from such things as planet positions and the Aspects (angles) between them. Planetary Aspects are described in the chapter [NUMEROLOGY].

The Signs at a basic historical level relate to the "weather" and activities of the agricultural year. As an archetypal set of 12 they relate to The Cycle of Growth at all levels of manifestation.

ZODIAC SIGNS AND HEALTH

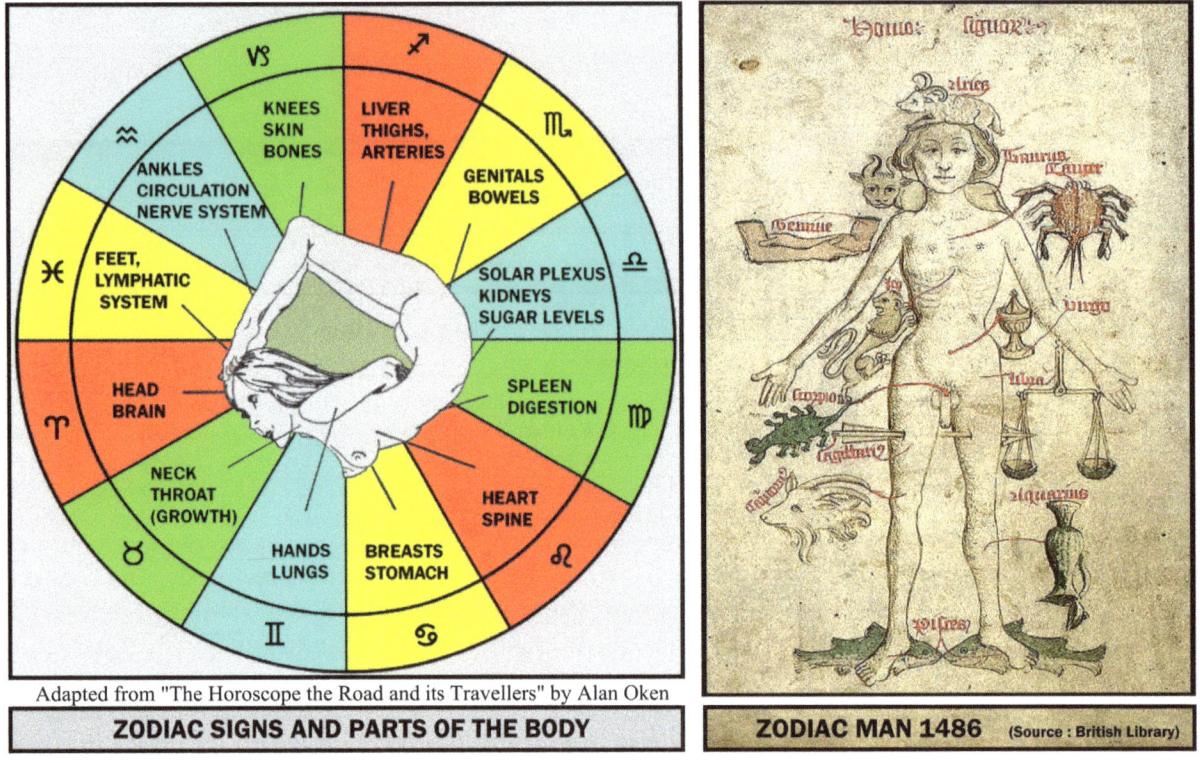

Figure 30 : Astrology : Zodiac Signs and parts of the body

Each Sign relates to a different part of the physical body. The link between the physical body and Zodiac Signs (different forms of Solar energy) is via the Chakra Energy System (Fire) of the body. The (roots of) the 7 Chakras are situated on the spine as energy "transformers" and they have a relationship with the physical body via the Endocrine Gland system (Earth) which produces hormones (Water), which, in turn, control all body functions. The pattern of the Chakra System is that of the "Tree of Life". The Air Element relates to their connection with the nervous system. [THE CHAKRAS].[THE KABBALAH TREE OF LIFE].

Each Chakra has a relationship with each of The 4 Elements. Fire – Energy, Water – Emotions, Air – the Nervous System, and Earth – the physical gland. In addition, The 4 lower Chakras each relate to one of the 4 Elements {EC}. So, for example, with the Fire-related 3rd. Chakra (The Solar Plexus, relating to the Adrenal Glands) we have Fire of Fire, Water of Fire, Air of Fire, and Earth of Fire.

Each Zodiac Sign, as a form of energy, naturally relates to a different part of the body. It follows that the relationship between the Archetypal Tree of Life and the actual positions of Signs in the Birth Chart of an individual have a bearing on general health. In fact, we could say that most of us are out of alignment in this sense because we do not have Aries rising.

Individual health also varies depending on the locations of planets in the Signs of a Birth Chart and aspects between them. If a planetary energy is not in harmony with that of a Zodiac Sign there is a negative health effect. There is a table of Planet relationships with the Signs in the chapter [ASTROLOGY : PLANETS].

ASTROLOGY : SIGNS

At a general level we can say that health problems are a result of stress which manifests itself by affecting the weakest part of the body. In my case, several planets in Gemini gave rise to numerous breathing problems when I was young – including a collapsed lung, and later on Mars in Cancer led to stomach ulcers. You will see from [MY STORY] that my mid Life Crisis forced me to learn how to handle stress ("hard" planet aspects), the result of which is that I have not had to visit a doctor for a medical problem since then.

The diagrams above show the relationship of Zodiac Signs with various parts of the body. It is notable that if we consider the whole cycle, as here, the head (Aries) and feet (Pisces) come together. We are aware of the fact that the brain has overall control of body functions, with different areas responsible for the activity of specific activity. Reflexology works on the principle that the feet (and hands) have similar specific areas that relate to certain parts of the body.

We must also note the more modern concept that Pisces has association with the unconscious mind, specifically The Personal Unconscious and The Collective Unconscious. The traditional links are statements that Pisces relates to "the back of the head", and the feet are our "under-standings".

It has been discovered that our DNA strands have similar head to toe relationships within them- so things get put into the proper place.

THE ZODIAC SIGNS

The following are brief descriptions of the individual Astrological Signs.

We ALL consist of all 12 forms of energy as symbolised by the 12 Zodiac Signs. The difference between us is that some Signs may be emphasised in our Birth Chart by House position (Angular Houses 1, 4, 7, and 10 are the important ones), and Planet positions. We see in [ASTROLOGY : PLANETS] that ,although our Sun Sign is important, we have to learn to consciously use it to balance the other energies.

We understand The Signs better by comparing each one with their complementary , balancing, Sign. Eventually the energies of every cycle cancel out to make a Zero Balance in preparation for the next.

ARIES AND LIBRA

ARIES (Cardinal Fire. The Ram. Personal Projection of Energy)

1. Fire Signs are related to Intuition. Intuition and Sensation are Irrational Functions that perceive experience as a whole – that is, without any analysis.
2. The seed is lying dormant in the Earth waiting for favourable conditions to germinate.
3. This is the first sign of Spring. The Spring Equinox. Equal Day and Night.
4. Aries is pure instinctive energy symbolised by The Ram. It is energy in its simplest form, basically concerned with personal survival. Rutting Rams fight each other to establish the "pecking order" of later access to the females – although this latter purpose is not in their consciousness yet. This enables "survival of the fittest" at Genetic level.
5. The lesson of Aries requires that one become a Pioneer or Leader in some field of endeavour.
6. Aries is concerned with Phallic Symbols – an erect penis with potential for creativity. In this we see the "reason" for the building of structures like Stonehenge, The Pyramids, and Ziggurats during The Age of Aries. They were status symbols. "Mine is bigger than yours".
7. Relating to Cycle of Growth Stage 1 (Seed), this is the time of birth. We observe Aries (Fire. Intuition) in its purest form in new born babies. Here it is uncontaminated by Thinking, Feeling, or Sensation – "Reasons" (Thinking Function) for actions do not yet exist.
8. The related 1st. House is that of The Ascendant, and "Personal Projection of Energy", while the 7th. House is concerned with "Social Projection of Energy".
9. The 1st. House is our natural way of beginning new projects, new life. As with other Houses, it is activated when transit planets pass through giving extra energy to the possibility of developing new projects – albeit in the form of ideas rather than practice.

ASTROLOGY : SIGNS

10. Aries people are simple and direct, perhaps childlike in some ways. Unsophisticated. They prefer occupations that enable them to do their own thing without too much external control.
11. Aries in our Birth Chart shows where we might become a Pioneer in preparing the ground for some new "field" of endeavour. To "make a name for our self".
12. Aries relates to the planet Mars "God of War".
13. The Tarot Cards 0.The Fool (the "April Fool" of April 1st.) is symbolic of innocence being prompted by pure animal instinct (the dog in the picture). I.The Magician shows the potential for development of use of The 4 Elements on the table (Mind) before him (Intuition, Feeling, Thinking, Sensation).
14. In Genesis, "man and woman" were created on Creation Day 6 at Cycle of Growth Stage 12 (Confinement) (no Eve yet) which is the end of Genesis Chapter 1. Chapter 2 begins Cycle of Growth Stage 1 (Seed. Aries/Mars) where man was formed "from dust". That is, gets a more physical shape – which is completed later on. We can see this as a new born child first becoming consciously aware of itself via a physical body, and in later Stages recognising its own sexual identity as a prelude to awareness of the world outside the parental home at Stage 4 (Transplanting. Cancer) and onwards.

LIBRA (Cardinal Air. The Scales. Social Projection of energy)

1. We note that Signs on opposite sides of a chart are of the same Quality – Cardinal, Fixed, or Mutable.
2. Air Signs are related to the Jungian Thinking Function, which is Rational (from "ratio") in that it is analytical and able to evaluate and describe experience.
3. The Scales symbol is the only one that depicts an inanimate object.
4. This is the turning point of the year. We have the Vernal Equinox – once again equal day and night, but now it is more noticeable that The Light is getting dimmer. The Year is preparing for its Death. The Sun has reached the limit of its outward journey. From now on the progression of Signs, and outer life, tends toward Rebirth and Zero.
5. Libra, The Scales, is the Sign of Balance. In the description here we see that each Sign has its complement at a later time. In this case the individualistic drive of Aries requires a mate to enable the survival of its genes. It therefore has to give up some of its hard-won independence.
6. The Lesson of Libra is to achieve Inner Balance. The method is to use Diplomacy to achieve aims, whilst not giving in to negative pressure.
7. As an Air Sign Libra is concerned with the Thinking Function, and mental concepts. Like Aries this tends to be at a simplistic level – here we have the conflicting mental concepts such as "Right and Wrong" or "Good and Bad". This is the place of mental dilemmas. Until there is resolution there will be no progress – only worry.
8. Libra is the beginning of Jungian "Resolution of Opposites".
9. The ruling planet of Libra is Venus –Beauty, Desire - which also rules earthy Taurus. In the Air element she operates at a mental level. At one level this is the universal attraction of "opposites" – the aim of which is to regain the original state which occurred before The Big Bang – a state of equilibrium and "peace". However, things are now more complicated than just Positive and Negative forces.
10. We are at the 7th. House and Cycle of Growth Stage 7 (Partners) of The Cycle of Growth, which refers to the time of life at age 23 when we seek a mate so that our genes will survive our death. It has to be someone who has the necessary complementary physical organs. At a psychological level we have become a personality based on our early life experience of parents and peers – mainly of the same sex. We have to seek outside this area of society for a mate. Someone of the opposite sex who is not a blood relation. It is better at this stage to control the Aries/Mars "Selfish Gene" force.
11. In the previous Cycle of Growth Stage 6 (Service to Self) we have begun to develop as an Individual. However, we cannot do everything our self.
12. At a Spiritual (energy) level, to survive so far we have had to adapt our personality to the demands of the external world. However, this may be to the detriment of our own Inner Balance. We are therefore unconsciously attracted to people who demonstrate our "missing parts". Perhaps abilities we have not yet used. Anyone who has "fallen in love" will recognise the power of this attractive force, and the fact that it is not a conscious process. If there are many "missing parts" it may require numerous partnerships to discover them – no single person would be an exact "Match".

ASTROLOGY : SIGNS

13. Libra people are peaceful because they can always see the merits of both sides in any conflict. Unfortunately the result can be stalemate - so nothing gets done. Maintaining the Peace can be a form of cowardice in the face of real threat – which might require Aries/Mars action. An example of the resolution of the impasse is our legal system which gets both parties together and an impartial judge to make the final decision – when everyone can move on.

14. When resolving our own inner, psychological, conflicts we can use the same method – which requires that we raise our consciousness to see the merits of both sides and take the position of "impartial judge" to make some decision for action (or not). Often our inner selves relate to experiences of the past, and do not have up to date physical evidence. There is Prejudice. As we become better at the process our inner "family" learn to trust us more, and we find a truer Inner Peace.

TAURUS AND SCORPIO

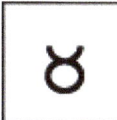  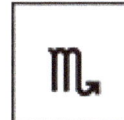 

TAURUS (Fixed Earth. The Bull. Personal Collection of Energy)

1. The Earth signs are related to the Jungian Sensation Function. (The 5 Senses).
2. Each successive Sign is a challenge to the previous one. Her we have the "Irresistible Force" of Aries meeting the "Immovable Object" of Taurus.
3. In the Annual Cycle the seed has been dormant waiting for the Earth to become warm and moist so it can germinate.
4. In Cycle of Growth Stage 2 (Germination) at age 7 months to 2 years the child gradually becomes aware of, and learns to control, its physical body – mainly because there is discomfort from hunger it did not feel in the womb. There is now a delay between needs arising and their satisfaction.
5. This is the development of the Jungian Sensation Function.
6. With Fixed Earth we have the principle of Inertia – a resistance to movement and change. Although Taurus people are said to be Patient, if we observe them closely it is rather that they are slow to act. In fact, the more they are pressured the more stubborn they become. The Lesson of Taurus is concerned with the management of physical resources, such as money and property – which includes care of the physical body. There is also the need to learn the benefits of having fixed routines – as in Nature.
7. Planets in Taurus have their energy "slowed down". For example, I have set up charts for several people with Mercury (Mind) in Taurus who could be described as having a "dour" personality. Being "slow witted" does not mean that they are stupid. Remember the story of "The Hare and Tortoise".
8. The ruling planet of Taurus is Venus. Here the Desire for equilibrium is focused on physical comfort. The focus on money mentioned elsewhere is really a means to this end.
9. The 2nd. House is that of "Personal Collection of Energy" and Personal Resources which includes all possessions, the human body, and personal skills and abilities. This is balanced by "Social Collection of Energy" in Scorpio.
10. The Tarot Card II.The Priestess refers to the "blank sheet" of the brain and unconscious mind. The cold ground. Card III.The Empress (Mother Nature. Mother Earth. The Garden of Eden) shows the now 'pregnant' Priestess where The Earth is responding to the Sun (consciousness) and supporting the growth of the seeds. Things of The Earth are forming pictures in the mind. We create our own "inner world" as a reflection of the outer one.
11. In Genesis we have the creation of The Garden of Eden
12. I have first-hand knowledge of the effect of Taurus/2nd. House by having natal Moon in the 2nd. House. I was once asked by a lady with Taurus Sun husband if I am Taurean – which, partially, I am. I again note that Taurus and the other Signs are in all of us. The difference is where certain signs are emphasised in a Birth Chart. Moon is a powerful influence. You can see how I try to keep this book as "down to Earth" as possible, and focus on factual information.

SCORPIO (Fixed Water. Scorpion/Serpent – Eagle – Dove)

ASTROLOGY : SIGNS

1. Water Signs are related to the Jungian Feeling Function, which is Rational (from "ratio") in that it analyses experience on a variable scale of degrees between "Pleasant – Unpleasant".
2. Having formed a relationship in Libra it is necessary to control one's emotions. A lesson of Scorpio is that of Negotiation, or Courtship.
3. The stages relate to the purpose of our union with others – for sex, gain, or more universal ideals.
4. The Scorpion/Serpent stage is that of pure satisfaction of selfish desires. Attention to Earthy matters.
5. To resolve the dilemmas of Libra it is necessary to investigate the true facts of the matter in question. This will take one into previously uncharted areas. Scorpio is concerned with investigating The Unknown.
6. The Eagle stage is where one can observe a situation objectively, without reacting in a habitual self-serving way. If we give a little, we get a little and resolve the Stalemate.
7. The Dove stage is where one understands and works from higher Ideals rather than mere achievement of personal or group desires. With its ability to seek out hidden emotional problems, Scorpio can become The Healer – such as by using psychoanalysis as well as other methods. Attention to Heavenly matters.
8. The co-rulership of Scorpio by Pluto is said to be related to in-depth research into the secrets of Nature. This gives rise to new Concepts and Theories (Sagittarius, Cycle of Growth Stage 9 (Conception).
9. Whereas the 2nd. House refers to Personal Possessions, the complementary 8th. House refers to Other People's Possessions. It contains the message that we cannot exist alone. The 2nd. House refers to the development of the human body, and the 8th. House its final deterioration and Death.
10. Cycle of Growth Stage 8 (Sex. Death. Intercourse) shows ways of relating to others where the Whole becomes greater than the parts. Intercourse is the normal give-and-take of human life. As we give from our Taurus store, so we receive. We each find our place in a wider society.
11. Fixed Water is the emotional control that Scorpio has to teach. The Traditional ruling planet is Mars, God of War and Sex, that was required to bring new life in Aries. Here its Fire is controlled by Water. One of the dangers of Water Signs emphasised with Scorpio is the tendency to "stagnate" from lack of external stimulation.
12. Scorpio people have great self-control and rarely reveal their inner thoughts or feelings – although they will seek out yours. They are the Researchers and Detectives of The Zodiac. Their Mars weapon, or Scorpion Sting, is the ability to attack us at a deep emotional level with seeming neutral questions or statements that somehow hurt. Whilst Cancer withdraws into its shell, Fixed Water Scorpio will spend a lot of time planning how to repay real or imagined hurts without revealing themselves.
13. In The Scorpion we find the use of psychologists by advertisers to sell their products by manipulating our feelings and desires rather than by logical persuasions.
14. The Tarot Card XII.The Hanged Man shows the Stalemate achieved by XI.Justice. A "hung jury". To resolve the Dilemma requires the raising of Consciousness above the situation so that one can see the merits of both sides (Positive/Negative. Good/Evil). XIII.Death shows that, in the end, we are all Equal – that is, searching for the same thing.

GEMINI AND SAGITTARIUS

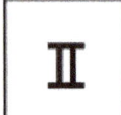   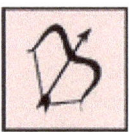

GEMINI (Mutable Air . The Twins. Personal Mental Concepts)

1. We are at Cycle of Growth Stage 3 (Experiment. Communication) at around age 2 to 4. Early Childhood.
2. Having developed control of a physical body, the next stage is that of Mental Development. This first begins by associating physical objects (which, from II.The Priestess and III.Empress now exist in memory) with words. Things – including people, and the child itself – get Names. The child therefore also becomes an "object" as the beginning of self-awareness..
3. Being related to the Jungian Thinking Function, Mutable (Changeable) Air is concerned with mental concepts, or Ideas. Gemini is concerned with Communication of all kinds – such as Speaking and

ASTROLOGY : SIGNS

Writing – also mental manipulation of objects, such as by using Mathematics. This is the commonly described "Rational Mind" which is based on information that is verifiable by using The 5 Senses (Sensation).

4. The symbol of The Twins is one of the two human figures - related ones. Traditionally, it refers to the twin stars Castor and Pollux. It is a symbol of Duality. We can see this as a function of the universal law that if something is created – even just an idea in the mind – its complement is also created to maintain the universal Zero Balance of energy. The Twins are of the same sex (or sexless). At this age there is no conscious differentiation.
5. One "Twinning" function of Gemini is to relate a mental concept to a physical object – to give it a Name that can be manipulated in the mind.
6. Another "Twinning" function is in the simplistic division of experience into "Opposites" such as "Right and Wrong", "Good and Bad" – manmade rules and laws which do not exist in Nature. However, they are suitable for retention by the young mind which cannot yet handle complicated explanations. At this age it therefore enables survival. We see in Libra, the next Air Sign in the sequence (mentioned above), that there is a need to re-evaluate these simplistic notions in the light of broader consciousness of life.
7. Gemini people have a continually active thinking mind, and are said to be "Jack of all trades, and master of none" due to their wide range of interests. They retain their child-like curiosity throughout life. However, they are not likely to get bogged down into fixed ways of thinking, and can act as "cross-pollinators" – such as by writing books like this.
8. The ruler of Gemini is Mercury, which relates to everything described here.
9. The related Tarot cards are IV.The Emperor (Power. Control) and V.The Hierophant (intellectual, moral, Right and Wrong) which together symbolise the masculine influences of the father who now becomes a conscious figure at this age.
10. In Genesis Eve was created from the "side" – or bias – of Adam whilst he was asleep (unconscious). Here we have the first creation of the "Gemini Twins" who are, as yet, sexually unaware. The seeds of the Jungian unconscious Anima and Animus.

SAGITTARIUS (Mutable Fire. The Archer. Social Mental Concepts)

1. This refers to Cycle of Growth Stage 9 (Conception). The Beginning of every thing.
2. In the Zodiac, Sagittarius The Archer/Hunter (The Centaur, half man, half horse) is the time of the conception of new life that may or may not eventually reach material form in the future. We note that Lady Diana Spencer described by her brother as "Diana The Huntress" had a Sagittarius Ascendant.
3. "I shot an arrow in the air, it fell to earth I know not where". [Henry Wadsworth Longfellow- albeit Sun Pisces]. (That's how I lose all my ***** arrows".)
4. Sagittarius makes numerous "New Year Resolutions" that never manifest.
5. "Conception" can be applied to the fertilisation of an egg which will eventually become a physical human, or the fertilisation of the human mind with an Original Idea. A "brain child" that might also, eventually, become a physical reality.
6. Sagittarius differs from Gemini because the concepts are abstract Theories, or guesses, – that is, not yet verified in one's own or group human experience. Gemini is "hands on" and concerned with personal experience. We note that all human inventions have a combination of both. This is the realm of Research, Religion, and Philosophy, as well as areas of life where such things are commonplace, such as churches, schools, universities, and books. We see another connection with Gemini in the use of written and spoken words. "In the beginning was The Word".
7. At a higher level, Sagittarius is a search for meaning to life. However, the tendency is to restlessly search in the external world rather than within the self.
8. With Mutable (Changeable. Active) Fire we also have the fields of Foreign Travel, Sport, and Entertainment, which take us out of our habitual surroundings to broaden our perception of the world around.
9. Sagittarius people have an abundance of energy and love of Change. They fill their lives with activity. They do not like any sense of restriction of their activities. Horse riding is a favoured activity – controlling the "animal" with the mind. Negatively, like Gemini, they can take on too many activities and

ASTROLOGY : SIGNS

not achieve any of their goals, or, worse still, overwork the physical body, which eventually fails in some way.

10. Sagittarius Fire is able to motivate, excite, and inspire. This is Novelty in its purest form.
11. The ruling planet is Jupiter (Expansion) which mainly operates at a social level and embodies the traits mentioned.
12. At a higher level we have Pluto in Sagittarius which relates to Sephirah 2 (Chockmah. Wisdom. Force) which refers to the original Big Bang of Creation which created Hydrogen and began to convert it to all the heavier physical elements we have today. The same nuclear reactions are still occurring in stars today – principally that of our Sun.
13. Whereas the 3rd. House of Gemini relates to "Personal Mental Concepts" the 9th.House relates to "Social Mental Concepts".
14. The related Tarot Card is XIV.Temperance. The figure has one foot on Earth and the other in Water and is pouring water from one cup to another. At one level this is a picture of The Higher mind's ability to impartially stand above "The Opposites" to evaluate their usefulness in relation to the current situation. At another it is the Plasma state of Matter where atoms are at extremely high temperatures and move around in random fashion – such as at the centre of stars.
15. At deeper levels this refers to the "separation of the waters" in the Biblical Story of Creation which produced Light (consciousness) and gave rise to the recognition of Day and Night.
16. The Element Fire (Intuition) is never far away from basic Archetypal Principles.

CANCER AND CAPRICORN

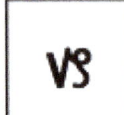

CANCER (Cardinal Water. The Crab. Personal Security. Shell. Roots)

1. We are now at Cycle of Growth Stage 4 (Transplanting. Roots) of The Cycle of Growth which refers to the around 4 to 7 years of age Play Age of Psychology when a child broadens its horizons and begins to relate to things and people outside the family home. Children discover their sex organs and discover boys and girls are not the same.
2. In Genesis, this is the time of "The Fall" when Adam is tempted by Eve to taste the fruits of The Tree of (carnal) Knowledge. They use fig leaves to cover their differences – which can be considered a symbol of the psychological Persona mask. They now become fully incarnate by being given "coats of skin" (another form of "shell"). Having separated from The Tree of (everlasting) Life they now have a body that will eventually wear out and die – The Tree of Knowledge, rather than The Tree of Life which regenerates itself. They are removed (Transplanted) from The Garden of Eden.
3. Stage 4 and the 4th. House is one of the 4 Crisis, or Stress Points of a chart which promote development and change. A step forward.
4. In the annual Sun cycle this relates to The Summer Solstice when, despite the warm conditions, the Light of The Sun begins to wane as days get shorter. The 4th. House is the lowest point of a Birth Chart. Having put down Roots (in the subconscious) the progress (of consciousness) is now upwards towards a broader viewpoint..
5. The symbolism of The Crab refers to the "Shell" of the home, as well as the "Shell" of the psychological Persona "mask" which enables us to operate in society without revealing our inner thoughts and feelings. We learn to "play parts" like an actor.
6. This is also the time of The Oedipus Complex when the child flirts with the parent of the opposite sex, and is rejected – and so is forced to find completion elsewhere.
7. The traditional Tarot Card VI.The Lovers is a depiction of the oedipal son being rejected by the mother to find "completion" outside the home. VII.The Chariot shows a man making safe progress inside his "persona shell" with his animal nature (Black and White Gemini "twin opposing horses") under conscious control.

ASTROLOGY : SIGNS

8. *... therefore doth a man leave his father and his mother, and hath cleaved unto his wife, and they have become one flesh."* [Genesis 2 verse 24]

9. Although Cancer is a Cardinal, Active, Sign (hence Transplanting) it is emotionally very sensitive. Like The Crab it does not face the world "head on" like Aries. It "makes progress sideways". Cautiously.

10. Cancer people have strong concerns for safety and security, and prefer to be in the "shell" of their own home. In Astrology this is related to Motherhood, where the "shell" is extended to give support and protection to others.

11. Cancer is related to The Moon, which has associations with Water inner feelings and emotions, as well as the Personal Unconscious, and women's menstrual cycle.

CAPRICORN (Cardinal Earth. The Mountain Goat. Social Security)

1. Cycle of Growth Stage 10 (Social Peak. Harvest) of The Cycle of Growth is opposite Stage 4 and therefore complementary in activity. The Birth Chart Houses contain the same meanings. This is best described as the common dilemma of "Career versus Home" which has become more prevalent in modern life with the change in traditional social male and female roles. It is like an actor having to perform 2 roles at the same time. In essence, this brings stress to relationships. Greater choice brings greater responsibility.

2. The Mountain Goat symbol refers to the time and effort required to "climb to the top" in one's Career. Despite being an Earth Sign, it traditionally has a fish's tail symbolising its unconscious content.

3. Whereas Cancer and the 4th. House refer to The Mother and "Personal Security", complementary Capricorn and the 10th. House refer to The Father and "Social Security".

4. This is the time of Christmas which celebrates the birth of the SON, Jesus, who, as The Messiah, also promised new life. Unfortunately people did not get the right message.

5. In the Annual Cycle this is the time of rebirth of the SUN at the Winter Solstice when despite the colder weather, the Light of the Sun is growing - with the days getting longer. The "dead" Winter time is promising new Life to come. This is emphasised at New Year's Day with the "rebirth" of a calendar year.

6. In a human lifetime, after Stage 9 (Conception) this is the beginning of our time of gestation in the womb. It is an expansion of awareness of the mother to now realise that she is pregnant, and the reaction of the father to the news, now and later on, is now known to have an effect on the developing foetus. Their relationship will never be the same again.

7. In the Christmas Story, when The King learned that there might be a new King to challenge his authority he ordered all new born children killed. This theme repeats that of the earlier birth of Moses, as well as the mythical tales of gods and goddesses, when fathers tended to swallow or otherwise try to do away with their young. The resolution in all cases was to resort to subterfuge and hide the children away until they were old enough to fend for themselves. In Jesus' case they fled the country, and after a brief appearance at age 12 where he was asking questions in the temple, he retired to seclusion until he made a public entry into Jerusalem at the beginning of his short ministry around age 33 where he was received joyfully by the crowd who were expected him as their Messiah. They wanted him to use his powers to solve all their problems for them, and do away with Roman rulership. At Cycle of Growth Stage 1 (Seed) his crucifixion is remembered at Easter Time which is at the beginning of Spring. That is, when the Spirit is "crucified on the cross of matter" by being forced to take material form.

8. At another level, the mental concepts ("brain children") symbolised by Cycle of Growth Stage 9 (Conception) are exemplified by the making of New Year Resolutions at this time. Because they contain the seeds of Change, many of those too do not survive. Perhaps they should just be preserved until Spring brings more favourable conditions.

9. After Cycle of Growth Stage 9 (Conception. The coming of The Messiah foretold) the lesson of Capricorn is concerned with the ability to make "long range plans" and work towards the envisioned goal over a long period of time. This is the ability to focus energy, and ignore side-issues that may divert one from the path. An image is that of the floor-sweeper that eventually becomes Chairman of The Board – rising to the top like "The Mountain Goat".

10. Capricorn is ruled by the planet Saturn/Satan which embodies all the properties mentioned. . The "Scapegoat" of those who suggest we have no free will.

ASTROLOGY : SIGNS

11. Tarot Cards XV.The Devil (Satan/material power) and XVI.The Tower (Lucifer, Bringer of Light. Consciousness) relate to the principle.

12. Capricorn rules all large organisations that have taken a long time to develop, such as big businesses and government. The common factor being the requirement of rules and regulations to organise large social structures. At another level it covers the unwritten traditions and laws which govern society. A problem with those structures is that they are so complex that it is difficult to adapt and change to different circumstances. Both Cancer and Capricorn share this trait. There is a certain fear of new influences, as if a small change will bring the whole structure tumbling down – as depicted in XVI.The Tower.

13. In individual terms, there can be the same attitude from older people who have become set in their ways. They have formed habits that are difficult to change. We see in the biblical story above the same resistance to Change.

14. In the following Sign, Aquarius, we see a challenge to Capricorn social structures where the individual finds his or her self too restricted. Examples of this in history are in the fall of great empires such as the Roman and British empires when the subjects rebelled because they were being taxed and getting nothing in return.

15. At a personal level, Capricorn/Saturn governs the rules and laws we make for ourselves, and the self-discipline required to maintain them. We have to form good habits and be prepared to change them when they have outlived their usefulness.

LEO AND AQUARIUS

LEO (Fixed Fire. The Lion. Personal Control of Energy)

1. Leo follows Cancer in the annual cycle. Having established a Persona, or psychological defensive "vehicle", we are able to develop the Ego Consciousness of "I Am".

2. Leo is the time of year when the Sun is at its hottest. We have the image of a male Lion surrounded by his lionesses (who do all the hunting) and cubs.

3. We are now at Stage 5 of The Cycle of Growth (Power. Creativity) which is the beginning of The 3rd. Octave at age 7 to 12. This is the Latency Stage of personal development, Erikson's "School Age" which contains no major physical changes. At this stage work is put before pleasure and we are evaluated by being compared with our peers.

4. In Genesis, this is the time of the birth of Cain and Abel and the first demonstration of sibling rivalry for God's favour. We note the story is concerned with God's judgement of what they produced as the fruits of their labours, in common with the social attitude at this time of life. Later on they will be judged relating to their ability to earn a living.

5. This is the beginning of the development of personal Ego Consciousness apart from what has been learned from parents. One has developed a Persona mask in Cancer and is able to Play (one's part). As time goes on, there will be the need to learn how to play other parts depending on the circumstances – whilst keeping one's inner integrity intact. To "render unto Caesar what is Caesar's, and to God what is God's".

6. Leo is ruled by The Sun which controls and is controlled by Nature in the changing of The Seasons. Its energy is filtered and transmuted by the Zodiac Sign of The Time. It is related to areas of life over which we have control, such as businesses and hobbies which we do for love rather than personal gain. Like The Sun, Leo people prefer to be the centres of attention and power.

7. The Tarot Card VII.Strength depicts a young woman, a feminine force, controlling a Lion. She has an infinity symbol above her head which symbolises the Higher (Creative. Fire) Mind controlling the lower elements. This symbol is in common with I.The Magician related to Aries, another Fire Sign at the beginning of The 2nd. Octave. The other Fire Sign, Sagittarius, at Cycle of Growth Stage 9 (Conception. The Archer, half man, half horse) has a similar symbolism where the figure has angelic qualities.

ASTROLOGY : SIGNS

8. The Symbols of The Time refer to masculine power and creativity being controlled by Mother Earth. With Leo people a little flattery goes a long way.

9. In Wicca they now take the fruits of "The First Harvest" of the year, make bread, and eat it – thus symbolically taking on godlike powers from the fruits of their labour – in effect, being co-creators with God.

10. The 5th. House is that of "Personal Creativity", which is balanced by 11th. House "Social Creativity" - which is the realm of "Friends" and acquaintances of like mind.

AQUARIUS (Fixed Air. The Water Carrier. Social Control of Energy)

1. Aquarius comes as a challenge to the structures and traditions of Capricorn. Sometimes Capricorn/Saturn overcomes Uranus and nothing changes.

2. Tarot XVI.The Tower (of Destruction) at Cycle of Growth Stage 10 can be considered as part of Stage 11 too. A "realisation" comes as a flash of lightning which destroys the structure built up by past efforts. New ideas are formed. Cards XVII.The Star and XVIII. The Moon are the conscious and unconscious reactions to the realisation that to express those ideas would invite social stigma. We see this symbolised in the escape of Jesus and his parents from Bethlehem, and his withdrawal from society until the right time.

3. The ruling planets of Aquarius are Saturn, which is concerned with traditional methods, ideas, and beliefs - and Uranus, which is concerned with new inventions and improvements. Saturn is the furthest planet visible to the unaided eye (consciousness), Uranus was discovered by the use of technology. Advanced Consciousness.

4. As an Air Sign Aquarius is related to Mental Development and the nervous system of the body (which carries "messages"). Its "Water Carrier" symbol can be considered as a "Cloud" which carries rain Water to all parts of the Earth. It is related, among other things, to Communication in Fixed form, such as writing and computer messages. We note the correspondence with The Computer Age of Aquarius, Mobile Telephones, and the Internet "Cloud". We can see how traditional Astrology would have difficulty understanding The Sign in its relationship with The Computer Age of Aquarius – especially as it was then ruled by Saturn.

5. The symbol of Aquarius is that of 2 electronic wave forms in harmony as seen on a spectroscope or computer. The "brain waves" of 2 people are synchronised. The symbol of Uranus is very similar to the "H" shape of the first television aerial. [ASTROLOGY : PLANETS]

6. The new planet co-ruler Uranus is concerned with the development of Will and related to Jungian Individuation.

7. In Leo we, and our roles, are the creations of our parents. In Aquarius we re-invent ourselves.

8. "Broadcasting" is a method of sowing seeds in Agriculture.

9. The Sign is related to Cycle of Growth Stage 11 (Discontent. Individuality. Will) . In The 1st. Octave, while we are in the womb, it is controlled by Saturn in the development of an individual human body, separate from the mother and The Collective – especially the nervous system. At this Stage there is no Will. In the Transcendent Octave it is concerned with the development of Will, and Individuation.

10. In The Kabbalah Tree of Life The Leo Sun is at Sephirah 6 (Tiphareth. Beauty) on The Middle Pillar where it is the centre of consciousness. Stage 11 Uranus is related to the previously un-numbered Sephirah Daath, above Tiphareth, also on The Middle Pillar - which we can now relate to Uranus Will and Individuation as the path across The Abyss.

11. In traditional Astrology the 11th. House is that of "Friends" – who are the people we relate to as a matter of personal choice, and treat as equals (Aquarius) rather than subjects (Leo). There are associations with the growth of Civilisations and Democracy.

12. Many rebels set out to destroy Capricorn/Saturn social structures and fail because they have nothing real to replace them. They want control rather than Democracy.

ASTROLOGY : SIGNS

VIRGO AND PISCES

  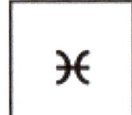 

VIRGO (Mutable Earth. The Virgin. Personal Service. Health)

1. Following the Leo period of creativity we are able to evaluate the results in terms of practical usefulness and survival. As Earthy Taurus restricts the impulses of Aries and forces the seed to put down roots, Virgo restricts the creations of Leo to what is more socially acceptable. Leo, Sign of "The Actor" enables us to experiment with different roles whilst still being supported by the family.
2. Virgo is the time of year when man begins to see the fruits of his labour. Although the Virgin is a feminine, earthy, symbol, she contains the seeds of potential for new growth.
3. This is Stage 6 of The Cycle of Growth (Service to Self. Health and Erikson's Adolescent Stage (Freud's Genital Stage) – the beginning of puberty at age 13. We have the onset of hormonal sexual drives – the potential for bringing new life – as yet, virginal. The focus of activity is among peer groups and finding one's social role apart from what parents may expect.
4. Virgo, as is Gemini, is ruled by Mercury. Here the mind is focused on the physical body, and Sensation rather than more abstract Thinking.
5. Among other things, Virgo is the Sign of "The Craftsman" - symbolising one's choice of occupation to earn a living, and developing appropriate skills, and "The Critic" – which indicates the mental attention Virgo subjects give to minute details in a search for "perfection". Often they worry themselves into ill health over minor details that most of us would feel to be insignificant. This is the Sign of Hypochondria.
6. The 6th. House is related to "Personal Service" (we can see the connection with Health). The complementary 12th. House is related to "Social Service", and The Collective Unconscious. The balance is in achieving a sense of vocation, or idealism, in one's daily activities in service to others. Balancing The Individual with The Collective. It is a highly personal issue. Without social support we would all have to be hunter gatherers or farmers.
7. It is interesting to compare the association between Health (Virgo) and the use of drugs (Pisces).
8. The Tarot Card IX.The Hermit refers to "isolation by a secret" and Erikson's stage of the formation of an inner personal identity. "Who Am I ?". The focus is more on the Feeling Function.
9. Virgo is our first awareness of our Personal Unconscious (as distinct from the Pisces Collective Unconscious) which will tend to inwardly challenge our conscious aims.
10. In Genesis, Cain killed his brother and was eventually driven out of the family home to make a life for himself. Scholars say that this relates to the time of man's evolutionary migration from Africa and the beginning of the first civilisation in Babylon and Mesopotamia. In psychological terms, the child separates further from its "roots" and expands consciousness to include the human civilisation of which it is a part.
11. The story of Cain and Abel describes the personal scenario of choosing a suitable job – or role - to make a living. Like Gemini, they are the same sex – however, the roles are different.

PISCES (Mutable Water. The Fishes. The Collective Unconscious)

1. If Uranus is successful in overcoming Saturn resistance to Chang in Aquarius, the old structures and habits of Capricorn/Saturn must be allowed to dissolve in Pisces. Long established habits are hard to break.
2. Pisces is the time just before Spring when preparations are being made for the rebirth of the natural world. The seeds are lying dormant waiting for warmth and moisture to help them germinate.
3. In the human Cycle of Growth Stage 12 (Withdrawal. Confinement) this is the time of confinement of the mother in preparation for the birth of her child. She is less physically able to move around, and is more in psychic communication with her child than she will ever be again.

ASTROLOGY : SIGNS

4. Pisces rules places of confinement and retreat such as Hospitals, Prisons, and Monasteries – and Mental Institutions. It is also concerned with Art, Music and Dance as expressions of The Spirit – as distinct from rational logic and words.

5. In the Tarot we have XIX.The Sun as symbol of the birth of consciousness, and XX.Judgement as symbol of release from bondage and answering the "call" to new life.

6. Jesus entered Jerusalem to the welcoming crowd on "Palm Sunday" – eventually to be rejected by them and crucified on the Cross of Matter.

7. The traditional ruling planet of watery Pisces is Jupiter (Expansion) which relates to the expansion of consciousness via external collectives such as human Societies and Civilisations. Jupiter also rules Sagittarius at Cycle of Growth Stage 9 (Conception. Fire) - so it is active at the beginning and end of pregnancy. Churches and religious bodies are more related to Sagittarius/Jupiter (academic, theoretical knowledge), and places of teaching and social entertainment than Pisces (Water. inner retreat).

8. The new ruling planet, Neptune, is concerned with enlightenment from within, and our connection with the "sea" of The Collective Unconscious. Although, traditionally, Pisces is said to be highly "spiritual", we note that all Zodiac Signs have lessons to teach as integral parts of the whole. In fact, there are dangers with Neptune/Pisces in that they should not be contacted without having a firm sense of Self Integrity (as described in Virgo above). The pure energy here is opposed to individuality of any description. It is continually attempting to draw everything back to the Number Zero state before the Singularity which resulted in The Big Bang. It can be symbolised as a "Black Hole" in space. Pisces/Neptune is the source of Imagination and Illusion.

9. We see the relationship between the Sea of Pisces and its Fishes symbol.

10. Neptune is related to Sephirah 1 (Kether. Crown. Number Zero) of The Tree of Life, which is the state of balance that existed before The Big Bang set Creation in motion. At that stage everything in the universe existed in one undifferentiated form. We see a relationship with the concept of The Collective Unconscious of C.G.Jung. It is suggested that this is the source and final goal of Creation.

11. This is the realm of Psychology. In human terms, Pisces/Neptune is concerned with attempts to reach altered states of consciousness (or escapism from the conscious material world) by meditation, or the use and abuse of alcohol and other drugs. At another level we have psychic development which contains similar dangers. I have experience of that field, where a main discipline is developing the ability to "switch off" when required. We also have mental institutions for people who have lost contact with Virgo. Are they more spiritual ?

12. Pisces people are sensitive and retiring, and not particularly strong willed. Because of their sensitivity they can be "taken over" by stronger personalities, and will absorb the "atmosphere" of their surroundings – so they need to choose their environment with care. They will take on lowly or menial jobs, such as caring for others, from a sense of obligation or empathy with those concerned – even though those people could or should do things for themselves. Lacking Virgo discrimination, and from their psychic ability for natural empathy, they can easily be swayed by a sad story.

13. We see a similarity between Pisces and the other Water Signs, Cancer and Scorpio, which are also concerned with self-protection from The Collective Unconscious. Without the Shell of Cancer, or the Control of Scorpio, Pisces can only retreat.

14. As the end of a cycle, the "dissolving" effect of Pisces/Neptune is to clear away the decayed, no longer useful, remains of the past ready for a new Spring. It has association with Karma and "forgiving and forgetting" past problems, with, perhaps, some form of atonement in the institutions mentioned above.

15. In Pisces is the principle of Forgiveness of self and others in order to put the past behind, and go forward. We can all promise to do better next time. Mistakes, after all, are a necessary part of the learning processes of life. Some organisations spend millions of pounds employing people to make mistakes.

16. In the same way that we are normally unaware of the Air that surrounds us, despite using it for Communication, also, like fishes, we are unaware of "The Sea".

ASTROLOGY : SIGNS

ASTROLOGY : THE ZODIAC AGES

AGES	ELEMENT	FROM	TO	HISTORY	CYCLE OF GROWTH STAGE
Leo	Fixed Fire	11720 BC	9550 BC	Summer heat. End of the last Ice Age	Stage 5 (Power. Creativity)
Cancer	Cardinal Water	9550 BC	7380BC	Farming and small communities.	Stage 4 (Transplanting. Roots)
Gemini	Mutable Air	7380BC	5210 BC	Mesopotamia "experimental city".	Stage 3 (Experiment. Communication)
Taurus	Fixed Earth	5210 BC	3040 BC	The plough. Mining. Cuneiform. The wheel	Stage 2 (Germination. Earth. Nature)
Aries	Cardinal Fire	3040 BC	870 AD	Pyramids. Stone circles. Conquest. Iron	Stage 1 (Seed. Status symbols)
Pisces	Mutable Water	870	1300	Monotheism. Roman Empire fall. Church rulership	Stage 12 (Withdrawal. Confinement)
Aquarius	Fixed Air	1300	3470	Printing. Electronic communication. Democracy	Stage 11 (Discontent Invention.Thinking)
Capricorn	Cardinal Earth	3470	5640	World Government ("1984" ?)	Stage 10 (Social Peak. Harvest)

Figure 31 : Zodiac Ages Summary

This chapter is written :
1. To show the presence of cycles beyond the scope of this book.
2. To give another viewpoint on the symbolism of the Signs.
3. To dispel some of the nonsensical information that appears on the subject. To examine the effects of past Ages we merely need to observe what was happening at the time. This is made difficult by lack of records from the past, but we only need to look out of our window to see what is happening today.
4. In researching this chapter it has become very noticeable that the Zodiac Ages have a strong connection with the development of the Calendar that we use today. (please see the [THE CALENDAR] chapter). The Calendar is one thing that, apart from the measurement of time, is global in effect.
5. To continue in our examination of the activity of the Archetypes. By seeing what humans were/are doing during the Zodiac Ages we can get an idea of what "The Spirit of the Time" was. It is a fact that at certain times the same new inventions appear in different, unconnected, parts of the world at the same time. There is often conflict as to who "discovered it first". One example of this is of Charles Darwin's "Origin of the Species" which he delayed publication whilst seeking improvements. He was prompted to publish earlier than he wished because Alfred Russel Wallace had arrived at similar conclusions. I wonder who else is writing this book now.

When examined in this context a pattern emerges of the stages of human development from hunter gatherer, to settler, to warring individuals, to warring nations and conquest, to differences settled by democratic methods. When we follow the routes of Homo Sapiens in the migration from Africa 90,000 years we see that, somehow, the places last colonised – such as Britain, Europe, and America, are now the most advanced. Other places in the world seem to still be "catching up" – going through phases the others have passed. The prime example of this is Africa itself, which still contains tribes of Bushmen of the hunter gatherer type, and Mesopotamia\Babylon - now Iraq – which was the first stopping place out of Africa, and the first ever large city (said to be first settled by Cain), and has now regressed to the earlier stage of dictatorship and internal conflict.

It must be something in the genes. Scientists have mapped the migration journey by collecting DNA samples on a global basis and checking for mutations from those of the original source. The further away from the African source, the greater number of mutations are found – different ones depending on the routes followed.

ASTROLOGY : THE ZODIAC AGES

PRECESSION OF THE EQUINOXES

Precession of the Equinoxes occurs because the spinning Earth has a regular "wobble" rather like a gyroscope. Its axis is tilted, and rotates anti-clockwise, taking around 26,000 years to make a full rotation - which allows an average of 2,170 years for each of the 12 Ages. The "Earth's Axis" is a purely imaginary line connecting, and extending beyond, the North and South poles. At present the North pole is pointing to the star now called Polaris (originally called *Cynosura*) but this has not always been the case.

OVERVIEW : FIXING THE WHEEL IN TIME

Due to precession the Sun no longer rises at 0 degrees of Aries on the day of the Spring Equinox. At present the Sign rising at the equinox is Aquarius, but the exact degree is not known. We are therefore currently within the "Age of Aquarius". My research has not uncovered any consensus of the actual timing of the Ages – nor any reasons for the choices made - so my estimate will be as good as anyone else's . We can use some historical information and symbolism of the Signs, as well as look what is happening today, to get a better idea.

Some people have used this fact to suggest that Astrology is not accurate. Apart from their obvious practical ignorance of the subject, they miss the point that the Zodiac Signs have nothing to do with anything outside the Solar System. They are imaginary divisions of Time and Space RELATIVE TO EARTH AS A CENTRAL POINT which enable us to accurately place the planet positions at any moment in time. The original purpose was to define a Calendar, which has evolved into our 12 month system. The Zodiac "space-time clock" is reset to zero degrees of Aries each year at sunrise on the Spring Equinox, and the annual cycle divided into 12 x 30 degree parts using that as the base. . The proof of this is that this is always the beginning of Spring and Nature's annual Cycle of Growth on Earth.

We note that the principle of the Zodiac Signs of Astrology is that they are symbols of the variations of solar energy as experienced on Earth. The energy of the Sun itself is always constant.

The Zodiac system is, in effect, an arbitrary system on the same principle as the division of the Earth by imaginary "lines" of Latitude and Longitude where zero degrees of each has been fixed by "common agreement". Like the Lines, the Signs do not actually exist.

The popular song "The Age of Aquarius" has no meaning in Astrological context. For example :

1. "The Moon is in the Seventh House" - refers to an astrological chart of some sort. The Moon goes through a complete cycle every 29 days. In theory 1 in 12 Birth Charts would have Moon in 7th. House. The Transiting Moon is in the 7th. House of any chart every 29 days.
2. "Jupiter aligns with Mars" – as the faster planet with a 2 year cycle, Mars aligns with Jupiter (Conjunction Aspect) in its 12 year cycle every 2 years or so.

I have used the following basic pieces of information to define dates for the Ages :-

1. I have looked for the earliest dates possible. A difficulty is that changes at the beginning of an Age occur in one place on the surface of our planet and can take hundreds of years to spread to the rest. The final results of an Age seem to be at the end, when its influence is finally global in extent. As with our annual seasons, there are no sharp or clear divisions between Ages.
2. We know that, following earlier beginnings, the 12 Zodiac star patterns were fixed and named when Aries WAS rising on the day of the Spring Equinox. By knowing when modern Astrology originated, we can give an approximate date to the Age of Aries. The best consensus is between 3000 and 2000 BC.
3. With an overall 26,000 year cycle the average length of each Age is 2,170 years. Adding this to Aries above brings us to somewhere between 1000 BC and 170AD for the beginning of the Age of Pisces. It is tempting to use the birth of Jesus in 1 AD, but, as we shall see, he is part of a bigger picture – and it would mean that we are not yet into Aquarius.
4. The Age of Aries coincides with the period of the building of earth monuments such as pyramids and henges – including Stonehenge – and the sudden abandonment of the activity. In Mesopotamia they built Ziggurats from 2200 to 600BC, and Egyptian pyramids were built from 2630 to 664 BC. In keeping with the general historical pattern, the practice spread to other parts of the world. This was also the beginning of the smelting of metals that require high temperatures, and The Iron Age, which is a feature of Aries. You will see how this fits in with the symbolism of Aries below.

The oldest part of Stonehenge was built during the period from 3000 to 2935 BC [EB]

ASTROLOGY : THE ZODIAC AGES

5. The following Age of Pisces is mainly characterised by the replacement of numerous gods and goddesses by The One God – Monotheism - and the birth of Jesus which gave the world a consensus for the counting of Years for the first time. Its beginning coincides with the fall of The Roman Empire – which was based on the military conquest methods of the previous Age – Aries/Mars "God of War". FROM THIS TIME WE SEE A GRADUAL TRANSFER OF GLOBAL POWER FROM KINGS AND EMPERORS TO THE CHURCH.

6. With the development of the Calendar being an important connection to the changing ages, the introduction of the Gregorian Calendar in 1582 is another important marker for the beginning of the Aquarian Age. As the One God replaced the many in the Age of Pisces, the One Calendar replaces the many and the Individual person – symbolic of the Sign - becomes more important in the Age of Aquarius.

7. There is agreement that we are now at the early stages of the Age of Aquarius. We can readily observe that we have entered a new Age with rapid change driven by growth in Technology, and Computers, with a focus on improved methods of Communication causing industrial and global revolution – all of which is in keeping with the ancient symbolism and meaning of the Sign. I remember it described in an early Astrological text as a time of "telepathy" – or thought transference – which, in effect, it is. "Being on the same wavelength".

8. Although there is more historical data from The Age of Pisces, I use the Age of Aquarius as the basis of timing the others because the dating of The Renaissance (rebirth) Period around 1300 AD seems much more reliable, and in keeping with the symbolism of the Age. The printing press was invented in 1453 AD, which is in keeping with the idea of Communication and Broadcasting information in words (an agricultural method of sowing seeds) and "The Water Carrier" carrying information by the "airwaves" – as is the later growth of electronic communication from the Telegraph, through Radio and Television, to Computers.

9. We have evidence of the beginning of the "New Age" of Aquarius at the end of the "Middle Ages" and beginning of the "Renaissance Period" which arose in Italy in the 14th. Century and spread to the rest of Europe by the 16th. and 17th. Centuries. The Middle Ages began in 500 AD with the fall of the Roman Empire. Rome was sacked by Alaric the Visigoth in 410 AD - which began "The Dark Ages" or "Early Middle Ages" which lasted until around 1000 AD. With the fall of Rome there was a return to the old feudal principles and method of government and a fragmented agricultural lifestyle. The intellectual and cultural life was again dominated by the Church (Pisces). We can see that, despite the gloomy view of some scholars, the Age of Pisces was not as "dark" as they paint it – unless it really means "hidden in the background". Its history is entirely in keeping with Cycle of Growth Stage 12 (Withdrawal. Confinement) and its symbolic association with Winter and the time preceding birth. The Aquarian Renaissance that followed was concerned with breaks with ancient tradition. Its main focus was "Humanism" which was concerned with the dignity and worth of the Individual, rather than subservience to Church or State - all of which is in keeping with Aquarius, which brings revolution and change, and has a connection with Jungian Individuation and his Thinking Function (Air Element). Following this was the "Reformation" which involved radical changes in the Christian church, and the growth of the Protestant church as a challenge to Roman Catholicism – especially concerning the use of "normal" languages instead of Latin (Communication).

10. John Wycliffe began translation of The Bible into English. He was accused of heresy by the Pope, and had to escape to Germany to avoid being burned at the stake. He translated parts of The New Testament into English in 1378 and "the word" (Aquarius) was later spread further by the invention of the Gutenberg printing press in 1453 AD. These events, again, are related to Aquarius as an Air Sign. The Air Signs are concerned with the Jungian Thinking Function and Communication. With the growing availability of more, and cheaper, books, the common person would now begin learning to read and develop their Thinking Function. There are only few remaining copies of his Bible because the church destroyed all they could find. Despite the suggestion that the later King James Bible was the work of a committee of experts, students of the subject, having access to some of Wycliffe's translations, are satisfied that they used his translation wherever possible.

11. Arriving at the present day we have "The Computer Age" – which, at base level, is concerned with Communication. Even though the ancients could have no idea of how this would actually manifest itself, we find that their symbolism is appropriate. Even the image of "The Water Carrier" is appropriate when we consider the development of radio and television, which carry information by using "the air waves".

We also now have the Internet. In Nature, another "water carrier" is a cloud, which stores and distributes water. In 1970 the "Cloud Diagram" was first used to picture telephone networks, and the computer "Cloud" is gradually becoming a greater part of our lives as a medium of information storage.

12. Finally, we can make some guesses about what the future might bring in the next Age of Capricorn.

PSYCHOLOGY OF THE AGES

We must take note of the fact that, as well as there being a difference in lifestyle, the psychology, or mentality, of the people of the Ages would have been very different to that of today. Scientists make this point when studying the physical brain sizes of our ancestors – although not in the same way. Recent DNA evidence [DNA] – Dr. Spencer Wells 2003 - has shown that a tribe of bushmen living a hunter-gatherer life in Africa today have DNA which must be very similar to that of the very first man. It contains markers that everyone alive today has, but not the later ones.

A focus of the current Age of Aquarius has been the development of the Jungian Thinking Function which has been accelerated by the ability to communicate by means of the written word (Aquarius. Fixed Air Sign). We have "The 3 Rs" – Reading, wRiting, and aRithmetic which have developed from this. We first had the development of the printing press, so common people gained access to books and schools, and we now have computers with Emails, Twitter and Facebook. It has been recently said that in China there is now a new "Nerd Generation" who do not meet in person at all, and that this has contributed to a fall in their birth rate.

INTUITION

Dealt with in more detail in the chapter [PSYCHOLOGY : THE 4 FUNCTIONS]

From C.G.Jung we learn that **how the brain is used** is more important than size. We all have the 4 Functions inbuilt but use them in different ways. There is a natural personal bias towards using a main Function with the others as subsidiaries. A main point here is that, whatever our natural bias, we tend to be forced by our upbringing and society to favour the development of one or two Functions rather than others – which may be contrary to our natural bias. In modern times the Thinking Function is highly regarded. Because of their way of life, the bushman's psychology has changed very little over time. They have no books or computers to develop their Thinking Function. There is an idea that they do not need mobile phones because they communicate at a different level. We can also consider modern day Aborigines in the same context.

The point here is that, from this, there is evidence today that in mankind's early days the Intuition Function was the main one. Further evidence is from observation of babies, and the recognition that their development in the womb and soon after birth mimics the whole process of Evolution, beginning with "blobs of jelly". So in a child's early days on earth we get an idea of what early man was like. At this time we have pure animal Instinct (Freud's "Id") – The Fire Element that develops into Intuition, as the other 3 Functions develop, depending on the environment. Further evidence is in some countries where children that lose their parents, and have to fend for themselves, they remain in an animal-like state where survival is the main aim.

G.J. Jung stated that the Mid Life Crisis, the beginning of Individuation, at age 42 was the time when the "inferior Function" (complement to the main Function) – still undeveloped from not being used fully – needed to be developed. We note that our early ancestors rarely lived much beyond age 30.

GENESIS

We therefore cannot understand why our ancestors did things because there was, actually, no "reason" as we know it today, because this relates to the rational Thinking Function. Their actions were more intuitive and instinctive. Animal – like. This proposition brings us to a better understanding of the coming to awareness of Adam and Eve in The Garden of Eden, in the Book of Genesis. [THE GENESIS STORY].

AGE OF LEO 11,720-9,550 BC

Cycle of Growth Stage 5 (Power. Creativity)

The symbolism of Leo is related to the full power of the Summer Sun in July and August. In our history the last ice age (Last Global Maximum) was around 20,000 years ago from which time global warming began to melt the ice to eventually increase sea levels by over 400 feet and, although there was a brief 1,000 year drop in temperature ("The Younger Dryas") beforehand, reached more liveable temperatures around 10,000 years ago. DNA and archaeological evidence shows that, after a slow recovery, the world population of Homo Sapiens then increased at a faster rate, which eventually forced them to leave their ice age refuges to find new areas to settle - Cycle of Growth Stage 4 (Transplanting).

AGE OF CANCER 9,550-7,380 BC

Cycle of Growth Stage 4 (Transplanting. Roots)

THE SYMBOLISM OF CANCER – CARDINAL WATER

The symbolism of The Crab basically refers to our need for a "shell" or some form of protection. A safe place to retire to. Its other meanings relate to such things as inherited characteristics and genealogy. At another level are our early Roots – our home and family in childhood including our mother or other protective figures. At still another level this refers to our persona, or "mask" (or shield) that we need in everyday life to enable our psychological self-defence and overall Sense of Security. The Cycle of Growth Stage 4 with its more dynamic nature, is called "Transplanting" which emphasises the need to occasionally move home and put down new roots in surroundings that will give better opportunity for growth beyond that which has been achieved so far. We can see that this Age is entirely in keeping with this concept as the warmer climate encouraged Homo Sapiens to multiply, and forced him to find new places to live.

Mankind was also enabled to stop a life of continual wandering and settle down (transplant) in groups, build dwellings, and put down the roots that later on evolved into larger civilisations. The beginnings of greater co-operation. The formation of clans. Transplanting was still necessary as the growth in population forced movements to new areas of settlement. This corresponds to the Psychological "Play Age" from 4 to 7 years of age when we begin to separate from our birth home and explore more of the outside world.

There is also a focus on the building of fences and walls which perform a dual purpose – keeping things in, and keeping things out. At one level this aids development by providing a safe environment for growth to occur, as well as provide a focus of control. At another level, when growth does occur, walls can prove to be a restriction to expansion. Hence the need for periodic Transplanting – especially as children grow up and need their own "space".

I have to make note here of a seeming connection between the Sign of Cancer, which is the element of Water in its Active state (being a negative polarity element it tends to withdraw rather than expand outwards) and the growth of Mesopotamia which historians emphasise was largely due to its position between two large rivers which could be used for irrigation. In any mention of growth in civilisations – such as the Romans building of aqueducts – Water control is a key factor in human development. The decline of this area in modern times was mainly a result of reduced rainfall.

Once again there is a focus on the Mesopotamian fertile crescent area as a point of origin for new developments. Possibly due to the warmer climate there. Possibly due to a more advanced civilisation better equipped to survive. This was the beginning of the geological Holocene Epoch which continues today. At this time the giant mammals became extinct. The suggestion is that they were hunted to extinction by the increasing human population – which had to find new food sources, although such large collections of bones have been found to suggest that it was slaughter for the sake of it. Archaeologists believe that the first settlements appeared in Mesopotamia around 10,000 BC.

Archaeological evidence indicates that the transition from food-collecting cultures to food-producing ones gradually occurred across Asia and Europe from a starting point in the Fertile Crescent. Cultivation and animal domestication first appeared in south western Asia by about 9000 BC, and a way of life based on farming and settled villages had been firmly achieved by 7000 BC in the Tigris and Euphrates river valleys (now in Iraq and Iran). [EB]

THE MESOLITHIC AGE. HUNTER GATHERER TO FARMER

As we proceed in our investigations it becomes very noticeable that archaeologists have great difficulty in deciding what their Ages are, and when they start and finish. With our Zodiac Ages we can be a little more accurate and focus on specific issues. Within Cancer is contained the principle of Enclosure as a means of focusing energy and defence. People build fences and walls to enclose land and build homes to enclose themselves - so enabling a focus and concentration of energy.

> *..... Eventually, the term "Mesolithic" (Middle Stone Age) was coined to cover this period in Europe, and by the 1880s some cultures which spanned the period had been identified, from about 8500 to 7000 BC in*

the Near East but lasting till the 4th millennium in Britain (when Neolithic technology arrived from the continent). [MSE]

*The Mesolithic hunter achieved a greater efficiency than did the Paleolithic and was able to exploit a wider range of animal and vegetable food sources.[EB]

*Because the Mesolithic Period is characterized by a suite of material culture, its timing varies depending upon location. In north western Europe, for instance, the Mesolithic began about 8000 BC and lasted until about 2700 BC.[EB]

AGE OF GEMINI 7380-5210 BC

Cycle of Growth Stage 3 (Experiment. Communication)

THE SYMBOLISM OF GEMINI – MUTABLE AIR

The Gemini symbol of The Twins, as with the other Air Signs, is one of the few non-animal or more human images in the Zodiac. It therefore suggests that it contains more human traits than instinctive, animal ones. Gemini also suggests duality and separation.

Gemini is an Air Sign. Among numerous other things, the Element of Air is concerned with mental development and the Jungian Thinking Function. Its main function is that of Communication. We can readily see how Air is used when we communicate directly with one another using sound and words, it is not quite so apparent when we communicate electronically or in writing – which relates more to the (Fixed Air) Aquarian Age.

Another concern of Gemini is "Short Journeys" and roads – an important means of local communication and trade.

Gemini is especially concerned with Thinking, Logic, and practical "hands on". The Sign rules the hands and arms, and brain, of our body which as seeming left/right "opposites" enable work to be done. Scientific and practical experimentation. At another level Gemini contains the mental concepts of "Opposites" – such as good/bad, right/wrong – which at that level enable mental work to be done. Its complementary sign, Sagittarius, a Fire Sign, has more academic concerns, and relates to Abstract Thinking. Gemini tests Sagittarian concepts and theories by communication and action. From the higher, broader, viewpoint of Sagittarius the "Opposites" lose their separate identity and become "Complements". Sagittarius has association with "Long Journeys" and "foreign travel".

Research shows that some Astrological writers have fallen into the trap of ascribing the beginnings of writing to this Age. It is clear, however, that writing did not begin until Cuneiform appeared around 3000 BC in the Age of Aries. During the Age of Gemini people would not have had much to write about, considering that the first city, Uruk, was not formed until its end in 5000 BC. Gemini is Mutable (Changeable) Air, Aquarius is Fixed Air.

In my chapters [THE GENESIS STORY] and [PSYCHOLOGY : DEVELOPMENT MODELS] there is evidence that one of the main concerns of Gemini in human child growth is that of mental development, and, in particular, naming things and developing a vocabulary with which to communicate. Mental concepts must arise before the need to write them down.

In our historical journey we can see that freedom from the continual need to hunt for food gives us time for other pursuits. We can also see that large numbers of people gathering together need ever more sophisticated methods of communication, new concepts and ideas in order to become organised, new words for objects that never existed before.

Once again, rather than trying to give examples from a subject I know very little about, I offer this extract from a book by Paul Kriwaczek called "Babylon – Mesopotamia and the Birth Of Civilisation". Written in 2010, it really sums up the meaning of the Age of Gemini and Cycle of Growth Stage 3 (Experiment. Communication) :-

*It cannot be denied that the riverine environment around the two great Middle Eastern streams did demand collaboration in irrigation works to ensure its settlers. And that somehow this led to the invention of city life. The rest is history, as the cliché has it. From its mysterious, shadowy beginnings until its final, well documented in the end, ancient **Mesopotamia acted as a kind of experimental laboratory for civilisation**, testing, often to destruction, many kinds of religion, from early personifications of natural forces to full blown temple priesthood and even the first stirrings of Monotheism; a wide variety of economic and production systems, from (their own version of) state planning and centralised direction to *(their own style of) neo-liberal privatisation, as well as an assortment of government systems, from primitive democracy and consultative monarchy to ruthless tyranny and expensive imperialism. Almost every one of these can be paralleled with similar features found in our own more recent history. It sometimes seems as if the whole ancient story served as a dry run, a dress rehearsal, for the succeeding civilisation, our own, which would originate in the Greece of Periclean Athens after the demise of the last Mesopotamian empire in the sixth century BCE, which has brought us to where we stand today.*

Though the experimenters of antiquity or long dead, their names largely forgotten, their homes buried, their possessions scattered, their fields barren, their temple towers ruined, their cities interred under mounds of dust, their empires remembered, if at all, by name only, this story still promises to teach us much about how we arrived at the way we live now. History may not repeat itself but, as Mark Twain said, it does rhyme. [BAB]

The Tarot card residents of the Cycle of Growth Stage 3 are IV.The Emperor (King) and V.The Hierophant (Priest). As we have seen, both these powers appeared for the first time during this Age. The solitary hunter gatherer had no need for them – or time to become one.

POPULATION GROWTH. CO-ORDINATING EFFORTS. COMMUNICATION. TRADE.

With people gathering together and learning to co-operate there is expansion of population. Villages become towns, towns become cities. The roles of individual people have to change. One does not now need to be Hunter and Soldier and Farmer to survive – so there is greater specialisation in the tasks required for daily living. One takes on a job that benefits everyone, perhaps more suited to one's individual preferences and abilities, and receives other services in return. Specialisation of tasks leads to greater efficiency, with technological development a natural outcome.

In addition, large scale projects can be undertaken that would be impossible (and unnecessary) for an individual. Mesopotamia had Public Works, such as water supply and sewerage. Here we have the example of irrigation improving efficiency in food production still further. Being a hot country, and their rainfall being unreliable, Mesopotamia had to use its two nearby rivers, the Tigris and Euphrates. This, in effect, forced co-operation.

*The need for irrigation and self-defence led the ancient Mesopotamians to organize and build canals and walled settlements. After 6000 BC the settlements grew, becoming cities by the 4th millennium BC [MERL]

As a product of this growth a new social structure is required. Whole new classes of people evolve who do not need to spend time seeking food or shelter for themselves – it was supplied by others.

We also get whole new sets of people who do not have to do any manual labour to make a living. Large groups of people require some kind of organisation. So we get such as the "Ruling Classes" and bureaucrats. The Kings, Priests and Thinkers. Not only do such people make a living without a normal job, they are able to mobilise huge numbers of people to take part in projects that have no bearing whatsoever on mere survival – such as the building of palaces, temples, and tombs. As a Sun Gemini I often wonder that I have survived so far without having to grow my own food or make anything to barter or sell.

At this time there was also a limited use of copper metal which was improved later on with the addition of tin to make bronze alloy.

*An earlier phase (in the 5th and 4th millennia BC or even before), when copper metallurgy was being adopted by Neolithic cultures in the Near East and south-eastern Europe, is sometimes called the Copper Age (or "Chalcolithic" or "Eneolithic"). Copper, obtained from nodules of locally available copper or from copper ores, was used to make ornaments and weapons (such as flat axe-blades), but was too soft or brittle to be truly useful. [MERL]

AGE OF TAURUS 5210-3040 BC

Cycle of Growth Stage 2 – GERMINATION

The Earth has been ploughed and sown. The Earth nurtures the Seed. Man learns to control the Earth. The Child learns to control its physical body and environment. The Freudian "Anal Stage". The first city has been formed ready for further development. At another level this is the realm of Business Management.

ASTROLOGY : THE ZODIAC AGES

THE SYMBOLISM OF TAURUS – FIXED EARTH

Our basic source of energy is our Sun. It is the relationship between the Sun and Earth that brings energy to physical manifestation, and enables growth. Each of the Zodiac Signs is an expression of a different FORM of energy. Taurus, as the most stable, material Sign, is concerned with using energy to build physical structures that enable escape from the confines of Earth and reach towards "heaven". Examples of such structures are the stems of plants and the human body – as well as, it seems from evidence of this time, temples and other constructions built for religious purposes. A message from ancient times has been that the human body is a temple. We can also see that the "message" of a Sign can be misinterpreted. This is also the Sign of the miser, where human energy is converted into money or other property which is locked away rather than being used for further growth. Even today we have evidence from the growth of terrorism that religious "messages" can become misinterpreted or corrupted when translated into form.

The Zodiac symbol of The Bull is of a masculine animal, full of creative energy. The seed impregnates the earth and uses it as a "womb" to gain sustenance and grow. In Stage 2 of The Cycle of Growth (Germination) the Tarot virgin Priestess becomes the pregnant Empress. Mother Nature.

Taurus is the Fixed Earth Sign. This is energy in its most stable form. It is concerned with physical human possessions which include the human body as well as money and property – which require the expenditure of energy to become "fixed assets". The main lesson of Taurus is concerned with the wise management of resources. At one level this is the infant learning to use and maintain its human body. In later life this can be extended to work related to the same principle. Its principle skill is Organisation. From its Fixed nature there is a tendency towards inertia. Taurus is difficult to get moving. There is, however, a strong inner link with the cycles of Nature. Taurus is best at occupations that require attention to fixed routines, and have a practical, earthy, basis - so make excellent farmers and tradespeople. They will undertake tasks that would be too repetitive and boring to most.

At another level, a symbol of Fixed Earth is the cube. We do not need to change this much to get to the shape of a building brick. To build with bricks takes a strong discipline and adherence to a routine. One of the Taurean symbols is "The Builder" and stonemason.

PHYSICAL DEVELOPMENT AND GROWTH

In our progress through the Ages we see that mankind has come from hunter gatherer to farmer and by so doing started to increase the population. Mankind as a living organism is increasing in size. Farming output is being improved by such methods as irrigation and ploughs.

> *4500 BC THE PLOUGH : Early forms of plough were being used by the end of the Neolithic period. They feature on Mesopotamian seals. By the Bronze Age, their use had spread across Western Asia and into Europe. [MERL]

> *A Sumerian (Erech) pictograph, dated about 3500 BC, shows a sledge equipped with wheels. [EB]

New earthly resources are being uncovered and exploited – taking the place of the original focus on stone (which is the most fixed "element" of Earth). Bricks are being made from clay. Ever larger, taller, buildings are appearing. Men are digging mines to harvest metal and semi-precious stones from the earth. At another level there the skill of human management is arising to organise and control the "human body". Organised labour. Cities need to eat, drink, work, and get rid of their waste.

This Age has a profound effect on the development of mankind. Even though the physical evidence of all that effort has since died – as the Laws of Nature decree it must – solid foundations have been built in human experience. Roots for further growth to occur.

> *All of the materials used by modern society are either themselves made of mined materials or require mined materials in their production. It is a truism to say that if it did not grow, then somebody, somewhere, dug it out of the ground. Even the other primary industries, agriculture, fishing, and forestry, would be helpless without tools and machinery made from the products of mines. It can be argued that mining is the most basic industry of human civilization. Mining always involves the physical removal of materials from the crust of the Earth, frequently in huge amounts for the recovery of only small amounts of the desired product. [MERL]

Farming is another 'feeding process' and could be considered a form of mining the earth. Take from the earth. Process to extract the required content. Discard waste products.

Having changed lifestyle from hunter-gatherer to farmer, there is now increasing pressure on mankind to move into larger cities. In 5000 BC Uruk in Mesopotamia was the only true city on earth. This 'monopoly' was to change with time.

There is still a focus on agriculture, with the need to feed an ever growing population. There is evidence to show that field workers in Mesopotamia lived in towns and walked to their work each day. Part of the reason for this is that the soil was becoming less fertile and individual farmers were unable to support themselves. Paul Kriwaczek [BAB] suggests another reason – that city dwelling was more pleasant. Soil erosion increased. This could be due to over farming, or the soil becoming drier due to climate changes.

While Mesopotamia was beginning to build cities, England was barely emerging from the hunter gatherer stage. According to The Encyclopaedia Britannica, agriculture was not introduced in England until 4000 BC by immigrants from Europe. 2000 years after Mesopotamia. They literally brought the seeds for future growth with them in the form of tried and tested cereals which are not indigenous to Britain and are so essential for obtaining satisfactory crops. We note that archaeology has not discovered any evidence of large cities in Britain similar to those in the East. Most development here seems to come from later Roman occupation – such as building of roads and public buildings. Rome is comparatively closer to Mesopotamia. A good reason for this is that, until the end of the last Ice Age 10,000 years ago, there were very few people here – Homo Sapiens, that is. Any earlier settlers had been forced into "cold storage". At that time Mesopotamia was much further advanced as a result of their warmer climate.

THE BRONZE AGE

The earthy Age of Taurus is also marked by the beginning of The Bronze Age which developed out of the earlier "Chalcolithic" – or Copper Age. During this time came the invention of the wheel.

We have to take note that, again, the effect of the Age did not reach Europe until much later :-

   *the Bronze Age began before 3000 BC, whereas in Britain it did not start until about 1900 BC. [EB]

In this Age the focus moves away from Babylon/Mesopotamia. Because of the growth in population there, it now became prey to human ambition. Various factions split away from the main group to form their own communities or groups. Although there are no actual internal wars, there was competition rather than co-operation. Efforts at improvement are mainly focused on the building of fortifications and developing bronze weapons.

CUNEIFORM SCRIPT – THE BEGINNING OF WRITTEN LANGUAGE

We can see the use of a stylus to make marks in a clay (Earth) tablet as similar to a plough making furrows in the Earth.

   *The earliest texts in cuneiform script are about 5,000 years old, having antedated the use of alphabets by some 1,500 years. [MERL]

Cuneiform was first used in Sumeria, Southern Mesopotamia in 3000 BC, for recording numbers as in business transactions and developed from there. One of Taurus' rulerships is Business Organisation. Cuneiform's last usage is recorded in 1 AD by which time other countries had adapted it to their own language. The Sumerian language mainly consisted of monosyllables and cuneiform was easy to misunderstand. Greater sophistication was required.

Written language can be considered the physical manifestation of abstract ideas.

AGE OF ARIES 3040 - 870 BC

Cycle of Growth Stage 1 (Seed)

PSYCHOLOGICAL INFLATION

According to Jung, Inflation occurs when we identify our Ego with the Self – or the power of God. The symbolism of The Age of Aries is entirely in keeping with this manifestation. When we are first born we are entirely contained and identified with the Self (God. Instinct. Intuition). The process of our earthly human development gradually separates us from the Collective to recognise our Ego as a separate being, and eventually individualise.

This Age was characterised by the building of pyramids, ziggurats, temples and stone circles, all of which are sexual symbols. Single monuments are representations of an erect penis. A potential for intercourse not yet realised. This refers to the animal rutting season when males compete for dominance and choice of the females – so enabling survival of the fittest. Putting them in circles gives a more feminine connotation – as in the "shell" settlements of Cancer mentioned earlier.

In order to build them it was necessary that people did not have to spend all their time looking for food. The "Tower of Babel" (Babylon\Mesopotamia) is a significant example. A lot of energy was put into activities with no actual physical survival value, but related to obtaining some form of harvest in the future. Symbols of fertility. We will see that these activities changed somewhat in the following Age of Pisces where the temples became focal points of mental study and learning rather than trying to reach God physically. Keeping closer to the Earth by studying the Laws of Nature and Philosophy.

Related to the time of the birth of a child, we can see the added symbolism of Spirit entering a physical body as a "temple of the soul". Another way of reaching God physically, but by internal, rather than external, means.

SYMBOLISM OF ARIES – CARDINAL FIRE

Aries is the Cardinal Fire Sign of impulsive, instinctive, action as symbolised by the Zodiac image "The Ram" in its competition with others for mates. The Fire Element relates to the Jungian Function of Intuition, which is also related to instinct. The ruling planet of Aries is Mars, God of War. Its time is Spring with the beginning of new life on Earth. It is related to activities concerned with intuitive or instinctive action rather than thought. So Sport, War, sex drive, and "the selfish gene" are related to it. At another level we have "The Pioneer" – "bravely going where no one has gone before". Conquering new worlds. Its principle is "Personal Projection of Energy". Aries is connected with the use of metals and sharp instruments. The forging of the legendary "sword of selfhood". The legends of King Arthur and Siegfried. The Bronze Age was eventually replaced by the Iron Age during this time. As the first Zodiac Sign, Aries is the simplest of all. Its action can be summarised as "The Law of The Jungle". Might makes right. It is this that has enabled survival of animal and human species until recent times. When one is alone this works very well. With increase in population we are often outnumbered in our aims - which extend beyond mere survival – so more co-operative skills are required.

Its complementary Sign on the opposite side of the Zodiac is Libra, related to Partnerships and "Social Projection of Energy". The Scales of Balance, Justice, and Partnerships. Even The Ram needs a mate.

EVENTS OF THE AGE OF ARIES

ASTROLOGY AND THE CALENDAR

Of main importance to us here is that the Age of Aries is the beginning of Astrology, which was still allied with Astronomy, and the Calendar as we know them today. The need for humans to "tell the time" (of year) in order to co-ordinate activities properly.

> *The earliest records of advanced, organized mathematics date back to the ancient Mesopotamian country of Babylonia and to Egypt of the 3rd millennium BC. There mathematics was dominated by arithmetic, with an emphasis on measurement and calculation in geometry and with no trace of later mathematical concepts such as axioms or proofs.[MSE]

USE OF METALS AND WAR

With the increase in human population there is focus on the mining and use of metals for tools and weapons and the conquest of one nation by another by force (related to Aries/Mars/Fire). We were gradually coming to the end of the Bronze Age and entering the Iron Age. In the paragraph below we see the Aries/Ram impatience modified by the Libra/Scales of Justice. The beginnings of a legal system and rule by social power. War could not be invented until after the invention of cities.

> *As city-states began to grow, their spheres of influence overlapped, creating arguments between other city-states, especially over land and canals. These arguments were recorded in tablets several hundreds of years before any major war - the first recording of a war occurred around 3200BC but was not common until about 2500BC. At this point warfare was incorporated into the Mesopotamian political system, where

a neutral city may act as an arbitrator for the two rival cities. This helped to form unions between cities, leading to regional states. When empires were created, they went to war more with foreign countries. King Sargon, for example, conquered all the cities of Sumer, some cities in Mari, and then went to war with northern Syria. Many Babylonian palace walls were decorated with the pictures of the successful fights and the enemy, whether desperately escaping, or hiding amongst reeds. A king in Sumer, Gilgamesh, was thought two-thirds god and only one third human. There were legendary stories and poems about him, which were passed on for many generations, because he had many adventures that were believed very important, and won many wars and battles.

[http://www.search.com/reference/Mesopotamia]

2000 BC ABRAHAM

Abraham (the first Hebrew patriarch) led his people out of Ur, Mesopotamia, to Canaan on the Sea of Galilee - in keeping with the pioneering symbolism of the Age and Cycle of Growth Stage 1 (Seed). The Jews were later captured by the Egyptians who used them as slaves to build pyramids.

1290 BC MOSES

Moses led the Israelites out of Egypt to the Promised Land – again in keeping with Cycle of Growth Stage 1 (Seeding. Pioneering).

1200 BC THE IRON AGE

Another important development was the increasing use of iron. The technology for the control of Fire (as symbolised by Aries) was being improved to obtain the higher temperatures necessary.

* *Iron is dated as early as 2800 BC; Egyptian records of iron ore smelting date from 1300 BC. Found in the ancient ruins of Troy, lead was produced as early as 2500 BC. [EB]*

* *The date of the full Iron Age, in which this metal for the most part replaced bronze in implements and weapons, varied geographically, beginning in the Middle East and south eastern Europe about 1200 BCE but in China not until about 600 BCE. [EB]*

MONUMENTS : PHALLIC POWER SYMBOLS UNITING EARTH AND HEAVEN

During the Age of Aries we have an interesting phenomenon which probably gives us a closer insight into the Archetype than anything else. It is the building of monuments such as pyramids and stone circles which have a similar symbolic meaning as temples and churches today. The principle seems to be to try and get as close to heaven as possible – although they were mainly status symbols of the rulers.

1. It answers the question of why the pyramids and other monuments, such as stone circles like Stonehenge, were built during this period. It was just "the in thing".
2. We have further evidence from the building of similar, smaller, monuments in the present day.
3. It is an indication of how the activities of Archetypes in the Collective Unconscious cannot be subjected to rational analysis. They are quite illogical to us. We cannot fully understand them. This idea is related to the Jungian Function of Intuition\Element Fire. Intuition\instinct is the least understood Function because it is not, in itself, rational. Symbolism is a way of understanding, when physical things take on a meaning beyond their appearance.
4. It is an indication of the power of Archetypes on a collective level. The activities here have absolutely no value for survival purposes. They require a vast expenditure of time, labour and resources to build. They are global in scope.
5. When we observe the Zodiac archetypes, their prime function seems to be to produce physical manifestation (of themselves ?).
6. We see the same forces at work in the creation of Astrology and The Calendar at this time. The common factor is that of co-ordinating human activity with that of the heavens.
7. The Element Fire (Jungian Intuition) and Earth (Jungian Sensation) are complementary. They are both Irrational (being concerned with Perceiving in different ways), rather than Rational (concerned with Judging, which is the concern of Thinking (Air) and Feeling (Water)).

ASTROLOGY : THE ZODIAC AGES

PHALLIC SYMBOLS

1. A phallic symbol is a symbolic representation of an erect penis. It contains potential energy for creativity in the act of sexual intercourse, but requires an object for release. It is a symbol of fertility, but is not, itself, fertile – entirely in keeping with the Aries Ram symbolism of competing males to establish a "pecking order", and war.

2. In the context of monuments, we can see that, although most act as indicators for the Winter Solstice some relate to the time of the Spring Equinox when the most important religious rituals occurred with the aim of producing a good food crop for the coming year. Solstices and Equinoxes relate to the crisis\change points on the Cycle of Growth – Stages 1, 4, 7 and 10.

3. The symbolism is entirely in keeping with the time of Aries. Cycle of Growth Stage 1 (Seed). The Ram has not yet mated, he competes with other males to eventually achieve that goal. Mars, God of War, is included in the symbolism of the Archetype. This is pure, instinctive force. Many war memorials are phallic symbols which honour those who died in wars.

4. In the Christian calendar this includes the time of Easter with its message of the self-sacrifice of Jesus on the cross and his later resurrection and ascension into heaven. Just prior to this he instituted the ritual of Holy Communion with bread and wine being used as symbols of his body and blood. Before beginning his ministry he attended a wedding where he turned water into wine (Blood. Fire. Spirit. Alcohol. "Fire Water"). A symbol of marriage and sexual intercourse. Spirit bringing creative energy to inert material.

5. There is a focus on the symbolism of Resurrection and Rebirth rather than simple Birth. New life coming from Death. Archaeological excavations of pyramids, ziggurats, and stone circles, have found many human bones in the foundations – mostly they seem to be burials rather than the human sacrifices which were the focus of those of the Mayans and Aztecs in South America. We can consider Archaeology itself as providing another form of "rebirth". A similar modern day practice is Cryonics where human bodies are stored in liquid nitrogen pending possible "resurrection" at a later date when medical research has reached a stage to enable it.

6. The building of pyramids, ziggurats, and stone circles, ceased, without logical reason, at the end of the Age of Aries. The following Age of Pisces focused more on the building of temples and churches instead. Civilised enclosures to contain people rather than just the priest. The next chapter shows that the later Age brought the births of the pioneers of all the monotheistic religions alive today – when the worship of animals and multiple gods was replaced by the One God.

2630 – 600 BC PYRAMIDS

Built in Egypt from 2630 to 600 BC, The Egyptian pyramids have pointed tops and were used as tombs for their kings and other important people that could afford them. They had no external steps. They were principally symbols of the power of the king and built by paid workers. After the huge expense of time and energy of the first few they deteriorated in size to become more affordable. The relics found with the bodies were clearly meant to serve the occupant in their afterlife in heaven – again emphasising new life after death.

ZIGGURATS

Although the term is strictly related to the ones built in Mesopotamia between 2200 and 600 BC, the term Ziggurat is used it to describe pyramid-like structures with flat tops that had temples built on them. They also used convenient hilltops as a cheaper method. They have steps on the outside to enable a priest to reach the top. Hundreds have been discovered all over the world. Later examples are found in such places as South America, China, Greece, and India. They have similar shape to pyramids because, due to the laws of Physics, this was the only way to build tall structures with the materials and technology to hand at the time. The principle is the same as making sand castles on the beach.

With both types of building there was often some form of human and/or animal sacrifice. The Aztec and Mayan ones were used to sacrifice thousands of humans to the gods to ensure a good harvest. The focus is on blood (Fire). Often the heart was removed. We note a similarity with the celebration of Mass or Holy Communion in churches today, with the **symbolic** body and blood of Christ. In this case the sacrifice is of God for Man, rather than Man for God – a main difference between the Old and New Testaments. The ziggurats' main purpose was to support the temple as high as possible, although some had rooms or tunnels inside they were relatively small because of the heavy weight above.

ASTROLOGY : THE ZODIAC AGES

As with churches and temples today, pyramids and ziggurats were aligned to geographical co-ordinates, some so that the Sun highlighted certain points at certain times of year, especially at sunrise at the annual Spring Equinox – which is the time of Aries and Spring.

THE TOWER OF BABEL - BABYLON

The Ziggurat Tower(s) of Babylon/Mesopotamia were the origins of the "Hanging Gardens" – one of the ancient Wonders of the World. We have a better idea of the reason for the monuments because of the record in The Bible in the Book of Genesis Chapter 11 :-

Verse 1: And the whole earth was of one language, and of one speech.

Verse 2: And it came to pass, as they journeyed from the east, that they found a plain in the land of Shinar; and they dwelt there.

Verse 3: And they said one to another, Go to, let us make brick, and burn them thoroughly. And they had brick for stone, and slime had they for mortar.

There is an inner meaning to Verse 3. Brick is a manmade object whereas stone is natural (of God). So we see that, here, man is replacing God's meaning with his own. We can see this as the beginning of multiple religions, where the worship of One God takes different forms. It is also suggestive of the development of the mind, with verbal communication (Thinking) replacing Intuition – as in the growth of a child.

Verse 4: And they said, Go to, let us build us a city and a tower, whose top [may reach] unto heaven; and let us make us a name, lest we be scattered abroad upon the face of the whole earth.

So we see another relationship with Aries and phallic symbols. "Making a name for one's self" is one of the stages of development of the Ego – when we can first say "I Am". We are then individuals, no longer just a part of collective humanity. There is no possibility of guessing when men and women first had individual names – but we must note that the most important name is that of God – so having a name makes us more godlike. We see something of this in John 1 Chapter 1: "*In the beginning was the Word, and the Word was with God, and the Word was God.*" At one time the name of God was considered too holy to be spoken aloud.

This is all in keeping with the meaning of psychological Inflation and trying to "become like God" (our condition at birth).

Verse 5: And the LORD came down to see the city and the tower, which the children of men builded.

Verse 6: And the LORD said, Behold, the people [is] one, and they have all one language; and this they begin to do: and now nothing will be restrained from them, which they have imagined to do.

Verse 7: Go to, let us go down, and there confound their language, that they may not understand one another's speech.

Verse 8: So the LORD scattered them abroad from thence upon the face of all the earth: and they left off to build the city.

Verse 9: Therefore is the name of it called Babel; because the LORD did there confound the language of all the earth: and from thence did the LORD scatter them abroad upon the face of all the earth.[KJV]

Babel is the root of the city name "Babylon" and the term "babbling" to mean speaking meaningless words. We can also see the phallic undertones, and the relationship with ego development. In the chapter [GENESIS AND THE CYCLE OF GROWTH] we note that "the LORD" (Jehovah) name for God finally replaced "God", and later "Jehovah God", after The Fall. I take this to mean that even though the worship of God failed at The Fall, his LAW remains.

1900 BC WRITING

During this period we have evidence of other changes to written communication - away from clay tablets.

Cuneiform was gradually phased out because it could easily be misinterpreted. Around 2100 BC the sexagesimal number system (based on number 6) came into being in Sumer Mesopotamia. We still use this system for counting hours and minutes, and angles (degrees) – all of which are related to the 360 degree circle/cycle. Wheels within wheels.

1900 BC – First evidence of Egyptian semi-alphabet characters [MERL]

1850 BC – Semitic alphabet adaptation of Egyptian characters. Consonants only.

1760 BC - The first Laws written down (Hammurabi's Laws of Babylonia on a stone pillar)

1700 BC – First known alphabet in Palestine & Syria

1000 BC - Greek adaptation of Phoenician variant of the Semitic Alphabet – adding vowels

500 BC - Greek written left to right

1 AD   - The last known use of Cuneiform.

3000 - 2000 BC STONE CIRCLES – STONEHENGE

We again have evidence of an extremely time and labour consuming practice that began and ended during the Age of Aries. A circle is a feminine symbol, whereas the others are masculine. We can, however, consider the individual stones as masculine phallic symbols. We can here, again, see the combined relationship between Aries and the Sun Cycle of Nature.

There are hundreds of stone circles around the world, the most famous being in Stonehenge, England. Although archaeologists have discovered (in the present car park) the remains of some wooden post holes dating back to 8000 BC (Age of Cancer – when people started building enclosures), Stonehenge itself was first dug out in 3000 BC as a circular earth bank enclosing a ditch, but was later remodelled to include wood. It is important to recognise that it began in the Neolithic Age (New Stone Age) when tools were made of stone. Later on it underwent numerous other rebuilding operations. Various varieties of stone were added and removed until they finally left it alone in 2000 BC – seemingly incomplete.

Whereas the Egyptian pyramids were mainly built as tombs, and were aligned geographically, it is established that Stonehenge served the same purpose of indicating the Winter Solstice and Equinoxes as the ziggurats. Although there is some disagreement among authorities on the subject as to the details, there is consensus that it was used for some kind of worship, and many burial sites have been uncovered in the close proximity. So we can see a similar purpose to the pyramids as well. Also, as with the Ziggurats, there is evidence of bones being used as foundations for the posts and stones, as well as the surrounding area being used for human burial and cremation remains. Although human sacrifices were common with the South American ziggurats, there is no evidence of it at Stonehenge.

Despite a huge amount of research, although there is agreement that Stonehenge served some religious purpose, there is no agreement as to why it was built. Another mystery is why it was not finished. At a logical level, related to our information here, we could surmise the possibility that its alignment was somehow related to factors affected by the Progression of Equinoxes, so during the course of 1000 years it gradually became less accurate. This does not explain the gradual conversion to stone. We are on firmer ground when considering a deeper psychological level, and the Age of Aries. In searching for a logical reason we are using the Jungian Thinking Function whereas the Age is concerned with undeveloped people using Fire\Intuition\Instinct and stone tools– which cannot be explained or rationalised. My suggestion is that the people did it simply from unconscious inner motivation. It was "the thing to do" and stopped when it was not, as the "Spirit of The Age" declined in power.

We see that the basic purpose of building these structures was to align man's activities with those of the heavens – which is exactly that of Astrology. We also see a development of the human mind where it becomes possible to experiment by thinking symbolically and draw plans, rather than keep physically building things and tearing them down.

AGE OF PISCES 870 BC-1300 AD

Cycle of Growth Stage 12 – (Withdrawal. Confinement)

SYMBOLISM OF PISCES – MUTABLE WATER

Pisces ("The Fish") is the Mutable (changeable/flexible) Water Sign with the principles of "Social Service". And "Obligation" (Karma). Until Psychology came into being it was difficult to understand, but we now have the concept of "The Collective Unconscious" which aligns perfectly with its symbolism. We can see why early astrologers had so much trouble without such a concept, although the "image" they offer is exactly as C.G. Jung describes. Basically, the Collective Unconscious is like a "sea" in which we all exist and share. Like the "Fishes" (symbol of Pisces) in their water, we have no conscious awareness of it. The Collective Unconscious, which is the same for everyone, affects us via our "Personal Unconscious" which contains our personal memories, and which is described to be like an "island" or "iceberg" in the sea. We are closer to it when normal, physical, consciousness is reduced during sleep. [PSYCHOLOGY : DEVELOPMENT MODELS]

Pisces is active in everyone's Birth Chart. The individual difference is if it, or the 12th. House, is somehow emphasised by having a planet present at birth, or if Neptune is somehow emphasised by its position (such as in Lady Diana Spencer's Birth Chart [ASTROLOGY : CHARTS EXAMPLES]. It can be given more importance by wilfully attending to its related activities, or the abuse of alcohol or other drugs producing altered states of consciousness.

People with Pisces emphasised in their Birth Chart are more conscious of the "sea" and are more sensitive to it, and so tend to prefer living in the background of life, away from the inner "noise". Lady Diana had Neptune in her 10th. House (Peak. Public View) and we note the problems she had with this as she was the focus of public, collective, image projections of the "princess" archetype. If properly trained it can be developed into mediumship or other artistic pursuits. This is the source of true Art and Music. Negatively (depending on the rest of their Birth Chart), subjects can seem to have little will of their own, tending to be overshadowed by positive or negative influences in their surroundings. Again, we can see evidence of this with Lady Diana, who gave us an objective indication of how collective forces (Pisces) can challenge our individuality (Aquarius). The Sign covers areas of life to which people can "retreat", and where there is opportunity for isolation and lives are organised by external rules - such as monasteries and convents, hospitals and prisons (repaying karmic debt).

This is also the realm of altered states of consciousness – including those attained by use of art, music, religion, meditation, prayer, and alcohol or other drugs. This is the realm of Philosophy, Psychology, and Theology – although the "-ologies" themselves are more related to the Element Air (the Jungian, rational, Thinking Function). Pisces, being a Water Sign is related to the Jungian (also rational) Function of Feeling).

It is important to note that Pisces is one of 12 equal Signs, so, despite many astrologers' attempts to state otherwise, it has no special spiritual importance of its own. Its tendency, as with the earthly sea, and the Collective Unconscious, is to "dissolve" and absorb everything with which it comes into contact. To remove the separation of individuals. In that sense it works against Individuation and Free Will. We observe the inability of people to function when under the influence of excessive alcohol or other drugs. One of the principles of Pisces is "Service to Others". Its complementary sign is the Earth Sign Virgo, with its principle of "Service to Self". Everything requires balance.

EVENTS OF THE PISCEAN AGE

We are now on firmer ground for dating our Ages from having better historical data. The principle inner focus of this Age was the birth of monotheism – the belief in One God, as distinct from the earlier belief in many gods and goddesses, and the worship of animals. To deny this focus makes no sense whatsoever in the face of the global changes that occurred, especially concerning our calendar, and the fact that those changes are now fundamental to our daily lives – whether one is "religious" or not. At the beginning of this Age we have the births of many of the great pioneering philosophers and mathematicians whose work came to define later human progress. A deeper observation and study of Natural Law. At that time there was not much difference in the disciplines, and many were also astrologers.

We have to note that the archetypal ancient gods and goddesses have not disappeared, but faded into the Collective Unconscious. Perhaps, from becoming invisible they have greater power. Some are still active in having planets named after them.

800-200 BC THE AXIAL AGE

German Philosopher Karl Jaspers coined the term "Axial Age" to describe the period 800 – 200 BC. He said that :-

> *"the spiritual foundations of humanity were laid simultaneously and independently in China, India, Persia, Judea, and Greece. And these are the foundations upon which humanity still subsists today." [KJ]

ASTROLOGY : THE ZODIAC AGES

753 BC - 1453 AD RISE AND FALL OF THE ROMAN EMPIRE

As one of the most important events of the Piscean age we must take note of the rise and fall of the Roman Empire. It symbolically shows the transfer of power from Aries/Mars to Pisces/Church. We note that its "lifetime" coincides closely with that of the Piscean Age. Although it had a global effect of bringing civilisation and order to many countries of the world, one of its main influences was that of assisting the birth of Christianity. The Vatican and the Pope still survive to this day in Italy. Although their power is somewhat diminished nowadays, the control is global in effect. So we see the gradual transfer of world power from militant Aries to religious Pisces – which was later challenged in the Age of Aquarius.

753 BC - Rome was founded by (king) Romulus.

509 BC - The last king deposed and Rome became a republic

300 BC - Began world conquest

27 BC - The Roman Empire was established.

200 AD - General rebellion of conquered people required effort to maintain order

410 AD - Capital Constantinople – split with Rome. Byzantine Empire.

Around 410 AD the Roman Empire was transformed into the Byzantine Empire which was oriented to a more Greek culture and Christianity rather than Roman paganism. It had expanded too far into the world and was unable to support its armies to maintain control.

> *It was the Church, more than anything, that was the real heir of the empire, and which was able to provide a measure of continuity after the collapse of temporal power and civil administration. The papacy continued to be based in Rome and to exert enormous authority over most of Europe, keeping alive not only many of the ideas of the Roman world but also a sense of a wider community which looked to the ancient city for support and leadership.[MSE]

          610 AD - End of the classical Roman Empire. Greek influence.

1453 AD - Capture by Ottomans (Turks). Coincides with the end of the Age.

RELIGION – THE BIRTH OF MONOTHEISTIC RELIGIONS EXISTING TODAY

During this age the *5 main world monotheistic religions were founded (among others).

586 BC   - *Judaism : Ezekiel. Fall of Jerusalem. Jews exiled to Babylon
570-490 BC   - Daoism : Lao Tzu (China) – instructed Confucius
579-551 BC   - Confucianism : Confucius (China) – founded
563-483 BC   - *Buddhism : Buddha (India) – beginning of Buddhism
6 BC – 30 AD - *Christianity : Jesus of Nazareth.
250 BC   - *Hinduism : Upanishads (sacred Hindu texts). Rebirth. Karma.
570-632 AD   - *Islam : Muhammad–recognized other monotheistic religions
630-550 BC   - Zoroastrianism : Zoroaster (Persia)
650 AD   - Koran compiled (Islam)
1209 AD   - Francis of Assisi founds the Franciscan Order.
1215 AD   - St. Dominic founds the Dominican Order

PHILOSOPHY. MEDICINE. MATHEMATICS

Here we see the first attempts to study and uncover the natural Laws of Nature. The "rules" that govern the lives of everyone on earth. This could be considered a reaction to The Tower of Babel mentioned earlier, with its effect of dividing the "one language" into many. There was focus on finding philosophical common denominators.

625-539 BC   - Neo-Babylonian Empire (Babylon="Gate of God")
620-560 BC   - Aesop - Fables
582-500 BC   - Pythagoras (Greece) – "the first mathematician"
539 BC   - Babylon/Mesopotamia conquered by Persia
470-399 BC   - Socrates (Greece) -
428-347 BC   - Plato (Greece) – followed Socrates' teaching
420-350 BC   - Hippocrates (Greece) – Medicine
384-322 BC   - Aristotle – taught by Plato

ASTROLOGY : THE ZODIAC AGES

304-250 BC   *- Erasistratus – Medicine (Anatomy)*
300 BC   *- Euclid (Greece) – mathematician - especially geometry*
287-212 BC   *- Archimedes (Greece) mathematician & inventor*
250 BC   *- Septuagint. Greek translation of the Old Testament*
190-120 BC   *- Hipparchus (Greek astronomy. Work later used by Ptolemy)*
70-19 BC   *- Virgil (Rome) - poet*
65-8 BC   *- Horace (Rome) - poet*
20 BC- 50AD   *- Philo Judaeus (Egypt) (Greek philosophy + Jewish scripture)*
100-170 AD   *- Ptolemy (Alexandria) Astronomer. Mathematician (geocentric universe)*
129-199 AD   *- Galen(Greece). Anatomy. Physiology*
523 AD   *- Boethius. "Consolation of Philosophy". Second to the Bible in Middle Ages*
1154-1485   *- "The Middle Ages"- religious & cultural stagnation(end of the Iron Age)*

OTHER EVENTS

270 BC   *- Ctesibius – accurate Water Clock*
300 BC   *- Hindu Number system in India - via Arabia became our global system.*
44 BC   *- Julius Caesar Calendar revision (Julian Calendar)*
500 AD   *- The Iron Age ends. The 'Middle Ages' begin (lasting to 1500AD [EB])*
976 AD   *- Arabic numbers developed from the Hindu system still used today*

CALENDAR AMENDMENTS

There was a revision to the Astrological "calendar" invented during the Age of Aries and which by now the Egyptians had formalised into 12 lunar months, and the Romans 10, later 12, months. The Roman Calendar, being based on lunar months was found to be too inaccurate, and in 45 BC Julius Caesar made changes to base it entirely on the position of the Sun. The Julian Calendar lasted until 1580 AD (Aquarian Age) when Pope Gregory revised it again, adding rules such as "leap years" so the calendar accurately matched the equinoxes.

I point out here that nowadays there is nothing more "global" in scope than the calendar and clock time. If nothing else, it is the one thing that all people of all nations agree on. Despite efforts to change measures to a digital base 10, time measurement is still based on Number 12 as initiated by the Sumerians in Mesopotamia in the Age of Aries, which is also the time when Astrology as we know it today began. It is from examples like this that we can observe something of the working of the Collective Unconscious in our lives. As our common psychological "root" its effect makes us all the same at fundamental levels.

CHRISTIANITY. THE BIRTH OF JESUS. COUNTING YEARS

MONOTHEISM

A fundamental change to the calendar that occurred at this time, affecting us all resulted from the birth of Jesus, which has fixed the counting of Years for the foreseeable future. Until that time Years were variable from country to country, or non-existent, mainly depending on the lives and reigns of kings and other rulers. As an event causing major global change (and conformity) the birth of Christianity must be a defining factor of The Age of Pisces. In effect, Jesus did become a "king". In this respect he replaced many others. There is the ritual of baptism by water.

We note the strange reluctance in many areas to use "BCE" ("Before the Common Era") instead of "BC". This could be because this Age included the births of all the other main monotheistic religions of our world today, replacing the multitude of "gods" that were worshipped before. Once again we see that the "message" of an Age can be interpreted into many different forms. It gives a hint of how the Archetypes of the Collective Unconscious operate in our lives, and why we need symbolism to get closer to the true meanings – which are not really able to be expressed in rational terms or language.

THE NEW COVENANT

An important point that seems to be missed is that, apart from the replacement of worship of many gods and goddesses, and animals, Jesus came to REPLACE the Jewish religion's adherence to the 10 Commandments. The resistance of the religions of mankind to change is demonstrated by their adherence to the Old Testament – and only the first 5 books at that. There is mention of earlier Covenants made between God and Man, the latest being with Moses with the Ten Commandments. The New Testament came to replace the Old Testament.

ASTROLOGY : THE ZODIAC AGES

As noted in my chapter [THE GENESIS STORY], it does seem that from this time God evolved into a much more benign figure, with the promise of forgiveness rather than punishment. We also bear in mind that Edgar Cayce states that Jesus was a re-incarnation of Moses.

In the Book of Matthew Chapter 22, Verses 35 to 40 (These short verses embody the symbolism of Pisces) :-

35: Then one of them, which was a lawyer, asked him a question, tempting him, and saying,

36: Master, which is the great commandment in the law?

37: Jesus said unto him, Thou shalt love the Lord thy God with all thy heart, and with all thy soul, and with all thy mind.

38: This is the first and great commandment.

39: And the second is like unto it, Thou shalt love thy neighbour as thyself.

40: On these two commandments hang all the law and the prophets. [KJV]

Hebrews Chapter 8, Verses 8 to 13 recognises that the first Covenant was not working, and states that each individual person now has access to "inner guidance" – and forgiveness.

*8: For if that first covenant had been faultless, then should no place have been sought for the second. For finding fault with them, he saith, Behold, the days come, saith the Lord, when I will make a new covenant with the house of Israel and with the house of Judah:

9: Not according to the covenant that I made with their fathers in the day when I took them by the hand to lead them out of the land of Egypt; because they continued not in my covenant, and I regarded them not, saith the Lord.

10: For this is the covenant that I will make with the house of Israel after those days, saith the Lord; I will put my laws into their mind, and write them in their hearts: and I will be to them a God, and they shall be to me a people:

11: And they shall not teach every man his neighbour, and every man his brother, saying, Know the Lord: for all shall know me, from the least to the greatest.

12: For I will be merciful to their unrighteousness, and their sins and their iniquities will I remember no more.

13: In that he saith, A new covenant, he hath made the first old. Now that which decayeth and waxeth old is ready to vanish away. [KJV]

Jeremiah Chapter 31, Verses 31 and 32 :-

*31: Behold, the days come, saith the LORD, that I will make a new covenant with the house of Israel, and with the house of Judah:

32: Not according to the covenant that I made with their fathers in the day [that] I took them by the hand to bring them out of the land of Egypt; which my covenant they brake, although I was an husband unto them, saith the LORD: [KJV]

Another main effect of his life was the consolidation of the concept of "One God" (that replaced many others) which is now the basis of the world's main religions. In effect, uniting the world as a kind of "classless society". We have direct contact with God, having no need for priests or other intermediaries.

The Pisces Fish symbol is one that is very prominent in its connection with Christianity. Not only were miracles involving fish performed by Jesus, but he informed his disciples, at least 4 of whom were born fishermen, that they would be "fishers of men" related to the image of casting nets – as distinct from the methods of military conquest of the time. In addition the symbol of a fish was used as a secret sign of recognition by Christians during the time of their persecution after his death.

ASTROLOGY : THE ZODIAC AGES

We can see this as a manifestation of the Pisces/Neptune principle activity of "dissolving" differences, and attempting to return to the original "Number Zero" state before Creation.

PHILOSOPHY

At this time we see another force appearing to challenge organised religion. People are becoming less satisfied with "blind faith" and studying the world around them for themselves.

> *philosophy (from Greek, by way of Latin, philosophia, "love of wisdom"), the critical examination of the grounds for fundamental beliefs and an analysis of the basic concepts employed in the expression of such beliefs. Philosophical inquiry is a central element in the intellectual history of many historical civilizations [EB]*

> *As used originally by the ancient Greeks, the term "philosophy" meant the pursuit of knowledge for its own sake. Philosophy comprised all areas of speculative thought and included the arts, sciences, and religion. As special methods and principles were developed in the various areas of knowledge, a specific philosophical aspect separated one from another, with each concerned to answer the most basic questions about the field. This gave rise to the philosophy of art, of science, and of religion. The term "philosophy" is often popularly used to indicate a set of basic values and attitudes towards life, nature, and society—thus the phrase "philosophy of life". Because the lines of distinction between the various areas of knowledge are flexible and subject to change, the definition of the term "philosophy" remains a subject of controversy.[MERL]*

AGE OF AQUARIUS 1300-3470 AD

The Age in which we are living now is characterised by Revolution, mainly driven by rapid advances in Technology (the application of Science) which has resulted in greater freedom from manual labour – not only by the practitioners themselves, but for those who use the new tools and machinery provided. Although it had beginnings in Mesopotamia, the term "Science" itself was invented at the beginning of the Age. The world was "becoming smaller". Evolution is occurring at the mental level. People are demanding more control over their personal lives. With greater choice comes greater responsibility.

The Age also includes development of electronic communications from the beginnings of the Telegraph followed by Radio, Television, telephones, and computers.

Cycle of Growth Stage 11 – Discontent

SYMBOLISM OF AQUARIUS – FIXED AIR

The Air Signs Gemini, Libra and Aquarius are the only ones to have human, rather than animal, symbols.

As with Gemini, above, the Element Air is concerned with the Jungian Thinking Function, and mental development and communication. In this case in its Fixed, or most stable, state. In the case of Gemini the communication is based on personal experience and experimentation (Cycle of Growth Stage 3 - Experiment). Gemini (which rules the arms and hands) is more of a "hands-on" experience. Aquarius has a more global, or group, function which challenges traditional methods and structures. New Ideas. At this level it is Revolution. Apart from the more violent ways of introducing new ideas and changing the existing order, it has a more benign method via the introduction of new technology – from stone tools to the Internet.

The symbol of Aquarius is the Water Carrier who pours "water" on the Earth. There is much confusion with the image, some even say, incorrectly, that it is a Water Sign. The best known "water carrier" is, of course, a cloud - which brings rain. It stores Water (Information. Meaning) and distributes it over the globe. At the time of writing, one of the newest inventions is actually called "The Cloud" as a means of using the Internet to store and exchange information.

The symbol of Aquarius shows 2 "waves" acting in harmony. The wave form is similar to that on an oscilloscope. Information is carried electronically over the radio "air waves" by combining a message wave with a fixed frequency "carrier wave" at the source - which is removed by the receiver. When 2 or more people are on the same "wave length" they can communicate with one another. We speak to one another by vibrating the air and decoding the vibrations. We can also consider the transfer of written (fixed) ideas in this context.

ASTROLOGY : THE ZODIAC AGES

Traditional Astrology has Saturn/Satan as ruling Aquarius. This is more symbolic of the restrictive practices of church and state which are Saturn/Capricorn structures which actively restricted the search for new knowledge. The Biblical example is the attempt by Herod to kill the new born Jesus.

The new ruling planet of Aquarius is recently discovered Uranus. The symbol of Uranus is similar to the original television aerial shape. [ASTROLOGY : PLANETS]

Aquarius and Uranus are concerned with the challenge of past traditions and methods by the Individual, and separation of the Individual from the Collective in the Jungian Process of Individuation. There is connection with the development of new technology, from stone tools onward.

In the outer world Aquarius is concerned with changing the balance of power from traditional rulership, such as kings, church, and state, to enable the individual person more control over their destiny. In the inner, personal, world there is connection with the Jungian process of Individuation. There is a strong connection with the principle of Democracy.

THE MIDDLE AGES

The time of transition between The Ages of Pisces and Aquarius 500 – 1500 AD is said to be "The Middle Ages" which began at the fall of the Roman Empire. Having lost that central control there was a lapse back to local control by separate warlords and therefore a reaction to the classic teachings of the early Piscean Age, with a sense of cultural stagnation which lasted until the "Renaissance" period – or "rebirth" of interest in the arts and classical past.

The emphasis on Communication is exemplified by invention of the Gutenberg printing press in 1453 AD which would begin the process of making books (typically, beginning with The Bible) available to people other than "the chosen few" – as well as encouraging more people to learn to read and write – the beginning of general Education.

Human Rights. The mass uprising of people against tyranny and slavery

The Age has been characterised by numerous internal mass uprisings by populations against its rulers throughout the world which have resulted in the rise of Democracy. This has occurred at various levels beginning with release of agricultural labourers (serfs) from bondage to their land lords – where they were basically owned slaves with no rights – followed by resistance against unfair taxation ("No taxation without representation") as the larger states were formed and took over control from the local aristocracy. There were similar scenarios across the world. Examples are the rise and fall of the Roman and British Empires, The English Revolution, The French Revolution, The Russian Revolution, American War of Independence (from British control), American Civil War (North versus South abolishing slavery and uniting the country as The United States).

1600 - 1900 AD THE BRITISH EMPIRE

The control of "The Crown" is symbolised by the Sign of Leo – the complement to Aquarius. Here we see evidence of the form of conflict between them. The struggle of Aquarius in joining with others to achieve some form of autonomy and self-rule. Democracy. Revolution has numerous forms.

The impact of Britain on the rest of the world was great – especially considering its relatively small size. This is an indication of the great power of the Archetypes, and how acting at the right time produces results. We note that it started at the beginning of the Age very soon after the end of the Roman Empire. It eventually covered 20% of the Earth's land area, with over 400 million people [MERL].

The method of growth was very different to that of Roman times – more Aquarian in principle. Overseas colonies were set up as commercial trading ventures rather than by conquest and used local chiefs as figureheads. The British Crown maintained minor supervision until it began to recognise the high volume of possible revenue. Gradually more British people emigrated to take over control. Not the military, note. The main driving force was the improvements in shipbuilding and navigation subsequent to the discovery of America in 1492 by Christopher Columbus.

Although Homo Sapiens had reached North America around 20,000 years ago, progress was delayed by the last ice age, so the Americas were finally colonised following global temperature rise 10,000 years ago – which was about the same time as Britain. Although Sir Walter Raleigh attempted settlement on Roanoke Island on the American coast in 1585, there was not much progress until there was peace with Spain in 1602. America was populated by the American Indian at the time. They had a lifestyle similar to that of the African Hunter Gatherer.

ASTROLOGY : THE ZODIAC AGES

We note the big difference in cultures. There are some that bemoan the changes to the cultures of groups such as the American Indians and the Aborigines. However, this is just an indication that Evolution has its own methods. If we observe the history of global national development over the ages we see that it follows the same pattern. As I write this today most countries are democratic. Those that still have some remaining form of dictatorship are under intense pressure to change – the people are still in revolt.

Apart from supplying commodities otherwise unobtainable in Britain, such as sugar, tobacco, silk and spices, a main commodity was slaves. It is interesting to consider that Britain, and America, as the last places in the world to be colonised by Homo Sapiens in the migration from Africa, were now a main instrument in the enforced "migration" of thousands of other Africans. Later on, Britain sent colonists to America and Australia – both of which are now world powers. Africa somehow seems to have missed out in bringing its population into the 21st. Century.

The beginning of the end for the British Empire was the American War of Independence (1775-1783) and finally around 1900 when British military and nautical dominance began to decline in the face of growth of, and challenges from, Russia, Germany, and Japan, and the populations of the Empire countries demanded freedom from British Rule. The Boer War in Africa (1899-1902) showed that, as with the Roman occupations, it was too costly to maintain control of areas overseas – especially as they now expected something in return for taxation.

It seems to be the pattern that the natives of "conquered" countries, once "civilised", eventually forced the foreigners out so they could have complete home rule. This is in keeping with Cycle of Growth Stage 11 (Discontent) and Aquarius. The Romans were forced to leave Britain in around 64 AD under similar circumstances.

Reduction in the power of the church (Discontent)

One main focus of the Age of Aquarius is the fall of the power of the Church, in particular that of The Pope, which, in the Piscean Age, took over control from Aries Age autonomous kings. The pattern here was the resentment from the king of the country, and recovery of control of his domain, followed by the loss of power of the king to a more democratic government.

The complementary Sign to Aquarius is Leo, the Lion "King of the Jungle". Among other things, we see below the challenge of individual inventiveness and resourcefulness to the power of the monarchies, and the evolution of Democracy.

An example was in England in 1533 when Henry VIII (King. Leo) broke the control of the Pope over religious practices (set up in the Age of Pisces) and founded "The Church of England" under his control. Later, the power of the monarchy was overcome by democracy.

> *Although these philosophical developments were important, the spirituality of the late Middle Ages was the true register of the social and cultural turmoil of the age. Late medieval spirituality was characterized by an intense search for the direct experience of God, whether through the private, interior ecstasy of mystical illumination, or through the personal scrutiny of God's word in the Bible. In either case, the established Church—both in its traditional function as interpreter of doctrine and in its institutional role as conveyor of the sacraments—found itself not so much embattled as dispensed with. [MERL]

We note the importance of the common man becoming able to read the scriptures for himself, in his own language brought another form of Democracy.

Reduction of bondage to Nature Cycles and physical effort – The Industrial Revolution

A symbol of the Age was the scientific discovery that the Sun is the centre of our solar system and not the Earth, as previously believed.

Technology began when the first man picked up a stone to kill an animal – or another man that got in his way. The rise of technology since then has followed a similar pattern, where it has initially been driven by needs of defence or war, or other forms of national competition.

We could say that the Aquarian Age is "The Scientific Age", "The Age of Invention", or "The Age of Global Communication" with focus on more down to earth matters rather than the earlier philosophy, or study for its own sake. Again, the process has involved the gradual transfer of power – this time, of Knowledge - from the chosen few to the common man.

ASTROLOGY : THE ZODIAC AGES

1760 INDUSTRIAL REVOLUTION

The greatest effect in more recent times has been The Industrial Revolution which began in Britain with the invention of the steam engine in the 17th. Century, and which effectively began to replace animal and human energy with that obtained from coal. The main effect was moving away from agricultural products as the main basis of social wealth. Again, to begin with, there was exploitation of human labour, with the general movement from farms to factories. Even children of 8 years of age were forced to work 14 hours a day with low pay in dangerous conditions - until the human rights human revolution began with the slogan "A fair days work for a fair day's pay", which forced new legislation. The main influences were :-

1. New materials iron and steel,

2. New energy sources. Coal, Steam, Electricity, Petroleum.

3. New machines such as the spinning jenny and the power loom

4. Increased division of labour and specialization of function. Mass production.

5. Developments in transportation and communication, including the steam locomotive, steamship, automobile, airplane, telegraph, and radio.

EVENTS OF THE AQUARIAN AGE

Here are just a few events to illustrate progress. We see the beginnings of conflict between Science (Aquarius) and Religion (Pisces). We note the difference in theme and content to that of The Age of Pisces. An especial noteworthy trend is that from the early beginnings of the 5 main religions in the Age of Pisces there is now a separation, not only from control by the various states and monarchies, but also within themselves, with the formation of numerous sects with their own doctrines :-

1160	University of Paris separates from church control
1170	University of Oxford founded because English pupils were banned in Paris
1209	University of Cambridge founded
1247	Roger Bacon unites science and religion
1310	Persian (?) Abu Musa Jabir ibn Hayyan ("Geber") introduces Alchemy
1370	Nicholas Oresme argues for heliocentricity
1453	Gutenberg printing press (movable type) and first Gutenberg Bible
1492	Columbus discovers America
1534-1540	Henry VIII - removes control by the Pope and heads the Church of England
1543	Copernicus (Polish) –established the Sun as centre of solar system.
1564	William Shakespeare (English poet and playwright)
1571-1630	Kepler (Germany) - Laws of planetary motion b.27-12-1571
1600 – 1900	Rise and fall of the British Empire
1608	Hans Lippershey applies for telescope patent
1612	Foundation of the Baptist Church in England
1620	The "Pilgrim Fathers" found New England in America.
1627	Johannes Kepler (Germany) tabulates accurate planet positions
1633	Galileo forced to recant belief in Copernicanism (1543) by the Inquisition
1642-1727	Isaac Newton (Britain) Mathematics. Physics. Optics b.25-12-1642
1656	Christiaan Huygens (Dutch) invents the pendulum clock
1660	English preacher George Fox founds the Society of Friends (Quakers)
1661	Sir Isaac Newton in Cambridge
1697	Foundation of the Amish – a conservative Christian group
1738	John Wesley founds (Christian) Methodism
1760	Beginning of the Industrial Revolution
1768	Captain Cook voyage to the South Pacific
1775-1783	American War of Independence

ASTROLOGY : THE ZODIAC AGES

1781	* Discovery of Uranus by telescope (Britain) W.Hershel b.15.11.1738
1787	United States Constitution drafted – separates church and state.
1789	Discovery of Uranium (element)
1789-1799	French Revolution
1791–1867	Michael Faraday-Electromagnetism. Chemistry b.22-9-1791
1822	The Rosetta Stone enables interpretation of Egyptian religion.
1823	Charles Babbage "Difference Engine" (beginning of computers)
1831	Charles Darwin 5 year cruise on HMS Beagle
1833	Charles Babbage "Analytical Engine" b.26-12-1791
1843	First telegraph line (Philadelphia to Washington) America
1846	* Discovery of Neptune by mathematics (Leverrier b.18-3-1811)
1856-1939	Psychiatry pioneer Sigmund Freud (Austria). b.6-5-1856
1859	Charles Darwin " …… Origin of Species".
1863	Seventh Day Adventist Church founded in America.
1875-1961	C.G.Jung (Switzerland) Psychiatry. Psychology b.26-7-1875
1877	Phonograph. Edison (America) b.11-2-1847
1878	William Booth foundation of The Salvation Army.
1879	Christian Science Church founded in Boston, America.
1887	Motion picture camera
1892	Beginning of radio (electromagnetic waves) Nikola Tesla (Croatia)
1893	Ghandi in S.Africa campaign against racism later British rule in S.Asia
1898	Radium discovery (Marie & Pierre Curie- France)
1899-1902	Boer War – challenge to the British Empire
1899	Sigmund Freud book "The Interpretation of Dreams"
1901	Marconi (Italy) transatlantic radio message b.25-4-1874
1903	First aeroplane - Wright Brothers(America)
1905	Einstein Relativity Theory b.14-3-1879. Published 1916.
1926	First Television (Baird) b.13-8-1888
1929	BBC begins broadcasting
1930	* Discovery of Pluto using photography 18-2-1930
1932	Discovery of the Neutron (James Chadwick)
1938	Discovery of nuclear fission (Hahn & Strassman)
1940	Discovery of Neptunium (element).
1941	Discovery of Plutonium (element)
1943	"Colossus" first programmable computer (England)
1947	Discovery of The Dead Sea Scrolls
1948	Nation of Israel established in Palestine.
1953	Double helix structure of DNA
1955	Martin Luther King bus boycott in Alabama
1957	Sputnik (Russia) first satellite
1960-1980	First use of the term "The New Age" and "Age of Aquarius"
1968	Intel Corporation founded to make "computer chips" (America)
1970	"Cloud" diagram used for Telephone networks diagrams
1973	First Mobile Telephone (Motorola)-weighed 1 kilogram
1975	Microsoft Corporation founded (America)

1975	*Benoit Mandelbrot discovers fractals*
1977	*Apple computers sold to home users (America) (Steve Jobs b.5-10-1955)*
1979	*First automated cellular network (Japan)*
1980	*Sir Clive Sinclair ZX80 home computer (England) b.30-7-1940*
1981	*IBM first "Personal Computers"- founded 1911 (America)*
1981	*BBC\Acorn Micro Home Computer*
1982	*Microsoft MSDOS Version 1 (Bill Gates b.28-10-1955)*
1983	*The Internet opens*
1985	*Microsoft Windows Version 1*
1989	*Development of the World Wide Web CERN Switzerland*
1989	*Norman Ramsey Nobel Prize for the Atomic Clock*
1990	*Microsoft Office Version 1 for Windows*
1990	*The Human Genome Project*
1990 +	*Growth of radical Islamic movements.*
1997	*Term "Weblog" by Jorn Barger.*
2000	*Development of "The Cloud" personal data services on the Internet*
2004	*Facebook social networking service*
2005	*Human genetic code found to be 98% chimpanzee*
2006	*Twitter social networking service*
2011	*Apple iCloud launch – remote storage of data.*

AGE OF CAPRICORN 3470-5640 AD

Taking the Sign of Capricorn as a guide, we can speculate about the future. Capricorn is mainly concerned with hierarchical structures and large organisations of people. This refers to such areas as Church, Government, and large business organisations. One effect of The Age of Aquarius has been to make the world a "smaller place". Apart from Computers and other methods of communication we have had massive growth of AIR travel. The growth of science and technology has also resulted in a huge growth in world population – not just because more babies are being born but also because medical science has improved our life expectancy. Because of this, the resources of the Earth discovered in the Industrial Age are becoming depleted. We have Global Warming.

Capricorn is concerned with Control. As the population grows this becomes more difficult. So, following from the previous paragraph, there could be some form of World Government. It may be that George Orwell's book "1984" with "Big Brother" government control may be more predictive than we imagine today. We are seeing the beginnings of restrictions to our "democratic rights" by increased public surveillance from traffic and other cameras "for the greater good". Our pets can have microchip implants to identify them, this could easily be extended to individual humans – with added functionality for location and personal accountability. Money could cease to exist as internet control of our bank account becomes more automated. The electronic tags like those contained in our rail tickets or security cards could be incorporated.

From the above we see the balancing effect of the complementary Sign of Cancer (Shell. Security).

Control of the world's resources by a single body is more likely to enable the colonisation of other planets. Global problems require global co-operation.

ASTROLOGY : PLANETS

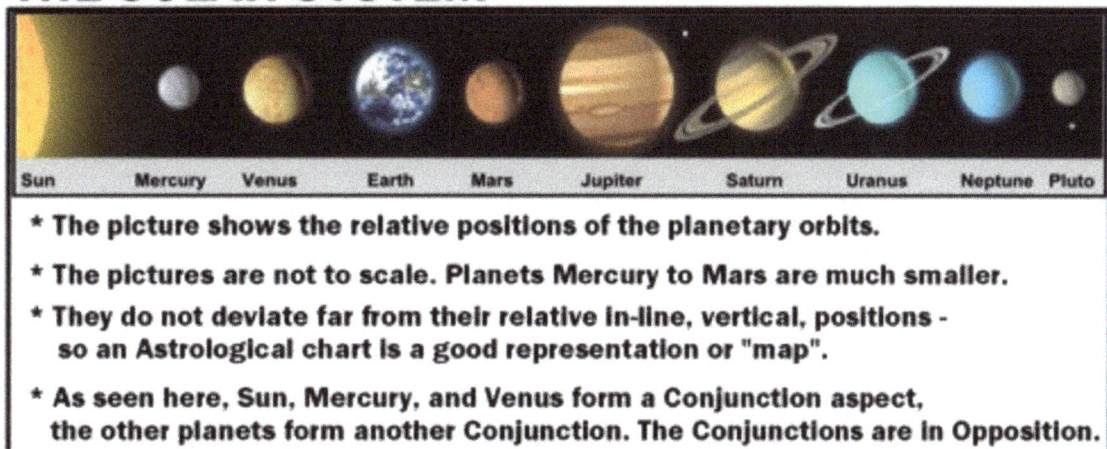

Figure 32 : The Solar System

PLANET RULERS OF ZODIAC SIGNS AND HOUSES

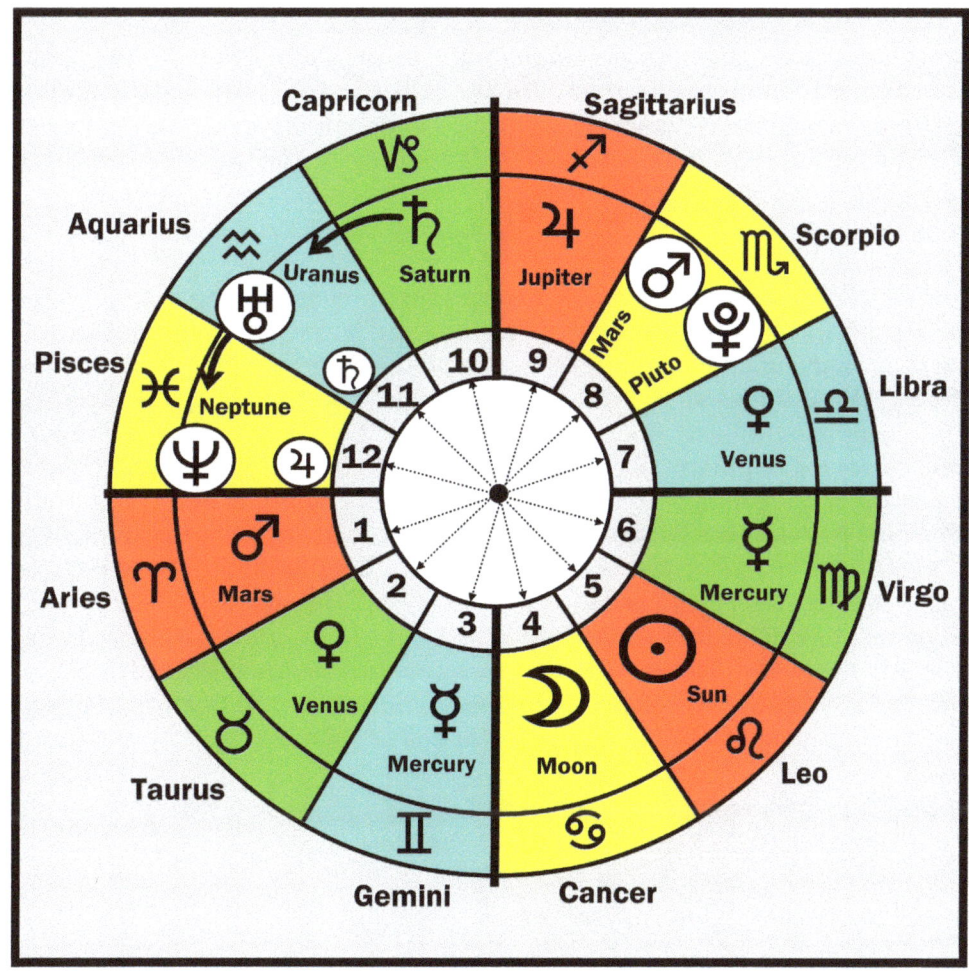

Figure 33 : Planet Rulers of Zodiac Signs and Transcendence

ASTROLOGY : PLANETS

OVERVIEW

The wheel diagram above summarises the archetypal rulership pattern of the planets by House and Sign, you will note that some of the planets have relationships with more than one House and Sign. The table at the end of the chapter summarises the information of the wheel diagram with additional details.

In keeping with the spirit of this book, we are here attempting to understand the basic or archetypal principles at work.

1. The field of Astrology is a study of the actual manifestations of the archetypal energies in physical form on Earth. However, at this level it is possible to get the right answers for the wrong "reason" because we are far away from the non-material motivating principles.
2. We therefore compare the traditional planet meanings with those described in [THE KABBALAH TREE OF LIFE] and [NUMEROLOGY] which deal with life at a more basic, evolutionary level.
3. For the purposes of this book it is only necessary to give a broad outline of the functions of the planets in a chart. The main text gives a brief description of each, and there is additional detail in a wheel diagram and a table. I only include planets discovered up to that of Pluto in 1930. Some Astrologers consider the positions of other bodies discovered in our solar system, some of which are undecided as to whether they are planets or asteroids (for example, Chiron). As far as I am concerned we still have a long way to go in examining and understanding the effects of the recent discoveries of the major bodies Uranus, Neptune, and Pluto. Pluto has not yet made a complete cycle of 248 years since its discovery.
4. The planets all get their basic energy (light and heat) from the central Sun.
5. In Astrology, Sun and Moon are treated the same as the other planets.

[THE KABBALAH TREE OF LIFE] SUMMARY

1. Please see the diagram in [THE KABBALAH TREE OF LIFE].
2. My arrangement departs slightly from the traditional Tree of Life where the 3 Sephirah at the top ("The Supernals") have no planetary relationships. We can now add the 3 Transcendent Planets mentioned.
3. The Tree of Life places planets in the same relative positions that they occupy in the Solar System beginning with the furthest at the top – which are the relatively newly discovered Pluto, Neptune and Uranus - and ending with Earth at the bottom.
4. With this arrangement as intermediary we can accurately associate Planets with Numbers Zero to 9 [NUMEROLOGY].
5. We can also associate Planets with Chakras, and see that it is not a simple 1 to 1 relationship. Some Chakras have 2 associated planets with activities that traditionally tend to oppose one another. This complies with their body functions in that the associated endocrine gland produces hormones that have opposing effects. [THE CHAKRAS]
6. The Kabbalah Tree of Life transfers energy from Sephiroth 1 (Kether. Crown) to Sephirah 9 (Malkuth. Earth) via the intervening Sephiroth in numerical order. This is termed "The Lightning Flash". When we consider the planetary rulerships of the Astrological Houses and Signs and compare them with the planet relationships to the Kabbalist Sephiroth we find that The Lighting Flash follows the same sequence as the Stages of The Cycle of Growth, and the order of planets in our Solar System.
7. The traditional Lightning Flash only describes the transfer of energy from "Heaven to Earth" – although implied by Kabbalist practices, there is no explicit transcendental return journey. Using The Cycle of Growth Stages and the newly discovered planets we can now rectify this omission.

This arrangement differs from Edgar Cayce's planetary associations with The Chakras. However, in keeping with the spirit of this book, we have to consider the actual material evidence we have. Here we can see 4 sets of relationships :–

1. The planet positions as they are in the solar system.
2. Their traditional associations with the Sephiroth of The Tree of Life.
3. The Cycle of Growth relationship with The Lightning Flash.
4. The positions of The Chakras in the human body.

ASTROLOGY : PLANETS

PLANETS IN BIRTH CHARTS
[ASTROLOGY : CHART EXAMPLES]

In this chapter we are mainly considering the positions of planets in a Birth Chart, which are fixed for the lifetime of an individual person, and only relate to that person. In a chart the function of a planet is not always exactly the same. Its behaviour is modified by :-

1. Its own specific nature.
2. Its position by Zodiac Sign which might make its expression easy or hard.
3. Its chart House position – which, in a Birth Chart, is more specific or personal to the subject.
4. *(Therefore, with 12 Signs and 12 Houses there are 144 possible interpretations for each planet).*
5. Its aspects, or angular relationships, with other planets in the Birth Chart.
6. The Will and Consciousness of the subject.

PLANET ASPECTS
[ASTROLOGY : PLANETARY ASPECTS]

Aspects are angular relationships between any 2 planets in their orbits depending on their positions by Zodiac degree and Sign. They are calculated by drawing lines between planets in a chart and its central point. Some angular relationships are more important than others in terms of their effect. We therefore have a Number 3 triangular relationship with any 2 planets producing an effect at The Centre.

PLANET TRANSITS
[ASTROLOGY : PLANET TRANSITS]

The positions of planets in a Birth Chart are fixed at the time of birth. The planets continue in their orbits around the Earth afterwards, and according to their positions at any later time, make aspects with all the planets in a chart, including the birth position of the planet itself. In a complete transit cycle of a planet through all the Houses of a Birth Chart and return to its place as at the time of birth it makes every possible aspect with all the other planets in the chart, both "easy" and "hard" – so the overall effect is Zero. For example, the orbit of The Sun takes 1 year and returns to the birth position on each birthday.

When we compare the later transit positions of a planet with its own birth position we call them Generic Transits because, no matter where they begin, the relative positions are always the same through any lifetime. For example, Saturn returns to its birth position every 30 years. This is what makes the overall structure of a human lifetime the same for us all.

When we compare a planet transit with other planets in a Birth Chart we call them Personal Transits because no one is exactly the same in this respect.

PLANETARY EFFECTS
[THE CHAKRAS]

It is generally understood that the planetary energies relate to our energy centres (Chakras) which form a link between our physical bodies and other forces of The Collective Unconscious. Each one vibrates to a particular frequency – like a musical note. The planets do not control them or us, they act as an physical indicators of the forces at work – like a twig dropped into a stream. Each Chakra operates at 4 different levels which relate to The 4 Elements. Some Chakras have 2 associated planets.

MYTHOLOGY

1. Despite efforts to choose other names, when the Transcendent Planets (with orbits outside that of Saturn) Uranus, Neptune, and Pluto were discovered it was finally decided to name them after mythological gods in keeping with the other planets. The names are in keeping with their Astrological activities – so this is an example of how The Collective Unconscious affects us.
2. *(For example, in [THE ZODIAC AGES] I suggest that the building of pyramids, ziggurats, and stone circles in The Age of Aries is a manifestation of "The Spirit of The Age" rather than having any particular "reason". We do not have as much control over life as we would like to think.*

3. It is from Mythology that we probably get the best idea of the workings of some Archetypes of The Collective Unconscious. We have to remember that in ancient times the psychology of the people was based more on Intuition (Right Brain) than Thinking (Left Brain). The Thinking Function includes such abilities as Reading, Writing, and Arithmetic which had not developed to the level of today – the Hunter Gatherer had no use for them. There was no Science and no "Big Bang" in consciousness.

4. In considering planets it is useful to consider them in terms of living beings with basic forms of energy and likes and dislikes. For example, some planets get on reasonably well together, others do not (depending on their environment - or Sign).

5. When we read the stories of Mythology we see a picture of continual change and conflict – especially between the male gods and their offspring – who were considered challenges to their authority and status. There was no fidelity in relationships, gods and goddesses mated more or less indiscriminately, even with their own siblings – there was much jealousy despite both parties in relationships being unfaithful. This is not a lot different to the modern Soap Opera. We have examples of the challenging and co-operative aspects planets form with one another during their orbits.

6. Part of the reason for incest was that there were not that many gods at the beginning. It all began with Gaia (Mother Earth. Mother Nature) being formed out of primeval chaos who gave (virgin) birth to Uranus ("Sky". "Heaven"). The first "family" (The Titans) only consisted of parents and 12 (NB!) children, so it is not surprising that they began mating with one another – including father and mother.

7. We note the universal law that when something is created out of Primeval Chaos its complement is created too – thus keeping the universal balance at the original Zero state. Hence the "even-ings" of Genesis.

8. In the Bible, Heaven was created on Creation Day 2. [GENESIS AND THE CYCLE OF GROWTH].

9. We note that the Genesis story is not a lot different from modern scientists' description of the formation of planets from the debris of The Big Bang.

10. For some reason, or lack of it, the male gods tended to fear that they would be ousted from their positions of power by their offspring and a habit developed whereby they swallowed or devoured their children at birth – later on in the stories, they would be forced to regurgitate them alive. The stories continue with variations on mothers' attempts to hide their new-born and/or fool the father into eating something else.

11. The stories hold a similar theme to the birth of Moses in Egypt who survived pharaoh's command to kill all new born Hebrew children. It is also similar to the survival of Jesus when Herod commanded the killing of all children under 2 years of age. The "Immaculate Conception" relates to Cycle of Growth Stage 9 (Conception. Sagittarius. Pluto. The Big Bang)

12. We also note that, apart from planets, we can consider the gods as being the chemical elements that evolved, beginning with Hydrogen (Atomic Number 1) which is the "father and mother" of all others. This relationship is considered in the chapter [NUMEROLOGY]. Chemical elements "mate" with one another to form various compounds. For example Hydrogen and Oxygen give birth to Water, Hydrogen and Sulphur give birth to Hydrogen Sulphide ("bad egg gas"). The increase in "population" is explained by the evolution of new elements which produce new compounds which combine with other compounds.... and so on.

13. Another relationship is with the "Gaia Hypothesis" proposed by Henry Lovelock in the 1970s that the Earth behaves like a self- regulating, living organism. At the bottom of The Tree of Life, Sephirah 10 (Malkuth. Earth) is on The Middle Pillar of Balance and Equilibrium, and therefore benefitting from direct relationship with Kether (Crown). It has no will of its own and therefore gives a material, concrete, example of the Original Plan. As Above, So Below, As Below, So Above.

PLANETARY RULERSHIPS

Like people, the Planets are able to express themselves better in some environments (Zodiac Signs and Birth Chart Houses) and are inhibited by others.

RULERSHIP (DIGNITY) AND DETRIMENT

The Rulership position is the natural "home" of a planet (House or Sign) where it works most easily because its basic energy is the same as the Sign. Detriment occurs when a planet is in the complementary Sign to that of its rulership (on the opposite side of a chart). A Planet is said to "Disposit" (transfer) the energy of its Rulership Sign to wherever it is placed – just like an individual person. Its most positive position would therefore be in the Sign of its rulership. Having the same energy, if placed elsewhere in a chart it connects its position to its Sign rulership position even though there may not be a planetary Aspect.

Possible permutations and combination possibilities are virtually endless. For example, in my birth chart, with Libra rising, I have several planets in their rulership Houses but in detriment by Sign.

Some planets rule more than one Sign.

EXALTATION AND FALL

Exaltation has a similar effect as Rulership, and Fall as Detriment. A planet in Exaltation gains supporting energy from its Rulership position.

THE TRANSCENDENT PLANETS

We begin a more detailed description of the Planets by dealing with them in order of Evolution as depicted in The Kabbalah Tree of Life. From the simple to the complex.

1. Evolution and Transcendence will eventually take us back to our roots in Heaven.
2. The recently discovered Transcendent Planets take mankind beyond the earlier boundaries imposed by man's physical senses and abilities (Saturn). In Astrology this is symbolised by the replacement of the old, traditional Rulers of Aquarius, Pisces, and Scorpio with new ones. The Transcendent planets are more related to the use of individual Will. Until Will is operating, the individual is still controlled by Saturn's social traditions, and cannot go beyond its boundaries.
3. Saturn does not give in easily. Its very nature has built up a strong position based on firm foundations. Battering at his thick castle walls has no effect. We can only make changes from within. In fact, using Saturn Discipline to enable Saturn to grow.

NEPTUNE

This planet is dealt with first because it relates to Sephirah 1 (Kether. Crown). Although Pluto is the outermost planet of our Solar System, its orbit does sometimes take it inside that of Neptune. As we shall see, Neptune is the beginning.

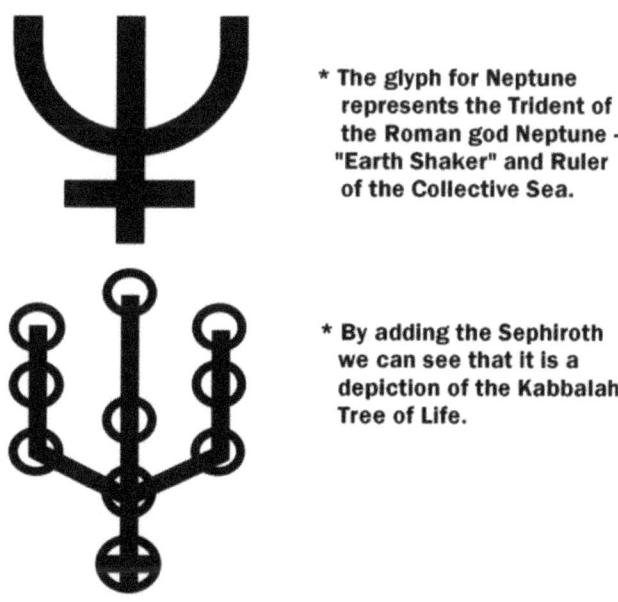

* The glyph for Neptune represents the Trident of the Roman god Neptune - "Earth Shaker" and Ruler of the Collective Sea.

* By adding the Sephiroth we can see that it is a depiction of the Kabbalah Tree of Life.

Figure 34 : Neptune and The Tree of Life

1. NEPTUNE IS KARMA. The universe tends toward a Zero balance.
2. "Cause and Effect" is a simplified concept at a human level, but complex at the archetypal level. There are too many words. However, the sum of the words is Zero.

ASTROLOGY : PLANETS

3. A Principle of Neptune is Dissolution, which is activity to return everything to the original state of primeval chaos where everything is Zero. The "sea" of The Collective. Some people return too soon, when they lose consciousness of their Personal Identity. There is no Will.

4. Neptune was discovered in 1846 due to variations in the orbit of Uranus. After a lot of discussion the decision was made to name it after a Roman god in keeping with the other planets. Its orbit of The Sun takes 165 years.

5. The glyph of Neptune is the simplified, basic, version of The Kabbalah Tree of Life. It depicts the original concept, idea, or plan, of the universe before the Creation. It also looks like a Trident – a 3 prong fishing spear. Neptune rules Pisces (The Fishes).

6. Neptune relates to Number Zero, the (empty) Circle of Life which contains everything else. The Ideal.

7. Sephirah 1. Kether (The Crown. Number Zero) is the basic source of The Tree of Life from which all other Sephiroth have developed. Together with Sephiroth 2 (Force. Number 1) and 3 (Form. Number 2) it exists outside all possible human physical, mental, and emotional experience – except via the "filters" of the other Sephiroth. Here we have the state of the universe before "The Big Bang" that began the formation of Matter as a Singularity (Saturn), together with the release of a large amount of energy (Pluto).

8. This is the state of the universe before the development of the Singularity (Number 1) which gave rise to The Big Bang. The same state of chaos exists today in stars – including our Sun – which consist of Plasma – mainly Hydrogen - at extremely high temperature. The Hydrogen is being converted to Helium and other heavier chemical elements by nuclear reaction, as with The Big Bang.

9. Plasma, only recently discovered, is the 4th. State of Matter which precedes Gas, Liquid, and Solid.

10. In Mythology Poseidon/Neptune is God of the Sea, "creator of waters" and "Earth Shaker" – bringer of earthquakes as an indicator of earthly chaos. As we see below, his activity is more by psychological confusion than overt action. He was given rulership of the sea by his brother Zeus/Jupiter after Zeus returned and overthrew their father Kronos/Saturn who thought that he had swallowed him at birth. (His mother Rhea had substituted a stone). Hades/Pluto, another (actually swallowed) brother, was disgorged and given rulership of the Underworld of the dead at the same time. In this story we have an enactment of the same principle which is implied in the concept of Astrological Transcendence, involving the need to overcome Saturn (symbol of social order) – who also castrated his father Uranus (incidentally giving life to Venus, Desire when the genitals were thrown into the "sea"). We also see the "brotherly" sibling relationship between Jupiter, Neptune and Pluto.

11. The principle of Neptune is Dissolution and can be related to Aqua Regia ("Royal Water") – the mixture of Sulphuric and Nitric Acids that can dissolve gold. Its main function is that of dissolving old Saturn structures that have outlived their usefulness into their basic elements so they can be re-used. In Nature this refers to the process of decay which occurs each year during Autumn and Winter. In the human mind this is "forgetting" – allied with "forgiveness". As "top of The Tree", we can see that some of the work is delegated to Pluto who releases Force from Matter in Sephirah 2 (Chockmah, Force. Number 1). $E = MC^2$.

12. Neptune rules Pisces, which is concerned with the "sea" of the Collective Unconscious. On Earth, the sea contains all physical elements in solution, including gold. Pisces is the realm of Psychology, Mysticism, Music, and The Arts, and any other activity that attempts to manifest contents of the Collective Unconscious in physical form. Until Neptune's discovery in 1846 Pisces was originally ruled by Jupiter (Expansion), which is concerned with expanding existing Saturn hierarchical structures. As examples we have the global expansion world trade and the rise of population producing the great global Civilisations and Empires. Like the earlier dinosaurs, there is a tendency to grow too large to be able to sustain themselves in the face of global (and internal Uranus) challenges, and be forced to break down into smaller "elements" (individual people).

13. We see examples of this in the rise and fall of the Roman and British Empires, and the National Health Service today in the United Kingdom that has become too big for its own good. It would seem that we are ready for individuals Uranus) to start taking responsibility for their own personal health rather than relying on The State (Saturn).

14. Neptune is in detriment in the Earth Sign Virgo which requires precise attention to detail. Neptune blurs things, and prefers an imaginary world to practical reality. Although they are both necessary to The

Cycle of Growth, we can see how their energies are antagonistic to one another when together at the same time and place.

15. Neptune/Pisces is related to Cycle of Growth Stage 12 (Withdrawal. Confinement) which is the time when the mother withdraws in preparation for the birth of her child. It is connected with Hospitals, Prisons and other areas of retreat. As the last stage of The Cycle It also has concern with Karma that must be repaid (to make a zero balance) before further progress can be made.
16. Astrological Neptune cannot act positively until Uranus has performed its task of Individuation. Only then can the Individual survive collective forces. It is clear that to connect with the power of the Collective Unconscious in a positive way one needs a high level of personal integration.
17. We see the negative effects of Neptune in people that use unnatural methods of raising consciousness with alcohol and drugs. A form of escapism from practical living (Saturn). The development of Will allows no shortcuts. We note that Will Power is required for addicts to return to a stable state and the physical reality we all share. We note that complementary Virgo's (Service to Self. Health) main concern is that of maintaining physical and mental health, so the 2 "sides" are not really "opposites".
18. There is correspondence with the Hindu God Shiva (The Destroyer) who is depicted with a trident.
19. A negative aspect of imaginative Neptune is the tendency to avoid material reality and live in an imaginary dream world. At a positive level such activities as The Arts, Music, and Mysticism can relate to Transcendence. Authors have "The Power of God" over the worlds they create.
20. We have to especially note that all of the lower Sephiroth on The Tree of Life are contained in Sephirah 1 (Kether. Crown) albeit in undeveloped state – without any form.
21. Neptune/Sephirah 1 (Kether. Crown) relates to The Crown Chakra.
22. At the level of Neptune we are all one and the same – hence its effect on The Age of Pisces giving birth to many philosophers ("lovers of wisdom" – for its own sake/without specific purpose).

PLUTO

* The glyph of Pluto is a symbol of involution with the Circle of Spirit being received by the Semi-circle of Soul and transmuted into the practical reality of the Cross of Matter.

* It is also a symbol of evolution where matter is transmuted to Spirit. $E=Mc^2$

1. The principle of Pluto is Regeneration.
2. In the Tree of Life it is the beginning of downward journey of The Involutionary Lightning Flash, and the Evolutionary journey of the return – and the expansion of the universe that is still occurring today.
3. In the absence of a traditional planet for Sephirah 2 (Chokmah. Wisdom. Force) in The Kabbalah Tree of Life, I have associated it with Pluto which relates to its principle of unlimited Force, or the energy of nuclear reaction . In the glyph we see the Spiritual Zero of Sephirah 1. Kether (Crown) being eventually converted into The Cross of Form (here abstract, as an Idea). At this level of manifestation we are in the abstract spiritual realms above any possibility of mental concept or physical form. The next stage of Creation therefore is the appearance of Sephiroth 3. Binah (Understanding. Saturn. Satan) which is the spiritual concept of Form not yet realised.

ASTROLOGY : PLANETS

4. Pluto relates to Number 1, which is a phallic symbol. Pure energy with, as yet, no object of release. In Mathematics it is a single point having no dimensions. The Singularity of The Big Bang. The dot within the circle.

5. At our lower level, we can see this as the drive required for the Sperm (dot) to penetrate the Egg at Cycle of Growth Stage 9 (Conception. Sagittarius). Another form of Big Bang. Still lower down we have the similar rutting of The Ram at Cycle of Growth Stage 1 (Seed. Aries. Mars) – both Stages are connected with the Fire Element and energise the beginning of the 1st. and 2nd. Octaves of The Logarithmic Timescale respectively. The former is the beginning of a human life in the womb (circle/shell). The latter is the beginning of life on Earth (circle/shell).

6. Chockmah (Sephirah 2, Wisdom. The Father) at the top of the Pillar of Mercy (Force) is the principle of Positive Polarity. As a result of the creation of Chockmah, Binah (Sephirah 3, Understanding. The Mother) at the top of the Pillar of Severity (Form) became the principle of Negative Polarity. We note that on Creation Day 1 in Genesis God created Day (Chockmah. light. consciousness) and Night (Binah. dark. unconsciousness). As with the other Creation Days, the creation of something required the creation of something else to complement it ("opposite") which, in turn, required an "evening" process to adjust the universal balance of energy to the original Zero State of Kether (Crown). No-Thing.

7. From Einstein we learned that Energy and Matter are the same "thing".

8. Pluto is concerned with the Involution of Spirit into Matter, as in the early formation of our material universe. On the Return journey it is Evolution of Matter into Spirit, such as Research that brings the secrets of the universe into the "light" of human consciousness – which includes "taboo" subjects such as Freud's consideration of sexually related problems, and Jung's recognition of The Collective Unconscious (itself related to Neptune). It relates to such things as The Laws of Physics in the outer world, and Psychology, Alchemy, and Mysticism in general as forms of "inner search" – all resulting in increased consciousness (light).

9. Pluto has especially close symbolic association with nuclear physics and Einstein's Relativity Theory which were in their infancy at the time of Pluto's discovery. $E=MC^2$ states that energy and matter consist of the same thing, and gave rise to the atomic bomb - which releases energy from matter. The stars of the universe, including our Sun, are still carrying out this nuclear reaction which converts Hydrogen to heavier elements.

10. This gives us a further association with the concept of "Critical Mass" when atomic particles (and people) gather together in gradually increasing numbers until they reach a state where they "explode" – thus destroying social and material structures. We see some examples in such activities as war, the ancient Roman arena, sport, and political demonstrations (all related to Mars) that can erupt into violence when large numbers of people gather together.

11. In Astrology, Pluto has been given co-rulership of Scorpio and the 8th.House which are concerned with "Sex, Death, and Regeneration". I give Scorpio (and Cycle of Growth Stage 8) 3 traditional symbols – The Scorpion, The Eagle, and The Dove – which are related to stages of development of consciousness beyond the material world. As with Aquarius and Pisces, Scorpio had a more mundane ruler – in this case Mars - until the discovery of its transcendent planet. Pluto is therefore connected with Uranus and Individuation, and begins to take over from Mars - God of War and (Freud's concept of) Sex - unconsciously when we die, or when we <u>consciously</u> begin to explore the secrets of life and death – and our own personal\collective "underworld". This suggests a connection with Reincarnation.

12. To Transcend an existing state requires Death to the first Dimension and Rebirth into the next.

13. We can actively use Pluto by investigating the secrets of life which requires application of Will and meditation – which gives rise to Regeneration.

14. The Sign following Scorpio is Sagittarius related to Cycle of Growth Stage 9 (Conception) which traditionally has relationship with academic knowledge. Cycle of Growth Stage 9, which relates to Number 1, is the actual place where The Cycle of Growth Begins. Sagittarius as the Mutable (changeable) Fire Sign relates to Plasma exactly.

15. At a mundane level, Pluto\Scorpio refers to such areas as the 3 stages of development of a caterpillar, to chrysalis, to butterfly (Metamorphosis) each of which requires complete reorganisation of its physical structure – although the life-giving Spirit is the same. We also have decomposition of the physical body into its basic elements after death - following the release of the life-giving Spirit . Those "dead" elements

ASTROLOGY : PLANETS

are then available to form the basis of new structures. So, once again, we have an example of the equivalence of Energy and Matter.

16. Pluto was discovered on February 18th. 1930. Originally 1,000 suggestions were made worldwide for its name which was eventually decided in favour of that of an 11 year old English schoolgirl who was interested in Mythology. Despite original efforts to the contrary, the 3 Transcendent Planets have ended up with mythological names. It has two glyphs, one of which consists of the initials of its discoverer Percival Lowell. The other glyph is based on that of Neptune, with the centre prong of the trident replaced with a circle relating to Number Zero (Kether. Crown). The Centre Pillar of [THE KABBALAH TREE OF LIFE] is re-formed when Uranus/Daath (Will) is reactivated.

17. In Mythology Hades/Pluto is God of Wealth and Ruler of the "Underworld" (Scorpio, Fixed Water, is concerned with emotional self-control) , the abode of the dead, which contains two areas that we can consider as "heaven and hell" (Elysium and Tartarus). There is an implication of judgement and reward or punishment for our actions in life (Karma). He was a brother of Zeus/Jupiter and Poseidon/Neptune. Having been swallowed at birth by his father Kronos/Saturn, he was released by Zeus/Jupiter who overthrew their father to become "King of the Gods and Men". This action also suggests the mundane rulership by Jupiter of Pisces (now also transcendent Neptune) taking over from the mundane rulership by Saturn of Aquarius in The Cycle of Growth Stages 11 and 12. The motivation here being of worldly domination rather than Transcendence (Individuation. Uranus). The common scenario of godly fathers "swallowing" their offspring at birth and later being "overthrown" suggests some form of repression by Authority (Saturn), with the possibility of releasing the blocked psychosexual energy – reference Cycle of Growth Stage 10 (Peak. Social Position).

18. Sephirah 2 (Pluto. Chockmah. Wisdom. Force) is related to God, Heaven, Light, Consciousness. Sephirah 3 (Saturn. Binah, Understanding, Form) is related to Satan, Hell, Darkness, The Unconscious. Together they are the roots of all Positive and Negative polarities. We note that God and The Devil, as seeming opposing forces, are not at the top of The Tree, where they are united to total Zero.

19. Pluto, with its long orbit cycle, works slowly in The Underworld – beneath the surface of life – until its results become public (Critical Mass). Its position in a Birth Chart indicates how the individual comes into contact with larger social changes. Its 248 year cycle is very erratic, sometimes coming closer to earth than Neptune. It can be in a Zodiac Sign for anything between 12 to 36 years – and affects everyone born in that period in a similar way. So it is more like "The Spirit of a Generation".

20. Most of us connect to Pluto by experiencing the results. In my case I have Pluto in the 10th. House (Social Peak. Career), which, among other things, is concerned with the kind of organisation one is part of to earn a living. From the beginning of my working life I have been subject to redundancy situations as a result of company takeovers – some of which I "survived" and some not – each time I had to find another job, some with the new company, some not. Those involved in negotiating possible company takeovers are legally obliged to carry them out in secret in case share prices are affected. When revealed, they come as a shock to those affected.

21. Pluto is also related to Regeneration of the physical body that can occur during meditation. It is related to Spiritual Healing. The Resurrection of Jesus after his crucifixion is an example.

22. One effect of Pluto is to bring about violent activities (Critical Mass) in groups of people who feel that their interests are being restricted or ignored. Energy is repressed until it reaches explosive power.

23. When Pluto was discovered in 1930 in the Sign of Cancer it was a time of global financial depression following a stock market crash.

1995 – 2007 Pluto in SAGITTARIUS (Jupiter. Expansion. Academic Mind. Religion. Universities)

Sagittarius has association with academic study and religion. We have seen an increase in suicide and other bombings (Pluto explosions) by Islamic extremists resulting in increased social security (Saturn control, restrictions to Jupiter expansion).

2008 – 2024 Pluto in CAPRICORN (Consolidation. Government. Traditional Structures. Hierarchies. Saturn)

Capricorn is concerned with government organisations and big business. One of its main functions is to curb excessive Sagittarius/Jupiter Expansion. At the time of writing in 2014, apart from measures to counteract terrorist threats – which affect the general public - there is global unrest with protests and rioting against governments concerning such things as unfair party elections, and restrictions and cutbacks due to a downturn in global economy. The big banks were paid billions of pounds to avoid another depression, and they have been

ASTROLOGY : PLANETS

under attack for mis-selling PPI insurance (security) - being forced to pay back billions of pounds. Capricorn is the complement to Cancer, and we see similarities to the 1930s. This time government intervention has prevented families losing their savings and livelihood.

URANUS

Uranus is mentioned here although it does not become active until the "return journey" – if at all.

* The glyph of Uranus (Sky) is similar to that of Mars with the Cross of Matter above the Circle of Spirit, but has the addition of two receptors.
* Personal drive is modified by information from the super conscious - like the television aerial receiving sound and pictures.

1. We note the similarity of the glyph of Uranus to the first letter in the surname of its discoverer William Hershel on March 13th. 1781. Pluto also has a glyph based on its discoverer's name. The planet axis of Uranus is odd in that it is almost at right angles to that of the other planets, so each of its poles is in darkness for 42 years, and light for 42 years (half its 84 year orbit).
2. There is no traditional appearance of Uranus in The Kabbalah Tree of Life because they did not know it existed. However, I have related it to Daath (the un-numbered Sephirah), which, itself, has no traditional planet association. The link is justified by the relationship, by different authorities, of Uranus and Daath with Will and The Throat Chakra. We also include the modern Jungian concept of Individuation. There is more information in the chapter [THE KABBALAH TREE OF LIFE].
3. Daath is on the Middle Pillar of The Tree as the path across The Abyss. However, it does not exist on the same dimension as the rest of The Tree (which has 4 Kingdoms of its own). It links Sephirah 6 (The Sun) at the centre of the Middle Pillar and Sephirah 1 (Neptune, Number Zero) at The Crown.
4. In The Kabbalah, Daath refers to "Learning By Experience".
5. In Mythology Ouranus/Uranus means "Sky" or "Heaven". Its rulership of Aquarius, the Fixed Air Sign, gives it relationship with all kinds of communication that use "air waves", including speaking, radio, television, and computers. Ideas are "fixed" into words for transmission and reception. The mythological account of Creation says that at first there was nothing, and the first manifestation was feminine Gaia (Earth) who was formed out of the primeval chaos. We see that this relates to Sephirah 2 (Binah. Mother) on The Tree of Life. From the seeming paired balance that Nature requires, Ouranus/Uranus was later formed as her masculine consort and they mated together to produce further gods. In terms of the creation of our physical elements it could mean, among other things, such as Uranus relating to the gaseous elements that make up most of our solar system – such as Hydrogen, Helium and Oxygen.
6. Uranus is related to Cycle of Growth Stage 11 (Discontent) and The Age of Aquarius.
7. Saturn ruled Aquarius in addition to Capricorn until the discovery of revolutionary, inventive, Uranus in 1781, now both planets have rulership. Until that time the tendency was for individuals to follow in the footsteps of their parents in following traditions and ways of making a living - and large nations had grown by using Saturn's order and discipline. The problem now arose that the hierarchical structures built up over a long period – the State and The Church, with one man at the head – were becoming irritating to the general population who were paying ever increasing taxes and getting nothing in return. Here is the growth of Democracy where the Individual gets some say in his destiny. Uranus is in

ASTROLOGY : PLANETS

detriment in Leo where the energy for Change is restricted by "The King" – or channelled into disruptive behaviour to be "different" and bring attention – being destructive rather than creative. Uranus requires destruction of past structures, but there must be something created to take its place. Change is Stability. Stability, Change.

8. In simplified terms of the Individual person, dual rulership of Aquarius means that one follows the path of either Saturn or Uranus in the Transcendental Octave of the Birth Chart. It is a matter of personal choice to follow a traditional Saturn path or find a personal one. For the individual person, Uranus relates to the Jungian Process of Individuation. This does not necessarily mean that one becomes a revolutionary, challenging everything Saturn stands for. Those who do that are still bound to Saturn in a more subtle way. Rather one must undertake the hard work of examining one's life and experience, and follow the way that one is best suited for.

   *............ *Render therefore unto Caesar the things which are Caesar's; and unto God the things that are God's. [KJV Matthew 22 : 21]*

9. We note that in the story of the gods, above, Uranus precedes the others as the father, and is castrated (creative force removed) by his son Saturn. In effect this confirmed his fears that his children would replace him when they were born. We also see the symbolic relationship between the planets Uranus (Individuality. Integrity) and Saturn (Tradition) which more or less inhibits Uranus activity. We see how Saturn "castrates" Uranus in Astrological terms too - at Cycle of Growth Stage 11 (Discontent).

10. In Mythology, the genitals (creative energy) of Uranus were thrown in to the sea (Collective Unconscious. Neptune/Pisces). By returning energy to the original source the universe is required to rebalance. The result was that Venus appeared from out of the sea. In effect, Venus (Desire. Need. Dividedness) replaced Uranus (Individuality) which is always seeking its "missing parts". Venus is associated with "Venereal" diseases.

11. We can see how this led to misinterpretation by the "Hippy Generation" and "New Age" movement of the 1960s and 1970s giving attention to The Age of Aquarius and relating it to the "Free Love" of Venus rather than the Individuality of Uranus. For the source of this activity, which has since tended to die out, we would have to consider the Transcendent Planet positions in the Birth Charts of those who were involved – that is, born around 20 – 30 years earlier. With the general idealistic confusion and involvement with drugs we would expect to find challenging aspects with Neptune being activated by planet transits at the time. [THE ZODIAC AGES]

12. There is another relationship - that with The Fall of Adam, who went against his "father's" wishes in choosing The Tree of (carnal) Knowledge above The Tree of Life (creative force of The Chakras, which were "sealed" as a result).

13. Both Trees of Genesis refer to the same Chakra system. They are alternatives for the use of the Chakra System.

14. The Sephiroth Daath is said to be the aim, and position of, God's creation before The Fall. In effect, it was never meant to reach the material manifestation of Earth [EC].

ASTROLOGY : PLANETS

THE OUTER PLANETS

The Outer Planets that orbit between Earth and the Transcendent Planets, are those that take us into the exterior, public, world to relate to other people, and eventually to the Greater Collective, on the return journey of life.

There is a more practical in-depth study in [ASTROLGY : PLANET TRANSITS].

SATURN

* The components of the glyph of Saturn are the same as those of Jupiter. Here the Cross of Matter rises above the Semi-Circle of Soul.
* The abstract concepts of expansive Jupiter are forced into practical use – demanding physical evidence.
* The principle of Saturn is Consolidation.

1. The Principle of Saturn is Consolidation and Bringer of Form. Alchemy symbol for Lead – among the heavier metals.
2. From the appearance of Creative, Positive, Expansive energy (The Father) in Sephirah 1, the balancing force of Negative, Consolidating energy (The Mother) appears. Saturn/Satan challenges and complements God.
3. Here at the beginning we have to recognise that "opposites" are different aspects of the same thing. The path to Jungian Individuation requires "The Resolution of Opposites" – which is a return to the original balanced state of Neptune – albeit at a conscious rather than unconscious level. This is a hidden secret contained in the New Covenant brought by Jesus which refers to inner as well as outer practices. We see how this replaced the old Ten Commandments (Saturn) with "Love thy neighbour as thyself" (Uranus) .
4. Saturn relates to Number 2 as the second part of the Binary System – for example Positive and Negative, God and The Devil, Good and Evil – among which are contained the greatest universal dilemmas. In Mathematics a single point with another added becomes a line with 1 dimension, Length. A line has zero breadth.
5. The new String Theory of Science says that one dimensional strings (Number 2 lines. 1 dimension. Length) are the building blocks of matter rather than atoms (Number 1 points. Zero dimension). This is exactly in keeping with [KABBALAH TREE OF LIFE] and [NUMEROLOGY] principles mentioned here.
6. We see in the chapter [NUMEROLOGY] - which shows how the chemical elements develop from Hydrogen – that Nature can only count up to Number 2.
7. In The Kabbalah Tree of Life Saturn is at the top of the Pillar of Severity (Form) as Sephirah Number 3 Binah, Understanding, of which she has overall control. There are connotations with The Great Mother as the bringer of all Form as a result of impregnation by higher power (Chockmah. Pluto). Virgin Birth. The abstract ideas of God become manifest – albeit, at this level, still not in physical material form. The Concept, or Plan, must still be processed by Mind, The Builder, lower down The Tree [EC].
8. In this depiction we have the seeming opposition between Father/God (Pluto) and Satan/Saturn The Devil. If we observe human practice carefully we see that, as with all "opposites" there is a sliding scale of activity somewhere between.
9. In the physical atoms of Matter, positive Protons (static) are balanced by negative electrons in orbit (moving) – which, to our limited senses, gives the illusion of some thing. We see how the inert nucleus gives structure to the atom by preventing the electrons flying away into space.
10. In Astrology, a principle of Capricorn/Saturn/Satan is "Long Range Plans".

ASTROLOGY : PLANETS

11. Saturn is "God of Time".
12. Saturn takes around 30 years to orbit The Sun.
13. Saturn has 2 main symbols – Satan, The Devil, and Lucifer "Bringer of Light".
14. Saturn rules Capricorn, relating to Cycle of Growth Stage 10 (Social Peak) and has its Fall in Cancer, The Home – Cycle of Growth Stage 4 (Transplanting). It is exalted in Libra (Partnerships).
15. Saturn relates to the 10th. House of a Birth Chart and "Social Security" – which is mainly concerned with the tradition, rules, and laws that maintain order among large number of people.
16. Saturn is related to the ambition and focus of energy required to reach the peak of social power and position. Rising to the position of a "Father Figure" (lawgiver) as a result of a lifetime of labour.
17. Saturn is Concentration of Energy into Form, which occurred after the Big Bang, and supplies a focus for human Ambition. It embodies the Gravitational Force that attracts physical bodies.
18. Saturn is the furthest of the traditionally known planets visible to the unaided eye – as such it was considered the final goal of development. Its principle is "Consolidation", demanding practical results for all activity. In terms of evolution it is concerned with the hierarchical structure, rules, and laws that are required in large groups of people – such as government and big business. Its nature is to focus energy into achieving some future goal with the tendency to reject or ignore side issues. "Burning Ambition".
19. In Mythology the 12 Titan children were encouraged by their mother Gaia (Earth) to overthrow their father Ouranus (Sky). Kronos/Saturn was the only one with the courage to do so. He castrated his father with a sickle (feminine Moon symbol) and threw the genitals into the sea (Neptune), from whence appeared Aphrodite/Venus (Desire) – (to re-balance universal energies to zero). Apart from the apparent "demotion" of Uranus as indicated here, we can see this as another depiction of the "Fall of Adam". It also suggests that Individuation requires that the essential energy "stolen" by Venus (Desire for Completion) is transferred to Uranus (Individuality). That is, it will be found within. Psychology tells us that, until we do so, it will be projected on to the people and objects of the external world, which will never fulfil their seeming potential.
20. We can see this as a negative scenario for the Oedipal Complex which is contained in Cycle of Growth Stage 4 (Transplanting. Tarot VI.The Lovers) when the mother should reject the advances of her sons.
21. From the mythological story we see a depiction of the conflict between Saturn and Uranus in Cycle of Growth Stage 11 (Discontent) which can revert back to the earlier satisfactions of Venus (Desire) or forward to Transcendence.
22. The rulership of Capricorn is symbolised by "The Mountain Goat" climbing to reach the peak. Saturn "The Builder". The goat symbol I use has a fish's tail indicating that there is an unconscious motivational content. Saturn is negative in insecure Cancer where it can transform the energy into building secure structures that become prisons. Exalted in Libra it builds constructive partnerships – which tend to be practical, or upwardly mobile, rather than loving. Its fall in Aries tends to make it try to be first and best in every activity – a collector of status symbols - and impossible in practice. It tends to restrict the more creative energies from continual negative criticism. A fear of making mistakes (which are necessary to the learning process).
23. Although Saturn also ruled Aquarius until the discovery of Uranus, it was really a negative effect because the growth of Science and Medicine over the ages was restricted by the rules and hierarchies of Church and State. If activities did not fit into the traditional doctrines they were banned – and even punished by death. "Witches" and other "heretics" were forced to recant or burned at the stake. We can re-read the Mythological story of Kronos/Saturn castrating Ouranus, and the gods swallowing their children, in this light. We can also see something of the challenge that Aquarius (The Individual) gives to its complementary Sign of Leo (The King) – which is concerned with individual rulers.
24. There is more detailed information about Saturn in [ASTROLOGY : PLANET TRANSITS]

ASTROLOGY : PLANETS

JUPITER

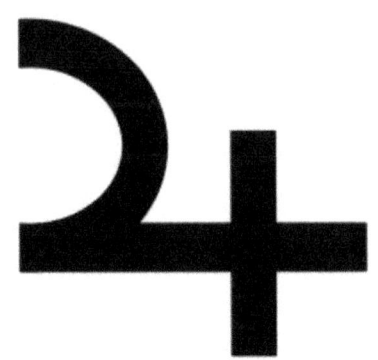

* The glyph of Jupiter consists of the Semi-Circle of Soul combined with the Cross of Matter.
* It shows how the higher mind can create abstract concepts beyond the limitations of physical constraint. Or *Illusion*.
* Its principle is Expansion.

1. The principle of Jupiter is Expansion. Alchemy symbol for Tin – which, like Gold, does not corrode.
2. Jupiter as traditional ruler of Sagittarius relates to Cycle of Growth Stage 9 (Conception) – which is concerned with Conception before birth, as well as conceptions that occur in human minds.
3. In the Kabbalah Tree of Life Jupiter relates to Sephirah 4 (Chesed. Mercy), and is balanced by Sephirah 5 (Mars) on The Pillar of Form. On the Pillar of Force, below Chockmah (Wisdom. Force) it differentiates energy into numerous channels.
4. Jupiter therefore relates to Number 3, which in occult terminology is "an initial completion". From balancing Chockmah (Father. Force) and Binah (Mother. Form) comes a child. From Zero beginnings there are now 3 forces in the universe. In Mathematics 3 points define a 2 dimensional plane, so we now have Length and Breadth. There is no 3 Dimensional matter yet, only a "plan" in 2 dimensions like a blueprint. Jupiter produces concepts and theories that may or may not work in practice.
5. After the creation of the Heavens (Air) in Creation Day 2, Creation Day 3 resulted in the separation of Earth and Sea (Water).
6. In Astrology, Jupiter is also related to Saturn, the next planet outwards, which challenges and limits expansion by insisting on organisation and control. The 2 planets are in continual struggle with one another. Too much Expansion leads to wasted energy (and possible death), too much control means stunted growth (and possible death).
7. If unchecked by Saturn the expansion of Jupiter can produce chaos. Examples are the Roman and British Empires that expanded beyond the ability for the ruling powers to control, so the whole structures collapsed and died.
8. In Mythology we have Zeus/Jupiter, "King of the Gods". As one of The 12 Olympians he was a son of Kronos/Saturn and Demeter – an Earth goddess something like Gaia but more concerned with fertility. It was she that introduced 3 months of Winter to Earth because, to cut the story short, her daughter Persephone had been abducted by Hades/Pluto, "God of the Underworld" - and she took time off each year to search for her. In true godlike form, Zeus survived being killed by his father (who had similarly survived his father Ouranus) and divided rule of the Cosmos between his brothers Poseidon/Neptune (The Sea) and Hades/Pluto (The Underworld).
9. Jupiter rules Sagittarius, Mutable Fire where its energies are unrestricted with concern for academic rather than practical results – and having fun. Its Gemini detriment probably relates to the stress of a too busy mind. Heated Air tends to lose contact with Earth, so ideas become a matter of opinion rather than fact. At another level, this could lead to forming a personal, practical, philosophy of life.
10. Jupiter is also the traditional ruler of Pisces (The Sea of The Collective Unconscious) – a Water\emotional Sign - takes it into the realms of Philosophy and Imagination and other forms of raised consciousness, such as Art and Music, places of seclusion and retreat, prisons and hospitals, alcohol and drugs. Its fall in Virgo (Mutable Earth) is from the tendency to be hypercritical, and demanding "perfection". The Ideals of Jupiter are meant for guidance rather than practice.
11. We note that Sagittarius and Pisces are at the beginning and end of the 1st. Octave of The Logarithmic timescale which is concerned with Gestation in the womb and Transcendence.

ASTROLOGY : PLANETS

12. Although the connection of Jupiter with Pisces – Cycle of Growth Stage 12 (Withdrawal. Confinement) is still valid, we must observe that Pisces is now co-ruled by Neptune, which takes effect in the Cycle of Growth Transcendent Octave if Uranus overcomes Saturn in the Cycle of Growth Stage 11 (Discontent). [ASTROLOGY : LOGARITHMIC TIMESCALE]

MARS

*Here are two representations of Mars with the same meaning. A reversal of the passive Desire symbol of Venus.

*The first is an Orb - Material status is uppermost.

*The second is an indicator of Desire transformed into positive action to achieve its object.

1. The Astrological Principle of Mars is "Self Projection". Alchemy symbol for Iron.
2. Mars relates to Cycle of Growth Stage 1 (Seed) and Stage 8 (Sex. Death) which mark the beginning and end of a human lifetime on Earth.
3. In The Kabbalah Tree of Life Mars relates to Sephirah 5 (Geburah. Severity), on the Pillar of Severity/Form. It is balanced by complementary Sephirah 4 (Chesed. Mercy. Jupiter) on the Pillar of Mercy/Force. In this pairing are contained lessons of Personal versus Social activities. They are balanced and reconciled on The Middle Pillar by The Sun (Consciousness). Mars is the focusing of energy at a personal level (the principle of which is borrowed form Binah at the top of The Pillar of Form).
4. Mars focuses the multiple channels of Jupiter (Expansion) energy into form. As we are nowhere near physical manifestation yet, this occurs in the mind. Some form of action begins to take place towards the Goal.
5. Mars also has a paired function with Venus lower down on The Tree of Life. The glyph of Venus is the reverse of that of Mars. At that level Mars tends to focus on achieving the desires and needs of Venus – and is therefore controlled at that level.
6. Mars relates to Number 4 which adds the dimension of Height to the other 3 – so we now have a very stable 3 dimensional world (Form). With Number 4 we get 2 sets of Number 2 – such as The 4 Elements which consist of 2 positive and 2 Negatives in balance. Nature counts in pairs. Odd numbers seek an other.
7. Number 4 is symbolised and represented by a cube.
8. Creation Day 4 saw the creation of physical Sun, Moon, and Stars.
9. Mars is the first planet outside the orbit of Earth, taking us out into a wider universe. Even though called "The Red Planet", with its symbolic Fire association, it is actually much colder than on Earth.
10. In Mythology, Mars is "God of War", with an allied connection with forging metal and using sharp instruments (focused force). His father was Zeus/Jupiter, King of the Gods (as depicted in the previous Sephirah of The Tree), and mother Hera, Queen of the Gods. When uncontrolled he is "bloodthirsty rage".
11. Mars is associated with masculine sexual energy and adrenaline – despite being on The Pillar of Form where it is focused - rather than The Pillar of Force (as is Venus). Desire is a powerful motivator.
12. Mars is the "Selfish Gene" posited in a book on evolution by Richard Dawkins in 1976, developing ideas about Natural Selection. It relates to "the survival of the fittest" in Evolution. Without Mars our human race would not exist. In Aries Cycle of Growth Stage 1 (Seed. The beginning of life on Earth) it enables

ASTROLOGY : PLANETS

(genetic) survival in life, in Scorpio Cycle of Growth Stage 8 (Sex. Death. The end of life on Earth), through procreation, DNA survival of Death.

13. Mars rules Aries, the Fire Sign of 'The Ram' – which, in Spring, is an excellent representation of martial energy. At this time rams are more concerned with fighting one another for supremacy than mating. Gaining status in the "pecking order". The Age of Aries was that of building Pyramids and Ziggurats – principally as status symbols. "Mine is bigger than yours !" It is in Detriment in Libra where is continually forced to compromise in close partnerships, and becomes less decisive. It also traditionally rules Scorpio, concerned with Sex and Death, where its energies are more aligned in co-operation with others – albeit not so much in the public eye. Its Detriment in Taurus relates to its impulsive energy being restricted to practical, repetitive, routines – such as in farming, or the 9 to 5 office commute. Mars often finds a form of independent action by taking occupations where one is given a task and left to carry it out in its own way – such as in Arts and Crafts, Van Driver, and seeking the Golden Fleece. Mars is the individual soldier, while The Military is structured more on Saturn/Capricorn hierarchical concepts. Mars is exalted in Capricorn, where it is disciplined, and in detriment in Cancer, enclosed in a defensive shell.

14. The traditional Mars ruler of Scorpio (Sex. Death) has been complemented by the discovery of Pluto (Regeneration). To obtain transcendence at a new level we must die to the old.

ASTROLOGY : PLANETS

THE INNER (PERSONAL) PLANETS

The Personal Planets are those that have orbits between that of the Earth and Sun. In Astrology they relate to one's inner self. The Sun is the point of balance.

THE SUN

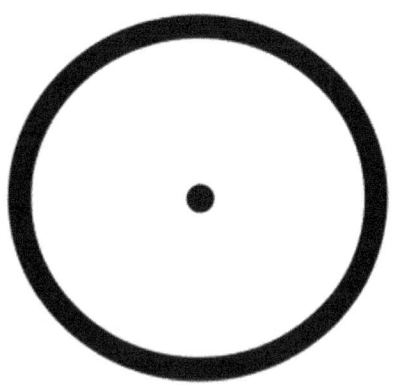

* The glyph of The Sun consists of two representations of the Circle of Spirit - symbol of Wholeness and Completion.

* The outer circle is the point at the centre made manifest.

* As Above, So Below.
  As Below, So above.

1. The Sun relates to Leo and Cycle of Growth Stage 5 (Power. Creativity). It is a symbol of creative energy and Consciousness. Alchemy symbol for Gold.

2. The glyph of The Sun is a symbol of the Singularity that appeared out of No-thing at the time of The Big Bang, and an atom of Hydrogen. Hydrogen was the first chemical element formed, which has a single proton orbited by a single electron. From this beginning all other chemical elements formed. Helium came from Hydrogen, followed by the heavier elements. The universe today consists of 98% Hydrogen – mainly at high temperature in the form of stars like our Sun. Our Sun is still converting Hydrogen into Helium – albeit at a much slower rate of evolution.

3. Our physical Sun, and others, is performing the same function of converting Hydrogen plasma to heavier elements as in Sephirah 1 (The Big Bang) albeit at a much slower rate.

4. The Sun is also a symbol of the psychological Ego, Ego Consciousness, or Self Consciousness, which mainly develops during The 3rd. Octave of The Cycle of Growth beginning with Cycle of Growth Stage 5 (Power. Creativity. Leo. The Sun).

5. In The Kabbalah Tree of Life The Sun relates to Sephirah 6 (Tiphareth. Beauty) which is at the centre of the Middle Pillar where it balances all the higher and lower Sephiroth of The Tree. In particular it forms a Triplicity more closely concerned with reconciling the energies of Sephiroth 5 (Geburah, Severity, Mars, Personal Activity) on The Pillar of Form and Sephiroth 4 (Chesed, Mercy, Jupiter, Social Activity) on The Pillar of Force.

6. This is a physical manifestation of Sephirah 2 (Chockmah. Wisdom. Force. Pluto. Number 1) which is higher up The Tree of Life and is concerned with the actual nuclear reaction at the centre of The Sun rather than its light.

7. The Sun relates to Number 5 (1 + 4) which is best symbolised by the human hand - which has an "opposable thumb" which acts against the other 4 fingers. This development was an important stage in human evolution. The symbolism relates to the concept of "Mind Over Matter" – that is, Mind in control of the 3 Dimensional world created by Number 4. This also relates to Consciousness controlling the 4 Elements Fire, Air, Water, and Earth – which are not in fully material form at this level.

8. The Sun relates to The Heart Chakra. Edgar Cayce stated that The Heart Chakra controls the lower 4 Elements of our being.

9. The Sun is the highest limit of normal human consciousness (Light).

10. As the masculine centre of our Solar System the Sun provides energy (Light and Heat) to all the other planets – which have none of their own. We can easily recognise this in the case of the Sun\Moon relationship. They do, however modify it according to their nature. We therefore find that The Sun is

ASTROLOGY : PLANETS

quite simple in nature, it is a powerhouse supplying the whole range of electromagnetic frequencies of light and heat for differentiation and use by the other planets.

11. In Astrology The Sun is concerned with Power and Light (Consciousness). Its position in a Birth Chart by Sign, House, and Aspects is an indicator of one's main life task or lesson – something that will often take a lifetime to develop. Each of the 12 Zodiac Signs carries its own particular lesson. To be fully whole we have to master them all over several lifetimes. No Sign is more "spiritual" than another. We do not truly begin our "Sun Sign Lesson" until free of parental control at Cycle of Growth Stage 5 (Power. Creativity).

12. The Sun rules the regal Fire Sign of Leo, where it displays self-confidence, and is in detriment in cold, rational, Aquarius where it can disrupt things merely to be "different". It is exalted in Aries where it has more freedom of action, and fall in Libra where it has less self-confidence and defers to its Partners.

13. Although of prime importance to us, Helios is relatively low down in the hierarchy of gods. Ouranus and Gaia gave birth (among others) to Hyperion(Lord of Light, Titan of the East) and Theia (Titan goddess of sight), the siblings mated and gave birth to (among others) Helios (Sun) and his sister Selene (Moon). We are familiar with their pairing as the personal Conscious and Unconscious. In traditional Astrology they BOTH have a pairing with Saturn (Consolidation. Form) – although, as we have seen, Uranus can replace Saturn as an act of Will.

THE MOON

*The glyph of The Moon represents Soul as a reflection.

*She is a Circle like The Sun, but reflects its light in phases depending on how the shadow of The Earth falls on her surface.

*We can therefore see The Sun, and learn its lessons, without the risk of being blinded by its light.

1. The Moon is a feminine planet, sensitive, nurturing, and withdrawing. Its principle is Reflection. Alchemy symbol for Silver.

2. In The Kabbalah The Moon relates to Sephirah 9 (Yesod. Foundation) low down on The Middle Pillar of The Tree, and therefore balanced. She transfers energy from higher realms to The Earth by regularly "going through phases".

3. The Kabbalah relates it to the Astral Realm. It has a more powerful definition in Kabbalism than elsewhere, where one of its symbols is Atlas – supporter of the Celestial Sphere.

4. In the past, in some ways The Moon tended to replace The Earth in human consciousness, and give the illusion of Earth being the centre of the universe. It performs this function in a Birth Chart, where the Earth is just a spot at the centre. Until astronauts got a better outside view its actual appearance was very much a matter of speculation. In early times they believed the Earth was flat - there is still a Flat Earth Society alive and well (?). At psychological levels The Moon is concerned with the human brain, and Personal Unconscious, which stores every detail of our experiences. It also contains images related to our personal "world view".

5. In its Waxing (growing) Phase the Moon is an Inner Planet, moving away from the Sun towards Full Moon. In its Waning (declining, more public) Phase it behaves like an Outer Planet – so it connects with both inner (Sun, Mercury, Venus) and outer worlds (and outer planets).

6. The Moon is also a symbol of Soul. It relates to the Navel Chakra which Edgar Cayce relates to The Cells of Leydig and calls "The Seat of the Soul".

ASTROLOGY : PLANETS

7. In the physical world The Moon has no light of its own and reflects the light of the Sun. The Personal Unconscious is the same, where it reflects the Light of Consciousness, and reacts according to its own (developed) nature.

8. Our Personal Unconscious is our link with The Collective Unconscious. They are really parts of the same thing. The latter is Neptune at the top of The Middle Pillar where it is reached via The Sun and Uranus.

9. Although the Sun and Moon are constant in their relationship in the heavens, the relationship seems to change when viewed from an Earth viewpoint. The Moon seems to "go through phases" each month, and have a daily effect on the sea tides (as symbol of the "sea" of The Collective Unconscious). The monthly cycle of The Moon is described in [ASTROLOGY : PLANETARY ASPECTS]

10. In the universe, the various cycles keep positive and negative energies apart, which prevents them meeting and annihilating one another to return to the original state of chaos.

11. We become aware of The Moon at night when the light of consciousness is dimmed. We "reflect" on our conscious experiences of the day through sleeplessness or dreams. A way of relating more consciously is by Meditation. Listening to what our inner self has to say. The daily and monthly shapes the Moon seems to form are shadows of the Earth. A kind of photographic negative.

12. The position of The Moon in a Birth Chart is an indicator of the experiences we have gained from past lives – what our Soul has already developed. Its energy is something that we tend to fall back on in times of life's problems. To withdraw into our "shell".

13. The Moon is a symbol of our Personal Unconscious that contains all our memories – despite the fact that we may not be able to recall them to consciousness. The Moon forms the hidden "Roots" or "Seeds" of all our re-incarnations – each of which is planted in the Earth to grow and die.

14. The Moon rules Cancer, the Crab Shell - the Sign of The Mother, The Home, Roots, and domestic security and the psychological Persona mask that hides our inner thoughts. Its occult purpose is to build a "shell" of psychic self-defence to be able to retain personal psychological integrity in the face of surrounding collective energies, avoiding the mood swings of the "tidal" ebb and flow. It has its Detriment in more publicly-oriented Capricorn. Its Taurus exaltation brings ability to collect and manage material resources – especially money (with a danger of hoarding). In Scorpio the personal integrity is disturbed from seeking intimate personal relationships. The control of Fixed Water enables feelings to be hidden.

VENUS

* The glyph of Venus consists of the Circle of Spirit above the Cross of Matter.
* She is Beauty of form and passive Peace in Action.
* She is Desire for whatever represents Wholeness and Completion to the individual at all levels, low to high. Inner Magnetism. The 'Missing Part'.

1. The symbol is that of combining the circle of "The Ideal" with the Cross of Matter. So we achieve Beauty. It is the Alchemy symbol for Copper which is a good conductor of heat and electricity, and Antimony which was originally used as a cosmetic.

2. Relates to Cycle of Growth Stage 2 (Germination. Taurus) and Stage 7 (Partners. Libra).

3. On The Kabbalah Tree of Life Venus (Feelings. Emotions) complements Mercury (Rational Mind). The Jungian Functions Feeling and Thinking are complementary to one another. They are both "Rational Functions" in that there are varying grades or levels of consideration, with Feeling, between Comfort versus Discomfort. Thinking makes its own, more objective, conscious, divisions.

ASTROLOGY : PLANETS

4. Venus relates to Number 6 which is symbolised by the 6 pointed Star of David – which, in turn, consists of the upward pointing triangle of Fire and the downward pointing triangle of Water. Thus we see Desire as "Fire-Water" – which also has associations with Blood and Sex. In Psychology this is "E-motion" which promotes Action.
5. Venus is the Inner Planet closest to The Earth. Its Principle is "Desire" – a form of magnetic attraction. It is concerned with normal survival needs as well as what we put the highest values on in life.
6. Venus/Aphrodite is Goddess of Love, Beauty, and Sexual attraction and related to Aphrodisiacs and Venereal Diseases. She had no parents but was created when Kronos/Saturn was persuaded by his mother Gaia to castrate his father Ouranus. Gaia was fed up with Ouranus's numerous infidelities – despite having had her own. Saturn threw the genitals into the sea (Collective Unconscious) and Venus came out. Here we have an extreme example of the Oedipus Complex before Oedipus was even "born".
7. It would seem that until Uranus begins to act in a Transcendent way by overcoming Saturn (Form. The Old), the creative energy is contained in, or symbolised by, Venus.
8. In ancient times there were temples built to honour Venus where men could have sexual intercourse with the priestesses as a religious practice. A point being that the priestesses gave their services freely and were not possessed by any one man. They were not considered prostitutes.
9. In a Birth Chart Venus is an indicator of what we desire or value most in life. Its paired planet is Mars, which indicates how those desires might be achieved (or not). In Synastry, where the charts of 2 people are compared, Mars and Venus are cross-compared to see how one satisfies the desires of the other. In this we see the mechanics of attraction. From partnerships we find the missing (unconscious) parts of our self.
10. Venus (Feelings) also has a paired relationship with Mercury (Rational Mind). They are both termed "Inner" or "Personal" planets. Their orbits are between The Sun and Earth.
11. Venus rules the Fixed Earth Sign of Taurus, where it brings physical attractiveness and a basic desire for physical comfort and beautiful surroundings – there is also a suggestion of desire for money, but this is really a means to an end (physical comfort). Its rulership of Libra is a basic desire for beautiful relationships and a perfect mate. In the less helpful Signs – Scorpio tends to use relationships for personal gain, and end them if non-productive, Venus in Aries is similar to that of Scorpio (both being ruled by Mars) with the tendency to have impetuous, short lived, relationships – mistaking sexual attraction or romantic idealism for love. At another level, there is the tendency to try and keep the peace when direct action is necessary. (Scorpio will plot in secret).
12. The true Partner is to be found within, in Jungian terms, the Anima of a man and the Animus of a woman.

MERCURY

* The glyph of Mercury is made up of the Circle of Spirit mediating between the receptive Semi Circle of Soul and the Cross of Matter.

* It is The Messenger that receives abstract Ideas and converts them into recognisable form - and converts Form into Ideas - as we are doing here.

1. The Principles of Mercury are Communication and Experimentation. Rational use of The Mind. It has the Alchemy symbol of the metal Mercury which is liquid at normal temperatures and easily amalgamates with other metals (except iron) without changing its independent form.
2. The symbol shows how "The Ideal" mediates between Moon and Earth.

ASTROLOGY : PLANETS

3. Mercury is the closest planet to our Sun.
4. In Numerology Mercury relates to Number 7. Odd numbers challenge the previous even ones. We can see how the Number 7 Rational Mind challenges the emotional imaginings of Number 6 (Venus) by demanding physical evidence.
5. Symbols of Number 7 are the Jewish Menorah 7 branch candlestick ,and the 7 days of the week. The symbolism is based on the Sabbath being the most important day of the week when "higher knowledge" (light, consciousness) is given and transferred to practical observance for the other 6 days. So this also refers to any form of Teaching.
6. On the Kabbalah Tree of Life Mercury relates to Sephirah 8 (Hod. Glory) at the bottom of the Pillar of Severity (Form. Material Reality). Its complement on The Pillar of Force is Sephirah 7. Venus – so basically we have Mind opposing Desire. They are balanced by The Moon on the Middle Pillar.
7. Mercury (Rational Mind) and Venus (Feelings) are Personal Planets orbiting between The Sun and Earth.
8. In Astrology the Planet is also paired with Jupiter, which is concerned with global or social issues rather than personal ones. Mercury experiments with the theories of Jupiter to see if they can be made practical.
9. With benefit of modern psychological concepts and terminology, we can ascribe Mercury to "The Rational Mind" and Jupiter to The Abstract, or Theoretical Mind.
10. Mercury rules the Signs of Gemini and Virgo. With Mercury's rulership of the Air Sign, Gemini, manifestation of ideas is at a more mental level, and is concerned with Communication - whereas with Earthy Virgo manifestation is at a practical, physical level. Virgo pays attention to physical detail through mental criticism and attention to detail, and production of physical objects such as by arts and crafts. Virgo also rules physical and mental health.
11. Mercury symbols and associations are extremely numerous. Like its metallic namesake, it can adapt and "amalgamate" with other planets. Some suggest it changes too easily with the "Jack of all trades and master of none" effect. However, we can see that part of the individual condition will depend upon which planets Mercury has close relationship (aspects) with in a Birth Chart. There is also the overriding factor of how we use our Will to discipline our thoughts and ideas.
12. In Mythology, masculine Mercury is principally "The Messenger of the gods" or "The Winged Messenger" – naturally related to the Element Air. This relates to the human ability for Communication in all its forms - bringing abstract mental ideas into forms that can be appreciated by the 5 physical senses, such as words we can hear, or words brought to the physical level on paper – or even ideas communicated through Art and Music, which appeal to our feelings and emotions. Also, nowadays, by computers.
13. The symbolism of Mercury also includes the Caduceus, which was the rod carried by a messenger. It is also related to the staff of Asclepius, the Greek god of healing ,which seems to be a representation of the Chakra system.
14. In typical mercurial fashion, Mercury has many additional functions - such as Patron of tricksters and thieves, trade and good fortune, and conductor of the souls of the dead to the lower world. He is also an early fertility symbol and "God of Crossroads" . In early times they combined the latter functions by erecting "Hermae" - phallic monuments – at crossroads. Mercury is "The Busy Bee" cross pollinating as he goes about his daily tasks.

ASTROLOGY : PLANETS

EARTH

* The glyph of Earth shows the Cross of Matter enclosed in the Circle of Spirit.
* It shows that, on Earth, there is no separation between Matter and Spirit.
* By observing the Seen we can also observe the Unseen.
* As Above, So Below. As Below, So Above.

Earth tends to be neglected by Astrologers because it is only implied as the centre of a Birth Chart. In fact, we do tend to lose sight of the totality of the Earth – as a symbol of our human body - as we focus attention on the details of our daily lives. That is, until something goes wrong. The Zodiac Sign Virgo gives us another perspective on the concept of "self-ishness".

Going back in time, it was not realised that Earth was a planet like the other visible ones, and was considered to be the centre of the universe around which everything else revolved. The Moon supports this illusion. We can see that, strangely, like the Transcendent Planets, spherical Earth was not a part of conscious reality until relatively recently – it was originally believed to be a flat plane which if travelled far enough we would fall over the edge.

When interpreting a chart it is correct to treat Earth as the centre because all observations are taken from this perspective. In modern day parlance, with Relativity, it does not matter if the Sun travels round the Earth or vice versa, the combined effect is the same.

1. "As Above, So Below. As Below, So Above" means that there are (more or less) physical manifestations of all the energies of The Tree of Life on Earth.
2. Some books about The Kabbalah say this symbol is that of The Sun, which is clearly not the case. Sephirah 10 (Kingdom. Earth) is at the bottom of The Middle Pillar where it is the result of the re-combination of all the archetypal undifferentiated energies from Sephirah 1 (Crown. Neptune. Number Zero) – albeit now in a diversity of material forms.
3. The Earth is the material, physical, world within which we live. Our Planet is the only one in the solar system to have water as liquid, and so able to support human life. The inner ones are too hot, the outer ones too cold.
4. The related goddess is Gaia, who was the first - formed out of the primeval chaos, and who created Uranus (Heaven) as a mate – which complies with the Genesis story of Creation – on Day 2 Heaven was created (as an idea). Modern day science states that matter gathered together and solidified to form the planets around 4,500 million years ago. The "Gaia Hypothesis" proposed by Henry Lovelock in the 1970s proposed that the Earth behaves like a living, breathing, organism.
5. Although the story of Gaia tends to conflict with other information here, we must remember that it is trying to describe archetypal energies, not physical forms. We have "an Idea in the mind of god".
6. In terms of the creation of our chemical elements it could mean, among other things, that Uranus (Heaven) relates to the gaseous elements that make up most of our solar system – such as Hydrogen, Helium and Oxygen.
7. The Earth relates to the Root Chakra, and Gonads (Sex Organs). The Kabbalah also relates The Chakra to Decomposition.

ASTROLOGY : PLANETS

PLANET DESCRIPTIONS – TABLE

ASTROLOGY : THE PLANETS IN ORDER OF NUMBER AND KABBALAH TREE OF LIFE RELATIONSHIP

NUMBER	TREE OF LIFE	GLYPH	ROMAN PLANET	*CHART ORBIT	TRADITIONAL PRINCIPLES	MODERN RELATIONSHIPS	GREEK	MYTHOLOGY	RULER OF	DETRIMENT	EXALTED	FALL
0	1 Crown (& 12)	♆	Neptune	165 years	Selflessness. Dissolution. Delusion	The Collective Unconscious	Poseidon	(Discovered 1846). God of The Sea. Bringer of earthquakes, confusion, and chaos. Splits earth and rock with his trident. Brother of Zeus and Pluto. Relates to artistic pursuits, alcohol and drugs. Neptune tries to return us to primeval chaos. It acts as an unconscious challenge to Individuality. We become aware of our common roots.	Pisces	Virgo	-	-
1	2 Wisdom. Force	♇	Pluto	248 years	Regeneration Revolution	Critical Mass	Hades	(Discovered 1930). God of The Underworld. Rules the shades of the dead and all minerals. Brother of Zeus and Neptune. Hades consists of both Tartarus (heaven) and Elysium (hell) - suggesting reward or punishment. Pluto gathers energy in secret until Critical Mass is achieved - when it comes to light as the "atomic explosion" of Revolution.	Scorpio	Taurus	-	-
2	3 Under-standing. Form	♄	Saturn	29 years	Consolidation. Tradition	Discipline. Structure	Kronos (Cronus)	Titan Son of Gaia & Uranus. Castrated Uranus whose genitals became Venus. Replaced by his son Jupiter. Saturn 'The Builder' is the basis of Order, Tradition, and hierarchical social structures - including those of the Family. Saturn is Control at all levels.	Capricorn (Aquarius)	Cancer & Leo	Libra	Aries
3	4 Mercy	♃	Jupiter	12 years	Expansion. Growth	Social Productivity	Zeus	King of gods and men. Overthrew his father Saturn & divided rule of the cosmos between sons Poseidon & Hades. Married sister Hera goddess of childbirth. One of his sons was Ares/Mars. Jupiter brings expansion and growth.	Sagittarius (Pisces)	Gemini & Virgo	Cancer	Capricorn
4	5 Severity	♂	Mars	2 years	War	Self Projection. Survival	Ares	God of War. Son of Jupiter/Zeus & sister Hera. Had an affair with Venus/Aphrodite who was married to Hephaestus - a metal craftsman.	Aries (Scorpio)	Libra & Taurus	Capricorn	Cancer
5	6 Beauty	☉	Sun (Apollo)	1 year	Power Love	Consciousness. Will	Helios	God of The Arts, Oracles, Plague and Medicine, Light and Knowledge. Creative energy. The Sun is the centre and source of life.	Leo	Aquarius	Aries	Libra
6	7 Victory	♀	Venus	1 year	Peace Beauty	Desire Feeling Emotion	Aphrodite	Goddess of love, beauty, and sexual attraction. Mated with many. Came out of the sea (Collective Unconscious). Aphrodisiacs. Venerial Diseases	Taurus & Libra	Scorpio & Aries	Pisces	Virgo
7	8 Glory	☿	Mercury	1 year	Communication Experiment	Rational Mind	Hermes	Messenger of the gods. Patron of tricksters and thieves, trade and good fortune. Early fertility symbol (Hermae phallic symbols) God of crossroads.	Gemini & Virgo	Sagittarius & Pisces	Virgo	Pisces
8	9 Foundation	☽	Moon (Luna)	29 Days	Receptivity Reflection Mirror	Personal Unconscious	Selene	Fell in love with Endymion (a beautiful eternal youth) and got Zeus to make him permanently sleep so that she could caress him undisturbed. The Moon has no light of its own, and reflects whatever light there is. It "goes through (monthly) phases" related to tides and the female menstrual cycle.	Cancer	Capricorn	Taurus	Scorpio
9	10 Kingdom	⊕	Earth (Terra)	Not Applicable	Stability	Natural World. Human Body	Gaia	Formed from primeval chaos. Gaia bore & mated with Ouranus to produce the Titans, Cyclopes and Hekatonchires. Later resented Ouranus and incited her sons to revolt. Saturn was the only one brave enough to act. Here is manifestation into Physical Form.	-	-	-	-
Daath	(11)	♅	Uranus (Caelus)	84 years	Individuality. Invention	Higher Mind Individuation Will	Ouranus	(Discovered 1781). Personification of The Sky. First male. Son and mate of Gaia. Jealous of his sons, Imprisoned his children in Tartarus below Hades/Pluto. Dethroned by his son Saturn/Kronos. Uranus is the basis of Individuation.	Aquarius	Leo	-	-

* Astrology Birth Chart orbits. Mercury and Venus orbit with the Sun. [The colours refer to the Pillar of The Tree of Life : White = Force. Gold = Middle. Balance. Black = Form]

Figure 35 : Table - Planet Descriptions

ASTROLOGY : PLANETS

ASTROLOGY : PLANETARY ASPECTS

This chapter is to explain the basic principles of Astrological aspects – which are the angles between lines drawn to connect any 2 planets and the centre of a chart. Planets are considered in pairs. There are several aspects which are considered important, but here we only deal with the main ones. The monthly cycle of the Moon's relationship with the Sun is used as an example of a complete cycle of relationships, and another diagram shows views of the 3 main aspects.

Traditionally, aspects were considered to be "Good" or "Evil". Nowadays we recognise that some stress is necessary in life to promote change and growth, so we call them "Easy" or "Hard" aspects.

Here we are mainly considering the fixed aspects between planets in a Birth Chart. In [ASTROLOGY : PLANET TRANSITS] we consider the aspects between planets in a Birth Chart and the planets at later times as they continue moving afterwards. As an example in this chapter, we can consider The Moon in this context. During the course of a month it transits through all the Signs – and therefore makes a complete circuit of a Birth Chart.

In the complete Transit Cycle of each planet it makes all possible aspects with all the other planets, including Easy and Hard ones, so, in the end, everything balances out to Zero.

Aspects are also considered in the chapter [NUMEROLOGY] where they have archetypal relationships with numbers.

ASPECT EXAMPLES DIAGRAM

The diagram shows how aspects should be indicated in an Astrological Chart to show that Hard (stressful) Squares operate at The Centre. The less stressful Trines tend to avoid conflict. The planets are in the Signs and Houses of their Rulership.

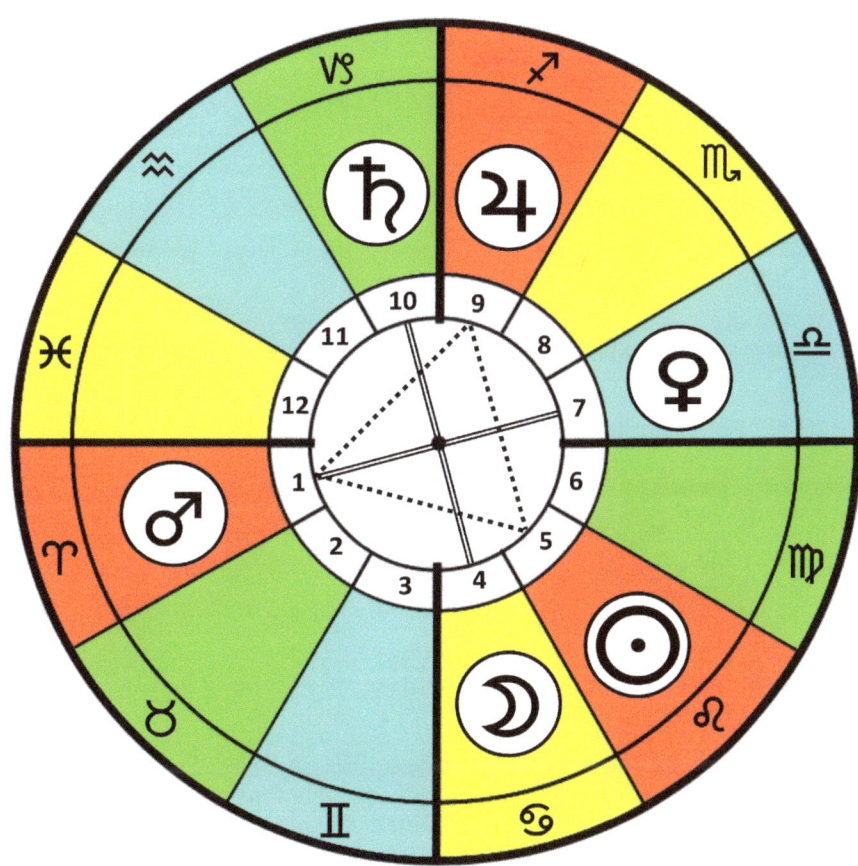

Figure 36 : Astrology Aspects - Examples of Planet Aspects

ASTROLOGY : PLANETARY ASPECTS

1. The basis of the Life Lesson of this example "chart" is "a Moon Cancer person trying to become Sun Leo" – so, early in life, we have a rather retiring, maternal, figure able to control domestic life (Moon in 4th. House) learning lessons to gain self-confidence such as by taking up creative pursuits or controlling children – perhaps even running a small business, especially if working from home (Sun in 5th. House).
2. The diagram keeps to the archetypal format with Aries rising on the Ascendant. In practice any Sign can be rising and Planets can be in any position in the wheel.
3. Here the planets are placed in the Signs and Houses of their rulership. That is, where they act most powerfully. The diagram therefore gives an idea of the natural relationships between the Signs and Planets by observing the Aspects between them.
4. It is extremely rare to have planets placed in such exact positions or Aspect relationships.
5. Even with no planets to emphasise the Aspects between Zodiac Signs, they also have natural Aspect relationships with one another "Easy" or "Hard".

CONJUNCTIONS (Zero degrees)

Here 2 planets are very close together. Depending on their separate natures, they may "get on" with one another or bring conflict. (In terms of Transiting Planets returning to their birth positions, we can treat conjunctions (Returns) as "Hard" because they encourage some form of Change).

There are no planets in Conjunction aspect here. The closest they come to that is where 2 planets are in adjacent Signs – in this case they are 30 degrees apart which is a Semi-Sextile (30 degrees) Aspect outside our scope here although we note that the Semi-Sextile is somewhat stressful in that the planets are in incompatible Elements of different polarities. Here Fire/Earth. Fire/Water.

TRINES (120 degrees)

The Trine Aspect relates to Number 3 (Jupiter). This is an "Easy" aspect. Planets in Signs of the same Element support one another.

Our Birth Chart example with a Grand Trine (3 Trine aspects) could lead to a life of relative ease from the ability to avoid difficult issues. In this case the intense stress of the Grand Cross (4 Square aspects) will bring issues to light, but the Trines will tend to mitigate the problems – perhaps by getting help when needed.

Beginning with the "Easy" aspects we note that the planets Mars, Sun, and Jupiter are all in the same Sign Element – in this case Fire Signs – as is common with the Trine.

We have 3 sets of double Trine Relationship (a total of 6 aspects) for consideration - Mars Trine Sun and Jupiter, Sun Trine Mars and Jupiter, Jupiter Trine Mars and Sun.

You will note that I have drawn the aspect lines (in the traditional way) joining the planets in a way that does not connect with The Centre. "Easy" Trines allow us to ignore events (for a time) or help overcome the stresses of Squares.

With Fire there is a great deal of positive energy involved.

OPPOSITIONS (180 degrees)

The Opposition Aspect relates to Number 2 (Saturn). The 2 planets are in complementary Signs on opposite sides of a chart. This relates to "The Libra Scales" and "The Resolution of Opposites".

We have 2 Oppositions here. They give an indication of the kind of close relationship that might be habitually formed.

1. VENUS OPPOSITE MARS - gives the dilemma "Peace or War". The emphasis on Aries Opposite Libra gives the dilemma "Me or You".
2. MOON OPPOSITE SATURN - Any hard aspect to Saturn brings a sense of insecurity, and need to exert self-discipline in the area of its position – otherwise the discipline comes externally. The Moon (The Past) position here brings ability to handle domestic affairs. In this case the Opposition emphasises, and therefore brings attention to, a shyness and difficulty with expressing emotions (Moon) - probably from negative criticism by an ambitious parent. The subject would tend to seek mature, stable, partnerships (Saturn). Perhaps "father figures". The additional Opposition by Houses 4 (Home) and 10 (Career) emphasises the dilemma "Home versus Career". This person could be a bit of a recluse, but find partnership with those in the public eye.

ASTROLOGY : PLANETARY ASPECTS

SQUARES (90 degrees)

The Square Aspect relates to Number 4 (Mars). This is a stressful "Hard" aspect.

Traditionally, astrologers only give a single interpretation to Square Aspects. You will see in the Moon example below that The Cycle of Growth enables 2 different interpretations depending on whether the faster planet is in Waxing Phase (separating from the slower planet) or Waning Phase (approaching a Conjunction – "Return" - with the slower planet).

Square Aspects are formed by planets in incompatible Signs and Houses – which are in the same triplicity. Signs – Cardinal, Fixed, or Mutable. Houses Angular, Succedent, or Cadent. There is always "disagreement" between the participants.

We have Square Aspects to 4 planets which are the result of the 2 Oppositions above. This rare arrangement is called a "Grand Cross" which brings tremendous inner stress to its subject throughout life. The normal Square Aspect tends to cause stress to 2 participating planets, in this case activation of one of the participating planets (such as by a Transiting planet making contact) will cause stressful activation of the other 3.

We get a clue to what will happen from observing the Oppositions. In this case the crosses are all formed by planets in Cardinal, Initiating, Signs and Angular Houses. So the tendency is to start several conflicting projects at once, or be prone to opening "cans of worms" (they can never be put back again).

So we can treat the Cross as one unit, or as 2 Oppositions, or 8 Square Aspects depending on the activated planet (such as by a Transit planet. For example, each planet will be activated by The Sun's transit once a year). This gives some idea of the complex issues when interpreting a Birth Chart :-

Mars Square Saturn and Moon, Moon Square Mars and Venus, Venus Square Moon and Saturn, Saturn Square Mars and Venus..

Taking the chart as a whole, the stresses involved by the Squares would be largely mitigated by having boundless Trine Fire energy. The individual has the ability to enlist the help of others, but may try to do everything themselves – when "burn out" could occur. He/She could be their own worst enemy. With a Grand Trine the problems could be ignored altogether for a time, in which case there are likely to be health problems arising later in life – especially at the time of The Mid Life Crisis. We cannot ignore our own inner needs indefinitely.

ASTROLOGY : PLANETARY ASPECTS

THE CYCLIC INTER-RELATIONSHIPS

We use the monthly cycle of the Moon as an example. It makes all possible aspects with The Sun during this time (ending with Zero energy balance). In the chapter [ASTROLOGY : PLANET TRANSITS] we use the same principles to compare the orbit positions of a single planet with its own position in a Birth Chart.

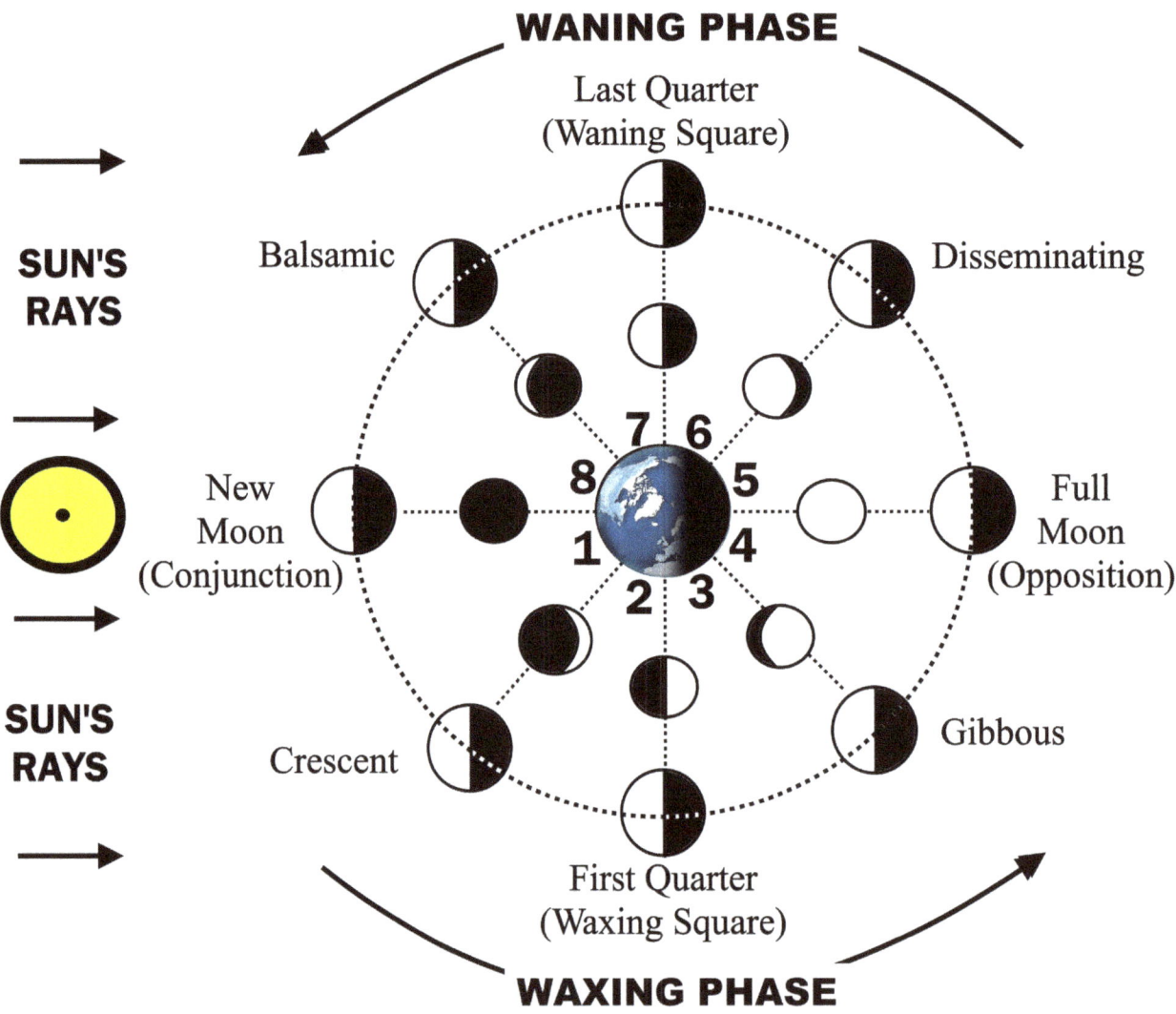

Figure 37 : Astrology Aspects - The Monthly Moon Cycle

1. The relationships can be applied to any 2 planets.
2. The diagram shows Earth at the centre with the main monthly positions of The Moon around it. The Sun position is at the left. The actual size of The Sun makes it too big to fit on to the page in proportion, so we shrink it down to its symbolic glyph as we would in a chart. Although it is at the left here, in practice it could be anywhere in a chart depending on the time of day.
3. The first principle of examining aspects is to observe the relationship between the slower moving planet and the faster moving planet. In this case we use The Sun (1 year cycle) and Moon (29 day cycle). The Cycle of Growth principle stated here is exactly the same for any pair of planets – or even a Transit planet position in relationship to its own (fixed) position in a Birth Chart.
4. For our purposes here we assume The Sun does not move, although it actually moves 30 degrees from one Zodiac Sign to the next during this time.

ASTROLOGY : PLANETARY ASPECTS

5. Although there are 8 positions of The Moon here, and we could consider 8 aspect types, we are only concerned with examining 4 Hard Aspects (a Conjunction, Opposition, and 2 Squares) in detail. These are the ones that tend to manifest themselves in the material world by forcing change.
6. The diagram shows the Moon cycle in 2 perspectives. The outer circle shows The Moon as it is actually lit by The Sun (always from the left here). The inner circle shows how The Moon is seen from Earth.
7. The diagram is oriented in accordance with The Cycle of Growth with the birth position at the left. We could divide the Cycle into 12 Stages and apply The Cycle of Growth meanings, but here we use the better known 8.
8. Although we use the exact degrees of aspects here, in practice small allowances are made called "Orbs".
9. Aspects are calculated by drawing (imaginary) lines from the planets to the centre of a chart.
10. All aspects in this diagram are based on the Number 4 (Mars) which is the most stable number, and therefore the most difficult to change. The aspects are called "Hard" ones in that they produce stressful situations. The 90 degree Square Aspect and its derivatives – 45 (Waxing), 90 (Waxing), 135 (Waxing), 225 (135 Waning), 270 (90 waning), 315 (45 Waning) are those that bring about opportunities for actual events to occur as well as making us more conscious of our "inner centre".
11. The Sun symbolises Consciousness. The Moon symbolises the Personal Unconscious.

THE MOON AND THE CYCLE OF GROWTH

This description misses out the interim 45 degree aspects which coincide with the Fixed Signs/Houses of The Cycle of Growth. Stage 2 (Crescent. Germination. Taurus), Stage 5 (Gibbous. Power. Leo), Stage 8 (Disseminating. Death. Scorpio), Stage 11 (Balsamic. Dissatisfaction. Aquarius). We see how Fixed Signs bring minor stress.

There is more detail in [NUMBERS – Number 8].

CYCLE OF GROWTH STAGE 1 (SEED) : CONJUNCTION ASPECT

The Cycle of Growth of a planet cycle begins when 2 planets are exactly aligned as seen from the Earth. This is the "New Moon" position. In the case of The Moon it is virtually invisible because we cannot see the side lit by The Sun. This alignment gives us a Conjunction Aspect of Zero Degrees.

At this time, in symbolic terms, The Moon receives a "seed message" from The Sun which grows and dies through the cycle – to receive a new "seed" at the next New Moon.

The faster planet now moves away from the Conjunction to begin its "Waxing", or growing, Phase, which continues until the Full Moon Opposition.

In this example there is little or no stress caused because The Moon is completely obedient to The Sun. The effects of Conjunctions between other planets depend mainly on the natures of the two involved as well as the Zodiac Sign and Chart House in which they occur – i.e. whether the "environment" is more favourable to one or the other.

Relationships to Stage 1 are those of the time of Spring – the birth of a child, the Sign of Aries (The Ram), and Mars God of War. The April Fool.

CYCLE OF GROWTH STAGE 4 (TRANSPLANTING) : WAXING SQUARE ASPECT

We are exactly half way through the Waxing Phase of The Moon which ends at the Opposition.

Traditionally, astrologers gave only a single interpretation of the Square Aspect, you will see that we now give 2 depending on whether it occurs in the Waxing Phase here, or the Waning Phase later on – or, more specifically, where it appears in The Cycle of Growth. This is the same for other aspects. Although there is stress in both cases, they have a different meaning or purpose.

We have arrived at the First Quarter phase. The line drawn from The Moon position to the centre now makes a 90 degree angle to that of The Sun. At the Transplanting Stage the "seed" planted at the Conjunction should have put down roots and be ready to go into a less sheltered environment. An example from the Logarithmic Timescale is that of Erikson's Play Age of a child age 3 years 6months beginning to relate to people other than just mother and father. This meaning is identical for all cycles at this Stage.

ASTROLOGY : PLANETARY ASPECTS

CYCLE OF GROWTH STAGE 7 (PARTNERS) : OPPOSITION ASPECT

Again missing out intervening stages, we arrive at the "Full Moon" position in the Cycle.

This is exactly half way through the complete Cycle when the Waxing (Growing) Phase gives way to the Waning (Dying) phase. This does not happen instantly. Depending on the speed of the planet involved the transition can take more or less time.

1. The Aspect is that of the 180 degree Opposition. The Opposition Aspect is symbolised by the Full Moon in that it is the time of greatest conscious awareness. In terms of Sun (conscious) and Moon (Personal Unconscious) we now become most aware of our inner thoughts and feelings. Whether we take action or not depends on our Will, and Decision.
2. The Opposition Aspect is stressful in that it brings awareness of one's "Centre". However, this occurs more in the mind – or objective consciousness. One is aware of "both sides".
3. We see this in the related symbol of Tarot Card XI. Justice, trying to come to a decision.
4. Although associated with the Sign of Libra, traditionally related to human partnerships, at a more archetypal level the Opposition Aspect is concerned with relationship between our outer, conscious, self and inner, unconscious, self.
5. In [ASTROLOGY : OVERVIEW] there is a copy of a BBC news article related to an increase of crime at the time of the New Moon.
6. The Opposition Aspect also refers to the Logarithmic Timescale age 23 years entry into the Erikson "Young Adulthood" Stage of development, at this Stage one has had some life experience since Cycle of Growth Stage 1.
7. The Opposition is also between Cycle of Growth Stage 1 and Cycle of Growth Stage 7 as indicated by both lines connecting to the centre. We become aware of our actions during the cycle so far.
8. At the Opposition Stage we become aware that that the Waxing Phase is over, and decline is about to begin. "Death" will eventually follow.

CYCLE OF GROWTH STAGE 10 (PEAK. PUBLIC VIEW) : WANING SQUARE ASPECT

Now we have another stressful Square 90 degree Aspect. The decline continues.

This is the "Harvest" position of the Cycle where one has the material results of all one's activity since Cycle of Growth Stage 1 (Seed). As with the other aspects mentioned, it is a time of Change. The decision now is whether to make a futile attempt to maintain one's position in the face of future declining influence on one's surroundings, or to prepare for the beginning of a new Cycle later on.

This is symbolically the time of the Winter Solstice rebirth of THE SUN - or the Christmas rebirth of THE SON (and challenge by existing Authority). A time of New Year Resolutions. Events may occur at this time to force the decision.

The decision to plant new seeds later on or continue as before.

ASTROLOGY : PLANET TRANSITS

The activities of each of the 12 Houses later in this chapter is common for all applications of The Cycle of Growth.

YOUR LIFE DIARY

At the end of this chapter is a Generic Transits "Life Diary" so you can test the theories for yourself.

Diana Spencer's Life Diary is in the next chapter [ASTROLOGY : CHARTS EXAMPLES].

In order to keep things simple, everything in this book refers to Natal Astrology, which is concerned with Birth Charts of people. In Astrology, Transits are concerned with the movement of planets after birth and comparing their positions at any later time with the Houses and planet positions in a Birth Chart, which is fixed. In this chapter we are only concerned with the meanings of the 12 Houses, the actual Zodiac Signs vary from person to person . Please see the [LADY DIANA SPENCER] and [MY STORY] chapters for examples of Birth Chart and Transits interpretations.

Transits themselves do not exactly "predict the future", they rather set up different kinds of external conditions depending on their aspect relationships with one another, and with the planets of a Birth Chart. They should be approached more with the attitude of being a "weather forecast" for farmers for use in sowing, reaping, and harvesting crops. Making use of Nature's Time takes less effort to achieve the desired results. Everything is subject to Free Will concerning what seeds are sown and what effort is made in their cultivation. Sometimes it is best to do nothing, or simply submit to "fate", in order to survive difficult external conditions. EVERYTHING IS SUBJECT TO PREVIOUS ACTIVITY – for example, if new "seeds" are not sown at the right time there will be no harvest later on.

BIRTH CHART

The Birth Chart is where everything starts. It is a snapshot, or map, of the planet positions at the time we were born. The Earth is the central point. This can be considered the "seed" of an individual. Rather like the egg which was fertilised at conception, it contains all the information required for future growth. So at this stage Astrology does not predict the future, but merely indicates potential possibilities. The principle is very similar to that of one's genetic DNA characteristics from which scientists are trying to predict future behaviour. Once we are born, despite our inner characteristics, our activities and experience begin to be shaped by our environment.

HOUSES

The basic overall House STRUCTURE of a chart is dealt with in detail in the chapter [ASTROLOGY : HOUSES].

PLANETS

The planets, and Earth, are continually orbiting the Sun. The time taken for each planet return to its original position in a Birth Chart is different. The further away the planet is from the Sun, the longer the time taken. Because we see everything from the viewpoint of Earth we treat the Sun and Moon like any other planets. This is valid, and conforms with the concept of Relativity because all our observations and measurements are taken from this earthly perspective. The orbit times vary from the monthly 29 day cycle of the Moon, and the annual cycle of the Sun, to that of the furthest planet, Pluto, which takes around 248 years.

TRANSITS

The planets continue moving in their paths after the time of birth. At any time we can compare their positions with a Birth Chart. Those positions, called "Transits" (to the Birth Chart) give indication of external influences on the subject at the time, and can indicate when events are likely to occur. I am mainly interested in examining the 12 year cycle of Jupiter and the 30 year cycle of Saturn because it is those that mainly determine the course of a lifetime. Transits of the faster planets tend to "fire off" events set up by the slower planets, and are not so important in this respect. The Sun, Venus, and Mercury, for example, transit their natal (Birth Chart) positions every year and make every possible aspect, "Easy" and "Hard". Mars transits last 2 years. For example, before I knew about Astrology I wondered why changes in my life often occurred around August. I later discovered that I have Pluto (planet of "Death and Regeneration" or "Change") in the Sign of Leo which the Sun transits every year from mid-July to mid-August.

In a complete Transit Cycle of a planet its relationship with the other planets makes every possible aspect (angular relationship) with every other planet – "easy" or "hard", positive or negative. This means that the sum total of effects comes to Zero. We see this as the meaning of Karma where we start from Zero and eventually return to Zero.

TWO TYPES OF TRANSIT CYCLES

There are two types of transit cycles GENERIC and PERSONAL. The position of a planet can be considered in relationship to both at the same time. The House meaning is the same in both cases, although related to the separate cycles., and conforms to The Cycle of Growth. The House meanings of a Birth Chart are similar, but not identical because they are fixed and refer to the totality of an individual, whereas here we are concerned with the dynamics of external influences.

It is an interesting exercise to consider if one's life experiences relate more to the Generic or Personal cycles.

PERSONAL PLANET CYCLES

The PERSONAL cycle of a planet depends upon its journey through the 12 Houses of the Birth Chart the positions of which are fixed at birth. This calculation requires an accurate Birth Chart. The 12 Houses of the Birth Chart are determined by the Zodiac Sign rising on the Eastern horizon at the time of birth - which is called the Ascendant Sign, and defines the beginning of the 1st. House. In a 24 hour day the Rising Sign (one of 12) changes every two hours and depends upon the rotation of the Earth. A planet does not tend to start acting in a personal way until it crosses the Ascendant and moves into our natal 1st.House for the first time. Until then it is mainly a function of past traditions and parental control. The "Quarters" of a Personal Cycle are the 1st.,4th.,7th, and 10th Personal Houses. As defined in the Birth Chart. The Placidean method of setting up a Birth Chart that I, and others, use has unequal sized Houses (i.e. are not all 30 degrees).

GENERIC PLANET CYCLES

It is this effect that makes a cycle of a lifetime similar for us all.

Each GENERIC cycle of a planet begins from its position at birth and continues until returns to that position, and repeats thereafter. We do not need an accurate Birth Chart to calculate them. The 1st. Generic Transit House begins at the Zodiac position of the planet in the Birth Chart and, starting from that position, we divide the cycle/circle into 12 x 30 degree Transit Houses to make up the 360 degree circle. Therefore each planet has its own separate "set" of 12 Generic/Transit Houses. The first event of each Generic cycle is the birth of the individual. The "Quarters" of a Generic Cycle are the cusps (starting points) of the 1st.,4th.,7th, and 10th Transit Houses which are 90 degrees apart. These are the main "crisis points". Events are most likely to occur when a planet makes a transit to each one.

4 QUARTERS : THE MAIN TRANSIT 'CRISIS' POINTS

Main life events tend to be triggered as a transiting planet enters the House – Personal or Generic - at the beginning of a quarter. It is at such times that actual external events are more likely to occur. In effect it is producing a challenging aspect with its starting position. The period from then until the beginning of the next quarter being adjustment to the change and preparation for the next. Everything is relative to the activity of the individual under free will. As in Nature, circumstances and climate provide opportunities for growth – they do not plant seeds or cultivate the soil to produce a crop.

We can see that at in the course of its 360 degree cycle any transiting planet will make every possible harmonious or challenging (easy or difficult) aspect to each planet in the Birth Chart (including its own starting point) and each of the other transit planets. Aspects between transit planets affect everything on earth, the difference for individuals is how they are affected through the aspects to their Birth Chart. The same external circumstances or conditions in life can be easy or beneficial to some, but affect others in seeming negative ways.

ASTROLOGY : PLANET TRANSITS

HOUSE & PERIOD MEANINGS

THE FIRST THING TO EMPHASISE IS THAT THIS DESCRIPTION OF ACTIVITIES OF THE 12 HOUSES IS COMMON TO ALL APPLICATIONS OF THE CYCLE OF GROWTH.

We have 12 Houses, and Astrology gives each House a separate meaning. This works to some extent, but we cannot fully understand the function of a House unless we take into account its position as PART OF THE OVERALL CYCLE. Whether considering such cycles as a calendar year, or a lifetime, each can be considered as having a Spring, Summer, Autumn, and Winter. The House meanings at a base level are identical to those of the 12 Astrological Signs, but differ in effect. The Signs describe various forms of energy available from the Sun that are used in turn to produce the cycle of seasons over time. The Personal Houses, are "fixed" in a Birth Chart and refer to the inner and outer "structure" of an individual person - the form, or results, of the energy as manifestation in Space. Each planet has its own set of Generic Houses defined by its starting position at birth.

The 12 House meanings correspond to the 12 stages in The Cycle of Growth.

The focus here is on a division of the Cycle of Growth into 4 Quarters of 3 Houses each. This is the realm of physical manifestation. We must not lose sight of the 3 Octaves of 4 Houses each which refer more to psychological development.

1ST. QUARTER : SPRING

1st. HOUSE TRANSIT – BIRTH. SEED TIME. SEEDS FOR FUTURE GROWTH

Cycle of Growth Stage 1 (Seed). Beginning of the 2nd. Octave.

(Aries : The Ram. Fire. Spring) Rebirth. Beginning of a new cycle. New interests. New ideas.

What was conceived at the Stage 9 time of Conception becomes a more tangible, physical reality.

After the 1st. Cycle, on entry into its 1st.House the planet has completed its transit of the 12th. House which has the function of clearing away the debris of the past to make room for new life. The 12th. House is mainly concerned with psychological preparation and rest, so there may or may not be actual events occurring during that time.

This is the beginning of a new cycle. Some decision is, or has been, made - consciously or unconsciously - which will establish future direction. This becomes the "seed". There may be the need to re-organise one's life in the face of current changes. The "child" is born.

At this time it is advisable to keep one's ideas to one's self. "Seeds", like babies, need to develop where they are protected. If revealed too soon they are likely to be distorted or destroyed. Nothing is clear yet. If one's own doubts and fears are not resolved inwardly they may not be expressed in the proper way. At this time the aim is to do as little as possible. Any actions are likely to concern the old cycle, resulting in the same seeds being sown again. The new cycle will then be a repetition of the earlier one.

2nd. HOUSE TRANSIT – GERMINATION. USING PERSONAL RESOURCES

Cycle of Growth Stage 2 (Germination).

(Taurus : The Bull. Fixed Earth. Resources. Money. The human body).

"Seed" ideas develop and become practical. There is a need to reassess use of resources of time, money, and effort to take the new trend into account as it begins to take root in the "subsoil" of the past. Failure to take into account this, and other stages, will mean repetition of the past.

This is a test of responsible reorganisation and management of all one's resources relative to the new area of growth. Providing support to the "new born". Not a time of much external activity. As one moves away from this phase there will be need to spend time, money, and effort, in relationship to the new possibilities that have been revealed, however limited this might be to begin with. One may find that new talents or abilities are revealed that require attention. The child learns to control the physical body.

3rd. HOUSE TRANSIT – EXPERIMENT. TRIAL & ERROR. COMMUNICATION

Cycle of Growth Stage 3 (Experiment. Communication).

(Gemini : The Twins. Mutable Air. Mind).

Testing the theory. Caution. Trial & Error. Study. Experiment. Mental activity. Communication with those close.

ASTROLOGY : PLANET TRANSITS

The seed begins to sprout. This is a time of experimentation. There is now the need to take some tentative action to see what sort of reaction one gets from others around. One must expect some negativity from those close because their lives will be affected too. They may not be ready for the possible changes required. There may also be the need to adapt one's "product" to the realities of social needs. This requires "market research". It is unlikely that what you have to offer has global appeal, so you need to find your target consumer. Also to discover where your focus of activity should be. This may require investigating areas of society that you may not have considered before.

There may be the need for some form of study or reading of books. Perhaps communication in speech or writing. This is the home of Scientific method. Experiment. Trial and error. Testing your "product". At this stage expect more failures than successes. The child learns the "rules" and begins to question the parents.

2ND. QUARTER - SUMMER

4th. HOUSE TRANSIT – CRISIS. TRANSPLANTING.

Cycle of Growth Stage 4 (Transplanting. Roots). End of the 2nd. Octave. We have to note that the 3 Stages related to Water Signs are concerned with dissolution of the past to make a new future. The 12th House before the beginning of a new cycle. The 4th. House leaving the "home" or place of inner development, and The 8th. House of Sex and Death in preparation for contact with broader principles. They bring times of Transition.

(Cancer : The Crab. The Shell. Active Water)

Break from the past. New roots. New "home". Personal foundations. A step forward.

The new plant (or child) requires strong roots. This may require transplanting to allow necessary space to grow further. Greater security. A bigger "shell" than the original. Preparing foundations.

This transit can be considered a time of "crisis" when actual events are likely to occur. One now has some concrete results from the earlier experiments, and needs to form a more stable base of operations following on from the earlier phase of the cycle. So "transplanting" may be necessary. Experiences now may take the form of things like moving house, divorce, marriage, or a new job. In effect "establishing a new home" – which can mean any area of life over which one has some control. Even a desk in an office. Building new foundations requires giving up relationships and activities that have outlived their usefulness. Symptoms of this are considering home improvements or extensions, or simply moving furniture around. It would be well to consider what is the real need.

Results now are those achieved inwardly rather than outwardly, so it may be that no actual event occurs. In fact there may be the sense that one's experiments have resulted in defeat. There may be numerous reasons for this, perhaps based upon being unable to discover the right "market". One's ideas may be "ahead of their time". It may be one's karma. However, if one has acted positively from the beginning of the cycle there will be a sense of growing self-confidence, which may be the real reason for the experiences offered. There is a sense of power from settling one's inner doubts about what may or may not work.

One is becoming "The Master of one's Own House". New attitudes are established. A new routine and way of life. A new Purpose.

The child recognises the difference between inner and outer life, and forms a "persona" ("mask" , or "shell") as a defence against the outside world.

5th. HOUSE TRANSIT – POWER. SELF EXPRESSION. CREATIVITY

Cycle of Growth Stage 5 (Power. Creativity). Beginning of the 3rd. Octave.

"All the world is a stage". (Leo : The Lion. Fixed Fire. Power)

Growth from stable roots. Controlling others. Self-confidence. Centre of activity. Personal domain. Action from love of the activity rather than material rewards. Hobbies. Sports. Caring for "children". Creativity from within one's self rather than trying to affect society.

If all has gone well so far in the cycle there will be a renewed sense of power and purpose to life. An increased self-confidence. Perhaps a sense of "promotion" from having direct, personal control of some area of life. The test is how this power is expressed and used. The necessity is that one acts out the new purpose or activity. If other people are not in accord then go forward alone. The danger is that one may believe the final goal has been achieved. When one demonstrates self-confidence there is less opposition from other people. Those that might challenge us move away, and we may attract weaker people ("children") looking for something or someone to believe in. This can offer a false sense of security because we become surrounded by people who seem to agree with us, and give us our own way. There will always be people for or against us.

Actual events would be related to the establishment of one's self as the centre of a sphere of operation. This could be in the sense of becoming the leader of some group, or family - such as when forming one's own business, starting a family, or taking up some occupation, sport, or hobby that one does for love, rather than gain.

The importance here is what principles we express through our personality rather than allowing the energies to inflate our ego. To become a creative channel. With power comes responsibility. The test is that of overcoming one's own human nature and not allowing this sense of power to be used simply to get one's own way in everything, or to prove the strength of one's ego in a battle of wills. The symptoms of this include such things as a yearning for fame or glamour, a powerful need to beget children, or suspicion of other's motives. Activities that are intended to make a personal mark in the outside world. Such behaviour indicates that one is not fully integrated inwardly, and it is still controlled by external appearances. Seeking outward pleasures and recognition rather than inner development. Leading by power, rather than by example. "Keeping up with the Jones's".

The child becomes an "actor" playing his or her newly designated role. He or she has developed a persona or "mask" as a reaction to life experiences so far. This can be considered a form of defence, or vehicle, from which to approach a wider experience of life. Within those limits, or boundaries, the individual is "master of his/her house".

6th. HOUSE TRANSIT – SERVICE TO SELF. HEALTH

Cycle of Growth Stage 6 (Service to Self. Health).

(Virgo. The Virgin. Mutable Earth. Needs something to become complete.)

Balancing service to self and others. Choice of work. Maintaining personal health. Development. Specialisation. Division of labour. Developing talents.

Experiences during transit of the 6th. House will depend upon how power has been used previously. The basic activity of this period is the refinement and development of one's skills before entering a more public environment. One needs to focus energy and specialise in some field of activity. This is a test of humility in recognising one's failings and need for further development. Although this may suggest a more subservient role, and a return to a more childish state of existence, the difference here is that we consciously choose the subject and teacher. One may also become a teacher. Paradoxically, in serving others we also serve ourselves. They enable us to focus on, and further develop, a particular set of skills.

Negatively, a common scenario occurs when the expansive transit of the 5th. House has been used for egocentric motives, and one's field of control has expanded too far beyond the foundations established during the transit of the 4th. House . Things get out of control. The individual attempts to personally be the centre of all activities of the "kingdom" which grows beyond the capabilities of one person to control. In such a situation one would normally appoint helpers. However, the price of able helpers is a share of the power, which includes being able to make decisions without having to seek the prior agreement of the "King" or "Queen" each time. If one has attracted "yes-men" and flatterers, who by definition are weak, they will fade away, or be of no use when help is really needed. In this scenario the result is often ill health from overwork, when the physical body or mind can no longer take the strain. The result is often a symbolic, and real, "heart attack". Misuse of power at that time could result in authority being removed altogether and the acceptance of a position in life with little or no opportunity for decision-making.

Although there is generally an increased workload as a result of the 5th. House period of expansion, we can also see a possible ego-centric motive for overwork - "I am the only one who can do the job properly" . Unrealistic pride.

We must also not lose sight of the fact that many people are destined for a lone path at this time, when the test is to not become over-burdened by taking on too many responsibilities or accept other people's tasks unnecessarily. "Service to Others" does have its limitations. This can contain a sense of humility too. One cannot solve everyone's problems. If others are not doing things correctly, they can be trained – and will want to do so. Otherwise we can leave them in the care of karma. Again, this means giving up some of one's power and control – and sense of "knowing what is best".

The child learns that survival depends upon maintaining physical health and the services one offers to others and varies from person to person.

3RD. QUARTER - AUTUMN

7th. HOUSE TRANSIT – FLOWERING. SOCIAL ADVANCE. PARTNERSHIP

Cycle of Growth Stage 7 (Partners).

(Libra : The Scales. Cardinal Air. Balance. Adjustment. Seeking a mate)

New partnerships. Seeking common goals. Step forward into more public role. Social service

With the transit of a planet through the 7th. House we reach half way through the cycle of the Houses of the Birth Chart. The focus at this time is on one to one relationships, and beginning to make a bigger contribution to the society in which one lives. Personal development so far has been in the more private areas of life behind the scenes. Further growth requires the acceptance of a more public role in a wider sphere of activity. Here one has even less control over the environment and therefore needs to have a more flexible approach.

One comes into contact with people who can provide support for the next stage of the process. The first step away from the past "home" towards a broader, more public, lifestyle. This could mean divorce and/or marriage, but the scope also includes business partners and other relationships. It could mean accepting an occupation that involves more responsibility for offering some service to others. So job changes are likely – perhaps as a result of the training received during the 6th. House transit. It also includes "enemies" – people who seem to obstruct our progress – but could give a more objective viewpoint.

Results also indicate that this can also mean that the subject is affected by changes in the life of a close partner – such as from his or her illness or redundancy.

Much depends upon the age of the subject when this transit occurs. During childhood this will be mainly under the control of parents. Later on the goal is still largely unconscious, more related to reproducing (or escaping from) the circumstances of the traditional parental home during early life and establishing one's own separate place in the world. The creative function related to that of producing children. It is worth noting here the extreme power of the inner, psychological, forces that are exerted. If this were not the case we would probably all still be living with our parents.

One of the problems is that if there is an existing relationship, it will need to adapt to the new circumstances or die. There needs to be some common goal that transcends the personalities of both parties. It could mean that our existing partner can accept a different role. Unfortunately in today's society the "call" is often misheard or misinterpreted. In the face of the prospect of an uncertain future, the need for new growth is translated into the biological terms of past experience. If there is a change of partnership it is often an attempt to regain the blissful ignorance of the past (" a newer model"). Sex is a powerful magnet.

The 7th. House is opposite the 1st. House. Here we have to remember that if the seed is to fulfil its destiny it must eventually reproduce. It cannot achieve this alone.

The developing "child" learns the need for co-operation with others – especially where reproduction is concerned.

8th. HOUSE TRANSIT – INTERCOURSE. TEAM EFFORTS. SHARED RESOURCES.

Cycle of Growth Stage 8 (Sex. Intercourse. Death).

(Scorpio : The Scorpion, Eagle, or Dove. Fixed Water. Sex. Death & Regeneration. The selfish ego must 'die' to fulfil its needs for relationship with others)

Scorpio has 3 different symbols depending on where the focus of motivation lies, and is ultimately concerned with the transcendence of the material world – especially after death. This is also symbolised by the transformation of a caterpillar into a butterfly. We can see that one can be in any state at any particular time.

1. The Scorpion/Serpent (Caterpillar) is the lowest level where one's attention is on sex and selfish earthly pursuits.
2. The Eagle (Chrysalis) where one has control over the emotions and is able to remain objectively still in the flow of life around. At this level is the possibility of manipulating others without seeming to take any action. One still expect something in return for one's efforts.
3. The Dove (Butterfly) where one is focused on more humanitarian pursuits.

ASTROLOGY : PLANET TRANSITS

Sharing. Teamwork. Adapting to the needs of others. Synergy. Courtship. Cross-pollination. Sex.

Plants produce flowers, sweets and perfume to help them reproduce. So does the human world.

Traditionally this is the House of "Sex and Death". Although life events now can be quite literal in meaning – there is the possibility of coming into contact with death as a reminder of our impermanent existence on Earth - we can nowadays offer a wider interpretation. The "Death" is actually that of the untamed, selfish ego that needs to co-operate with others in order to survive. The past must die to make room for new life.

The 8th. House of one's Birth Chart is concerned with "shared resources", and is opposite the 2nd. House which is concerned with "personal resources". Now we are concerned with the lesson that there is always some sort of price to pay for co-operation. Not always money - and the fact that we can achieve more from teamwork than acting alone – to mutual benefit. Synergy is where the whole becomes more than the sum of its parts. However, some form of sacrifice is necessary.

The simplest level is that of normal commercial interchange. The lesson that we have to give something to get something back. Consider how far mankind has evolved from the need for each of us to make or grow or barter goods to survive. Such things as science and technology and other intellectual pursuits would not exist today ("they neither sow nor reap"). The House is also concerned with taxes and inheritances. The joint resources of a Family, Society, or Country. So there is also the possibility of being involved in legal activities and disputes during this transit – especially those concerned with wills, inheritances, and divorce settlements. Private events can become public knowledge.

Another level it is concerned with sexual intercourse that produces children. At another, the division of labour such as where one partner works to earn money while the other takes care of the home. A division that has become a little blurred and complicated nowadays. The principle is based on each individual using their specialised abilities on behalf of the whole. Rather like a football team that has a goalkeeper, and various attackers and defenders. Each contributing to the "goal" in their own way. The main point being that the goal is an achievement of something that transcends individual or personal achievement. All participants share the results. Each being enabled to develop their special skill further. The price is that we have to give up part of our selfhood, and some of our selfish desires, to achieve something bigger.

When a planet transits the 8th. House such matters need to receive the focus of our attention. The primary need is to keep focused on one's goals in the face of difficulties or distractions that arise – especially that of maintaining or achieving a stable economic and financial base. It may be a time where the care of children is required – certainly an additional expense, and a requirement to apportion responsibilities for care. There may be financial or taxation problems. There may be a need to get out of debt or otherwise stabilise finances. On another level we may need to obtain funding or support for a venture that has been developing "behind the scenes" of life and is becoming ready to be launched on a wider basis. Another kind of "baby". Sometimes it is just practical help, or moral support that is needed rather than money. Perhaps we need to employ a professional helper.

The main aim here is survive the period and end up in a position of physical, financial, and social "health" - having discovered one's real priorities for expenditure of time, money, and effort.

The child learns the need for give-and-take. Especially where getting help is concerned.

9th. HOUSE TRANSIT – CONCEPTION. CONCEPTS. BROADENING THE MIND

Cycle of Growth Stage 9 (Conception). Beginning of the 1st. Octave.

(Sagittarius : The Archer. Mutable Fire. Conception. Mental conception. Seeking beyond one's-self to find greater meaning. Life after "death")

Mind broadening. Study. Travel. Religion. Broader social viewpoint. Foreign influences. "In laws". Law.

It is possible that the previous 8th.House "Sex and Death" experience now leads us to explore possibilities of life after 'death'. Sexual reproduction is one way of achieving this at a genetic level. What else one leaves behind in passing is another way. This is also a time that may require attention to legal matters, especially those concerned with taxes, wills and inheritances. Perhaps a wider view of how disputes can be settled. Becoming acquainted with the wider, impersonal, laws of our existence.

One of the traditional concerns of the 9th. House that is often missed by modern astrologers is "in laws". This is quite important when we consider it as part of the cycle. In general terms, having come into partnership in some way, such as by marriage, we begin to meet people who they know, and we have not yet met. They have a life and activities outside the partnership. Such activities are often outside the scope of our personal experience. They are "foreign" to us. This takes on more meaning when we consider the more universally accepted concerns of the 9th House. Which are related to "long distance travel". It is natural that we be invited to share in these "alien" activities, and thus broaden our experience.

A more modern association with the 9th.House is that of Conception. This can relate to our own physical conception, or mental conception. The symbolism of each House has a natural relationship with that of a Sign, in this case the 9th. Sign Sagittarius. In the annual cycle this is the preparation for the Christmas and New Year period.

We need to make special note here that our journey of life begins at Conception, the experiences of the later weeks we spend in the womb being as significant as any other. Perhaps they could be more important than we realise. Exploration of this area of knowledge has, in the past, been limited to times when things go wrong. As with other areas nowadays, new technology is opening up new possibilities for exploration.

Although travel or moving house is likely around the time of this transit we must not lose sight of the fact that its purpose in terms of the cycle is to broaden our mind and outlook for future possibilities, as well as gain a broader understanding of the laws that govern Nature, Society, or the Universe in general.

This brings us to other concerns of the 9th. House, which are directly related to broadening of the mind. Abstract knowledge - outside personal experience. This is the natural domain of schools and universities, churches, or other areas where training and education takes place. It is unlikely that earlier life experience gives all the knowledge needed to fulfil our purpose. So we often decide that some sort of training or study is important at this time. Important subjects are those that relate to understanding ourselves in relationship to the rest of humanity such as Law, Religion, Philosophy, Psychology and Astrology. Unfortunately, for many, there is an irrational fear of exploring such areas. In any such situation it is a help to realise that thousands of people are involved in such areas on a daily basis. This transit brings the lesson of needing to remove the prejudice and fear that blinds us to the broader realities of life. To put the traditions of our birth into a wider perspective. "Know Thyself". An example is the new evidence arising from the study of Evolution and DNA being challenged by established religions which will need to expand their horizons – exploring the Spirit, rather than the Letter, of the Law.

4TH. QUARTER : WINTER

10th. HOUSE TRANSIT – PEAK OF ACHIEVEMENT. HARVEST
Cycle of Growth Stage 10 (Social Peak).

(Capricorn : The Mountain Goat. Cardinal Earth. Climbing the material "ladder of success". Higher aims. New Year Resolutions)

Harvesting fruits of past efforts for good or ill. Promotion. Responsibility. Duty. Prestige. Limelight.

Transit of the 10th house is probably the one that is most easily remembered, and therefore most useful for checking that the birth time is correct. This is because one now reaps the harvest of all one's efforts throughout the cycle. Whereas previous activity has tended to be in the background of life, the fruits of one's labour are now in concrete form and evident for all to see. For good or ill. One's popularity and social standing, or otherwise, is at its highest. If nothing significant was noticed during the 1st. House transit it now may be possible to look back at that time to see how everything started.

Since the 1st. House transit one has learned how to fit one's personal aims in with those of others. The task now is to take some public or professional stand in full public view as a result. One reaches a position of power and responsibility RELATED TO ONE'S PAST EFFORTS. This can mean things like job promotion, or invitations to join governing bodies of organisations. Perhaps teaching or otherwise reporting on one's activities. This can also mean social ostracism as a result of attempting to be too independent, separating oneself from society, or being involved in anti-social activities. In the School of Life bad examples can be as useful as good.

It is important that one now focuses on the job at hand. This will probably mean taking on added responsibilities, and therefore time for other activities will be limited. This is a time of consolidation rather than further expansion. The period of transit is limited and will be followed by a "Winter" decline in preparation for the new cycle which starts when the planet transits the 1st. House once again. It is also important that one does not allow one's integrity to be compromised. A strong moral stance must be maintained. We have only observe the media to realise that, when coming to public view, much can be revealed that we would rather have kept hidden. It also arouses jealousy and other negative emotions in some people who do not understand the hard work that has been put into achieving the position, and we become attacked by them.

ASTROLOGY : PLANET TRANSITS

A danger at this time is that we may let success "go to our head" and push aside new "Conceptions", ideas for future growth. "Killing our brain-children". At least "bear" in mind that this experience is temporary. We can now see the symbolic relationship of the meaning of this time to the story of the "Virgin Birth" which contains more than reference to normal human reproduction. The 10th House relates to the sign of Capricorn with its symbolism of rebirth at Christmas and the Winter Solstice. Extending the symbolism, human conception requires that just a single sperm fertilises the egg. Once one penetrates, defences are put up so others are rejected.

In terms of the Birth Chart this is the Personal House wherein the mother first becomes aware of her pregnancy and the possible birth to come. Perhaps this is really when our life ambitions are set, positive or negative, from her attitude to the coming new life . At least until we find our own life pathway.

I have noticed that female subjects are likely to bear a child around this Transit time. Usually their first.

The 10th House of Career is opposite the 4th. House of Home and Roots. The conflict between the two areas is a common life experience. One usually has to be neglected in favour of the other. Therefore the draw towards the Home can be very powerful at this time as a form of compensation. At its peak the planet in question has begun its return to the 4th. House.

11th. HOUSE TRANSIT – DISSATISFACTION. INVENTION.

Cycle of Growth Stage 11 (Discontent).

(Aquarius : The Water Carrier. Fixed Air. Communication. Invention. Change. Independence. Rebellion.)

Social decline. Re-assess aims. Challenging outmoded ideas & traditions. Inventing new.

Having achieved social position and prestige in the 10th House we could assume that we would be satisfied with the current situation. However, to arrive at this destination we have had to focus energies on achieving the goal over a considerable period of time. Not only has this required that we ignore interesting side issues that may have arisen, but we also have had to adapt our original aims to fit in with the social climate. So at this time, apart from positive and negative responses from those around, we have a personal mixture of feelings of success and failure.

If successful, we may attempt to prolong the situation for as long as possible. However this is often counteracted by an inner sense of being a 'slave' to one's position or office. There is a sense of "noblesse oblige", and maintaining one's position takes continual effort. In the midst of success one is at everyone's beck and call. Privacy becomes limited. One becomes surrounded by people who, apart from flattery, take more than they give. To appear in public makes one vulnerable to attack from all and sundry with their own agendas to carry out. Perhaps one's health begins to suffer, or perhaps a sense of boredom sets in. One's emotional energy becomes drained.

If failures outweigh successes at this time, there is the likelihood that one might attempt to stir up trouble in revenge. Blaming other people or society for one's own failure. Perhaps joining groups involved in anti-social behaviour. This is a futile waste of time and energy because we gradually stir up increasing opposition and become hopelessly outnumbered. While fighting against, rather than for, something we can lose sight of possibilities for positive growth.

There is, however, a middle path where one may be called upon to use one's public position to openly challenge outmoded or unfair forms of tradition or government. Perhaps joining a group of people dedicated to such a purpose – or undertaking some form of self development. We often see "celebrities" offering support to charitable organisations during this period. Law, Tradition, Order, Routine, and Habit are necessary to our survival, so we need to replace bad structures with good one's rather than trying to eradicate them altogether. That would lead to anarchy.

Another manifestation we see frequently is when an individual becomes a "celebrity". They seem to give up their chosen career to become a host in television quiz or chat shows, or similar. Only the results of time will tell if this is a positive or negative activity. Have they lost their way, or sense of purpose, or got lazy? If new seeds are sown at the proper time later on then it would seem to be opportunity for growth to continue. We must also note that, because the 11th. House is opposite the 5th. House, similar ego issues can appear here too.

Eventually, whatever the situation, the cycles of life continue to draw us forward to further new experience. This could also be forced by actual events. In this modern age there is no such thing as a "job for life". Redundancy is a possibility during this transit. Now is an opportunity to look at one's original aims and see if there is something that can be revived or improved upon. Nowadays new technology is advancing very quickly – perhaps new and better tools are available. Perhaps one invents the tools that can help build a new future. Greater freedom.

We see this time demonstrated in the lives of famous people when they are in public view for a period and later fade into the background.

12th. HOUSE TRANSIT – WITHDRAWAL. CONFINEMENT. DECAY

Cycle of Growth Stage 12 (Withdrawal. Self-Sacrifice).

(Pisces : The Fishes. Sacrifice the past to move forward. The Collective Unconscious rules everything).

Each of the Houses relating to Water Signs carries the necessity to give up the past to make way for a broader future. Here we have Confinement awaiting birth/new cycle. Clearing of past. Settling debts. Rewards or penalties. Karma.

In relationship to the Birth Chart this is the time of confinement when the mother has to reduce physical activity and retire into the home in preparation for the birth, which is the concern of the following 1st.House transit.

In Nature it is late Winter - nearly Spring. Seeds are in the ground waiting for the right time to germinate. The waste products of the past have been converted into fertiliser for future growth. The ground prepared for new growth. Death has made space for new life. Even if one is still carrying out normal daily tasks there is a sense of isolation. This is a time of transition.

Although one can be receiving rewards for past services, the task now is one of self-analysis. The planet has gone full cycle and one has had concrete results from one's efforts. Before one can begin a new one there is a need to re-evaluate one's successes and failures - especially in the light of one's original aims at the beginning of the cycle. Destroying the "weeds" and making space for "new crops" to grow.

This is a time of working on matters inwardly rather than outwardly. The external world needs to become less focused. There may be participation in artistic, religious, musical, or other non-practical activities like entertainment and travel to aid this process. Taking holidays, or spiritual retreat. Perhaps taking courses or joining groups involved in some form of self development - such as religion, psychology, meditation, Astrology, or Yoga. Perhaps, finally, completing tasks that have been left undone. Or simply resting.

Attempts to ignore this requirement could result in being forced into "retirement" from external activities by illness or some other form of "imprisonment". This House traditionally rules Prisons, Hospitals, Monasteries, Convents and other areas of personal isolation as well as "underground" structures such as sewerage and drainage. Even God rested after the Creation.

This is a time of repayment of debts – to one's self and others. Giving and receiving forgiveness. Sometimes it is easier to forgive others than one's self. We can see positive reasons for allowing one's self to "forget it" now. The task is to enter into the next cycle free of "baggage" from the past. One will try to "do better next time".

One now realises that the interminable process of life is more important than one's practical achievements, which are "transit-ory". Another danger at this time is that of becoming self-satisfied with one's achievements and assuming that this is the end to one's struggle in life. There is a need to realise that all structures require regular maintenance. The body and mind need exercise, otherwise they collapse. Prepare for the new "Spring".

The 12th. House is opposite the 6th. House which is concerned with one's health and physical well-being. If we have neglected maintenance to our homes or other possessions – especially the physical body – this would be the time to have problems forcing them to our attention.

Despite the symptoms, accidents or health problems at this time are more likely to have psychosomatic than physical causes. We can see how seeming negatives of ill health, and even abuse of alcohol and drugs (also traditional concerns of this House) can actually assist the 12th. House "forgetting" process. Indeed, some form of exploration in the field of Psychology may be especially beneficial at this time.

At another level, this is the "House of Karma" where debts are repaid for good or ill. "As You Give, So Shall You Receive". The final harvest and judgement of our past actions.

THE GENERIC CYCLES OF JUPITER

Experiments show that the 12 year cycles of Jupiter are more individual or personal in their effects, which are more noticeable, whereas Saturn concerns our relationships with others in more social terms. There is a "Life Diary" at the end of the chapter to test the theory for yourself.

ASTROLOGY : PLANET TRANSITS

THE GENERIC CYCLES OF SATURN

Originally this chapter was to be about Saturn alone, with another about Uranus, but I came to the realisation that we cannot consider one without its relationship to the other. At base level Saturn gives us the overall structure of a physical lifetime without which we would be unable to function. It is the Cycle of Nature that has brought us to our current evolutionary state, and which defines the stages in the Cycle of Growth. However, on its own it demands that we are all born, grow, and die according to a fixed routine, or timetable. In fact, back in the stone age very few humanoids lived beyond a single Saturn Cycle of 30 years.

If we need any further evidence in life today we only have to observe (or become) people over this age to see a distinct physical depreciation has set in. The best examples being those whose life activities are based on physical prowess. It is a well-known fact, for example, that those who indulge in sport become no longer able to compete with those younger than themselves. For a sportsman, life generally ends at 35. This also applies to reproduction, as men's physical energy declines and women are beginning to approach menopause. Uranus technology has overcome this to some extent – but not the psychology.

We have all evolved out of the animal kingdom, so it is not surprising that this is the case. Looking outside ourselves into that area we note that various species are more or less dependent on an annual cycle. Although the life expectancy is not so long, the same principle of the young continually attempting to replace the old applies. Somehow we have managed to gradually extend our lifespan beyond this time.

Looking back at the process of evolution, we see that what sets us apart from animals is "brain power" which gives us the ability to communicate and co-operate with one another. Can you imagine the possibility of millions of "higher animals" living in one place as we do? Ants seem to manage it, but not lions and tigers. Whenever I consider it, I am always amazed that I have come through life without having to grow my own food, or physically make anything to sell or barter.

As we study Astrology we realise that "brain power" comes from the planet Uranus, which has a similar form of energy to the Zodiac Sign of Aquarius. More specifically, when we study Psychology we realise that Uranus and Aquarius are both physical/psychological projections of the same Archetype from the INNER world of the Collective Unconscious. It is rather like seeing the "face" of "the man in the Moon". In fact, they do not have any energies themselves, but they do allow us symbols to give our limited minds something to work with. Other archetype examples are those which control Saturn/Capricorn and the other astrological symbols.

We can now also see how the development of "mind" enables us to survive beyond 30 years. Despite weakening physically we survive by being more crafty and cunning. The young work in co-operation with the old. The old are able to pass on the fruits of their experience and so save the young making the same fatal mistakes. So they do have some value after all. Another function of Uranus/Aquarius is that of its facility for Invention and Technology. At base level the manufacture of tools that serve to reduce the need for physical strength – even to multiply it. The continual improvement of weapons to survive against physical attack. Even amongst humankind the nation with the best technology usually wins against force of physical numbers.

So Uranus/Aquarius takes us beyond the earthly confines of Saturn. It does have another influence at a personal, individual, level. That of part of the psychological process of Individuation. If we try to see how it actually works in life we might understand the process better. Like the ancient "Gods" the various archetypes do not always get along with one another. There is conflict and struggle between them.

SATURN'S FUNCTION

The influence of Saturn extends to every facet of our lives. It exists wherever we see law, order, structure, and attention to physical detail. It also includes the structure of the physical body, which is the same for each of us, and the need to support it.

Saturn is symbolically "The Taskmaster" of the horoscope. He requires structure, order, and practical results - and often appears to be a block to our conscious desires. In some systems of thought he is "The Devil" that forces us to achieve material aims. We are never free of its influence during our lifetime. Like it or not, we still need to eat to live. If we observe this one effect on our lives we probably get an understanding of his main purpose. He also has another name ,"Lucifer" – " The Bringer of Light". In Astrology his function as the bridge between the inner 'personal' planets and the outer 'transpersonal', slower moving, planets (Uranus, Neptune, and Pluto) which separate our solar system from the wider Universe, and, symbolically, expand our consciousness. These three were discovered in 1781, 1846, and 1930 respectively. Saturn is the furthest planet visible to the naked eye. The others were discovered by technological and mathematical methods (a result of man's expansion of consciousness beyond the 5 senses). There is the suggestion that the ancient astrologers did not know about these planets because mankind was not ready to use them.

Saturn is concerned with Law wherever we find it. We are all subject to Law – whether of Family, Community, Society, "Human Nature", or any of the Natural Laws studied by science and technology.

THE FAMILY STRUCTURE

Saturn determines the overall structure of our lives, the levels of social hierarchy, and their rules and laws. Our first contact and controlling influence is (usually) that of our Mother, and from there our consciousness expands to include other members of our family inside the home, which has its own structure and rules. Depending on the social climate there, we gain experience of other people who visit the home. Later on we begin to explore the world outside. Some go on explore a wider Universe.

Within the family, Saturn's structural influence is over the hierarchy, or "pecking order" and how the members relate to one another. Some members, usually the older ones, have more power and control than others. It is also concerned with the traditions that the family has established and inherited over generations, such as social standing and working traditions. This has become less fixed nowadays, but not too long ago it was accepted that we take on and continue the lifestyle and occupation of our parents. The individualising effect of The Age of Aquarius has made life more complicated.

SOCIAL STRUCTURE

As we come into contact with a widening Society containing a greater number of people Saturn is concerned with the laws and traditions which govern that society. These can differ depending on the country we are born into, and even the region of that country.

IT IS NECESSARY TO RECOGNISE THAT WE MUST ALL FIT OUR ACTIVITIES INTO SOME FORM OF SOCIAL STRUCTURE OR TRADITION. THE PARADOX IS THAT, AS WE DISCOVER OUR TRUE INDIVIDUALITY, WE FIND OUR TRUE POSITION IN SOCIETY – SERVING OTHERS WITHOUT LOSING OUR SELFHOOD.

SATURN STRUCTURE OF A LIFETIME

The basic structure of all our lives, as humans, from birth to death is the same depending on our age. We are born incapable of supporting ourselves and requiring help from others to survive. The price for this is that we are under the total control of external forces. As life progresses we attain more control of our physical world, including our bodily functions, and destiny. A major factor in this is how much we can support ourselves and how much we need to depend on others. What we need to do to house ourselves and earn our "daily bread".

From birth onwards we tend towards a gradually widening viewpoint as our perceptions expand further from mother, to family, towards a widening experience of society outside the home. At the beginning of life we develop abilities according to the requirements of our parents and other authority figures. Certain energies we have are developed, and others are suppressed depending on what kind of behaviour is deemed appropriate. For example, the competitive nature of Mars is generally deemed appropriate to men but not women even though the planet has the same effect in any Birth Chart.

Gradually life, and time, takes us away from our parents towards a more individual lifestyle. However, the basic pattern still tends to mimic theirs. It is interesting to note that not too long ago it was usual for children to "follow in the footsteps" of their parents – even to continuing the same daily occupations. Although this seems to have changed a lot nowadays, people who rebel against their upbringing are not always as free from this effect as they think. By deliberately following a different lifestyle they are still governed by its influence because it still determines what to rebel against. At another level it is very difficult to change our basic psychological nature - which psychologists tell us is well established by 6 years of age as a result of the relationship between personal traits and environmental influences.

THE INNER PERSONAL SATURN – SELF DISCIPLINE

At an individual, personal, level Saturn's laws first take the form of external discipline, often a seeming blockage to our plans and desires. This comes in the form of people and things outside ourselves such as parents, older people, social laws, and government. Society in general. Perhaps lack of money – which is usually due to failure to supply some kind of service to society. It will remain at this level until we realise that we have some form of duty or task to perform in life – and begin to undertake it. Saturn then becomes the internal force of Self-Discipline. We begin to embody "Saturn the Teacher" within our self. This does not mean that we do a lot of work for people who are quite capable of performing tasks for themselves. In fact it makes us more selective in choosing what we do because we have to satisfy both inner and outer needs at the same time. What we do for others also benefits our self.

SATURN'S OPPOSITION TO OUR LIFE PURPOSE. NECESSARY EVIL

It is important to keep in mind the fact that Saturn is not the indicator of one's Life Purpose which is more related to the position of the Sun in the Birth Chart. SATURN ACTUALLY SEEMS TO OPPOSE OUR LIFE PURPOSE. We can see from the symbology that Saturn "The Devil" actually tends to be a resistance to, or even block, the energy of the Sun. Together, the Sun and Saturn symbolise the seeming opposing forces of "Spirit" and "Matter". We can see the results of the activity of these forces every calendar year during Spring, Summer, Autumn, and Winter when the basic power of the energy of the Sun is controlled and modified.

We therefore see the true purpose of Saturn "The Adversary" [YLT]. We gain strength and knowledge from learning the rules of, and competing in, "The Game of Life".

SATURN TRANSITS : 30 YEAR CYCLES

The basic structure of all our lives, as humans, from birth to death is the same. We all go through similar growth experiences during our life from birth to death which take on a more personal meaning when we consider the Birth Chart position of Saturn as a "seed time", and follow its cycles of growth from then onwards. We have similar daily routines. Until now Astrology has only considered two cycles, taking us up to age 60. This is because it used to be rare for people to live so long. Now people are living longer with the possibility of living to 100 years of age or more we need to consider the meaning and possibilities of a third cycle. We can see that each of the 3 cycles has a different focus. However, not everyone takes advantage of them.

The First Cycle (0-30 years) is concerned with an individual becoming established as a result of parental upbringing.

The Second Cycle (30-60 years) should start with the individual becoming established in society away from the parental home. However, at that time, the life circumstances and expectations are likely to be very similar to those of the past. This cycle includes the "Mid-Life Crisis" which prompts towards a more personal, individual, pathway - separate from one's past traditional or social upbringing. You will see below that I suggest the Mid-Life Crisis is more related to the influence of Uranus whose energy challenges that of Saturn.

At the beginning of this cycle I became aware of occult knowledge [MY STORY] , but returned to a normal life whilst studying the various subjects.

The purpose of the Third Generic Saturn Cycle (60-90 years) is not so clear, considering the lack of suitable subjects. Perhaps this writing will supply the structure to find out. It seems to be related to our "Second Childhood". As with all aspects of life, we can only reap what we have sown previously. It appears that the majority of people nowadays are not able to cope with 2 Saturn cycles, and consider their (creative) lives ended at age 60 with the coming of retirement from daily work and a seeming relief from many of Saturn's external disciplines.

The state, or condition, of our physical body at age 60 can be considered the result of personal Karma. We reap what we sow.

After retiring at age 65 I now have time to write this book.

With the natural degeneration of the physical body, it would seem that this third cycle would be related more to mental or spiritual, rather than physical, development - however, considering the advances in medical science over the last few years and what might be coming in future, this might not be the case. Future generations could find their physical bodies lasting much longer - assuming that they could make use of the extended time on earth. We do, however, need to consider if there is some purpose to life other than physical creativity and decline.

We note that, as I write this, as a result of Uranus technology and invention, the current generation can expect to live beyond 100 years. This defines Quantity of life, but not Quality.

SATURN AND JUPITER

We gain a better understanding of planetary energies when we examine them in relationship to one another. The energies of those in adjoining orbits tend to conflict with one another., and require us to find some sort of balance between them in our lives. Saturn tends to be a "block" or limitation to all energies of the Birth Chart. This especially refers to the energies of Jupiter, the next planet orbiting between itself and the Sun. The main principle of Jupiter is "Expansion". With too little expansion there is no growth. Too much expansion, and without structure, there is disintegration and wasted energy. Examples of this are the rise and fall of the great empires such as the Roman Empire and British Empire that expanded far beyond the ability to control them.

SATURN AND URANUS

Uranus is the next planet away from the Sun. Uranus energy tends to challenge Saturn structures by such means as open rebellion or the introduction of new methods and structures. It is strongly related to the growth of science and technology. As with all other factors, we need to take into account its INNER activity – which, whilst allowing more individual freedom, has meant that we have to take more responsibility for our actions. We can no longer blame our parents or society for our situation.

The Generic Cycle of Uranus takes around 84 years. The planet has only recently been discovered and it seems that mankind is not yet ready to take full advantage of its energy. Its cycle period does correspond with what we can now consider within the scope of a normal human lifetime nowadays – as distinct from the beginning of the 20th. Century when the average length of a lifetime was much less, and before which 42 years was a "ripe old age".

> *The life expectancy of new born children in 1999 is 75 years for boys and 80 years for girls. In 1901 baby boys were expected to live for 45 years and girls 49 years. [HOUSE OF COMMONS RESEARCH PAPER 99/111. (21st. December 1999) "A Century of Change: Trends in UK statistics since 1900"]*
>
> 42 years happens to be related to :-
> 1. The time of a half a Uranus cycle, and therefore the beginning of Generic Uranus Cycle Stage 7 (Partners. New social role).
> 2. Beginning of Logarithmic Timescale Stage 8 (Sex. Death).
> 3. The Mid-Life Crisis age. Perhaps more aptly named than expected.
> 4. We can also add the 40 week gestation period in the womb, and the 40 days and nights Jesus spent fasting in the wilderness which, although numerically different, relate to the same Stages in The Cycle of Growth.

Looking closely, it seems that Uranus offers some form of "life after death". I relate the cycle of Uranus to the C.G.Jung concept of the Individuation Process, which he suggests is "a task for the second half of life".

MID LIFE CRISIS AGE 42 – TRANSITING URANUS OPPOSITION TO ITS BIRTH CHART POSITION

It is nowadays recognized that, around the ages of 30-40 (beginning of the 2nd. Saturn Cycle), a decline of physical energy begins to occur, followed by a Mid Life Crisis. Many people deny it occurred in their life. This could mean, of course, that this was not an issue for them. However, it generally means that they did not recognise it, or may have missed out a necessary stage in personal development. Although prompted to change they are still acting according to the programming of their early life experience (Saturn). This is an intensely personal experience when the individual begins to feel an inner discontent, despite the fact that to all intents and purposes the exterior (Saturn) life may be going well. Actual changes to the lifestyle may not occur until triggered by some external event. Such events are - death of a parent, breakdown of a relationship, growth of children beyond the need for parental care, or other forms of 'redundancy', especially that of facing the now closer reality of one's own death.

Not too long ago people did not live much beyond the age of 40. Even today the effects of 'old age' are felt at this time. Physical decline is more apparent, especially in such areas as sport - where athletes become unable to complete with those younger than themselves, and women come to the end of childbearing possibility. This can result in attempts to recover past youth by seeking new partnerships, or have more children, rather than face the uncertainty of an unknown future. "Making a comeback.". If this is the case it is futile, because it merely postpones the event to a later stage of life. At such a time one may be less able to cope with it. Another factor to be taken into account is that of society in general which has still not come to terms with "life beyond 40" - the publicity which we are faced with daily tending to glorify youth over old age – such as a from a huge cosmetic industry geared to making us look younger (and "more attractive").

Although it is not fully clear what is happening at this time, it seems that, psychologically, the previously suppressed parts of our individual character are now coming forward to be recognized and put to use. With the decline in our physical state we need to be able to have full use of all our resources – not just the ones that have enabled our survival so far. Especially the ones that involve development of the Mind. Previously held attitudes and beliefs are challenged with the need to consider opposing arguments. Our children are making a New Society. The firmer these beliefs, the more difficult the process. This is a time requiring a reappraisal of all one has experienced in the past so that one can go forward using all one's faculties rather than having to waste energy fighting one's true self. As we get older it becomes more apparent that each one of us is ultimately alone. The psychologist C.G.Jung called this process, which lasts a whole lifetime, "Individuation". It contains the strange paradox that as we become more of an individual we grow into a wider perspective and experience of life.

A main area of study of this process is Psychology. A difficulty here is that there is a tendency to spend time considering problems rather than healthy solutions. The symptoms are seen as a disruption to life with an attempt to return to an earlier state, rather than a step towards a later goal. As with society in general, there is little consideration of the future and what goals might be in later life. This attitude is being forced to change as a result of people living longer.

Another area of study is that of Religion. In Western countries religion does not seem to have come to terms with the possibility of life after physical death. In Eastern countries there are millions of people who accept Reincarnation as fact. There is also Spiritualism as the only area of practical study of the subject. It is a worthwhile exploration. Because any results are a matter of personal belief and experience I make no further comment. We are considering factual evidence here. However, it is a simple observable fact that whatever stops growing dies – even in the human world. As we get older , what we actually reap becomes more a matter of Personal Responsibility. We are less able to blame our parents or upbringing – or Society. This brings a different slant to general concepts of "Karma", which tend to be the sole concern of re-incarnation. By studying the cycle of Saturn in relationship to our Birth Chart we can see the process of our own "sowing and reaping".

GENERIC SATURN CYCLE

With a 30 year cycle Saturn's movement is very slow, so related changes also occur slowly over a long period of time. As with the other cycles there are "crisis points" when Saturn transits the 4 quarters of its orbit in relationship to its position in a Birth Chart. These correspond with Spring, Summer, Autumn and Winter, and are times when actual events are most likely to occur. At these times is the opportunity to "get out of the rut" and take a step forward in development and growth. Saturn always requires hard work and attention to one's duty, so everything is relative to whatever one has been doing since the seeds were sown at the beginning of the cycle when Saturn last transited its position at birth, and how they have been cultivated since.

GENERIC SATURN CYCLE : 1st. QUARTER. SPRING.

SEED PERIOD. REBIRTH. NEW IDEAS AND OPPORTUNITIES.

Cycle of Growth Stage 1 (Seed)

Begins at approximate ages 0, 30, 60, 90.

When Saturn returns to its position as at birth there is a repetition of the personal Saturn birth principle as defined in the Birth Chart which will direct and colour the whole of the following cycle. In the previous few years there would have been a sense of re-evaluating the results of the activities of life in terms of success or failure, and making plans for the future. Having achieved some results, there is now the possibility of taking advantage of changing conditions which will define one's social position and pathway for the next 30 years.

After the initial changes, activities over the next few years will be concerned with establishing new daily routines, and re-organising resources of time, money, and effort. Although there may be new possibilities now is not the time for too much action because there is more likelihood that they will be related to the previous cycle and result in sowing the same "seeds", and therefore merely repeating the previous cycle. This is a time for making plans for the future.

Age 0 : THE BIRTH POSITION

The Seed position of Saturn in a Birth Chart by House, Sign, and Aspects determine the whole cycle.

ASTROLOGY : PLANET TRANSITS

AGE 30 : FINDING A PERSONAL LIFE PATH

With the Saturn Return to its birth position at age 30 one has probably been following in the footsteps of family expectations or traditions. Now there is the opportunity to finally break away from conscious or unconscious parental control to take an occupation more suited to one's personal abilities and preferences. To plant new seeds.

AGE 60 : RETIREMENT FROM THE PERSONAL LIFE PATH

Jupiter has its 5th. Return at this age.

Coincides with Cycle of Growth Stage 1 (Seed) of the 5th. Generic Jupiter Cycle.

One reaps the harvest of the last 30 year cycle, for good or ill. If one has worked diligently there is opportunity for further growth – otherwise there is a sense of having to start over again from the beginning.

One "harvest" to consider is whether one has had the foresight to make provision for a pension – and done something about it. It is interesting to note that, with the Aquarian/Uranus drive for "freedom", this has become more of a personal responsibility, which will increase as people are living longer. Governments are already finding it difficult to support an ageing population. Greater freedom invokes greater personal responsibility. The situation is exacerbated by the fact that there is now no such thing as "a job for life", so employers are less responsible for organising pensions.

There seems to be a difference at around age 60 - the beginning of a 3rd. Generic cycle – when Society decides that we have "done our bit" and rewards us according to our conformity. In effect, at this time, we begin to gather the harvest of the whole of our working life and "reap what we have sown" – especially in terms of our bank balance, which will STILL govern our lifestyle. There is now generally no need to earn a daily living and one is free of family encumbrances. At one level, this is what a lot of people seem to consider as their life goal. Indeed, some seem to (try to) achieve this state earlier at the beginning of the previous cycle. We must, however, take note of the fact that whatever stops growing will die.

If we observe closely, at age 60 there also seems to be an attitude from younger people that we have outlived our usefulness, and that we are just waiting for physical death. I remember a similar attitude from my children and their friends when I was 30. This attitude tends to be confirmed by many people of this age. A certain collusion between individuals and society as a whole. I have had many work colleagues who have not lived very long after their retirement.

This new cycle often seems to be the entry into a "second childhood" phase when one needs to be "looked after". A regression all the way back to the first Saturn position at Birth. Unfortunately this is often confirmed by one's state of health. There is, however, a big difference between giving control of one's life over to the "experts" and "father and mother" in the disguise of younger relatives, or society, and making one's own decisions about how one is treated. I discovered this during my mid-life crisis around age 40 as mentioned in the chapter [MY STORY].

Interestingly, how young people, and society, actually treat their elders now will have a strong bearing on how they will be treated when their turn comes. Once again, reaping what is sown.

Once more the challenge is to choose between conformity to tradition or to sow fresh seeds for growth – despite the possibility of not being around at the time of harvest. Perhaps training younger people or somehow otherwise conveying the fruits of one's experience to the "fertile soil" of the next generation.

Rather than trying to relive the past, and being free of the need to earn one's daily bread, this could be the opportunity for spiritual development.

GENERIC SATURN CYCLE : 2nd. QUARTER. SUMMER.

ACTION. BREAKING FROM THE PAST TO MAKE NEW FOUNDATIONS

Cycle of Growth Stage 4 (Transplanting. Roots)

Approximate ages 7, 35, 65

This is the Waxing (growing) Square Aspect (90 degrees) of Saturn to its birth position.

Following on from the past quarter, one should have taken time to explore the possibilities offered by the, then new conditions. Giving up relationships and activities that are no longer required or useful to the new cycle.

This can be a difficult time because the individual is now required to actually take action to separate from the past and establish his or her own foundations. Social and Personal. To find the place where they really belong as an individual.

AGE 7 : STEPS OUTSIDE THE FAMILY HOME

At age 7 we are still under parental control. However, one begins to find more individual expression from the friends and acquaintances one chooses to associate with. This is the beginning of Erikson's "School Age". "
[ASTROLOGY : LOGARITHMIC TIMESCALE]

AGE 35 : A BIGGER HOUSE ? INDIVIDUATION ?

At this age one has an established social position in life – for good or ill. One's children are probably in their teens (Saturn 3rd.Quarter) - hopefully, more self-supporting, and rebelling in preparation for their departure from parental influence. However, this is a time where challenges arise to enable changes of direction. Saturn's influence is a tendency to bind one to a fixed earthly routine. With this opportunity to take a step forward the tendency will be to repeat and expand on whatever has been done in the past – so is likely to be expressed in terms of a bigger house or car, or a better job.

An important consideration now is the decline of one's physical energies. This is best seen in the cases of athletes or other pursuits that rely on physical activity. It is clear to everyone concerned that at this age there is no longer the ability to compete with younger people. A sporting career or other physical work may be prolonged, but eventually must be given up.

At this time we are also approaching the age of 42 which is that of the mid-life crisis prompted by the opposition of Uranus with its Birth Chart position. Its pressure is toward the separation of one's self from the rest of humanity towards Individuation.

GENERIC SATURN CYCLE : 3rd. QUARTER. AUTUMN.

SUPPORT. JOINT ACTIVITY TO A WIDER VIEWPOINT

Cycle of Growth Stage 7 (Partners. Social Role)

Approximate ages 15, 45, 75

This is the Opposition Aspect of Saturn to its position in a Birth Chart.

Generally after developing in the background of life there is a clearer understanding of one's true purpose. Half way through the cycle there is now a need to carry this to the service of a wider public. One now has concrete results of the new trend by which progress can be judged. For development to continue it is necessary to accept some role involved in offering service to society and/or join with others of like mind.

AGE 15 : NEW RELATIONSHIPS. JOINT REBELLION

When this occurs at age 15, neither child or quite yet adult, one rebels against the rules and authority of the parental figures around – trying to become one's own "authority". Most of us have to conform to the role we are expected to at this age. Some run away from home to escape it. Finding a job, or early marriage, is another way. Greater freedom = greater responsibility.

This is Erikson's Adolescent Stage concerned with emancipation from parents and finding a place in one's peer group.

AGE 45 : NEW RELATIONSHIPS

At age 45 what was just a possibility or idea at the beginning of the Age 30 cycle has now become more real. One can now compare progress with what one's expectations were earlier on and make necessary adjustments before taking a more public pathway. If the opportunity to make a new start based on one's own personal values was missed previously there is the possibility to do something about it now. This may be forced by the need to develop a healthier lifestyle. The illnesses to which we are personally prone are not random. One may now have an aged or sick parent to care for. If so, this role reversal allows the opportunity to examine their condition in the light of how they have lived their life.

If the earlier call was not heard, and one is still living according to traditional parental rules or social expectations this urge can be misinterpreted. This is an age of decline in sexual activity. One's physical appearance (in society's terms) is deteriorating. Rather than considering one's own inner personal values, there can be an attempt to recover the lost youth so highly valued by the general public. There can be an attempt to regain this earlier state by seeking a new, younger, partner or running away from home to "start afresh". As this is towards the end of woman's childbearing years there can be the attempt to have another child "before it is too late". It is helpful if one's existing partner is of the same age, and therefore at the same state.

This is a time of increased social contact. One should be choosing new relationships in the light of new growth rather than old habits. Even doctors and therapists perform a role in this context - widening one's viewpoint. The problem here is that they tend to see only problems. They do not have the time or inclination to consider matters of soul development, so often drugs will take the place of the use of Will - treating symptoms rather than the root causes. Trying to get back to a previous state rather than moving forward. Some doctors also adhere to popular social concepts concerning old age and believe that they are wasting their time treating older people. We cannot entirely blame them because they are confronted daily with physical evidence that seems to confirm this belief.

The point to consider here is that once one has travelled far in the wrong direction it is very difficult to find one's way back to a truer pathway. If one missed the side turning before, it is more likely to be rediscovered in what is new at this time rather than get too bogged down with past regrets. In the continual struggle between Spirit and Matter it is our task to find solutions that are practical at the time. Often this requires compromise. Perhaps this is the main reason for our earthly existence.

Going forward, one's main life purpose develops further from support of others. Relationships must serve some purpose within a larger structure or framework beyond home and family. Goals that transcend all those involved. This may require several readjustments to achieve concrete results, but will also lead to wider possibilities not previously imagined.

GENERIC SATURN CYCLE : 4th. QUARTER. WINTER

HARVEST. PEAK OF DEVELOPMENT TO TEMPORARY RETIREMENT

Cycle of Growth Stage 10 (Peak of Social Achievement)

Approximate ages 21, 51, 81

This is the Waning Square Aspect (90 degrees) to the birth position. Saturn has travelled 270 degrees in its cycle.

One has reached the peak of the cycle and is beginning a decline in preparation for the beginning of a new cycle.

AGE 21 : COMING OF AGE. ADULT RESPONSIBILITY

It is interesting to note that Age 21 is also the beginning of the Second Quarter (Cycle of Growth Stage 4 - Transplanting) of the Generic Uranus Cycle.

One now reaps the harvest of all one's efforts throughout the cycle. The fruits of one's labour are now in concrete form and evident for all to see. For good or ill. At this time one's past indiscretions also come to a wider public view. This could mean some kind of job promotion or offers of a more leading social role - such as sitting on a committee or acting as a spokesperson. It could also mean ostracism from failure to fit into some social role.

Although nowadays Age 18 is some preparation (Generic Jupiter Cycle of Growth Stage 7 (Partners)), Society rewards the attainment of age 21 by officially promoting us to adult status. We now legally become free of parental control and responsible for our actions.

AGE 51 : SOCIAL PEAK

At 51 it could be that one's children form the basis of this effect as part of the "fruits". There is an urge to enter a wider world free of responsibility for them. As this tends to be the peak of one's earning years too, there may be the opportunity to travel or take up new hobbies and interests. This is a reminder that we are all ultimately alone. As one progresses beyond this point success or failure are now more clearly a matter of one's own personal responsibility.

Negatively one could be trying to maintain social position rather than accepting its decline in preparation for the new cycle at age 60.

Although one may be fulfilling a more public role, perhaps having gained some kind of promotion or moved into an area offering wider social services, there is a gradual decline in external activity over the next 7 years in preparation for the next cycle. One moves from "centre stage" to a role more "behind the scenes". Perhaps responsibilities outweigh the benefits of the position. There is a need to consolidate one's gains rather than seek further expansion. To conserve resources of time, money, and energy rather than increasing expenditure. Future results will be dependent on your ability to do this, as well as hold on to new possibilities that could act as seeds for future growth.

As one nears the end of the cycle there is need to spend some time in isolation and make a personal re-evaluation of one's past life so far. The task is to clear the ground for new growth. Getting rid of any outworn things, ideas, and feelings that might hold to the past. What is done is done. Forgive one's self and others for past misdeeds. Take time to rest – perhaps Music, Dance, or some form of Spiritual Retreat may be of benefit. This is a time of "altered states of consciousness" – one's attention is on inner, personal, matters rather than outer material ones.

If not, at least to some degree, undertaken voluntarily, this could be forced by circumstances to enable as clean a start as possible. Saturn is a hard taskmaster and cannot be resisted entirely. This is a time of receiving rewards, so one may gain certificates and prizes. It is also a time of repaying debts, so it could mean imprisonment or other forms of separation from society - such as those due to health problems that finally need correction. Physical symptoms are not always due to physical causes. Looking to the examples set by more famous people, we can see that this is also often forced by alcohol and drug abuse. We can now see such matters in a more positive light. If involved too much in public matters one can "lose one's Self".

At age 60, the end of such a period, and the beginning of a new cycle, even society concurs that there is some need for a fresh start – often free of the need to earn a living, and free of family responsibilities.

AGE 81 : LIFE PEAK

At 80 one's physical and mental condition is clearly a big indicator of how life has been lived so far. The "fruits of one's efforts" are never clearer. One reaps what one has sowed. This is Karma. There is no-one else to blame. One may be concerned about what one will leave to posterity.

PERSONAL SATURN CYCLE

The Personal Saturn Cycle can often be used to correct a Birth Chart where the exact time of birth is not known. The 4 "crisis points" transits of 1st, 4th, 7th and 10th Houses are more distinct, as is the general progress of life in the intervening periods.

Saturn does not operate on a personal, or individual, level until it transits our Ascendant (1st. House Cusp) for the first time after birth. Periods can vary in duration due to apparent variances in Saturn's orbit as seen from Earth. The computer gives us the correct position. The transit of each of the 12 Houses takes around 2-3 years. The focus of the Generic Cycle and that of the Personal Cycle may or may not relate to one another - making matters easier or more difficult to handle. The meaning of each Stage of the cycles is the same – just the timing may be different. Please bear in mind that we are only considering the effect of one planet of 10 here. The others have continual influence too. Trying to "Keep up with the Jones's" means one is a slave to external social pressures rather than following one's true path.

1st. HOUSE (Ascendant) TRANSIT – NEW SEED. REBIRTH

Cycle of Growth Stage 1 (Seed).

This is the beginning of a new cycle of Personal Responsibility and consideration of a social role more suited to one's own abilities and preferences. At that time some decision is made consciously or unconsciously which will establish the direction of the new cycle. This becomes the "seed" of the new cycle. Outwardly there will be little or no change to the routine of life already established. One cannot undo what has already been done. The aim is to use the experiences of the previous cycle and the position now established as foundations for future growth. There may be a sense of "starting at the bottom again".

Because this is the beginning of a time of inner, rather than outer, development - which will last around 7 or 8 years (a First Quarter transit) - there will tend to be a lack of related outer events. Perhaps a sense of isolation. Such events that do occur will tend to be related to the past cycle and therefore be more of a distraction.

ASTROLOGY : PLANET TRANSITS

Attempts to maintain the routines of the old cycle at this time could result in the same "seed" being re-sown again, so the new cycle will be a mere repetition of the old. The aim is to continue one's normal routine whilst being alert for new possibilities that may be presented. All that is required at this stage is a change of attitude rather than actions. We are concerned with an expansion of conscious awareness here - especially that of one's own internal discomfort with the present lifestyle. Listening to one's "Inner Voice(s)". There could be health problems to aid the process. Everything starts with an Idea.

At this time it is advisable to keep one's ideas to one's self. "Seeds" need to develop underground where they are protected. If revealed too soon they are likely to be destroyed. If one has not resolved one's own doubts and fears before proceeding, at least to some small extent, one is not likely to be able to overcome those of others around who may be affected by possible changes. Because of lack of clarity now, possible consequences may be distorted.

SATURN TRANSIT OF HOUSES 2 TO 12

The transits of the other 11 Houses follows the meanings of Stages 2 to 12 of The Cycle of Growth.

To summarise :

The 1st. Quarter refers to new developments in the background of life whilst continuing the habitual lifestyle.

The 2nd. Quarter refers to a more social expression of the new influence.

The 3rd. Quarter refers to new one to one friendships, partnerships, and perhaps marriage.

The 4th. Quarter refers to the achievement of some form of social standing and decline.

ASTROLOGY : THE LIFE DIARY

Check out your own Generic Transits.

On the next page is a form that you can use to see how you fit into the Planet Transits scenario.

1. Fill in the "Year" column starting with your year of birth. This makes it easier to add the Events.
2. Enter important or memorable events in your life. Each Generic House covers birthday to birthday, so it is more accurate to put them against the Year of Age that they occurred, failing that, use the Calendar Year. Changes are usually gradual.
3. Such events are house moves, partnership changes, job changes, health problems, child birth, beginnings and endings of activities in life – and so on.
4. If you cannot remember clearly – they were probably not important enough.

To the right of the form are indicated the beginnings of each Quarter of the generic cycles of Jupiter, Saturn, and Uranus. As "stress" times they are those when changes are more likely.

Changes are more likely to occur at the beginning of a cycle, especially that of Jupiter, so they are starred (*) in the "Events" column. If there are no changes there you can consider whether there was an opportunity which was missed or declined at the time. Please note that a cycle "Seed" time may be more a time of planning for the future. Internal rather than external activity. Often the actual change (such as moving house, giving up the past) occurs at Cycles of Growth Stages 4 (Transplanting) and 12 (Withdrawal. Confinement).

MAIN GENERIC PLANET STRESS POINTS SUMMARY

To summarise the main stress points when events are most likely to occur. The meanings are identical for all planets. Stress points can occur for more than 1 planet at the same time.

CYCLE OF GROWTH STAGE 12 (WITHDRAWAL. CONFINEMENT)

A time of clearing away the past ready for new life. Sometimes events occur at this time in preparation for further development in Stage 1.

CYCLE OF GROWTH STAGE 1 (SEED. NEW BEGINNINGS)

Beginning of a new cycle. The 1st. Quarter. New activities. If the new impulse is not acted on – a repetition of the past. There may not be actual outer events. This is psychological preparation. Perhaps study of a new subject or discovery of new talents or abilities.

CYCLE OF GROWTH STAGE 4 (TRANSPLANTING. A STEP FORWARD)

Depending on what activity occurred since Stage 1 a step forward. If the 1st. Quarter inner results were positive, a step forward in social expression. Perhaps group activity. A symptom of this is rearranging furniture, or thinking of moving or building a home extension – which could just relate to the previous cycle rather than the new one. The "home" may not be the domestic one. It could, for example, relate to one's place of work or working knowledge. Experience of a new social area - perhaps developing into a new role at Stage 7.

CYCLE OF GROWTH STAGE 7 (NEW PARTNERSHIPS. NEW SOCIAL ROLE)

If the Stage 1 impulse has reached this stage, there is a need to take the results to a wider society. If we observe the dramas in television and films, this is generally a sense of boredom with the existing partner and an attempt to find a new one. "The Eternal Triangle". There was no change at Stage 1, so the old cycle is being repeated yet again. I had a colleague at work who married for the 4th. time and was obviously not very happy, once again.

CYCLE OF GROWTH STAGE 10 (SOCIAL PEAK)

This is the harvest of all one's efforts throughout the cycle since Stage 1, followed by a decline of interest in preparation for the new cycle. The decline may be ignored, or the lesson not learned, resulting in a repetition of the cycle beginning at Stage 1.

ASTROLOGY : PLANET TRANSITS

LIFE DIARY FORM showing planet cycle Quadrants

Years with yellow highlights are when events are likely to occur – depending on what "seeds" are planted.
2 page PDF and Excel XLS versions are available from my web site www.cycleofgrowth.com

| 1. Fill in the 'Year' column starting with your year of birth. |
| 2. Fill in the main events or changes in your life against the years |
| 3. Read my books "Your Personal Life Diary" and "The Cycle of Growth" to see how to use the information. |

KEY TO TIMES WHEN MAJOR CHANGES ARE LIKELY (highlighted in yellow)

| 1 | (Seed) | New beginnings | 7 | (Partners) | Change in relationships |
| 4 | (Transplanting) | A step forward | 10 | (Peak. Harvest) | Public results of your efforts |

#	Age	Year	Event	Ju	Sa	Ur	#	Age	Year	Event	Ju	Sa	Ur
1	0		* * * BIRTH	1	1	1	43	42			7		7
2	1			2	1	1	44	43			8		
3	2			3			45	44			9		
4	3			4			46	45			10	7	
5	4			5			47	46			11	7	
6	5			6			48	47			12		
7	6			7			49	48		*	1		
8	7			8	4		50	49			2		8
9	8			9	4	2	51	50			3		
10	9			10			52	51			4		
11	10			11			53	52			5	10	
12	11			12			54	53			6	10	
13	12		*	1			55	54			7		
14	13			2			56	55			8		
15	14			3		3	57	56			9		9
16	15			4	7		58	57			10		
17	16			5	7		59	58			11		
18	17			6			60	59			12		
19	18			7			61	60		* *	1	1	
20	19			8			62	61			2	1	
21	20			9			63	62			3		
22	21			10		4	64	63			4		10
23	22			11	10		65	64			5		
24	23			12	10		66	65			6		
25	24		*	1			67	66			7		
26	25			2			68	67			8	4	
27	26			3			69	68			9	4	
28	27			4			70	69			10		
29	28			5		5	71	70			11		11
30	29			6			72	71			12		
31	30		*	7	1		73	72		*	1		
32	31			8	1		74	73			2		
33	32			9			75	74			3		
34	33			10			76	75			4	7	
35	34			11			77	76			5	7	
36	35			12		6	78	77			6		12
37	36		*	1			79	78			7		
38	37			2	4		80	79			8		
39	38			3	4		81	80			9		
40	39			4			82	81			10		
41	40			5			83	82			11	10	
42	41			6			84	83			12	10	

Figure 38 : LIFE DIARY FORM

ASTROLOGY : PLANET TRANSITS

TIMING OF MAIN PLANETARY EVENTS THROUGH A LIFETIME

Squares of Jupiter occur roughly every 3 years. "Easy" Trines occur between Squares.

Age 7   Waxing Square of Saturn to its natal place. [COG 4. Transplanting]

Age 12	First Return of Jupiter to its natal place. [COG 1. Seed]. Puberty.
Age 15	Saturn Opposition natal Saturn. [COG 7.Partnerships (male and female). School Age]
Age 21	Waning Square of Saturn to its natal place. [COG 10. Peak] "Coming of age"
	Waxing Square of Uranus to its natal place. [COG 4. Transplanting (Adult)]
Age 24	Second Jupiter return. [COG 1. Seed]
Age 28	Uranus Waxing Trine natal Uranus. [COG 5. Power]
Age 30	Saturn Return to its natal place. [COG 1. Seed]
Age 36	Second Waxing square of Saturn to its natal place. [COG 4. Transplanting]
	Return of Jupiter to its natal place. [COG 1. Seed]
Age 42	Uranus Opposition natal Uranus. [COG 7. Partners. One to One Friends]
	Neptune Waxing Square to Natal Neptune. [COG 4. Transplanting]
	Jupiter Opposition natal Jupiter. [COG 7. Partnerships]
Age 45	Second Opposition of Saturn to its natal place. [COG 7. Partners]
Age 48	Fourth Return of Jupiter to its natal place. [COG 1. Seed]
Age 51	Second Waning Square of Saturn to its natal place. [COG 10. Peak]
Age 56	Uranus Waning Trine to natal Uranus. [COG 9. Conception]
Age 60	Second Return of Saturn to its natal place. [COG 1. Seed]
	Fifth Return of Jupiter to its natal place. [COG 1. Seed]
	Pluto Waxing Square to its natal place. [COG 4. Transplanting]
Age 63	Waning Square of Uranus to its natal place. [COG 10. Peak]
Age 66	Third Waxing Square of Saturn to its natal place. [COG 4. Transplanting] Retirement
Age 72	Sixth Return of Jupiter to its natal place. [COG 1. Seed]
Age 80	Third Waning Square of Saturn to its natal place. [COG 10. Peak]
Age 84	Uranus Return to its natal place. [COG 1. Seed]
	Seventh Return of Jupiter to its natal place. [COG 1. Seed]

BECAUSE IT IS IMPORTANT TO NOTE, I REPEAT THE OBSERVATION THAT IN THE COURSE OF EVERY CYCLE OF EVERY PLANET EVERY POSSIBLE ASPECT IS EXPERIENCED – EASY AND HARD.

This negates traditional Astrological concepts concerning "good" or "evil" times.

ASTROLOGY : PLANET TRANSITS

ASTROLOGY : CHARTS EXAMPLES

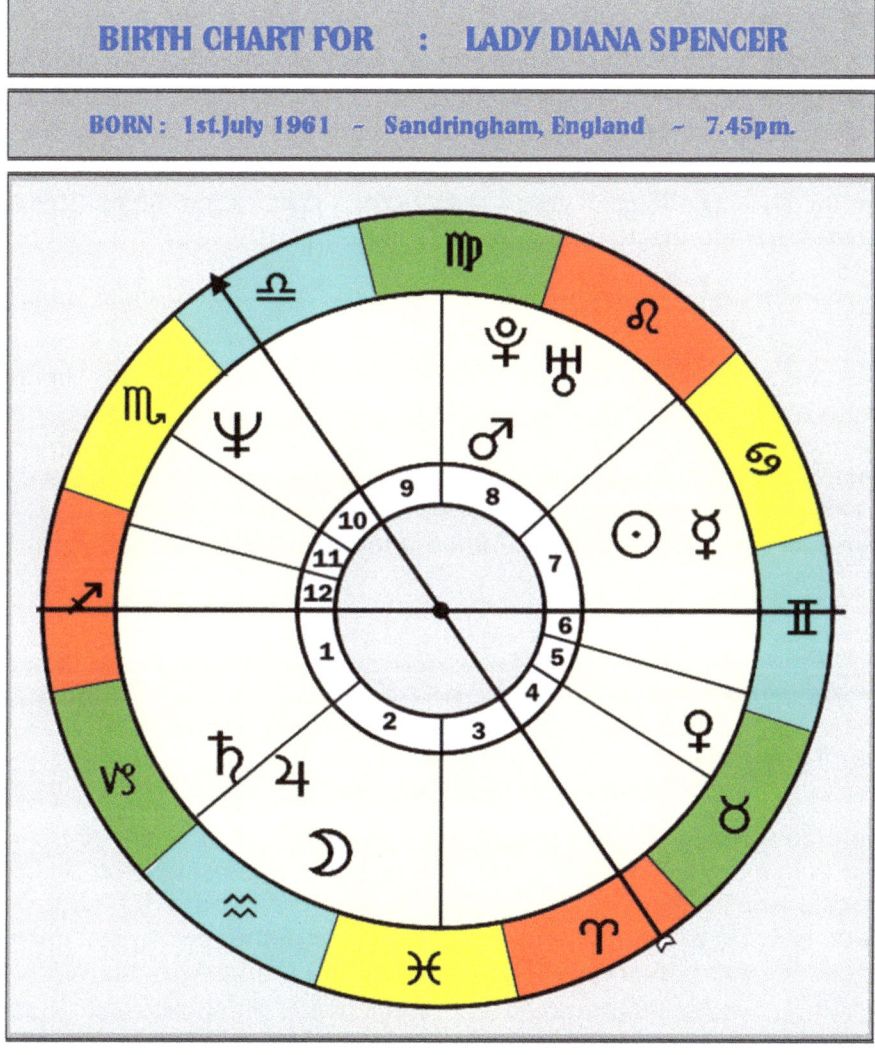

Figure 39 : Birth Chart of Lady Diana Spencer

PLANET POSITIONS OF THE EXAMPLE BIRTH CHART

1st. House – Self Projection (Seed) – Saturn in Capricorn (Cardinal Earth)

2nd. House – Personal Resources (Germination) – Jupiter & Moon in Aquarius (Fixed Air)

5th. House – Personal Creativity (Power. Creativity) – Venus in Taurus (Fixed Earth)

7th. House – Social Projection (Partnerships) – Sun and Mercury in Cancer (Cardinal Water)

8th. House – Social Resources – Uranus in Leo (Fixed Fire) . Mars & Pluto in Virgo (Mut. Earth)

10th. House – Social Security (Peak. Career) – Neptune in Scorpio (Fixed Water)

ASTROLOGY : CHART EXAMPLES

BIRTH CHART EXAMPLE : COMMENTARY

The lives of famous, or infamous, people are good sources for astrological analysis and study – although we cannot always know everything that goes on in the background. Here we have the additional benefit of knowing the exact time and place of birth.

The following is a brief example of Birth Chart interpretation. It is not extensive, but does show the principles involved. An in depth interpretation would include an analysis of positions of all the planets by Sign and House together with consideration of the Aspects (angles) between them as well as consideration of the Signs "ruling" each House – that is, the Sign in which the cusp – or beginning – of the House occurs.

The rotary movement of the chart is anti-clockwise in order of the Houses and Signs. This Birth Chart uses the Unequal House System attributed to Placidus. Quotations marked [DHTS] are from the book "DIANA - HER TRUE STORY" by Andrew Morton.

THE PAST : MOON IN AQUARIUS (Fixed Air)

The Moon position shows the past of the individual in terms of past lives, and family conditions and traditions - especially the relationship with the mother. In Aquarius it gives a difficulty with sharing emotions and individuals tend to be fiercely independent or loners. At another level it enables the early escape from family structures and traditions that have outlived their usefulness. It brings an inventive, if not erratic, tendency. Comfortable with, and liking for, modern technology. The Rebel. The Revolutionary. The Criminal. The Bohemian. Friend rather than Lover. Diana's mother left the family when she was 6 years of age.

*Diana's mother ..... "was fiercely proud, combative and tough minded" [DHTS].

*"There was frustration in the family that she had not produced a male heir to the title. Diana said that she (herself) ["should have been a boy" [DHTS].

*"She was the only girl I knew whose parents were divorced. Those things just didn't happen then." [DHTS]

We can see the effect on Diana with her continual battles with "the establishment" and making her own decisions against considerable opposition. We can see the "revolution" Diana caused to the monarchy. This was mostly "unconscious", in that, although she made her own decisions against opposition, she did not actually do anything directly to attack it (she had Sun in Cancer. "The Crab" retreats rather than attacking). The effect even continued after her death, with her funeral. It was a full state affair demanded by the public. There was no prior protocol so they had to use the one prepared for The Queen Mother (Innovation. Cancer, mother).

She is believed to have influenced the international ban on the use of anti-personnel landmines after her death. Again, she achieved it without any direct confrontation. One of her roles was almost that of a 'martyr'. (Neptune in Scorpio in 10th. House).

THIS OPENS UP A WHOLE NEW AREA OF SPECULATION. HOW IS IT POSSIBLE THAT A BIRTH CHART CAN DESCRIBE NOT ONLY LIFE IN THE WOMB, BUT PARENTS, FAMILY RELATIONSHIPS AND CONDITIONS . Perhaps this will be explained via Genetics.

There is an Opposition Aspect between her Moon in Aquarius and Uranus (ruler of Aquarius) in Leo where it is in Detriment. So she would have to balance her true Aquarian Moon Individuality with a tendency to try to be "different" to get attention. The latter is then very subtly controlled by other people.

MOON IN 2nd. HOUSE – PERSONAL POSSESSIONS

Individuals have good practical ability, and are happy performing routine "down to Earth" tasks. Good at handling money and property. There is a connection with, and love of, Nature.

*Coleherne Court ....the happiest time of her life....She always had the rubber gloves on as she clucked about the place." [DHTS]

THE FUTURE : SUN IN CANCER

(Cardinal Water). Crab. Tortoise. Shell. Mother.

The Sun position, source of basic energy and power, shows the main lessons of life that the individual has come to develop and learn. This is development of Ego Consciousness.

ASTROLOGY : CHART EXAMPLES

Water emphasis brings strong emotional sensitivity, and therefore a retiring nature. Like The Crab Diana needed to learn to build a "shell" around herself to protect her soft inner parts. In human terms the "shell" is symbolised by

1. the human body (as "Temple of the Spirit")
2. the personal home in which we live, to which we can retire to recover from contact with the outside world.
3. In psychological terms it is the "Persona" which comes from the mask which Greek actors used on stage. Survival in our world depends upon the ability to play parts, or take on different roles. It is not always useful to reveal our inner feelings. Sometimes people have difficulties when the Persona becomes too fixed, for example, always trying to be "the leader" or "a follower". One's persona needs to be flexible depending on circumstances, and who we are dealing with.

The "shell" can also be symbolised by the motor car, enabling travel outside the home (like the related Tarot "Chariot"). It is also related to one's aura, or energy field, surrounding the body, and psychological "psychic self-defence".

The lesson often includes the need to become a "Mother" - with the ability to extend the personal "shell" to include others that need protection and security. Not necessarily within one's own family. Negatively, like The Crab, individuals can find it hard to "let go" at the proper time, or become over concerned with safety and security - when the "shell" can become a prison. Because of the tendency to repress, or "bottle up" energy, people with Cancer emphasised in a Birth Chart are prone to psychosomatic illness - especially stomach ulcers ("can't stomach it").

We note Diana's interest in, and concern for, children in her life. Animals can become a substitute.

> *"Like her elder sisters, Diana was on horseback at three and soon developed a passion for animals, the smaller the better. She had pet hamsters, rabbits, guinea pigs, her cat marmalade, which (brother) Charles and Jane loathed, and, as her mother records "anything in a small cage." DHTS]*

> *"Diana today still revisits her former home, even though it has been turned into a Cheshire Home holiday hotel for the disabled." [DHTS]*

> ["In contrast to the eerie splendours of Althorp, Diana's rambling ten-bedroomed home Park House was positively cosy …. .Screened from the road ….." [DHTS]

(The reference to horseback is more related to Diana's Sagittarius Ascendant).

SUN IN 7th. HOUSE – PARTNERSHIPS. FRIENDS AND ENEMIES

Opposite to the Ascendant 1st. House (Self Projection) this Sun position is not very strong. The individual has to learn how to get on in one-to-one relationships (friends or enemies), giving and receiving support or receiving opposition. This House is the first step away from the home into a wider social world. Mutable (Changeable) Gemini on the cusp of this House indicates the need for numerous such relationships -which can be friendly, platonic, or sexual. It also tends to apply to one-to-one sibling relationships. Diana's brother was more like a close friend too. Each relationship could require a different Persona, or role. The danger, then, is that one can lose contact with one's inner, true, Self from playing so many parts.

8Th. HOUSE EMPHASIS – INTERCOURSE. DEATH

Intercourse. Death and Regeneration. Sex. Using other people's resources.

I have to mention here that Diana has Mars ("God of War") in conjunction (combination) with Pluto and Uranus in her birth Chart – all in her 8th. House. The combination gives an extreme sense of power and drive towards an individual, independent approach to life. A drive to "change the world". An element of "The Dictator". A powerful sex drive. We can see that this was not overtly expressed in her (public) life, although she came into contact with many such powerful people. We saw her psychological problems and struggle with depression and bulimia which can be related to turning energy inward against one's self rather than expressing it outwardly. (I have experience with my Mars in Cancer causing stomach ulcers). Competitive sport may have been a way of expressing the energy.

In traditional Astrology The 8th. House and Scorpio treated Sex and Death as "taboo" subjects that were not discussed in open society – which gave the House/Sign its connection with "Secrets". There is still a similar

ASTROLOGY : CHART EXAMPLES

association with in depth research and detective work which uncovers the "secrets of life". We note that this is not itself a creative act in that it uncovers facts of life that are already there and brings them to consciousness. Psychoanalysis is also related.

In addition there is a major "Constellation" called a Grand Cross in her Birth Chart. The aspects concerned are not exact, very loose in fact, so it is not as intense as it could be. You will note that there are planets in the 4 Fixed Signs Aquarius, Taurus, Leo and Scorpio. If we draw a line between Aquarius and Leo (in Opposition), and another between Taurus and Scorpio (in Opposition), the 2 lines make a cross consisting of 4 "Square" aspects at the Centre where the planetary energies challenge, or seem to block, one another. This makes for a great deal of inner tension for an individual because an attempt to express energy in any of the 4 directions indicated sets off challenges from the other 3. There is a tendency to "open cans of worms" (the point being that they can never be put back again). In simplistic terms, the subject is forced to become aware of the inner conflict and learn to think and plan carefully before taking action. The aim is to become "Captain of one's ship" and get a consensus of agreement between the inner energies first. Like children, internal psychological complexes only tend to become negative and obstructive when there is an attempt to ignore them. Successful resolution of this problem gives rise to highly gifted, successful individuals. The question then arises – "who is this Captain ?"

ASCENDANT (1st. House cusp). SELF PROJECTION

SAGITTARIUS - Mutable (Changeable) Fire. The Archer. The Centaur – half human, half horse.

Defining the point of birth, this shows how individuals most easily and naturally project themselves into life. The symbol of Sagittarius is The Archer, Centaur, or Hunter. At her funeral, Diana's brother referred to her as "Diana The Huntress" - the female version of The Archer. He would have seen more of this aspect of her character than most. They were inseparable when young and spent a lot of time together away from parental view.

Here, Mutable Fire gives problems of self-control - there is always a need for the stimulation of continual changes. Continual travel and activity. Difficulty with concentration of mind (Diana's Moon would modify this depending on circumstances). Individuals can be competitive and blunt to the point of rudeness. Full of energy and mischief - not always good natured in motivation. Here we see this combined with Cancer sensitivity :-

*["..and she pinched, (brother) Charles complained. Soon he realised that he could wound with words, teasing his sister mercilessly..." [DHTS]

(We see how Charles attacked via her sensitive, Water, Cancer, Feeling, nature).

Its lesson relates to the development of the Higher Mind to control the instinctual "animal nature". A Sagittarius emphasis draws individuals to horse riding, or other forms of animal training. Dog trainers say their real job is to train the owners. Sportsperson and Entertainer are other preferred activities. Activities based on Intuition (Fire) rather than practical (Earth) or mental (Air).

Combined with her Moon position, this gives a highly assertive, even aggressive, character trait. This is modified by the rest of her Birth Chart as well as external circumstances. Her Sun in watery, retiring, sensitive, Cancer pulls in a different direction. "Bottled up" energy brings health problems.

["As with all siblings there were fights which Diana, being bigger and stronger, invariably won." DHTS]

["Although quiet and demure in her first term she was no goody-goody, she preferred laughter and skylarks to solid endeavour ..." DHTS]

ASTROLOGY : CHART EXAMPLES

SATURN IN 1st. HOUSE – SELF PROJECTION

Controlled Self Projection.

This is mentioned because of its important, powerful, position in her Birth Chart. One function of Saturn is to control and focus energy in order to achieve long term goals. Negatively it can stifle life to the point of extinction. When things stop growing they decay. It demands Conformity and Discipline. Early in life its energy comes from external discipline from parents and grandparents, later on it is met through social rules, laws and traditions - which may or may not be appropriate to the present situation. The aim in life is to accept Saturn's restrictions ("render unto Caesar...") and take control of its energy by exercising Self Discipline. One can then take control of one's self and focus energy on the job at hand. This is indicative of one's Career, and the ability to rise through the levels of society to a position of social power. Using social rules to progress. "Long range plans".

In the 1st.House this gives rise to what we call "shyness" in a character. It is indicative of a psychological uncertainty that occurs when, at an early age, one's self assertion is continually, negatively, criticised. This results in conditioning to expect criticism in advance of everything one does. Although seemingly all negative, it does force the individual to stop and think before acting. Early discipline and responsibilities.

With undisciplined Sagittarius Ascendant and rebellious Moon in Aquarius, we can never be sure how much of this criticism was actually warranted - or even invited. Perhaps to get attention. Especially when young, even negative attention is better than none at all.

> *Diana's first mistake, as far as parents were concerned, was in being born a girl.["..."the feelings of guilt that she wasn't born a boy ..." [DHTS]
>
> *"..the growing girl did not see as much of her mother she would wish, and less of her father." [DHTS]
>
> *"Diana's upbringing reflected the values of a bygone age." DHTS]
>
> *"There was a formality and restraint to their childhood, a reflection of the way Diana's parents were raised." [DHTS]
>
> *"...Another nanny beat Diana on the head with a wooden spoon if she was naughty....." [DHTS]
>
> *"While Prince Charles sympathised with his tearful wife he insisted that the royal road show had to go on." [DHTS]
>
> *"However well she did, however hard she tried, she never earned a word of praise from her husband, the Royal Family or their courtiers." [DHTS]
>
> *The ability to become this smiling persona in public is helped by the nature of bulimia... there is unhappiness underneath because they are frightened to express their anger." [DHTS]

Saturn (Old Age. Tradition) here (and if otherwise emphasised by birth chart position) also brings responsibilities more appropriate to older people during the early years of life. Perhaps being the eldest child having to take care of siblings, or, for whatever reason, missing parental control. Perhaps spending a lot of time with grandparents.

Diana was born into a family with a long tradition of service to the Crown.

> *"While Diana was in awe of her grandfather, she adored the grandmother, Countess Spencer. "She was sweet, wonderful and very special. Divine really." says the Princess. The Countess was known locally for her frequent visits to the sick and the infirm and never at a loss for a generous word or gesture. While Diana has inherited her mother's sparky, strong willed nature she has also been blessed with her paternal grandmother's qualities of thoughtfulness and compassion." [DHTS]

Here we see an unbalanced idealistic viewpoint. We know that everyone has their faults. We see below how the extremes of "self-sacrifice" (Pisces/Neptune. Martyrdom) can lead to suicidal tendencies. Pisces rules Diana's 4th. House - Cycle of Growth Stage 4 (Transplanting. Age 3 to 4 years) - which archetypally is ruled by her Cancer Sun Sign, and defines early life experiences.

ASTROLOGY : CHART EXAMPLES

SATURN IN CAPRICORN - Cardinal Earth

The symbol of The Mountain Goat relates to the ability to climb to high position in life. Capricorn's wintery modification of energy is symbolic of the structure of the society in which we live - with its laws and traditions. The Establishment. Its effect is as described above for Saturn. Saturn is the natural planetary "ruler" of Capricorn. So, at birth, Diana was naturally well equipped to take advantage of her social position (although other aspects of her Birth Chart might not agree, or want to conform).

Although Diana was born into the "Upper Classes" this could equally apply to someone who starts out as a floor sweeper. The "upward" movement is relative to the starting position and one's will and circumstances. She almost refused to marry Prince Charles at the last minute. Saturn won. There can be the tendency to "marry one's father " (or mother, for men). Small wonder so many marriages eventually end.

NEPTUNE ("God of the Sea". The Unconscious)

in SCORPIO 10th. HOUSE – THE PEAK. CAREER. SOCIAL POSITION

This planet deserves a mention because the 10th. House position gives it more emphasis in a birth Chart. The tendency of this Neptune position is to bring the individual - and inner, private, "secrets" - to public view. Public Service. Charisma. Here it is in the Sign of Scorpio, with its symbolism related to Sex and Death (Suicide. Self-sacrifice. Regeneration) - and other socially "taboo" subjects (eg. AIDS). There was a lot of "conspiracy theory". Prince Charles has Sun in Scorpio in his Birth Chart. So we see something of Scorpio's influence on her "Career" – added to her Sun in the house of Partnerships. Also that she died almost as a martyr - a "living symbol "- which forced more changes in the monarchy.

We must also take note of her tendency towards suicide - directly, and health-wise, and her psychological problems.

*"Graveyards held a sombre fascination. (brother) Charles and Diana frequently visited ….." [DHTS]

*"Standing on top of the wooden staircase she hurled herself to the ground …" [DHTS]

10TH. HOUSE CUSP : LIBRA

Her 10th. House is actually under the rulership of Libra - Sign of Balance and Partnerships. Again, her Career and social status involved Partnership. The "natural" archetypal ruler of the 10th. House is Capricorn which is positioned in her 1st. House which brings a strong connection between them.

There are other planets and details in her Birth Chart which are beyond this brief sketch.

ASTROLOGY : CHART EXAMPLES

GENERIC TRANSIT CHART EXAMPLE
We now see how the later movement of planets affected Diana's life.

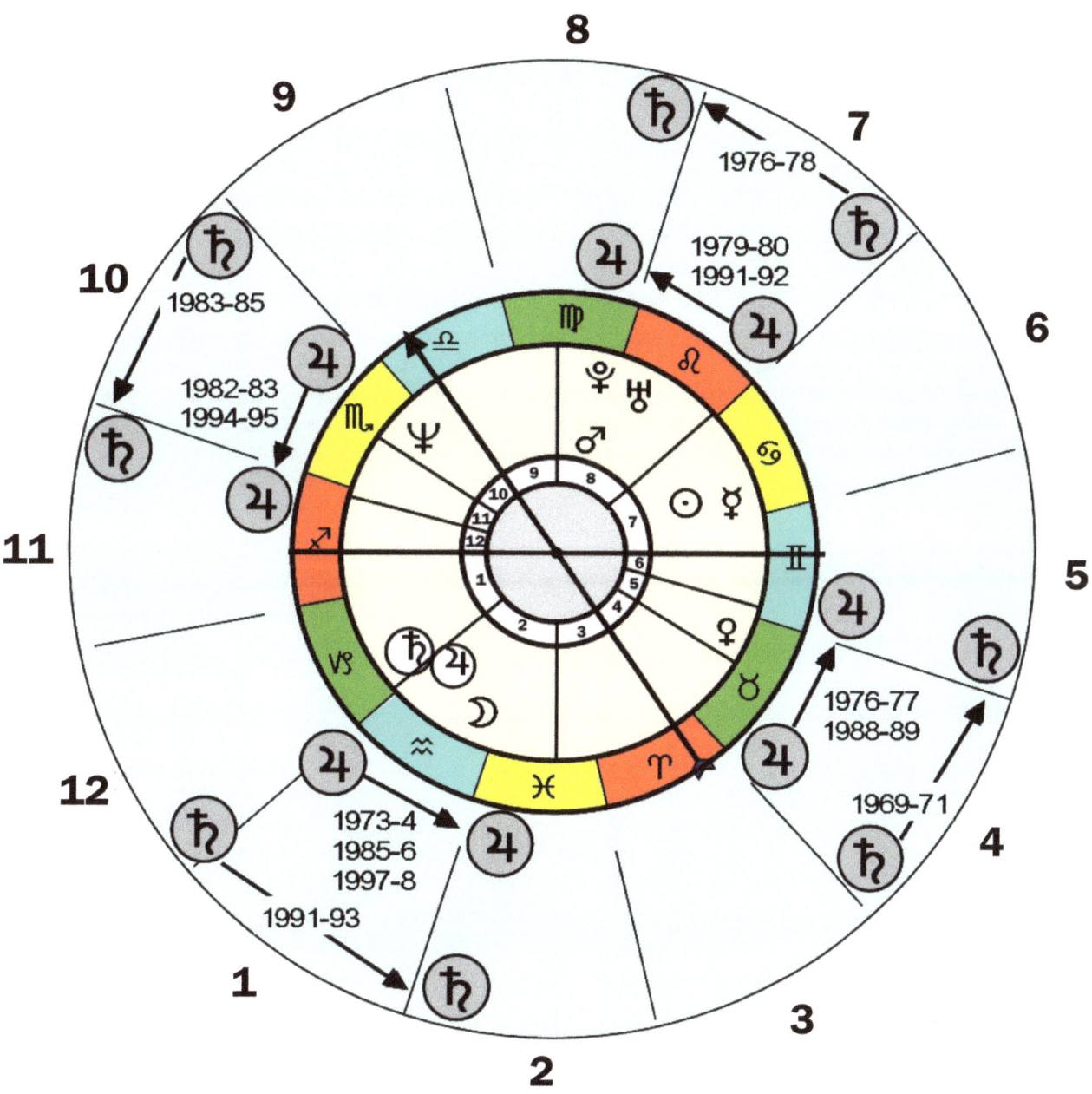

Figure 40 : Transit Chart of Lady Diana Spencer

GENERIC TRANSIT CHART DESCRIPTION

1. The central circle shows Diana's Birth Chart with its planet positions. Outer Houses 1 to 12 (coloured blue) are the Generic Jupiter Houses. The Birth Chart positions of Jupiter and Saturn are the starting points of their Generic Cycles.

2. The outer transit circle is divided into 12 houses of 30 degrees with the cusp (beginning) of the Generic 1st.House at the birth position of Jupiter. Jupiter makes a complete cycle every 12 years. Saturn 30 years.

3. It is normal to take into account the positions of transiting planets (Personal Transits) in relationship to the Personal Houses of the Birth Chart too. I have not done so here. Diana's birth Saturn position is (just) in her Personal 1st. House so there would not be a great difference anyway. Jupiter is (just) in her Personal 2nd.

209

ASTROLOGY : CHART EXAMPLES

House. The close proximity does not seem to affect results much. In any case, my experiments so far show that the Generic positions are better indicators of external events. The Personal ones seem to be more of an inner response to them.

4. Because Saturn is conjunct (adjoining) Jupiter in Diana's Birth Chart, we can conveniently use the same Jupiter Generic Houses for Saturn for this example.

5. The Transit circle shows the years when Jupiter and Saturn transited Diana's 1st., 4th., 7th., and 10th. Generic Houses. These are chosen as being at the beginning of the "quarters" - which are times of stress or conflict of energy when changes are most likely to occur (Spring, Summer, Autumn, Winter). I also include the 12th.House transits because events tend to happen at this time to clear the way for the new cycle.

6. I have based my commentary on the Jupiter transit cycle. Its 12 year cycle gives it approximately 1 year in each House. Jupiter's energy is broadly related to one's social standing. Its main keyword is "EXPANSION".

7. Saturn's actions tend to oppose those of Jupiter. It's main keyword is "CONSOLIDATION". It tends to seek practical or tangible results. Order and Structure.

8. Too much Expansion brings chaos. Too much Consolidation brings standstill.

9. Because planets appear to travel backwards through the Zodiac at times ("retrograde") the transits of planets through the Houses is very irregular. Periods of retrogradation are said to be times of "reconsideration". I have based my dates on periods when the planet movements were Direct (forward). Their activity in a House is not ended until they finally leave it during an orbit. The dates in the transit diagram are not exactly accurate in that they suggest January to December positions, whereas there could be some months difference either way. Correct dates are in the commentary where I have taken the first house entry direct and last house exit direct.

10. I have not included the first 12 year Jupiter cycle because parents have greater control of circumstances - usually until the first Saturn Return (to its birth position) around age 30 – or later at the Mid Life Crisis.

11. I have added comments about Saturn where it seems appropriate.

10. I have noticed that women often give birth during 10th. House transits by Jupiter or Saturn. Here we see both.

12. You will note that we use the same keywords for a House transit no matter what planet we are referring to, or whether the transit is Personal or Generic. The difference is the activity of the planet under consideration. They are similar, but not identical, to those used for the Birth Chart houses, which refer to internal, personal, individual factors rather than external ones. The Birth Chart refers more to one's natural, instinctive, reactions to external circumstances until one gains more self-discipline and development of Will. Any Birth Chart trait of character or personality, can be changed by use of Will, as can the outcome of events. Acting from decisions based on objective here-and-now data processing rather than gut reaction (unless one has learned to trust it) or hearsay.

13. Diana died at age 36 which is the beginning of a new 12 year Jupiter cycle - Cycle of Growth Stage 1 (Seed). Neptune was making a PERSONAL 1st.House transit at the same time (Seed). We can see that she was beginning to make a new life for herself.

14. Any planets placed in the main Personal houses at the 4 quarters of a Birth Chart (Houses 1,4,7,10) have a greater influence than others. Because Diana's chart has Neptune in the 10th. House of Career I have added a commentary at the end.

15. I have not made any judgements here. I have merely recorded the relationship between transits and events. If any judgements were to be made it would have been for Diana to do so.

ASTROLOGY : CHART EXAMPLES

DIANA'S LIFE DIARY

This gives a summary of Diana's Generic Planet Transits. She was born in July so the Years cover July to June. There is a blank form in the chapter [ASTROLOGY : PLANET TRANSITS] for you to try this for yourself.

GENERIC HOUSES

	Age	Year	Event	Ju	Sa	Ur
1	0	1961	* * * BIRTH. Park House, Norfolk	1	1	1
2	1	1962		2	1	1
3	2	1963		3		
4	3	1964	Brother Charles born	4		
5	4	1965		5		
6	5	1966		6		
7	6	1967	Mother moved away as a trial separation	7	4	
8	7	1968	Sent to Riddlesworth girls' boarding school	8	4	
9	8	1969	Parents' divorce	9		2
10	9	1970	Sent away to school	10		
11	10	1971		11		
12	11	1972		12		
13	12	1973	* West Heath Boarding School	1		
14	13	1974		2		
15	14	1975	Death of grandfather. Move to Althorp - family ancestral home	3		3
16	15	1976	Went to finishing school in Switzerland.	4	7	
17	16	1977	First met Prince Charles. Left school	5	7	
18	17	1978	First job as nanny. Moved to London	6		
19	18	1979		7		
20	19	1980	Met Charles at Balmoral	8		
21	20	1981	First public appearance with Charles. Married	9		
22	21	1982	Prince William born	10		4
23	22	1983	Visit Australia and Canada. Took William. Represented The Queen	11	10	
24	23	1984	Prince Harry born	12	10	
25	24	1985	Suicide attempt. Audience with the Pope. Visited AIDS victims	1		
26	25	1986	Visit British Columbia. Charles with Camilla Parker-Bowles	2		
27	26	1987	Portugal. Germany. France	3		
28	27	1988	Separation from Charles	4		
29	28	1989	Charles and Diana living apart	5		5
30	29	1990	Diana linked with James Gilbey	6		
31	30	1991	*	7	1	
32	31	1992	Father died. Official announcement of the separation	8	1	
33	32	1993		9		
34	33	1994	Leaked telephone calls made public in the press	10		
35	34	1995	Queen asked them to end marriage. Charles agreed. Diana disagree	11		
36	35	1996	Official divorce. First holiday with Dodi Al Fayed. Sold dresses.	12		6
37	36	1997	Visited Angola land mine victims. DIED	1	4	
38	37	1998		2	4	

Figure 41 : Diana Spencer's Life Diary

ASTROLOGY : CHART EXAMPLES

1ST. GENERIC JUPITER CYCLE 1961 – 1972
Although this period is under parental control, there are life changes ar the crisis stages.

2ND. GENERIC JUPITER CYCLE 1973 - 1984

Cycle of Growth Stage 1 : SEED TIME (Dec.1973-March 1974)
1974 Age 13 - Went to West Heath School

Cycle of Growth Stage 4 : TRANSPLANTING (May 1976-April 1977)
****

(SATURN : also first Generic Saturn Cycle of Growth Stage 7 : Partnerships May 1976-June 1978)

1977 Age 16 - Finishing school in Switzerland. Met Prince Charles for the first time. Left school.
****

JUPITER

Cycle of Growth Stage 7 : PARTNERSHIPS (June 1979-June 1980)

1980 Age 19 - Met Prince Charles again at Balmoral and began their relationship.
****

(NEPTUNE : Also .. Transiting Neptune had crossed the Ascendant of Diana's Birth Chart to enter her Personal 1st.House on 1st. January 1979. When a transiting planet enters the Personal First House the call is to consciously begin using the energies of the planet. With Neptune in the 10th. House of Career in Scorpio in her Birth Chart we could summarise this as "Charisma", "Glamour", "Deception". The influence of Scorpio leading to sexual, secretive, undertones. Prince Charles has Sun in Scorpio.)

Neptune was in her Generic 2nd. House (Germination).
****

Cycle of Growth Stage 8 : SEX. DEATH. INTERCOURSE (July 1980-July 1981)
1981 Age 20 : Married 29th. July 1981

Cycle of Growth Stage 10 : PUBLIC PEAK OF ACHIEVEMENT (January 1982-September 1983)
We see a powerful combination of Saturn and Jupiter both in their Generic 10th. Houses. I have mentioned the tendency for women to give birth during this transit.

We note the symbolism of the 10th. House and Capricorn includes the rebirth of the SUN at the solstice, and the SON at Christmas.

1982 Age 21 : Prince William born 21st.June 1982

(SATURN : also first Generic Saturn Cycle of Growth Stage 10 : Public Peak December 1982-October 1985)

Cycle of Growth Stage 11 : DISSATISFACTION. REBELLION (October 1983-October 1984)
1983 Age 22 : Official visit to Australia. Diana insisted on taking William against advice.
1984 Age 23 : Prince Harry born 15th.September 1984 (Jupiter Generic 10th. House)

(SATURN : Prince Harry's birth was still within her Generic Saturn 10th.House transit.)

Cycle of Growth Stage 12 : WITHDRAWAL. CONFINEMENT. (November 1984-March 1985)
We see the activity of 12th House "clearing the past" in preparation for a new cycle. Receiving "punishment" or rewards for past efforts (Karma).

1985 Age 24 : Charles & Diana audience with the Pope. Official visit to America. Made honorary army colonel in Berlin. Visited AIDS victims upsetting The Palace. Diana's suicide attempt.

ASTROLOGY : CHART EXAMPLES

3ND. GENERIC JUPITER CYCLE 1985 - 1996

Cycle of Growth Stage 1 : SEED TIME (March 1985-March 1986)

1986 Age 25 : Charles & Diana visited British Columbia. Charles' relationship with Camilla Parker-Bowles continues.

Also .. This is an especially important period in Diana's life because SATURN is also transiting her Personal 1st. House (Seed time). (February 1987-November 1988) approaching the beginning of its 2nd. Cycle at age 30 – so there is a double emphasis, Personal and Generic, when the "call" is to take charge of one's own life and begin to form one's own personal "tradition" or life structure distinct from that of the parents.

Cycle of Growth Stage 4 : TRANSPLANTING (April 1988-April 1989)

Symbolic of the child leaving the family home to explore the outside world. The Oedipus Complex. A new Persona (social mask).

(also Generic SATURN Cycle of Growth Stage 12 : Withdrawal 1989-1991)

1989 Age 28 : Charles and Diana now living in separate apartments.

Cycle of Growth Stage 7 : PARTNERSHIPS (May 1991-May 1992)

Diana linked with James Gilbey in the press.

****

SATURN : FIRST SATURN RETURN AGE 30

Saturn Cycle of Growth Stage 1 : Seed Time (February 1991-December 1993))

Saturn returned to its position in Diana's Birth Chart. The beginning of the 2nd. Saturn cycle is the first opportunity of real, internal, freedom from parental control. Self-discipline rather than external discipline. Here she is "free" of her father AND Prince Charles.

1992 Age 31 : Father died (Saturn).

Official (external Saturn) announcement of the separation from Prince Charles (Saturn)

****

Cycle of Growth Stage 10 : PUBLIC PEAK OF ACHIEVEMENT (January 1994-January 1995)

(Neptune in 10th. House by birth or transit tends to make public what we would wish to remain private).

1994/1995 Age 33/34 : Press leakage of taped telephone calls. Queen Elizabeth officially asked Charles and Diana to end their marriage. Charles agrees. Diana delayed decision for 3 months.

"Leakage" sounds very watery (Neptune/Pisces. The Sea).

Cycle of Growth Stage 11 : DISSATISFACTION. REBELLION (February 1995-January 1996)

1996 Age 35 : 28th. August Charles and Diana divorced (officially).

Transiting Neptune was conjunct Diana's Natal Saturn (Official) in April 1996 and twice in 1997, after retrogradation, in the month of her death.

Cycle of Growth Stage 12 : WITHDRAWAL. CONFINEMENT. (February 1996-February 1997)

1997 Age 35 : January - Visited Angola to see land mine victims.

First holiday with Dodi Al Fayed.

4TH. GENERIC JUPITER CYCLE 1997

Cycle of Growth Stage 1 : SEED TIME (March 1997-February 1998). Age 36

In February - Jupiter returned to the same position as at birth (Jupiter Return)

ASTROLOGY : CHART EXAMPLES

June   - Met Mother Theresa (who died 6 days after Diana, and after losing her faith)
August   - Visited Bosnia concerning land mines
August   - Died in car accident 31st. August 1997.

Transiting Neptune, moving Direct, came in conjunction with Diana's Natal Saturn in January 1997, and again moving Retrograde (backwards) on the 19th. August. It was still within 1 degree of her natal Saturn on the day she died.

She is believed to have influenced the signing of the Ottawa Treaty after her death, which created an international ban on the use of anti-personnel landmines

LADY DIANA SPENCER : NEPTUNE PERSONAL HOUSE TRANSITS

A 4TH. QUADRANT JOURNEY FROM 10TH. HOUSE (PEAK) TO 1ST. HOUSE (REBIRTH)

With birth Neptune in the Sign of Libra (Partnerships) in the 10th. House of Career /Social Position we see a heightened effect of "Glamour" in these areas. There was a difference between the "real" Diana and the archetypal images that were projected on her by the general public. A danger is that the individual can believe the illusion to be real and become psychologically "inflated" – that is, take on a "god-like" identity. Adolf Hitler - whose Neptune was powered by a Conjunction/Combination Aspect with Pluto (Sephirah 2 – Force. Power. Critical Mass) both in his 8th. House (Sex. Death) - is an example.

Diana's Pluto in Virgo, also in her 8th. House, formed an almost exact Sextile (60 degree) Aspect with Neptune. The Sextile Aspect is similar to the "easy" Trine (120 degree) Aspect but takes a little more work to combine energies.

Diana's Neptune story is in conformity with the meaning of the Logarithmic Timescale "1st./4th. Octave" (Gestation/Transcendence) and its symbolic relationship with the life of Jesus and his birth, crucifixion, and death. Both figures had similar relationships with authority figures and the general public. Both figures died at about the same age after seemingly completing a difficult "life mission". Both were subjected to projected images by the general public. In Jesus' case he was expected to solve everyone's problems for them. We can also see how he avoided Inflation by acts of humility such as washing the feet of his disciples. Hitler gave in to it and therefore lost his touch with reality – and his true inner Self.

Diana's life experiences have a strong link with the transit of Neptune through the Personal Houses of her Birth Chart. Neptune "God of the Sea" is related to the Collective Unconscious and Water of all kinds. The realm of Psychology. Its energy is concerned with dissolving boundaries between the seen and unseen worlds. It produces floods to clear away materials of the past. It produces altered states of consciousness such as from a sense of idealism, or drugs. It is active through such channels as religion, music, and art of all kinds, and alcohol or drug induced states and dreams. It acts through watery Feeling and emotion rather than logical Thinking. One's perception of "Beauty" as an (emotional response to the) "ideal", although the main province of Venus, is related to Neptune. Negatively it brings external deception and self-deception – although there is a tendency towards eventually bringing such matters to full public view. The "Freudian slip". "Self-undoing". "Carelessness". "Forgetting". "Forgiveness".

It is closely related to the Sign of Pisces and the 12th. House concerns for "Social Service", "The General Public" and "Karma" as well as being the realm of Psychology. ". It insists that all debts be repaid or forgiven before we can move on. "Forgive us our trespasses" (exactly in proportion to) "as we forgive those that trespass against us". So it works both ways. It is often hardest to forgive our self.

This short life does suggest that Diana had some form of Karmic debt to repay, or mission to accomplish, and moved on having completed it. The strong influence of Neptune on her life is exemplified by :-

1. The unrealistic aura of "glamour".
2. The projection on her by the public of the "fairy tale princess (marrying Prince Charming)" archetype.

Here is an example of the problems that arise when attempting to match events with planet transits.

Neptune moves very slowly, around 1 degree a month, and takes 165 years to make a full orbit, so any particular effect or aspect is spread over a long period of time. It does not make a complete cycle in anyone's lifetime. This is emphasised with retrogradation. In this example it took 36 years to travel 79 degrees from 8 degrees Scorpio to 27 Degrees Capricorn.

ASTROLOGY : CHART EXAMPLES

1961. At birth Neptune was in Diana's Personal 10th. House of Career, a time of peak public view, but the beginning of a decline and withdrawal in preparation for a new cycle.

1964. Neptune entered Diana's Personal 11th. House (Dissatisfaction. Rebellion) for the first time.

1971. Neptune entered Diana's Personal 12th. House (Withdrawal. Confinement. Awaiting rebirth) for the first time.

With Neptune on its own this could mean her entering a convent or hospital - or other form of solitary confinement until the 1978 entry into her Personal 1st. House. However, all the other planets will be drawing in their individual directions. Her Sagittarius Ascendant would not support this, although some form of philosophical or psychological study might be indicated. We can see some relationship with her natal Sun in Cancer and its main life lesson related to the need to build a "home" or, more correctly, an inner psychological "shell" for "psychic self-defence". The Persona.

> *1977. Age 16 Diana met Prince Charles who had been dating her sister. She was too young to date. [DHTS]*

1978/1979 - NEPTUNE ENTERS DIANA'S PERSONAL 1st. HOUSE (SEED. SELF PROJECTION)

Cycle of Growth Stage 1 (Seed). Age 17.

We can see the importance of Neptune in Diana's Birth Chart from its strong influence on her life circumstances.

In essence, we see her now entering the "Career" which is predicted by the birth position of Neptune in Scorpio ("Sex. Death & Regeneration"). Her life was also a "soap opera" on this subject too – giving the public an opportunity to view it objectively and review their own attitudes.

December 1978. Neptune crossed her Ascendant direct and entered her Personal 1st.House for the first time. It remained in this House for the rest of her life apart from some retrograde ("reconsideration", "delay") periods when it re-entered her 12th. House, and later moved Direct again. With any planet at this time there is a call to express one's own personal version of its energy. With Neptune one can give in to pressure to conform to established beliefs and practices, enter a convent, or simply "follow the crowd". We see that Mother (Cancer symbol) Teresa was a personal heroine of Diana - perhaps a role model of someone fulfilling a similar destiny, but without the continual public scrutiny. Mother Teresa was born in August 1910 with Sun in Virgo (Mutable Earth. Self Service. Health) requiring a more practical, down to earth, expression. Virgo is opposite Pisces (Social Service).

1979. Neptune crossed her Ascendant retrograde and re-entered her 12th.House. and later crossed her Ascendant direct and entered her Personal 1st.House for the second time.

1980. Diana met Prince Charles for the second time and they began their relationship.

1981. Diana was married to Prince Charles

(With Neptune now in its GENERIC 3rd House. (Experiment. Communication) there is additional emphasis on the need for her to communicate her philosophy. There were a lot of "leaked" (very watery ! Neptune natal 10th. House) telephone conversations during this time.

1996. Neptune made a conjunction with Diana's Natal Saturn. Retrograded (reconsideration) in May and moved Direct in October. One of Neptune's main functions is attempting to dissolve structures and traditions built by Saturn. Clearing the past to allows space for new growth – as in Winter.

1996. Charles & Diana divorced (Neptune/Pisces "dissolved" relationship)

1997. Neptune moving Direct made a conjunction with Diana's Natal Saturn again and moved on, then retrograded in May.

Age 35. 1997. August. Neptune retrograde made an exact conjunction yet again with Diana's Natal Saturn on August 19th. 1997. At this time she visited Angola and had her first holiday with Dode Al Fayed (continuing her Neptune in Libra influence on close relationships).

Diana died on the 31st. August in typically Neptune-confused circumstances with suggestion of involvement with alcohol or drugs (Pisces/Neptune).

We note that Age 35 is entering the Mid Life Crisis period which can lead to Individuation (Uranus) or a return to a traditional lifestyle (Saturn). With Moon in Aquarius we would expect Diana to have the required energy to take a more individual lifestyle. However, it seems that Saturn habit/Neptune glamour was about to win again. If she had not been with Dode El Fayed she may not have died.

Edgar Cayce suggests that a shortened lifetime helps us avoid repetition of sin.

A SIMILAR STORY – MICHAEL HUTCHENCE (22nd. Jan. 1960 – Sept. 1997)

Strangely, as I completed this chapter, there was a documentary about his death on television.

Michael Hutchence was lead singer and member of a rock band INXS in Australia. He became a world famous pop icon. He was heavily involved in sex and drugs, and his name was connected with those of numerous glamorous women including Kylie Minogue. There was controversy concerning whether his death from asphyxiation was suicide, an accident, or the result of a large "cocktail" of alcohol and drugs found in his blood.

His Birth Chart is similar to Diana Spencer's by having Libra (Partnerships) on his 10th. House Cusp and Neptune in 10th. House in Scorpio. Apart from the 10th. House position, his Neptune had additional influence by being in conjunction with his Moon in Scorpio (Sex. Death).

There are similarities between his Birth Chart and Lady Diana's (remembering that they were born only 18 months apart, so the slower planets had not moved far). However, the House positions are significant considering the 24 hour rotation of the Earth.

We have the following similarities :-

1. He was a famous personality.
2. His life was constantly given media attention.
3. He had Libra (Partnerships) on the cusp of his 10th. House
4. He had Neptune in Scorpio in his 10th. House.
5. His Neptune was Sextile Pluto in Virgo in his 8th. House.
6. He died age 37 (Diana 36).
7. There was mystery concerning his death.

ASTROLOGY : SYNASTRY

This chapter has several purposes :-
1. *To give an example of how the comparison of 2 Birth Charts can give an insight into the relationship between two people in the process called Synastry.*
2. *To show something of the history of psychoanalysis and how Jung's process of Individuation developed from that.*
3. *To give an example of the effects of the Generic life cycle of Jupiter and Saturn.*
4. *Please also see more information about Freud and Jung Birth Charts in [THE PURPOSE OF LIFE].*

I have to oversimplify here in order to be brief. This also seems to be 2 examples of Individuation. Both Freud and Jung separated from "The Collective" as a result of their experiences – challenging the ideas of their peers. Jung also, later on, challenged and separated from Freud who he initially treated as a "father figure". There are some surprising similarities in their Birth Charts.

There is more detail concerning their methods and philosophies in [PSYCHOLOGY DEVELOPMENT MODELS].

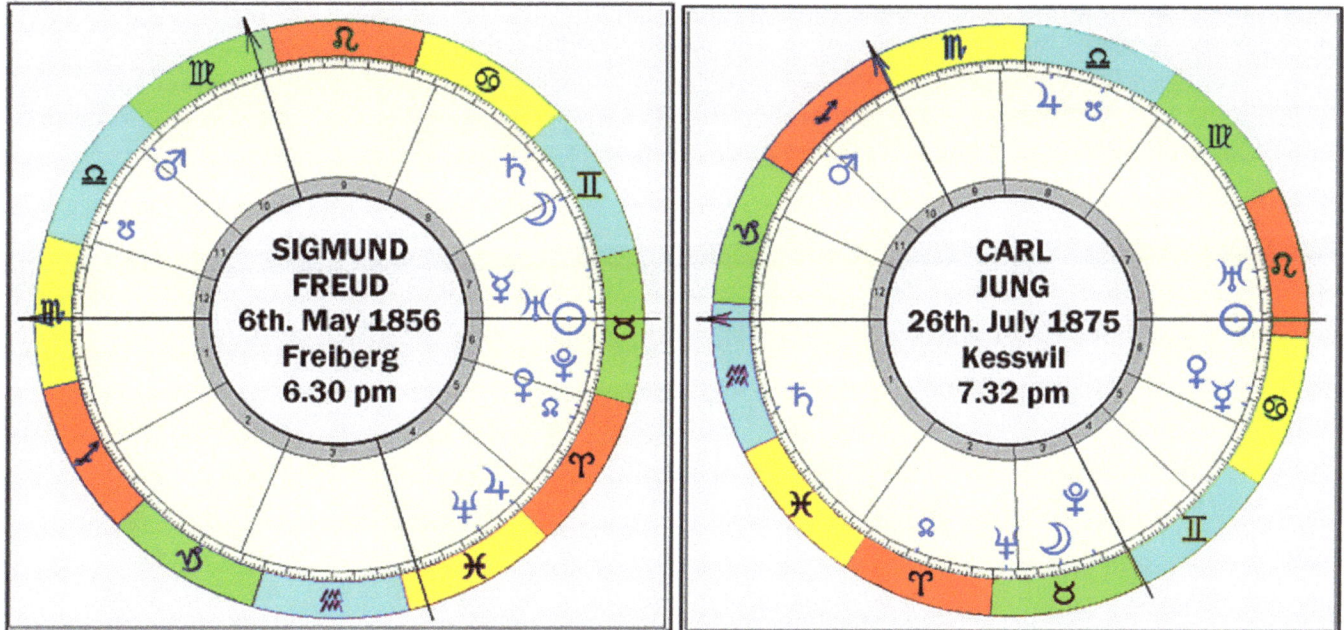

Figure 42 : Freud and Jung Birth Charts

FREUD : JUNG - THEIR GENERAL RELATIONSHIP

My view of the lives of Freud and Jung is based on the biographies contained in the books "Jung, Man and Myth" by Vincent Brome, and Sigmund Freud's "The Interpretation of Dreams" which has a chapter "A Sketch of His Life and Ideas" by James Strachey.

Because both were born at even-tide they have Sun on the cusp of the 7th. House of Partnerships ("Friends and Enemies"). This is not a very strong position for any planet in human terms, being in Opposition Aspect to the Ascendant (Personal Projection of energy). We also see this in the Birth Chart of Lady Diana Spencer [ASTROLOGY : BIRTH CHART EXAMPLES]. There is therefore the tendency to seek co-operation in one to one relationships when undertaking any project. Being exactly on the angle of a Quadrant of the Birth Chart gives it an especially strong affect over the personality and life experiences. It is interesting to note that the practice of Psychoanalysis consists of numerous one to one relationships. There is also the tendency to make enemies – another form of close partnership. The Opposition Aspect is that of the "Full Moon" which allows conscious awareness of whatever is on the complementary "other side" of a chart. From the detail below we can see how this affected the different viewpoints of both men, which eventually led to their split. (Freud had the additional emphasis by having Mars in the Partnership Sign of Libra (Again, a weak position from tending to seek reconciliation rather than "War" - and Jung, had Jupiter in Libra – "Expansion within one-to-one relationships").

In the early days of the practice of Psychology there was a lot of academic competition between the various groups and factions brought about by conflicting ideas and theories – very similar to that in the various religions over the ages. This is probably because there were so few recognised, named, mental illnesses. Disputes over the correct treatment of symptoms were possibly due to completely different causes (of the symptoms). We see something of this in the relationship between Freud and Jung which began extremely amicably and finally ended with Jung publicly condemning Freud's conclusions and methods. There seems to be something in the Collective Unconscious that attracts certain people together – ESPECIALLY where Psychology is concerned. In this case, Freud and Jung parted because they were successfully using completely different approaches and methods. It did not occur to them that they were each attracted to the (different) "right kind" of patient.

To add to the focus of their Sun positions, both have Uranus (Individuality. Unconventional. Invention) in the 7th. House (Partners) in Conjunction Aspect (close to) to the Sun, giving a strongly individualistic, unconventional, personality and desire to serve humanity in some way. During the years between the birth of Freud and that of Jung Uranus had moved from Taurus to Leo. The 7th.House position of Uranus brings individualistic "unusual, or unconventional, partnerships". Equal friendships rather than sexual level. We see in both their lives how the strong Uranian influence led them to depart from convention into the "cutting edge" of inventing new methods when they found old ones did not work. Eventually, even from one another.

They both have Mars, God of War, near the cusp of their 11th. House (Social Creativity. Friends) on the Transcendent Octave [ASTROLOGY : LOGARITHMIC TIMESCALE] – which is related to Aquarius/Uranus. The position of Mars in a Birth Chart indicates where battles will be fought.

MOON'S NODES

I would not normally have included this point, but we have the fact that that both Freud and Jung have North Node in the Sign of Aries, and South Node in the complementary Sign of Libra - so we have 2 similar people as examples of their activity. The Moon's Nodes are treated like planets although they are imaginary points where the orbit of The Moon crosses the path of the Earth's orbit around The Sun. They are used to determine eclipses of The Sun or Moon. They are always in Opposition Aspect to one another on opposite sides of The Earth, so are dealt with as a pair.

On its own the Zodiac Signs of the Moon's Nodes is not usually very significant at a **personal** level. The House positions are more important. With an 18 year nodal cycle everyone born within a 1 ½ year period of that will have the Nodes in the same Signs. The aim of the Nodes in a Birth Chart is to encourage individuals to focus attention on the energies symbolised by the North Node by Sign and House rather than the complementary ones of the South Node. In their case we can see that they both acted in accordance with this by pioneering new areas of life (Aries) rather than relying on the resources of close relationships (Libra). This gives additional focus to their Opposition aspects between their Sun in the 7th. House (normally ruled by Libra) and Ascendant (normally ruled by Aries) - already mentioned.

This is a good example of how to work with Opposition aspects in Birth Charts which focus consciousness on "Opposites". The aim is to find the "still centre" and creative resolutions from both sides of the "arguments". We can see that Freud and Jung were able to maintain their individuality despite having numerous intimate personal relationships (including one another) - albeit of a professional rather than sexual level.

SIGMUND FREUD "Father of Psychoanalysis"

With Moon in Gemini (past life) and Sun in practical Taurus (current lifetime) Freud was basically a "Gemini (Mutable Air) trying to be more Taurus (Fixed Earth)". Therefore having a developed mental ability for communication, study, and experimentation ("Jack of all trades") but learning new lessons about down-to-earth practical affairs and organisation, especially of money and other physical resources. We see combination of these factors in his early years :-

> *In Vienna during the whole of Freud's childhood the family lived in the most straightened conditions; but it is much to his father's credit that he gave invariable priority to the charge of Freud's education, for the boy was obviously intelligent (Gemini) and was a hard worker (Taurus) as well. The result was that he won a place in the 'Gymnasium' at the early age of nine and for the last six of the eight years he spent at the school he was regularly top of his class. [IOD]*

The same factors are evident in his "choice" of career. In true "curious" Gemini fashion he rather drifted into a career as a doctor as a result of his interest in the physical, natural world (Taurus).

Freud insisted more than once that at no time in his life did he feel any particular predilection for the career of a doctor.' I was moved, rather', he says, 'by a sort of curiosity, which was, however, directed more towards human concerns than towards natural objects'. Elsewhere he writes 'I have no knowledge of having had any craving in early childhood to help suffering humanity. In my youth I felt an overpowering need to understand something of the riddles of the world in which we live and perhaps even to contribute something to their solution'. [IOD]

Gemini is curious. Uranus likes solving puzzles.

In time he qualified and spent some time in a hospital for nervous diseases in which field he set up a private practice. Until that time he was solely concerned with physical science and the brain (physical Taurus Fixed Earth), but having failed in using electro-therapy, began using hypnotism (Gemini, experimentation) which was not yet fully accepted in the field. He developed into the treatment of neuroses, and included dream interpretation in his work. His systems and methods were so effective that he split away from established ones, and developed what was to be the basis for Psychoanalysis. His theories were based on the concept that all mental problems are caused by repressed sexual energy – "Libido". This is not surprising - he lived at a time when sex was a taboo subject and many people got married with no knowledge of the physiology of the other sex.

Returning to his Birth Chart and the Opposition Aspect with his Taurus Sun and Ascendant, we now note that he has Scorpio (Fixed Water. Sex. Death) rising which gives an interest in uncovering the secrets of life. The Ascendant shows our most natural way of self-expression. The Sun Opposition Aspect therefore gave him a unique awareness by being able to objectively observe his own psyche – in particular his own sexual impulses, which are controlled (perhaps repressed) in Fixed Water Scorpio – but did not stop him fathering 6 children.

I have noticed in my psycho analytical work that the whole frame of mind of man who is reflecting is totally different from that of the man who is observing his own psychical processes..... [IOD]

His (Taurus, Fixed Earth) fixation on this concept was what finally led to the split with Jung, who, as we will see, had a different viewpoint. Taureans can be very stubborn. As a pioneer in the early days of Psychoanalysis Freud had to endure a ostracism from friends and colleagues who did not understand his concepts on sexual pathology – especially as he was dealing with a subject that invited ostracism if mentioned in "polite society". Homosexuality was a criminal act at that time.

G.G.JUNG "Discoverer of Individuation"

Jung did some investigations of Astrology [ref. "The Portable Jung": chapter "On Synchronicity"]. One experiment was that of comparing Birth Charts of married couples where, among other things, such as Mars and Venus, he found a 10% match between Sun and Moon.

With Moon in Taurus (Fixed Earth) and Sun in Leo (Fixed Fire) Jung was basically a "Taurus trying to become more Leo". Later in life he was considered arrogant by his colleagues – who obviously did not realise that he had 2 stubborn Fixed Signs to deal with inwardly. He therefore had developed down to earth abilities and was able to cope with practical affairs requiring attention to routine. He would have been a good business manager. At 21 years of age he actually took over the handling of family resources when his father died. There was very little money, and his mother was unable to cope. His father was a pastor of the Swiss Reformed Church, his mother from a wealthy family. She suffered from chronic unexplained illness, so was never close to Carl. He was the only survivor of 4 children.

His birth chart has Saturn in his 1st. House (including the Ascendant)– concerned with individual self-expression. (Similar to Lady Diana Spencer [ASTROLOGY : BIRTH CHART EXAMPLES]. This brings the Discipline of Saturn into effect at a very early age, with very little of the freedom of a normal childhood. In particular one's attempts at self-expression and appearance are continually negatively criticised. Never being "perfect" enough. This leads to a repressed, "shy" character – always expecting rejection. In addition, he was a lonely child spending much time playing in isolation. His birth Sun (Father) and Moon (Mother) - both in Fixed Signs - are in Square (Challenging) aspect to one another. His loneliness was increased by his father and mother continually quarrelling.

ASTROLOGY : SYNASTRY

At school he was forced to mix with children of uneducated peasants and farmers where his loneliness increased from being bullied because of his "fancy manners". Nevertheless, he was deeply affected when unable to go to a school outing with the other children because he was too small. This affected him for the rest of his life.

There was no explicit reason why he began to study medicine – he originally wanted to be an archaeologist. He had Venus (Desire. Likes) in Conjunction with Mercury (Mind) in the Sign of Cancer (ruled by Moon. Past. Family. History) in his 6th. House, which governs what we do to make a living. Cancer, which rules Cycle of Growth Stage 4 (Transplanting) has great interest in "digging roots". Perhaps he did become an "archaeologist" at a psychological level in his studies of mythology and allied subjects. Psychologists are often accused of being "archaeologists" in their exploration of the early years ("past life") of their patients. He changed to psychiatry at the end of his medical studies as the result of reading a textbook on the subject. He met Freud in 1907 when Freud was 50. They developed a close association, albeit mainly by correspondence, which was almost like father and son. In 1909 at a conference Freud said that he was adopting him ....

>   *"...... as an eldest son, anointing him as successor and Crown Prince" ["The Portable Jung " - Joseph Campbell].

In turn Jung regarded Freud as a "father figure". Here we note that Jung had Moon (Past) in Taurus and Freud had Sun (Future) in Taurus. In comparing two birth charts this factor is common in relationships in that the Sun, in its lifetime "mission" to develop the attributes of its birth Sign, is attracted to a birth Moon of that Sign person who has the attributes already developed.

>   (As Sun Gemini I married a Moon Gemini. I once did a Birth Chart for a Moon Leo lady who said that she now realised why her close men friends were all Leo Sun). This is, of course, not a strict rule. Close relationships are more often based upon Mars to Venus cross-relationships. That is, the Mars of one party satisfies the Venus desires of the other.[BTB])

Although they corresponded for 10 years, the close relationship between Freud and Jung lasted only 6 years. The final split in 1912 was due to Jung finally rejecting Freud's fixation on repressed sexuality being the cause of all nervous disorders. Although Jung challenged it from the beginning of their relationship, he had nothing else to replace the theory with. We recall the challenging Square Aspect between Jung's birth Sun in Leo and Moon in Taurus. This would also follow as a challenge to Freud's Sun in Taurus. In the intervening period he even defended Freud against growing opposition from his peers. Jung had become more stable in his concept of Individuation, and called his methods Analytical Psychology to distinguish from those of Psychoanalysis. He described Libido as a more general form of psychic energy, rather than just sexual. We could say that he reconised several different planetary energies other than that of Mars.

Returning to Jung's birth Chart, we have noted Jung's 7th. House Sun, which, as with Freud is in Opposition "Full Moon" Aspect with his Ascendant. Whereas Freud was objectively aware of sexuality, as symbolised by his Scorpio Ascendant, we see that Jung was aware of Individuation as symbolised by his Aquarius Ascendant. In addition, I have noted that both men have Sun in Conjunction Aspect with Uranus in 7th.House, which is the ruling planet of Aquarius – so the influence of the archetype of the Planet and Sign is very strong in both Birth Charts.

Looking back over their lives we can see examples of Individuation in action. Both, because of their adult life experiences, separated from their peers and accepted early ostracism to become individual exponents of their concepts. In Jung's case with Saturn in 1st. House the experience of being alone came at an early age – so it could be considered a kind of preparation.

A strong Saturn in a Birth Chart gives rise to a "bruised Ego" and being subject to strong discipline, or needing to take on more adult responsibility in early life. Being the eldest child is often a manifestation. There is often the sense of an "absent father" with the need to fulfil the "controlling" role for one's self at a normally inappropriate age. We see that Jung had the experience twice in his life, once with his own father, and later with Freud. The sense of loneliness can be a crushing defeat or lead to being able to establish and develop one's own concepts and beliefs "behind the scenes". It also gives rise to a strong sense of "self-consciousness". Jung's writings include evidence of much self-analysis, often related to his early days ("archaeology ?") – very similar to that of Freud mentioned above.

GENESIS AND THE CYCLE OF GROWTH

CYCLE OF GROWTH		GENESIS		TAROT	ZODIAC		PLANET	KABBALAH	PSYCHOLOGY
1ST. OCTAVE (ABSTRACT LEVEL) - PHYSICAL VEHICLE (DEVELOPMENT OF BODY AND BRAIN)									
Stage Zero	-	Day Zero	preparing heavens and earth	-	-	0	Neptune	1. Kether Crown	-
Stage 9	Conception	Day 1	Light appears (Conscious recognition of "opposites".	XIV. Temperance	Sagittarius. Fire Abstract Mind	1 ♇	Pluto Regeneration	2. Chockmah Force	Conception
Stage 10	Peak. Harvest		Dark -> Night (Satan)	XV. The Devil	Capricorn. Earth The Builder	2 ♄	Saturn Consolidation	3. Binah Form	LIFE IN THE WOMB Human Evolution
			Light -> Day (Lucifer)	XVI. The Tower					
Stage 11	Dissatisfaction	Day 2	Separation -> expanse					Daath/Abyss	
			expanse -> Heavens (Sky)	XVII. The Star	Aquarius. Air Water Carrier	♄	Saturn		
		Day 3	Earth and Sea	XVIII. The Moon					
		Day 4	Stars, Sun, Moon	XIX. The Sun					
		Day 5	Fish and Birds						
		Day 6	Land creatures and "man"						
Stage 12	Withdrawal Confinement	Chapter 2 Day 7	Day of rest (final even-ing) (Sleep. Unconsciousness)	XX. Judgement	Pisces. Water Collective	3 ♃	Jupiter Expansion	4. Chesed Mercy	
				XXI. The World					
2ND. OCTAVE (PHYSICAL AND PSYCHOLOGICAL LEVELS) - PHYSICAL VEHICLE. CONTROL OF BODY									
Stage 1	Seed 11 Lunar Month	Man made "from dust". "the man" is born		0. The Fool I. The Magician	Aries. Fire Projection	4 ♂	Mars Self Projection	5. Geburah Severity	Physical Birth (Oral)
Sephirah 6 (Tiphareth. The Sun) has no effect on the evolutionary "Lightning Flash"						5 ☉	The Sun Ego Consciousness	6. Tiphareth Beauty	
Ego Consciousness is only in embryo form until "born" to start the 3rd. Octave.									
Stage 2	Germination From 7 months	Man moved to Eden/Earth to Serve. The 2 Trees		II. The Priestess III. The Empress	Taurus. Earth Organisation	6 ♀	Venus Earth Desire	7. Victory Feeling	Infancy (Anal. Physical)
Stage 3	Experiment From 2 years	Companionship. Formation of animals. Eve/counterpart creation Naming of animals and Adam.		IV. The Emperor V. The Hierophant	Gemini. Air Thinking	7 ☿	Mercury Communication	8. Glory Thinking	Early Childhood (Mental)
Stage 4	Transplanting From 4 Years	The Temptation and Fall. Ejection from The Garden of Eden. "Coats of skin".		VI. The Lovers VII. The Chariot	Cancer Shell	8 ☽	Moon Subconscious	9. Foundation Unconscious	Play Age (Oedipus. Persona)
3RD. OCTAVE (SOCIAL LEVEL) - SOCIAL "VEHICLE" (PERSONA & EGO) : STARTS THE "RETURN JOURNEY"									
Stage 5	Power. Creativity From 7 Years	Cain presents his "gift" to God and is disappointed at seeming rejection		VIII. Strength	Leo. Fire Creativity	5 ☉	Sun Ego Conscious	6. Beauty Consciousness	School Age (Productivity)
Stage 6	Service to Self From 13 Years	Cain kills Abel		IX. The Hermit	Virgo. Earth Health. Work	7 ☿	Mercury Practical Mind	8. Glory Self Conscious	Adolescent. Puberty (Identity)
				X. The Wheel					
Stage 7	Partners From 23 Years	Cain leaves the family to mate and form his own clan		XI. Justice	Libra. Air Balance	6 ♀	Venus Air Desire	7. Victory Desire	Young Adult Intimacy : Isolation
Stage 8	Sex. Death From 42 Years			XII. Hanged Man XIII. Death	Scorpio. Water Control	4 ♂	Mars Self Projection	5. Severity	Adult & Old Age
						♇	Pluto Regeneration	2. Force	

Figure 43 : Genesis and Evolution Summary Table

GENESIS AND THE CYCLE OF GROWTH

We first note that chapters 1 to 3 of Genesis, in turn, relate to Octaves 1 to 3 of the Logarithmic Timescale.

The chapter begins with some overviews and ends with detailed comparison of the stages of The Cycle of Growth with the Biblical Book of Genesis – which is the first book of The Bible and contains the story of Creation.

I have included the full biblical text of Genesis Chapters 1 to 4, with my commentary mainly using Young's Literal Bible translation [YLT] to enable a contrast with the better known King James Version [KJV]. I have also included some repetition of material elsewhere in this book to save having to refer back and forth. The IMAGES of the Tarot cards seem more relevant than their interpretations in this context. Perhaps they contain more than we realise.

Special note is made of the fact that each stage requires an "even-ing" which appears to be a balancing of the elements of the universe to maintain a total of Zero. A form of "Cosmic Accountancy".

We also note that at certain stages the creations are given names (as "children") – which is a high level mental reproduction of a physical manifestation. This is, in itself, another form of even-ing. The mental level "creation" is also an even-ing process – we get (the named object. Earth. Sensation) and (its name equivalent in another dimension. Air. Thinking). The process gets more complicated as the number of creations increase. God eventually gets bored and delegates the naming process to Adam which gives him something useful to do in the absence of anything else apart from a bit of gardening (Until his Fall, that is, which occurs after he runs out of things to name. "The Devil makes work for idle hands.")

We note that this story is not restricted to the Christian Religion, but is similar to those found in others.

ROBERT YOUNG'S LITERAL BIBLE TRANSLATION AND CONCORDANCE

I have attempted to get as close to the original meaning as possible by using "Young's Literal Translation" of the Bible where Robert Young has, as far as possible, translated word by word without concern for meaning and without changing the tense as other translators do. The task, actually, is impossible because, according to Robert, there are numerous cases where *"ten or twenty" Greek/Hebrew words only have a single English equivalent, and one Greek/Hebrew word can translate to "ten or twenty" English words* [YLT]. It makes for a strange English text in places.

Further study can be done by using a "concordance" which lists all the words used in the translated Bible together with the original Greek and Hebrew words and their literal meaning. Robert Young's *"Analytical Concordance to the Bible"* (a monumental work containing "about 311,000 references") not only contains every word in the Bible but shows it each time it is used, in the relevant paragraph (in Book/Chapter/Verse order), and with the paragraphs separated according to the original Hebrew/Greek words used.

NUMBERS

At the root of The Story we have an example of one of the basic factors of Universal Law that [NUMEROLOGY] indicates :-

1. Everything comes from No-Thing – Zero. We see below that there was, in fact, a Zero day of Creation. Although the Number Zero did not appear until modern times the story does include it. In modern terms this makes 8 days of Creation (Zero to 7). This is in accordance with the meaning of Number 8 which is symbolic of high level organisation Number 4 (including "Naming") of Natural Law, over Number 4 Organised Material Structure. There is a similar situation with [THE CHAKRAS] where we can add the previously undiscovered Hypothalamus gland which controls the 7 others.

2. When something is first created from No-Thing (Zero) it becomes Number 1, which is naturally followed soon after by Number 2 – which is the complement (not "opposite") to whatever Number 1 consists of. This keeps the universal balance at Zero. (i.e. At Universal Level $0 + 1 + (-1) = 0$).

3. Newton said "Every action has an equal and opposite reaction".

4. After that, as numbers increase, things become more complicated. The Zero Balance is harder to maintain.

5. We note from our studies of The Kabbalah, Number Zero, Pisces/Neptune, and the Entropy of Physics, that there is a universal force which is acting to return everything to the Zero State of inertia, or primeval chaos, that existed before The Big Bang. In human terms, to make each one of us a nameless part of The Collective (from which we came).

6. It seems that the expansion of the universe – which, in effect, creates Time – ensures that when something is created its complement is created too. The amount of time that elapses in between (which might be a microsecond) is enough to maintain the separate complementary energies which would otherwise meet and cancel each other out. Scientists suggest that at some time in the future the expansion of the universe will stop, when it will contract back to its original Singularity. When that begins, Time will run backwards.

7. Perhaps time runs backwards anyway when at mid-life we return to "a second childhood" in preparation for death and rebirth.

Evidence here is that in Chapter 1 each day cycle of Creation is followed by an "even-ing" which suggests some form of interchange between the members of the "partnership" created each day. This also answers the riddle of why the description of Creation Day 7 occurs at the beginning of Chapter 2 rather than the end of Chapter 1. Having done all that work, God too needed a "day of rest" to do his own "even-ing" – as we do at the end of every daily cycle, and Nature does at the end of each annual cycle. We could add this concept to that of Karma .

A cycle of Number 6 creates Number 7 – which then has its own cycle (the days of the week).

Later on, Adam needs Eve and Cain needs Abel. Although different, they are Complements, not Opposites. They are separate, independent, individuals in their own right, but relate to the other.

We see a relationship in our own lives, which requires sleep at the end of each day cycle during "even-tide" (that is, the even-ing of a Day Cycle, Earth rotation). It also shows the source of the church's dilemma in deciding whether our Sunday "day of rest" is the first or last day of the week. "Chicken or Egg ?" (actually, in evolutionary terms, the egg came first as a development of the bacterial reproductive method, and later marine animals and birds. Chickens came much later).

GENESIS OVERVIEW

Genesis is the first book of The Bible Old Testament. *A notable feature of Genesis is that "man" is created twice – and adapted again afterwards in accordance with the scientifically accepted concept of human Evolution.*

We can consider the story in terms of :

1. Cycle of Growth Stages beginning at Stage 9 (Conception) – which include :-
2. The 3 Octaves of [ASTROLOGY : LOGARITHMIC TIMESCALE] which relate to human physical psychological development.
3. Zodiac Sign associations and the Annual Cycle of Nature.
4. Tarot Card associations.
5. Human Evolution as accepted scientifically from "Big Bang" to present day.
6. Human physical development (Gestation of a foetus, birth, early physical and psychological development in human life).
7. The life of Jesus.

According to Edgar Cayce, after several interim incarnations, Adam and Eve became Jesus and Mary.

THE NEW TESTAMENT AND EVOLUTION OF GOD

Although I have not included details in this book, we note that [THE KABBALAH TREE OF LIFE] includes a "God Name" to correspond with each of the 4 "Kingdoms" (Elements) of each of the 10 Sephiroth – which adds up to 40 names. There are more names, some of which are mentioned here. This does not imply different gods, rather it is a functional title as suggested here.

We note that even in this short narrative God gets different names at each of the 3 Logarithmic Cycle of Growth Octave stages.

When we compare the Old and New Testaments we get 2 entirely different views of God. In the Old Testament we have The Ten Commandments written by God on to tablets of stone and given to Moses (another incarnation in the line Adam to Jesus [EC]). We note that this was an entirely one-way transaction in that the written Covenant (contract) was one-sided in God's favour, and seemingly based on "Reward or Punishment". His promises to Moses ("Party of the Second Part") were not written down, and seem to not been kept. I have come across this sort of thing in my working life with employers making unkept promises at a job interview, and "forgetting" later. Nowadays we usually get a Contract of Employment.

GENESIS AND THE CYCLE OF GROWTH

In the New Testament it is admitted that the Old Covenant was not working (I have suggested the reason) so Jesus, in his final incarnation, brought a much simpler New Covenant.

Mark 12:30: And thou shalt love the Lord thy God with all thy heart, and with all thy soul, and with all thy mind, and with all thy strength: this is the first commandment.

Makk:12:31: And the second is like, namely this, Thou shalt love thy neighbour as thyself. There is none other commandment greater than these.[YLT]

[Hebrews Chapter 8, Verse 8] : For if that first covenant had been faultless, then should no place have been sought for the second.

GENESIS – 3 DEPICTIONS OF GOD

In Genesis, the One God is described using 3 different names, and has 3 different roles during the process. The King James Version translates them into "God", "the LORD God", and "the LORD" respectively. (When reading The Bible I often find it more understandable to use the word "LAW" in place of "LORD").

1. "God" (Hebrew : Elohim – an object of worship) [KJV=GOD]. who made the universe and prepared man ("male and female"). The first Creation up to Creation Day 7. Cycle of Growth Stage 9 (Conception) to Stage 12 (Confinement awaiting birth) and the "First Octave" of the Logarithmic Timescale.
2. "Jehovah God" (Hebrew : Yahweh - which is the "name of God" [KJV= the LORD GOD] separating the one Hebrew God from the other deities of the time. Allowed to be written, but not spoken. The combination seems to mean "The Named God to be worshipped" - who created the Garden Of Eden and gave Adam the task of naming everything. "Woman" was created out of Adam. Cycle of Growth Stage 3 (Experiment. Communication) which gives another meaning to the related "Gemini Twins". Recognition of different sexes appears in the next Stage.
3. "Jehovah" [KJV=the LORD] alone (can be written, but is too holy to be spoken – although Eve seems to say the name). The name does not appear until Genesis Chapter 4 where "The Tree of Knowledge of Good and Evil" reveals an association with the "knowing" of sexual intercourse and other material desires. I take this to mean that even though the worship of God failed at The Fall, his LAW remains – which includes The Cycle of Growth.

We see later developments of this principle :-

Yahweh the God of the Israelites, his name being revealed to Moses as four Hebrew consonants (YHWH) called the tetragrammaton. After the Exile (6th century BC), and especially from the 3rd century BC on, Jews ceased to use the name Yahweh for two reasons. As Judaism became a universal religion through its proselytizing in the Greco-Roman world, the more common noun elohim, meaning "god," tended to replace Yahweh to demonstrate the universal sovereignty of Israel's God over all others. At the same time, the divine name was increasingly regarded as too sacred to be uttered; it was thus replaced vocally in the synagogue ritual by the Hebrew word Adonai ("My Lord"), which was translated as Kyrios ("Lord") in the Septuagint, the Greek version of the Old Testament.[EB]

GENESIS CHAPTER 1 – LOGARITHMIC TIMESCALE 1ST. OCTAVE
CYCLE OF GROWTH STAGE 9 (Conception) TO STAGE 12 (Withdrawal. Confinement)

Here the work is done by "God". At the beginning of the Bible in the Book of Genesis we have the biblical account of the Creation of the Universe out of "waste", and "darkness", in 6 days. Although no "big bang" is mentioned, progress does seem to follow the now scientifically accepted scenario of the gradual condensation and solidification of matter, and the evolution of plants, animals, and man - although the timescale actually covers 13,700 million years.

It corresponds with the First Octave of the Astrological Logarithmic Timescale beginning at Cycle of Growth Stage 9 (Conception. Sagittarius. Fire) which covers the 10 lunar months of our life in the womb (and later Transcendence). There was no Adam or Eve yet, and Edgar Cayce states that this coincides with a non-material Creation as an Idea in the mind. In terms of a human lifetime, the baby is still in the womb - not yet born (physical).

Edgar Cayce stated that this refers to the incarnation of Amilius in the lost civilisation of Atlantis, the first of several incarnations of the entity that would eventually become Jesus. It seems to me that, if this is true, it is a waste of time searching for Atlantis on Earth as we know it because the inference is that Chapter 1 deals with another dimension - which is not fully material until Chapter 2. This is in accordance with Kabbalist concept that the un-numbered Sephirah Daath was the original (concept of) Sephirah 10 (Malkuth. Kingdom. Earth) before The Fall. So we have to remember we are here dealing with the mental world of ideas rather than the physical one. ("The Word")

GENESIS CHAPTER 2 – LOGARITHMIC TIMESCALE 2ND. OCTAVE
CYCLE OF GROWTH STAGE 1 (Seed) TO STAGE 4 (Transplanting)

Here the work is done by "Jehovah God". Chapter 2 begins with the 7th. Day of Creation when God rested. This coincides with Cycle of Growth Stage 12 (Withdrawal. Confinement) – the time of a mother preparing for birth of her child. Later, despite the 6 days of Creation that occurred in Chapter 1, we are explicitly told in Chapter 2 :-

> *Chapter 2 : Verse 5: and no shrub of the field is yet in the earth, and no herb of the field yet sprouteth, for Jehovah God hath not rained upon the earth, and a man there is not to serve the ground.

We see the correspondence with the concept of a "Seed" Stage.

We next have the creation of The Garden of Eden containing The Tree of Life, and The Tree of Knowledge of Good and Evil. This is a complex symbol which is able to be interpreted at several levels. For example :

1. Another stage in the evolution of physical Earth, or "physical" human body.
2. The beginning of the Second Octave of the Logarithmic Timescale at Cycle of Growth Stage 1 (Seed. Aries. Fire).
3. The birth of a human baby – now in visible in physical form (in consciousness) as a vehicle for the soul.
4. Planting a seed in the Earth enabling its further development into maturity.
5. The Chakra\endocrine gland system of a human body. This is the physical Tree of Life which is capable of regenerating a human body to allow human lifetime of thousands of years [EC]. Using it as The Tree of Knowledge - sexual reproduction of the body instead - causes the body to deteriorate and die. (The Chakras are sealed. A description of their opening being in Revelation – the final book of The Bible).

In the first chapter of Genesis there seems to be the strange anomaly that vegetation, animals and man ("male and female") were created – but not woman! Eve does not appear until the 'second creation' in Chapter 2. However, with Young's translation it is clear that the first step was PREPARATION (a planning stage). This also fits in with current understanding of human evolution that the mechanism of sexual reproduction in plants, then animals, occurred before the appearance of man. A baby in the womb develops both sets of sexual organs. It is not until later on in the pregnancy that it becomes predominantly, physically, male or female.

It is interesting to note that scientists concerned with Evolution show that the various parts of the human body were first developed in fish and animals before they came together to make the first humanoid. We could say that God experimented with animals first – as scientists do today – in conformity with the description of Cycle of Growth Stage 3 (Experiment).

Following the creation of The Garden of Eden, we now have that of Adam and Eve. Once again, the suggestion is that they do not have actual physical form until the next Chapter when, after their Fall, they are given "coats of skin".

GENESIS CHAPTER 3 – LOGARITHMIC TIMESCALE 3RD. OCTAVE
CYCLE OF GROWTH STAGE 5 (Power. Ego Consciousness) TO STAGE 8 (Death)

"Jehovah God" is still in charge. We now have the story of the Temptation of Eve by the Serpent, and Adam by Eve. Having chosen The Tree of Knowledge they realise that their physical bodies are different and cover them up. We can see this same revelation in early childhood today. After this they are given "coats of skin" and cast out of The Garden of Eden to fend for themselves – that is, to experience the karma of their choice. This explicitly locks away access to The Tree of Life. The Chakra\endocrine system is sealed until we have an example of the opening of chakras by John in Revelation – the last book of the New Testament, and of The Bible – suggesting the final stage of spiritual development.

Cycle of Growth Stage 4 (Transplanting) stage of human development includes :-

1. Logarithmic Timescale 3 to 7 years, which is Erikson's "Play Age" when children begin to explore the world outside the family home, and discover their sexual organs as they become more active.

2. The psychological Oedipus Complex which occurs at this time. The Temptation is clearly related to the flirting with the parent of opposite sex at this age which is also the development of Jung's psychological Anima in men, and Elektra in women.
3. The development of a psychological Persona (Mask. Shell. Skin).

GENESIS CHAPTER 4

Now "Jehovah" takes over. Outside The Garden of Eden Adam "knew" Eve, and Cain was conceived and born, and, later, Abel (as a complement). We now have a common occurrence of sibling rivalry when Cain kills Abel because he believes that his "gift" (Daily occupation. Job) is not acceptable to God, and Abel is favoured.

Cycle of Growth Stage 6 (Service to Self. Virgo) corresponds, with its focus on choosing an occupation with which to earn a living.

Cain is cast out of the family to make his own way in life, and do some "knowing" of his own. (He eventually formed his own clan, which scholars today suggest eventually became the first civilisation in Mesopotamia). Cycle of Growth Stage 7 (Partners) is the time of seeking a mate outside the family of birth.

Despite the negative tone of "casting out" we note that this is a normal stage of human development. This is also part of animal development, such as in lions and wolves where the young male is forced out of the family group to live a lone existence until he forms his own pride.

We now seem to leave The Cycle of Growth, although we note the tendency for increase in population of the Earth in physical terms of human evolution, as well as accordance with the psychological concept of expansion of consciousness of a young adult to include increasingly wider social relationships outside the family home.

FURTHER CONSIDERATIONS

Here are some general observations before detailed comparison with stages in The Cycle of Growth. We first have to note that each stage of the story of Creation takes 1 day. That is a COMPLETE CYCLE OF TIME (Wheels within wheels). Evolution tells us that they would not be days as we know them. There are various versions of this quotation :-

*[2 Peter Chapter 3 Verse 8] And this one thing let not be unobserved by you, beloved, that one day with the Lord [is] as a thousand years, and a thousand years as one day; [YLT]

We can also observe that, in the mind, we can conceive ideas in an instant – although they might take years to develop into a finished product in actual practice. The 2 processes are contained in Octaves 1 and 2 of the Logarithmic Timescale.

Although much of the Bible is an historical record, it can also be interpreted at deeper symbolic levels, as well as a superficial, logical, level – especially in the New Testament when we come to the teachings of Jesus. One of the problems is that the translation into English from the original Hebrew and Greek was done by people who were probably only concerned with the objective layer of interpretation, and the same holds true for later, more modern, translations (of the translations). We can uncover additional meaning by comparing the text with the Cycle of Growth stages.

EDGAR CAYCE AND GENESIS

I also have to take into account the teachings of Edgar Cayce concerning the Old Testament. Because he was a channel of so much other verifiable evidence about people he never met we have to take notice of his other information. I maintain the focus on The Cycle of Growth because it provides a more continuous cyclic overview of what would otherwise be a series of disconnected subjects. It also gives a view of possible Universal Law that even God is subject to. An important point is that Edgar states that humans were not fully in a material state until Adam and Eve were given "coats of skin" in Genesis Chapter 2 Verse 21.

From the viewpoint of Cayce's unconscious sources we get a theme of man's continuing "disobedience " to the Will of God - which avoids some important questions :-

GENESIS AND THE CYCLE OF GROWTH

1. Why did God create us in the first place ? The general suggestion is that he wanted companionship (!?) and we got it wrong (?). The Cycle of Growth poses the question of why God got involved in fulfilling material ambition rather than spiritual development – as we are supposed to.
2. If God is so omnipotent, how could he have made such errors ? Most written material blames us and our Free Will. However, The Cycle of Growth gives a picture of continual development through the millenia – learning by experience.
3. Who is The Devil, who seems to have power to oppose God's wishes? From Jung's work we understand that we all have an unconscious Shadow. To me, it is clear that The Devil is God's Shadow. This is in accordance with Universal Law stating that whenever something is created, or comes into being, its exact complement is created at the same time or soon afterward (everything adds up to Zero). So we have things like Male and Female, Matter and Antimatter, Adam and Eve. This also seems to shed light on God's seeming irrational behaviour at times – such as from not keeping his covenant\agreement with Moses by protecting the righteous who keep his laws. This is especially emphasised by his bet with the Devil that Job would not curse him, no matter what misfortune he experienced. [THE PURPOSE OF LIFE\God's Covenants and Treatment of Job]. Even God's religious ministers get personal and health problems.

THE CYCLE OF GROWTH STAGES

We now consider The Creation story in more detail. We are here attempting to describe how physical things come into being from No-Thing in an Abstract, non-physical Dimension. To do so requires reference to images that can be recognised by the human Mind. This is valid in that the images, and he related physical objects, all ultimately come from the same "seed" source. For example, although The Cycle of Growth is mentioned here, in reality it does not exist until much further down the Kabbalist Tree of Life.

The process is made valid by the fact that The Cycle of Growth exists at all levels, which themselves now exist at one and the same time, and summarised by the ancient words "As Above, So Below – As Below, So Above". We use convenient diagrams to separate ideas, but, in fact, everything is contained within the universal "sea" of the collective unconscious – as it was at the beginning.

To fully understand, we must eventually discard the images.

GENESIS AND THE CYCLE OF GROWTH

CYCLE OF GROWTH STAGE ZERO

This is the "DNA" of The Cycle of Growth which contains all the information required for later development.

Relating our study of [THE KABBALAH TREE OF LIFE] and modern scientific theory about how the universe began, we find agreement between them that, at this stage, there was No-Thing. A "Zero State".

[THE KABBALAH TREE OF LIFE] consists of 10 Sephiroth of increasing density of form, they evolve from the "The Ain" (Absolutely Nothing) via Sephirah 1 (Kether. Crown) which relates to Number Zero, No-Thing at a more "physical" level. As we analyse Genesis we take note of how the Chapters and Verses are divided.

Chapter 1 : Verse 1: In the beginning of God's preparing the heavens and the earth

Chapter 1 : Verse 2: the earth hath existed waste and void, and darkness [is] on the face of the deep, and the Spirit of God fluttering on the face of the waters,

Sephirah 1 (Kether. Crown. Number Zero. Neptune)

Out of Absolutely Nothing comes the glimmerings of An Idea. Zero is The First Whole Number which has only become recognised as such in the Computer Age. It did not exist in ancient times [NUMEROLOGY].

From now on, if Some-thing is created, its complement must be created too in order to maintain that balance.

"The Deep" is suggestive of The Abyss just below Kether which is crossed by the Sephiroth Daath on the "Return Journey" up The Tree. It could also refer to the "sea" of The Collective Unconscious.

We have the beginning of Kabbalism's "Lightning Flash" where energy is transferred to each of the Sephiroth in numerical order.

NEPTUNE

1. With the discovery of Neptune we can associate it with Sephirah 1 (Kether. Crown. Number Zero) as beginning and "container" of every thing.
2. We first note that the symbol of Neptune is a simple, basic, depiction of The Kabbalah Tree of Life with its 3 Pillars. At this Stage the Planet is just an idea and there are no other Sephiroth.
3. Neptune/Pisces relates to Cycle of Growth Stage 12 which is at the end of The 1st. Octave of the Logarithmic Timescale which itself is concerned with our Gestation in the womb – creating a physical body – and, at another level, Transcendence. We can envision Stage Zero as Stage 12 of an earlier Cycle.
4. The symbolism of Pisces relates to Earth's "Sea" which contains all chemical elements in solution. It is also The Collective Unconscious, which contains every-thing yet to come (to consciousness). The evolution of man is based on bringing to Consciousness what is already there.
5. Pisces has 2 rulers - Neptune (Dissolution. The Collective) and Jupiter (Expansion). For normal human beings, Pisces and Cycle of Growth Stage 12 (Withdrawal. Confinement) is ruled by Jupiter which also rules Sagittarius at Cycle of Growth Stage 9 (Conception).
6. To avoid too much repetition of what is elsewhere in this book, we note that Neptune does not become active at a human level until Uranus (Individuation) becomes active first. If this were not so, we would simply be absorbed (dissolved) back into The Source. This is evidenced by those who achieve altered states of consciousness – such as by using (or abusing) - alcohol and drugs and lose contact with the material world and their Self.
7. When Jupiter is active at Cycle of Growth Stage 12, The Transcendent Octave is bypassed and we arrive back at Cycle of Growth Stage 9 (Conception) which is another beginning in the endless cycles of physical birth and rebirth.
8. The traditional rulership of Sagittarius AND Pisces by Jupiter creates a kind of "short circuit" between Cycles of Growth Stages 9 and 12 which bypasses The 1st. Octave in its Transcendent phase. I have attempted to describe this in more detail in [THE KABBALAH TREE OF LIFE].

DAY 1. CYCLE OF GROWTH STAGE 9 (CONCEPTION)

"Light" (consciousness) comes from the original Stage Zero "Dark".

GENESIS AND THE CYCLE OF GROWTH

Genesis 1 : Verse 3: and God saith, `Let light be;' and light is.

Conception. The beginning of the Creation story. The work of "God". From now, until Chapter 2, and Creation Day 7, we are only in "The Mind of God" (or The Womb). There is no physical manifestation yet. This is The 1st. Octave of The Cycle of Growth. We have several related images :-

1. Cycle of Growth Stage 9 relates to Creation Day 1 when the first thing to appear is Light from No-thing. (To redress the universal balance of Zero "God divided the Light from Darkness". The newly-created Darkness relates to Cycle of Growth Stage 10).
2. At the top of The Kabbalah Tree of Life we have the division of Sephirah 1 (Kether. Crown. Number Zero) into Sephirah 2 (Chockmah. Wisdom. Force. Light. Consciousness. Number 1) and Sephirah 3 (Binah. Understanding. Form. Dark. The Unconscious. Number 2).
3. Number 1 is related to the single Point of Mathematics that has no dimensions.
4. Number 1 becomes the point/dot in the centre of the Circle of Zero – which becomes the symbol of The Sun on The Middle Pillar lower down The Tree of Life. The Zodiac occurs later when the energy of The Sun is differentiated into 12 different "forms".
5. Sephirah 2 (Chockmah. Force) is The Principle of Consciousness (as distinct from The Principle of The Unconscious). The Sun is actual human Consciousness (which is usually focused on objects still lower down The Tree).
6. The Sperm (dot. Number 1) fertilises the Egg (circle. Number Zero) to begin the process of growing a physical body. All the required information to achieve it is present in the combined DNA – which now is a representation of "the whole" Number Zero.
7. In modern Science, the beginning of the physical universe required the presence of a "Singularity" in the midst of "No-Thing".
8. The first physical chemical element Hydrogen, Atomic Number 1, consists of a single central Proton with a single Electron in "circular" orbit around it. Hydrogen still makes up 98% of the matter in the universe.
9. We now have a single Cell containing a Nucleus.
10. The process continues by division of that cell into equal parts each of which contains the same DNA information (which is a physical representation of The Tree of Life at Stage Zero). As cell division continues, and numbers grow, some cells separate from the others to undertake different functions on behalf of The Whole.
11. Another example of this Process is the development of a fully functioning human body from a single cell in the womb – which repeats the stages of Human Evolution.
12. Another example is the evolutionary development of a human from isolated Hunter Gatherer to participating in groups of people who perform different functions on behalf of the whole.
13. Another example is The Cycle of Growth which depicts the same sequence of stages in the development of a single human from Conception, to Family, to participation in a gradually widening Social Consciousness.

Zodiac Sign : Sagittarius

Mutable (Changeable. Chaotic) Fire. The Centaur – half man, half beast. The Archer. The Higher Mind. Academic knowledge. Conceptions. Theories. "Foreign" influences. Pluto.

At the beginning of Creation The Big Bang produced Plasma which consists mainly of Hydrogen and Helium at extremely high temperatures, and still forms the basis of the active suns in our universe. The temperature is maintained by nuclear reaction as Hydrogen is converted into heavier elements. This is the symbolic province of the planet Pluto (Regeneration). Lower down The Tree of Life Sagittarius is ruled by Jupiter (Expansion) which is similar in activity but merely expands what is already existing, rather than creating something new.

The Kabbalah : Sephirah 2 (Chockmah. Wisdom. Force. Number 1. Pluto)

Sephirah 2 (Chockmah. Force. Consciousness. God) is the pure energy released by the appearance of a Singularity at the time of The Big Bang which is still expanding our universe. Together with Sephirah 3 (Binah. Form. The Unconscious. Saturn/Satan) we have Einstein's relativity that states Energy and Matter are (different forms of) the same thing. $E=MC^2$

GENESIS AND THE CYCLE OF GROWTH

Tarot Card : XIV. Temperance

We have Separation and Mixing. (temperance="moderation". "mixing")

The image is of an angel with one foot in water, the other on earth, mixing water between 2 jars. Tossing ideas in the mind to and fro. (fluttering ? evening ?). The "angel" is a representation of The Tree of Life. We have 3 levels of activity in descending order:-

1. The Energy in the mind of the angel (its halo).
2. The activity of the 2 cups.
3. The Water and Earth at "the bottom".

The sperm finds its distant target, and penetrates the egg which begins to adapt. The sperm dies. The process of cell division begins. Although the traditional description of Temperance relates to "mixing", our Stage 9 also suggests "separation" – which is emphasised by the image in the next card, The Devil.

THE CALENDAR TIME

That of foretelling the coming birth of Jesus . The Magi see a new star in the East. The Virgin Birth. Conceptions, or "virgin births", occur in the Mind.

We now have our first binary separation.

DAY 1. CYCLE OF GROWTH STAGE 10 (PEAK. AMBITION)

Having first perceived "Light" the still existing original Stage Zero - Darkness - also becomes conscious, so both states can now be named (given form as a mental concept). An "even-ing" occurs as each separate manifestation takes its place in consciousness – AND IS NAMED. We have simple "Black and White" thinking.

Verse 4: And God seeth the light that [it is] good, and God separateth between the light and the darkness,

Verse 5: and God calleth to the light `Day,' and to the darkness He hath called `Night;' and there is an evening, and there is a morning – day one.

It seems that even God has materialistic ambition. Is this prompted by his Jungian 'Shadow' (Satan. The Devil)? We note that Darkness and Light are related to the 2 faces of The Devil – the "Fallen Angel" Saturn/Satan, and Lucifer "Bringer of Light". Sephirah 3 (Binah. Understanding) repeats the latter association.

The 2nd. Level of [THE KABBALAH TREE OF LIFE] is the separation of Sephiroth 2 (Wisdom. Force) at the top of The Pillar of Force, and 3 (Understanding. Form) at the top of The Pillar of Form out of 1 (Kether The Crown) at the top of The Middle Pillar. We now have more "physical" representations, or conceptions, of Light and Dark – IN CONSCIOUNESS. The idea is not the "thing".

Zodiac Sign : Capricorn

Cardinal (creative. active) Earth. Ruled by Saturn/Satan. The Mountain Goat (climber) – using earth to ascend to heaven – and also suggesting the next Tarot card which contains "The Tower of Babel", built for the same purpose. The search for "Stardom" on Earth. "Long range plans". The symbol of The Goat with a fish's tail suggests its unconscious connotations.

Capricorn is a desire for material and social achievement (Harvest. Social Status). Later on, after creating the Earth, God seems to require obedience from - or later in the time of Moses and The Commandments, worship - by humans (Capricorn), rather than just their company – which was the stated original reason (Conception) for our creation. It shows how high ideals can be modified when coming down to practical reality. This concept is entirely in keeping with Capricorn.

In the cycle of a year Capricorn is the time of the Winter Solstice celebration of the rebirth of the SUN - and the Christmas birth of the SON of God. The promise of new life to come.

Tarot Card : XV. The Devil (Dark) – Unconscious

The Devil image is that of Inertia (Sephirah 3 - Binah. Form)– resistance to the movement of Change (Light. Consciousness of Cycle of Growth Stage 9). History shows how "The Establishment" has resisted the growth of Knowledge, and Science.

The Devil is Temptation to use spiritual energy for material purposes. Yet it seems necessary.

GENESIS AND THE CYCLE OF GROWTH

The Devil replaces the Temperance "angel" (so he has "fallen" – more explicit in the next card) the human figures replace the 2 cups of Temperance. He also has another function as Lucifer "Bringer of Light" – explicit in the next verses. The Devil is related to "the dark side of life". We note that there is no such "thing" as Darkness, so it can be considered as an "image" of No-Thing. Perhaps darkness can be considered as the "space" which gave rise to the Singularity of The Big Bang – or was the Singularity the "sperm", and Space the "egg"?

As mentioned above, it seems that The Devil is God's Jungian "Shadow". With the creation of Light Universal Law states that its complement must appear as well. As Darkness was there already, this seems to be an evolution in consciousness. We now get Day and Night. The Light has made the Darkness conscious too.

Tarot Card : XVI. The Tower (Light) – Conscious

The Tower is the result of "The Immovable Object" being the focus of "Irresistible Force" – something has "got to give".

A flash of lightning brings the 2 people "down to earth". The theories of Sagittarius must be proven by material evidence. They are the same ones depicted in The Devil card, now released from bondage. Realisation. A new spark of consciousness – not yet fully realised (= made real. materialised). Release from the bondage of a restricted viewpoint. Beware of what you wish for. You may get it. This is the other manifestation of Satan as Lucifer "The Bringer of Light". Is this the original "Fall" (to Earth) before Adam? Who fell ?

We have the beginning of "The Lightning Flash" of The Kabbalah Tree of Life.

There are stories of those who "do deals with The Devil" in return for their immortal soul – usually The Devil craftily gets the upper hand. For example, in one deal a man wishes to be the happiest man in the world with all his physical needs catered for – so The Devil makes him mad and he is sent to an asylum.

The Kabbalah Sephirah 3 (Binah. Understanding. Saturn/Satan. Number 2)

Sephirah 3 contains the Principle of Form and is at the head of The Pillar of Form.

CREATION DAY 1 – DAY AND NIGHT

1. From The Tarot association we can now associate this stage with the universal "Big Bang "- with the Singularity from Day 1 exploding into life. Somehow taking on a life of its own.
2. We have a "spark" of Consciousness that may develop into material form. A "New Year Resolution".
3. In terms of [THE KABBALAH TREE OF LIFE] this is the creation of the complementary Twin Pillars of Mercy (Force. Positive) and Severity (Form. Negative) - as distinct from The Middle Pillar with Kether (Crown. Zero) at the top, where everything is in balance.

Consciousness and Unconsciousness. Good and Evil. Continuing the theme of division and separation, this refers to everything we recognise by pairs of "opposites", which are really complements. One cannot exist without the other. This is an example of the law – repeated numerous times - which states that if something is created its complement must come into being too, so the sum is always Zero – keeping the Universe in balance, as it was originally. Each day of Creation ends with an "even-ing".

We therefore have the basic Cycle of Growth divided into 2 parts. We have the idea of "taking turns", and the beginning of linear Time. Dark and Light cannot re-unite, so they each have their separate times which they rule – making the first Day (Cycle of Time). At one level – Consciousness (awake) and Unconsciousness (asleep).

CYCLE OF GROWTH STAGE 11 (DISSATISFACTION)

This Stage covers Creation Day 2 to Day 6 which eventually sees the creation of land animals and man – but not yet Adam ("the man"). This coincides with the traditional function of Aquarius that is concerned with "Invention".

At this level of development there is no Ego Consciousness and no Free Will (everything is controlled by God), so Cycle of Growth Stage 11 (Discontent. Aquarius. Uranus) is under the rulership of Saturn (Binah. Form).

Daath, the previously un-numbered Sephirah which relates to Uranus ("Sky") does not yet exist either – although Day 2 suggests its appearance in embryo form.

CREATION DAY 2 – SEPARATION OF THE WATERS. HEAVEN

Once again we return to the "waters" that existed at Creation Day Zero (Verse 2).

GENESIS AND THE CYCLE OF GROWTH

This gives credence to the Jungian concept of the Collective Unconscious "sea" as the prime source of everything. We note that, as indicated by Edgar Cayce and The Kabbalah, there is nothing material until Chapter 2. Until then, everything is at a psychological or mental level.

*Verse 6: And God saith, `Let an expanse be in the midst of the waters, and let it be separating between waters and waters.'

*Verse 7: And God maketh the expanse, and it separateth between the waters which [are] under the expanse, and the waters which [are] above the expanse: and it is so.

*Verse 8: And God calleth to the expanse `Heavens;' and there is an evening, and there is a morning – day second.

We now have 3 levels :-
1. Water above The Expanse, which is the (unused) original source (Sephirah 1. Kether. Crown. Neptune. The Collective Unconscious).
2. The Expanse – which is "Heavens" (Element Air. Daath). Another "form" of NoThing.
3. Water below The Expanse – which is also of the original source and, by further separation, to become Earth (Element Earth) and Sea (Element Water) on Creation Day 3.

The Fire Element appeared at Sephirah 2 (Chockmah. Force. Pluto. Plasma. Hydrogen) and is being converted to lower Elements. So prima materia - the original "waters" - also contains Fire.

We note that "above" and "below" are relative terms which, at lower levels, manifest in different places. At this level they co-exist in the same "space" at different frequencies of vibration like - but not the same as – Plasma (Fire of Earth), Gas (Air of Earth), Liquid (Water of Earth), Solid (Earth of Earth). That is, different frequencies of vibration of the same "thing".

Zodiac Sign : Aquarius

(Fixed Air). The Water Carrier. (Communication. Invention. Rebellion)

Uranus, planet ruler of Aquarius, which means "Sky" (Heaven).

We are told that this makes Heaven – which fits in with the symbolism of Aquarius, which is ruled by the planet Uranus, meaning "Sky" or "Heaven". Aquarius rules communication using audible or electronic "Air Waves". In many ways Air and electromagnetic waves act like fluids – and therefore water. Here Aquarius has its traditional ruler Saturn. As yet there is no possibility of Uranus (Will) becoming active as matters take their natural course. Saturn wins.

Edgar Cayce likened the process of an idea becoming material reality to pouring material into a mould.

Tarot Card : XVII. The Star

We now have a sequence of Tarot cards that actually depict stages in Evolution. However, they are not in the same sequence as the scientific account, and the meanings of which are not clear in relation to the traditional ones. It would seem that more study is required.

To begin with, XVII.The Star clearly depicts "separation of the waters".

The image is of a "Water Carrier" figure, like Temperance, with one foot in Water, the other on Earth. Temperance was tossing water from one cup to another (an initial separation) and refers to the "ruffling of waters" at the beginning of Creation. The two containers are now being emptied, one into water, the other on to the earth. The "separation of the waters" is occurring. The Star in the background now has a more geometric, material, form.

The image is very similar to that of "The Water Carrier" symbol of the 11th. Zodiac Sign of Aquarius.

Tarot Card : XVIII. The Moon

This card, and The Sun following, appear to be out of sequence compared to the scientific story of evolution where heavenly bodies were created 4.6 million years ago as matter began to cool and solidify.

(Ruler of Night. The Unconscious Mind. The Soul. Before the Dawn). Water creatures begin to evolve further and move on to land. The "Dark Night of the Soul". The Temptation of Jesus in the wilderness. Nightmares.

GENESIS AND THE CYCLE OF GROWTH

We are reminded that, at some stage in evolution, sea creatures began to move on to land. Human foetuses still develop gills that later disappear.

Tarot Card : XIX. The Sun
(Ruler of Day. The Conscious Mind. The Spirit. The Dark Night of the Soul is past). The image of a child on a horse (controlling the "animal"). On the first Palm Sunday, just after his temptation, Jesus rode into Jerusalem on a donkey to be welcomed by the crowd (a short time before his crucifixion).

The Kabbalah (Daath. Uranus)
Is only in embryo form, and therefore has no effect.

THE TIME :

Winter. Not much life on earth. The time of the Christian fast of Lent, commemorating the 40 days and nights temptation of Jesus by Satan in the wilderness before his entry into Jerusalem. (Which may also relate to the 40 week Gestation in the womb).

CREATION DAY 3 – EARTH AND SEA. VEGETATION.

The work of Tarot Card XIV.The Star is completed when the water from one cup reaches the earth, and the other cup reaches the water.

*Verse 9: And God saith, `Let the waters under the heavens be collected unto one place, and let the dry land be seen:' and it is so.

*Verse 10: And God calleth to the dry land `Earth,' and to the collection of the waters He hath called `Seas;' and God seeth that [it is] good.

Water and Earth are both negative Elements.

*Verse 11: And God saith, `Let the earth yield tender grass, herb sowing seed, fruit-tree (whose seed [is] in itself) making fruit after its kind, on the earth:' and it is so.

*Verse 12: And the earth bringeth forth tender grass, herb sowing seed after its kind, and tree making fruit (whose seed [is] in itself) after its kind; and God seeth that [it is] good;

*Verse 13: and there is an evening, and there is a morning – day third.

This is a further "separation of the waters" from Creation Day 2

We have to note that Chapter 2 Verse 5 after Creation Day 7 explicitly states that **"and no shrub of the field is yet in the earth"**.

CREATION DAY 4 – STARS – SUN – MOON

*Verse 14: And God saith, `Let luminaries be in the expanse of the heavens, to make a separation between the day and the night, then they have been for signs, and for seasons, and for days and years,

*Verse 15: and they have been for luminaries in the expanse of the heavens to give light upon the earth:' and it is so.

*Verse 16: And God maketh the two great luminaries, the great luminary for the rule of the day, and the small luminary – and the stars – for the rule of the night;

*Verse 17: and God giveth them in the expanse of the heavens to give light upon the earth,

*Verse 18: and to rule over day and over night, and to make a separation between the light and the darkness; and God seeth that [it is] good;

*Verse 19: and there is an evening, and there is a morning – day fourth.

Although slightly out of step with the scientific description of evolution, we are still fairly well synchronised with the Tarot with XVII.The Star, XVIII. The Moon, and XIX. The Sun. Although I put The Sun into Cycle of Growth

Stage 12, it can be considered to be in Stage 11 too. The Sun is one specific Star, symbol of Consciousness. In terms of The Cycle of Growth, The Sun does not begin development until Stage 5 (Power. Ego Consciousness). Stage 11 and Stage 5 are on opposite sides of the "wheel".

At Level 4 of [THE KABBALAH TREE OF LIFE] Sephirah 6 (Tiphareth. Beauty. The Sun) is related to the Astrological Sun on the Middle Pillar. The Heart Chakra.

We also have the concept of the ability to measure Time and the beginning of Astrology.

CREATION DAY 5 – FISH AND BIRDS.

Verse 20: And God saith, `Let the waters teem with the teeming living creature, and fowl let fly on the earth on the face of the expanse of the heavens.'

Verse 21: And God prepareth the great monsters, and every living creature that is creeping, which the waters have teemed with, after their kind, and every fowl with wing, after its kind, and God seeth that [it is] good.

Verse 22: And God blesseth them, saying, `Be fruitful, and multiply, and fill the waters in the seas, and the fowl let multiply in the earth:'

Verse 23: and there is an evening, and there is a morning – day fifth.

In line with Evolution, the creation of more complex water creatures followed that of the plants. The development of a human foetus includes a fishlike stage, with gills that eventually disappear, a birdlike stage, and an apelike stage with a tail that disappears. In line with the concept of gradually increasing material density, the creation of animals starts with Air and Water. Earth follows.

CREATION DAY 6 – LAND CREATURES. THE MAN. MALE AND FEMALE

Verse 24: And God saith, `Let the earth bring forth the living creature after its kind, cattle and creeping thing, and beast of the earth after its kind:' and it is so.

Verse 25: And God maketh the beast of the earth after its kind, and the cattle after their kind, and every creeping thing of the ground after its kind, and God seeth that [it is] good.

Verse 26: And God saith, `Let Us make man in Our image, according to Our likeness, and let them rule over fish of the sea, and over fowl of the heavens, and over cattle, and over all the earth, and over every creeping thing that is creeping on the earth.'

"Us" is an interesting suggestion of multiple creators. "In our image" again suggests development from a prior plan, or conception – which is the Creation Day Zero Neptune image of The Tree of Life at Sephirah 1 (Kether. Crown. Number Zero). It also suggests that things are not fully material yet – only images.

Verse 27: And God prepareth the man in His image; in the image of God He prepared him, a male and a female He prepared them.

The beginning of Sexual Reproduction instead of cloning of cells by division enabled diversification of species. There is no "woman" until Eve appears in Chapter 2.

Verse 28: And God blesseth them, and God saith to them, `Be fruitful, and multiply, and fill the earth, and subdue it, and rule over fish of the sea, and over fowl of the heavens, and over every living thing that is creeping upon the earth.'

Verse 29: And God saith, `Lo, I have given to you every herb sowing seed, which [is] upon the face of all the earth, and every tree in which [is] the fruit of a tree sowing seed, to you it is for food;

Verse 30: and to every beast of the earth, and to every fowl of the heavens, and to every creeping thing on the earth, in which [is] breath of life, every green herb [is] for food:' and it is so.

Verse 31: And God seeth all that He hath done, and lo, very good; and there is an evening, and there is a morning -- day the sixth.

GENESIS AND THE CYCLE OF GROWTH

CYCLE OF GROWTH STAGE 12 (WITHDRAWAL. CONFINEMENT)

GENESIS CHAPTER 2 – RESTING FOLLOWED BY THE GARDEN OF EDEN

CREATION DAY 7 – RESTING (ANOTHER EVEN-ING)

We note that Creation took 6 days and there is no human yet.

Chapter 2 : Verse 1: And the heavens and the earth are completed, and all their host;

Verse 2: and God completeth by the seventh day His work which He hath made, and ceaseth by the seventh day from all His work which He hath made.

Verse 3: And God blesseth the seventh day, and sanctifieth it, for in it He hath ceased from all His work which God had prepared for making.

Verse 4: These [are] births of the heavens and of the earth <u>in their being prepared</u>, in the day of Jehovah God's making earth and heavens;

Verse 5: and no shrub of the field is yet in the earth, and no herb of the field yet sprouteth, for Jehovah God hath not rained upon the earth, and a man there is not to serve the ground,

This Stage in the Cycle of Growth is that of the time when the mother becomes confined to the home in preparation for the birth of her child. The child has developed "in secret" and is ready to show itself (come to consciousness) in the world.

In The Bible we have a similar scenario where God rests – which gave rise to the traditional Christian day of rest each Sunday. This also corresponds with the concept of "even-ing" of a daily cycle.

In keeping with Edgar Cayce's information, actual physical manifestation has not yet occurred. Everything preceding has been preparation and planning. There is no material Man or Woman yet, despite now having male and female ! There was a stage in early evolution when sexual reproduction began for the first time in plants and animals. Prior to that the method was by cell division (into identical cloned pairs).

Although both sets of sexual organs begin to develop in the womb, a foetus does not physically become of male or female sex until later in pregnancy. The physical organs (Chakras) do not become active until children reach 3 to 4 years of age.

We see the evolutionary concept of man "ruling" the lower animals – that is, the animal parts of self. The 4 Elements. The lower Chakras.

Zodiac Sign : Pisces

Mutable (adapting. Changing) Water. The Fishes. The Sea. Collective humanity. The Collective Unconscious. Humanity as a whole.

Tarot Card : XX. Judgement

Image of humans appearing from "tombs" under the earth. Answering the "Call" of the trumpet. New life. Escape from bondage. Vocation. Release from confinement (including that of the womb). Rebirth.

Tarot Card : XXI. The World

The World is a transition stage between Cycle of Growth Stage 12 (Confinement) and Stage 1 (Seed) as the birth of a child.

The picture is of an androgynous figure moving forward through a "doorway". Although present, our sex organs do not begin to develop functionally until The Cycle of Growth Stage 4 (Transplanting) and afterwards– (Freud's Phallic stage 3 to 6 years of age, Erikson's Play Age). We now have the end of one cycle and the beginning of a new cycle within The Cycle of Growth. The gateway of birth. Leaving the womb. At the conclusion of this human stage we have the "breaking of the waters" and an "individual" person coming out of the "sea" of the Collective to undertake new and more personal experiences in a physical world.

GENESIS AND THE CYCLE OF GROWTH

The Kabbalah Sephirah 4 (Chesed. Mercy. Jupiter. Number 3)
Cycle of Growth Stage 12 is here ruled by traditional Jupiter.

CYCLE OF GROWTH STAGE 1 (SEED)

We are now leaving the 1st. Octave of the Logarithmic Timescale which is concerned with the manufacture of the human body in the womb defined by past evolution, and entering the 2nd. Octave of development concerned with the birth of a child and its "appearance" on Earth, and later development in terms of learning to control its body and mind as an infant.

We note that, in human terms, this is a repetition of the 1st. Octave pattern in that organs continue to develop in the same order that they were created. We can see that this makes sense in that The Cycle of Growth Stages continue in the same order of The 4 Elements – Fire, Earth, Air, Water.

Having developed a physical "vehicle" in which to travel Earth, we now enter a stage of psychological development to be able to control the "vehicle" by using the mind. At the end of this 2nd. Octave we will also have developed another psychological "vehicle" - which is the Persona, "shell", or "mask," that enables us to function in a wider society outside the family home.

In terms of planetary evolution, although the Earth was present as a blob of molten rock, it was still not in a state that would sustain any sort of life. The planet had to cool down to a temperature at which water is liquid – and maintain it. This property is extremely rare among universal bodies. But at least we now have Earth.

GENESIS : FORMATION OF "THE MAN"

*Chapter 2 : Verse 6: and a mist goeth up from the earth, and hath watered the whole face of the ground.

The sentence describes exactly what scientists today believe occurred. In the early evolution of the Earth it was too hot to have liquid water – even the rocks were partially liquid. The atmosphere actually came "up from the Earth". It was a mixture of water vapour and gases which were the result of volcanic activity. As Earth cooled to its present temperature there were thousands of years of rain which carried other dissolved elements and washed away chemical compounds to make seas of hot "primordial soup". In Chemistry, mixing chemicals in water enables many reactions which would otherwise not take place. The chemicals split into their positive and negative constituents, which, in effect, takes them back to a state similar to that before the elements differentiated. This stage in evolution eventually gave rise to simple carbon based chemical Amino Acids that can combine in numerous ways to make complex proteins. Here is our, and the Earth's, "first breath".

*Verse 7: And Jehovah God formeth the man – dust from the ground, and breatheth into his nostrils breath of life, and the man becometh a living creature.

Evolutionary theory suggests that, following the creation of the seas, the first life form on earth (Prokaryotes) was a hollow spherical cell membrane with no nucleus. Its hollow spherical form came about by water becoming attracted to the surface of minute colloidal particles of clay ("dust"). The membrane could then absorb chemicals from its surroundings. This has recently been reproduced under laboratory conditions. This was the original "seed shell".

In accordance with Cycle of Growth Stage 1 (Seed), we have the similar image of planting a seed.

We have the added symbolism of rebirth with the 1st. House/Ascendant of a Birth Chart "rising" on the Eastern horizon.

*Verse 8: And Jehovah God planteth a garden in Eden, at the east, and He setteth there the man whom He hath formed;

Astrology Log Timescale : Birth – 7 months
The first stage of Infancy. The child is pure Instinct (Intuition). There is no Thinking or Feeling Function and Sensation is at a very basic level.

Zodiac Sign : ARIES (The Pioneer) Planet : MARS (Personal Drive)
Cardinal Fire. Impulsive, instinctual energy. The Ram. Spring. The 1st. Octave also began with a Fire Sign – Sagittarius (Mutable, Changeable Fire) – the state of superheated Plasma, or "disorganised energy". Now the energy is focused and directed towards survival.

GENESIS AND THE CYCLE OF GROWTH

Tarot Card : 0. The Fool
He enters a new world of which he has no knowledge or prior memory. He carries baggage of the past at the back of his head (unconscious), and is encouraged by a dog (animal instincts) - also from 'behind', in the unconscious – but nearer the earth.

Here we have association with Number Zero which began the 1st. Octave.

Tarot Card : I. The Magician
He has the power of Will to use the tools of Fire, Earth, Air, Water (Intuition, Sensation, Feeling, Thinking) on the table before him (Latin : mens = "mind". mensa= "table"). He waves his magic wand and objects (mental images) appear from "thin air". There is the suggestion of sensory or information input with the tools for data processing. Putting ideas to practical use. A potential for creativity but no actual results yet.

Here we have association with Number 1, which refers to Sephirah 2 (Chockmah. Force. Nuclear Energy) – albeit at a lower level.

The Kabbalah Sephirah 5 (Geburah Severity. Number 4. Mars)
The focus of energy on The Pillar of Form.

CYCLE OF GROWTH STAGE 2 (GERMINATION)

Now the Winter ice has melted, the application of water enables the seed to sprout and put down Roots into the Earth – which is being warmed by the Spring Sun. We note that, in the material world, this development is underground, not yet visible. This adds to the suggestion that, in the human world, we are dealing with <u>psychological, unconscious, development</u>. We have pictures in the mind taking form as new memories. The Earthy nature of the symbols suggests this occurs in the physical brain.

The child has left "The Garden of Eden" of its mother's womb, where all its needs were instantly gratified to enter a new "Garden of Eden" where there is a delay.

There is no actual physical human body until Adam and Eve get "coats of skin" [EC]– at Cycle of Growth Stage 4 (Transplanting) - which emphasises that we are dealing with psychological, rather than physical, development. The infant has no concept or mental image of its body yet – let alone sex.

We create our own "inner world" as a subjective version of the outer one – based on personal experience.

GENESIS : FORMATION OF THE GARDEN OF EDEN

Verse 9: and Jehovah God causeth to sprout from the ground every tree desirable for appearance, and good for food, and the tree of life in the midst of the garden, and the tree of knowledge of good and evil.

Verse 10: And a river is going out from Eden to water the garden, and from thence it is parted, and hath become four chief [rivers];

Verse 11: the name of the one [is] Pison, it [is] that which is surrounding the whole land of the Havilah where the gold [is],

Verse 12: and the gold of that land [is] good, there [is] the bdolach and the shoham stone;

Verse 13: and the name of the second river [is] Gihon, it [is] that which is surrounding the whole land of Cush;

Verse 14: and the name of the third river [is] Hiddekel, it [is] that which is going east of Asshur; and the fourth river is Phrat. (Euphrates [KJV])

Verse 15: And Jehovah God taketh the man, and causeth him to rest in the garden of Eden, to serve it, and to keep it.

There is agreement among scholars that the 4 rivers refer to the Fertile Crescent nowadays bounded by the Tigris and Euphrates rivers, where Cain settled after his expulsion from The Garden of Eden, and where he became the founder of a new group of people which eventually grew to become the first civilisation in

GENESIS AND THE CYCLE OF GROWTH

Mesopotamia. However, the other 2 rivers no longer exist, although aerial searches have suggested the possibility of dried out water courses.

We note the association with archetypal Number 4, suggesting the development of the Jungian 4 Psychological Functions - Intuition (Fire), Sensation (Earth), Thinking (Air), Feeling (Water) – which, in turn, relate to the 4 Stages of each of the 3 Octaves of The Cycle of Growth. Here, the "rivers" become "streams", or flows, of psychological (Water) energy.

GENESIS CONTINUED

"Jehovah God" creates the Garden of Eden in the East (from where the Sun rises - The Ascendant beginning of the 1st. House is the East of the Birth Chart) into which he puts "the man" with two additional trees – 'The Tree Of Knowledge Of Good and Evil' and 'The Tree of Life'. It seems necessary to "re-create" all the plants and animals here. "The man" is creating a mental image of the world, and eventually putting himself there too – when he becomes Adam.

The Garden of Eden is a complex symbol that can be interpreted at several levels. It can be considered to represent such things as the human body, The Chakra system of endocrine glands, a child's early family home, or the human brain. Edgar Cayce states that The Tree of Life refers to the system of physical hormone-producing endocrine glands that control all of our body functions. In turn, the endocrine glands are related to the Chakras, or energy centres of the body. [THE CHAKRAS]. By choosing The Tree of Knowledge instead of The Tree of Life we have lost conscious control of the Chakras, and so the body gradually deteriorates and dies instead of being regenerated. By choosing sexual reproduction instead we have lost the ability to regenerate at a personal level. Edgar Cayce states that at the time of Atlantis (which is also a representation of The Garden of Eden [EC]) men lived for thousands of years.

Psychologists say that the early relationship of a child with its parents is as if they are "Godlike" figures with the power of life or death, supplying its every need – but demanding obedience in return. There is also the tendency for the child to consider itself as godlike at this age (psychological 'Inflation'). It achieves "godhood" by disobeying, and thus becoming equal to, "God". At this stage the Jungian 4 Functions are not differentiated. The experience of the infant is of pure Fire energy – animal Instinct. Intuition. The child is also developing a psychological inner world.

Astrology Log timescale Age 7 months – 1 year 8 months.

Psychologists do not recognise this as a separate stage in human development. It is included in Freud's first, Oral, stage – Erikson's Infancy. Erikson's Infancy Stage includes our Cycle of Growth Stage 1 and Stage 2. (Autonomy vs. Shame/Doubt).

This stage concerns development of conscious recognition of the mother, and, later, other parental persons - as well as learning to control a physical body.

Zodiac Sign : TAURUS. Planet : VENUS (Feeling. Desire)

Fixed Earth. The most material and stable Sign. Possessions. Physical Resources of Body, Talents, and money. Seeds are germinating deep in the earth. Taurus, as the most stable Earth Sign, is that of the "immovable object" resisting the "irresistible force" of the Aries Ram. The result of this challenge is physical Growth. Taurus is a Feminine, Negative, Sign.

Here we have association with Sephirah 3 (Binah. Form. Number 3) which has the same dynamic. Here the Earth Body resists the child until it learns to use it by an act of Will.

The Tarot now has 2 feminine, receptive, watery, images.

Tarot Card : II. The Priestess

The virgin priestess with potential resources to mate with any masculine force (The Magician) and produce fruits accordingly (The Empress). She is the "blank sheet" - the brain - ready to record any information. The computer hard drive. The Personal Unconscious.

Tarot Card : III. The Empress

We note there is a river in the background in accordance with the Genesis text. The single source is separating into 4 channels.

GENESIS AND THE CYCLE OF GROWTH

Mother Nature. Growth. The Priestess has become impregnated and is (NB !) pregnant in the image. The event of the Original Conception is being repeated at another level – within the human mind. A New World is taking form. The Garden of Eden on Earth (The family home and unconscious mind).

From a state of being asleep, unconscious, most of the time, the child is becoming conscious of the daily rhythms of its body and mind – which mimics the daily rhythm of the Earth's day.

CYCLE OF GROWTH STAGE 3 (EXPERIMENT.COMMUNICATION)

We begin mental development – in particular, the Thinking Function. Words.

We now have Masculine Tarot images here. The child recognises father figures with a function distinct from that of the mother, and receives simple instructions . The text shows the importance of naming things at this stage of a child's growth. That is, the formation of mental structures – ideas – that can be communicated to others. A Name is a mental equivalent of a physical object. It is also the beginning of self-realisation. If I have a name, I exist - "I am".

GENESIS : TREE OF KNOWLEDGE. NAMING OF ANIMALS. CREATION OF EVE

The man is forbidden to eat the fruit from the Tree of Knowledge with the warning that if he does he will die. Children do not fully recognise that many parental commands are for their own protection. Their understanding is not developed enough for them to be given reasons. Here is correspondence with the power and authority of The Emperor, and The Hierophant passing down "the Law of God". We note that, despite common belief, there is no mention of an apple.

The "knowledge" referred to clearly has a basic sexual meaning, as we shall see later on. This is borne out by Jung's concept that a man has to re-discover his inner feminine Anima in the process of Individuation following the Mid Life Crisis. Until this time he is "split" internally, and the image is projected on to (external) women as a (missing) object of desire (Venus). With women it is her masculine Animus that is projected on to men. However, in The Cycle of Growth it also includes any strong attraction to material things generally.

>*Verse 16: And Jehovah God layeth a charge on the man, saying, `Of every tree of the garden eating thou dost eat;*

>*Verse 17: and of the tree of knowledge of good and evil, thou dost not eat of it, for in the day of thine eating of it – dying thou dost die.'*

>*Verse 18: And Jehovah God saith, `Not good for the man to be alone, I do make to him an helper – as his counterpart.'*

>*Verse 19: And Jehovah God formeth from the ground every beast of the field, and every fowl of the heavens, and bringeth in unto the man, to see what he doth call it; and whatever the man calleth a living creature, that [is] its name. [YLT]*

>*Verse 20: And the man calleth names to all the cattle, and to fowl of the heavens, and to every beast of the field; and to man hath not been found an helper – as his counterpart. [YLT]*

Adam's first task is to give names to every living creature. In the King James Bible he also finally gets his name. (Young's Literal Translation differs from The King James Bible in not giving Adam's name until later on when he "knows" Eve to give birth to Seth).

>*Verse 20 : And Adam gave names to all cattle, and to the fowl of the air, and to every beast of the field; but for Adam there was not found an help meet for him.[KJV]*

It seems that, originally, God expected these creatures to be companions for Adam, but somehow it did not work out. Pets are not necessarily a good substitute for other humans. So God made a mistake ? (It is clear that God does make mistakes. There is admission in The New Testament that the second Covenant (this is the first, equally one-sided "Covenant") made with Moses was not working, which required the incarnation of Jesus with a new Covenant. As usual, we humans are blamed).

We are, however, reminded that every act of creation requires the creation of a "counterpart" to maintain the universal Zero Balance.

GENESIS AND THE CYCLE OF GROWTH

Astrology Log Timescale 1year 8 months to 3 years 6 months

We have Freud's Anal stage, Erikson's Early Childhood, concerned with learning control of the human body and objects in the immediate environment.

Zodiac Sign : GEMINI. Planet : Mercury (Mind)

Mutable (adaptable) Air. The Sign is concerned, among other things, with mental development and communication. "The Twins" Castor and Pollux are both male, suggesting two equal principles (complements) originating from the same "root" with the creation of tension/attraction between them. This fits in with the creation of Eve from "the man". Although there was "male and female" from Creation Day 6, there is no "woman" until now.

Children of this age do not yet recognise "man" as different to "woman".

Another twin relationship (marriage) is a physical object and its name – combining Sensation and Thinking levels of perception.

Tarot Card : IV. The Emperor

He rules by established power without reason or explanation. "Do as you are told". A Father Figure. Traditionally and psychologically a "godlike" personality. For example, The Roman emperors were regarded as "gods" by the population.

Tarot Card : V. The Hierophant

We note that this card is very similar in appearance to that of The Devil. The Hierophant rules according to rules and laws and intellectually with words. ("Do because I know better"). He is a teacher of moral law and defines (Twin Pillars of) "opposites" such as "Good and Evil" – thereby perpetuating the Original Sin of Knowledge of Good and Evil. History shows us how one person's "good" can be another's "evil" – especially when motivated by a religion.

We are now in the realm of Thinking, Ideas, and Words – which are mental representations of the world around, as distinct from the actual reality. Names. He relates to the Transactional Analysis concept of "The Parent". [PSYCHOLOGY : DEVELOPMENT MODELS].

You will remember we started the Creation with "God" who became "Jehovah God" (KJV "LORD God"). We now have "Jehovah" " (KJV LORD - Law) as the "NAME of God" developed to differentiate the One God from the numerous other "gods" of the time. The use of a child's first name is of identical purpose. We see something like a (child of) Smith becoming "John Smith", later to have a personal identity separate from his parents as just "John" – especially outside the home.

GENESIS : THE CREATION OF EVE – WOMAN

This stage gives an interesting insight into the symbols of this Stage 3 of The Cycle of Growth, and the next. Here we have relationship with the Gemini Twins – who are of the same sex (or sexless). We have the implication here that Adam and Eve are created as equal "twins" until the "Knowledge" of Stage 4 (Transplanting).

The next act of God was to create Eve as a companion to Adam. Although the King James Bible says from Adam's "rib", Young's Literal Translation from the Greek repeats "counterpart". Some modern scholars suggest the word "side" or bias is a better translation, as Eve was created as an equal (and later demoted) . Once again we have the concept of creation of "opposites" which is repeated throughout the story of Creation. We can add to the interpretation the idea that this can also mean "bias" in that Eve as a female complemented Adam's masculine bias (in accordance with universal law that if anything is created its complement comes into being to keep the "Zero Total" balance). The method required that Adam be put into "a deep sleep" (unconsciousness) so that part of him could be separated out. Undivided "male and female" from Creation Day 6 now becomes more physical "man" and "woman". <u>The text does not explicitly state that Adam returned to consciousness – confirming Jung's concept of a man's unconscious Anima.</u> This suggests that in getting an external counterpart he loses sight (consciousness) of his own, inner, feminine Anima. We again remind ourselves that, according to Cayce, we are still dealing with non-material beings. However, we are learning that things can be both Conscious and Unconscious (as "counterparts").

GENESIS AND THE CYCLE OF GROWTH

A "counterpart" is in keeping with Jung's concept of the Anima which is the PERSONAL inner complement to whatever a man considers masculine. The Anima and Animus to some degree are personal. We again see an example of the Universal Law that once something is created its complement comes into being soon after (the sum total is Zero).

*Verse 21: And Jehovah God causeth a deep sleep to fall upon the man, and he sleepeth, and He taketh one of his ribs, and closeth up flesh in its stead.

*Verse 22: And Jehovah God buildeth up the rib which He hath taken out of the man into a woman, and bringeth her in unto the man;

*Verse 23: and the man saith, `This [is] the [proper] step! bone of my bone, and flesh of my flesh!' for this it is called Woman, for from a man hath this been taken;

(suggesting a contraction of Womb + Man).

"Eve" is not named by Adam until after the Temptation in Verse 20 of the next chapter.

We next see the creation of fathers and mothers. This, again, fits in with our development at this age when the child learns the different roles they perform, sexual and otherwise, and therefore its own expected role. One game played now is "Mothers and Fathers". "Only girls play with dolls."

*Verse 24: therefore doth a man leave his father and his mother, and hath cleaved unto his wife, and they have become one flesh.

"Cleave" means "split apart" as well as "stick fast, adhere" [Oxford Dictionary]. There is no mention of a woman leaving her parents. "they have become one flesh" suggests that the text is not referring to separate people, in keeping with my psychological interpretation. We need to interpret at 2 levels. Aleister Crowley's Tarot Card "VI. The Lovers" [THE TAROT] depicts the dynamics very well.

*Verse 25: And they are both of them naked, the man and his wife, and they are not ashamed of themselves.

Too young for an actual wife at this Stage, this is clearly related to the current stage of development which is before a child is taught – explicitly, or implicitly from the reactions of those around - about the different sexes, and the related social taboos, as another step to recognising its separateness from other people – a sexual identity and role. Nevertheless, the "opposites" do have a relationship. Later on, the male child will seek his inner Anima in the external world by projecting it on to female figures.

We note that we cannot tell the sex of the subject of a Birth Chart – at that level men and women are identical. i.e. "Nature" – which gives us an insight into the later effect of "Nurture".

CYCLE OF GROWTH STAGE 4 (TRANSPLANTING. ROOTS)

This Stage is a "crisis stage" concerned with the necessity of breaking away from a stable position to take a step forward in development. Moving away from past conditions. Putting down new physical\psychological roots. At one level it could be considered as "moving house" – although the external act can occur anywhere else in the Cycle.

GENESIS CHAPTER 3 – "THE FALL"

We now have the story of the Temptation of Eve by the Serpent, and Adam by Eve. Many assume the Serpent to be The Devil in disguise, however there are additional considerations.

The Serpent has long been associated with Kundalini ("Serpent Fire") which is spiritual energy "coiled", or locked, at the base of the spine and is involved with the 7 Chakras energy centres (The Tree of Life).

We note that Freud stated that psychological problems were due to repressed sexual energy. He was living at a time when sex was a taboo subject, and people often married with no knowledge of the anatomy of the opposite sex. So their problems were at a very basic level. Later on, Jung took a more sophisticated approach and called it "Psychic Energy" which has connotations with the possibility of it taking different forms.

I therefore conclude that The Bible is merely describing what we experience as normal "arousal of energy" when confronted with an attractive member of the opposite sex. This is, in effect a "raising of Kundalini" (creative life force) – albeit to a relatively low level.

GENESIS AND THE CYCLE OF GROWTH

When we understand that The Tree of Life refers to the human Chakra system, we recognise that there is only 1 Tree, not 2. The difference is how the creative energy is used. We learn in Genesis that the Tree of Life Chakra\endocrine system is sealed because the energy was used for sexual "knowledge" rather than spiritual purposes which requires Regeneration of self by successive physical incarnations. In the biblical book of Revelation we have an account of the opening of Chakras. The writer may be the same John that wrote this, which, as we can now see, has nothing to do with snakes :-

* John Chapter 3, Verse 14: And as Moses lifted up the serpent in the wilderness, even so must the Son of man be lifted up:

* John Chapter 3, Verse 15: That whosoever believeth in him should not perish, but have eternal life. [KJV]

We can see that the earlier separation into Adam and Eve - physical and unconscious counterparts - produces a powerful attractive force between the sets of positive and negative polarities. Both unconsciously trying to rediscover their "missing" parts in the external world. Anyone who has "fallen" in love will have experienced this almost irresistible force.

We have yet another example of something created in the universe giving rise to the creation of its counterpart\complement to maintain Zero Balance. The tension is an attempt to return the separate energies to the original Zero balance.

"Jehovah God" banishes them from the Garden of Eden. There are some strange incidents where JG does not seem to know what is going on. The Cycle of Growth theme of Transplanting is clearly in evidence as they are both ejected from the Garden. Adam and Eve, now having their complementary counterpart split away, begin to feel the tension of the attraction of the "opposite" polarities created. We therefore see the Serpent as a symbolic representation of sexual attraction (or, indeed, the focus of Desire – Venus - on any material object). Each is "the apple of the eye" of the other – although The Bible says "fruit" which contains a less objective meaning covering numerous interpretations. We note that, usually, to produce a fruit requires a form of sexual reproduction. A fruit contains seeds of new growth.

We see the same scenario repeated in childhood development when a child flirts with the parent of the opposite sex and is rejected, and therefore forced to find the "missing part" elsewhere – outside the original home.

*Verse 1: And the serpent hath been subtile above every beast of the field which Jehovah God hath made, and he saith unto the woman, `Is it true that God hath said, Ye do not eat of every tree of the garden?'

(Young's English equivalent for "subtile" as used here is "crafty". The Serpent is activating unconscious desires in a similar way that sex (and other unconscious motivations) are used in advertising today.)

*Verse 2: And the woman saith unto the serpent, `Of the fruit of the trees of the garden we do eat,

*Verse 3: and of the fruit of the tree which [is] in the midst of the garden God hath said, Ye do not eat of it, nor touch it, lest ye die.'

The next verse is suggestive of reincarnation ...

*Verse 4: And the serpent saith unto the woman, `Dying, ye do not die,

*Verse 5: for God doth know that in the day of your eating of it -- your eyes have been opened, and ye have been as God, knowing good and evil.'

*Verse 6: And the woman seeth that the tree [is] good for food, and that it [is] pleasant to the eyes, and the tree is desirable to make [one] wise, and she taketh of its fruit and eateth, and giveth also to her husband with her, and he doth eat;

*Verse 7: and the eyes of them both are opened, and they know that they [are] naked, and they sew fig-leaves, and make to themselves girdles.

We note the word "wise" has associations with Sephirah 2 (Chockmah. Wisdom. God Force. Love).
<u>This is in keeping with the Cycle of Growth Stage 4 relationship with Erikson's Play Age - when we first discover our sex organs, and learn that men and women are different.</u>

GENESIS AND THE CYCLE OF GROWTH

Being naked in a dream suggests that one is revealing one's inner self for all to see. Here the fig leaves are taking the place of the Persona mask. Later JG gives them "coats of skin" to cover themselves instead – at which time Cayce says they are now in physical form. This too could be symbolic of the Persona "mask". The fig is a sweet fruit (of The Tree of (sexual) Knowledge ?) containing hundreds of seeds (sperm?).

Astrology Log Timescale : 3 years 6 months – 7 years

We now have Freud's Phallic stage and Erikson's Play Age, which is primarily concerned with the discovery of our physical sexual organs. Erikson states the main dilemma to solve at this time is "Initiative versus Guilt". We have the Oedipus/Electra competition with the same sex parent for the attentions of the complementary sex parent. In mythology, Oedipus discovered that he had accidentally (unconsciously) married his mother after being separated from his early family. The main social environment is still within the immediate family, so, having discovered our own physical body in the previous stage, we become more aware of the surrounding environment in our gradual expansion of consciousness.

Zodiac Sign : CANCER. Planet : Moon (Home. Roots. Security. Mother. Personal Unconscious)

Cardinal (active) Water. The Crab. The Tortoise. The Chariot (Motor Car). Psychic self-defence. The Home. Roots. Security. The Mother. The Persona.

Here is a very complex set of symbols. In a Birth Chart the 4th. House, and the positions of the Sign of Cancer and the Moon, which has relationship as "ruler" of both, is an indicator of one's mother (please see the example Birth Chart analysis for Lady Diana Spencer). The Serpent\Scorpion (both poisonous) that appears here is also one of the symbols of the Sign of Scorpio (Fixed Water) concerned with Sex, and Death – stated in The Bible account as the penalty for disobedience. In addition we can take into account the complementary House and Sign on the opposite side of a Birth Chart. In this case it seems appropriate here to mention that our Cycle of Growth Stage 10 (Peak. Career) contains the Devil Tarot card. If we compare its image to that of The Hierophant, The Lovers, and The Chariot, there are distinct similarities. In our Genesis story the Serpent – Desire aroused - appears more or less openly.

Tarot Card : VI. The Lovers

Male and Female. Positive and negative polarity attracted by Desire. Early Tarot images show a man between two women, one old, one young, the man moving toward the younger - as if separating from the mother to his beloved. In the Oedipal battle the father (of a male child) should win, so the subject has to search elsewhere for his "missing" part. Cupid/Eros (root of "erotic") is above with bow and arrow. The Waite image is very like The Garden of Eden, with 2 trees hidden in the background. Aleister Crowley's card shows the Hierophant performing a "marriage" – the detail of which is a clearer depiction of what is happening at outer and inner levels.

On the surface it looks like the stage of life where, after teenage rebellion, a couple get married and leave their respective families. However, in our set of Stages in The Cycle of Growth this does not occur until later on (Stage 7). We are not yet fully in the physical world yet – so we remain with Oedipus as an interpretation.

Tarot Card : VII. The Chariot

The image depicts a male figure driving a vehicle drawn by two "animals". The vehicle has 4 pillars supporting an overhead canopy, so the driver is partially enclosed (in his shell/persona). The animals differ from one another. One is black, the other white. The rider has no reins to control them – it is as if he controls them with his mind. He has the wand or rod of The Magician and Emperor in his hand which symbolises Power and Will. In Waite's card he is leaving a village or city behind. It basically means "progress from the home into a wider world". Will in action.

'The Chariot' is a 2 wheeled vehicle requiring control of "opposing psychic forces" in order to make progress. The Cancer Crab has an external shell of protection which, apart from a house or home, symbolises the "persona" or "mask" used by actors in the past. The individual is taking on a new "role" in life. The child recognises "I am" and begins a wider experience outside the family home. A step forward in ego development. He has learned to keep some things secret from others in order to fit in. We note that, at this age, much depends on the situation in the family home – which may not relate to the "real world" out there.

GENESIS AND THE CYCLE OF GROWTH

Within the context of Genesis, we also see that this also means that the child has learned to control a physical body as a "vehicle", so it no longer needs conscious attention to move around – the same principle as learning to ride a bicycle, or drive a car.

THE PERSONA

in psychology, the personality that an individual projects to others, as differentiated from the authentic self. The term, coined by Carl Jung, is derived from the Latin persona, referring to the masks worn by Etruscan mimes. According to Jung, the persona enables an individual to interrelate with the world around him by reflecting the role in life that the individual is playing. In this way one can arrive at a compromise between one's innate psychological constitution and society. Thus the persona enables the individual to adapt to society's demands. [EB]

GENESIS : DISCOVERY AND BANISHMENT. EVE IS NAMED

A strange scenario - although, as a parent with 2 children, I can relate to it. JG seems to be discovering what any parent knows – if you want something done tell your children not to do it - and they are likely to blame one another when discovered. Omnipotent JG (who we are told elsewhere knows everything in our minds) cannot find them. Have they invented the game "Hide and Seek" as we play with our children? It all seems a bit hard, considering that JG's actions caused the tension in the first place.

*Verse 8: And they hear the sound of Jehovah God walking up and down in the garden at the breeze of the day, and the man and his wife hide themselves from the face of Jehovah God in the midst of the trees of the garden.

*Verse 9: And Jehovah God calleth unto the man, and saith to him, `Where [art] thou?'

*Verse 10: and he saith, `Thy sound I have heard in the garden, and I am afraid, for I am naked, and I hide myself.'

*Verse 11: And He saith, `Who hath declared to thee that thou [art] naked? of the tree of which I have commanded thee not to eat, hast thou eaten?'

*Verse 12: and the man saith, `The woman whom Thou didst place with me – she hath given to me of the tree – and I do eat.'

*Verse 13: And Jehovah God saith to the woman, `What [is] this thou hast done?' and the woman saith, `The serpent hath caused me to forget – and I do eat.'

*Verse 14: And Jehovah God saith unto the serpent, `Because thou hast done this, cursed [art] thou above all the cattle, and above every beast of the field: on thy belly dost thou go, and dust thou dost eat, all days of thy life;

*Verse 15: and enmity I put between thee and the woman, and between thy seed and her seed; he doth bruise thee – the head, and thou dost bruise him – the heel.'

*Verse 16: Unto the woman He said, `Multiplying I multiply thy sorrow and thy conception, in sorrow dost thou bear children, and toward thy husband [is] thy desire, and he doth rule over thee.'

*Verse 17: And to the man He said, `Because thou hast hearkened to the voice of thy wife, and dost eat of the tree concerning which I have charged thee, saying, Thou dost not eat of it, cursed [is] the ground on thine account; in sorrow thou dost eat of it all days of thy life,

From now on, sexual reproduction is the only way of replacing a human body, which wears out and dies. [EC] suggests that the reason for this is that it cuts short the length of time we are in a state of sin. We note that, in occult terms, a child is a physical representation of the abstract relationship between the 2 parents. In Numerological terms, 2 + 1 = Number 3.

*Verse 18: and thorn and bramble it doth bring forth to thee, and thou hast eaten the herb of the field;

GENESIS AND THE CYCLE OF GROWTH

Verse 19: by the sweat of thy face thou dost eat bread till thy return unto the ground, for out of it hast thou been taken, for dust thou [art], and unto dust thou turnest back.'

"The man" gives Eve (="life, life-giving") her name. I wonder if this also relates to "Eve – ening".

Adam continues his naming task. Eve is now a (named) physical object.

Verse 20: And the man calleth his wife's name Eve: for she hath been mother of all living.

We have another depiction of the feminine archetype which includes The Priestess, The Empress, Mother Earth, Mother Nature etc.

Verse 21: And Jehovah God doth make to the man and to his wife coats of skin, and doth clothe them.

The "man and his wife" are given "coats of skin" to replace their fig leaves. This gives rise to other interpretations :-

1. THE PHYSICAL BODY as a physical "vehicle". Edgar Cayce states that this mean that they were "clothed in flesh" and finally became material, physical, human beings. It is this covering\vehicle which dies because it is related to the animal world (Earth Element). Although Eve re-appears later on, the text does not explicitly say she is sent from the Garden too, which suggests she is Adam's unconscious Anima.
2. Once again we have a similar meaning to Chapter 2 Verse 24 *"therefore doth a man leave his father and his mother, and hath cleaved unto his wife, and they have become one flesh."*
3. THE PERSONA – a psychological "mask", "shell" or "vehicle" as described above.

Verse 22: And Jehovah God saith, `Lo, the man was as one of Us, as to the knowledge of good and evil; and now, lest he send forth his hand, and have taken also of the tree of life, and eaten, and lived to the age,'

Verse 23: Jehovah God sendeth him forth from the garden of Eden to serve the ground from which he hath been taken;

Adam has become "godlike" ("one of us") in his ability to create – entirely in keeping with the meaning of the next Cycle of Growth Stage 5 (Power. Creativity).

Adam has to leave "home" and find a job to support himself. Again, "the ground" also refers to the physical body. He is sent to the EAST of the garden where new cycles begin). Cycle of Growth Stage 5 is the beginning of the 3rd. Octave of the Logarithmic Timescale concerned with beginning to explore the world outside the family home at Age 7 until Death. After their inflated, episode of disobedience to God, and therefore becoming like "gods", they are brought back down to earth – to start again.

Verse 24: yea, he casteth out the man, and causeth to dwell at the east of the garden of Eden the cherubs and the flame of the sword which is turning itself round to guard the way of the tree of life.

THE CHERUBS OR CHERUBIM

Finally in this stage a guard is put on the Garden of Eden. That is, the Chakra\endocrine gland system is sealed. We have to wait until the last book in The Bible, Revelation, to have an example of the Seven Seals being reopened. The Cherubim re-appear in "The Vision of Ezekiel" and in Revelation when the Chakras are opened.

The Cherubim appear in various "disguises" in The Bible. We can reveal them by observing that they appear as various "sets of 4". They are depicted in the Tarot cards X.The Wheel of Fortune and XX.The World.

We therefore have a set of associations with Number 4 which reveal their hidden meaning :-

1. [THE 4 ELEMENTS] and [THE 4 FUNCTIONS]
2. The 4 lower Chakras.
3. Sephirah 5 (Severity. Mars)
4. etcetera

So the "sealing" is by where we focus our conscious attention, rather than deliberate closure.

This gives new meaning to the next Stage of The Cycle of Growth – which refers to Number 5, and which appears as a challenge to Number 4 [NUMEROLOGY]. Without Number 4, Number 5 would not exist. Number 5 is the dawning of Ego Consciousness which controls the lower 4 Elements.

GENESIS AND THE CYCLE OF GROWTH

CYCLE OF GROWTH STAGE 5 (POWER. CREATIVITY)

This Stage refers to The Sun and the development of Ego Consciousness.

We are now at the beginning of the 3rd. Octave of the Logarithmic Timescale. We reached the lowest part of "the wheel" in the previous Stage (Roots) and are now moving "upwards" in our journey. Observing closely, we see similarity with the theme of Adam's departure from The Garden of Eden. Jehovah God now becomes plain Jehovah (KJV "LORD") – which we take to mean the rule of LAW (Nature).

The story continues the theme of development in the home followed by experience of a gradually widening society outside the home, and finally leaving it.

We note another "binary" pairing of Cain and Abel with different, complementary, characteristics - which might give us a clue to the psychology at this age. There is focus in Genesis upon "the fruits of their labours" – that is, the choosing of an occupation to earn a living (after experimenting in Cycle of Growth Stage 5 (Creativity).

GENESIS CHAPTER 4 – CAIN AND ABEL

We note that we have the beginning of a new chapter in The Bible – as we have the beginning of a new "chapter" in The Cycle of Growth – The 3rd. Octave.

We see a similar theme with the dilemma of Cain in offering the fruits of his labour. We note that, in the story, Jehovah seems puzzled as to why Cain was upset and suggests that he was actually pleased that Cain had produced something.

We could read this in the light of an inner, psychological, choice that is made between different occupations. Here between a more practical one of "serving the ground" (farming ?) compared with "feeding a flock" – which, in Biblical terms, usually refers to some kind of ministry over people.

We also note the similarity of the theme repeated elsewhere in The Bible concerned with inheritances by the eldest son, and the story of The Prodigal Son where he leaves and wastes his inheritance. He finally returns and is received with great rejoicing, and "killing the fatted calf". His brothers who stayed behind and toed the line were most upset that they had not received such attention.

Although "knowing" is here given explicit sexual connotations, we have not yet reached the Stage 8 (Sex. Death. Intercourse) Stage of The Cycle of Growth. We therefore have an inner meaning which refers to Cycle of Growth Stage 5 (Personal Creativity. School Age).This could therefore have bearing on the psychological concept that we all have "Sub-Personalities" – that is, different Personas that play different roles on The Stage of Life.

> *Verse 1: And the man knew Eve his wife, and she conceiveth and beareth Cain, and saith, `I have gotten a man by Jehovah;'
>
> *Verse 2: and she addeth to bear his brother, even Abel. And Abel is feeding a flock, and Cain hath been servant of the ground.
>
> *Verse 3: And it cometh to pass at the end of days that Cain bringeth from the fruit of the ground a present to Jehovah;
>
> *Verse 4: and Abel, he hath brought, he also, from the female firstlings of his flock, even from their fat ones; and Jehovah looketh unto Abel and unto his present,
>
> *Verse 5: and unto Cain and unto his present He hath not looked; and it is very displeasing to Cain, and his countenance is fallen.
>
> *Verse 6: And Jehovah saith unto Cain, `Why hast thou displeasure? and why hath thy countenance fallen?
>
> *Verse 7: Is there not, if thou dost well, acceptance? and if thou dost not well, at the opening a sin-offering is crouching, and unto thee its desire, and thou rulest over it.'

Astrology Log Timescale : Age 7 to 13 years of age

We can see a parallel with the productivity of Cain and Abel being judged. This is Erikson's (Primary) School Age when there are no major physical changes. In the field of the local neighbourhood and school, the dilemma is "Industry versus Inferiority" with a fear of "not knowing how". The reward is "Competence". Work is put before pleasure. We are judged by what we produce or create – which is entirely in keeping with the story of Cain (the farmer) and Abel (keeper of sheep).

Zodiac Sign : LEO .   Planet : Sun (Ego Consciousness)

Fixed Fire. Instincts "lie fallow" – which is similar to the state of Aries (Cardinal Fire) when The Seed is planted in new ground and striving to germinate. This Cycle of Growth Stage, with its relationship to The Sun (Light) is an important step in the development of Ego Consciousness, and Will. "Fixed" Fire, creative energy, is under personal conscious control rather than being directed by parents.

The importance of the Stage is that this is the first step in the development of Ego Consciousness, with the need to make personal decisions. At base level, as we become personally creative in producing objects of our own making we become "co-creators with God".

Tarot Card : VIII. Strength

We have the Tarot image of a female figure controlling a lion. She has the Number 8 Infinity Sign of Higher Mind above her head. In the Agricultural Cycle we have the activity of The Sun (God) bringing forth new life on Earth – another form of "practical achievement" – albeit forced to abide by The Laws of Mother Nature and the annual cycle stages of The Zodiac.

CYCLE OF GROWTH STAGE 6 (SERVICE TO SELF. HEALTH)

We see relationship with Cycle of Growth Stage 3 (Mercury in Gemini. Mutable/Changeable) Air. The Hierophant. Age 2 to 4) and this stage –(Mercury in Virgo Mutable/Changeable Earth) when practical reality begins to conflict with "God's Laws" as symbolised by IV.The Emperor and V.The Hierophant of the earlier stage. Both are concerned with mental development – first at a symbolic level of using words to communicate, and now at a more practical level.

GENESIS : CAIN KILLS ABEL

Here is the story of Cain killing his brother (male peer) because he thought that God rejected his gift (creative talent from Cycle of Growth Stage 5) in favour of Abel's. We can see this as man's continued tendency towards a physical, practical, lifestyle. However, we have seen that Abel was born as a "counterpart" to Cain (relating to Gemini/Air/MERCURY Twins of the same sex). By killing Abel he is forced to seek the "missing part" elsewhere (Virgo/ Earth/MERCURY)– that is, with a female "counterpart". Despite the earlier attitude that males and females are the same, the physical reality is different.

The story therefore depicts the "homosexual " Adolescent Stage among peer groups when males relate to males, and females to females. The next stage requires male/female relationships – which occurs in the next phase at Cycle of Growth Stage 7 (Partners).

The story contains the message that to achieve certain things in life we have to give up (kill) other things and focus our energies in a particular direction.

> *Verse 8: And Cain saith unto Abel his brother, [`Let us go into the field;'] and it cometh to pass in their being in the field, that Cain riseth up against Abel his brother, and slayeth him.*

We have a seeming repetition of the Adam and Eve scenario where Jehovah does not seem to know what has happened.

> *Verse 9: And Jehovah saith unto Cain, `Where [is] Abel thy brother?' and he saith, `I have not known; my brother's keeper – I?'*

> *Verse 10: And He saith, `What hast thou done? the voice of thy brother's blood is crying unto Me from the ground;*

> *Verse 11: and now, cursed [art] thou from the ground, which hath opened her mouth to receive the blood of thy brother from thy hand;*

> *Verse 12: when thou tillest the ground, it doth not add to give its strength to thee – a wanderer, even a trembling one, thou art in the earth.'*

GENESIS AND THE CYCLE OF GROWTH

This suggests that, even though Cain wanted to be a farmer, he would not making a living out of it. (His fruit was no good, and rejected). He was better as a hunter-gatherer – or founder of a new civilisation (Mesopotamia).

*Verse 13: And Cain saith unto Jehovah, `Greater is my punishment than to be borne;

*Verse 14: lo, Thou hast driven me to-day from off the face of the ground, and from Thy face I am hid; and I have been a wanderer, even a trembling one, in the earth, and it hath been – every one finding me doth slay me.'

*Verse 15: And Jehovah saith to him, `Therefore – of any slayer of Cain sevenfold it is required;' and Jehovah setteth to Cain a token that none finding him doth slay him.

Astrology Log Timescale : Age 13 – 23 years

This is Erikson's Adolescent Age and which, internally, is mainly concerned with Puberty when sex hormones start pumping. The aim here is the establishment of Personal Identity as distinct from our parents and peers. Externally it is the stage of peer group relationships at Secondary School – mainly with those of the same sex. The Gang.

We now have more freedom from parental control and our main interpersonal activities relate to a group of our peers – that is, people of our own age and sex. In fact, there is a certain competition with the opposite sex which is encouraged in secondary schools.

Zodiac Sign : VIRGO. Planet : Mercury (Mind)

Mutable (Changeable) Earth. The Sign of Virgo is related to the annual time when the fruits of past labour are ready for harvest. The fruits also contain the seeds for new growth in a future cycle. This Earth Sign is concerned with "Service To Self" which includes having an occupation to support a physical body and attention to Health.

There is a Mercury focus on training the mind at this time.

Tarot Card : IX.The Hermit

The Tarot Card IX.The Hermit shows a lone figure on a dark, narrow path navigating with a faint light. At base level this is "isolation by a secret" as the beginning of awareness of our inner self whose energies may conflict with what we perceive externally.

The Hermit relates to Virgo in that they are both lone "Virgins".

The inner sex drive is beginning to focus attention to a new area of life – which includes the opposite sex. There is growing awareness of being "alone in a crowd" and, because of the competition between the sexes, the next step will require leaving that "crowd" behind.

CYCLE OF GROWTH STAGE 7 (PARTNERS)

At this stage one finds a partner and finally moves away from both the early family home and the peer group into a wider Society.

We are at the beginning of the second half of The Cycle of Growth. From now on we have to meet and reconcile the "opposites" of the first half so the life cycle totals Zero at its end. To begin with we have to give up some of our hard-won individual selfhood from Cycle of Growth Stage 1 (Seed. Aries. Mars. War) and learn lessons of Venus (Desire. Peace) in order to procreate.

As was Adam, Cain is forced to move away from The Garden of Eden. He has killed his male "counterpart" and so is forced to find a female one which will enable him to generate his own family. Leaving the protection of his home he is naturally concerned about his survival. This is somewhat a repetition of the opposite Cycle of Growth Stage 1 (Seed) which is also concerned with survival in a new world.

At an inner level, this is a further expansion of Consciousness to incorporate a wider view of Society than that described by his early family. He will begin to meet challenges to his earlier teachings.

GENESIS : CAIN STARTS A NEW GENERATION

*Verse 16: And Cain goeth out from before Jehovah, and dwelleth in the land, moving about east of Eden;

GENESIS AND THE CYCLE OF GROWTH

Movement to the East again suggests a new beginning. The King James Version says this, with mention of the land "of Nod" which two words do not appear in the original Hebrew/Greek text:-

Verse 16: And Cain went out from the presence of the LORD, and dwelt in the land of Nod, on the east of Eden.[KJV]

Verse 17: And Cain knew his wife; and she conceived, and bare Enoch: and he builded a city, and called the name of the city, after the name of his son, Enoch.

The East of Eden, remember, is where the Cherubim are on guard. The Chakras are closed. The "Concise Oxford Dictionary" defines "the land of nod" as meaning "sleep" (that is, a state of unconsciousness). So Cain seems to have moved closer (back) to the position of childish innocence (unconsciousness) – or the condition of The Fool beginning a new cycle of life in the East. The situation now is that Abel is dead, and Cain is a wanderer. When we compare this with our now known stages of human evolution, the meaning appears to be that Cain was not yet ready to be any kind of a farmer, so instead became a wanderer – or Hunter Gatherer – under protection of The Law.

The Book continues with Cain finding a wife and settling to become the father/founder of a new civilisation. We are not told where she came from, but Edgar Cayce stated that Cain was a leader of a clan or group. We have a similar situation in the mythical stories of the Greek and Roman gods where incest was normal (and necessary for procreation) - there were not many around to mate with. In that scenario I can see a similarity with Chemistry where positive and negative elements "mate" to produce chemical compounds, which, in turn, break down to "mate" and produce new chemical compounds.

Historians believe that Cain, was one of the first actual settlers in Sumer, later Mesopotamia. His fear of being killed was realistic in that the dwellers in the area at the time were nomads – mainly robbers. The story is that members of Cain's clan had some tribal mark. The nomads learned to avoid them because those bearing the mark fiercely and ruthlessly avenged any attack on one of their clan. The suggestion is that Enoch relates to the Sumerian city Unug (Akkadian Uruk).

Adam and Eve continued their genealogical line with the birth of their third son, Seth, who possibly replaced Abel and had similar characteristics. There is agreement with other religions that this occurred when Adam was 130 years old. They say that Adam died aged 936.

We note that Edgar Cayce stated that Adam was one of the incarnations of Jesus, and Eve of Mary, his mother.

Astrology Log Timescale : 23 – 42 Years

Erikson states the Young Adulthood stage to be concerned with "Intimacy versus Isolation" and the formation of Partnerships. There are no major physical changes. Isolation is the state of the previous Virgo/IX.The Hermit.

Zodiac Sign : LIBRA. Planet : Venus (Desire. Need)

The Cardinal air Sign of Libra is in opposition to the Cardinal Fire Sign of Aries at Cycle of Growth Stage 1 (Seed. Aries. Mars) at the beginning of our earthly life. We see influence of the Cardinal, Creative, Initiating, influence in both. We are now at the beginning of the second half of The Cycle of Growth. The "Return Journey" begun at Cycle of Growth Stage 4 (Transplanting. Cancer. Cardinal/Initiating Water) is continuing.

Cain has faced death for the first time and realises his own vulnerability. Whereas Mars enabled survival of his genes at the beginning of life, he now needs a mate to enable their survival after his death.

Tarot Card : XI.Justice

"The Scales" card is basically concerned with the resolution of dilemmas. The Sword of Mars has to be balanced with peaceful methods (Venus). Justice tempered with Mercy.

CYCLE OF GROWTH STAGE 8 (SEX. DEATH)

The Genesis Story continues with increase in population by lots of "begetting".

Astrology Log Timescale : 42 Years of age to death

The Adult and Old Age stage of Psychology, which ignores the Mid Life Crisis Uranus Opposition at age 42, tends to suggest that life from now on is "downhill" with physical/mental senescence in preparation for death.

GENESIS AND THE CYCLE OF GROWTH

THE CALENDAR

This chapter gives a brief the history of our annual calendar, and relates it to the Cycle of Growth by noting the symbolism and dates of various festivals observed each year.

Nowadays, despite differences in nationalities and world religions, there is nothing more "global" in scope than the calendar and clock time. If nothing else, it is the one thing that all people of all nations agree on. Despite efforts to change measures to a digital base 10, time measurement is still based on Number 12. It is from examples like this that we can observe something of the working of the Collective Unconscious in our lives. As our common psychological "root" its effect makes us all the same at fundamental levels. We note that, despite being used to co-ordinate human affairs, the original purpose was to co-ordinate man's efforts with God and Nature. It is also interesting that, despite efforts to divide time into smaller and more accurate units, even to subatomic levels, Nature never seems to fully agree. There is always a slight difference. This means that that, despite every effort, the calendar can never match the solar and lunar cycles exactly. There will always be the need to make odd adjustments. The Circle cannot be "Squared" exactly. It is probably this "friction" between them that makes the diversity in The Cycle of Growth. The 4 Seasons are not exactly the same length.

This quotation gives some hint of the involvement of The Collective Unconscious :-

> *A calendar is like a chain that emerges out of the waters of oblivion and holds the ship of history to its moorings. Beneath the surface of the waters, there must have been sunk some kind of an anchor.[P.W. Wilson, "The Romance of the Calendar"].

The development of the Calendar is also a mark of man's development in consciousness. Our first level is of the daily solar cycle of dark and light, then the monthly lunar cycle, followed by an annual solar cycle. Despite millions of years of human evolution we only, finally, reached the last stage – that of being able to accurately count Years - in 1 AD – 2,013 years ago as I write this.

This book also includes mention of the 26,000 year cycle of the Zodiac Ages [ASTROLOGY : ZODIAC AGES] of which examination has so far been limited by the lack of records. More about this should come to light (consciousness) as we progress.

ASTRONOMY\ASTROLOGY AND THE CALENDAR

Perhaps this was the first calendar. In "An Introduction to the History of Astrology" (which agrees with other sources) Nicholas Campion states :-

> *Evidence of the recording of lunar phases has been revealed by notches carved on animal bones dating back to 15,000 BC during the Stone Age and before the development of agriculture. Such recording would have become far more important as a result of the development of agriculture between 10,000 BC and 5000 BC and <u>evidence from many early cultures shows that the heliacal rising of the stars was used by 2000 BC to give a more precise timing to the agricultural year.</u>[IHA]

We can safely assume that the constellation Aries was named at a time when it was rising at the Spring Equinox , which not only gives us an idea when "modern" Astrology began, but also, gives an idea when the Age of Aries began, i.e. before 2000 BC, – which agrees with Nicholas Campion's statement above. This gives added evidence that the measurement of Time is intimately related to the symbolism of the Zodiac Signs. We have a kind of "Birth Chart" for The Calendar with an Aries Ascendant.

EGYPTIAN CALENDAR

The Egyptians measured years beginning with the reign of King Menes (3100-3066 BC)

> *The ancient Egyptians were the first to replace the lunar calendar with a calendar based on the solar year. They measured the solar year as 365 days, divided into 12 months of 30 days each, with 5 extra days at the end. About 238 BC King Ptolemy III ordered that an extra day be added to every fourth year, which was therefore similar to the modern leap year. [MSE]

> *At the end of the 4th millennium BC, when King Menes, the first king of a united Egypt, started his reign, the ancient Egyptians began to name each year by its main events, presumably to facilitate the dating of documents. [EB]

THE CALENDAR

We note that the Egyptians did not use the solar year as we know it today. They were mainly interested in when the annual flooding of the river Nile would take place, which was the source of their soil fertility. They realised that it was always close to the time Sirius "appeared" each year.

*Theoretically, the Egyptian civil year began when the Dog Star, Sirius (Egyptian Sothis), could first be seen on the eastern horizon just before the rising of the Sun (i.e., 19/20 of July). As the civil calendar of the ancient Egyptians consisted of 12 months (each of 30 days) [EB]

MESOPOTAMIA

In my research I have continually met references to the Babylonian Empire of Mesopotamia (now Iraq), which seems to have pioneered all kinds of activities in the Arts and Sciences at this time. Mesopotamia is located in what was once the "fertile triangle", or Levant, on the Eastern Mediterranean. There is speculation that, due to its position in relationship to various rivers in the area which seems to correspond with Biblical text, this is the original location of The Garden of Eden. Interestingly, Levant was the destination of the first migration of Homo Sapiens (who appeared 200,000 years ago) across the then fertile Sahara Desert, from the equatorial (zero degrees latitude) centre of Africa 115,000 years ago. The pioneers all died in the following ice age, which turned the Sahara into desert. The original community survived in Africa – the Equator runs through its centre, giving reliable high temperatures to survive the numerous ice ages - to make a later, more successful, exit 85,000 years ago across the Red Sea.

We can see that Mesopotamia has a human history going back to the beginning of Stone Age existence. In "An Introduction to the History of Astrology" we find :-

*It seems probable that the learning which was acquired in the megalithic cultures was communicated to Mesopotamia, perhaps between 3000 and 2000 BC and it was in Mesopotamia just after this last date that we find evidence of the emerging combination of astronomy, mathematics and mythology which was to become the basis of astrology.[IHA]

In Microsoft Encarta :-

*The earliest records of advanced, organized mathematics date back to the ancient Mesopotamian country of Babylonia and to Egypt of the 3rd millennium BC. There mathematics was dominated by arithmetic, with an emphasis on measurement and calculation in geometry and with no trace of later mathematical concepts such as axioms or proofs.[MSE]

*The ancient Babylonians had a lunisolar calendar of 12 lunar months of 30 days each, and they added extra months when necessary to keep the calendar in line with the seasons of the year. [MSE]

The Babylonians and Assyrians measured years by using the reigns of their kings. It begins with the birth of King Sargon I (2335-2279 BC).

GREEK CALENDAR

A year is actually 365 ¼ days in length.

*In ancient Greece a lunisolar calendar was in use, with a year of 354 days, the Greeks were the first to intercalate extra months into the calendar on a scientific basis, adding months at specific intervals in a cycle of solar years. [MSE]

45 BC JULIAN CALENDAR – based on the Sun

There was a revision to the astrological "calendar" invented during the Age of Aries and which by now the Egyptians had formalised into 12 lunar months, and the Romans 10, later 12, months. This was a Christian calendar mainly intended to observe the various special holy days.

The Egyptian Calendar was found to be too inaccurate, and, for a time, the Romans used "intercalary" months of varying lengths to make adjustments during the year. There were no rules about it – so the priests had control. It reached a stage where the calendar was 3 months adrift from the seasons, so in 45 BC Julius Caesar made changes to base it entirely on the position of the Sun. It had 12 months - Martius, Aprilis, Maia, Junius, Quintilis, Sextilis, September, October, November, December, Januarius and Februarius. We note Quintilis to

THE CALENDAR

December use Latin numbers 5 to 10 to name the months. There was an intercalary month Intercalaris that had variable days to balance the calendar which was abolished in the new method.

They did not count the days as we do. The first day was called Kalendis (from which comes "calendar"), The Nones was the 5th. day (or 7th. for long months Martius, Maia, Quintilis, October), The Ides was the 13th. day (or 15th. for long months). Apart from Kalendis, they counted the days as being prior to the next named day.

There was still an error because, as today, an intercalary day is required every 4 years and they were applying it every 3 years. Augustus Caesar corrected this.

1582 AD GREGORIAN CALENDAR

The Julian calendar lasted until 1582 when Pope Gregory revised it again, adding rules such as "leap years" so the calendar accurately matched the equinoxes.

Despite all this effort, our calendar today is still inaccurate by around 26.8 seconds each year, which makes a day every 3200 years. The correction will not be our problem then.

As with other countries, Britain was slow in accepting the new calendar for religious rather than factual reasons – principally the formation of The Church of England at the time and the split from Catholic Rome. Anything connected with Catholicism was "bad news". We used the Julian Calendar for another 170 years until 1751. Whilst Scotland used January 1st., the English year began on March 25th.

ISLAMIC CALENDAR

As an indication of the problems caused by mismatched calendars, the Islamic Calendar is still based on the cycle of the Moon with each year having 12 lunar months. The beginning of each month is at the time of the Crescent Moon – which must be observed, not calculated. So far no reliable rule has been established to calculate when this will occur – not even by using computers.

JEWISH CALENDAR

The Jewish Calendar measures from the date of Creation. Since the 9th. Century AD this has been accepted by Jewish scholars as being October 7th. 3761 BC. [EB]

THE PAGAN CALENDAR

Because there are no set rules there are a wide variety of practices, so this can only be a generalisation.

Paganism is a term mainly used by Christians of ancient Rome as a label for any religion other than a monotheistic one. It therefore is somewhat derogatory. In essence, Paganism puts Mother Earth, or The Goddess, on equal rank with The Sun God and celebrates their inter-action as displayed in the annual cycle of Seasons. Apart from observing set festivals, the actual form of observance is generally left to individual or personal preferences. Although there may be leaders, there are no actual priests. Or, more correctly, in some groups each one is a priest. At deeper levels there is the working of "Magic" which is concerned with bringing about changes according to Will. It relates to the Tarot Card I. The Magician. There is a similarity with the concepts of the old Alchemists. There is also a similarity (as we would expect) with The Cycle of Growth. At its most simple and logical level the "secret" is that if we wish to produce a certain crop, or result, we have to sow the proper seeds, and nurture them until they bear fruit. The Laws of Nature will do the rest.

As I see it, Paganism, being concerned more with physical ritual, is related to the feminine Jungian Functions Feeling and Sensation whereas the Christian religion, with its focus on words, written and spoken, and logic, is related to the Jungian Thinking Function. The Pagan Festivals and rituals are there to help individuals relate to the Cycle of Growth at a nonverbal level.

THE DIAGRAM OF PAGAN FESTIVALS

Here is a diagram below showing the 8 main Pagan festivals oriented to match the Annual Zodiac Cycle. You will see from this, and elsewhere in this chapter, a correspondence with Christian ones. Although I have included the Zodiac Signs they are not used as such by Paganism. There are 4 festivals which celebrate the Equinoxes and Solstices, and another 4 which celebrate the exact half-way points between them. To observe them a modern calendar is required because they are on February 1st., May 1st., August 1st. and October 31st. – so the form is not as ancient as some would believe.

THE CALENDAR

They therefore divide the year into 8 equal portions. An essential point to recognise is that my diagram shows the inner (whole) circle divided as such. Other sources draw it as an 8-pointed star which loses its meaning.

SYMBOLISM OF NUMBER 8

The symbolism of Number 8 [NUMEROLOGY] is related to its symbolic representation as 2 joined circles which can be drawn as the Infinity symbol or the Arabic Number. In effect, they depict 2 inter-related cycles of Number 4. The I Ching symbol shows a similar representation which produces a more harmonious whole as a "union of opposites".

Number 8 therefore refers to 2 kinds of order in the universe which are inter-related, one above the other. "As Above, So Below. As Below, So Above". At a human level it can refer to such things as the laws and people that control human affairs. At another level, Number 8 in [THE KABBALAH TREE OF LIFE] refers to Sephirah 9 (Yesod. Foundation. The Moon) which itself has 8 distinct phases in its monthly cyclic relationship with The Sun. From this relationship we get the Calendar that controls human affairs.

My diagram which follows can also be considered as 2 sets of Number 4, albeit in the same space. The Equinoxes and Solstices relate to the actual positions of The Sun throughout the year, the others relate to month dates, and therefore The Moon.

Figure 44 : The Pagan Cycle and Number 8

THE CYCLE OF GROWTH AND THE PAGAN CYCLE

Here we are concerned with the relationship with The Cycle of Growth. With my combined diagram we can see that the other festivals coincide with the centres of the 4 FIXED Signs of the Zodiac – Taurus, Leo, Scorpio and Aquarius- which are the most stable forms of their Elements. In essence, this 8 Stage cycle is a simplified version of the 12 Stages of The Cycle of Growth based on the limitations of Number 4.

When we observe Pagans in action there is a distinct focus on The Earth, Mother Nature, and Material manifestation. Whilst not wishing to devalue this in any way, we must recognise that the focus is on an earth-bound existence. This was obviously a necessary stage in our evolution. With the coming of Jesus and the

THE CALENDAR

Christian religion, and his 12 disciples, the focus has changed to a much more complicated way of life. Few of us have to worry about where the next meal is coming from nowadays. However much we may bemoan the loss of "The Simple Life", Evolution has its own way of moving forward. We have to use the lessons learned by "The Farmer" and apply them to a different level of existence.

Many of our annual festivals refer to events in the life of Jesus.

Jesus' life was the fulfilment of Old Testament prophesies concerned with the coming of The Messiah – which described the circumstances of his birth and later life, followed by his betrayal and death. He therefore knew exactly what his fate would be, and we can understand his temptation to avoid it. We have his continual references to "it is written" to verify this. Speculation as to the part that Judas played in his betrayal seems to ignore that fact. As further evidence, we see in John Chapter 13 during the Last Supper that that Jesus announces his betrayal, when there are questions from the disciples who would do such a thing, his reply was thus :-

*Verse 26: Jesus answered, He it is, to whom I shall give a sop, when I have dipped it. And when he had dipped the sop, he gave it to Judas Iscariot, the son of Simon.

Verse 27: And after the sop Satan entered into him. Then said Jesus unto him, That thou doest, do quickly. [YLT]

THE FIRST OCTAVE OF THE CYCLE OF GROWTH

(GESTATION AND TRANSCENDENCE)

Each of the 3 "Octaves" in The Cycle of Growth [ASTROLOGY : LOGARITHMIC TIMESCALE] contains 4 Stages of The Cycle of Growth, which makes 12 Stages altogether. We are somewhat limited in our investigation of the First Octave because it has associations with areas of life with very little historical or scientific evidence.

THE "FIRST OCTAVE" (one third) OF A MONTH

We can relate the annual cycle to that of a single month cycle via The Cycle of Growth. Wheels within wheels. There is an additional monthly pattern in that the beginning of months of the modern Annual Calendar is not exactly synchronised with the transit of the Sun through the Zodiac Signs. The entry of the Sun into a Sign occurs around the 21st. day of each month – 10 days before the 1st. day of the following month. If we consider this as Cycle of Growth Stage 9 (Conception), and a month as having 30 days, this makes up the "First Octave", or one third, of the passing of the Sun through a Sign – with the actual "manifestation" on the first day of the new month (in the Earth calendar) occurring at Stage 1 (Seed). There is a diagram of this in [ASTROLOGY : LOGARITHMIC TIMESCALE].

(In terms of human physical and psychological growth, the Second Octave follows the same order of development as that of the First Octave of life in the womb. The Third Octave is not so clear in this respect).

For example, we have Jesus being born at the time of the Winter Solstice in December at Cycle of Growth Stage 10 (Peak. Harvest) when the ancients celebrated the rebirth of the Sun, and his crucifixion and death and resurrection at the time of Easter - just after the Spring Equinox – Cycle of Growth Stage 1 (Seed). Jesus appeared to the disciples several times afterwards until his final Ascension celebrated in May, 40 days after Easter Sunday. The number 40 appears again, as it did before the Crucifixion as the time of Jesus' temptation.

The symbolism is related to the "Crucifixion of The Spirit in Matter" – the formation of a "Seed", or human body, which is a "vehicle" enabling a soul's experience on the Earthly level of existence. We can consider the state of the soul, or spirit, of a new born baby as being related to that of crucifixion – imprisoned in matter. At some later stage in our evolution we may find that it also refers to experiences before and after an earthly lifetime – which itself is related to Cycle of Growth Stages 1 (Seed) to 8 (Death).

Easter Sunday is not a fixed date, it is based on Astrology. It is defined as the Sunday after the first Full Moon following the Spring Equinox (at sunrise on the day of the Equinox the Sun enters the first Zodiac Sign, Aries, which marks the beginning of the Zodiac year). If the Full Moon is on a Sunday then the following Sunday is used. Easter Sunday (the Resurrection day) is used to fix other dates in the annual church calendar, such as Good Friday, which is the previous Friday – the day of The Crucifixion.

THE CALENDAR

CYCLE OF GROWTH STAGE 9 (CONCEPTION)

November 22nd. Sun enters Sagittarius (Mutable Fire. Pluto. Number 1 or Jupiter Number 3). The Archer. Tarot Card XIV.Temperance.

Among other things, Sagittarius rules the academic field of knowledge - theories and ideas transmitted by words. Its complementary Sign, Gemini, is concerned with rational knowledge gained by practical experience.

ADVENT

Of prime importance in its relationship with The Cycle of Growth is that this is the "New Year" of the Christian Church as a result of the life of Jesus. It is regarded as the birth of the Christian Church.

Advent begins on the closest Sunday to November 30th. and lasts until Christmas Eve, December 24th and is concerned with the conception of and preparation for the birth.

Returning to the beginning of Cycle of Growth Stage 9 (Conception) we have the prediction of the birth to come :-

> *Isaiah Chapter:7:14: Therefore the Lord himself shall give you a sign; Behold, a virgin shall conceive, and bear a son, and shall call his name Immanuel. [KJV]

(Immanuel or Emanuel = "God with us")

The story of his earthly life begins with the Angel Gabriel coming to Mary and prophesying that she will give birth to a son. This was in the 6th. month of the pregnancy of her cousin Elisabeth, wife of Zacharias, who conceived as a result of their prayers because she was unable to conceive normally. He was old and she was barren. Their son grew to become John The Baptist who was important in prophesying the coming of Jesus, and actually baptised Jesus before he began his ministry.

> *Luke Chapter 1: Verse26: And in the sixth month the angel Gabriel was sent from God unto a city of Galilee, named Nazareth,
>
> Verse 27: To a virgin espoused to a man whose name was Joseph, of the house of David; and the virgin's name was Mary. [KJV]

The story of Jesus begins with his conception by the Holy Spirit of Virgin Mary. There was therefore no physical sexual intercourse. "Brain Children", or ideas, are conceived this way in the mind all the time. This is all in accordance with the predictions of The Old Testament.

CYCLE OF GROWTH STAGE10 (SOCIAL PEAK. HARVEST)

On December 22nd. The Sun enters Capricorn (Cardinal Earth). Saturn. Number 2. The Mountain Goat. Tarot Cards XV.The Devil and XVI.The Tower.

Earth is closest to the Sun at this time.

Capricorn is concerned with making long range plans to achieve practical goals. The development of what was conceived in Sagittarius. The following of a practical Career and rise to fame and fortune. The Lesson includes a certain ruthlessness or focus of effort that is required to pursue such a goal and keep to a narrow path – in other words, ignoring or cutting out, side issues that may arise.

The ruler of Capricorn is Saturn\Satan. The Jungian Shadow. The "evil" is that of using spiritual energies to achieve material ends. We note that, in our story of Creation - which is related to the First Octave [GENESIS AND THE CYCLE OF GROWTH] - God was guilty of just that. Just before his crucifixion Jesus was tempted by The Devil to do the same thing to escape his fate. We can see Temptation as a general part of The Cycle of Growth.

Stage 10 is related to 2 Tarot Cards. XV. The Devil, where the association is obvious, and XVI. The Tower which symbolises man-made structures to reach the Heavens and "godhood". There are physical ones, such as The Tower of Babel - and symbolic ones, such as the hierarchies of the Church and Armed Forces, and other large organisations, which are also the province of Capricorn.

Stage 10 is concerned with Harvest in terms of human achievement and public recognition - that is, reaping the practical harvest of one's work as well as the public or social position one achieves by so doing. We all achieve relative public fame in The Cycle of Growth. It can mean success or failure, depending on how well one does the job. Even failure can be used as an example to indicate the "right way".

THE CALENDAR

In the story of Jesus we have an immediate entry into the limelight (the "new star in the East"), and the subsequent attempt by king Herod to kill him – by killing all the new born at the time. We note that this theme is repeated in classical mythology on numerous occasions - when the male Gods swallow, or otherwise dispose of, their new born children because they fear that they will be replaced by the "new king". The stories usually continue with the survival of the child by their being hidden away – or, if they are swallowed, the king eventually being forced to regurgitate them alive. In Jesus' case they were forewarned of the coming purge and ran away.

In this story we have the symbol of the continual conflict between old and new ideas. Jesus was born in a stable because "there was no room at the (public) inn". Although there were no inns at that time, the story is consistent with the fact that people of the time had spaces in their homes to house their animals over winter. New ideas are not easily accommodated into a busy, already ordered, lifestyle.

**We need to remember that this Stage in The Cycle of Growth is not concerned with the actual birth of a physical human child, which comes at Stage 1 (Seed) as the beginning of the next Octave. The human child is still in the womb. In an Astrological Birth Chart the 10th. House is at the "Midheaven" position, and refers to the human father and the actual confirmation of pregnancy - which, until now, was just a "theory". It is now that he realises he will no longer have first claim to the mother's attention.

In the Calendar we have the New Year replacing the old one during this Stage. Traditionally a time of making "New Year's Resolutions" – which may or may not survive to reach physical maturity. The actual Resolution is more related to the next Stage in the Cycle of Growth.

** Having said that I have noticed that women often give birth when Jupiter or Saturn passes through (transits) their Generic 10th.House [ASTROLOGY : PLANET TRANSITS].

DECEMBER

21st. Pagan "Yule" festival. Rebirth of the SUN. Was Pagan New Year.
21st. Winter Solstice. Shortest Day. Rebirth of the Sun. Day length begins to increase.
25th. Christmas Day. Celebration of the Birth of Jesus.

JANUARY

1st. - New Year's Day. The "birth" of the Calendar Year – but not yet the Nature Year.
5th. - 12th. Night after Christmas – the end of Christmastide. Decorations are taken down.
6th. Epiphany – the first public appearance of baby Jesus. The 3 Wise Men.

In recent times "epiphany" has come to mean that one has had a sudden inner revelation or realisation of truth or understanding. We have reference to Tarot Card XVI. The (lightning struck) Tower.

CYCLE OF GROWTH STAGE 11 (DISCONTENT)

January 20th. The Sun enters Aquarius (Fixed Air). Saturn Number 2 or Uranus Number 11. The Water Carrier. Tarot Cards XVII.The Star and XVIII.The Moon.

This is the actual time related to New Year's Resolutions. Aquarius is the Sign of Rebellion and Invention when new things and methods begin to replace the old. Ideas begin to "crystallise" and take a more tangible form. It is also concerned with Communication – especially of the more public kind. It is connected with modern methods of broadcasting – such as by radio, television and computers using the "air waves". In older terms, Broadcasting referred to a method of hand-sowing seeds over a wide area of ground.

With Cycle of Growth Stage 10 being "The Peak", this is the first stage of decline. The time of Winter is that of withdrawal from outer life to await the rebirth of Nature in Spring – despite the rebirth of the Sun at the Solstice having promised new life to come. Having realised her pregnancy, the mother begins to broadcast the fact and make practical and psychological preparations for the coming birth.

In the story of Jesus he now disappears from public view. There is no record of his existence from age 12, when he was asking questions of the elders of the temple, until his appearance at a wedding feast where he is reluctantly persuaded to turn water into wine by his mother [John Chapter 2]. In verse 4 he states ".. mine hour is not yet come". It may not have a bearing here, but we note the watery nature of the images in the relevant Tarot Cards here – XVII The Star and XVIII The Moon. Later in the chapter he shows his rebellious tendencies by turning the money changers and animal sellers out of the temple of Jerusalem.

During this period Jesus broadcasted his gospel to small and large gatherings of people and also performed his other miracles – including feeding 5000 people using 5 loaves and 3 fishes.

THE CALENDAR

His public ministry only lasted around 3 years before his death at age 33. We note a correspondence with the 30 year cycle of Saturn. In Astrology the event brings changes that enable us to depart from the traditional occupations of our parents and other family to take a more personal or individual path, because we are now no longer under their direct control. It would seem that Jesus was forced into the traditional mould chosen for him before he was born.

FEBRUARY

1st. (Midway between Winter Solstice and Spring Equinox) Pagan Sabbat "Imbolc" or "Candlemas". The goddess and Returning Light. Harnessing divine energy for harvest. A time of making resolutions and initiations

2nd. Christian Candlemas –Presentation of baby Jesus to the temple. Purification ritual of Mary after the birth.

40 days before Easter - Shrove Tuesday and Ash Wednesday –this is the beginning of Lent 40 days (excluding Sundays) of fasting ending at Easter. Marks 40 days of Jesus' fasting and temptation prior to his ministry and crucifixion. Could also refer to the 40 weeks of development in the womb after conception and prior to birth.

CYCLE OF GROWTH STAGE 12 (WITHDRAWAL. CONFINEMENT)

February 19th. The Sun enters Pisces (Mutable Water). Jupiter Number 3 or Neptune Number Zero. The Fishes. Tarot Cards XIX.The Sun and XX.Judgement.

Pisces is where we have contact with the "sea" of the Collective Unconscious. When we withdraw from activity in the external world, the Unconscious becomes more active (Jung). Among other things, Pisces is related to places of confinement such as prisons, hospitals, monasteries and convents. Places where people "meditate" about their past. Pisces has relationship with alcohol and drugs. We can sum all this up as relating to altered states of consciousness where consciousness is turned inwards, rather than outwards towards the external world. The 12th. Sign and 12th. House of a Birth chart are associated with the concept of Karma "As ye sow, so shall ye reap". The Cycle of Growth shows that our personal spiritual journey obeys the same laws as those that make up the annual cycle of Nature.

At this Stage we have the Tarot Card XX. Judgement the image of which suggests release from imprisonment and rebirth.

It is important to recognise that, whereas the Old Testament with its original covenant with Moses and God, and The Ten Commandments, suggested forms of punishment for transgressions against The Law, the New Testament, with the New Covenant with God and Jesus, promises Forgiveness. The point being that we inwardly judge ourselves. The aim is not to make the same mistakes again.

We have relationship with the cycle of Nature with :-

> *Be not deceived; God is not mocked: for whatsoever a man soweth, that shall he also reap. [KJV Galatians Chapter 6:7]

There is additional relationship with Water (as for washing) in the Christian practice of Baptism for the forgiveness of sins which was introduced by John The Baptist, and who baptised Jesus prior to his ministry.

This is the final Stage of The Cycle of Growth prior to rebirth. Its main concern is the clearing away of what remains of the past to make way for new growth. At this stage the mother with child becomes gradually less able to move around and is forced to greater introspection. She becomes in greater psychological contact with her child so the birth can be timed correctly.

In the story of Jesus it relates to the time where he fasted in solitude for 40 days and nights in the desert, and was tempted by the Devil to use his spiritual powers to escape his coming crucifixion. We spend around 40 weeks in the womb.

Also in the story, Jesus returns from the desert after his temptation and enters Jerusalem riding on a donkey (fulfilling another prophecy) when he is enthusiastically welcomed by the people who spread palm leaves in his path (Palm Sunday) – something usually reserved for important people. This seems very similar to the image of Tarot Card XIX. The Sun where we have a child riding triumphantly on a horse.

This could refer to our experience prior to reincarnation.

THE CALENDAR

MARCH
3 weeks before Easter : Mothering Sunday. A non-fasting day in the middle of Lent remembering the feeding of 5,000 people by Jesus.

THE SECOND OCTAVE OF THE CYCLE OF GROWTH

(CHILDHOOD and PSYCHOLOGICAL DEVELOPMENT)

At the beginning of the Second Octave we have the paradox of the death of Jesus at 33 years of age occurring at the time of new life on Earth – referring to Spring in the Annual Cycle, and that of a new born baby. The birth position of an Astrological Birth Chart. This is symbolic of the crucifixion, or imprisonment, of the Spirit in Matter, or physical form – which refers to the physical bodies of plants, animals, and humans, all of which return to "dust" at Cycle of Growth Stage 8 (Death. Intercourse).

Festivals in the Calendar refer to the Crucifixion of Jesus, his entombment in a cave, his Resurrection, and some events leading to his Ascension.

We have a repetitive symbol of Transition from one state of being to another – which here includes release of the Jews from slavery in Egypt, and their Exodus.

On the day before Good Friday, Maundy Thursday celebrates The Last Supper which has become the Holy Communion of the Christian Church. Being Jewish, Jesus and his disciples observed the Feast of The Passover, which itself celebrated the release of the Jews from slavery in Egypt. "Passover" refers to the final punishment of the Egyptians by God for not releasing the Jews from their bondage. On a particular night the first born of each family in Egypt was to die. The Jews marked their doorways so that they would be "passed over". This event finally forced Pharaoh to release the Jews. During the Last Supper Jesus recognises that Judas will later betray him to the authorities, and actually tells him to do so. Although not explicit in the story, the suggested reason for this is that Judas expected Jesus to use his powers to escape, and so reveal them. Considering that Jesus had already been tempted by The Devil in this matter, it was unlikely to happen. Everybody knew Jesus anyway, so there was no need for Judas to identify him. It really seems that the betrayal was there to fulfil an Old Testament prophecy concerning the coming of the Messiah, and that he would be betrayed.

It also seems that one purpose of the life of Jesus was to act out the symbolism of the Agricultural Year and The Cycle of Growth – which has defined the Calendar still in existence today. You will see elsewhere that I have found it useful to replace the word "Lord" with "Law" to aid understanding of The Bible. His main message is that everyone has direct contact with God, with no need for priests or other intermediaries. We are all subject to Law, which includes the possibility of forgiveness of sins. To be forgiven we must first recognise the "sin" (problem) and then take action not to continue doing what we are harming ourselves with. We see a relationship here with making "New Year's Resolutions". I have experience in healing of people feeling better after a session but returning later with the symptoms returned. It is difficult to give up old ways. He continually suggests that physical illnesses are the result of disobeying God's Laws. At one level this could mean eating and exercising properly. Psychologists today recognise psychosomatic illness where psychological factors can introduce physical symptoms. There is some evidence of this in the chapter [MY STORY].

Jesus was crucified on Good Friday. This is the First Day of Easter. On the Second Day his body is placed in a cave (a symbol of the womb). On the Third Day (Easter Sunday) his followers find that the cave has been opened and the body gone. Later he appears alive to some of his disciples in his resurrected body, which still carries the marks of his crucifixion. Sometime afterwards is his final Ascension into heaven. The final evidence of his ministry is said to be when his disciples are given "The Gift of Tongues", when the words they speak are understood by people of different countries. Of note is the fact that this is celebrated on Whit Sunday – or Pentecost – 50 days after Easter, which is just after the Sun enters Gemini in May each year – which itself refers to Cycle of Growth Stage 3 (Experiment. Communication). The image of one of its associated Tarot Cards V. The Hierophant is clearly that of a preacher.

In summary, the "Coming of The Messiah" is (at least) an annual event – depending on the Cycle under consideration. The offer of new life to come.

CYCLE OF GROWTH STAGE 1 (SEED)

The Spring Equinox. Sunrise is zero degrees of Aries. The first day of Spring.

THE CALENDAR

MARCH

March 21st. –The Sun enters Aries (Cardinal Fire). Mars. Number 4. The Ram. The Tarot Cards Zero.The Fool and 1.The Magician.

Aries "The Pioneer" relates to Nature by clearing the ground and ploughing fields ready for planting.

Aries is principally a phallic symbol. An erect penis full of potential creativity not yet released. We see that, in the Age of Aries [ASTROLOGY : THE ZODIAC AGES], a lot of time and effort was put into such symbols - pyramids, temples, and henges – which were abandoned later on. In the Calendar Year on May 1st. we have the symbol of the Maypole where, in the Sign of Taurus, the pole is now clothed by Nature.

    Pagan Lesser Sabbat "Ostara". Planting of seeds of the (Sun) God within the (Earth) Goddess to be reborn at Yule (Christmas). "Spring cleaning". Painting eggs.

Last Sunday - Clocks go forward.

March 25th. –Lady Day marking the announcement of the coming birth of Jesus by Gabriel to Mary.

APRIL

Palm Sunday. One week before Easter Sunday celebration Jesus' triumphant entry into Jerusalem – also a symbol of possible rebirth. A step forward into social recognition.

1st. - All Fools Day (ref. Tarot Card Zero, The Fool)

Thursday before Easter Sunday : Maundy Thursday – Last Supper of Jesus and his disciples, which was then the Jewish Passover. Betrayed by Judas.

Friday before Easter Sunday : Good Friday – Crucifixion and death of Jesus

Saturday before Easter Sunday : Holy Saturday – Jesus' body placed in a burial cave.

Easter Sunday : Sunday after the First Full Moon after March 21st. (Sun's entry into Aries). The resurrection of Jesus.

Easter eggs. Another symbol of new life to come.

CYCLE OF GROWTH STAGE 2 (GERMINATION)

April 20th. The Sun enters Taurus (Fixed Earth). Venus. Number 6. The Bull. The Tarot Cards II.The Priestess and III.The Empress.

Taurus as Mother Nature is the most stable of the Earth Signs. Its inertia resists the head-butting Ram of Aries.

MAY

1st. May Day – Celebration of the coming of new life promised by warmer weather. Maypole dancing. Long ribbons are tied to the top of the pole and dancers hold the end of each one. Men and women dance in opposite directions around the pole which plaits the ribbons to eventually cover it top to bottom. The Maypole is the phallic symbol of Aries. The covering of ribbons is symbolic of the new growth beginning to cover the bare earth at the time of Taurus.

Pagan Sabbat "Beltane" festival. Crowning of the May Queen. Division between Winter & Summer. (Dark\Light). Fire celebrations & rituals.

CYCLE OF GROWTH STAGE 3 (EXPERIMENT. COMMUNICATION)

May 21st. The Sun enters Gemini (Mutable Air). Mercury. Number 7. The Twins. Tarot cards IV.The Emperor and V.The Hierophant.

Gemini is concerned with mental development and communication in words. Among other things it rules the (twin) arms and hands, and lungs.

1. We note the connections here with the related Tarot card V.The Hierophant depicted as a priest of the church, and also Number 7 which relates to Mercury (Communication. Rational Mind), ruler of Gemini. Number 7 is concerned with the "opposition" between 1 and 6 as exemplified by "The Sabbath" being more important than the other 6 days of a week, and its function of a teacher "bringing light". We therefore have Moral Law.

THE CALENDAR

2. Cycle of Growth Stage 3 is concerned with the "Early Childhood Stage" of psychology (at age 2 to 4 years) when a child is developing its mental abilities and learning to name things in particular. Ref. The Gift of Tongues below.
3. We also have the association of the first task of Adam in the Garden of Eden being to name things, followed by the creation of Eve as "counterpart".

MAY : ASCENSION DAY – Number 4

1. Refers to The New Testament.
2. Ascension Day, or Holy Thursday, is 40 days after Easter and 10 days before Whit Sunday. It celebrates the final physical Ascension of Jesus into heaven. The connection with Number 4, and therefore Mars, refers to Cycle of Growth Stage 1 (Seed) and Cycle of Growth Stage 8 (Sex. Death) – the beginning and end of our physical life on Earth.
3. Number 10 is also suggestive of New Beginnings at a higher level or dimension. Cycle of Growth Stage 9 (Conception).
4. We note the recurrence of the Number 40 as indicating a fixed period in time, or stage.

PENTECOST – Number 5 (Tarot VIII.Strength)

1. We here have a different Numerological association.
2. Pentecost, which basically means "The 50th. Day", is essentially an older Jewish (and Pagan) agricultural festival which celebrated the "first harvest" of barley – a kind of Harvest Festival which was variable because it depended on when the barley was ripe. It was celebrated 50 days after Passover – which is now the day before Good Friday. In the Christian Religion it is now celebrated 50 days after Easter Sunday.
3. Mentioned first because it is older in origin, relating to The Old Testament – and demonstrates the attitude of the original "Old Covenant" with Moses.
4. In the Old Testament Jewish Religion it commemorates God giving The 10 Commandments to Moses on Mount Sinai. Again we can see the activity of the Stage-related Tarot card V.The Hierophant as "giver of the law" and "giver of food".
5. The 10 Commandments were inscribed on 2 tablets of stone, 5 on each.
6. Apart from the Tarot Card number, we have the added Numerological association of (5 + 0) Number 5 with "1 versus 4" and "Mind over Matter".
7. Number 5 refers to The Sun as bringer of Consciousness – which itself refers to Cycle of Growth Stage 5 (Power. Creativity) and happens to include a similar Pagan festival, Lammas, mentioned above which celebrates "First Harvest" in Britain. It includes Tarot Card VIII.Strength (gentle control of "the animal"). Mind over Matter.
8. There is further association with The Torah (= "To guide, or Teach"), which is the traditional Jewish "Bible" consisting of the 5 books which eventually became the first 5 books of The Old Testament".
9. We therefore have a strange mixture of symbols.

WHIT SUNDAY – Number 7 and Number 4 (Tarot V.The Hierophant)

1. We are now concerned with The New Covenant with Jesus and The New Testament.
2. Whit Sunday is a New Testament Christian festival which occurs each year on the 7th. Sunday after Easter Sunday - which itself celebrates the Resurrection of Jesus after his crucifixion, the beginning of a new year at Spring, and the physical birth of a child – Cycle of Growth Stage 1 (Seed).
3. We actually have 7 times 7 days, which in Numerology reduces to 4 + 9 =1 + 3 = 4 and therefore, once again, refers to Mars and its associated Stages – in particular, backwards to Cycle of Growth Stage 1 (Seed) and Easter.
4. The reader may like to follow the associations of interim Number 13 on the theme of Death and Rebirth, which I have omitted.
5. Whit Sunday celebrates the "Gift of Tongues" (Gemini. Communication) when the disciples were able to speak to the people in their own languages. In essence, this was the "physical" birth of the Christian Church.

It was also somewhat a reversal of God's reaction to The Tower of Babel attempt to reach Heaven by building a tower in Genesis when the original one language became numerous languages ("babble") as people were spread over the Earth – so they lost the ability to communicate with one another.

CYCLE OF GROWTH STAGE 4 (TRANSPLANTING)

June 21st. Sun enters Cancer (Cardinal Water). The Crab. Tarot Cards VI.The Lovers and VII.The Chariot.

The Pagan Midsummer Festival was concerned with saying "farewell" to the Sun as day length becomes gradually shorter after the Summer Solstice.

We note that "Midsummer" is a misnomer because Spring has only just ended. This is the beginning of Summer. However, it is the half-way point of The Cycle of Growth. From now on the movement is upwards in The Cycle towards Cycle of Growth Stage 9 (Conception).

The relationship with this and The Cycle of Growth is concerned with our psychological development and development of the crab-shell or mask of the Persona as a mediator between our inner and external self that enables us to function in the outer world. It includes the realisation of "I am".

JUNE

June 21st. - Summer Solstice –Longest Day. Beginning of decrease in length of days.

Pagan Midsummer "Litha" festival. The Sun God is at his strongest. (Many ancient monuments were aligned to catch the rays of the rising sun at this time).

June 24th. – "Midsummer" Day (3 days after the Solstice).

THE THIRD OCTAVE OF THE CYCLE OF GROWTH

(DEVELOPMENT TOWARDS ADULTHOOD AND INDIVIDUALITY)

CYCLE OF GROWTH STAGE 5 (POWER. LOVE)

July 23rd. the Sun enters Leo (Fixed Fire. The Sun. Number 5). The Lion. Tarot Card VIII.Strength.

Despite the now waning light of the Sun, the weather is at its warmest and we can allow Nature to take its course. The image of a lion among his pride. The first grains are harvested, baked into bread, and shared.

With the now, more real, indication of the death of the "Sun God" we are reminded of Jesus and The Last Supper, just before his death, who used bread and wine as symbols of his body and blood. The "Sun God" having given us the bread of life is now "dying" after giving power to The Goddess, Earth.

The symbolism is repeated in the corresponding Tarot Card VIII. Strength with the image of a female\virgin controlling a lion. Negative Earth combining with Positive Sun.

AUGUST

1st. Pagan Sabbat "Lammas" or "Lughnasadh". Time of the first grain harvest. "Slaying of the God". Voluntary sacrifice to the Goddess. Time of contests & tests of strength.

CYCLE OF GROWTH STAGE 6 (SERVICE TO SELF. HEALTH)

August 23rd. Sun enters Virgo (Mutable Earth). Mercury. Number 7. The Virgin. Tarot Card IX.The Hermit.

Virgo is the time of final harvest. Its results are dependent on what has been done beforehand – and which will have to support life until the next harvest. The Earth is now Virgin until the "Sun God" returns to bring new life. However, her fruits bear seeds with the potential for new growth later on.

It is the complementary Sign to Pisces, which also has relationship with sowing and reaping – in this case, of Karma. In Virgo we have the karmic lesson in Earthy terms. The seeds from Virgo are still dormant.

Virgo as "Service to Self", among other things, is concerned with how we earn our daily bread and maintain the Health of our physical body.

THE CALENDAR

CYCLE OF GROWTH STAGE 7 (PARTNERS)

September 23rd. Sun enters Libra (Cardinal Air). The Scales. Venus. Number 6. Tarot Card XI.Justice.

In Libra "The Opposites" meet and balance. At the Autumn Equinox Day and Night are again equal in length as the light of the Sun continues to wane. We are reminded that there are no Opposites in Nature. Everything has its Season. Balance means Stagnation. As the Spring Equinox was a time of sowing seeds in the Earth, the Autumn Equinox is the time for "sowing new seeds" among people. A time of sharing one's harvest.

The complementary Sign to Libra, when the year is "dying", is Aries, the beginning of Spring.

SEPTEMBER

21st. Autumn Equinox. Pagan "Mabon" second harvest of fruits and nuts. Life (light) is continuing to leave the land. The sharing of Nature's gifts. A time for reflection.

CYCLE OF GROWTH STAGE 8 (DEATH. INTERCOURSE)

October 23rd. Sun enters Scorpio (Fixed Water). The Scorpion/Serpent, Eagle, and Dove.

Mars Number 4 or Pluto Number 1.

Scorpio is concerned with Death and Rebirth. In Nature there is decay, but the products will be used to enable new life to come. New seeds have been sown, and hidden in the Earth until the outer circumstances are more supportive in the next year. The complementary Sign is Taurus – when germination occurs.

As a time of long nights, this is traditionally when we are most likely to see spirits of the dead.

OCTOBER

31st. October – Halloween (="All Hallows Even"). Trick or treat "Mischief Night"

The veil between this life and the next is at its thinnest.

31st. Halloween Night. Eve of Catholic All Saints and Pagan Samhain (New Year)

Last Sunday in October - End of British Summer time. Clocks go back 1 hour.

NOVEMBER

1st. Catholic All Saints (All Hallows)

2nd. Catholic All Souls Day – prayers for the dead.

4th. Nov. Pagan Sabbat "Samhain". New Year (only from 19th. Century). In Cycle of Growth Stage 9 (Conception) we have the beginning of the Church year.

5th. Bonfire Night (1605 gunpowder plot). Original festival to scare off spirits of the dead.

11th. Martinmas – celebration. Feasting.

MONTH MEANINGS

We see that the months are generally named according to the planet ruling the Zodiac Sign which the Sun enters around the 21st. day of the month.

NOVEMBER - "Ninth" month. 9th. Sign Sagittarius. Cycle of Growth Stage 9 (Conception).

DECEMBER - "Tenth" month. 10th. Sign Capricorn. Cycle of Growth Stage 10 (Peak).

JANUARY - From Janus, God of gateways, doorways, and beginnings. Depicted as 2 faces looking in opposite directions. In Britain, especially the North, there was a ceremony of the eldest member of the family going out of the main door of the home, and the youngest entering with symbolic objects such as salt and coal. We can see the connection with New Year. Matches with the Zodiac Sign Aquarius (Water Carrier). New Year Resolutions. Cycle of Growth Stage 11 (Discontent).

FEBRUARY - Februa was a Roman festival of purification. We can see the correspondence with the symbol of Pisces (Fishes) where it relates to clearing the past to make a new future, and Baptism. Cycle of Growth Stage 12 (Confinement).

MARCH - From Mars, God of War, ruling planet of Aries (Ram). The phallic Sign. Cycle of Growth Stage 1 (Seed)

THE CALENDAR

APRIL - From Greek Aphrodite\Roman Venus. Venus rules Taurus (Bull). Cycle of Growth Stage 2 (Germination)

MAY - From Maia, a fertility goddess, daughter of Atlas (who bears the heavens) and Pleione (an Oceanid nymph). Maia gave birth to Greek Hermes (Roman Mercury) – Messenger of the Gods. Mercury rules Gemini (Twins). Cycle of Growth Stage 3 (Experiment. Communication).

JUNE - From Juno (Greek Hera), Queen of the Gods. Goddess of marriage and married women. Wife and sister of Jupiter (such a relationship was common among the older Gods because at the beginning there were so few of them to go round). Her festival was celebrated on March 1st. in Rome (she was mother of Aries\Mars). With Cancer (Crab) being ruled by the Moon, the relationship with Juno is a bit obscure. However, the Sign is related to Mother and the Home. Cycle of Growth Stage 4 (Transplanting) makes thing a little clearer with a relationship with Tarot Card VI. The Lovers – also coincidentally (or synchronistically ?) Number 6 (Venus. Desire) - the same as the month.

JULY - Julius Caesar, the Roman Emperor who reformed the calendar, named this month after himself. Symbolically, this seems to be no accident. The Sign is Leo (Lion. King of the jungle) ruled by the Sun – related to Cycle of Growth Stage 5 (Power. Creativity).

AUGUST - Augustus (="consecrated. Holy") Caesar amended the calendar and named this month after himself. The symbolic relationship is with Virgo (Virgin) – who shares Mercury as ruling planet with Gemini. Cycle of Growth Stage 6 (Service to Self). Again, the connection is not clear, however, we can note that the Encyclopaedia Britannica says :-

> *With unlimited patience, skill, and efficiency, he overhauled every aspect of Roman life and brought durable peace and prosperity to the Greco-Roman world. [EB]*

Virgo is a practical Earth sign containing the principles of Analysis to create Order. Virgo is "The Filing Clerk" of the Zodiac - as at Harvest Time, "sorting the wheat from the chaff". What is practically useful from what is not.

SEPTEMBER - "Seventh" month. 7th. Sign Libra. Cycle of Growth Stage 7 (Partners).

OCTOBER - "Eighth" month. 8th. Sign Scorpio. Cycle of Growth Stage 8 (Death. Intercourse).

THE TAROT

The chapter contains an overview of The 4 suits of the Minor Arcana and, at the end of the chapter, the individual 22 cards of the Major Arcana being described in relation to the 12 stages of The Cycle of Growth. There is more detail in other chapters.

Here is another subject surrounded in mystery and superstition – both of which are based on ignorance of the subject. In keeping with the overall nature of this book I am making no attempt to examine the subject in depth, but to extract the principles involved – especially where they relate to other areas of study such as Astrology, Psychology, The Kabbalah, and The Cycle of Growth.

There is mention of [THE KABBALAH TREE OF LIFE] because it plays a part in the more recent symbolism. There is a table comparing the 10 Sephiroth with the 40 numbered cards of The Minor Arcana at the beginning of that chapter.

If you wish to study the Tarot, it is of utmost importance that you do it in your own personal way. Consider it to be like a "tool" that can be used in many different ways.

Of relevance is my personal practical experience of using these cards in giving readings to people who, apart from friends and family, include hundreds of reading for people unknown to me, and who I never met before or since. This was my personal evidence that they do "work". As mentioned in the chapter [MY STORY] I first approached the subject with a high level of scepticism, and then only because I was encouraged by a friend who bought my first set of cards for me.

TAROT READINGS

My first experience of using the cards was from being given a set by a friend. Being sceptical, I decided to try them out first, so I sat down with my wife to give her a "reading", laid out the cards and referred to their meanings by looking them up in a book. To my surprise she understood the experience I was talking about – even though I did not.

When giving readings I always use the 10 card layout called "The Grand Cross" which, for me, gives a good balance of content between being too general or too complicated. The important factor being that it includes information about the past and present, as well as the future - so it is possible to first establish that the reading is accurate. Sometimes things do not seem to work. It may be due to my misreading, but a few times I have had clients say afterwards that they get the same problem with any form of clairvoyance or other reading. I usually get everyone to write things down. Quite often people come back to say they understood afterwards. On one occasion at a "Psychic Fair" I found out later that the person had then gone to my wife, who was giving clairvoyant Spirit Communication readings at the same time, and who gave her the same information she had written down - and could still not understand.

Every Tarot reader develops their own style, but they tend to fall into two main types with variations between. Like me, although the cards tend to "tell a story", some explain the meaning of each card and allow the client to make the associations with their life circumstances. At the other end of the scale, others use the cards as a link with the client and then give a clairvoyant reading – which, to me, borders on "cheating". I feel that the method I use gives less opportunity for my own personal views and beliefs to interfere. In fact, the less I know about the subject, the better seems to be the reading. It is very difficult to give a reading for myself. At another level I have discovered that the more specific a client is with the subject of the reading, the more accurate it is. Past and present circumstances are easier to check too. I do not need to know what the subject is, but the client needs to decide beforehand.

It is interesting to note that repeating a reading on the same question usually results in the same essence of meaning. Often the same few cards keep appearing. We note that once a reading is given the circumstances are not exactly the same.

As with the interpretation of a Birth Chart, I do not believe that the outcome predicted by a reading is what will necessarily happen. If, perhaps as a result of the overview provided by the reading the client decides to take a different course of action, then there will be a different outcome. As Edgar Cayce says "everything is subject to the Will".

THE TAROT

HISORY OF TAROT CARDS

Tarot cards were originally used for playing card games in the same way as modern ones. As in the modern day, there were numerous versions – possibly depending on what game they were used for. According to the Encyclopaedia Britannica the earliest reference to playing cards occurs in Chinese literature of the 10th. century. Although they invented block printing in the 6th. century the reference seems to be more related to mah-jongg and dominoes – both of which use tiles rather than card. The modern set of Tarot cards appeared in Italy in the 1430s by adding 21 "trump" cards.

Several references say that The Joker, which refers to Tarot card Zero, The Fool, was added to the normal deck in the 19th. century in order to play a game called eucre, making the point that it did not replace the 21 trumps. I tend to disagree. Although historically this may be correct The Joker does actually - in the timeline, and symbolically - replace the trump cards. As a "wild card", it takes the place of others in many games, and can cause disruption in the expected, logical, chain of events. In our examination of Number Zero in the chapter [NUMEROLOGY] and elsewhere we note that :-

1. Everything comes from Zero – or No-Thing.
2. The Number Zero is a relatively new discovery.

In the absence of the Tarot Major Arcana, there is also a modern tendency to allocate one of the 4 suits to be "trumps" in some games which aligns with the tendency for bias, for example, toward one of the 4 Jungian Functions, or Element Fire, Air, Water, and Earth, that they represent in the Tarot. The 22 trumps of the Major Arcana are none the less active by being relegated to the realms of the Unconscious. The act of giving a Tarot reading is basically similar to playing a game of cards (or reading a Birth Chart). One is "dealt a hand" at the beginning and we have to "play it out".

It is interesting to note that, whereas there were numerous versions of playing cards and Tarot cards at the beginning, nowadays there is very little variation in the, now standard, formats. There seems to have been some form of "organisation" at work.

HOW TAROT CARDS WORK : SYNCHRONICITY

COINCIDENCE

Coincidence is when events coincide in a rational or empirical way but without any seeming cause and effect relationship. I could, for example, see a coincidence of five black cars stopped at traffic lights. It could be considered coincidence that tossing a coin 10 times resulted in 10 tails, even though the chance at each toss is even. The point is that the result is one of an extremely large number of possibilities. Anything that can happen will happen, in time.

An area of the study of Coincidence is that of Statistics where certain properties hold the same proportions for large numbers of people. People make money out of statistical data in such areas as gaming – in roulette the odds are fixed so that over a period of time the house always wins. My brother is involved in the Insurance industry and says it is uncanny how they can calculate premiums for individuals, depending on their sex and lifestyle, and predict they will make a profit on a premium over time.

SYNCHRONICITY AND DIVINATION

When we give a reading for someone using Tarot cards we use synchronicity, which somehow connects events together in a <u>meaningful</u> way. Even though we shuffle the cards to make a seemingly random selection the ones chosen make a meaningful story. Good results, however, require a good method. The clearer the original question, the clearer the answer. There is also the necessity to use a layout that has fixed named card positions. A simple one for 3 cards would be "Past", "Present", and "Future".

C.G.Jung defined Synchronicity to mean the connection of two or more events by Meaning rather than Coincidence. A psychological link. Something different to what we would expect as a result of randomness or chance.

There is the example of a woman ordering a red dress and receiving delivery of a black one by "mistake". She then finds that a relative has died and she needs a black dress for the funeral. The relationship between black and death is a symbolic one. I suppose it would need to be a white dress in China.

THE TAROT

THE I CHING AND OTHER ORACLES

There are numerous examples of Divination like the Tarot that relate to the same principle. One is the Chinese method of referring to an oracle called the I Ching. One asks a question and then randomly chooses one of 64 Hexagrams each made up of 6 lines which can be Ying or Yang, or "changing" Ying or Yang. This was originally by separating stalks of a yarrow plant, nowadays by tossing 3 coins 6 times. We then look up the meaning in "The Book of Changes". I can find no relationship between the order of the 64 hexagrams and The Cycle of Growth, but the method does work. C.G.Jung used the I Ching, and wrote the foreword to the book "I Ching Book of Changes" which was translated from Chinese to German by Richard Wilhelm, and from German to English by Cary F. Baynes.

Other examples of divination would be the examination of the entrails of a freshly killed animal, or the analysis of a Birth Chart. In each case there is a relationship between an inner, psychological event, a "question", and an outer one. Another example is Numerology [NUMEROLOGY].

At another level there seem to be universal laws in operation that we are not yet aware of. When we look at the world of Nature carefully enough we can always see order, not chaos. Farmers make use of this all the time. We are told that we evolved as humans as a result of "mistakes" made in copying DNA. However, scientists are happy to note that mutations occurred at roughly 10,000 year intervals, and use it to calculate when they happened. When we study The Cycle of Growth we note that "mistakes", or deviation from fixed routine or structure, are part of the process in the Transcendent Octave. In my chapter [THE PURPOSELESS LIFE] is the result of a computer algorithm that starts off in a seeming random fashion and ends in an orderly fashion that continues ad infinitum – the point being that it is produced by a regular repetitive "programme".

ARCHETYPES

C.G. Jung in his work with dream analysis found that people often spontaneously produced the same images or themes no matter what their race or creed. He came to the conclusion that there are universal psychological forces operating that affect us all in the same way. The forces exist in The Collective Unconscious – an area that we all connect to via our own Personal Unconscious, and share. It seems that the meanings of such things as the Zodiac Signs and Tarot cards have arisen as a result of this. When we study The Cycle of Growth we find that these same forces affect all areas of our universe. The Astrological planets do not control our lives, but the laws that govern the movement of the planets also govern our lives. For example, a human lifetime has the same overall pattern as a calendar year – Spring, Summer, Autumn, and Winter.

From the example of Synchronicity earlier in this chapter, the interesting fact is that it does not matter whether the dress is black or white, both Eastern and Western races go to funerals. There have been recent discoveries to show that even stone age people had their graveyards. Why would this be so in such "unevolved", 'not quite human' beings? Burial of the dead clearly has no value for purposes of survival.

THE MINOR ARCANA

SUITS CORRESPONDENCES

Tarot	Modern	Element	Function	Perception	Polarity
Wands	Clubs	Fire	Intuition	Light/Sight	Positive
Cups	Hearts	Water	Feeling	Feelings	Negative
Swords	Spades	Air	Thinking	Hearing	Positive
Pentacles	Diamonds	Earth	Sensation	Touch	Negative

COURT CARDS (above)

	Page	Knight	Queen	King
Wands	Earth of Fire	Air of Fire	Water of Fire	Fire of Fire
Cups	Earth of Water	Air of Water	Water of Water	Fire of Water
Swords	Earth of Air	Air of Air	Water of Air	Fire of Air
Pentacles	Earth of Earth	Air of Earth	Water of Earth	Fire of Earth

Figure 45 : Tarot Minor Arcana

THE TAROT

There is a more detailed table of descriptive names for each card in [THE KABBALAH TREE OF LIFE].

The Minor Arcana is directly comparable with the modern deck of playing cards as having 4 suits each with 10 numbered cards plus some Court Cards with pictures - Knight (instead of Jack), Queen, and King. The main difference here is that each of the Tarot suits has an extra Court Card called a Page. This makes 14 cards to a suit – 56 cards overall. It is related to the objective world. Without the Major Arcana in modern packs it is concerned with gambling and chance.

4 SUITS

The 4 suits coincide with [THE 4 ELEMENTS] and [THE 4 FUNCTIONS] Fire (Wands), Air (Swords), Water (Cups), and Earth (Pentacles or coins) - from top to bottom in the diagram.

We can see the association with the modern suits :-

1. With Wands (Fire. positive polarity), the instinctive, mindless, basic, Club weapon of the early Tarot is here reduced to a stick, or staff, of wood. The Jungian Intuition Function.
2. The association of Swords (Air. positive polarity) with the Spades image is obscure. There is a suggestion that it developed from the Italian "spada" which means sword. There is another old pack that depicts them as the leaves of a tree. However, the association with Words and the symbol of Justice transformed into (s)words is clear. The Ace of Spades is traditionally the "death card", as is The Ace of Swords. The Jungian Thinking Function.
3. Cups (Water. negative polarity) is more manipulative via emotions, feelings, desires, and attractions of Hearts. The Jungian Feeling Function.
4. We can easily see that the suit of Pentacles or Coins (Earth. Negative polarity) is related to Diamonds as the most stable, dense, form of crystallised Carbon, and a means of currency. The Jungian Sensation Function.

TAROT CARDS 1 TO 10

Although I do not include the Minor Arcana in the Cycle of Growth they do fit into a similar pattern. There is a beginning with number 1 and an end with number 10. When we get to 10 we start again at number 1. It is important to note that the Elements are all an expression of the same basic energy, the difference being the rate of vibration, or frequency, so Fire is fastest and related to light, and, at the lowest rate of frequency, we have Earth.

A.E. Waite was a member of "The Hermetic Order of the Golden Dawn" society and a Freemason so the structure of his Tarot is strongly influenced by The Kabbalah (or Qabalah) and based upon "The Tree Of Life" which is a symbolic image or diagram - in principle rather like a Tarot card – that is used for study and meditation. [THE KABBALAH TREE OF LIFE]

There are 3 important points to consider :-

1. Each of the 10 Sephiroth contains the same numbered cards of each of the 4 Tarot suits – so all 4 Elements are represented. This fits in with areas such as Astrology and the Chakras where, although the separate divisions are given various symbolic Elemental associations, each of the divisions contains each of the 4 Elements. The paragraph "Tarot Court Cards" below is another example of this principle.
2. The Aces of each suit refer to the Element in its purest, initial, form and the following cards relate to its development and increase in energy. In terms of The Tree of Life, its descent into a more material form from 1 to 10. In The Kabbalah Tree of Life the Aces refer to Sephirah 1 (Kether. Crown. Number Zero).
3. At the beginning the Element is weak in material terms until it reaches the balance point at card number 6. If you look at the Tree of Life figure [THE KABBLAH TREE OF LIFE] you will see that the Sephiroth 6. Tiphareth, Beauty, is in a state of balance at the centre, and has numerous paths, or points of communication with others. Here the Element is at its most harmonious, stable, form. It relates to the Heart Chakra. (This is not the same "heart" as in the suit of Hearts). As the growth, or power of a single Element, increases it becomes into conflict with other forces, and, paradoxically, becomes more limited. Energy is used to overcome opposition rather than expand further. The two Positive Elements – Wands and Swords – meet outer resistance. With negative Cups all energy becomes "watered down" to a state of dreamlike bliss, and Earthy Pentacles shows the lack of its complementary element Fire by entering

THE TAROT

a state of retirement, or inertia in the cold dark Winter of life. So one of the lessons of the Tree of Life is to remain at number 6. Here it is part of the mystical "Middle Path" – or Middle Pillar of The Tree of Life.

4. You will note that, in its balance position in the Centre Pillar, Tarot cards numbered 6 have direct contact (via Daath) with the highest Sephiroth 1.The Crown. This suggests the possibility of control by means of Will and Purpose – which can align all the Elements into a single goal. At this level people share the same Ideals – which may not be the same as a material goal.
5. Number 6 relates to Cycle of Growth Stage 5 (Power. Creativity. The Sun. Ego Consciousness) at the beginning of the 3rd. Octave.

TAROT COURT CARDS

Each suit has 4 court cards which tend to refer to actual people in a layout – and which could also be a depiction of the client. The 4 cards also refer to the 4 Elements in turn. The image and the Element suggest the type of person and the energies they express. We note that the Kings (Fire) and Queens (Water) are seated, and therefore more stable or established in their positions. The Knights (Air) are riding horses, moving in a manner appropriate to the Element. The Pages (Earth) are depicted as younger persons contemplating symbols of their Element.

You will note from the Minor Arcana diagram that each of the 4 Suits, or Elements, has 4 modes of operation with King (Fire),Queen (Water), Knight (Air) and Page (Earth). Partial descriptions can be :-

Wands (Fire) are concerned with creativity, action, and creativity.

King of Wands is Fire of Fire	(Power. Will. Lord Of The Manor)
Queen of Wands is Water of Fire	(Balanced Power. Lady Of The Manor)
Knight of Wands is Air of Fire	(Moving Power. Action. Competition. Negotiation)
Page of Wands is Earth of Fire	(Delegated Power. Service. $E = MC^2$)

The Swords (Air) show a more divisive, pictures of conflict of ideas, and loneliness.

King of Swords (Fire of Air)	(Intellectual masculine Power. Moral Law. Justice)
Queen of Swords (Water of Air)	(Intellectual feminine power. A lone woman)
Knight of Swords Air of Air)	(Movement. Conflict of ideas. Discussion)
Page of Swords (Earth of Air)	(Practical study. Science)

The Cups (Water) mainly relate to Pleasure or Desire (inner Feeling) and Sharing.

King of Cups (Fire of Water)	(Concealed Power. Secrets. Manipulation)
Queen of Cups (Water of Water)	(Maternal Power)
Knight of Cups (Air of Water)	(Cautious approach. Wooing. Offerings)
Page of Cups (Earth of Water)	(Imagination. Reflection. Investigation)

Pentacles or Coins relate to practical affairs

King of Pentacles (Fire of Earth)	(Practical businessman. Craftsmanship)
Queen of Pentacles (Water of Earth)	(Practical management. The Mother. Home)
Knight of Pentacles (Air of Earth)	(Routine work. The Ploughboy)
Page of Pentacles (Earth of Earth)	(Pupil. Practical Study. Knowledge)

THE TAROT MAJOR ARCANA AND THE CYCLE OF GROWTH

Here we adopt a more poetic tone on a subject that is given more practical detail in other chapters.

When considering associations with [NUMEROLOGY] it is instructive to compare cards I to IX with those of higher number. For example, card number VI.The Lovers (Number 6 – Venus/Desire) has association with card XV. The Devil – also Number 6. However, in The Cycle of Growth VI.The Lovers refers to Stage 4 (Transplanting. The Moon. Cancer) and XV.The Devil refers to Stage 10 (Peak. Harvest. Saturn/Satan. Capricorn). This is an example of how matters can become extremely complex, and so is avoided here.

THE TAROT

The Major Arcana is represented in some modern card games by choosing one of the 4 suits as "trumps" – giving it a higher value than the others. It is related to the hidden subjective realm of the Collective Unconscious.

I include the Traditional Meanings of A.E. Waite as historical examples – not because they are always correct. As with all occult or unknown subjects, we need to discern what is true or false for ourselves. There are always traps for the lazy or unwary and it is a fact that sometimes the writers of Waite's time deliberately set out to deceive (ref. [DFMQ]).

The Major Arcana is a set of 22 cards that are presented as a set of pictures that, until The Cycle of Growth, have no real logical linkage to one another, although, taken as a whole they do tell a story with a beginning and end – and then start over again. In psychological terms they appeal to the "Right Brain" which is concerned with Art rather than the "Left Brain", Science. They have no equivalence in a modern deck of playing cards – except, as mentioned, being represented in entirety by The Joker.

There is much controversy about them, much of which can be dissolved when we consider some facts :

1. Some writers put some cards in a different order to that in which they appear. This is an obvious error because they are explicitly numbered in sequence Zero to XXI. For some reason they are numbered using Roman numerals, perhaps to emphasise their difference to the Minor Arcana which clearly has a logical, numeric basis. There is one exception where A.E. Waite in his Tarot version (which I use in this book) has transposed, without giving a reason, the Strength card, originally XI with Justice, originally number V. This makes sense because the pictures clearly relate to the Zodiac Signs Leo (Lion. Sign 5) and Libra (Scales. Sign 7). This is clarified further in the relevant chapters.

2. It is pointless trying to understand the Art of the Tarot, or any other art, in a logical way using the Jungian Function of Thinking (Left Brain). Art uses the "language" of the Jungian Function Feeling (Right Brain) which tends to value things, such as in the broad sense of like or dislike. Because words are "Left Brain" it is also pointless trying to describe feelings in words – but we all know what they are.

3. Although I use A.E Waite's version of the Tarot - who used the artist Pamela Coleman Smith – I do not suggest that you try to read his book "The Key to the Tarot". At top level it is rambling and incoherent, and at another level there seems to be a deliberate attempt to mislead, and perhaps misinform. Or, perhaps, he was just not a Left Brain person. Although his books are not too good, the symbolism depicted in his cards has great depth. I am sure that they would not have survived to be so popular otherwise.

4. The language of the Tarot is symbolism. At one level it has personal meaning, at another, such as with the Major Arcana, it is universal.

5. Arcana means "hidden".

6. To understand each card fully we need to consider its position relative to the pattern of The Cycle of Growth.

7. I have included biblical text of the Genesis story of Creation relating to Cycle of Growth Stages 9 to 1 to emphasise the similarity between the images. There is more detail in [GENESIS AND THE CYCLE OF GROWTH].

Although some form of value judgement ("good or bad") may be implied in the description of the Major Cards, it is not intended. When dealing with The Cycle of Growth every stage is necessary. Indeed, modern psychology demonstrates that to seemingly miss a step leads to continual regression, or psychological interference, until its puzzle is solved.

The first thing to note is that 22 cards will not fit exactly into 12 Stages. However, when we keep everything in order and compare the meanings everything falls into place. There are occasions when a Tarot card on a 'cusp' might fit in to the earlier or following Stage, but this is a reflection of normal life. For example, although our calendar has a fixed structure, the seasons' climate does not always follow the exact same pattern each year. Apart from the calendar we cannot tell exactly when Spring becomes Summer. In this case, the challenge serves to deepen our understanding of the Cycle.

Another main point is that the true beginning of Creation is at Cycle of Growth Stage 9 (Conception) and relates to the Big Bang of human evolution. The Stage relates to Tarot Card XIV. Temperance. The intervening period between that stage and that of The Fool is concerned with the development of the foetus in the womb and the Transcendent Octave of the Logarithmic Timescale. Here we begin with 0. The Fool which is the actual arrival of a physical new-born baby, which until now has only been an 'abstract' possibility. In my chapter [GENESIS AND THE CYCLE OF GROWTH] we see that this, in turn relates to the creation of Adam in the Garden of Eden from dust - after God rested on the 7th. Day. We are then dealing with actual human development from Birth to Death and beyond.

Because The Cycle of Growth begins at Stage 9 (Conception. New Life) I begin with Card XIV.Temperance which follows Card XIII.Death.

CARD XIV : TEMPERANCE

Figure 46 : TAROT XIV - TEMPERANCE

THE IMAGE

We see a winged, angelic, figure, neither male nor female, standing with one foot on the Earth and the other in Water – symbolic of Earthly and Emotional Under-standings. The angel is pouring the contents of a cup from one to the other – a process of separation and combination. The figure has the symbol of the Fire Element on the breast and the symbol of the Sun in the centre of the forehead. In the background there is a narrow pathway – a seeming extension of the water on the ground – which leads between two hills (which replace the pillars of other cards), where the Sun is shining between. The Sun in the background is like that on the forehead of the angel. Both give the impression of a crown. They are not the same, although the latter is a personal image of the former. They are both acting in harmony.

All 4 Elements are depicted here – Earth, Water, Fire and Air. This could be a depiction of The Tree of Life with its several levels top to toe.

ASSOCIATIONS : CYCLE OF GROWTH STAGE 9 (CONCEPTION)

The 9th. House – Social Mental Concepts

Sagittarius, The Archer. The Centaur, half man half horse. Mutable (Changeable) Fire. The Higher Mind. Abstract Thinking. Expansion of Consciousness. Academic Study. Foreign Travel.

Cycle of Growth Stage 9 has 2 related planets – Pluto (Regeneration. Number 1) at the beginning of the Kabbalah evolutionary Lightning Flash, and Jupiter – (Expansion, Inflation. Number 3) if the Transcendent Octave is not activated.

In the calendar year this is the time of The Annunciation – the foretelling of the birth of Jesus by the Angel Gabriel to the virgin Mary - the coming of The Messiah.

Conception is the beginning of Life in the womb and occurs in secret. There are no external indications yet. The mother may become intuitively (Fire) aware – but physical evidence will be needed.

THE TAROT

In the chapter [THE GENESIS STORY] we can see that the current stages under discussion - Cycle of Growth Stages 9 to 12 - relate to the 7 days of Creation – which also, following the same evolutionary pattern, relates to the Creation of a human body in the womb. The story of The Adam and Eve actually relates to Cycle of Growth Stages 1 (Seed) to Stage 4 (Transplanting) because, until Stage 1 – physical birth – there is no physical Garden of Eden, and no Adam. However, we must take note of the fact that nothing comes into being in the material world without first becoming an image in the mind. "In The Beginning was The Word".

This is the beginning of Creation in Genesis Chapter 1 – which follows the now accepted scientific description from the Big Bang onwards :-

Verse 1: In the beginning of God's preparing the heavens and the earth

Verse 2: the earth hath existed waste and void, and darkness [is] on the face of the deep, and the Spirit of God fluttering on the face of the waters, [YLT]

COMMENTARY

1. The Number 14 equates to Number 5 (The Sun) – Mind over Matter. At this level there is relationship with the Higher Mind, Super Conscious, – or Jungian 'Self'.
2. As a Fire Sign, this is the beginning of the 1st. Octave of the Logarithmic Timescale. Cards relating to the other Fire Signs - Aries (2nd. Quadrant) I.The Magician and Leo (3rd. Quadrant) VIII.Strength have the infinity symbol above the heads of the subjects.
3. With Temperance we become our own Tarot V. Hierophant – connecting to the higher self.
4. It is said that after we die the whole of our past life passes before our eyes.
5. Hindsight is an exact science. New life offers a second chance. The previous Cycle of Growth Stage 8 (Death) has its uses.
6. The image is of Will and The Higher Mind in action, and has connotations with Card I, The Magician and his tools. Here, all 4 Elements are being separated and combined.
7. Temperance means separation and mediation. The resolution of conflict at a higher level. Justice could only see 2 alternatives. As we see below, this can also mean academic study to establish a wider viewpoint.
8. Real Life is complicated, and does not always conform to human rules. "The Opposites" are really only meant for guidance. *"Rules are for the guidance of wise men and the blind obedience of fools. "[Solon, the Lawmaker of Athens 559BC].* Justice is often depicted as blind, or blindfolded.
9. There are also connotations with Card XVII, The Star, to come, when the contents of the cups are emptied.
10. In human Conception the genes of the Sperm and Egg mingle to produce a child - which is different to both father and mother. Evolution favours Diversity.
11. When 2 people have intercourse, sexual or otherwise, a third entity is produced – which is the relationship between them. This is Synergy, where the whole is greater than the parts. This is part of the meaning behind the Holy Trinity – Father, Son, and Holy Ghost.
12. This is how the universe began. The Big Bang produced (separated) pure energy out of No-Thing (Number Zero). Some of the energy immediately became Matter. $E=MC^2$.
13. The related Planet is Pluto, which has the same connotations.
14. Sagittarius - Mutable (Changeable) Fire - relates to Sephirah 2 (Chockmah. Wisdom. Force) – the chaotic condition of Plasma which is 98% of our universe.
15. This is how life began on Earth millions of years ago with the combination of 2 bacteria. During the following months, until birth, the child will relive each stage of Evolution from that time - to fish, to ape, to human. The child then lives it over (and over) again as a human on earth, or a brain-child – an original idea.
16. This is also how ideas ("brain children") are created in the mind before they take physical form later on. This is a true "Virgin Birth". The timescale is usually much faster than Evolution or the birth of a human child, but the process is the same.

THE TAROT

17. The association of Sagittarius with Academic Study and the Higher Mind are entirely in keeping – as is the fact that this means gaining knowledge without any personal, practical, experience. (In-tuition)
18. Perhaps Cycle of Growth Stage 9 holds a secret of Reincarnation.
19. The "crowns" in the image bring to mind that in The Tree of Life we begin with Sephirah 1 (Kether. Crown. The Crown Chakra. Number Zero).

TRADITIONAL MEANINGS [AEW]

Economy, moderation, frugality, management, accommodation.

Reversed : Things connected with churches, religions, sects, the priesthood, sometimes even the priest who will marry the Querent; also disunion, unfortunate combinations, competing interests.

FROM MY PRACTICAL READINGS

Complications in life. The Querent is needing to combine several factors in order to reach a decision for action. There is warning to take no action yet. It is a time to think and plan in secret. This could also mean negotiations are taking place. The decisions now will affect the future.

CARD XV : THE DEVIL

Figure 47 : TAROT XV - THE DEVIL

THE IMAGE

In accordance with the traditional image, The Devil is here depicted as a half-human half-animal figure - with wings as an indicator of his heavenly origins before his fall. His right hand is raised in benediction like that of V.The Hierophant. Before him are male and female figures who are chained to a stone block.

We note that the image and that following are similar to that of The Hierophant and The Lovers.

The variations from the traditional image are that, firstly, The Devil has been given the horns and face of a goat (which, apart from being a traditional image, emphasises its relationship with Capricorn) and he has an inverted pentacle on his forehead. In addition, both human figures have horns and tails. The tail of the female has fruit, that of the male is alight with Fire, which seems to have been ignited by The Devil's torch – and which is pointed towards the Earth.

Both human subjects are chained to a block at the feet of The Devil, however the chains are loose - they could easily be removed.

THE TAROT

In this image, whilst not particularly frightening, The Devil has a stern, serious expression. The traditional images seem more benevolent, some even smiling. Stupid even.

The image resembles that of the Greek God, or Nature Spirit, Pan.

ASSOCIATIONS : CYCLE OF GROWTH STAGE 10 (SOCIAL PEAK. HARVEST)

The 10th. House – Social Security.

The Winter Solstice. The Rebirth of The SUN. The Rebirth of The SON of God at Christmas. Capricorn the climbing Mountain Goat (or half goat, half fish). Cardinal (Active) Earth – Career. Worldly Ambition.

Saturn /Satan (Consolidation. Discipline. Control. Number 2)

Life in the womb : The mother realises that she is pregnant. The foetus will repeat the stages of early Animal evolution into human form.

This is the "Birth in a Manger", that is, The Spirit requires an Earthy vehicle for Earthy experience among the common animals, as in The Garden of Eden. We do not yet have a human child who will be born later in Spring, at Easter, with his final crucifixion on the Cross of Matter.

The first reaction of the reigning King Herod was to treat the Birth as a threat to his authority, and to kill all the new born. This could be The Emperor or Hierophant in action.

In Genesis 1 we see another relationship between The Devil (Saturn/Satan) and The Tower (Lucifer/Bringer of Light) :-

*Verse 3: and God saith, `Let light be;' and light is.

*Verse 4: And God seeth the light that [it is] good, and God separateth between the light and the darkness,

*Verse 5: and God calleth to the light `Day,' and to the darkness He hath called `Night;' and there is an evening, and there is a morning – day one. [YLT]

COMMENTARY

1. We note that Darkness was the original state of the universe before The Big Bang.
2. In The Kabbalah Tree of Life we are at Sephirah 3 (Binah. Understanding. Form. Saturn/Satan. Number 2) which contains the principle of Inertia, forcing Chockmah Force to come to order. We see how this also relates to Tradition and Government.
3. The Devil is the first of two cards relating to Cycle of Growth Stage 10 (Social Peak. Harvest). After Stage 9 (Conception) comes the building of a human body in the womb which will become the Temple of the Soul.
4. This seems to be another representation of The Hanged Man where, after some mental analysis, the reason for the "blockage" may be coming clear.
5. After Temperance can discover no practical solution to the Dilemma the stone that the builder rejected becomes a cornerstone of future growth.
6. After academic Temperance, we have the possibility of a practical solution.
7. The position of The Devil in The Cycle of Growth Stage 10 (Social Peak) is opposite the cards V. The Hierophant and VI. The Lovers which have similar images. The Opposition Aspect is one of conscious awareness.
8. The Hierophant can appear as The Devil, and The Devil as a Hierophant.
9. Number 1+5 equates to Number 6 (Venus) – Desire.
10. The Devil is an essential part of The Cycle of Growth. He is a "Fallen Angel". He would not exist unless he serves some Holy (Whole. Health) purpose. In God is contained everything.
11. The Devil is the Jungian "Shadow". Light (consciousness) always casts a shadow (in the unconscious). The Archetypal version is God's Shadow. With Job in the Old Testament we see God's struggle with his Shadow. We each have our own Shadow which consists of all we hold to be "inferior", and which, with recognition and development, can become the source of new life.
12. In this case "Inferior" merely means undeveloped from lack of use.

13. The Devil reminds us of our animal origins and the fact that we are required to live an earthy existence - and support a physical body.
14. The chains of the Devil's subjects are loose. If they were aware of it, they would find them easily removable.
15. The Devil is a Capricorn Scape-Goat who is blamed for many human actions – as if there is no Will.
16. The Pentacle has 5 points which symbolise Mind, and Matter (the 4 Elements). With the downward-facing "triangle", as here, it is Matter Over Mind (when reversed it is Mind Over Matter). This is also the thumb opposing 4 fingers, so we can "grasp" things.
17. Even God had material ambition when he created everything – each "day" of Creation being a single cycle of The Cycle of Growth. During each cycle he created additions to the material world and rested on the 7th. Day. This is the same as the form of a human working week – which has been designed to specifically match this pattern. We could have chosen any other set of days, or none at all.
18. There is no evil that cannot include some good, or good that cannot include some evil.
19. The Hierophant decides what is good or evil without evidence, and therefore perpetuates the Original Sin.
20. The Devil is the result of eating from The Tree of Knowledge in The Garden of Eden. Without knowledge there is no good or evil – which is why many remain ignore – ant.
21. The Devil is also known as Satan, which means "The Adversary", or Pan, the masculine creative Nature Spirit akin to Mother Nature. Pan is also the generic family name of the Chimpanzee to whom all humans are related via a common ancestor.
22. The association with Capricorn, Career, and the chained figures, means that to achieve a worldly Harvest, or high position, requires being chained to The Wheel for a long period of time.
23. The "Temptation of The Devil" is whether to remain as we are, in a safe albeit, controlled, environment or to seek outside Tradition to find our own answers. In true mediation of "Opposites" we find a third option – we can do both.........
24. We can " ... render therefore unto Caesar the things which are Caesar's; and unto God the things that are God's." [Matthew Chapter 22 :21]
25. The Devil is "Temptation", The Serpent, as that of Adam by Eve in The Garden of Eden later on. Another connotation is therefore that sexual intercourse is the use of higher energies for lower purposes.

TRADITIONAL MEANINGS [AEW]

Ravage, violence, vehemence, extraordinary efforts, force, fatality; that which is predestined but is not for this reason evil.

Reversed : Evil fatality, weakness, pettiness, blindness.

FROM MY PRACTICAL READINGS

The Devil appears when the Querent is tempted to continue doing what is known to be wrong, or has known bad effects.

THE TAROT

CARD XVI : THE TOWER

Figure 48 : TAROT XVI - THE TOWER

THE IMAGE
We see a tall, narrow, tower structure with 3 small windows which is being struck by lightning at its top. At the top of The Tower is a crown which has been knocked off in the process. Two human figures have been ejected from The Tower and are falling headfirst to the ground.

ASSOCIATIONS : CYCLE OF GROWTH STAGE 10 (SOCIAL PEAK. HARVEST)
As The Devil, above.

COMMENTARY
1. In Genesis after Light (consciousness) comes from the primal Darkness, the Darkness becomes "visible".
2. The Tower is the second of two cards relating to Cycle of Growth Stage 10 . After seeing Satan/Saturn, "The Adversary" [YLT], which is one face of The Devil, we now see his other face – Lucifer, which means "Bringer of Light".
3. The Number of The Tower equates to Number 7 (Mercury. Communication) which we can relate to The Tower of Babel and its concern with "Babble" when numerous languages were created.
4. The 2 falling figures are those in the card of The Devil who have now been released from bondage. It is an indication of the effort required to dislodge them.
5. This is "divorce" from the Cycle of Growth Stage 4 (Transplanting) marriage of The Hierophant and The Lovers.
6. The narrow Tower with small windows is suggestive of a restricted viewpoint –and/or creative energy focused on a material goal over a period of time (Capricorn/Saturn). At least something has been achieved. Somehow, to reach this stage, the work has been necessary.
7. The lighting, striking the "head" of the tower, then becomes the light of new Consciousness or Revelation. Perhaps Realisation, or the perception of Reality, that one has not really reached the top. The continuing Cycle of Growth suggests that we never come to a Final Conclusion. The king has lost his crown.
8. Having achieved The Goal, perhaps there is something better.

THE TAROT

9. "The Lightning Flash" of The Kabbalah Tree of Life carries the raw energy of Sephirah 1 (Kether. Crown) down The Tree to the bottom Sephirah 10 (Malkuth. Kingdom. Earth). Each of the intervening Sephiroth stages reduces the frequency of vibration.
10. The Tower is a representation of the Twin Pillars seen in the cards at other stages – II. The Priestess, V. The Hierophant, and XI. Justice. They are disguised in cards VI. The Lovers, VII. The Chariot and XV. The Devil. They combine into a single support in Card XII. The Hanged Man which, through his sacrifice, later becomes The Tower.
11. The Tower is akin to The Tower of Babel and other manmade, phallic, status symbols such as spires, ziggurats, and pyramids – which are symbols of man's attempt to reach "Godhood" by material rather than spiritual methods (and were begun in Cycle of Growth Stage 1 (Seed) by The Magician). The Tower is built of manmade bricks rather than natural rock. Brick eventually crumbles to dust.
12. There is included the message that every human creation eventually becomes dust.
13. The Tower is the result of Icarus, with his manufactured wings, flying too close to the Sun causing him to fall back down to earth and be drowned in the sea (of common humanity or The Collective Unconscious). Cycle of Growth Stage 12 (Withdrawal).
14. Some suggest an allusion to the Fall of Adam. In the Cycle of Growth this occurs in the "opposite" Stage 4 (Transplanting). This is rather "The Fall" of God in His appearance as The Son.
15. The image is a demonstration of why human "Houses of God" – Temples, Churches and phallic towers - need lightning conductors to protect them from "acts of God".
16. The Tower, however, is part of The Cycle of Growth. The suggestion is, especially with The Devil here, that it is a "necessary evil". Until one has actually achieved something in the material world, and made it perceptible to the 5 Senses, it is all just academic imagination. With The Devil we finally have hard evidence. In The Tower is contained the secret of life that the destination is not really important. What is important is the journey required to get there. In time, everything we achieve passes away. But there is always a rebirth to come.
17. This is a realisation that Tradition and Authority, and other controlling figures, do not always offer the right answers. If one becomes famous, one becomes a slave to one's followers.
18. It is a realisation that the only common realities in life are Birth and Death – at which time we are ultimately alone.

TRADITIONAL MEANINGS [AEW]

Misery, distress, indigence, adversity, calamity, disgrace, deception, ruin. It is a card in particular of unforeseen catastrophe.

Reversed : According to one account, the same in a lesser degree also oppression, imprisonment, tyranny.

FROM MY PRACTICAL READINGS

The Tower appears at times of sudden, often unexpected, changes.

THE TAROT

CARD XVII : THE STAR

Figure 49 : TAROT XVII - THE STAR

THE IMAGE

The image is of a naked female figure kneeling with one knee on the ground and the other foot in a pool. She has a jug of water in each hand from which she is pouring water, one into the pool, the other on to the Earth. In the background there is a small bird sitting on a bush. In the sky we see 8 eight-pointed stars, one of which is larger than the rest. In Numerology Number 17 becomes Number 8.

This image is basically the same as the traditional one.

ASSOCIATIONS : CYCLE OF GROWTH STAGE 11 (DISCONTENT)

Discontent can mean "Divine Discontent".

The 11th. house – Social Creativity. Friends.

Aquarius The Water Carrier (Cloud. "The Air Waves"). Fixed Air. Positive.

The Sign has 2 related planets and, as individuals, we can relate to one or the other at any time. The Traditional Saturn/Satan (Number 2), also rules Stage 10 – so it can be a continuation of the control of The Devil, when there will be no later changes (The Transcendent Octave is not activated) – and the newly discovered Uranus - planet of Invention and Individuation where we learn to think for ourselves. It is a question of Will as to which is given attention.

The images of both related cards, The Star and The Moon, related to Cycle of Growth Stage 11 (Discontent) are of night time. This is when the inner Unconscious becomes active.

The main function of Uranus (Number 11) is Revolution, which can be brought about by peaceful or violent methods, such as negotiation or new technology. It has other associations such as Communication. Invention. Technology from stone tools to computers. Electronic communication, Radio, Television – all of which create "waves".

Life in the womb : The development of the nervous system. The attention of the mother is focusing on the child within.

With the relationship of the 2 Tarot cards with The Cycle of Growth Stage 11 we are reminded of the Greek myth of Pandora and her box, or jar, which has a theme vary similar to that of Adam and Eve in The Garden of Eden. Pandora was given a container which she was instructed by Zeus, King of The Gods, (who can be considered in the role of The Emperor, The Hierophant or The Devil) never to open. Of course her curiosity got the better of her and she did, and the result was that she released all the evils of the world (XVIII. The Moon).

THE TAROT

There was, however, one thing that remained, and that was Hope. In Pandora's case there was no punishment because Zeus knew what would happen. Perhaps God did too.

The Star clearly depicts the "separation of waters" (which first appeared in XIV. Temperance) of Creation Days 2 and 3 by the outpouring on to Earth and Water. We also have the creation of Stars in Creation Day 4.

Verse 6: And God saith, `Let an expanse be in the midst of the waters, and let it be separating between waters and waters.'

Verse 7: And God maketh the expanse, and it separateth between the waters which [are] under the expanse, and the waters which [are] above the expanse: and it is so.

Verse 8: And God calleth to the expanse `Heavens;' and there is an evening, and there is a morning – day second.

Uranus, ruler of Aquarius and Cycle of Growth Stage 11 (Discontent) means "Heaven".

Verse 9: And God saith, `Let the waters under the heavens be collected unto one place, and let the dry land be seen:' and it is so.

Verse 10: And God calleth to the dry land `Earth,' and to the collection of the waters He hath called `Seas;' and God seeth that [it is] good.

Verse 11: And God saith, `Let the earth yield tender grass, herb sowing seed, fruit-tree (whose seed [is] in itself) making fruit after its kind, on the earth:' and it is so.

Verse 12: And the earth bringeth forth tender grass, herb sowing seed after its kind, and tree making fruit (whose seed [is] in itself) after its kind; and God seeth that [it is] good;

Verse 13: and there is an evening, and there is a morning – day third.

Here we get the stars that appear on the card.

Verse 14: And God saith, `Let luminaries be in the expanse of the heavens, to make a separation between the day and the night, then they have been for signs, and for seasons, and for days and years,

Verse 15: and they have been for luminaries in the expanse of the heavens to give light upon the earth:' and it is so. [YLT]

COMMENTARY

1. The Star is the first of two cards related to Cycle of Growth Stage 11 (Discontent). We note the similarity of this card with that of XIV. Temperance which appeared in Stage 9 (Conception) . At that stage the Water of Life was being poured from one jug to the other. It was the "mixing of opposites" (as is physical Conception) in the attempt to discover a "solution" to a problem or dilemma. Worry. Apart from the obvious interpretation concerned with everyday matters, the suggestion is that it was asking the question "Why?". Or "What is the Purpose of Life". This problem did not arise out of nothing. The Process began with card XI. Justice and came to focus with the realities of Card XIII. Death.

2. XVIII = Number 8 (The Moon), the symbol of Infinity and The Higher Mind. As 4 + 4, it is that of worldly, material, control. Time and Nature controlling The 4 Elements. The Tarot Moon comes next.

3. After the realisation that the past, and what is accepted by external Society ("Caesar") - as symbolised by The Devil - does not supply the answers we need, we are prompted to seek within.

4. The image is of pouring life energy, or consciousness, into 2 different places. The outer and inner worlds. Here, the inner, Water, world is receiving conscious attention whilst continuing with the automatic routines of everyday life – on Earth - the cup in the left (sinister, unconscious) hand is "behind" the figure.

5. A Star is a Sun which is only visible at night – when the setting of the outer Sun reduces our consciousness of the Outer World of society, and transfers consciousness to the personal, private, Inner World.

6. The Star is the unconscious counterpart of our personal Sun, which is the centre of our Solar System.

THE TAROT

7. This card is often related to Hope (of new and better beginnings). At this time The Star is not yet revealed. The attention of the figure in the image is internal. In the Annual Cycle we are now in Winter Time, hoping for a new Spring – or fulfilment of a New Year Resolution.
8. Aquarius/Uranus also relates to the transfer of power from The Monarchy or Dictatorship to the Individual via Democracy.

*"Now is the winter of our discontent

Made glorious summer by this son of York;

And all the clouds that low'r'd upon our house

In the deep bosom of the ocean buried."

[William Shakespeare : Richard The Third Act 1, scene 1, 1-4]

The verse depicts a power struggle. Richard's brother Edward IV had taken the English crown from Henry VI and removed the oppression of the York family. Edward's emblem is the Sun. We see the image of The Star, previously concealed, now rising - and the Aquarian "Water Carrier" with his dark rain clouds pouring into the "sea" of the Collective Unconscious . There are also connection with The Media – advertising and broadcasting the news.

TRADITIONAL MEANINGS [AEW]

Loss, theft, privation, abandonment; another reading says-hope and bright prospects,

Reversed : Arrogance, haughtiness, impotence.

FROM MY PRACTICAL READINGS

A time of separation from society and consideration of one's inner world. Introversion. Perhaps meditation. Hope for a better future not yet realised in outer reality.

CARD XVIII : THE MOON

Figure 50 : TAROT XVIII - THE MOON

THE IMAGE

We see two dogs, or a wolf and a dog, howling at the Full Moon on which is projected the image of a human face. In the foreground is a crayfish or lobster which is climbing on to dry land from out of the sea. It has a narrow path in front of it. The image is a "snapshot" of time, or a moment of hesitation. For the crayfish to *continue on its journey it must pass between the animals, then the two pillars. We do not know if it will do so, or if fear will cause it to retreat back into the sea.*

ASSOCIATIONS : CYCLE OF GROWTH STAGE 11 (DISCONTENT)

We have an example of how difficult it is to separate stages of development. The Moon could equally be placed in Cycle of Growth Stage 12 (Withdrawal) together with XIX. The Sun – especially as we have the continuation of Creation Day 4 in Genesis 1, and Day 5 :-

Verse 16: And God maketh the two great luminaries, the great luminary for the rule of the day, and the small luminary – and the stars – for the rule of the night;

Verse 17: and God giveth them in the expanse of the heavens to give light upon the earth,

Verse 18: and to rule over day and over night, and to make a separation between the light and the darkness; and God seeth that [it is] good;

Verse 19: and there is an evening, and there is a morning – day fourth.

**Verse 20: And God saith, `Let the waters teem with the teeming living creature, and fowl let fly on the earth on the face of the expanse of the heavens.'*

Verse 21: And God prepareth the great monsters, and every living creature that is creeping, which the waters have teemed with, after their kind, and every fowl with wing, after its kind, and God seeth that [it is] good.

Verse 22: And God blesseth them, saying, `Be fruitful, and multiply, and fill the waters in the seas, and the fowl let multiply in the earth:'

Verse 23: and there is an evening, and there is a morning – day fifth. [YLT]

COMMENTARY

1. The Moon is the second card related to Cycle of Growth Stage 11. The meditation, or inner contemplation, of The Star is leading to the Unconscious becoming active and bringing forth new life. Like Pandora's Box, the release of Hope is coupled with other, more fearful, possibilities.
2. 1 + 8 equates with Number 9 (Sephirah 10. Malkuth. Kingdom. The Earth) – which is the end of a cycle of the rational numbers. One can go no further on the current path. The future is unclear.
3. The Moon (unconscious) meets the light of the Sun (conscious). This is Reflection when Conscious and Unconscious come together. Here the images are as of a nightmare.
4. The Moon refers to The Personal Unconscious.
5. Everything created must follow the evolutionary path, or process, of The Cycle of Growth. This is a picture of the (scientific) stage of Evolution when animals were first coming out of the sea on to dry land, to evolve further in the new habitat.
6. The Moon refers to Creation Day 5 when water creatures were formed. Later on they evolve to populate and survive on dry land.
7. This is "The Dark Night of the Soul", which one can only face alone and unaided – except for that inner glimmer of hope. One knows the past is dead, but the future is unclear. To begin with the images produced are negative ones based on the teachings of The Hierophant's "Heaven and Hell" (in Card V we can see he holds the keys to both, or believes he does). We then have to pass between his 2 pillars.
8. This is the time of Jesus facing his destiny. His lone Temptation by The Devil in the wilderness.
9. The Moon could relate to psychoanalysis.
10. The pictures in the mind are beginning to take form.

TRADITIONAL MEANINGS [AEW]

Hidden enemies, danger, calumny, darkness, terror, deception, occult forces, error.

Reversed : Instability, inconstancy, silence, lesser degrees of deception and error.

THE TAROT

FROM MY PRACTICAL READINGS

This is a stage of life where one seems to be going through a "tunnel". There is some hope of a better future, but nothing is clear. One can only take things slowly, a step at a time. A similar card to IX. The Hermit.

CARD XIX : THE SUN

Figure 51 : TAROT XIX - THE SUN

THE IMAGE

The central figure is of a naked child riding a white horse carrying a red banner of victory. Behind the child is a wall. In the background is the full Sun as at midday, when it is brightest. Its rays are of two types. The Sun image is echoed by sunflowers showing over the wall, and a crown on the head of the child.

The traditional image is of twin children (male and female ?), rather than a child on a horse. A child does not know its sex until The Hierophant tells it. Until then it is both- as indicated by foetal development and the Birth Charts of Astrology.

ASSOCIATIONS : CYCLE OF GROWTH STAGE 12 (WITHDRAWAL. CONFINEMENT)

Pisces The Two Fishes. Mutable (Changeable) Water. The Collective Unconscious.

Again we have 2 related planets – Jupiter (Expansion. Number 3) if The Transcendent Octave is not activated, and Neptune (Dissolution. Number Zero) when there is contact with The Collective Unconscious.

In line with the evolutionary development of sexual reproduction in plants and animals after that of cell division, in Genesis we have "man and woman" – which do not become human Adam and Eve until Chapter 2 :-

*Verse 24: And God saith, `Let the earth bring forth the living creature after its kind, cattle and creeping thing, and beast of the earth after its kind:' and it is so.

*Verse 25: And God maketh the beast of the earth after its kind, and the cattle after their kind, and every creeping thing of the ground after its kind, and God seeth that [it is] good.

*Verse 26: And God saith, `Let Us make man in Our image, according to Our likeness, and let them rule over fish of the sea, and over fowl of the heavens, and over cattle, and over all the earth, and over every creeping thing that is creeping on the earth.'

THE TAROT

*Verse 27: And God prepareth the man in His image; in the image of God He prepared him, a male and a female He prepared them.

*Verse 28: And God blesseth them, and God saith to them, `Be fruitful, and multiply, and fill the earth, and subdue it, and rule over fish of the sea, and over fowl of the heavens, and over every living thing that is creeping upon the earth.'

*Verse 29: And God saith, `Lo, I have given to you every herb sowing seed, which [is] upon the face of all the earth, and every tree in which [is] the fruit of a tree sowing seed, to you it is for food;

*Verse 30: and to every beast of the earth, and to every fowl of the heavens, and to every creeping thing on the earth, in which [is] breath of life, every green herb [is] for food:' and it is so.

*Verse 31: And God seeth all that He hath done, and lo, very good; and there is an evening, and there is a morning – day the sixth. [YLT]

COMMENTARY

1. The Sun is the first of 2 cards relating to Cycle of Growth Stage 12. Following The Moon, where everything was unclear and uncertain, we have the light of new consciousness. There is an air of victory and success from trials and difficulties overcome. Hope becomes a conscious possibility.
2. 1+9 equates to Number 10, which, in turn becomes Number 1 (Sephirah 2. Pluto. Regeneration. Force) – a new beginning. The physical Sun (Sephirah 6. Number 5. Power) is a lower manifestation of same nuclear reaction.
3. Following the unconscious nightmares of The Moon, The Sun is daylight Consciousness.
4. After the self-doubts of XVIII. The Moon, the path ahead has become clearer.
5. In common with the theme of Cycle of Growth Stage 12 (Withdrawal), the work is not yet fully completed. The wall between the child and The Sun suggests that some protection is still necessary. The child has some control of its "animal nature" but is not ready to advance.
6. This is still the time of Winter. The child in the womb will not be born into the outer world until Cycle of Growth Stage 1 (Seed).
7. After the temptation of Jesus in the wilderness he entered Jerusalem on a donkey to the cheers of the crowd. This became Palm Sunday. Later the crowd turned against him when it was clear that he could not magically solve all their problems for them.
8. Social Fame is only temporary.

TRADITIONAL MEANINGS [AEW]

Material happiness, fortunate marriage, contentment.
Reversed : The same in a lesser sense.

FROM MY PRACTICAL READINGS

Coming to light after a time of darkness. There is a sense of Vindication of one's inner beliefs or ideas, where one has found some kind of evidence in the face of inner opposition. The question is how to use it.

THE TAROT

CARD XX : JUDGEMENT

Figure 52 : TAROT XX - JUDGEMENT

THE IMAGE

The image is of an Angel (Gabriel the messenger) blowing a trumpet, which has a banner with a red cross on a white ground. In front, and repeated behind, are coffins each containing a standing human figure listening to the call – there is a man and woman with child between in the foreground. The coffins are depicted as being on water, rather than land, which suggests unconscious elements coming to light. Repressed energies being released.

The traditional image is similar in content except for only having 3 human figures.

ASSOCIATIONS : CYCLE OF GROWTH STAGE 12 (WITHDRAWAL. CONFINEMENT)

The 12th. House – Social Service. Obligation. Karma.

As for The Sun, above. With this card - and XXI. The World - we have a closer relationship with Creation Day 7 – a day of rest. This is the beginning of another chapter in Genesis. The work is not complete.

**Verse 1: And the heavens and the earth are completed, and all their host;

*Verse 2: and God completeth by the seventh day His work which He hath made, and ceaseth by the seventh day from all His work which He hath made.

*Verse 3: And God blesseth the seventh day, and sanctifieth it, for in it He hath ceased from all His work which God had prepared for making.

*Verse 4: These [are] births of the heavens and of the earth <u>in their being prepared</u>, in the day of Jehovah God's making earth and heavens;

*Verse 5: and no shrub of the field is yet in the earth, and no herb of the field yet sprouteth, for Jehovah God hath not rained upon the earth, and a man there is not to serve the ground, [YLT]

COMMENTARY

1. Following the Card of The Sun we have an indication that the task is almost complete.
2. XX equates to Number 2 (Saturn. Sephirah 3. Binah. Form. Cycle of Growth Stage 10). We see a similar release of energy to that depicted in XVI.The Tower albeit at a lower level.

3. The image is that of the Angel Gabriel blowing his horn at The Last Day of Judgement, when the dead rise to be judged. Perhaps this is reincarnation.
4. Here we have a paradox because, traditionally, the horn is blown when the world comes to an end and souls come to be judged by God on their past actions. It contains the idea of Karma. Here we have a child in the womb about to be born into the material world.
5. The figures rising from the coffins are a symbol of Resurrection from death – perhaps relating to that of Jesus. It was followed by his Ascension.
6. The whole is a symbol of a "Higher Calling", or Vocation, to pursue a particular form of life. The pursuit of an "Ideal".
7. The banner with a cross on Gabriel's horn suggests "Take up thy cross and follow me"
8. Jesus accepted his destiny prophesied in The Old Testament.
9. Perhaps the card may be summed up as follows :-

The Bible : Matthew Chapter 16

Verse 24: Then said Jesus unto his disciples, If any man will come after me, let him deny himself, and take up his cross, and follow me.

Verse 25: For whosoever will save his life shall lose it: and whosoever will lose his life for my sake shall find it.

Verse 26: For what is a man profited, if he shall gain the whole world, and lose his own soul? or what shall a man give in exchange for his soul?

Verse 27: For the Son of man shall come in the glory of his Father with his angels; and then he shall reward every man according to his works. [KJV]

XX. The World is the next card in sequence.

TRADITIONAL MEANINGS [AEW]
Change of position, renewal, outcome. Another account specifies total loss though lawsuit.

Reversed : Weakness, pusillanimity, simplicity; also deliberation, decision, sentence.

FROM MY PRACTICAL READINGS
The Card tends to denote some sort of Promotion, or rise to a higher rank in the hierarchy of life. It may not be in material terms.

THE TAROT

CARD XXI : THE WORLD

Figure 53 : TAROT XXI - THE WORLD

THE IMAGE

Although there is Duality, the image is that of total harmony, showing a figure dancing at the centre of an elliptical Victory garland and holding 2 wands, one in the (conscious) right hand, the other in her (unconscious) left. The figure is naked except for a sash, or scarf, which covers the sexual organs so the figure is androgynous. Masculine and Feminine forces are in balance (until The Hierophant or The Serpent interfere).

As with The Wheel of Fortune we have the 4 faces of the 'Beasts of Revelation' at the 4 corners. Here all 4 Elements are in balance. A still position in the midst of chaos.

As with cards IV. The Emperor and XII. The Hanged Man, The suggestion of the stable Cross of Number 4 and The 4 Elements is emphasised by the crossed legs.

ASSOCIATIONS : CYCLE OF GROWTH STAGE 12 (WITHDRAWAL. CONFINEMENT)

AND STAGE 1 (SEED)

Attention is drawn to Card X. The Wheel of Fortune which is similar in outline. As with that card we cannot ascribe this Image of Transition to a single Stage in The Cycle of Growth.

COMMENTARY

1. The World depicts a Child in The Womb.
2. A child does not fully recognise its sexual nature until Cycle of Growth Stage 4 (Transplanting. VI.The Lovers) – which is also that of the Temptation of Adam and Eve, and is Opposite the Temptation of XV.The Devil, mentioned above.
3. The image is that of a seed containing potential for new growth. Also a Shell.
4. The World is a card of Victory and Completion and New Life to come.
5. 2+1 equates to Number 3 (Jupiter. Expansion) which is symbolic of an initial completion – which is yet to materialise, or be born as Number 4. Like card III. The Empress at Cycle of Growth Stage 2 (Germination) where II. The Priestess is now pregnant.
6. We have to note that this might not mean "Success" in worldly terms. We learn from both Success and Failure – which therefore means that they are not "opposites" in the wider theme of evolution.

7. In the opposite Wheel of Fortune the figures were animal-like and outside The Wheel - and holding blank books. Here is just a single, integrated, figure "at the centre of The Universe". The lower energies have been transmuted and directed to a higher single – practical - purpose.
8. At the time of birth we forget our past.
9. There is a hidden meaning here. We have to note that the Victory Garland is elliptical instead of circular. From our study, the latter arrangement would seem to fit better, but all versions show the same "distortion". The difference between an Ellipse and a Circle is that the Ellipse has 2 focal points, whereas the Circle has one. This duality is echoed by the figure holding 2 wands - reminiscent of, and predicting, the single one of The Magician where they act as one unified source. The Victory Garland tied top and bottom also implies a division into Right and Left. I have mentioned that the figure at the centre is androgynous. Please see [NUMBERS : Number 2]
10. The 2 focal points could be suggestive of 2 complementary cycles – that of The Lunar, feminine, monthly, Menstrual Cycle and the Annual, masculine, Solar Cycle - or even of Number 8 and Infinity.
11. The suggestion of "Wheels Within Wheels", and the fact that this Card is sometimes named "The Universe" rather than "The World" could indicate the possibility of a wider expansion of consciousness which, for example, includes the cycles of the other planets of our solar system, and perhaps beyond. In order to achieve this we would need to pay attention to cycles longer than those of Days, Months, and Years.
12. Perhaps Statisticians, rather than studying The Wheel of Fortune, should be studying The Universe.
13. In our examination of The Cycle of Growth we can see how seemingly different cycles are really one and the same.
14. The next Card, The Fool, can be either male or female – perhaps, again, both. An infant does not know its sex until it is told ("pink or blue ?"). At the time of birth a bias is introduced ("Pink or Blue ?"). This is one of the facts of life.

TRADITIONAL MEANINGS [AEW]
Assured success, recompense, voyage, route, emigration, flight, change of place.

Reversed : Inertia, fixity, stagnation, permanence. It will be seen that, except where there is an irresistible suggestion conveyed by the surface meaning, that which is extracted from the Trumps Major by the divinatory art is at once artificial and arbitrary, as it seems to me, in the highest degree. But of one order are the mysteries of light and of another are those of fantasy. The allocation of a fortune-telling aspect to these cards is the story of a prolonged impertinence.

FROM MY PRACTICAL READINGS
The conclusion of the matter under question – or the end of a phase of life. This could mean "success or failure". It is in the nature of man to attempt the impossible. Either way we win by expansion of consciousness.

THE TAROT

CARD ZERO : THE FOOL

Figure 54 : TAROT 0 - THE FOOL

THE IMAGE

A young person stands in a high place on the brink of an abyss. He carries his few meagre possessions in a bag attached to a staff on his right shoulder. The staff is pointing to a pale sun behind him, so his pale shadow will be cast before him. From where he stands he could get a broad view of the landscape below, but his face is turned to the sky. Because he is looking upwards he cannot see where he is going. We can see he is heading for a sudden descent. He carries a White Rose held in his left hand behind him. A small dog is on his left, it is standing on its hind legs as if in imitation. (Or is The Fool imitating the dog ?). He is not presently conscious of possessions, rose, or dog.

ASSOCIATIONS : CYCLE OF GROWTH STAGE 1 (SEED)

The 1st. House – Rising Sign. Ascendant. Personal projection of energy.

Aries The Ram (Cardinal/Active Fire. Positive)

Mars (God of War. The Selfish Gene)

Logarithmic Timescale Age : Infancy 0-7 months. Oral Stage.

This is the beginning of the 2nd. Octave of The Cycle of Growth.

In terms of The Creation of Genesis we are now into Chapter 2 with the first appearance of a physical, earthy man made from "dust". The infant takes its first breath.

> *Chapter 2 Verse 7: And Jehovah God formeth the man – dust from the ground, and breatheth into his nostrils breath of life, and the man becometh a living creature. [YLT]

There is no Adam yet.

COMMENTARY

1. The Fool is a picture of Innocence. He is not foolish unless someone tells him so. However, both Fools and non-fools learn the same lessons.
2. The precipice is reminiscent of The Abyss of [THE KABBALAH TREE OF LIFE].
3. The Fool is a new born baby. He is at the stage of Evolution just before The Fall – so he\she is not conscious of sexuality.

THE TAROT

4. The Fool is the first of 2 cards related to The Cycle of Growth Stage 1 (Seed). At this stage, although masculine in potential, his sexual polarity is undetermined. In the next card, The Magician, he becomes more positive.
5. His staff is his sceptre. It is phallic in essence, as a Tarot Wand. It carries souvenirs from the past in a bag behind his head – so he is unconscious of them.
6. As with 'The Ram', the dog is a symbol of pure instinct which seeks only to be creative and multiply. It is the Element Fire. The Fool is also unconscious of the dog.
7. Because Will is not yet present, Instinct rules supreme. Here is the newly-born child. Evolution has reached that of Stone Age man.
8. The Fool is Number Zero, no-thing, yet with potential to be any thing. Everything comes out of no-thing.
9. Number Zero is the image shape of the previous Major Card – XXI The World and The Womb.
10. Number Zero also refers to the state of the universe before the Big Bang – which is related to Cycle of Growth Stage 9 (Conception) at the beginning at the 1st. Octave of The Logarithmic Timescale. This is a less explosive repetition.
11. This stage seems to be that of a more physical, material, Zero.
12. Number Zero has become of prime importance in the Digital Age, equal to The One. Until now it has tended to be devalued and remain hidden by The One. It is the Feminine Ying Principle that balances the masculine Yang. Acting together they make The Universe. In Numerology, unlike the numbers 1 to 9 that re-appear at every level, Zero only occurs once – so it is ignored. Card 0.The Fool shows that everything balances out to Zero at the end of each Cycle.
13. Zero is neutral Grey – containing both Positive (White) and Negative (Black) in balance.
14. The picture is of someone entering unknown territory. He carries high aspirations, but will soon be brought down to earth to make them practical. There is potential but no practical purpose yet.
15. Although depicted as a young person, The Fool is ageless. The external conditions are young.
16. The Time is that of Spring when hidden seeds begin to wake from their sleep deep in the Earth. This is the unconscious about to become conscious.
17. This is our state before reaching The Garden of Eden.
18. The Rose Flower is a symbol of future aspiration. The blooms of roses eventually wither and die. The Rose is not the seed or the flower. Strangely, the single flower is often valued more than the bush. It carries seeds of which very few germinate. The Rose is best propagated from the humbler woody portions – which will grow new roots.
19. The rose here is white, like the pale sun in the background.
20. Humans seek mates in the same way as Roses – with Honeyed Sweets, Flowers, and Perfume.
21. The staff is the Wand of The Magician in virgin form. A symbol of Will. In the modern day playing card version of the Minor Arcana suit it has become a crude Club. The bag at the back of his head carries the fruits of past experience, his only true possessions. The Fool is unconscious of the bag and its contents. He is looking to the distant future.
22. DNA is the seed of Evolution.
23. "Left" ("sinister") and "Behind" are both unconscious.
24. The whole is a symbol of Innocence. The Fool is not foolish – although he may be regarded as such by those who think they know better.
25. Only Fools can invent new things. Children invent new worlds as they grow.
26. Jesus said we must all become as little children [Matthew 18:2] – which means Fools.
27. *The Stone the builder rejected became the cornerstone* [Psalm 118:22, Matthew 21:42, Mark 12:10, Luke 20:17, Acts 4:11, 1 Peter 2:7]. A cornerstone was the first stone laid at the base of a new building. Stones are made by God, whereas men make bricks. Those who translate the cornerstone as a "head" stone, or use bricks, are foolish and think too much. This is the lesson of The Tower of Babel and unnatural gardens hanging from above.

THE TAROT

TRADITIONAL MEANINGS [AEW]
Folly, mania, extravagance, intoxication, delirium, frenzy.

Reversed : Negligence, absence, distribution, carelessness, apathy, nullity, vanity.

FROM MY PRACTICAL READINGS
The Querent beginning a new project, or new phase of life with no previous experience of the circumstances. A new phase of learning or spiritual development.

CARD I : THE MAGICIAN

Figure 55 : TAROT I - THE MAGICIAN and MENSA

THE IMAGE
The Magician stands behind a table which carries the tools of his trade. His right hand is holding his Magic Wand which points to Heaven, his left hand points to the Earth. His tools are those of the Minor Arcana. Wand (Fire. Intuition), Cup (Water. Feeling), Sword (Air. Thinking), Coin or Pentacle (Earth. Sensation). The Magician has the dual-circle symbol of Infinity and Higher Consciousness above his head. As Above, so Below. There are roses growing above and before him (with lilies). He wears a white robe underneath a red cloak. There is a serpent around his waist.

The Mensa High IQ Society logo is a simplified version.

ASSOCIATIONS : CYCLE OF GROWTH STAGE 1 (SEED)
As with The Fool, above.

COMMENTARY
1. The Magician is the second of 2 cards related to The Cycle of Growth Stage 1 (Seed) where the unfocused idealism of The Fool begins to find direction. The Seed is now ready to grow. Observe a new-born child to see him in action.
2. The Magician's right hand points to the source of the aspirations of The Fool. His left to the productiveness of the Priestess. Light (consciousness) comes to Earth.

THE TAROT

3. Although we are at Cycle of Growth Stage 1, and have symbolism of the birth of a child, which is the same as that of planting a seed in the Earth, the true beginning was at Cycle of Growth Stage 9 (Conception) under the control of another Fire Sign – (Mutable) Sagittarius.
4. Although agreeing that there is a period of psychological Inflation from birth, followed by gradual recognition of The Mother, psychologists do not recognise Cycle of Growth Stage 1 as being separate from Stage 2 – probably because of the short timescales involved, with Stage 1 lasting only 7 months from birth.
5. The Magician is pure, undifferentiated, Positive energy – which must seek the Negative in order to become creative. His Number is the Primal I (Pluto. Regeneration).
6. Until The Magician meets The Priestess his tools are unused, useless. He only uses his head as a "battering Ram".
7. Although The Magician is a masculine figure he can be active in men or women. In keeping with Astrology, The Tarot, and an overall principle of this book, he is representative of a particular form of energy rather than human male and female. In this case the energy is positive\extroverted rather than negative\introverted. Having said that, in this particular case it is in a static state. Like the positive pole of an electrical system nothing flows until it is connected to a negative. This is an example of how the Archetypes are limited.
8. The Magician is a phallic symbol, as is his magic wand. That is, of an erect penis full of potential creativity which is not yet released. His wand is his sceptre. A symbol of power, but not itself powerful.
9. Although we have sexual connotations, we cannot limit the Archetype to mere human behaviour – although the possibility is included. The meaning is concerned with inner potential . The external, material, object is subject to Individual Will.
10. The image is similar to, and a development of the previous one, The Fool. The right hand is still holding the staff, the symbol of Will, which is now a magic wand. It is still in the right hand and pointing to Heaven. The Magician is now looking forward instead of into the sky. His left hand points to a more practical aim. The Work has not yet begun, but it is about to take form in the mind.
11. He is about to utter the Magic Words that make things appear and disappear.
12. A meaning contained in the image is "As Above, So Below, As Below, So Above". We can do what we Will – but everything is subject to Law (The Lord).
13. The lilies in the picture are Madonna Lilies – symbol of chastity and the Virgin Mary. They are used in funerals as a symbol of the soul. So we have life and death shown as two versions of a single flower. The Magician is facing them as he faces the (Virgin) Priestess as the next step in his journey.
14. Rider-Waite's lilies come from Bible Book The Song Of Solomon, which, although part of The Bible consist of secular, rather than religious, poetry. In Chapter 2 :1 is " ego flos campi et lilium convallium " "I am the flower of the field and the lily of the valley" – which carries Kabbalistic symbolism.

*I [am] the rose of Sharon, [and] the lily of the valleys. As the lily among thorns, so [is] my love among the daughters. [KJV]

*As a lily among the thorns, So [is] my friend among the daughters! [YLT]

The modern Rose of Sharon is actually not a rose. Scholars suggest that the biblical one is a species of lily. So we here have "pure lilies" and "red lilies" with similar meaning to that of turning water into wine – a "magic trick" of Jesus. With The Wedding, this has connotations with Desire and sexual intercourse – here yet to come - exactly in keeping with the phallic symbolism of Cycle of Growth Stage 1 and Mars. Again, Aspiration becomes Desire.

15. Flowers tend to be mentioned in The Bible in this context :-

* The grass withereth, the flower fadeth: but the word of our God shall stand for ever. [Isaiah Chapter 40:8]

16. In Latin, Table is "Mensa", "Mens" means mind.

17. In the earlier Tarot versions The Magician was depicted as an ordinary workman with a wand in his left (unconscious) hand. His hat was shaped like the infinity symbol of this Magician. When one "wears different hats" one performs different roles in life.

18. A skilled workman may seem to work magic to the uninitiated in his transformation of raw materials to finished product. It takes repetition to learn. The principle of Repetition is contained in the Infinity Symbol.

19. The Infinity Symbol in the card means is similar to my serpent symbol in the endless Cycle of Growth. It contains an archetypal principle. The self-devouring serpent at the waist of The Magician relates to the same principle, and is that of the slightly more material image of the one in The Garden of Eden. Here it divides his body into upper and lower parts. As Above, so Below. The symbol refers to Number 8.

20 The Serpent of The Cycle of Growth offers the possibility of Transcendence.

21. In reality, over time, The Magician eventually only creates himself. The rest passes away.

TRADITIONAL MEANINGS [AEW]

Skill, diplomacy, address, subtlety; sickness, pain, loss, disaster, snares of enemies; self-confidence, will; the Querent, if male.

Reversed : Physician, Magus, mental disease, disgrace, disquiet.

FROM MY PRACTICAL READINGS

The Querent has the required skills to handle the situation in question. Alone, the card does not show if they will be used. It is potential only.

CARD II : THE PRIESTESS

Figure 56 : TAROT II - THE HIGH PRIESTESS

THE IMAGE

The Twin Pillars are the same as those in the Kabbalah Tree of Life. The Path of the Priestess is (on) the Middle Pillar.

A young woman is seated between two pillars, one black, inscribed B, the other white, inscribed J - they are representations of Boaz and Jachin which were the pillars of Solomon's Temple in Jerusalem. There is a cross at her breast which is also at the centre of balance of the two pillars. Her Cross is not yet a material one. She has a Crescent Moon at her feet – although it more resembles the New Moon it can also be considered a representation of Sephirah 9 (Foundation. The Moon) near the foot of The Middle Pillar. On her head she wears a horned hat with a globe at its centre – which can be considered a feminine representation of Sephirah 1

THE TAROT

(Kether. Crown). In her lap she holds a scroll inscribed with the name TORA (as "Book of the Law"). Behind her, supported by the two pillars is a veil with palms and pomegranates. Behind that, just visible, is the empty Sea. The traditional image contains only The Priestess with Cross, Book and Veil behind. Her book is already begun.

ASSOCIATIONS : CYCLE OF GROWTH STAGE 2 (GERMINATION)

The 2nd. House – Personal Collection of Energy.

Taurus The Bull. Fixed Earth. Negative.

Venus (Number 6) Goddess of Beauty and sexual attraction. Desire. Physical comfort. The Female Symbol. Magnetism.

Logarithmic Timescale Age : Infancy age 7 months to 1 Year 8 months. Trust vs. Mistrust. The Mother.

COMMENTARY

1. Number 2 (Saturn. Binah. Form) refers to The Great Mother who resists, and brings Form to, creative energy.
2. The Priestess is the first of the two feminine cards related to Cycle of Growth Stage 2 (Germination). The Seed from Stage 1 requires somewhere to put down its roots. It is the beginning of its development into its final earthly form. This is the Virgin Soil before planting. A potential support for growth, but nothing has happened yet to set it in motion.
3. The Priestess serves The Magician by visualising his aims. Her images are the first step towards bringing abstract ideas into physical manifestation.
4. Her appearance is a result of what we learn from Number 2 of [NUMEROLOGY]. Whenever something - like The Magician - is created in the universe, its complement is also created. The sum total is always Zero.
5. The pillars with the veil here represent the unwritten Laws of Nature which will be discovered in the next card. We can consider that her number II is a depiction of the 2 Pillars "Severity" and "Mercy".
6. Not yet conscious, the child meets unconscious feminine power for the first time.
7. The Priestess is the feminine Hierophant (High Priest). Her pillars represent energy in its simplest form, related to those of the Kabbalah. Those of The Hierophant are man-made.
8. One aspect of the symbol is that of the undeveloped Soul – which demonstrates its distinction from Spirit. Another, more modern concept, is the Personal Unconscious – so we can now understand Soul better.
9. The Priestess is pure negativity – which needs the stimulation of Positive energy to become creative. She is seated, indicating her stability and natural inertia - related to Taurus (Fixed Earth). She has The Moon (planet) at her feet, which is exalted in Taurus.
10. The Moon has no light of its own – we only see it by reflection of the light of the Sun (Consciousness). The Crescent Moon is the first phase of its cycle. It occurs in the Waxing (growing) phase half way between New Moon and first Quarter. When the cycle is superimposed on an Astrological Birth Chart with the New Moon in the Ascendant (Birth) position, the Crescent Moon position is 45 degrees away exactly in the centre of the 2nd. House – which refers to Taurus and Cycle of Growth Stage 2 (Germination).
11. We must note that Waite's Image is not of pure form, being a fruit of his understanding which is coloured by his study of Kabbalism and Freemasonry. The more complicated an image, the more it departs from its true essence. It is best that we make our own personal additions – which seems to be one of our tasks in life.
12. The Twin Pillars are found in sacred places and temples, and represent a gateway into the unknown. They are the outer ones of The Kabbalah. The path of II.The Priestess is on the Centre Pillar of Balance and Equilibrium. The original ones were said to be in Solomon's Temple – the first in Jerusalem. The Veil, or other barrier, is also found in temples behind which only initiated priests could perform their secret rituals in "The Holy of Holies". Here, the veil gives us a glimpse of the "hidden fruits" which are yet to come. All this is in keeping with Cycle of Growth Stage 2 (Germination).

THE TAROT

13. "TORA" can mean the Jewish Torah, Book of Law, or The Tarot. The pages of her book are being written upon. Her book is The Book Of Life. At another level she is the "Akashic Record" where everything is recorded at a mystical, non-physical, level. This could also mean The Collective Unconscious.

14. Waite's image itself is, as is any art form (including written material), a perfect example of the fruits of The Priestess – but is not The Priestess. She is an Archetype. We only ever see the Veil, not The Priestess herself, who is invisible – in common with all the other Archetypes who are pure energy, without form. We "see through a glass darkly".

15. *Perhaps this is a better clue to our existence in this part of childhood, when we are still mainly unconscious, and therefore closer to the Archetypes : *1 Corinthians Chapter 13 Verses 11 and 12 - When I was a babe, as a babe I was speaking, as a babe I was thinking, as a babe I was reasoning, and when I have become a man, I have made useless the things of the babe; "for we see now through a mirror obscurely, and then face to face; now I know in part, and then I shall fully know, as also I was known; [YLT]*

16. Among other things, The Priestess is image–ination in early days of life uncontaminated by material sensory input (Sensation) or Thinking.

17. We must take special note that at this stage there is no outer form. So far we only have the glimmerings of an Idea

18. At the highest level, the Priestess is the Virgin Mary who gave Virgin birth to the Son of God. Again. We are beyond human sexuality, which comes later in The Cycle of Growth.

19. Priestesses were female priests who were authorised to carry out religious rituals. They gradually disappeared from the time that the mono-theistic religions began. This dates from the Age of Pisces 590 BC – 1580 AD [THE ZODIAC AGES] when all of today's religions based on One God began, and men took over control of the temples (as in the following Cards). Perhaps this refers to the "demotion" of Eve who was created as an equal to Adam and subsequently "demoted" by God. This development is echoed by the later Major Card V. The Hierophant, who is a male priest(ess). There have been many types of priestess over the ages including the Roman Vestal Virgins, with their vows of chastity. Their sensitivity attuned to higher energies.

20. In older times some priestesses were concerned with offering sexual services. At that time there was a different attitude to sexual intercourse to that of today. A man could have intercourse with a priestess without being considered unfaithful to his wife. The priestess herself was not "controlled" by the relationship and retained her independence.

21. Nowadays, nuns with their "marriage to God" can be considered a modern version of The Priestess, as well as giving them association with the Virgin Mary. They are present in most of the main world religions today, but they certainly do not share the same status as before. We also need to view prostitution in a slightly different light. The Japanese Geisha, now an entertainer, had similar origins.

22. So far we have considered more superficial levels, and need to dig deeper. We note that all images of the Priestess show her with a book or scroll in her lap. Considering our analysis so far, we can note that this conveniently covers the region of her sexual organs.

23. In addition, with new psychological knowledge and our association with Cycle of growth Stage 2 we can take the symbolism a step further. It appears to me, especially as Waite's scroll has only a title, that the "book" is, in reality a "virgin" "blank sheet". The sheet will accept any image or writing impressed on its surface. This is pure negativity – without which the positive polarity would have nothing to work on. There would be no form possible.

24. We add to this the recent discovery that the brain records every experience we have something like an extended version of a video-audio recorder. Following Galvani's electrical stimulation of a frog's leg to make it twitch in the 18th. century, we have later experiments by scientists stimulating the brain directly (it has no sense organs) with weak electric currents when the subject relives past experiences in their entirety – with sights, feelings, tastes and smells. Perhaps above all, this experiment demonstrates a relationship between The Priestess and the brain in the role of recording memories.

25. The brain, in fact, does consist of a sheet of tissue that has been "screwed up" like a sheet of paper. I discovered this in a visit to the Natural History Museum in South Kensington, London. Strangely, it has been very difficult to find reference to this anywhere. Scientists seem more interested in dissection and analysis rather than considering The Whole. I did find this :-

THE TAROT

The cerebral cortex is essentially a sheet of neural tissue, folded in a way that allows a large surface area to fit within the confines of the skull. Each cerebral hemisphere, in fact, has a total surface area of about 1.3 square feet.

[http://www.news-medical.net/health/Human-Brain-Structure.aspx]

26. The Priestess therefore has connotation with unconscious Memory.
27. We have ascertained that The Priestess requires external stimulation. [TRANSACTIONAL ANALYSIS] mentions everyone's need for "Stroking" – an extreme example of which is sexual. This is also the case with babies. This is the first Stage of development of the 5 senses which provide different levels of information based on a spectrum of electromagnetic (Fire) frequencies. We can also equate this with the stage where the tools of The Magician begin their development.
28. The 4 Functions themselves are depicted in the 4 suits of the Minor Arcana – Wands, Swords, Cups and Pentacles. We note that the originators of The Tarot understood the 4 Jungian Functions intuitively before Jung recognised them objectively and scientifically.
29. The Priestess has relationship with XII.The Hanged Man on the return journey. The Middle Pillar is depicted in different forms.

TRADITIONAL MEANINGS [AEW]

Secrets, mystery, the future as yet unrevealed; the woman who interests the Querent, if male; the Querent herself, if female; silence, tenacity; mystery, wisdom, science.

Reversed : Passion, moral or physical ardour, conceit, surface knowledge.

FROM MY PRACTICAL READINGS

The Priestess appears when the Querent was a situation where there was no prior knowledge or experience – requiring study, or learning something new.

CARD III : THE EMPRESS

Figure 57 : TAROT III - THE EMPRESS

THE IMAGE

A woman is seated comfortably in the midst of rich natural growth. Her seat is based on firm foundations of rock. It is not of wood or stone, or even gold. If we observe carefully, we can see that she is pregnant. This is reflected in the ripe corn in the foreground which will feed her subjects as well as becoming the seeds of future growth. There is a flowing river with a waterfall behind her. Where she sits, the water has reached its lowest level. She has a shield which seems carelessly set aside. On the shield is the symbol of Venus, indicating that her method of growth is by peaceful means, rather than conquest. On her head is a diadem of 12 stars indicating that she has mastered the 12 practical tasks of the Zodiac and by so doing serves the Spirit. In her right hand she carries a sceptre showing that she is of royal authority. A feminine phallic symbol. A dispenser of Law. On top of the sceptre is a sphere, which is a representation of the world, which is her domain, and Number Zero where everything is in balance.

Traditional images of the Empress depict her as similar to the male Emperor – which is the following card in sequence. In this case her shield is in use, and her sceptre even has an orb (a sphere surmounted by a cross) which is the male symbol of Mars, God of War. As we will see, there are clear errors in this interpretation which are probably the result of the designers' experience of warrior empresses at the time. Our Empress has no need of force, she follows and dispenses Natural Law. In her realm her power, although delegated, is absolute. We disobey her Laws at our own peril. She is Mother Nature.

ASSOCIATIONS : CYCLE OF GROWTH STAGE 2 (GERMINATION)

As with The Priestess, above.

COMMENTARY

1. The Empress is the second of the two feminine cards related to Cycle of Growth Stage 2 (Germination). The Seed from Stage 1 has been planted and is beginning to put its roots down into the Earth, where it is fed and watered.
2. Her Number 3 is a demonstration of how the complementary Numbers 1 and 2 result manifestation as a "resolution of opposites". We are not at a fully physical level yet. Number 3 (Jupiter. Expansion) refers to Growth.
3. The Empress follows the unwritten Laws of Nature which are the province of The Priestess.
4. The Empress uses Earthy materials to build the things of The Earth. This includes money – which is a SYMBOLIC representation of time and effort (energy), as well as the objects it produces. A fifty pound note is merely a piece of printed paper.
5. The Empress is the feminine Emperor. The Mother.
6. This is the beginning of Consciousness. The veil of The Priestess suggests that the "fruits" already exist (as a result of Evolution), but we need to become aware of them in order to write our own personal Book Of Life. We create our own inner World in God's image. The first object in a child's consciousness is the face of its mother. It is an internal image of an outer object. This enables re-cognition.
7. To some extent this pregnancy, or seed growth in the 2nd.Octave of The Logarithmic Timescale is a repetition of Cycle of Growth Stage 10 (Peak) in the 1st. Octave - which was the beginning of creation of a physical human body under the control of another Earth Sign, Capricorn – Cardinal (Creative, Initiating, Earth). In Fixed Taurus, although we again have an earthy theme, the true, hidden, meaning is concerned with development of Consciousness and The Mind. Our experiences become fixed in the lower frequencies of Time and Space. It is a mark of the natural stability and inertia of Fixed Taurus that it needs the force of The Ram to start moving.
8. Despite the suggestion of the image, there are, as yet, no fruits - we are only at Cycle of Growth Stage 2 (Germination). This is the Rooting stage, where nothing much shows above the surface. To advance too soon would invite destruction. At the beginning of a project we must first get our-self organised. This is a stage of Physical Development.
9. The child is learning to use its physical body. So the mind is also developing along fixed channels.
10. The image shows that the virgin Priestess has been impregnated by the Magician's Fire of Spirit and is bringing new life to the Earth. The Laws of The Empress are a physical reflection of the spiritual Laws of The Priestess. We learn spiritual principles from practical experience which mimics The Cycle of Growth. As Above, So Below.
11. As The Priestess suggests Short Term Memory, the Empress suggests Long Term Memory. The main requirement for transferring memories to long term "storage" is repetition, which is an essential part of Training. Nature is always efficient, and Forgetting is similar to that of disposing of unwanted waste material.

12. Although a symbol of The Empress is Mother Nature, we need to recognise that we are also dealing with human development now. C.G. Jung stated that we begin to experience the Archetypes through our parents and later development depends upon their examples. A missing parent can create difficulties in life – especially the one of the same sex, who can supply us with a role model early on, which, although not necessarily an accurate representation of what we will become, does give us a stable starting point. Later on we note the increased anxiety of young people nowadays who are allowed greater freedom of action, and therefore incur greater responsibilities than they can handle. During my lifetime young offenders were given a "short sharp shock" of military-like training instead of prison. It was discontinued because of the suggestion that they enjoyed it too much.

13. Following on from our observations of The Priestess, with her psychological associations with the human brain and memory, we can be on firmer ground when we state that The Empress is the beginning of psychological growth. When newly born a child is pure Intuition or Instinct (Fire). At this stage in life it is beginning to develop the other 3 Functions. It seems that the first in order of importance are those of Sensation and Feeling. Thinking comes in Cycle of Growth Stage 3 (Experiment. Communication). Whereas, until now, the child's physical needs have been met immediately on demand, there is now a delay between the arousal of a need and its satisfaction. There is a greater experience of physical discomfort than before. The child is forced to recognise its own physical body, and its needs (Venus – Peace. Comfort - is ruler of Taurus).

14. This stage of life is related to the Sign of Taurus which is symbolic of our physical possessions – which includes our body and its talents. In traditional Astrology this was more related to money and property. If we look closer we can see that these outward objects are really just means to an end. The true purpose is that of maintaining basic physical comfort. People with Taurus emphasised in their Birth Chart like a stable home with a regular routine and soft things around them. This brings an attunement with the Archetype of Mother Nature where the daily cycle mimics that of the annual one. We note that our image of The Empress is entirely in keeping.

15. A key to Wholeness, or Holiness, in life is the maintenance of a physical body. The body is a "temple of the spirit". *"Mens sana in corpore sano"* – a sound mind and healthy body. The human body is our own private World, Garden of Eden, and Temple.

16. Although of a down-to-earth practical focus, this also includes one's inner "picture" of the world around and one's place in it. Included in this is the secret of achieving physical manifestation of one's ideas by using the Laws of Nature. We are all Farmers in life – with a variety of possible crops to plant, grow, and harvest.

17. At a psychological level The Empress is imagination in action.

TRADITIONAL MEANINGS [AEW]
Fruitfulness, action, initiative, length of days; the unknown, clandestine; also difficulty, doubt, ignorance.

Reversed : Light, truth, the unravelling of involved matters, public rejoicings; according to another reading, vacillation.

FROM MY PRACTICAL READINGS
When The Empress appears in a reading the matter in hand is growing and things are beginning to take shape. There are now some practical results of one's actions.

THE TAROT

CARD IV : THE EMPEROR

Figure 58 : TAROT IV - THE EMPEROR

THE IMAGE

A bearded man sits on a large, heavy, solid, plain, throne. The throne has rams' heads on the back and arms reminding us of the Zodiac Sign of Aries - but here set in stone. He holds a sceptre in his right hand in the shape of a Crux ansata, meaning "cross with handle", which is the same as an Egyptian Ankh (key). The shape has an overall allusion to the symbol of Venus rather than Mars. He rules by established power rather than War.

In his left hand he holds an Orb – which is missing the usual cross at the top, but which is included in the traditional card. He is wearing armour under his robe. Traditional images are simpler than this one with the orb, symbol of the Mars cross on a circle (Aries), on top of the sceptre and an empty left hand. As with cards XII. The Hanged Man and card XXI. The World, the legs are crossed, which alludes to the stability of The Cross of Number 4 (Mars) and his apparent control of The 4 Elements.

ASSOCIATIONS : CYCLE OF GROWTH STAGE 3 (EXPERIMENT. COMMUNICATION)

The 3rd. House – Personal Mental Concepts.

The Gemini Twins. Mutable Air. Positive.

Mercury (Number 7) The Rational, Practical, Mind.

Logarithmic Timescale Age : Early Childhood 1 year 8 months to 3 years 6 months. Development of muscular control and Will. Parental Persons. The Garden of Eden when Adam was put to work naming things. Words are mental concepts which represent objects. A time of mental development.

COMMENTARY

1. The Emperor's number IV relates to Mars (focused energy) which rules Aries Fire and Scorpio Water.
2. The Emperor is the first of the two masculine cards related to Cycle of Growth Stage 3 (Experiment. Communication) concerned with mental development.
3. The Emperor is the Masculine version of the Empress. She controls Nature and Nurture, he controls and co-ordinates the activities of people (and his physical body).
4. The Emperor is an overall symbol of worldly power tand control. The "Father figure".
5. The child is also learning to rule its physical domain.

6. The father does not necessarily give reasons for his commands because the child would not understand. At another level, Knowledge is Power – which he does not easily delegate.
7. The child's consciousness now includes The Father among its "objects".
8. Psychologists state that, at the beginning of life, from its complete dependency, the infant sees both parents as god-like figures who wield the power of life and death.
9. The association with Cycle of Growth Stage 3 is emphasised by its connection with Erikson's "Early Childhood" stage of psychological development which he states as being concerned with the development of Will.
10. The Ankh is often depicted as being in the hand of gods or pharaohs. It means "life", and appears in the name of the Egyptian king Tut-<u>ankh</u>-amon. It is also associated with a Key. We can see it as a similar symbol to that of Venus, which has a circle over a cross. This relationship is emphasised in the traditional image where the Emperor is sitting with legs crossed, when his body and legs form the same overall shape of the Venus symbol. The Emperor generally rules by peaceful methods – unless his rulership is challenged.
11. Without the circle, the sceptre becomes a Tau Cross (like, and associated with, the letter T) – which seems to combine the Christian Cross and the Ankh. This re-appears in the image of Card XII – The Hanged Man.
12. In effect, Waite has removed the Cross (world symbol) from the Emperor's traditional sceptre so that he now "holds the world in the palm of his hand". His sceptre is a phallic symbol. His throne retains images of "The Ram" - now in fixed material form – so he can also relate to the previous Cycle of Growth Stage 2 (Germination. Taurus. Fixed Earth).

TRADITIONAL MEANINGS [AEW]
Stability, power, protection, realization; a great person; aid, reason, conviction; also authority and will.
Reversed : Benevolence, compassion, credit; also confusion to enemies, obstruction, immaturity.

FROM MY PRACTICAL READINGS
The situation is under the control of someone who acts as "Father Figure". A figure of Power and Authority. It could refer to the Querent or someone else. Nowadays it could even be a female. The Emperor may not have all the right answers. Although the suggestion of absolute control could be accurate, the Querent could be projecting the Emperor image on to someone else, when that person would tend to (be allowed to) behave accordingly – thus emphasising the illusion. It is easy to allow others to control our life, when they can be blamed for whatever goes wrong. It is a question of who takes Responsibility.

THE TAROT

CARD V : THE HIEROPHANT OR HIGH PRIEST

Figure 59 : TAROT V - THE HIGH PRIEST

THE IMAGE

The image is of a High Priest blessing two postulants. He is seated, indicating his stable, earthly, status. He sits between two pillars, which, although reminiscent of those of The Priestess are not the same, being man made. He wears The Triple Crown and carries a sceptre with The Triple Cross at the top – which are both symbols of the Holy Trinity. Between the postulants at his feet are two crossed keys – they are the keys to Heaven and Hell. Good and Evil – which are the "pillars of the church" he represents.

Unlike those of II.The Priestess, His pillars are not exactly the same as those in The Tree of Life. Her focus is on The Middle Pillar, his focus is on the outer Pillars - those of Severity (Form) and Mercy (Force). So the symbols of Gemini (to which Sign he refers) – the written symbol, and that of The Twins – are both representations of The (outer) Twin Pillars.

ASSOCIATIONS : CYCLE OF GROWTH STAGE 3 (EXPERIMENT. COMMUNICATION)

As The Emperor, above.

COMMENTARY

1. The Hierophant is the second of the two masculine cards related to Cycle of Growth Stage 3 concerned with mental development. His authority is different to that of The Emperor, as is his realm of control. His weapon is words and manipulation of the imagination rather than force. At one level this is brain-washing, and its association with a 'cleansing' process. His sceptre has the triple cross.
2. His Number 5 (The Sun. Ego. Consciousness) is related to "Mind Over Matter". The Roman "V" being representative of a human hand with 4 fingers and an opposable thumb. Or is it "Matter over Mind" ? The hat of The Pope is a 5 sided Mitre.
3. The Hierophant is a partner of the Emperor. The Emperor leads by physical control, The Hierophant with moral ideas. He is usually honest and believes he has Right on his side.
4. The Hierophant archetype controls The Pharisees of The Bible and elsewhere.
5. The child reaches the age of higher knowledge based on abstract Academic or Moral rather than Natural Law or Power.
6. The child begins to challenge authority and ask "Why?".

THE TAROT

7. Outer objects have names. The name is not the thing, it is a mental concept. The higher is an image of the lower. As Above, So Below.
8. The Hierophant is representative of higher power and can be any "parental figure", including the natural parents. He need not profess any religion. He is concerned with the established hierarchical order of things. High and low. He can be such as a Lawyer or Teacher.
9. His sceptre is similar to that of the other masculine figures so far – The Fool, The Magician, The Empress, The Emperor. A symbol of Will. In Card IX to come The Hermit also carries a staff. In Card XI Justice it is replaced by a Sword - its twin pillars similar to those of The Hierophant – which may also suggest The Letter of The Law, rather than The Spirit. He says "it is the Will of God".
10. His attitude is similar to that of The Magician with the message "As Above, So Below" – albeit related to human concepts.
11. If we observe closely we see that the overall image is the same as the next Card VI The Lovers, and Card XV The Devil. Each one is concerned with a form of "Marriage".
12. We note that The Hierophant as representative of The Church, or Religion, has done, and is still doing, much evil in the name of good. Its tool over the years seems to have been terrorism – both at psychological and physical levels. It works especially on those with immature minds or little real experience of life. However, he is a necessary part of The Cycle of Growth. We have to start somewhere.
13. The Hierophant preaches Blind Faith (in his ideas). Here, perhaps, we can see examples of Possession (by an Archetype).
14. Card XV.The Devil appears in Cycle of Growth Stage 10 (Social Peak. Harvest). If we observe closely, it resembles the image here. Both that Stage, with one of its concerns with Career, and this, are concerned with hierarchical positions in life. The Hierophant's professed ones are more abstract, although the Church has its hierarchical career levels too. The Hierophant has high social position.
15. In the past, with rich families, the basic career alternatives were The Military, The Law, or The Church. The last was often the choice for the dunce who could not cope with either of the other two.
16. The pillars of The Hierophant are man-made – representing the "Black and White" of men rather than Nature. There is comparison with Card XVI The Tower, which follows The Devil. The Tower of Babel is manmade - of brick, rather than stone.
17. The Hierophant is concerned with Good and Evil. Good and Bad. Black and White. Simple "Opposites" that do not exist in the real world. He does not recognise that "one man's meat is another man's poison". There are no shades of grey.
18. The Hierophant is a teacher. The churches were the first schools. His lessons are those of simple commands and repetition. Reading and writing.
19. In Stage 3 of The Cycle of Growth (Experiment. Communication) the Emperor is the masculine version of The Empress, The Hierophant or High Priest is the masculine of The Priestess, with access to Higher Laws. The problem is that there is no physical Evidence. We are expected to have Faith (in his words).
20. Here is a reflection of Evolution. During the Age of Pisces came the birth of the monotheistic (One God) religions. At that time the male High Priest removed the power of female Priestesses over the temples.
21. The Twin Pillars (which appear in various disguises in The Tarot) and the twin postulants are the Twins of Gemini and Scales of Libra (both Air Signs).
22. The complementary Sign to Gemini (Personal, Practical Knowledge) is that of Sagittarius (Academic, Theoretical Knowledge). Despite his nature, The Hierophant does not differentiate between the two. Whenever one "Opposite" is active the other is too. This is an example of how the theoretical Opposites are useful to aid discrimination.
23. The Hierophant can be considered to be "The Parent" of Transactional Analysis.

TRADITIONAL MEANINGS [AEW]

Marriage, alliance, captivity, servitude; by another account, mercy and goodness; inspiration; the man to whom the Querent has recourse.
Reversed : Society, good understanding, concord, over kindness, weakness.

THE TAROT

FROM MY PRACTICAL READINGS

The Hierophant appears as someone who has knowledge of the situation at hand, or seems to. He may be as a priest, teacher or lawyer. Although he may be honest in his opinions, he may not be correct about the situation. He tends to abide by fixed rules and see things as "Black or White".

CARD VI : THE LOVERS

Figure 60 : TAROT VI - THE LOVERS

THE IMAGES

Rider-Waite

In the Rider-Waite Card we have a clear representation of Adam and Eve, naked in The Garden of Eden. A depiction of, among other things, the first awareness that there is difference between man and woman. Adam stands before The Tree of Life, Eve stands before the Tree of Knowledge and The Serpent. So the pair also represent the 2 Trees.

The 2 Trees can be considered to represent the Kabbalah Pillars of Form and Force – although, in reality, they are one and the same in the Chakra system. We also have a depiction of The Middle Pillar in embryo form here. We see it is developed by Consciousness and Will later on.

Above everything is a full sun, then an Angel, then a cloud. There is a seeming transmutation of energy from high to low. Adam and Eve are each only aware of the other. Their view of one another is not clear because of the cloud between. In the centre background is a hill. Pointing to Heaven it is a phallic symbol (natural, rather than man-made) reminiscent of the Magician and Aries, and The Middle Pillar .Physical arousal. We see Crowley's association with Gemini. Although I put The Sign to the previous Stage it emphasises that there are no real divisions between them.

Traditional

In the Traditional image we see a young man between two women, one old the other young. It is of a man leaving his mother in favour of his beloved. His mother seems reluctant to let go. This "beloved" does not yet have a physical form. Here we see the beginning of inner tension as he is forced to seek Completion elsewhere.

Above them is the Greek god Eros, "God of Love" (Roman, Cupid) both of which mean Desire. In this is contained the story of Cupid and Psyche. Their story is based on feminine jealousy. Venus, Goddess of Love (related to Card III The Empress) was annoyed by men turning away from worshipping her to worshipping Psyche – who was a beautiful human female. She sent her son Cupid to make Psyche fall in love with the ugliest man in the

303

THE TAROT

world. Eros fell in love with her himself, and visited her only in the darkness of night (in the Unconscious ?) with the proviso that she should not see his face. Psyche disobeyed and lit a lamp (consciousness) to see his face. Because of the disobedience Cupid abandoned her, when she was forced to travel the world in search of him. We note that Eros was not of the world. She was eventually united with Cupid and made immortal by Jupiter (King of the Gods).

The Greek Eros (root of "erotic") was similar to Cupid except that he never left his mother (Aphrodite/Venus). He is often described as being mischievous and depicted as being blindfolded. "Love is Blind" Unconscious.. Perhaps this is a demonstration of a psychological difference between Greek and Roman cultures. Here is an example of how Archetypes get "disguised" by human life. To get closer to the true basic meaning we have to consider the root of it all.

In Psychology The Psyche means the totality of the human mind, conscious and unconscious. In some areas this is synonymous with feminine "Soul" (as distinct from masculine Spirit). So we have an echo of Card II The Priestess. We note that each step in our Evolution INCLUDES (does not replace) the lessons of previous one. The bag of The Fool gets heavier. At this stage is a reminder that when we advance into a life away from our family we do not actually leave them behind.

Aleister Crowley

The Aleister Crowley Card shows a priest performing a marriage. It is of special note here because it emphasises the influence of the previous Card V. The Hierophant or High Priest, as well as suggesting the hidden, unconscious, psychology at work. The image is similar to that of Rider-Waite with the transmutation of power from "God" to The Lovers via an intermediary. This calls to mind the modern psychology statement that the attitude of a child to parental figures is as if they are "Godlike" – having the power of life and death. There is also sexual connotation, here with the rod and cup, and coiled serpent. This is the miracle of Jesus when he turned water into wine ("fire water") at a wedding.

This is the Oedipus (Male)/Electra (Female) stage of child development when the child competes with the parent of the same sex for the attentions of the parent of the opposite sex. In healthy families the advances are rejected. The child is therefore forced to seek "completion" elsewhere in the external world. The man's unconscious, feminine, Anima or woman's masculine Animus is projected onto people in the outside world until it is discovered within.

In the image we see the hidden marriage between the man's Anima and the woman's Animus – who are the true instigators of the relationship – in the Unconscious.

ASSOCIATIONS : CYCLE OF GROWTH STAGE 4 (TRANSPLANTING)

The 4th. House – Personal Security. Home. Roots

The Summer Solstice – the light of the Sun begins to diminish. Cancer The Crab. Cardinal (Active) Water. Negative.

The Moon (and its light- reflective properties – related to The Mother and The Personal Unconscious. Number 8).

Logarithmic Timescale Age : Play Age 3 years 6 months to 7 years. Initiative vs. Guilt. Genital development. Oedipus/Electra- attraction to the parent of opposite sex. Basic Family. Persona formation.

COMMENTARY

1. The Lovers is the first of 2 cards which include both masculine and feminine symbols in images. Although Cancer is a negative Water Sign it is here in its Cardinal, Active mode. Cancer is symbolic of the protective Mother and the crablike protective "shell" of the home. Hence we have "Transplanting" as the beginning of the child's need to build its own "shell" to explore a wider experience. There should be a partial rejection by the mother as the completion of the weaning stage. "You are not a baby any more". The "Shell" is also symbolic of the Persona, the symbolic mask we all wear.
2. In Cycle of Growth Stage 4 (Transplanting) we put down new roots. Make a new (inner) Home.
3. Number 6 (Venus. Desire) is the uniting of Fire and Water to produce Desire. Earlier, in Number 2 (Saturn. Form. Mother) we saw that the creation of Number 1 (Pluto. Force. Father) produced a complementary feminine force. In Number 6 (Venus) we see the universal principal that "Opposites Attract". The forces involved are attempting to annihilate one another and return to the original state of perfection - Zero.
4. The moral ideas of the Hierophant separate The Lovers into external and internal characteristics.

THE TAROT

5. The Lovers is both separation and joining together. Desire is the uniting force so created. Magnetism.
6. The Lovers means Desire in its widest sense. We have to distinguish between Desire and Needs. We discover ourselves from what we are attracted to. Our Motives (Motivations. Fire) are what is important, rather than the Object itself – but we do not see it at the time.
7. When we "Fall in Love" we lose conscious control to that of the Unconscious. The same experience may be repeated with various partners until the inner lessons are learned.
8. Desire is not Love. Will is Love.
9. Desire suggests that something is missing.
10. In Erikson's Play Age the child discovers its sexuality. We must note that an actual marriage is out of the question at this age – so here we have instinct, or spirit, driving us forwards. Positive Spirit is always seeking the Negative polarity to become creative. This is an echo of The Magician and The Priestess. The first object of Desire is the (Oedipus\Electra) desire for the parent of the opposite sex, which, when rejected, forces us out to find "another". This dilemma is depicted by the traditional Tarot card.
11. At this stage the Mother could become "The Devouring Mother" who keeps the child "tied to her apron strings" – not allowing any freedom of action.
12. We see the Negative Polarity as the force of Attraction. Need. An emptiness that wants to be filled. The universal "Black Hole".
13. Here we see instinctual impulses being controlled by the moral laws of Society, as depicted by The Hierophant/High Priest, with their influence on the child – via the parents.
14. The child is forced to seek satisfaction elsewhere. Therefore Transplanting.
15. The child will first seek in the objects of the outside world.
16. Because the bias is formed according to the dictates of the Parents and/or Society (Nurture), there will be a greater or lesser variance with the true, inner self (Nature).
17. The true aim of the child is to eventually discover and resolve the "missing" balances within. Often overcoming parental or social "taboos". Until then they will be projected into the outside world and the people in it. As we discover them through our love-objects we learn to love our-self. Nevertheless, we need to go through this stage numerous times to recover them from our unconscious.
18. At this stage we learn who we are from close contact with others – who we are not.
19. Transactional Analysts state that a child's initial "life position" is set by Age 6. Usually, because "I am small", it is "I'm Not OK - You're OK". It takes time and conscious effort to reach "I'm OK – You're OK". We cannot love our neighbour unless we love our-self. There are other possibilities discussed in [PSYCHOLOGY DEVELOPMENT MODELS : TRANSACTIONAL ANALYSIS]. Perhaps we can never be truly OK until we have found our true Self.

TRADITIONAL MEANINGS [AEW]
Attraction, love, beauty, trials overcome.
Reversed : Failure, foolish designs. Another account speaks of marriage frustrated and contrarieties of all kinds.

FROM MY PRACTICAL READINGS
A new attraction or desire in life. Perhaps some creative occupation. Often, the beginnings of a new relationship, or partnership, that need not be sexual.

THE TAROT

CARD VII : THE CHARIOT

Figure 61 : TAROT VII - THE CHARIOT

THE IMAGE

We see a young person, who can be of either sex, driving a chariot. He carries a rod in his right hand – which could be the representation of a phallic staff, wand, or sceptre. A symbol of Will.

On the shoulders are the Urim and Thummin. This is a strange continuation from the traditional, ancient, image considering that no-one really knows what they mean. There is a suggestion that they were used in divination by the priests of the Old Testament. There is agreement that the priests wore a form of breastplate, which is included here.

The Chariot has a canopy overhead supported by 4 columns, and is drawn by two beasts. In the traditional version they are horses, typically facing in different directions – or attempting to - and the wheels of the Chariot are depicted in a similar fashion. The Rider-Waite version emphasises their different polarity by making them black and white. The rider needs no reins to control the animals, he does it solely with the power of his mind.

The Chariot is moving away from a city in the background, and we can see that it has successfully crossed a river. A barrier overcome.

In addition, the Chariot of Aleister Crowley shows a suit of armour –a "shell" like that of The Crab on his helmet. His "horses" are the '4 Beasts' of Revelation. The 4 Elements. The Cherubim. We see his association with Cancer.

ASSOCIATIONS : CYCLE OF GROWTH STAGE 4 (TRANSPLANTING)

As The Lovers, above.

COMMENTARY

1. The Chariot is the second of 2 cards which relate to Cycle of Growth Stage 4 (Transplanting). Here our hero has discovered a suitable Persona, or mask, behind which he can travel in the world, and play his part. He has his masculine and feminine energies under control as instructed by The Hierophant.
2. With The Chariot, the Lovers are depicted as animal energies which act together to enable progress.
3. Our hero has successfully solved the dilemma posed by The Lovers and is leaving his old "home" to face an uncertain future. A clear representation of Cycle of Growth Stage 4 "Transplanting".

4. The relationship with domestic, security-minded, Cardinal (Active. Initiating), Cancer and its "shell" is continued with the canopy overhead, the breastplate, and the shoulder armour – which has crescent moons. We have the image of a "mobile home".
5. We can see a similarity with the modern motor car that resembles a shell and a chariot, and is powered by fossil fuel which has evolved from past Nature. It is often considered an indication of one's status.
6. The human body is another type of "vehicle".
7. The child develops a Persona. That is, a mask to mediate between its true inner self and the outside world of society. The "mask" is another "shell" of defence. A Shield. Armour.
8. The Persona must be flexible in order to act out different roles in life, otherwise there is no creativity or further growth.
9. In the absence of other specific information, we can speculate that the shoulder-plates represent "masks" of the Persona. The fact there are two beasts and two shoulder-masks, right and left, suggest the Jungian concept that in the first part of life we use and develop a Main Function, when the "opposite" Function remains unconscious and undeveloped. The "inferior", undeveloped, Function calls for attention and development at the time of the Mid Life Crisis.
10. The child has found a way of surviving, and making progress, outside the family home.
11. The Chariot is a mobile home.
12. We note that the direction of travel is determined by past experience – which has been limited in scope and understanding.
13. Number 7 (Mercury. Communication. Rational Mind) complements Number 6 (Venus. Feelings. Emotion).

TRADITIONAL MEANINGS [AEW]
Succour, providence also war, triumph, presumption, vengeance, trouble.
Reversed : Riot, quarrel, dispute, litigation, defeat.

FROM MY PRACTICAL READINGS
The Querent is making worldly progress with the ability to control circumstances.

THE TAROT

CARD VIII : STRENGTH

Figure 62 : TAROT VIII - STRENGTH

THE IMAGE

The image is of a young woman gently controlling the mouth of a lion (Leo). Above her head is the same dual-circle symbol of Infinity and Higher Mind as that of The Magician (and another Fire Sign, Aries). As Above, So Below. The differences between this and the traditional card is that in the latter the woman is wearing a hat shaped like the Infinity symbol (as has The Magician). The phallic symbol of a mountain is in the background, as it was in Card VI. The Lovers.

The Rider-Waite version has transposed this card, relating to the Sign of Leo, with card Justice, now card XI, which better relates to the Sign of Libra.

The Aleister Crowley card is entitled "Lust" – an intense form of Desire. His picture is very relaxed.

ASSOCIATIONS : CYCLE OF GROWTH STAGE 5 (POWER. LOVE. CREATIVITY)

The 5th. House – Personal Creativity. Ego Consciousness.

Leo, The Lion. Fixed Fire. Creativity. Intuition. Controlled Power/ Instinct.

The Sun (Number 5. Development of Ego Consciousness. I have a Name therefore "I Am").

Logarithmic Timescale Age : School Age 7-13 years of age. Identity vs. Identity Diffusion.

Instincts lie fallow in favour of practical Productivity. Traditionally the time of the annual First Harvest.

COMMENTARY

1. With a developed Persona, the charioteer is able to act out his chosen role.
2. We see here that the outward, expansive, motion of Card VII. The Chariot has been halted. Sexual instincts lie fallow. This relates to the psychological School Age where the lessons are related to putting work before pleasure and the completion of set tasks. It is a test of Competence. We note that there are no concerns about survival or security – which were established in Cycle of Growth Stage 4 (Transplanting). The Persona has become established – although activity in any Stage depends on the results of the previous one.
3. The actor is playing his part.
4. The figure in the card has the symbol of Infinity/Higher mind above her head. Number 8 (The Moon), one circle on top of another (or side by side as infinity), is the stability of earthy, material, organised,

THE TAROT

Number 4 on 2 different levels which denotes control of Earth (4) by an organised mind (4) – or The Laws of Nature. Stability is Change. Change, Stability.

5. At basic level the symbol has the same meaning as that of St. George or other Knights (Swords. Thinking Function) "saving virgins" from The Dragon (Fire. Desire), although the moderation depicted here is a gentler approach to one's "animal" Fire instinct – which, after all, is our main life force. He rides a horse, which is reminiscent of the previous card, The Chariot. His lance is a phallic symbol. His Sword is as the upper cross of 4 which controls the Lower Nature. In one version of the story St. George does not kill the dragon but takes the woman's girdle and binds the dragon with it. This is more in keeping with the symbol here.

6. Whereas we were previously contained by our family, here we learn to "contain our self" – and "keep our mouth shut" at certain times.

7. As Fixed (controlled) Fire, Strength also means Perseverance. Some writers say Perseverance is related to Taurus. Although partially true, the Fixed Earth Sign is naturally slow and deliberate with the problem of getting started. Here the lesson is knowing when to stop.

8. The association with Cycle of Growth Stage 5 (Power. Love. Creativity) is concerned with the power of The Sun and Creative Force. Here is energy devoted to pure Creativity uncontaminated by Purpose. It is the discovery of life by means of Play, which psychologists are discovering is the most efficient way we all learn. Later on in life this becomes our Hobbies – which means the things that we do, and games we play, for pleasure rather than monetary or other gain. We note that in schools today there is a focus on such activity at this age. A tendency towards Art rather than Science, which comes later.

9. Leo is also related to Personal Creativity. It includes such things as Sports - where one is in competition with others, but has to obey the Laws of the game. Although one trains for sports, at the time of playing there is no time to think. One must act instinctively, Intuitively (Fire). In a team, one learns to co-operate with others where all share in successes and defeats. Leo likes to lead the team.

10. Lust is Desire, here "The Ram" of Cardinal Fire impulsive Aries is under Fixed Fire Leo control. Finding a mate requires some form of courtship – which is a type of Number 4 ritual. Once again, needing to learn the "rules of the game" (Number 8).

11. Strength controls the excesses of the Chariot. Everything has limitations. This is self-control rather than that of the Emperor or Hierophant, which is external.

12. During Erikson's School Age there are no major physical changes. It ends at the age of Puberty at age 12 when there is further sexual development.

13. The Infinity symbol in this card and that of Card I. The Magician is the same as my Serpent symbol for The Cycle of Growth. It contains the archetypal principle that everything is subject to Higher Laws. Will. Both cards relate to Fire Signs, here Fire is under control and therefore in its most stable form. It is being directed into more practical channels.

14. Fire is related to the Jungian Function Intuition.

15. Leo is the time of Summer when The Sun is hottest. Nature is in full bloom. However, Light (consciousness) is declining with the now shortening days.

16. Leo, The Lion, is King of the Jungle (or thinks he is). With his air of lazy self-confidence many believe him. He has his "pride". His lionesses do the hunting.

17. The lesson is that of controlling the Fire of Spirit to some useful or creative purpose rather than extinguishing it, which would result in death, or allowing the Fire to spread to destructive purpose.

18. The Sun relationship indicates that we here have the beginning of development of Ego Consciousness. "I Am" becomes a co-creator with God. This is the time of the "First Harvest" of the agricultural year.

TRADITIONAL MEANINGS [AEW]

Power, energy, action, courage, magnanimity; also complete success and honours.

Reversed : Despotism, abuse of power, weakness, discord, sometimes even disgrace.

FROM MY PRACTICAL READINGS

Creativity. The Querent is using self-control and working co-operatively. "In charge" of the project.

THE TAROT

CARD IX : THE HERMIT

Figure 63 : TAROT IX - THE HERMIT

THE IMAGE
We see a lone male figure dressed in the habit of a monk. He carries a staff in his, (unconscious), left hand and a dimly lit lantern in his (conscious) right. Because it is dark externally and he cannot see far ahead, he makes his way cautiously. The future is not clear.

ASSOCIATIONS : CYCLE OF GROWTH STAGE 6 (SERVICE TO SELF)
The 6th. House – Personal Service.

Virgo The Virgin. Mutable (Changeable) Earth. Mental Analysis.

Mercury (The Rational Mind. Number 7)

Logarithmic Timescale Age : 13-23 years. Teenage. Adolescence. Puberty. Identity vs. Identity Diffusion.

COMMENTARY
1. The self-control of Strength leads to the beginnings of thinking for one's self. Matching inner ideas with practical reality. The price of increased consciousness is inner doubt. The Persona role of the child is becoming less appropriate.
2. The Hermit has become aware of his INNER self. He becomes conscious of contradictions within himself. He is somehow "different" to "the norm" of his peers – or thinks he is. By observing The Path from above we see that everyone is really the same.
3. The Hermit is "isolation by a secret"
4. The traditional associations with this card are not of much use to us here. The best that they can offer in some sense of consensus is that of Prudence – which basically means that one is walking an unfamiliar path and is taking care to avoid unknown pitfalls that may be ahead. Perhaps summed up by the term "walking on thin ice". This does include connotations of "putting something away for a rainy day" in the expectation of problems to come. We need to look to other related areas of knowledge to expand our understanding.
5. Following the Card VIII. Strength it seems that the Fire has dimmed to a small spark of focus. It is concentrated into a single place. It is inner consciousness.

THE TAROT

6. Number 9 (Earth) is the first stage of Completion in the sequence of numbers. It is the last whole number or Integer. It is a step away from Number 8 where everything is organised. Here the Individual (Number 1) has become aware of inner resistance to the established order (Number 8). Something new is developing internally. New seeds.
7. We now see a more individual, lone, path. This is the time of Erikson's Adolescence and "Identity Crisis".
8. In psychological terms the stage begins at puberty and lasts until age 23 when one takes up a role in society and probably gets involved in more permanent, intimate relationships. At puberty we have a time of major physical changes, especially one's concerned with more overt sexual development. With the increase in sex hormones one has to master new inner drives and emotions. The main social focus is on peer groups and role models. Finding a new "mask" based on one's peers rather than parents' ideas.
9. Virgo and the 6th. House have connections to the Health of an individual as well as the sort of job one does to earn a living (both supporting a physical body) – we can see the relationship between the two, and its concern with this age, when we need to consider such matters. We can see that it is our personal set of skills and abilities that make us different from our peers. It is also true of our proneness to certain types of illness.
10. The 6th. House is entitled "Service to Self".
11. Mercury, planet of The Mind, rules Earthy Virgo as well as Airy Gemini (Communication. Mind). Here it is concerned with more practical matters. We note that this is a time of school examinations the results of which will greatly affect career prospects.
12. At this time is the tendency of society to segregate the sexes. We see groups of boys and groups of girls with not much private inter-action between them. Competition between sexes is socially encouraged. Nowadays girls tend to do better academically than boys. The suggestion is that the former are more likely to bend to the new social pressures. It was the same in the past when it was thought unnecessary to educate women. The Pendulum swings.
13. During Adolescence we tend to relate more to a peer group of the same sex. The Gang. In effect we have a "homosexual" period. Here we have an inner feeling that we somehow do not fit in. In the following Cycle of Growth Stage 7 (Partnerships. Social Role) hormones force us to leave the group to seek our inner counterpart.
14. The association between Virgo and IX.The Hermit is that they are both Virgins.
15. The Hermit is Adam, having eaten of The Tree of Knowledge, cast out of The Garden Of Eden, and Cain who, having slain his brother, is banished to The East of Eden where he has to become self-supporting. (He has discovered a path that separates him from his brothers/peers).
16. With its Earth connotation, we are reminded that true Independence begins with Financial Independence. Here is the time of development of skills to eventually enable that. The realisation of the need to become self-supporting.
17. This could mean "Worry" or interference by the Unconscious to conscious activity. Sleepless nights. Forcing attention to inner needs. As do our illnesses.
18. As I write this in 2014 there is concern for an increase in teenage depression and suicidal tendencies related to poor self-image. Perhaps as a result of more permissive parenting providing no strong role models and greater freedom forcing young people to make decisions they are not yet equipped to make.

TRADITIONAL MEANINGS [AEW]

Prudence, circumspection; also and especially treason, dissimulation, roguery, corruption.

Reversed : Concealment, disguise, policy, fear, unreasoned caution.

FROM MY PRACTICAL READINGS

There is the sense of being "alone in a crowd" with the need to keep one's ideas and opinions to ones-self. The discovery of a new, more personal, pathway.

THE TAROT

CARD X : THE WHEEL OF FORTUNE

Figure 64 : TAROT X - THE WHEEL OF FORTUNE

THE IMAGE

At the centre of the image is a wheel in motion. In common with traditional images there are 3 figures at the circumference. The figure at the top suggesting more human qualities whilst the other two are animal - like. Assuming that the figures are travelling head first, The Wheel is rotating anti-clockwise – the same as the Earth does. Although there is suggestion that all 3 figures are fixed to the Wheel and are rotating with it, the interpretation of the symbol is that the one at the top is stable, and remains at the top – observing the other two. The one at the top carries a weapon, here it is a Sword in common with some versions, others have a club.

A.E. Waite has made some additions and changes.

The rising figure is a Hermanubis which is a combination of the Greek Hermes (Roman Mercury "Messenger of the gods") and Egyptian Anubis (who weighed the heart of the dead to determine their worthiness to enter the afterlife. We see a similar modern version in card XI. Justice, which follows). The descending figure is that of The Serpent. For Waite, this is Typhon. His image is a rather tame version of the mythical creature said to have 100 dragon heads and a serpent body. We can remain with our Serpent who first appears in The Garden of Eden.

Around the circumference of the wheel reading clockwise are the letters TARO, which is a play on words. The word ROTA means "wheel" in Latin, and is also associated with "Law". With the return to the first T we get TAROT. The letters can be read 'Rota, Tarot, orat, tora Ator', which Waite 'translated' as 'The Wheel of the Tarot speaks the law of Ator (=Hathor, or Love).

The Wheel has the appearance of a compass. Its arrow is pointing to (Astrological) West which is the position of the Card in our Cycle of Growth Stages 6 and 7.

4 BEASTS OR CHERUBIM

There is an important addition in the corners of the card of the symbols of the 4 Cherubim of the Book of Genesis. They were first set as guardians of the empty Garden of Eden, and later appear as 4 Beasts in Revelation. They refer to the 4 lower Chakras and 4 Elements [EC] as well as the 4 Jungian Functions – Bull (Earth. Sensation. Taurus), Lion (Fire. Intuition. Leo), Eagle (Air. Thinking. Aquarius), Man (Water. Feeling. Scorpio). They are the tools on the table of Tarot I. The Magician.

The 4 Beasts or Cherubim reappear in the last Card of The Tarot – XXI The World. Here they each have a blank book ready to be written, reminiscent of that of II. The Priestess. The tools on the table of I.The Magician have been incorporated into the previously undivided subconscious (II.The Priestess).

THE TAROT

THE THREE FATES - LIZ GREENE MYTHIC TAROT

In Liz Greene's (Psychologist, Astrologer, Tarot) Mythic Tarot her image is of the Morai, or "Three Fates", observing a Wheel Of Life with 4 human figures. The Fates are said to control the "thread of life" of each mortal. One spins the thread on to her spindle ("the things that are"), one measures the thread (in the sense of allotting fair proportions) ("the things that were") and the other cuts the thread to end life ("the things that will be"). The last Fate, with scissors, means the same as the figure with the sword, in our Cards.

ASSOCIATIONS : CYCLE OF GROWTH STAGES 6 AND 7

The Wheel of Fortune is the 10th. in the sequence which is exactly half way through The Tarot . Ignoring The Wheel of Fortune and The World, we have 10 outward-going and 10 returning cards. Stage 6 is exactly half way through The Cycle of Growth. The following Stages indicate a return to the beginning. The inner Wheel has the same structure as an archetypal Birth Chart with an arrow pointing to this Stage of The Cycle of Growth.

Cycle of Growth Stage 6 (Service to Self) is the last Stage concerned with the outward, growing, waxing, journey of The Fool from Birth/Ascendant into worldly life.

This is another card which is difficult to place in a particular Stage. The main reason is that it seems to contain all stages. This is in common with Card XXI. The World. In this image the undeveloped, animal like, creatures are outside The Wheel. In the final card, The World, a human figure is at the centre of The Circle, which resembles a womb – and is the Zero of The Fool. There, everything is in balance, with the promise of New Life to come. The Wheel of Fortune promises only Death. There is something here pertaining to the Tree of Knowledge, with its promise of death, and The Tree of (Everlasting) Life, in The Garden of Eden.

COMMENTARY

1. Psychologists say that Adolescence is a time of Recapitulation (Remembering. Re-assessing) before progressing further.
2. Here we enter the seeming chaos of life. Wheels within wheels. Having experienced Home and Family we are now about to enter into the more Public sphere of activity.
3. Number 10 is the end of a cycle and the beginning of a new one as Number 1 (Pluto. Regeneration. Force) at a higher level (1 + 0 = 1).
4. The figure holding the sword in this card is placed on The Wheel of Fortune at the position of Stage 10 (Peak of Social Achievement) on the wheel of The Cycle of Growth. At Stage 10 in The Cycle of Growth it is Winter when we can finally view the Harvest of past activity and begin to prepare for the new cycle to come. It is also representative of Career.
5. The Wheel of Fortune has similar meaning, and is also a card of Transition – as is XXI. The World. We are at the half way point.
6. The figure holding the sword in this card is XI. Justice in the next. From his position at the top he can see The Wheel, but may be able to do nothing with his knowledge.
7. There is suggestion that some do not escape from the animal "rat race" (hamster wheel) to reach the next Stage.
8. The central Wheel is an image of The Cycle of Growth as depicted in this book, although here it has 8 segments instead of 12. The number 8 refers to the monthly phases of the Moon cycle, rather than the annual one of The Sun. Also the co-ordinates found on a compass used for earthly navigation. So The Wheel of Fortune has consciousness limited to the monthly Lunar Cycle rather than the annual Solar Cycle. Such is the case, for example, in monthly bills, and women's menstruation when a single egg is produced – which may or may not become fertilised.
9. The Circle, or Cycle, can be subdivided into as many or as few segments as we wish, depending on what we are using it for, and what our state of consciousness can accommodate. Zero being the most difficult.
10. The image of The Wheel of Fortune has connotations with the board game (of chance) "Snakes and Ladders". It has 100 squares. The players take turns throwing a dice and move the indicated number of squares forward. If they land at the bottom of a ladder they go forward to the square at the top. If they land on the head of a snake (temptation) they go back to the square at its tail end. The winner is the one who finishes first. But it is just a matter of Chance, rather than ability.
11. The Wheel of Fortune can be applied to any game of Chance. There is no Will, only "Luck".

THE TAROT

12. The 4 Quarters of The Cycle are "crisis points" – with an opportunity to change.
13. A Message of The Wheel is "Change is Stability. Stability, Change". That which stops moving or growing dies.
14. There is suggestion that this is the Wheel of Karma. To the degree that we reap what we sow this is true. However, in psychological terms Jung continually made the point of the need to reconcile "The Opposites". In the Following, Waning, part of The Cycle of Growth we begin to meet the complementary energies of the stages in the opposite positions on the Wheel to the ones we met earlier. From "The Marriage of Opposites" comes new life. In normal human life, among other wheels, The Wheel is that of our everyday life. Normally, it is not until there is some crisis, when The Wheel comes to a "bump" in the path, that we have the opportunity to raise our consciousness to a new level. The normal tendency is to "solve the problem" and return to the comfortable routine of The Wheel as soon as possible.
15. An example of an Opposite at this age contrasts the age of Infancy with that of becoming a potential parent.
16. The Wheel of Fortune is physical reaping and sowing. Its contrasting Cycle of Growth Stage 12 and XXI.The World on the opposite side is concerned with spiritual Karma.
17. The Wheel of Fortune is the cycle of Earthly rebirth, albeit without physical death.

TRADITIONAL MEANINGS [AEW]

Destiny, fortune, success, elevation, luck, felicity.

Reversed : Increase, abundance, superfluity.

FROM MY PRACTICAL READINGS

This is an indication of Routine and Learning. Repetition eventually results in awareness. New consciousness. One message is that we often have to wait for changes in inner and external circumstances before we can move forward.

CARD XI : JUSTICE

Figure 65 : TAROT XI - JUSTICE

THE TAROT

THE IMAGE
Here is the well-known symbol of Justice with The Scales in the left (unconscious) hand and the upright Sword in the right hand. At this stage everything is in equilibrium – so there is no movement. Until there is imbalance in the Scales the Sword cannot move either. The figure is seated, indicating stability.

In Waite's Tarot we have repetition of The Twin Pillars found in Card II. The Priestess and Card V. The Hierophant. We also see a repetition of the veil of The Priestess. Here we are concerned with Human, rather than Universal Laws.

We could consider this beginning of the 2nd. half of life as similar to that before Creation, when everything was in balance.

ASSOCIATIONS : CYCLE OF GROWTH STAGE 7 (PARTNERSHIPS. PUBLIC ROLE)

The 7th. house – Social projection of energy.

The Autumn Equinox - equal Day and Night, Light and Dark balance. The days are still getting shorter. After this, the Unconscious time is on the increase.

Libra The Scales. Cardinal (Active) Air. Positive.

Venus (Desire. Goddess of Beauty, Peace, and sexual attraction. Number 6)

Logarithmic Timescale Age : 23 to 42 years. Young Adulthood. Intimacy vs. Isolation.

Cycle of Growth Stage 7 (Partnerships. Social Service) is the "Full Moon" stage of objective awareness – exactly opposite the Ascendant Stage 1 (Seed). From now on we enter the Waning Phase of return to the beginning of The Cycle – when all the past must be balanced to a final Number Zero. This is indicated by Card XI. Justice, who holds the Scales and The Sword.

The sequence of Stages is the exact reverse of the Waxing half of the cycle – except that here one is meeting the "opposite" polarity. Stage 1 is our entry into "the world". Stage 7 is the entry into an even wider world. Stage 8 complements Stage 2 – and so on.

COMMENTARY

1. From the repeated cycles of The Wheel of Fortune, The Hermit begins to become aware of contradictions WITHIN HIMSELF. This is the beginning of new consciousness similar to that of The Magician and following cards.
2. The outer world contains contradictions to the teachings of our parents and peers.
3. 11 is a depiction of Twin Pillars. They are clearer here than elsewhere.
4. The Number of this card is 2 (1 + 1. Saturn. Binah. Form. Mother). Whereas before it was simple "Yes" or "No" of a child, here the dilemma is at a higher level. Number 1 (Force. Father) is balanced by its "Opposite". The following journey is discovery that there is no such thing as "opposites".
5. This is the possible birth of a Higher Self.
6. The association between The Scales, Justice, and the Sign of Libra (Scales) needs no explanation.
7. There is a strange paradox that one discovers one's inner self in the Public sphere of interaction.
8. This is the Stage of Paradoxes – which C. G. Jung calls "the opposites".
9. The "opposites" are the Twin Pillars. Useful for simple understanding of life. They are also visible in Card II. The Priestess, Card V. The Hierophant and Gemini, and invisible in Card XV. The Devil – being reduced to a single "block".
10. This can be "Justice without Mercy".
11. The human symbol of Justice is often depicted as being blindfolded with the idea that justice should be impartial. It also suggests "blind obedience" to the Law. In addition there is suggestion of the need to give attention to one's inner feelings as distinct from external appearances.
12. With the rulership of Venus over the Stage, and her desire for Peace, we see the ability to harmonise seemingly "opposing" forces. However, Venus may just be beauty of form, without equivalent content. As Desire she reminds us that "opposites attract".
13. Cycle of Growth Stage 7(Partners) is one's first entry into the Public arena of life from the relative seclusion of the family home. Beginning to make "one's own way" in life.

THE TAROT

TRADITIONAL MEANIGS [AEW]

Equity, rightness, probity, executive; triumph of the deserving side in law.

Reversed : Law in all its departments, legal complications, bigotry, bias, excessive severity.

FROM MY PRACTICAL READINGS

The Querent has an important decision to make.

CARD XII : THE HANGED MAN

Figure 66 : TAROT XII - THE HANGED MAN

THE IMAGE

We see the body of a young person hanging from a gibbet – which, apart from being used as a gallows for execution, was a structure used to hang dead bodies of criminals after they had been executed. The figure in the Card is suspended upside down by one ankle, the other leg being bent to form a cross.

Gibbets were usually situated next to a public highway, often at cross-roads – the idea being to demonstrate the power of the law and to discourage other wrong doers. The various versions of The Tarot mainly depict two different types – here we see a T-shaped "Tau Cross", the other main type has two supports with a cross-beam at the top. Both types are authentic reproductions of the structures actually used, the difference in The Tarot being that they are constructed from living wood.

The common factor of all the images is that the subject is co-operating in the process, and is not suffering. Indeed often, as here, the subject is actually in a state of trance or ecstasy.

I have added associations with The Kabbalah Tree of Life. Here, The Sephiroth and associated Planets are those outside the orbit of The Sun, away from Earth. The Planets are the Outer Planets as distinct from the Inner, or Personal Planets. Having formed an Ego and Personality, the Middle Pillar is developing and we are now on the return journey of The Tree of Life.

ASSOCIATIONS : CYCLE OF GROWTH STAGE 8 (INTERCOURSE. DEATH)

The 8th. House – Social collection of energy.

Scorpio The Scorpion (Serpent. Eagle. Dove). Fixed Water.

Mars (God of War. Number 4) or Pluto (Regeneration .ruler of The Underworld. Number 1)

Logarithmic Timescale Age : 42 years to death. (includes Adulthood and Old Age)

Age 42 is the time of the Mid Life Crisis.

THE TAROT

COMMENTARY

1. This is the first of 2 cards associated with Cycle of Growth Stage 8 (Sex. Death)
2. Until now the symbolism of this card has been shrouded in mystery. Its associations in The Cycle of Growth and The Kabbalah Tree of Life reveals more of its meaning.
3. After Justice we have the image of a condemned criminal – who seems to be enjoying his fate.
4. The upside-down man is a symbol of the reversal of values that occurs at this stage. The consideration of "opposites" forced by Card XI. Justice. The first half of life is concerned with Material and Social Establishment. The second half with giving it up.
5. The Scales of Justice (which represent "The Opposites") are still equally balanced, and no decision has been made. No sentence passed. No action taken.
6. The "crime" is that of disobeying the rules of Society (or is it The Hierophant ? - perhaps The Devil). We are about to enter realms which Society says are forbidden, or taboo.
7. With Death impending, what is there to lose ? We leave this life as we entered it – alone.
8. Here we have "The Dove" Stage of Scorpio. In addition, there is an aspect of self-sacrifice. There is a reversal of life values. Everything eventually balances out to Zero.
9. The Number of this card adds to 3 (1 + 2. Jupiter. Expansion. Child) here, the possible resolution of a 2-sided dilemma. The Traditional card shows the man hanging between the 2 pillars of Justice (albeit natural rather than man made) – unable to decide. His body actually forms the "3rd. (Middle) Pillar" of The Kabbalah "Tree of Life". The combination of 2 "Opposites" enables the creation of a third possibility. The parents produce a child.
10. Because Psychology recognises 2 stages during this period, we can ascribe Adulthood (Age 35-65) to this card. The dilemma is Generativity vs. Stagnation where the challenge is concerned with the responsibilities of worldly leadership. Here we have Stagnation.
11. We see someone suspended on The Middle Pillar where everything is in balance. His head is at the position of Sephirah 6 (Tiphareth. Beauty. The Sun. Light. Illumination. Consciousness). There is a dawning of new consciousness.
12. The Middle Pillar does not begin to materialise until one begins to develop Ego Consciousness at Cycle of Growth Stage 5 (Power. The Sun). A personal view of The World.
13. Although, in childhood, we complain about lack of Freedom, Free Will brings the burden of decision and choice – which can be stressful.
14. Although Cycle of Growth Stage 8 (Sex. Death) includes all forms of Intercourse, the sexual type produces ecstasy. Meditation is said to do so as well.
15. We therefore have an added relationship to the practice of Meditation – forced by circumstances or otherwise.
16. Perhaps the Laws being broken are those of The Emperor and The Hierophant. In early days, sex was more of a "taboo" (socially prohibited) subject and carried out in secret – despite its necessity for human survival – and "everybody doing it".
17. The Cross, among other things, is a symbol of human mortality. The body dies.
18. The sacrifice alluded to here is Self-Sacrifice. Self-Control. Whereas in Card VIII. Strength one learns self-control in a secure location, here one develops it further by having little or no power over external (or inner) circumstances. (Cycle of Growth Stage 8 Intercourse).
19. One of the secrets of Scorpio is that we usually have to give, or sacrifice, something to get something in return.
20. With Card XIII. Death following this one, there is included the meaning that we are all subject to The Laws of Nature.
21. In simple human affairs the Card is a symbol of opposition. "Cross purposes". Until negotiation takes place there is stalemate. Progress is blocked. This forces a recognition and understanding of the "opposite" point of view – and therefore increases consciousness. This is the dawning of Diplomacy instead of War.

THE TAROT

22. Cycle of Growth Stage 8 is the resulting challenge from our Stage 7 entrance into the Public arena. The beginning of the Waning Phase of The Cycle. The Laws of Physics state that every action produces an opposite and equal reaction.
23. In Hexagram 38. "Opposition", the I Ching states :- *"The two elements Fire and Water never mingle, but even when in contact retain their own natures. So the cultured man is never led into baseness or vulgarity through intercourse or community of interests with persons of another sort; regardless of all commingling, he will always preserve his individuality"*. Its advice is to limit one's self to producing gradual effects.
24. Here one is learning the unwritten laws of social intercourse and co-operation.
25. This is a card of Meditation. Here it is forced. There is nowhere else to go. We gradually learn to do this as an act of Will – seeking answers within, rather than in the exterior world where everyone's opinions are in conflict. Finding our True Self.
26. The Hanged Man could mean boredom, where one has lost the inner drive to continue. Perhaps it is time to make changes.

TRADITIONAL MEANINGS [AEW]
Wisdom, circumspection, discernment, trials, sacrifice, intuition, divination, prophecy.
Reversed : Selfishness, the crowd, body politic.

FROM MY PRACTICAL READINGS
There is visible or invisible obstruction to the aims of the Querent. One can only submit to circumstances and make progress as opportunities arise. It is a test of patience and commitment. Attempts to use force could result in total failure.

THE TAROT

CARD XIII : DEATH

Figure 67 : TAROT XIII - DEATH

THE IMAGE

We see a skeleton wearing black armour riding a white horse. He is carrying a banner with a white rose on a black background. The rose signifies life. Although this skeleton has no weapon, where he passes there are dead bodies, there are people in front of him who are about to die. Some of the people are dressed in rich clothing, some are young, some old, which indicates that everyone is equally subject to higher law. In the background are two pillars between which the Sun is visible on the horizon. The promise of new life to come.

The traditional image of the card is of a skeleton with a scythe with human body parts – hands, heads and feet, on the ground before him. Some wear crowns, some do not.

ASSOCIATIONS : CYCLE OF GROWTH STAGE 8 (INTERCOURSE. DEATH)

As The Hanged Man, above.

COMMENTARY

1. This is the second of 2 cards associated with Cycle of Growth Stage 8 (Sex. Death. Scorpio. Mars/Pluto). To XII.The Hanged Man, Death comes as a release.

2. The theme of The Hanged Man's submission to his Fate, and Universal Laws, is continued in this card – as is the theme of Illumination, or growth of consciousness. The inner and outer Kingdom of IV.The Emperor is beginning to decay.

3. The Number 13 equates to Number 4 (Mars), but at a different level. Although a seeming destruction of what was achieved in the material stability of earlier Number 4, we now understand that everything is subject to the stability of higher laws. At Cycle of Growth Stage 1 (Seed. Mars) - the earlier Number 4 - the child was concerned controlling a human body, at this age we are concerned with its ultimate destruction.

4. Death is when structures break down into their simpler elements which return to their source. The card can also be considered a symbol of mental analysis where one considers "pros and cons". Some are more important than others.

5. Because Psychology recognises 2 stages during this period, we can ascribe Old Age (Age 65 to Death) to this card. The dilemma is Ego Integrity vs. Despair where the challenge is concerned with the fear of Death. We note that this is entirely in accordance with the card, so we need to make special note of the

term "Ego Integrity" in the face of the image, which depicts dismemberment of human bodies. The danger is when one looks back instead of forward. If this happens then, like Lot's Wife in The Bible, we are turned to a "Pillar of Salt". Petrified. Dead before our time.

6. As the human body starts "falling apart" at this age, we are forced to face the unavoidable reality of our final physical death to come.
7. The skeleton indicates that the essential hidden, inner, human structure is the same for all humans. The body is but an outer garment. This theme is repeated each year at the time of Scorpio when plants die, and trees lose their outer cladding of leaves to reveal their essential structure . Nature makes provision for survival of Winter, with seeds prepared for new growth to come. Decayed outer remains then become the food for that new life.
8. Scorpio is concerned with the physical "remains" passed on after death, such as inheritances from wills and genes.
9. Even Stone Age men buried their dead with expectation of new life to come.
10. In Scorpio one gets down to the "nitty gritty" – that is, the essential, basic, realities of life and death. In this is contained the "secrets" of occult subjects, which are, in reality, in plain sight for all to see. The only problem is "ignore-ance", and therefore lack of due attention or study. Reduced consciousness. We have to overcome the "taboos" of The Hierophant that prevent us even looking.
11. Even The High Priest is subject to Death.
12. At a normal day to day level we are here concerned with human Intercourse, sexual or otherwise, that can give rise to children or "brain children" to come. Life consists of numerous concurrent "layers", or levels of existence, other than the physical.
13. After Death, the following stage in the Cycle of Growth is Stage 9 (Conception). New life.
14. Death is the destruction of external, earthly, circumstances, which are subject to Change. The inner structure remains the same.
15. The suit of armour suggests the protective "shell" of the Persona Mask developed in Cycle of Growth Stage 4 (Transplanting. Cancer. Cardinal Water. Crab. Shell) that must now be discarded in order to undertake a new role in life.
16. This is emphasised by the symbols of the Fixed Water Sign of Scorpio. We have the Scorpion and Serpent which moult their outer shell/skin as they grow. Scorpio is associated with Metamorphosis of butterflies and moths which have the stages Egg, Caterpillar, Chrysalis, Imago where complete restructuring of the body occurs.
17. Cycle of Growth Stage 8 contains the secrets of Individuation.

TRADITIONAL MEANINGS [AEW]

End, mortality, destruction, corruption also, for a man, the loss of a benefactor or a woman, many contrarieties; for a maid, failure of marriage projects.

Reversed : Inertia, sleep, lethargy, petrifaction, somnambulism; hope destroyed.

FROM MY PRACTICAL READINGS

In normal human affairs Death refers to changes in outer circumstances - after which one is living a completely different routine, or form of life. This can be a release from past restrictions or obstructions to progress (symbolised by The Hanged Man). When we are seeking change we become more alert to external opportunities. We often need to wait for such a time before being able to proceed. Change is one thing that we can always rely on.

THE KABBALAH TREE OF LIFE

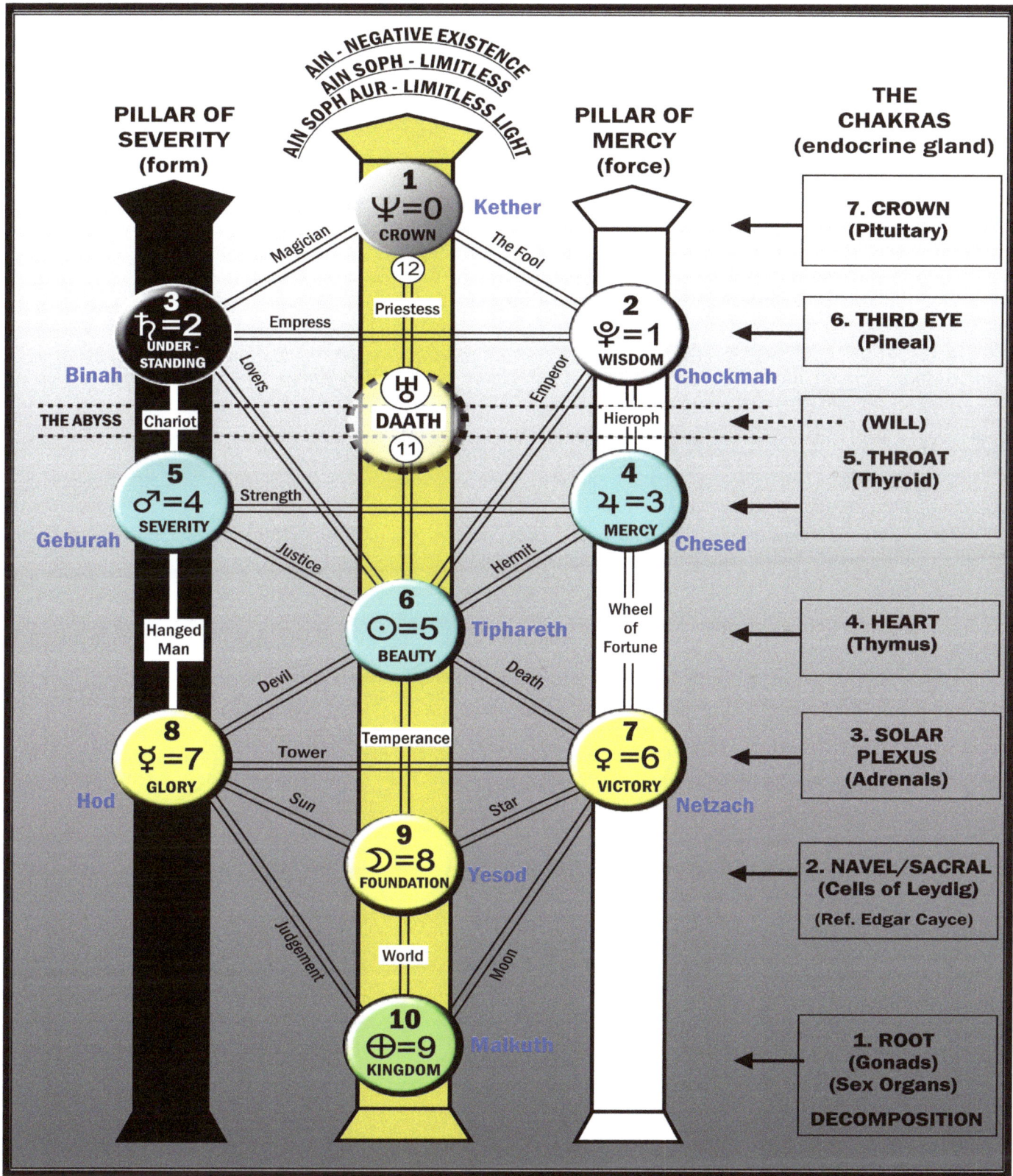

Figure 68 : TREE OF LIFE - NUMBERS, PLANETS, AND CHAKRAS

Please note that most of the detail of The Tree of Life is in the chapter [NUMEROLOGY] where we can get closer to the Archetypes.

THE KABBALAH TREE OF LIFE

Once again, The Kabbalah is much more complicated than this brief description. The Tree of Life is only part of the subject. For example, there is an additional ritualistic content. I attended a study group for 2 years, but many ideas, did not fit in with my Astrological concepts. You can see that now it does – especially when we can include Uranus, Neptune, and Pluto. There are also several variations of how Kabbalism describes The Tree of Life by considering the patterns of relationships between the Sephiroth.

There is a table at the end of the chapter summarising the relationships with the 40 numbered cards of The Tarot Minor Arcana to clarify The 4 Kingdoms (The 4 Elements) in which The Tree exists. Each Sephirah includes its own Tree of Life – Wheels Within Wheels.

Comparison of The Tree of Life with The Cycle of Growth at the end of this chapter.

My main reference here is Dion Fortune's book "The Mystical Qabalah" [DFMQ] because she encapsulated many of the traditional ideas – including A.E. Waite's. There is the added value of Dion relating to his version of the Tarot Cards – although, as mentioned in the chapter [THE TAROT] his images are of more value than his interpretation. She mentions the tendency for some writers on the subject to deliberately deceive. Some of them being her contemporaries, she was able to confirm this as fact with them directly.

WE ESPECIALLY NOTE THE SIMILARITY OF THE DEVELOPMENT OF THE MIDDLE PILLAR DESCRIBED BELOW WITH THE DEVELOPMENT MODELS OF PSYCHOLOGY'S TRANSACTIONAL ANALYSIS MODEL AND JUNGIAN INDIVIDUATION MODEL (which has an "Ego-Self" Axis" similar to The Middle Pillar) [PSYCHOLOGY : DEVELOPMENT MODELS].

THE TREE OF LIFE PARTIAL DESCRIPTION

1. The Tree of Life consists of 10 Sephiroth. Their association with the Tarot is the sets of cards numbered 1 to 10 of the Minor Arcana.
2. The separation between Sephiroth is a convenience to aid Mental (Thinking Function) analysis. In reality they co-exist in the same space.
3. Each Sephirah has a Hebrew name with an English translation.
4. In considering the basic Principles of The Tree we avoid much of the confusion that The Tree depicts. Evolution has developed from simple beginnings to more complex forms via Diversity.
5. Although I have omitted explicit information, it would be well to consider the relationship between the Paths between the Sephirah and [THE TAROT] Major Arcana – as shown in my diagram, and contained in Kabbalah Tradition.
6. In The Bible "The Tree of Life" refers to the Chakras and Endocrine Gland system of the body [EC] . Please note the planetary associations with Chakras here do not match with those of Edgar Cayce.
7. The Tree of Life is different for each separate human being. The same for all.
8. The roots of The Tree are in Heaven, The Ain, and it grows toward Earth, Kingdom, with decreasing rate of frequency and increasing materialisation, as Light becomes Matter.
9. The Tree of Life is supported by 3 Pillars. The Middle Pillar, colour Gold, is that of Equilibrium and Balance, beginning with Sephirah 1 (The Crown. Number Zero). The other pillars were created from this source on Creation Day 1 when Light and Darkness (Sephiroth 2.Chockmah and 3.Binah) appeared to create the basic positive and negative polarities.
10. In human terms we could say that the Middle Pillar depicts various levels of Will and Consciousness, with Sephirah 1 (Kether. Crown) having Zero Will and cosmic consciousness, and Sephirah 10 (Malkuth. Kingdom. Earth) having Free Will but almost no consciousness [THE PURPOSE OF LIFE].
11. At the beginning of involution Sephirah 1 (Kether, Crown. Number Zero) at the top of The Middle Pillar is coloured Grey which splits into Black and White Pillars. The return journey requires the "resolution of opposites" by solving the resulting dilemmas. Life is not just Black and White. At root level it is Grey.
12. So, in the beginning, Grey makes Black and White, not the other way round.
13. This is the Zero State at The Beginning and The End of existence. The pathway between is into Diversity, the Return is to Simplicity. The Process is called Karma.
14. Edgar Cayce also relates colour Grey to The Crown Chakra.

THE KABBALAH TREE OF LIFE

15. The Pillar of Mercy (Force), colour White, is headed and defined by Sephirah 2 (Wisdom. Force. Number 1), which encapsulates the First Law of Thermodynamics – "Heat is Work. Work is Heat". It is of Light, Masculine, Positive polarity.

16. The Pillar of Severity (Form) colour Black, is headed and defined by Sephirah 3 (Binah. Understanding. Form. Number 2) which is a natural consequence of Sephirah 2 emanating from and complementing Sephirah 1. It is of Dark, feminine, negative polarity. It absorbs the energy of Sephirah 1 and is one side of the equation $E=MC^2$ which summarises the considerable amount of energy contained, or locked up in, in Matter.

17. We note that paired Sephiroth at the same level on the pillars of Severity and Mercy involve the Jungian "resolution of opposites". Their resolution is based on the New Biblical Covenant – "Love thy neighbour as thyself".

18. Despite their appearance in the diagram, each Sephirah is a sphere, or "world" of its own – and contains its own cycles. Wheels within Wheels.

19. There is another Sephirah called Daath which exists in another dimension, albeit related to the Middle Pillar of Balance and Equilibrium.

20. Each Sephirah contains all 4 cards of the same number in each of the 4 suits of the Tarot Minor Arcana. So each of The 4 Elements is represented in each Sephirah - they each therefore exist at 4 different levels, so we could consider 40 Sephiroth. There is a detailed table in the chapter [THE TAROT].

21. In Kabbalist terms The 4 Elements relate to 4 "Kingdoms" each containing its own Tree - in descending order of vibration – Atziluth (Spirit. Fire), Briah (Mind. Air), Yetzirah (Astral. Water), Assiah (Material World. Earth).

22. With the association of a Planet to each Sephirah, we see that Astrology gives a much more sophisticated (albeit complicated) set of relationships - when a Sign can be in any one of 3 modes (Cardinal, Fixed, Mutable), of a single Element to make 12 forms of energy, and therefore 12 Kingdoms for each Sephirah.

23. In The Book of Revelation the Tree of Life is explicitly described as having 12 phases.

24. The transfer of energy from Sephirah 1 to Sephirah 10 is evolution from Conception to physical form (Magick). That is, from Simple to Complex (Darwin's Diversification). Movement from 10 to 1 is evolution from Complex to Simple (Mysticism). Some Kabbalists seem more interested in the former – thus attempting to put spiritual methods to material use – and therefore incurring the karma of Adam.

25. The Tree is associated with Jacob's Ladder of the Bible, which joins heaven and earth.

26. Energy is transferred from the top of the tree to the bottom in number order of the Sephiroth. Kabbalism calls this "The Lightning Flash" as it zigzags downwards.

27. Sephirah 1 (Kether. The Crown) is no-thing. Number Zero. The Abstract world of basic Archetypes. Here, among other no-things is found the set of 4 Aces of the Tarot Minor Arcana which are the archetypal Principles of [THE 4 ELEMENTS]. This is probably the closest we can get to a concept of God in our material life. Beyond is The Ain which is the unmanifest source of The Big Bang. Absolutely Nothing.

28. Sephirah 1 (Kether. Crown. Number Zero) is the source of everything manifest.

29. Sephirah 2 (Chockmah. Force) and Sephirah 3 (Binah. Form) are the highest Supernals that are able to be contemplated by the human mind. They represent God (Love) and The Devil (Form). In Kether, from which they emanate at the top of The Tree, there is no conflict.

30. We have the concept of Anti-Matter and Matter.

31. As we descend The Tree it is divided into triplicities, or triangles, each consisting of 3 Sephiroth. In Astrology there are 2 types of triplicity which give a better explanation of their relationship. The Zodiac Signs consist of a triplicity of each of The 4 Elements – Cardinal, Fixed, and Mutable. The Houses consist of Angular, Succedent, and Cadent. There are various ways of understanding the activity of a Triplicity (Number 3) – such as "Father – Mother – Child", however, apart from The Kabbalah, our knowledge of Creation [GENESIS AND THE CYCLE OF GROWTH] shows that the principle is that there is an original Initiating Force which creates ("something") . In order to

THE KABBALAH TREE OF LIFE

maintain the original universal balance of Zero, the Complement (of "something") - which some call an "Opposite" – automatically comes into existence. It is the relationship (space. attraction) between them that creates the Number 3 "child".

32. So the original 1 adds 1 which manifests as 2. The actual energy dynamics are 0 = 0 + (+1) + (-1) which maintains the Zero balance. The tendency is for the opposite polarities to attract and attempt to annihilate one another to regain the original state of perfection. As they are now separate manifestations in a different dimension (of the Space-Time Continuum) to the original this is not possible (we observe this at Earth level where one person cannot "absorb" another to become one). There is, however, a strong bond of relationship between them. That "magnetic" bond of relationship is a real force which creates its own universal imbalance, and therefore creates an additional 1 to make another odd number (Number 3) – which in turn requires balance – and so on.

33. We note that The Tree contains a "triplicity of triplicities" which itself follows the same principle. Each triplicity or Triangle has a Sephirah on each of the 3 Pillars. The Sephirah on the Middle Pillar harmonises and balances the other 2.

34. Sephiroth 1 to 3 are called the Supernals, and form the Celestial or Supernal Triangle. The initiating Triplicity. Other Kabbalah systems call it the "Celestial Triad" or "The Plane of Emanation". The realm of abstract Non-Form. We see the basic separation of The Crown into 2 complementary principles – first, of expansive Force - which then gives rise to contractive Form. We note that Sephirah 1 (The Crown) already contains the Principle of all 3 Sephiroth as described by the term "Father, Son, and Holy Spirit". Grey becomes Black and White.

35. There is a division between The Supernals and the lower Sephiroth called "The Abyss" which separates the Supernals from the other 7 Sephiroth. The un-numbered Sephirah, Daath, is the bridge across The Abyss on the Middle Pillar. Daath is said to be the original position of Sephiroth 10 (Kingdom) before The Fall of Adam. Its relationship with Uranus also suggests Jungian Individuation.

36. Daath is not in the same dimension as the rest of the Tree of Life, so it avoids The Abyss.

37. It is suggested that Wisdom, Understanding, and Daath also form a triplicity, although they have no visible connection. Some say this is "Learning by Experience" and Will. It seems that this activity brings the Daath bridge across The Abyss into manifestation.

38. The next triplicity/triangle is formed by Sephiroth 4, 5, and 6 which is called "The Moral Triad", or "The Plane of Creation". Here we are at the level of ideas and imagination. It is probably this level that Edgar Cayce refers to as "Mind is The Builder". This level is more social than personal. We could refer to it as "Collective Consciousness".

39. Sephiroth 7, 8, and 9 together form the "Mundane Triad" or "Plane of Formation". Which, again, refer to gradually reducing levels of energy frequency. We note that they relate to Mercury, Venus and Moon. Their orbits being between that of Sun and Earth – in Astrology they are termed "Personal Planets".

40. Sephirah 10 (Kingdom) is the realm of the concrete Material World. The final physical manifestations of the conception at Number 1 (albeit not exactly in accordance with the original "Ideal" – in common with the realisation of most concepts). It is Planet Earth and the physical human body. This emphasises the error of the commonly held belief in Numerology that number 10 is at a higher spiritual level than Number 1, which confuses material power and status with spiritual development – especially as the spiritual aim stated by Jesus is to " .. become as a child", which is the stage of the New Born, number 1.

41. Associating Number Zero with Sephiroth 1, we can now relate Sephirah 10 to Number 9, which is the Numerological limit of single numbers. Numerology reduces all numbers to the range 1 to 9 [NUMEROLOGY].

42. The Tree of Life has 7 levels which relate to the 7 Chakras – energy centres of the human body which form the surrounding electro-magnetic aura. (Ref. [DFMQ] Dion Fortune "The Mystical Qabalah" who refers to Aleister Crowley)

43. There are a total of 22 paths between the Sephiroth which relate to each of the 22 cards of the Tarot Major Arcana and the 22 letters of the Hebrew alphabet (which are also numbers).

THE KABBALAH TREE OF LIFE

44. The Sephiroth are Objective (insofar as they can be). The Paths are Subjective. The Sephiroth can be considered as paths in themselves, making 32 paths altogether. There seems some doubt with Daath, which is omitted from this scenario.

45. The Paths also exist in each the 4 Kingdoms (Elements), so there could be a similar multiplication as described above.

46. With the Middle Pillar all human dilemmas are resolved. Dilemmas arise as a result of increased consciousness. Increased consciousness arises from resolving dilemmas. (rising above them to another level, where both "opposites" become visible as manifestations of the same Principle). (ref. Jung's "resolution of the opposites"). It is a natural process. The only sin is ignore-ance.

47. Dilemmas resolve the seeming initial division, or seeming differences at one level, into a creative Whole at a higher level of understanding. The final solution is at the Supernals of The Tree of Life – thus arriving back at Zero. (At this level, among other things, we reconcile the seeming conflict between Good and Evil, God and The Devil (Sephirah 1 and 2) - everything on The Pillars of Severity and Mercy has its purpose.

48. On their own, Sephiroth 9 (Foundation. Moon) and 10 (Kingdom. Earth) also on The Middle Pillar have no conflict. Everything is in balance – albeit with no Free Will.

49. Sephirah 6 (Tiphareth. Beauty. The Sun. Consciousness) at the centre of The Middle Pillar, is one of the goals of human achievement. It has a path to every other Sephiroth except 10. Kingdom (Earth) where its energy is adapted by 9. Foundation (The Moon. The Personal Unconscious). Tiphareth has been likened to a spider in the centre of its web waiting to sense the vibrations of activity. Edgar Cayce says that the Heart Chakra (counted as the 4th.) is the top level of control of The 4 Elements, related to Air and Mind. Kabbalists state that this is normally the highest level reached on The Middle Pillar.

50. Like Daath, Tiphareth (Ego Consciousness) is only in embryo form at the first "Lightning Flash" of human incarnation.

51. Tiphareth is the highest level we can achieve on the Middle Pillar without building the Daath bridge across The Abyss (which is on another Dimension). It relates to the Sun of our Solar System and as depicted in a Birth Chart. As a symbol of Consciousness, it is not fully formed until later in the life of a human in the same way that it did not exist at the Creation of the universe. [PSYCHOLOGY : DEVELOPMENT MODELS].

52. On the downward journey of The Lightning Flash Sephirah 6 (Tiphareth. Beauty. The Sun. Number 5) is not fully formed. In The Cycle of Growth it begins development at Stage 5 (Power. Creativity) – which is the beginning of the 3rd. Octave when Ego Consciousness is achieved as a precursor to Individuality away from parental control.

53. In the Tarot Minor Arcana the 6s are at the balance point between 1s and 10s. Being on the Middle Pillar the 4 Elements can combine harmoniously with one another - having the additional benefit of Will, Purpose, and direct, uncontaminated, Higher Knowledge of Sephirah 1 (via Daath).

54. We note that the Tarot Minor Arcana should really be numbered Zero to 9.

55. From the position of Tiphareth one has everything Spiritual and Material in balance, albeit at a relatively low level. In that position, among other things, in Jungian terms, the "Opposites" have been reconciled. This is not quite (but almost) the same as the "beauty" of Venus (Desire) which occurs at a lower level as indicated. At this level The 4 Elements are co-operating under Mind and Will.

56. Tiphareth with its relationship to Number 5 is symbolised by the "opposable thumb" opposition of 1 to 4 others. (The 4 Elements). Mind over Matter.

57. The association of Sephiroth 6 with The Sun (Planet) is firstly indicated by its symbol of a point at the centre of a circle which is the same as the abstract depiction of Number 1 [NUMEROLOGY]. It is therefore Sephirah 2 (Chockmah, Wisdom, Force) at a lower level. Secondly, the physical activity of The Sun today in gradually converting Hydrogen to heavier elements is identical with the faster method which occurred at the time of The Big Bang . We have an example of a lower manifestation of a higher Ideal.

58. The other Sephiroth on The Middle Pillar (Moon and Earth) are also lower manifestations of the principles contained in Sephirah 1 (The Crown. Number Zero) - as are the other Sephiroth, but less directly.
59. The diagram shows different levels in order to be perceived by the Finite Mind. In fact there is no separation in time and space. It is a question of attunement. Consider the invisible information that is actually present in the space where you sit now – from such things as television, radio, mobile telephone signals, the 5 senses – each requires a different attunement to register in consciousness. The ancients understood the principles if not the methods.
60. We note that at our level of consciousness we can only perceive, or attune to, a single incoming "signal" at any one time.
61. Each Sephiroth has its own vibration frequency. For example, Visible Light in Sephirah 10 (Malkuth. Kingdom. Earth) has an infinity of possible colours but is only a small part of the electro-magnetic spectrum – which includes such things as invisible x-rays and ultra violet. The difference is frequency of vibration cycle perceptible to the physical eyes. The other senses attune to other frequencies.
62. The more Material Sephiroth 9 (Moon) and 10 (Earth) are in balance on The Middle Pillar according to the laws of Physics – and The Cycle of Growth. The positive and negative energies of their cycles balance to the original Zero. They avoid return to No-Thing by "taking turns" though the dimension of Space and Time.

THE TREE OF LIFE AND NUMBERS

This is considered in greater detail in the chapter [NUMEROLOGY].

It is a strange fact that Kabbalism does not normally include Numerology in connection with The Tree of Life, despite the Sephiroth and Paths being numbered. Working on the assumption that there must be a connection, I did not discover it until after I had written the chapter [NUMEROLOGY] and discovered the importance of Number Zero which did not exist in earlier times. The simple answer is that BOTH NUMEROLOGY AND THE KABBALAH BEGIN WITH NUMBER ZERO. In effect, the Sephiroth are mis-numbered. Despite this, it is not necessary to change that system – it is enough to simply register Numbers as another set of associations.

This is in keeping with the Spirit of this book where modern discoveries have led to new knowledge.

The accuracy of The Kabbalah and its Planet associations brings into question the accuracy of Numerology and its Planet associations. However, once again, this does no violence to Numerology – it merely clarifies and corrects the way the basic archetypal Spiritual Motivations are interpreted. It is possible to get the right answer for the wrong basic reason, especially as the higher (lower numbered) Sephiroth contain everything lower down The Tree. **This is an addition to the usual concept that higher numbers contain the lower ones. The lower numbers also contain the higher. Number Zero contains everything else.** We can understand this in a more material sense by considering the now accepted fact that all Chemical Elements evolve from basic Hydrogen with its single Proton and orbiting Electron, and the other elements are bound, or formed, by the same Laws of Physics that make it so.

THE TREE OF LIFE AND THE PLANETS

We remind ourselves that the Planets will behave differently depending on which of the 4 Kingdoms (4 Elements) of each Sephirah we are considering at the time.

We add new information to the traditional Tree of Life by including the newly discovered planets Uranus, Neptune, and Pluto. In ascribing them to Daath, Kether, and Chockmah I was able to fill "vacant spaces" which had no traditional associations.

To me as an Astrologer, the Tree of Life offers the only true set of associations with the Planets (and, therefore, Chakras, Evolution, etc.) in that, apart from their symbolic relationships with Sephiroth, they are arranged in according to their positions in the Solar System. If we take The Sun as centre and move toward the top of The Tree, the orbits of Mars and Jupiter are outside that of The Earth, followed by Saturn and the 3 Transcendent Planets. Likewise in the downward direction we have Moon, Mercury and Venus (the Personal Planets) between The Sun an Earth. This adds additional Astrological connotations to The Moon, which we know is sometimes between Sun and Earth, and sometimes not.

Having made new associations, it is well to justify my choices :-

THE KABBALAH TREE OF LIFE

1. **NEPTUNE**: It is immediately apparent that the glyph, or symbol, of Neptune is appropriate at the top because IT IS A SIMPLIFIED DEPICTION OF THE TREE OF LIFE (as shown below). We have The 3 Pillars meeting at Yesod (Foundation. Moon) with The Cross of Matter (Malkuth. Earth) at the bottom.
2. **URANUS**: Is clearly associated with the Sephirah Daath and The Abyss, which was previously without a number. There is a more detailed explanation below, but here it is worth mentioning its association with the Throat Chakra and Will because numerous authorities agree with it, including Edgar Cayce.
3. **PLUTO**: Concerning my association of Pluto with Sephirah 2 (Chockmah. Force. Wisdom. The Father), despite its non-appearance in Kabbalism ; this is confirmed by Dion Fortune's statement - included under Sephirah 8 (Hod. Mercury. Number 7) in her book - which describes the action of Pluto and its relationship with Nuclear Fission and $E = MC^2$ (Geburah is Sephirah 5 (Severity. Mars. Number 4)) :-

Chockmah, on the other hand, is the dynamic principle; it reflects into Geburah, which is the Cosmic Katabolist, representing the breaking - down of the complex into the simple, thus releasing latent energy; and this reflects a domain into Netzach, the life force of Nature. [DFCD]

4. In Astrology, Pluto is positioned as co-ruler of the fixed Water Sign Scorpio and Cycle of Growth Stage 8 (Death. Intercourse) before, rather than included in, the Transcendent Octave (relating to the Middle Pillar of The Tree). It is in a similar position in The Tree of Life, supplying motive power to the whole Tree and controlling a Pillar of its own.
5. With our Kabbalah association we can see that Pluto is archetypally associated with the Mutable/Changeable Fire Sign of Sagittarius and Cycle of Growth Stage 9 (Conception. New Life. Nuclear Reaction). We can see that Stage 8 Intercourse can lead to Conception.

THE TREE OF LIFE AND THE TAROT

This is dealt with in more detail below with a table of correspondences between the Minor Arcana and the Sephiroth at the end.

THE TAROT MINOR ARCANA

Please refer to the chapter [THE TAROT] for more details.

Kabbalism has always had an intimate association with The Tarot. The 10 Sephiroth each relate to cards 1 to 10 of the Tarot Minor Arcana in the 4 suits Wands (Fire), Swords (Air), Cups (Water), Pentacles or Coins (Earth).

In addition there is a "cycle" via the Sephiroth in numerical order Sephirah 1 (Kether. Crown) or Ace) to Sephirah 10 (Kingdom) which has a more direct contact with the top of The Tree. A.E. Waite stated that once Tarot Cards have progressed from Aces to 10s we arrive again at the Aces at the top of The Tree. In relating the 3 triplicities/triangles to The Tarot he said that, after the Aces as principles of The 4 Elements, Card/Sephirah numbered 2,3, and 4 refer to Cardinal Signs, 5, 6, and 7 refer to Fixed Signs, and 8, 9, and 10, to Mutable Signs.

There is emphasis on the importance of the 6s of the Tarot as being at the centre of The Middle Pillar where there is direct influence from Sephirah 1 (Kether. Crown).

THE TREE OF LIFE AND THE CHAKRAS

I also include the Kabbalist associations of Planets with [THE CHAKRAS] . As an Astrologer the Kabbalist arrangement and associations make more sense to me than other authorities which simplistically attempt to allocate a single planet to each Chakra. The Planet associations with Chakras add another dimension to the study.

THE CHAKRAS AND ENDOCRINE GLANDS

The endocrine gland system of the human body is the physical manifestation of The Chakra energies.

We can see that relationship between the Kabbalist Tree of Life and The Tree of Life of Genesis and Revelation is not a simple one. However, when we consider that the Endocrine System of the human body is a complicated inter-relationship which is not fully understood in medicine today we must expect it. This makes sense in that some endocrine glands produce different hormones that have opposite effects on the human body. For example Adrenaline and Noradrenaline which give the "flight or fight" effect, and the complex method used to produce ovulation in women just once each month (the mechanism is blocked by other hormones for the rest of the month).

THE KABBALAH TREE OF LIFE

1. The first principle is that The Chakras are rooted in the human spinal column, which is The Middle Pillar of The Tree of Life.
2. Each of the 10 Sephiroth receives its energy from the ones above. Those on the Centre Pillar act as balancers and co-ordinators. In particular you will note that there are 3 triplicities of Sephiroth coloured White, Blue, and Yellow in the diagram.
3. The Chakras are counted in reverse order to the Sephiroth.

7.THE CROWN CHAKRA – 1. THE CROWN SEPHIRAH

THE PITUITARY GLAND - NEPTUNE

This is the chakra at the highest level of vibration ("The Thousand Petal Lotus") and its association with the Pituitary Gland which controls all others (subject to the Hypothalamus). Its relationship with Neptune's meaning is clear. We have noted the similarity of structures of The Tree of Life and the glyph of Neptune.

6.THE THIRD EYE - SEPHIROTH 2 (CHOCKMAH. FORCE) AND 3 (BINAH. FORM)

THE PINEAL GLAND – PLUTO AND SATURN

Here is balanced Force and Form. At this level we can consider it in terms of Visualisation, or "Image-ination" at the level of Higher Mind. Every Thing begins with an Idea concept, and a mental picture.

5.THE THROAT CHAKRA - SEPHIROTH 4 (CHESED) AND 5 (GEBURAH)

THE THYROID GLAND – JUPITER AND MARS

The Thyroid is basically concerned with the growth processes of the body, which relates to the principle of Jupiter (Expansion. Society) on The Pillar of Force. It is balanced by Mars (God of War. The Individual) on The Pillar of Form. They carry the message that Expansion and Growth must be restricted in order to function. We can see historical examples in History from the great Empires which arose from martial conquest, and fell because the populations became too big to control.

DAATH - THROAT CHAKRAS – URANUS

There is more detail below. However, we can summarise :
1. Daath is on The Middle Pillar of Equilibrium.
2. Most authorities, including Edgar Cayce, relate Uranus to the Throat Centre.
3. Uranus relates to Jungian Individuation.
4. Most authorities relate the Throat Centre to Will.
5. Development of The Third Eye, together with Will, are goals of spiritual development.
6. Daath does not exist in the first downward "Lightning Flash".

4.THE HEART CHAKRA – SEPHIRAH 6 (TIPHARETH)

To avoid extreme complications, we merely observe the numerous path connections of Sephirah 6 in the diagram. It is the point of balance of the whole Tree Of Life. We note that, similar to Daath, it is only partially developed at the time of birth. It only really begins to develop at Cycle of Growth Stage 5 (Power. Creativity. The Sun. Ego Consciousness. School Age) when we begin to explore the world free of parental restrictions.

THE THYMUS GLAND – THE SUN (CONSCIOUSNESS)

There is no scientific clarity concerning the function of the Thymus Gland, although there is a suspected connection with the Immune System. The gland is at its maximum size at the time of birth, after which there is little further development. It tends to reduce in size later on, and atrophy in old age. Perhaps this is an indicator of a decline in our spiritual consciousness.

We see association with The Sun as centre of our Solar System and the heart as the centre of the body and its blood circulation system.

THE KABBALAH TREE OF LIFE

3. THE SOLAR PLEXUS – SEPHIROTH 7 (NETZACH) AND 8 (HOD)

THE ADRENALS – VENUS (DESIRE. EMOTION) AND MERCURY (RATIONAL MIND)

Although the Adrenal Glands are connected to the kidneys, we are now at the area of our body that contains several major organs such as Gall Bladder, Pancreas, Stomach, Spleen and Liver.

Once again, The Tree of Life requires the need to balance complementary forces. We are at the level of the inner Personal Planets Venus and Mercury which are basically concerned with Right Brain Feeling and Emotions (Venus. Art) and Left Brain Thinking, Logic and Ideas (Mercury. Science).

We note that "Solar" Plexus suggests the overall control of The Sun (Consciousness. Heart Chakra), which is the balancing influence of Tiphareth above on The Tree.

We see how imbalance (dis-ease. illness) occurs from stress between conflicting emotions and the rational mind.

2. THE NAVEL – SEPHIRAH 9 (FOUNDATION)

CELLS OF LEYDIG - THE MOON

We have to be impressed by the fact that Edgar Cayce "knew" about The Cells of Leydig and their function considering that, even today, they are not a subject of common knowledge. He is the only person to associate them with a Chakra.

I have used Edgar Cayce's association with The Cells of Leydig who describes it as "The Seat of the Soul" and relates it to human reproduction. It is mainly concerned with production of the male sex hormone Testosterone (which is present in both sexes). Its association here with The Moon – in turn associated with the Soul, and Personal Unconscious - is clear from the study of Astrology. As a result of this comparison it seems we must regard The Moon as more than the passive, negative, reactive planet of Astrology.

In a Birth Chart, the position of The Moon indicates what has been developed in past lives, and has associations with other inherited traits.

Kabbalists also describe the energy of the Sephirah in more powerful terms, especially due to its position on the Pillar of Equilibrium. It is related to the Titan god Atlas who bears the celestial sphere of the heavens on his shoulders. We are therefore reminded that a property of the planet Moon is to stabilise the Earth orbit and stop it wobbling on its axis. Without it our annual seasons would be even more unpredictable – as would be the sea tides and menstruation cycle in women. The regularisation of the "wobble" gives rise to [THE ZODIAC AGES].

Dion Fortune [DFMQ] also describes Sephirah 9 as "the reproductive centre".

1. THE ROOT CHAKRA – GONADS – THE EARTH

Most authorities relate this Chakra to the Gonads – the male and female sex organs. In the Kabbalah, and Eastern philosophy, it is also related to the anus and process of elimination of body waste, as well as the process of Decomposition that breaks down materials into simpler elements that can be re-used for growth. The Root Chakra is referred to as "The 4 Petal Lotus" (rate of vibration) which relates to The 4 Elements in material form- such as the physical Elements of Chemistry and Physics – and those that make up the human body.

Again we have connection with masculine Testosterone, as well as the female sex hormone Oestrogen (which are both present in both sexes).

There is association between the activity of Neptune and Sephirah 1 (which is the original source and therefore contains everything), and the association of Sephirah 10 and the concept of Elimination and Decomposition. The action of Neptune is often likened to the activity of Aqua Regia ("Royal Water"), which is a mixture of acids able to dissolve even gold. Its relationship with the annual time of The Cycle of Growth Stage 12 (Withdrawal), Pisces in the Natural Year, and life in general, concerns the breakdown and return of used growth material to the soil in preparation for a new cycle. Fertiliser. In some ways the spiritual activity of Neptune (Dissolution) seems antagonistic to material life. We have the further relationship of Neptune/Pisces with The Collective Unconscious which tends to challenge human Individuality – rather than the Personal Unconscious of Sephirah 9 (Foundation. The Moon).

The Moon also has relationship to the human brain – especially as a source of Memory – conscious and unconscious.

THE KABBALAH TREE OF LIFE

THE PLANETS AND SEPHIROTH

THE MOST IMPORTANT THING TO NOTE IS THAT THE GLYPH, OR SYMBOL, OF NEPTUNE HAS THE SAME BASIC STRUCTURE AS THE THREE PILLARS OF THE TREE OF LIFE, WITH THE CROSS OF MATTER (EARTH) AT THE BASE. BEING RELATED TO SEPHIRAH 1. KETHER, THE CROWN, WE CAN SEE THIS AS THE SIMPLE, ORIGINAL, PRINCIPLE OF EVOLUTION AS AN IMAGE IN THE MIND OF GOD – BEFORE THINGS BECAME MORE COMPLICATED.

The whole process describes a situation we are all familiar with. We get a bright idea, but the realisation of the physical goal takes a lot more effort.

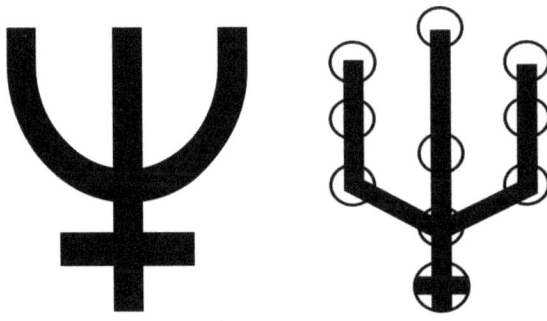

We view the planet positions from the Sephiroth 10. Kingdom – Earth. We note that the planetary associations on (my version of) The Tree include Uranus, Neptune, and Pluto which have been recently discovered and could not have appeared in the original Kabbalah - which has been developing for thousands of years. However, conveniently, there were Sephiroth with no associations which I have filled. Here are some brief correspondences in the working of The Tree that arise from this arrangement :-

1. The model includes all the planets of our solar system – Earth too.
2. The Sun is at Sephirah 6 (Tiphareth. Beauty) the centre of The Tree supplying it energy via multiple paths to the other Sephirah. This is in conformity to its position in our solar system.
3. We have the normally paired Inner Personal Planets Venus, Feelings (Sephirah 7) and Mercury, Mind (Sephirah 8) - at the same level – both orbiting The Sun between it and Earth.
4. The Moon (Sephirah 9) is lower down, between Sun (Sephirah 6) and Earth (Sephirah 10) in its normal position. The path of XIV.Temperance (Cycle of Growth Stage 9 (Conception)) on The Tree indicating that the effects of every cycle of the Moon – especially related to the female menstrual cycle - (and other planets) balance out to zero.
5. Paired Mars (Sephirah 5) and Jupiter (Sephirah 4) are both at the next higher level, both orbits being between that of Earth and Saturn. They basically apply to personal and social activities. The path between them is the Tarot Card VIII. Strength which suggests, among other things, social control (Jupiter) of Personal Projection (Mars) exemplified by Cycle of Growth Stage 5 (School Age. The Sun) to which the Tarot Card refers.
6. The Sun (Sephirah 6) on The Middle Pillar balances Jupiter and Mars.
7. The association of Pluto (Regeneration) the planet furthest from the Sun to Sephiroth 2, Wisdom (The Father) and Creative Force at the top of the pillar of Force, makes sense in its association with meditation, healing, and regeneration of body cells – and the development of the Atomic bomb. We note the use of radiation on cancer cells.
8. The Sephirah 2, Wisdom, relationship with Pluto is also explained by the Tarot path of 0. The Fool who is motivated solely by (animal) instinct or Intuition with no other "contamination" by Feeling, Thought, or practical consideration.
9. The Sephirah 3 (Understanding. The Great Mother. Form), relationship with Saturn is explained by the Tarot Path of I. The Magician who is more concerned with achieving physical manifestation of his ideas. The connection between Sephirah 3 (Saturn/Satan) and Sephirah 1 (The Crown) is explained by his role

THE KABBALAH TREE OF LIFE

as "The Fallen Angel" intent on Earthy, material, activity. Using spiritual powers for material purposes. This demonstrates his purpose and necessity. Satan is God's (Jungian) Shadow.

10. We see from The Tree that the normal human concept of God (Sephirah 2) and The Devil (Sephirah 3) as opposing, rather than complementary, forces is incorrect. The Dilemmas they bring force the necessity of Choice, and therefore develop consciousness.

11. The path connecting Wisdom and Under-standing (III. The Empress) reminds us that we are here dealing with archetypes at (above a) psychological level. She is active in Cycle of Growth Stage 2 (Germination) where the infant is forming inner images in the mind to match those in the outer world (later on we manipulate those images in our thinking/imagination processes).

12. At another level, the activities of planets Pluto and Saturn oppose one another on opposite Pillars. The "irresistible force" meets "the immovable object". Pluto is solely concerned with releasing creative energy in any way it can. Saturn is concerned with conserving and controlling energy by imprisoning it in various Forms – such as Ideas and Matter. So we have manifestations in terms of nuclear reactors and mob violence. Together, the 2 planets make the equation $E = MC^2$ which has connotations with Critical Mass. Energy and Matter are the same.

13. We see that the planets Neptune, Pluto, and Saturn are related to the "Three Supernals" of The Kabbalah and the Crown Chakra.

DAATH, URANUS, AND THE MIDDLE PILLAR

Several Kabbalist authorities relate Daath to the Throat Chakra, and some authorities – including Edgar Cayce – relate Uranus to The Throat Chakra and Will. So we summarise :-

1. Daath is high on The Middle Pillar between Tiphareth(Beauty) and Kether (Crown).
2. Daath exists in an entirely different dimension to the rest of The Tree of Life.
3. Daath begins to take form as the result of an effort of Will.
4. Before Daath can form, Consciousness, Ego, and Lower Will must develop in Sephirah 6 (Tiphareth, Beauty).
5. There are associations of Daath with the Throat Chakra and with Will.
6. Yet Daath is Silence.
7. There is clearly a relationship between Uranus and the Jungian Individuation process, which involves the building of an "Ego-Self Axis" (The Middle Pillar).
8. The Transactional Analysis psychological model involves development of "The Adult" [PSYCHOLOGY : DEVELOPMENT MODELS] – each of which is a kind of mediator, or channel of communication. This concept relates more to Sephirah 6 (Tiphareth. Consciousness) and The Sun.
9. In Psychology, neither the Ego-Self Axis (Jung) or The Adult [TA] exist at birth. They are developed during a lifetime. They both connect Lower Intelligence with Higher Intelligence. However, the potential must exist in "embryo" form for later development. This is not incompatible with the concept of the coming of a "new Messiah", the pattern of which is exemplified by the birth and life of Jesus and described by the Transcendent Octave of The Cycle of Growth. An INNER – not outer – process.
10. In Astrology, the Transcendent Octave indicates the need to activate Uranus (Individuality) to replace the traditional, repetitive, habit patterns of Saturn. This, in turn, has compatibility with Edgar Cayce's often repeated concept that "Mind is The Builder". Until Uranus becomes active, Neptune will tend to have a negative influence, being required to act unconsciously.

The mind uses its spiritual ideals to build upon. And the mind also uses the material desires as the destructive channels, or it is the interference by the material desires that prevents a body and a mind from keeping in perfect accord with its ideal. [EC Reading 357-13]

11. "The Ideal" is Sephirah 1 (The Crown. Neptune)
12. Daath is on the Middle Pillar of Balance and Equilibrium as a POTENTIAL bridge across The Abyss between Sephiroth 6. Beauty and Sephiroth 1. The Crown.
13. We see that Daath is on the path of II.The Priestess between Tiphareth and Kether. The Crown. In keeping with the characteristics of Daath, she is, basically, the "blank sheet" of the "brain" waiting to be activated with images. The brain has a capacity for use far beyond our present capability. The Personal

THE KABBALAH TREE OF LIFE

Unconscious and unconscious brain is symbolised by The Moon (planet) which is at the foot of the Tarot Card image, and The Tree of Life – still on the Middle Pillar, but where it has less freedom.

14. The Tarot Priestess sits balanced between 2 pillars. Behind her is an area hidden by a veil. The Moon (Sephirah 9. Yesod, Foundation) is at her feet.
15. The Priestess is as a Nun – married to God, not man – yet willing to have intercourse with any man whilst maintaining her own identity.
16. The Middle Pillar is the return journey from Malkuth (Kingdom. Earth) to Kether. Crown. Heaven) via XXI.The World, XIV.Temperance, and II.The Priestess. This is in keeping with the Biblical concept of "becoming as a child". Reading this, or any other occult book, is rather contrary to that principle.
17. Between Tiphareth (Beauty. Sun. Number 5) and Malkuth (Kingdom. Earth. Number 9) is Yesod (Foundation. Number 8) ruled by The Moon – symbol of The Soul, and The Personal Unconscious. Here we are in agreement with Edgar Cayce who calls the Sacral/Navel Chakra "The Seat of The Soul".
18. Attempts to reach The Crown via the other Pillars fail because when a Sephirah on one pillar is activated, its complement on the other pillar is automatically activated too – creating imbalance and doubt. This is an aspect of The Tower of Babel which attempts to reach Heaven using material methods.
19. Daath comes into activity when the other Sephiroth are silent. The Priestess is then not confused by the noise. This idea is compatible with the use of imagery in meditation – which is the same as Jung's "Active Imagination" – although even that may be a distraction.
20. This describes "The Middle Path" of the ancients.

THE TREE OF LIFE AND THE CYCLE OF GROWTH

With the addition of the newly discovered Transcendent Planets to the traditional 10 Sephirah Tree of Life we can now associate it with the 12 Stages of The Cycle of Growth.

Kabbalism does not explicitly treat The Tree of Life as a repetitive cyclic system. However, with the addition of the new planets of the Transcendent Octave we can see how it can be.

We have continual difficulty of equating the various occult systems with the 12 Stage Cycle of Astrology. Study of The Kabbalah shows it necessary not to be too simplistic in our approach – for example, it is stated that the whole Zodiac is contained in Sephiroth 2 (Chockmah. Wisdom. Primal Energy). The Tree of Life is referred to at the beginning and end of The Bible, so, apart from "Wheels within Wheels", we have the following Biblical verses which give us a firm basis for continued research. It is interesting to note that this is a more detailed description than that of Genesis. Perhaps we now have the end result :-

> *And he shewed me a pure river of water of life, bright as crystal, going forth out of the throne of God and of the Lamb:in the midst of its broad place, and of the river on this side and on that, [is] a tree of life, yielding twelve fruits, in each several month rendering its fruits, and the leaves of the tree [are] for the service of the nations; [Revelation 22 Verses 1-2 YLT]

The allusion to a river represents a "stream" of energy – albeit related to the Water Element.

1. Authorities of The Tarot state that when dealing with the Minor Arcana, together with its Kabbalah association, a principle is that the Aces of the 4 suits relate to the Principles of The 4 Elements. As the numbers increase we get closer to the bottom of The Tree. When we arrive at the bottom Sephirah 10 (Malkuth. Earth) we immediately "arrive at the top again". The important point here is A CYCLE IS IMPLIED – although it is not immediately evident, or detailed.
2. We first note that the addition of the new Transcendent Planets "filling in gaps" takes us closer to understanding. It is now clear that The Middle Pillar is that of a "Return Journey" – albeit at a more conscious, wilful, process than the unconscious one described by The Cycle of Growth.
3. We have the addition of Uranus (related to Aquarius and Cycle of Growth Stage 11. Individuation) and its association with the previously un-numbered Sephiroth Daath.
4. We have Neptune (related to Pisces and Cycle of Growth Stage 12) - and its now additional association with Number Zero – as both beginning and end of The Cycle.
5. Pluto is at Sephirah 2 of The Tree of Life as Cycle of Growth Stage 9 (Conception), also relates to the end of The Cycle of Growth at Stage 8 (Sex. Death) concerned, among other things, with human reproduction.

THE KABBALAH TREE OF LIFE

THE OCTAVES OF THE LOGARITHMIC TIMESCALE

We are now in a position to consider the subject in more detail.

Although the processes are here described in sequence order for simplicity, parts of the development stages can occur more or less at the same time depending on what currently occupies the focus of consciousness.

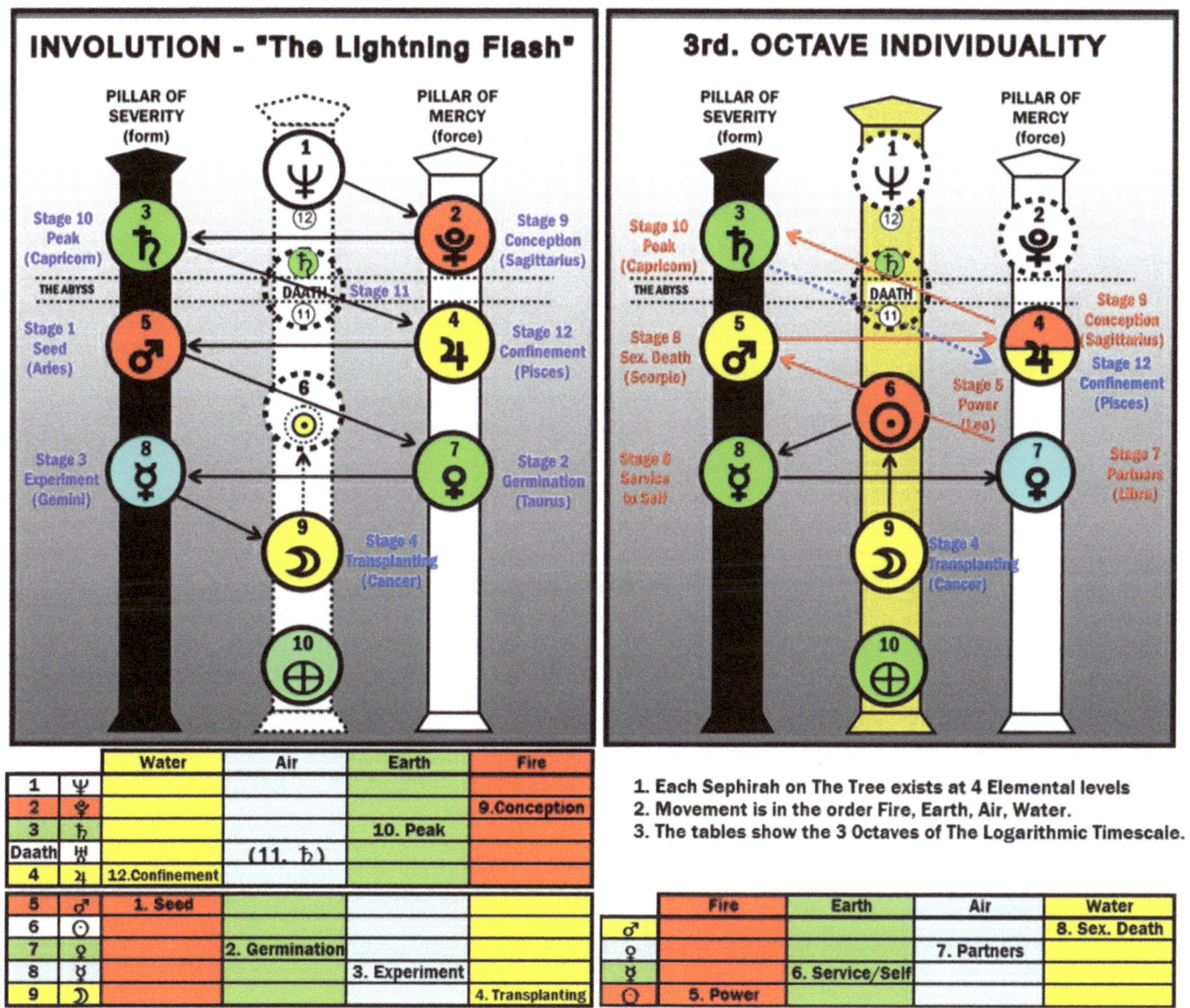

Figure 69 : Tree of Life and The Cycle of Growth 3 Octaves

THE 1ST. AND 2ND. OCTAVES – GESTATION AND CHILDHOOD

1. To begin with we take the traditional planet associations with The Kabbalah Tree of Life, and compare them with the natural planet rulers of the Zodiac Signs ruling each Stage of The Cycle of Growth.
2. The "First Conception" is of Pluto in Sagittarius at Cycle of Growth Stage 9 (Conception) which connects it to Cycle of Growth Stage 8 (Sex. Death) at the end of the previous Cycle.
3. We note that planets Jupiter, Mars, Venus, and Mercury, appear twice on The Tree and The Cycle of Growth. However, in accordance with Astrological Principles, at each Stage THEY TAKE ON DIFFERENT FUNCTIONS ACCORDING TO WHICH OF THE 4 ELEMENTS THEY ARE LOCATED.
4. IT IS IMPORTANT TO NOTE THAT WE ARE HERE MAINLY CONCERNED WITH HUMAN DEVELOPMENT AND EVOLUTION AT A PSYCHOLOGICAL LEVEL. The Tree has numerous other functions.
5. Traditional Kabbalism contains the concept of "The Lightning Flash" whereby energy is transferred down The Tree in Sephiroth number order. Daath does not yet exist on this dimension.

THE KABBALAH TREE OF LIFE

6. WE NOTE THAT SEPHIRAH 6 (Tiphareth. Beauty. The Sun. Lower Will) IS ONLY PRESENT IN EMBRYO FORM UNTIL CYCLE OF GROWTH STAGE 5 (Creativity. Power. Leo. The Sun).
7. We see an exact match with The Cycle of Growth beginning with Stage 9 (Conception) matching Sephirah 2 (Chockmah, Wisdom, Force). At the archetypal level this is the province of Pluto(Regeneration. Nuclear Reaction) where there is orgasmic energy release, followed by the sperm fertilising the egg. A "Big Bang".
8. Each Octave of The Cycle of Growth contains 4 Stages in order Fire, Earth, Air, Water.
9. The first Octave is concerned with development of a foetus in the womb (and Transcendence at a later stage of life). It ends with the completion of the "shell" of a physical human body as a "vehicle" for (or Temple of) the Soul.
10. The 2nd. Octave begins at Cycle of Growth Stage 1 (Seed) with Mars in Aries (Cardinal Fire) which is physical birth into the realm of The Family – an extended protective "shell".
11. The 2nd. Octave ends at Cycle of Growth Stage 4 (Transplanting) which is ruled by Moon in Cancer (Water). This Stage is that of resolution of The Oedipal Complex and the formation of a Persona (mask/shell). Cancer (Crab. Roots. Foundations. Shell) and The Moon are concerned with psychological "shells" and psychic self-defence.
12. Cycle of Growth Stage 4 (Transplanting. Moon) refers to Sephirah 9 (Yesod. Moon) which is the lowest point of human consciousness, and the lowest point of a Birth Chart. From now on the direction is upward through The Tree of Life.
13. We note that formation of a "shell" at this Psychological level mimics that of the combination of Sephirah 2 (Force) and Sephirah 3 (Form) at the top of the Tree of Life – such as the formation of a single atom of Hydrogen [NUMEROLOGY] Number 1 with a single Proton and Electron, and the formation of a human body "shell" for the soul (Moon) during Gestation – this is apart from the "shell" of the orbit of The Moon Planet around The Earth.
14. The Psychological Shell (Persona. Mask) is a "vehicle" to explore the social world outside The Family Shell as depicted in the Tarot card "VII. The Chariot".
15. The Middle Pillar of The Tree is only an abstract concept until energy has reached Sephiroth 10 (Malkuth, Earth, Final Foundation) at the end of the 2nd. Octave of The Cycle of Growth.
16. The Tree of Life refers to the human Chakra System rooted on the spine.
17. We note that with Cycle of Growth Stage 4 we are at the bottom of The Tree of Life and The Cycle of Growth, and the following stages take us back towards the top.

THE 3RD. OCTAVE – SCHOOL & ADULT - INDIVIDUALITY

1. The 3rd. Octave again begins with the Element Fire with Sun in Leo (Fixed Fire).
2. This is Cycle of Growth Stage 5 (Fire Element. Leo, Creativity. Power) which corresponds with the School Age of Psychology at age 7 when the child is beginning to explore the outside world with more freedom from control by its parents.
3. On The Tree of Life energy ascends to Sephirah 6 (Tiphareth. The Sun) and the Middle Pillar now becomes active for the first time. This is The Heart Chakra. Although already partially developed in "embryo" form, experiences are now focused more in this area of growth.
4. As the first time energy is being directed up the spine this can be considered a form of raising Kundalini as mentioned in [THE CHAKRAS].
5. The child is learning to drive its 2 concentric "vehicles" or "shells". Body and Mind (Earth and Moon).
6. The Sun is a complex symbol of the development of The Higher Mind, Ego, and Individual Will and Consciousness. Relating to Number 5 [NUMEROLOGY] with the "opposable thumb" (1 versus 4) it is also symbolic of Mind over Matter, or Higher Mind controlling The 4 Elements. As in our Solar system, the Sun is at the central point of The Tree of Life, which has association with The Heart Chakra [THE CHAKRAS] – also in accordance with Astrology.
7. The following stages of development occur in REVERSE ORDER to that of The Lightning Flash. By so doing they begin to turn the cycle back to the top of The Tree.

8. We note that the reversal of direction is achieved by maintaining the elemental Fire, Earth, Air, Water sequence, which enables revisiting the Sephiroth at different levels to that of the descending Lightning Flash.
9. As The Heart Centre gains control, development becomes less automatic or instinctive. The development of new Paths on The Tree - connecting Tiphareth to the others - corresponds with the concept of creating Neural Paths in the physical brain and The Tree of Life.
10. Cycle of Growth Stage 6 (Earth Element. Virgo. Self Service. Health. Adolescence. Age 13) is controlled by Mercury (Rational Mind) which was previously active at Cycle of Growth Stage 3 (Air Element, Gemini, Experiment, Communication. Early Childhood).
11. We are, therefore, once again at Sephirah 8 (Hod. Mercury) but now in the Earth Element.
12. Cycle of Growth Stage 7 (Air Element. Libra. Partners. Young Adulthood. Age 23) is controlled by Venus (Beauty. Desire) which ruled Stage 2 (Germination) in the Earth Element.
13. We are now at Sephirah 7 (Netzach. Victory) in the Air Element.
14. The next Stage of The Cycle of Growth, Stage 8 (Water Element. Scorpio. Sex. Intercourse. Death. Adult and Old Age. Age 42) is ruled by Mars (War), which ruled Stage 1 (Seed) in the Fire Element. We note that Mars controls the beginning and end of a human lifetime. At Birth, in Fire, it is instrumental in enabling earthly survival, at Death, in Water, it releases that function.
15. Cycle of Growth Stage 8 begins at Age 42, which is the time of the Mid Life Crisis and the mid-point of the 84 year cycle of Uranus.
16. We are now at Sephirah 5 (Geburah. Severity. Mars) at its Water level.
17. The next steps show the archetypal struggle between Cycle of Growth Stage 9 (Fire Element. Conception. Jupiter. Expansion) at Sephirah 4 (Chesed. Mercy), and Cycle of Growth Stage 10 (Earth Element. Saturn. Consolidation. Tradition. Habit) at Sephirah 3 (Binah) – which, with Daath inactive in Cycle of Growth Stage 11, Saturn wins.
18. Cycle of Growth Stage 10 and Sephirah 3 (Saturn. Binah. Form) is a natural block to all energy. In this case it accepts energy from Jupiter in Fire and transfers it to its Air level at Cycle of Growth Stage 11 (Discontent) . Saturn naturally rules both Stages. The next steps are easy because they follow the pre-existing order of The Lightning Flash. The energy is transferred to Sephirah 4 (Jupiter) at its Water level where it becomes Cycle of Growth Stage 12 (Withdrawal. Confinement) – and the end of the 1st. Octave as a preparation for a new Cycle.
19. Looked at in another way, Sephirah 4 (Jupiter) acts as a "short circuit" transferring energy from Cycle of Growth Stage 9 (Conception. Jupiter. Fire) to Cycle of Growth Stage 12 (Withdrawal. Jupiter. Water) – making 10 stages instead of 12.

THE TRANSCENDENT OCTAVE

Until Transcendence becomes active the Cycle of Growth effectively remains at 10 Stages instead of 12 Stages. We see that with energy rising up the Middle Pillar via Daath to Kether. A Cycle of 10 becomes a Cycle of 12. Sephirah 6 (Tiphareth. The Sun. Ego. Consciousness) has become more active with the potential to activate Daath (Uranus. Will).

THE KABBALAH TREE OF LIFE

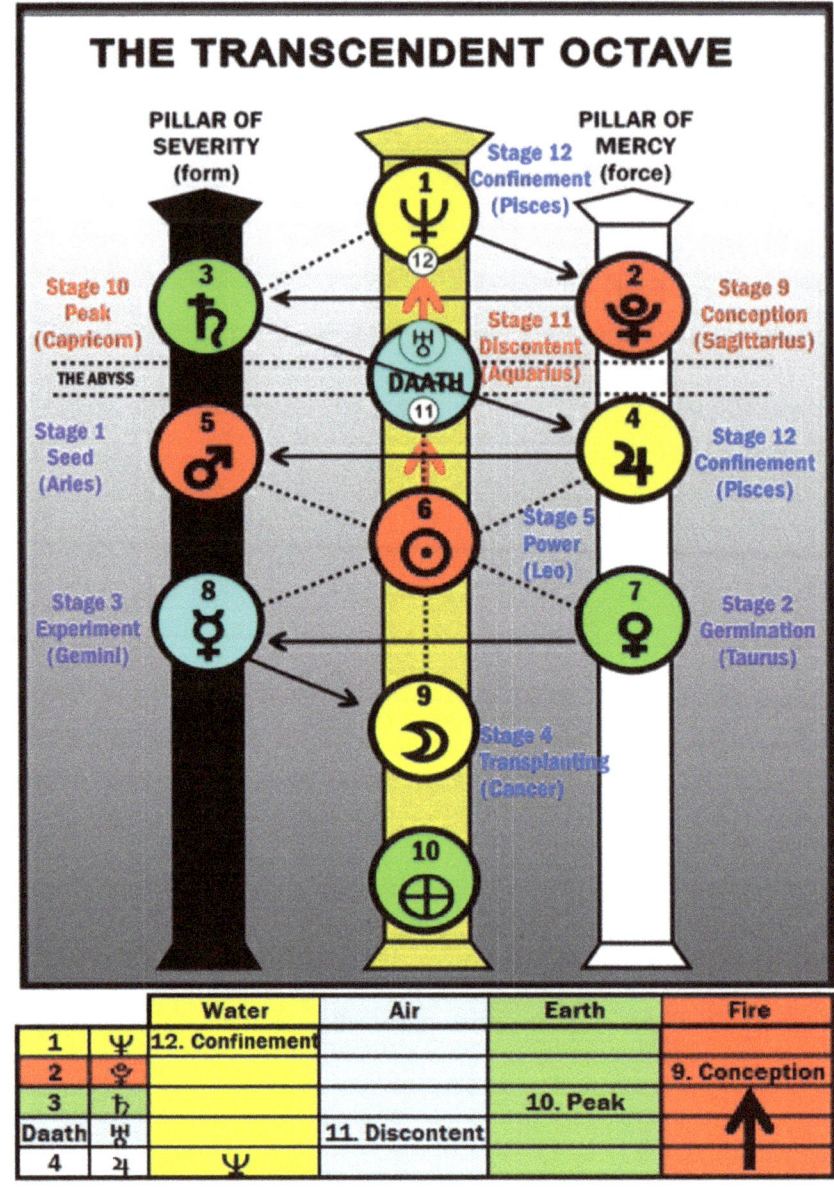

Figure 70 : Tree of Life and Transcendent Octave

1. We see that with Daath Active the natural transfer of energy from the Earth Element to Air at Cycle of Growth Stage 11 (Discontent) can be achieved in a different way. It provides an alternative channel, or release, which prevents Sephirah 3 (Binah. Saturn) controlling it.
2. Daath is the activity of Will, which Edgar Cayce states to be the sole controlling factor of life. "Everything is subject to Will " [EC].
3. Cycle of Growth Stage 12 (Withdrawal. Confinement) then occurs at the level of Sephirah 1 (Kether. Crown. Neptune) at the level of Water.
4. We have transcended the normal state.
5. Having reached that level we have a "New Creation" when energy follows the original evolutionary path of The Lightning Flash, and Sephirah 2 (Fire Element. Chockmah. Wisdom. Force. Pluto. Regeneration. Change) takes its place as Cycle of Growth Stage 9 (Conception).
6. We can now see how Sephirah 2 gets its name of Chockmah, Wisdom.
7. We note that Daath becomes active as a result of expansion of consciousness at Sephirah 6 (Tiphareth. Beauty. The Sun. Ego Consciousness) which is below it on The Middle Pillar.

8. We can see that if Pluto becomes active instead of Mars at Cycle of Growth Stage 8 in the Water Element it can transfer to the Fire Element to become Cycle of Growth Stage 9 (Conception) to begin a new Lightning Flash.

I feel it is once again important to revisit the [PSYCHOLOGY : DEVELOPMENT MODELS] diagrams. Once again we see the evolution of Daath (Uranus). Individuality and Tiphareth (Sun. Ego)

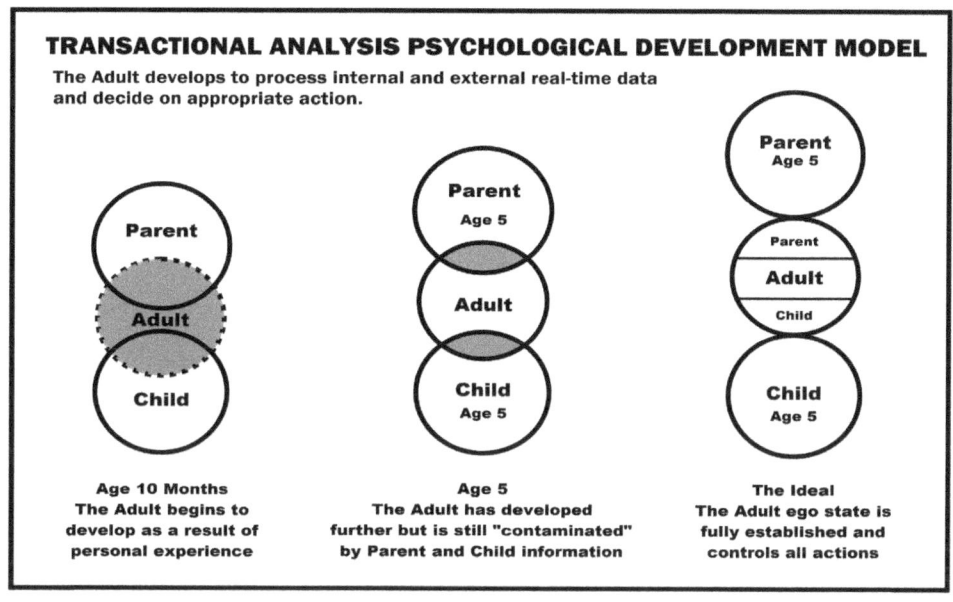

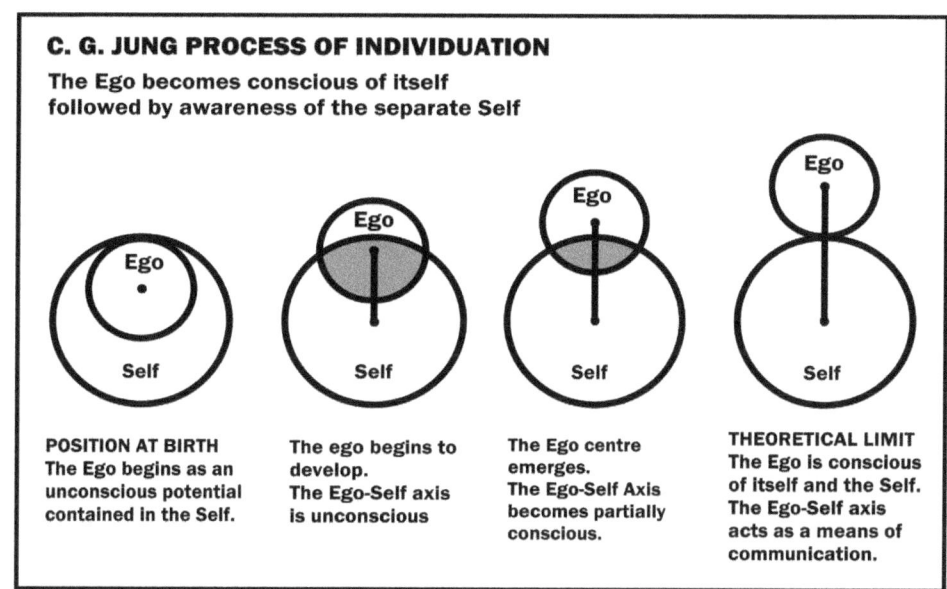

THE KABBALAH TREE OF LIFE

KABBALAH, NUMBERS, PLANETS AND TAROT

The Cycle of Growth 3+1 Octaves' processes occur in order Fire (Force), Earth (Form), Air (Mind), Water (The Collective).

The Element descriptions refer to the summary interpretations of the cards of the Tarot Minor Arcana numbered 1 to 10 [AEW et al].

Number 6 is an indication of the most positive, balanced, expression of the Element.

There is deterioration of meaning at the bottom of The Tree after Number 6 (Tiphareth. Sun) where activity finally loses connection with the Idealism and Hope of The Middle Pillar.

Number 1 Aces are the Principles or Ideals of The 4 Elements.

Numbers 2, 3 and 4 refer to the Cardinal (Initiating) phase of the element, (Creator)

Numbers 5, 6, and 7 refer to the Fixed (Organising) phase. (Preserver)

Numbers 8, 9, and 10 to the Mutable (Changeable. Adaptive. Child) phase. (Destroyer)

		Sephiroth and Tarot Minor Arcana		Numbers	Planets		Fire / Intuition / Spirit / Atziluth / Wands	Earth / Sensation / Matter / Assiah / Pentacles	Air / Thinking / Mind / Briah / Swords	Water / Feeling / Emotion / Yetzirah / Cups
THE SUPERNALS (Cosmic Consciousness)	1	Kether	Crown	0	Neptune	♆	Root of Fire	Root of Earth	Root of Air	Root of Water
	2	Chokmah	Wisdom	1	Pluto	♇	Dominion	Harmonious Change	Peace Restored	Love
	3	Binah	Under-standing	2	Saturn	♄	Established Strength	Material Works	Sorrow	Abundance
Will	Abyss	Daath	"Empty Room"		Uranus	♅				
CREATION (Self Consciousness)	4	Chesed	Mercy	3	Jupiter	♃	Perfected Work	Earthly Power	Rest from Strife	Pleasure
	5	Geburah	Severity	4	Mars	♂	Strife	Earthly Trouble	Defeat	Loss in Pleasure
	6	Tiphareth	Beauty	5	Sun	☉	Victory	Material Success	Earned Success	Joy
FORMATION (Objective Consciousness)	7	Netzach	Victory	6	Venus	♀	Valour	Success Unfulfilled	Unstable Effort	Illusory Success
	8	Hod	Glory	7	Mercury	☿	Swiftness	Prudence	Shortened Force	Abandoned success
	9	Yesod	Foundation	8	Moon	☽	Great Strength	Material Gain	Despair & Cruelty	Material Happiness
ACTION	10	Malkuth	Kingdom	9	Earth	⊕	Oppression	Wealth	Ruin	Perfected Success

Figure 71 : Table - Kabbalah, Numbers, Planets, and Tarot

THE CHAKRAS

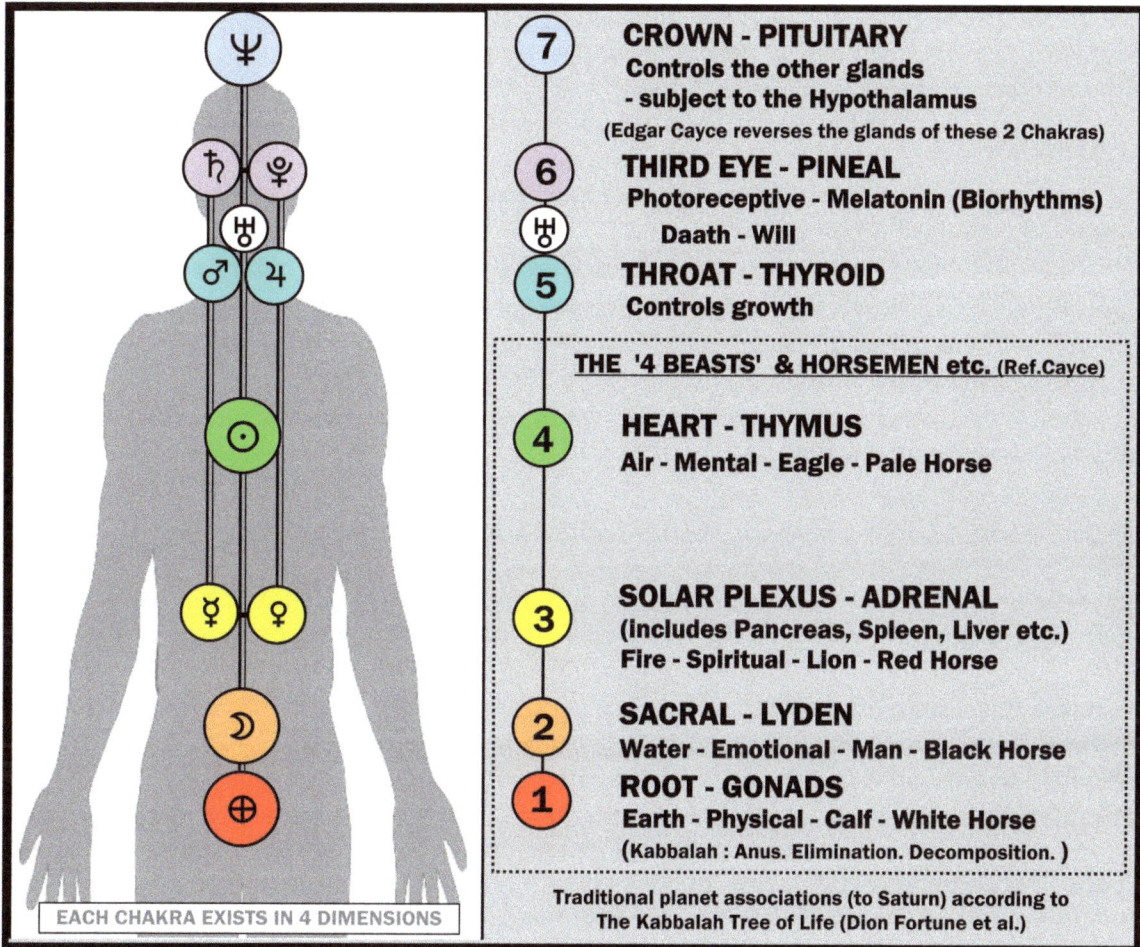

Figure 72 : The Chakras and Kabbalah planet relationships

The first thing to note is that written material concerning The Chakras ignores the physical functions of their related physical endocrine glands. This is possibly because their activity was generally unknown until recent times, and there are still uncertainties concerning their functions (especially the higher ones). I have tried to remedy this somewhat with the table at the end of the chapter, but a detailed study is not within the scope of this book. When studying The Chakras there is considerable disagreement among the authorities as to what their functions are. Hopefully a more holistic approach will shed more light.

We note that the Biblical "Tree of Knowledge" and "Tree of Life" both refer to the Chakra system. They are one and the same except that The Tree of Knowledge is the state where the Chakras are restricted (closed) in activity. That is because, at " The Fall", Adam and Eve preferred to regenerate themselves via Carnal "Knowledge" and reincarnation rather than spiritual methods. This is borne out by the, as yet unexplained, deterioration of some of the glands after birth.

Edgar Cayce states that Jesus was the last of a long line of reincarnations of Adam. Jesus demonstrated the possibility of spiritual Resurrection of the body after his crucifixion.

Exponents of Kundalini Yoga inform us that there are 3 energy channels that travel along the spine. The middle channel becomes active when the outer ones are balanced.

[THE KABBALAH TREE OF LIFE] has 3 Pillars and is clearly related to The Chakras. Edgar Cayce's associations differ from other authorities. When Edgar Cayce's source was questioned about this, the answer was that it was not concerned about other interpretations.

In The Book of Revelation, the Chakras both as a group (The Tree of Life), and separately, have various symbols applied.

THE CHAKRAS

We also note that The Tree of Life has "12 fruits" – and so is explicitly related to The Cycle of Growth.

*And he shewed me a pure river of water of life, bright as crystal, going forth out of the throne of God and of the Lamb:in the midst of its broad place, and of the river on this side and on that, [is] a tree of life, yielding twelve fruits, in each several month rendering its fruits, and the leaves of the tree [are] for the service of the nations; [Revelation 22 :verses 1 & 2]

THE 4 ELEMENTS

The first thing to note is that The Kabbalah shows that each of The Chakras\endocrine glands exist at the levels of The 4 Elements (4 Kabbalist Kingdoms):-

1. Fire : the spiritual energy level. Each Chakra has a different electromagnetic frequency.
2. Air (communication): They have a certain "intelligence" in performing their functions, and have connection with the nervous system of the body and brain. The hormones act as "messengers" which cause body organs with the appropriate receptors to react accordingly.
3. Water : Their hormone products are chemicals discharged directly into the blood stream. They are sensitive at an emotional level.
4. Earth : There is a physical body organ.

OVERVIEW

1. The Chakras are important in the overall scheme of spiritual development as well as normal healthy living. Here I just give an overview with a more detailed table of correspondences at the end of the chapter.
2. Each Chakra has a relationship with a planet in our Solar System, which indicates how an Astrological Birth Chart connects with its subject, especially in relationship to health. I have used those in [THE KABBALAH TREE OF LIFE.
3. In spiritual terms the Chakras are centres of energy, but each one is related to physical organs called Endocrine Glands which together secrete a large number of hormones that control all the body functions. The Endocrine Glands are "ductless glands" in that they release their products directly into the blood stream, rather than storing them – so they have immediate effect. We note that the glands produce several pairs of hormones that have an opposite effect on the body. Many illnesses are the result of imbalances in the Chakras and their associated glands caused by physical, psychological, or spiritual disharmony ("Stress").
4. Although, traditionally, Chakras are ascribed to specific functions, they do not work alone. The activity of one affects the others. In every case they are controlled by the "Master Gland" – the Pituitary - which is related to The Crown Chakra, which is itself controlled by the Hypothalamus which is not mentioned by tradition.
5. The Chakras have relationship with psychic abilities such as Clairvoyance and Clairaudience. Once again, several Chakras are involved in the phenomena.
6. In normal humans the Chakras are closed at a higher spiritual level. They have been in this state since the time of Adam and Eve being turned away from The Tree of Life (the Chakra System) in the book of Genesis. Their ejection from The Garden of Eden and exclusion from The Tree of Life is a symbol of the Chakras being sealed. The Biblical Book of Revelation at the end of The Bible is an account of an experience of the Chakras being opened.
7. This means that there is only one Tree. The Tree of Knowledge and The Tree of Life both refer to the same human Chakra system, the difference is in how they are used.
8. The Chakra information related to Revelation here mainly comes from the readings of Edgar Cayce. Like other early pioneers, his language –or, more correctly, that of his psychic source - is a bit difficult to understand. Again, we are indebted to the work of others in not only extracting them from his 14,000 readings on all subjects, but also working to interpret them into a logical format, and explain the symbology contained in the biblical Book of Revelation. If you are interested, I especially recommend *"The Book of The Revelation"* [TBOTR] published by Edgar's "Association for Research and Enlightenment" which is the result of a group, "The Glad Helpers", meeting with Edgar Cayce over the course of 7 years from 1936 to research that specific subject.

9. There are numerous explanations and descriptions of The Chakras elsewhere in literature. I am basing mine mainly on the teachings of Edgar Cayce's source, which sometimes differ. However, I include the Kabbalistic and Planet relationships because, as an Astrologer, I find them easier to understand. We have to note that the teachings of the East will be more appropriate to Eastern evolution, where the Chakras are understood more fully. We can expect that those of us in the West will need to travel a different path of understanding. At a personal level it probably equates to what religion we are drawn to, or born to – whether we practise it or not.
10. Edgar Cayce gives prime importance to the 2nd. Chakra – The Lyden, or Cells of Leydig, in terms of our physical & spiritual development. Because the physical gland and energy centre is not mentioned in any other literature, I have given it greater coverage here.
11. The activities of the endocrine glands are not fully understood in medical terms because they are so complex.

REGENERATION

It is important to note that, implied in Cayce's interpretation of Revelation and opening the Chakras is included the possibility of regenerating cells of the human body that have died, or lost (spiritual) functionality, as a result of "The Fall" of Adam and Eve, or misuse over eons of human existence. In physical terms, this seems especially noticeable with the Thymus Gland that actually reduces in size after birth, and is non-existent in most adults. There is also a possible similar correspondence with The Cells of Leydig. We also have the illness Diabetes related to the, so far unexplained, destruction of cells in the Pancreas. In addition, Revelation gives symbolic references to certain cells of the body. For example "Nations" are mentioned as meaning groups of cells of the body, but could equally mean groups of people who perform various practices. As Above, So Below.

THE BOOK OF REVELATION

Revelation treats the Chakras and body cells as one and the same. For example in Revelation Chapter 4 :-

***4 and 20 ELDERS** [mean]s 24 cranial nerves that lead to the 5 senses" :- [TBOTR]

*Chapter 4 Verse 4: And round about the throne were four and twenty seats: and upon the seats I saw four and twenty elders sitting, clothed in white raiment; and they had on their heads crowns of gold. [KJV]

"Seats" refers to the physical glands and senses. [EC]. The concept is that we are controlled by the physical 5 senses rather that the spiritual promptings. "Churches", apart from actual religious communities of the time also relate to the physical glands.

If we compare the evolution of the human body with the evolution of mankind there is a similar pattern. Everything begins with a single living entity, an amoeba or hunter gatherer, which begins to multiply. As the cells, or people, increase in number there is a need for greater efficiency - certain "cells", or people, evolve to perform specific functions on behalf of the whole. Evolution favours Diversification. So nowadays we have an extremely complex human body, and an extremely complex human civilisation – yet everything was in "Seed Form" in the embryo of 'The Big Bang'. Revelation takes us a step further - as does C.G.Jung with his concept of The Self.

Earlier in Revelation Chapter 4, the Overself, or Superconscious ("First Voice"), offers control to replace the old rulership by the physical (seats\thrones) 5 Senses we have reference to : -

*Chapter 4 Verse 1: After this I looked, and, behold, a door was opened in heaven: and the first voice which I heard was as it were of a trumpet talking with me; which said, Come up hither, and I will shew thee things which must be hereafter. [KJV]

THE CHAKRAS

THE CHAKRA STRUCTURE

The Chakras operate at 4 different levels – Physical gland (Earth), Emotional (Water), Mental (Air. Intelligence. Nervous), and Spiritual (Fire. Type of energy).

PHYSICAL (EARTH)

At a physical level The 7 Chakras are parts of the Endocrine System of our human body. The physical Endocrine Glands are "ductless" in that they release the hormones they produce directly into the blood stream, unlike other glands which store their products. Their effect on us is therefore immediate – like having a hormone injection. The Endocrine System controls every one of our body functions. Each of the Endocrine Glands is part of an inter-related system in that their products can enhance or restrict the activity of the others. It is important to note that, although some psychics can see the Chakras as coloured vortexes of energy at the front of a body, their roots are connected to the spinal column, making them somewhat conical in shape.

OTHER LEVELS

I will not pretend to fully understand the other levels, although it is clear that each chakra has its own form of "intelligence". They react at unconscious and conscious levels. Much depends on our mood and state of health. There is also a connection with higher universal spiritual forces such as "The 7 (Spiritual) Rays" which are under control of certain "angels", or intelligences whose job is to maintain each one. The link is symbolised by the colours of the visible colour spectrum which indicates that there is a difference in "musical note", or rate of vibration frequency, of each colour, ray, and Chakra. In Eastern symbolism the Base Chakra is " The Four Petal Lotus", colour Red, and The Crown The "Thousand Petal Lotus", colour Violet. We note that Red appears at the higher frequency too. Violet ,Chakra 7, is a mixture of Blue and Red – perhaps beginning a new cycle at a higher level.

PLANET RELATIONSHIPS

There is some disagreement between authorities as to which planetary energy relates to each Chakra. In this book I use the planet relationships of [THE KABBALAH TREE OF LIFE] to the Chakras. The Tree of Life Sephiroth are numbered 1 to 10 in descending order of vibration frequency and are placed at 7 levels, 3 of the levels have 2 Chakras each with one on The Pillar of Form and the other on The Pillar of Force. The others are on The Middle Pillar. The Chakras are numbered 1 to 7 from Base to Crown.

We note that Edgar Cayce states that our Earthly incarnations are only part of our development. We could have incarnations on any of the other planets. In considering this we have to be aware that our physical sense organs can only perceive vibrations within certain limits. For example, many animals can see or hear things that we cannot. They live at a more instinctive "Fire" level than we do. There are levels of perception beyond those of the 5 Senses. In effect, there is no division. In our search for life on other planets we assume that it will be at the same physical level of existence.

THE 4 LOWER CHAKRAS

Again, I mention the main points and leave the detail to the table at the end of the chapter.

1. We are on firmer ground (pun intended) when we consider the 4 lower Chakras because they relate to The 4 Elements - Air, Fire, Water and Earth. We are explicitly told in Revelation that the 4th. Horseman (Death) has control of "one fourth of the earth".
2. The 4 lower Chakras are "The 4 Beasts" and "The 4 Horsemen". There is no word "Apocalypse" in the Bible. They symbolise control of lower animal or instinctual energies and can be related to the 4 Knights of the Tarot Minor Arcana. The Horsemen are intelligences (of the Chakras) that control The Beasts.
3. As we see from The Tarot Knights of each suit, and Cycle of Growth Stage 4 (Transplanting. VII.The Chariot), "riders of horses" refers to the control of animal elements by higher intelligence.
4. We have to especially note that, in Revelation, the seals of the Chakras were not opened in order of their positions.
5. We can therefore associate the 4 lower Chakras with [THE 4 FUNCTIONS] of C.G. Jung.

1st. CHAKRA – BASE , OR ROOT

The Chakra is related to Planet Earth where everything is at the lowest rate of vibration.

THE CHAKRAS

We have the Gonads, which are the primary sexual organs of both men and women which also relate to the Earth Element. Its Beast in Revelation is The Calf, and Rider of the White horse, carrying a Bow and Crown (conquest).

The Gonads are mainly concerned with the production of Testosterone (male sex hormone) and Oestrogen (female sex hormone) which are both present in the blood of both sexes in varying amounts.

The Kabbalah also relates the Root Chakra to the anus and Elimination, and Decomposition – which both return waste products to the environment to be recycled. This process of breaking down into simpler elements seems to return us to the top level of The Crown Chakra (Sephirah 1), ruled by Neptune where everything is in "embryo" form.

The first stage of development for a new born baby is that of control of bladder and bowels.

REVELATION CHAPTER 2

As an example of the correspondence between Revelation and The Chakras :-

Revelation Chapter 2 refers to "the deeds of the Nicolaitans", which, although they actually existed, in the context here ALSO means the physical Gonads (sexual organs) – which give some insight into the overall meaning.

In researching "Nicolaitans" I was unable to find any reliable information. There seems to be a lot of speculation – but it is noticeable that most writers do not even spell the word correctly. *"Young's Analytical Concordance"* simply translates as "followers of Nicolas". Taking this a step further, we see verse 4 refers to "left thy first love" (God). We are now on firmer ground. We can see reference to "The Fall of Adam" (*"from whence thou art fallen"*) - when he disobeyed God (*"left first love"*) in favour of Eve - as the first misuse of the Gonads (male and female versions) and possibility of a return to The Tree of Life. "The 7 Churches", apart from the ones that used to exist in the world, refer to the physical endocrine glands – as the human body is "Temple of The Soul". Here we see that a single entity has control of all The 7 Chakras (7 Stars – higher versions of the 7 Candlesticks. Light. Consciousness). So we have instruction from The Overself. The Superconscious, or The Self (of John). "Take a letter ….".

> *Verse 1: Unto the angel of the church of Ephesus write; These things saith he that holdeth the seven stars in his right hand, who walketh in the midst of the seven golden candlesticks;*

We have reference to the Chakras as "stars" and "candlesticks". Ephesus relates to the Gonads [EC] so perhaps each physical church was focusing on development of a different Chakra.

> *Verse 2: I know thy works, and thy labour, and thy patience, and how thou canst not bear them which are evil: and thou hast tried them which say they are apostles, and are not, and hast found them liars:*

> *Verse 3: And hast borne, and hast patience, and for my name's sake hast laboured, and hast not fainted.*

"Patience" is the Virtue of the Gonads (sex organs). "Left First Love" is its Fault. [EC].

> *Verse 4: Nevertheless I have somewhat against thee, because thou hast left thy first love.*

> *Verse 5: Remember therefore from whence thou art fallen, and repent, and do the first works; or else I will come unto thee quickly, and will remove thy candlestick out of his place, except thou repent.*

That is, seal the Chakra again.

> *Verse 6: But this thou hast, that thou hatest the deeds of the Nicolaitans, which I also hate.*

> *Verse 7: He that hath an ear, let him hear what the Spirit saith unto the churches; To him that overcometh will I give to eat of the tree of life, which is in the midst of the paradise of God. [KJV]*

Although John is, on the surface, writing a letter to a church, he is also led to address, or meditate on, his own 1st. Chakra and its activity.

2ND. CHAKRA – LYDEN (3rd. to open)

This is one of the physical glands that deteriorates after birth.

THE CHAKRAS

The Planet relationship is that of The Moon. In the physical world The Moon stabilises the Earth orbit. The Kabbalah relates to Sephirah 9 (Foundation) as a function of bringing Sephirah 8 (Mercury. Mind) and Sephirah 7 (Venus. Emotion) energies into balance. The Moon also refers to the Personal Unconscious.

Special mention is required here because Edgar Cayce is alone in ascribing this Chakra to "The Lyden" or "Cells of Leydig" – being named after their discoverer. To some extent this is the most important endocrine gland for the individual because he describes it as "The Seat of The Soul" – which aligns with an Astrological association with The Moon.

His is the only source that refers to The Lyden, and it is not yet given a great importance, if any, in medical literature. Indeed, it is difficult to find information about it.

Its Beast, in Revelation, is The Man, and Rider of The Black Horse carrying a Pair of Balances (Karma)

Research so far shows The Cells of Leydig are concerned with the production of the male sex hormone Testosterone, and here are 2 types of Cells – foetal (determining the sex in the womb) and adult. Taken from a scientific paper "*Origin, Development and Regulation of Human Leydig Cells*" [HLC] written in 2009, the stages are :

1. <u>Cycle of Growth Stage 9</u> Precursors become functionally active after 6-7 weeks of gestation - when testosterone can be detected.
2. <u>Cycle of Growth Stage 10</u> Differentiation. 7 to 14 weeks of gestation.
3. <u>Cycle of Growth Stage 11</u> Foetal Maturation. 14-18 weeks of gestation.
4. <u>Cycle of Growth Stage 12</u> Involution. Further development until birth.
5. <u>Cycle of Growth Stage 1</u> The foetal cells increase during the initial 2-3 months after birth, and are stimulated by Pituitary gonadotrophin LH to grow in number and cell size to become Mature Cells.
6. <u>Cycle of Growth Stages 2, 3, 4 and 5.</u> Peak growth is at 7 months, with a decline afterwards **when some Cells regress to the foetal stage**.
7. There is further activity at puberty with increase of Mature Cells and development of secondary sexual characteristics that differentiate men and women in preparation for reproduction. (Cycle of Growth Stage 6) –Adolescence\Puberty.

(Q) The Leydig gland is the same as that we have called the Lyden, and is located in the gonads? (A) It is in and above, or the activity passes through the gonads. Lyden is the meaning - or the seal, see? while Leydig is the name of the individual who indicated this was the activity. You can call it either of these that you want to. [EC Reading 281-53]

(EC has given the correct location according to the medical description despite its relative obscurity elsewhere [BTB])

L-y-d-e-n is the sealed gland that is opened when copulation takes place in the uterus, or the body becoming impregnated with the germ necessary to produce childbirth, or child bearing, and with the correction of these conditions this body will be able to bring forth that of children see? [EC Reading 3816-1]

* *The Lyden, [Leydig] or 'closed gland', is the keeper - as it were - of the door, that would loose and let either passion or the miracle be loosed to enable those seeking to find the Open Door, or the Way to find expression in the attributes of the imaginative forces in their manifestation in the sensory forces of a body; whether to fingertips that would write, to eyes that would see, to voice that would speak, to the whole of the system as would feel those impressions that are attuned with those the infinite by their development and association or with those inter-between, or those just passed over, or as to the unseen forces; for the world of unconsciousness is not in a material change from the physical world save as to its attributes or of its relationships with. Whether the vision has been raised or lowered depends upon that height, depth, breadth or length, it has gone for its source of supply. [EC Reading on himself. Explaining the working of his own Lyden Gland 294-140]*

The spiritual arises from the centres in the Lyden or leaden [Leydig or Leydigian] glandular forces that are as hidden energies, or the very nature of the creative or reproductive forces. There are the abilities of each center, each gland, each atom to reproduce itself within the body - which is the very nature of glandular reaction. [EC Reading 1468-5]

THE CHAKRAS

> *There has been the opening of the Lyden (Leydig) gland and thus a disturbance through glandular system. Possession at times is the result. [EC Reading 3410-1]*

> *We find that there has been the opening of the Lyden (Leydig?) gland, so that the kundaline forces move along the spine to the various centers that open with this attitude, or with these activities of the mental and spiritual forces of the body - much in the same manner as might be illustrated in the foetus that forms from conception. These naturally take form. Here these take form, for they have not in their inception been put to a definite use. [EC Reading 3421-1]*

> *For as we find this entity has more than once been among those who were gifted with what is sometimes called second sight, or the super-activity of the third eye. Whenever there is the opening, then, of the Lyden (Leydig) center and the kundaline forces from along the pineal, we find that there are visions of things to come, of things that are happening. [EC Reading 4087-1]*

Edgar Cayce was able to describe the surroundings of subjects of his readings at the time even though they were unknown to him and living in other parts of the world. This is now termed "Remote Viewing". There have been attempts to use it for military spying purposes. I have a small experience of this when doing distant or "absent" healing.

We can see that the descriptions align with the idea that The Tree of Knowledge and Tree of Life both relate to the Chakra System, and are one and the same. It would seem that the use this Chakra is put to is the key. Regeneration can occur by means of sexual Intercourse ("knowing") and reincarnation, which requires the production of new human bodies (which eventually wear out), or Spiritual Regeneration - as demonstrated by the Resurrection of Jesus after his crucifixion.

We also see that the use of the Chakras can be developed by practice.

3RD. CHAKRA – ADRENAL\SOLAR PLEXUS\NAVEL (2nd. to open)

The 3rd. Chakra is the Solar Plexus, often called the Adrenal, and is related to the Adrenal Glands situated above the kidneys. However, we must take into account that other important hormone producing organs are also present in this area of the body - the Pancreas, Spleen, and Liver – which all work together.

Its Beast in Revelation is The Lion, and Rider of The Red Horse, carrying a Large Sword – which can be used for good or evil.

In The Kabbalah this refers to the level of the 2 Sephiroth which relate to the Personal Planets Venus (Sephirah 7. Desire. Emotions. Feeling. Right Brain) and Mercury (Sephirah 8. Rational mind. Thinking. Left Brain).

THE ADRENALS

The Adrenal glands produce two hormones – Adrenaline (Epinephrine), and Noradrenaline which has an opposite effect. They have several functions, such as controlling heart rate, and are related to the "flight or fight" bodily reaction which mobilise the resources of the body to respond to possible attack (or other urgent requirement). The body would normally return to normal when the danger is perceived to pass. The perceived danger may be psychological (unconscious) rather than physical, but the glands work in the same way. If they are continually stimulated over a long period of time the stress can adversely affect the physical body producing such imbalances of high blood pressure or ulcers (or any other illness). This is usually called "Stress".

THE PANCREAS

The Adrenal Cortex is concerned with several hormones called Steroids. Aldesterone increases water retention in the body by controlling the amount of salt in the urine, and Rennin has the opposite effect. Cortisone increases the level of sugar in the blood, which is balanced by Insulin from the Pancreas which has the opposite effect.

DIABETES

We have another gland that can deteriorate after birth.

The illness Diabetes is an inability for the Pancreas to produce sufficient Insulin- which is involved with converting glucose into energy. There are different types of the illness.

1. Mellitus (= "like honey") caused by destruction of Pancreas cells by as yet unknown causes – often occurring in children – and rectified by emulating the function of the Spleen with injections of Insulin extracted from animals.
2. A rare type called Insipus caused by a problem with the Pituitary.

3. The majority of diabetics have Senile Diabetes where Insulin production is normal but the tissues of the body cannot process the sugar – resulting in excessive sugar levels in the blood. My guess is that more exercise would use up the sugar.

Diabetes indicates the connection between the Spleen and Kidneys from its symptoms of excessive thirst and need to urinate frequently.

THE LIVER

The Liver is concerned with neutralising poisons and wastes. Related to our subject here, it produces 4 hormones :-

1. Angiotensinogen - works with Renin, secreted by the Kidneys, to maintain blood pressure.
2. Thrombopoietin – works with the bone marrow to produce blood platelets required for clotting.
3. Hepcidin – controlling levels of iron in the body.
4. Betatrophin – works with the Pancreas to produce Insulin.

4TH. CHAKRA – HEART – THYMUS

Another gland that deteriorates after birth.

Even in the lives of the general public The Heart is given special attention. We see from our study of Number 5 [NUMBERS] it refers to the opposable thumb of the human hand where 1 opposes 4. We also see that, in human life, and in this chapter, that 1 can rule 4 (The 4 Lower Elements), or 4 can rule 1. It is all a matter of Consciousness (The Sun) and Will (Uranus) as demonstrated by The Transcendent Octave of The Cycle of Growth.

In the Kabbalah this is Sephirah 6 (Tiphareth. Beauty. The Sun. Light. Consciousness. Number 5) located at the centre of The Middle Pillar. The decline of the organ later in life suggests a connection with Ego Consciousness

Edgar Cayce relates this Chakra to the Beast of Revelation at the highest frequency level, The Eagle, and Rider of The Pale Horse, having *"power over one fourth of earth"*, and of Death.

It is only within the last 20 years or so that the function of the Thymus has begun to be understood – although not yet fully, due to its complexity. Its basic function is the control of the Lymphatic System of the body, which circulates a fluid in a similar way to the blood circulation and is related to our resistance to disease. It is another organ that presents us with seeming anomalies. The first point is that, in relation to total body size, it is largest in infancy. It continues to grow quickly until age 7, then the rate of growth slows down until puberty. After puberty the organ begins to shrink in size until it becomes virtually non-existent in the elderly. It is related to the body's defence against disease, which is mainly the concern of Lymphocytes which firstly recognise foreign substances, and then produce antibodies to destroy them. A problem here is that the Thymus has to differentiate between "friendly" and "alien" substances.

One theory is that infancy provides us with a lifetime resistance to disease. The Thymus is involved in the production of antibodies and T-cells, and it is therefore my suggestion that it is this gland that is attacked by the HIV virus that causes AIDS. The HIV virus is known to affect the production of T-cells, which destroys the immune system and leaves the body open to attack from other diseases.

THE CHAKRAS

THE HIGHER CHAKRAS

5TH. CHAKRA – THROAT – THYROID GLANDS

The Kabbalah relates The Throat Chakra together with Uranus in the unnumbered Sephirah Daath – which exists in a different dimension to the rest of The Tree of Life.

This is the first of the 3 Mental Centres. We are now at a level above that of The 4 Elements, so there are no similar symbolic images. In Revelation, John is given "the key of the bottomless pit" – which is a symbol of the Unconscious (and perhaps The Abyss on The Tree of Life). The results are, firstly, a recognition of repressed memories and emotions, and, secondly, partial regeneration of the 4 lower chakras by releasing each of their "Angels" (higher spiritual forces).

We note that The Bottomless Pit appears in The Kabbalah as The Abyss which is (potentially) crossed by the Sephiroth Daath. It also relates to the Personal, and Collective, Unconscious. Although it is associated with the Throat Chakra, Daath, as we see here, is normally "sealed" – that is, repressed or unused. We therefore have a further relationship with Sephirah 9 (Yesod. The Moon. Personal Unconscious) which is an indication of the complexity of the system).

Cayce states that the Throat Chakra is related to Voice, and Will. He also relates it to the planet Uranus, which confirms my association of the planet, in turn, with Jung's process of Individuation [PSYCHOLOGY : DEVELOPMENT MODELS]. In the chapter [THE PURPOSE OF LIFE] we see the suggestion that the main purpose of our existence is the development of Will.

THYROID GLAND

Once again, medical science does not fully understand the function of this gland other than the fact that its correct functioning is vital to a healthy life, and that it is the only body part that uses Iodine, which it obtains from our food to produce the enzyme Thyroxine. It is under the control of the Pituitary, and concerned with supplying energy for growth to all the living cells of our bodies.

PARATHYROIDS

The 4 Parathyroids control the levels of Calcium in the body – which is involved in formation of bones and teeth, as well as muscle and nerve functioning.

6TH. CHAKRA – THE THIRD EYE – PINEAL

In The Kabbalah we are now in the realm of "The Supernals" at Sephirah 2 (Chockmah. Force. Positive Polarity. Pluto) and Sephirah 3 (Binah. Severity. Form. Saturn) which together give us $E=MC^2$ and are controlled by Sephirah 1 (Kether. Crown. Number Zero).

We now have a difference in Cayce's relationships between the Chakras and endocrine glands where he relates The Crown with the Pineal Gland. I am using the traditional Chakra association. This difference is only in physical position, not functionality.

He states that opening this Chakra gives us access to all of our soul memories. That is, the Pineal is like a recording device. We tend to relate this with The Personal Unconscious, which has other associations above. My suggestion is that the interconnection is via the Water Element version of The Tree of Life, which connects the Sephiroth at that level.

In Sanskrit there are "The Akashic Records" which are said to contain, among other things, all the memories of our past lives, and which exists on the Astral Plane which is described as a level of existence between the earthy and spiritual worlds – which fits with my Water suggestion. Some people can travel this level whilst in a dream state. One feature is that they come across seeming physical people who do not react to their presence. Mystics state that such entities are the discarded "shells" of the astral bodies (rather like our physical bodies) of those who have advanced to more spiritual realms. The astral shells eventually decay to nothing.

The Pineal, 6th. Chakra, releases, or activates, the Angels (higher spiritual intelligences. Fire) of the lower chakras.

Although Daath relates to the Throat Chakra, we can see that it also connects with The Third Eye.

> *Revelation 9:13: And the sixth angel sounded, and I heard a voice from the four horns of the golden altar which is before God,*

THE CHAKRAS

Revelation 9:14: Saying to the sixth angel which had the trumpet, Loose the four angels which are bound in the great river Euphrates. [KJV]

- although only a third part of the lower elements were purged we assume that the activated Will can control them :-

*Rev:9:18: By these three was the third part of men killed, by the fire, and by the smoke, and by the brimstone, which issued out of their mouths. [KJV]

PINEAL GLAND

Another gland that deteriorates with age.

The gland is situated in the centre of the brain. Again, little is known about its function. It is known to produce Melatonin which is secreted into the brain in darkness and inhibited in daylight. It affects sex hormone production and seems to control our daily body cycles, or biorhythms. It collects deposits of calcium as we age, which would affect it adversely.

In disagreement with [EC] the association with light seems to suggest more of a relationship to the Third Eye Chakra. Its activation at night could be connected with dreaming and mental activity whilst asleep. However, I remember reading a medical text which stated that Melatonin secretion is somehow affected by light "on the top of the head". [BTB].

This does not change the functions and associations of the Chakras, only their physical location.

7TH. CHAKRA – THE CROWN – PITUITARY

The Kabbalah relates The Crown Chakra to Sephirah 1 The Crown which is related to Neptune (Dissolution). The Sephirah also connects to Sephirah 2. Wisdom (Pluto. Regeneration) and Sephirah 3. Understanding (Saturn. Form). Together the 3 Sephiroth are referred to as "The (abstract) Supernals".

In Revelation Chapter 8, when the final 7th. Seal is opened there is silence for "about the space of half an hour", and then the 7 angels relating to the Chakras are given trumpets which they sound in turn – emphasising the physical control of the endocrine system by the Pituitary. The Chakras are thus purified.

The 'sounding of trumpets' relates to the Tarot Card XX. Judgement – "The call to higher things". Vocation. Promotion. This seems to mean that the Chakras are activated by means of vibrations generated at the appropriate frequency - such as when sounding a musical note can break a glass of water tuned to that note.

PITUITARY GLAND

Although stated to be "The Master Gland", the Pituitary is still under the control of the Hypothalamus – which is therefore the true Master. The physical functioning is not yet fully understood.

This is the "Master Gland" of the body that controls the others. It produces several substances the purpose of which are not fully understood, but are likely to be involved in controlling the other glands. It consists of 2 parts, the Anterior, and the Posterior which is effectively an extension of the Hypothalamus. In the literature, descriptions of the hormones produced can disagree. There is no need for the complication here.

THE "8TH. CHAKRA" AND OTHER ANOMALIES

We can see that, in order to be confident that our beliefs have some basis in fact, we need to be able to relate them to the physical world as we know it. This is the basis of my Cycle of Growth. In effect, The Chakras are an example of how this can come about, because they exist at several levels at one and the same time.

Another thing to note is that when we see diagrams of the Chakras superimposed on outlines of human bodies (my diagram included) the ones in the head, the Pituitary and Pineal, are widely separated whereas in reality they are close together inside the brain together with the Hypothalamus. Also, the Pineal is slightly above the Pituitary – a fact noted only by Edgar Cayce. However, this does not change the functionality and description of the organs. My diagram also adheres to the normal symbolic representation of increasing frequency.

THE HYPOTHALAMUS

This is in keeping with the symbolism of Number 8 [NUMBERS] which is concerned with higher level (mental) management of practical affairs (4 over 4) – and can relate to normal business management as well as The Laws of Nature.

When we examine the Endocrine System we are faced with the fact that everything is actually controlled by the Hypothalamus which forms a link between the Endocrine and Nervous systems, and, among other things, co-ordinates our inner and outer activities. The presence of this organ is not noted in any "occult" literature - in fact medical science is only now beginning to understand its function if not its methods. When I visited the *Natural History Museum* in South Kensington, London, in 2010, it was described as being like "the Chairman of a football team giving instructions to the Manager (Pituitary), who then passed them on to the players (other glands)".

The Hypothalamus is known to produce 2 hormones which pass to the posterior Pituitary.

ANTI DIURETIC HORMONE

This controls the water levels in the body via the kidneys, enabling them to extract more or less water from the urine. The Hypothalamus also has the power to make us feel hungry or thirsty if it decides we do not have enough food or water.

OXYTOCIN

The activity of this hormone is not clear because it alone seems to affect a wide variety of organs throughout the body. For example, it is present in high quantities in women during childbirth, and seems to have some role in producing sexual orgasm, and even other levels of bonding in our social behaviour.

Another effect of Oxytocin is to produce memory loss – which is why we do not usually remember our birth – which is at the end of The 1st. Octave at Cycle of Growth 12 (Pisces. Water. Withdrawal. Confinement).

It is also suggested that it is produced in larger quantities at other times in life, such as around 7 years of age (at the end of the 2nd. Octave at Cycle of Growth 4 (Cancer. Water. Transplanting) which is why we do not easily recall events of our earlier years.

It is a well-known fact that long term memory improves during old age, which is the end of the 3rd. Octave (Cycle of Growth Stage 8 (Water. Scorpio. Sex. Death), whilst short term memory reduces. We may remember events from years ago, but not what we had for lunch. Perhaps there is a connection with Oxytocin [BTB].

GENESIS AND REVELATION

The first and last books in The Bible have a bearing here. In Genesis we are told about The Fall of Adam which is related to his sexual intercourse with Eve. According to Edgar Cayce's source we were not supposed to actually enter incarnation at a physical level – so there would have been no Bible because the Creation would have concluded at the end of Chapter 1. Physical material, and Adam, do not appear until Chapter 2 [GENESIS AND THE CYCLE OF GROWTH].

The Kabbalah suggests that Daath was the original destination of mankind before The Fall to Sephiroth 10. Kingdom, with relationship to the lost city of Atlantis.

We lost the full use of our Chakras when Adam chose The Tree of (sexual) Knowledge and Death, rather than The Tree of Life (the spiritual Chakra energy system). With no physical body there would be no Death (and no endocrine system). The "Seven Seals" opened in Revelation were originally closed to Adam and Eve because they used the creative spiritual powers for material (lower, selfish, 4 Elements) purposes. We thus have the Cherubim "guards" set on The Garden of Eden, and Tree of Life, after their banishment. Each of The Cherubim has the 4 faces of the 4 Beasts (Elements). So our study of The 4 Beasts as guardians of the 4 lower chakras gives new meaning to Exodus Chapter 20 where we find :-

> *Verse 4: Thou shalt not make unto thee any graven image, or any likeness [of any thing] that [is] in heaven above, or that [is] in the earth beneath, or that [is] in the water under the earth:*
>
> Verse :5: Thou shalt not bow down thyself to them, nor serve them: for I the LORD thy God [am] a jealous God, visiting the iniquity of the fathers upon the children unto the third and fourth [generation] of them that hate me; [KJV]

We could say that the endocrine glands are material "graven images".

The Book of Revelation is written by someone who calls himself John. It is not clear if this was the apostle John. It is a record of his visions experienced whilst each of his 7 Chakras opened. As such, like dreams, the content would be entirely subjective to him alone, although based on archetypal images. Because Western religions do not recognise the Chakras, it is not surprising that they attempt to give other interpretations. It is strange that the Book was ever included in The Bible. In the Eastern world the Chakras are part of everyday knowledge.

In terms of "prediction of the future", this therefore suggests that at some future time we could have similar experiences. This also relates to "The Second Coming" of The Messiah – which would be experienced as a related INNER EVENT. If you reject this idea, then you have just killed "The Child" once again, as in the biblical story of the birth of Jesus.

"OPENING CHAKRAS"

There is much written elsewhere about "opening the Chakras". We must note that this is an extremely dangerous thing to attempt. I have noted my own small experience in [MY STORY]. Revelation mentions "Earthquake" which is the vibration of the physical body during the experience. In John's case not only would he have reached the necessary stage of spiritual development, the experience was overseen by his Super-conscious, or "Higher Self". This is in keeping with the Jungian concept that we eventually have to allow ourselves to be controlled by 'The Self'. Another consideration is that, as with any powers, spiritual or material, they have to be put to the proper use - otherwise they might destroy the individual physically, mentally, and spiritually. They have to be used, and used for the right purpose. From Adam's example we can see that misuse incurs a heavy Karmic burden – continuing through all later generations until now. In fact, EC suggests that we are all travelling this same path as Adam, and Jesus was the final incarnation of Adam.

In Adam and Eve's case Edgar Cayce traces them through several reincarnations until they redeemed themselves in those of Jesus and Mary. Thus, in effect, enabling redemption in us as their descendants.

A modern day example, or method, of opening the Chakras would be in the taking of drugs with the result of "raised consciousness". We see from Mark Thurston's work [THE PURPOSE OF LIFE] that although the experiences are somewhat similar to that described in Revelation, the participants are in no way enhanced by it. Mark states that this is because we originated in a super-conscious state, and the main reason for our "descent" into a more material state was so we could develop Will. With drug related experiences we regress to the earlier higher state of consciousness where we had even less Will than now. We can see evidence of the truth of this when we observe people who are addicted to tobacco, alcohol, or other drugs. Not only are they "without Will", but they have to use a considerable amount of "Will Power" to recover to their original state of self-control – and health (which word is rooted in "Wholeness" and "Holiness"). We can also, perhaps, see something of this in animals who, despite having limited mental powers and very limited Will, are able to survive by using their instincts.

The Kabbalah relates this state of "no will" with that of the Angels who have never incarnated, each of which carries out important single functions such as that of maintaining The Seven Rays, and maintaining each of the 10 Sephiroth. This is not out of keeping with the concept of The Patron Saints of the Catholic Church – although they actually incarnated into human form. Humans are intended to be "multi-tasking "and to evolve into gods. The concept is also in keeping with the ancient notion of numerous "gods" and "goddesses" – which seems to have a greater sense of Equal Opportunities.

KUNDALINI YOGA

Kundalini Yoga is concerned with methods of opening the Chakras. The exponents state that there are 3 energy channels connected to the spine. Their method requires balancing the 2 outer channels, which allows the middle channel to become active. They then raise Kundalini "Serpent Power" from the Base Chakra to The Crown Chakra.

The next page shows a summary table.

THE CHAKRAS - TABLE OF CORRESPONDENCES

THE SEVEN POWER CENTRES (CHAKRAS) AND RELATIONSHIPS

(* Edgar Cayce definitions)

	OTHER CORRESPONDENCES					* BOOK OF REVELATION (Cayce)					PHYSICAL ENDOCRINE GLANDS		
	Chakra	Kabbalah	* Colour	* Lord's Prayer	*Element	*Beast	*Church	* + Virtue - Fault	Chapter 6 : Horse rider	*Vision	Glands	Hormone	Notes
-	-	-	Grey* (Silver)	-	-	-	-	-	-	-	HYPOTHALAMUS (Master Gland. Controls Pituitary)	Oxytocin	Stimulates contraction of uterus & secretion of milk. (Produces memory loss). Stored in the pituitary.
												ADH	Anti Diuretic hormone Increases water absorption into the blood
												Controls daily body rhythms (ref. 3rd.Eye Pineal)	
7	Crown Sahasrara (*3rd. Eye)	1. Crown ♆	Violet	Father in Heaven	-	-	LAODICEA	(no virtue) - Neither hot nor cold (Lukewarm)	-	Silence	PITUITARY (controls the other glands)	ACTH.	Stimulates production of hormones in cortex of adrenal glands.
												TSH	Thyroid Stimulating Hormone Stimulates production of thyroxin by thyroid gland
												STH or HGH	Stimulates growth by increasing rate at which amino acids are built up
												FSH Follicle stimulating hormone	In women works with LH to stimulate development of ova & secretion of oestrogen & progesterone.
												LH	Lutenizing Hormone Stimulates ovulation. Puberty.
												Lactogenic Hormone	Works with LH to cause secretion of hormones by corpus luteum. Milk production after birth.
6	Third Eye Ajna (*Crown)	3. Form - 2.Force ♄ ------- ♇	Indigo	Name	-	-	PHILADELPHIA	+ An open door (no faults)	-	Earthquake perfect	PINEAL	Melatonin	Secreted in darkness. Levels vary on a daily/seasonal cycle. (sleep/wake). Treat Alzheimer's ? Affect sex hormone production. Biorhythms
5	Throat Vishudda	(Daath ♅) 5.Severity-4.Mercy ♂------- ♃	Blue	Will	-	-	SARDIS	+ Few not defiled. - Imperfect	-	Souls of faithful slain (martyrs)	THYROID	Thyroxin	Controls rate of growth and food breakdown
												TCT	Decreases calcium and phosphorus in the blood by reducing their release from bones
											PARA THYROID	PTH	Increases calcium. Decreases phosphorus.
4	Heart Anahata	6.Beauty ☉	Green	Evil	Air Mental	Eagle	THYATIRA	+ Charity. - Fornication	Death (power over one fourth of earth)	Pale Horse Propogation	THYMUS	T-cells. Antibodies	Immune system. Central Tolerance - cells non reactive to self. Works with Spleen, Bone Marrow, & White blood cells. Reduces in size after puberty.
3	Solar Plexus Manipura	8. 7. Glory --- Victory ☿ ------- ♀	Yellow	Debt (Karmic)	Fire Spirtual	Lion	PERGAMOS	+ Faithful. - Stumbling block	has Large Sword War Good and Evil	Red Horse Sustenence	ADRENAL (Kidneys)	Adrenalin & Noradrenalin	Stimulate liver glucose, heart rate, breathing. Constricts blood vessels
												Aldosterone	Increases sodium and water in blood via kidneys
												Cortisone	Stimulate an increase in the rate of food breakdown. Resistance to stress
											Pancreas (Digestion)	Insulin	Sugar control
												-	(Liver, Gall Bladder, Stomach, Spleen)
2	Sacral Swadhistthana (NAVEL)	9. Foundation ☽	Orange	Temptation	Water Emotion	Man	SMYRNA	+ Suffering - Insincerity	has Pair of Balances wages (& Karma)	Black Horse Self preservation	* LYDEN Seat of the Soul	testosterone	hormone-secreting cell of testis: a cell that borders the sperm-producing tubes in the testis and secretes testosterone and other male sex hormones
1	Root Muladhara	10.Kingdom ⊕	Red	Bread	Earth Physical	Calf	EPHESUS	+ Patience - Left first love	has Bow and Crown (conquest)	White Horse Self-gratification	GONADS (male & female sex organs)	testosterone	Male : testes and sperm (also some oestrogen)
												oestrogen	Female : ovaries and eggs (also some testosterone)

Figure 73 : Chakras - Correspondences Summary Table

THE CHAKRAS

NUMEROLOGY

The attempt here is to get as close to archetypal numbers as possible and see how they relate to The Cycle of Growth – which includes, among other things, Evolution beginning with The Big Bang. Apart from human evolution we consider how the Chemical Elements evolved from the first simple Hydrogen atom (Atomic Number 1) to the set of heavier elements existing today.

There is a short description of practical Numerology at the end of this chapter.

Numerology reduces numbers to the range 1 to 9 and ignores numbers 10 and 12 as having no particular importance.(11 is given importance as a higher octave of Number 2. 22 As a higher octave of Number4. This narrative shows how this occurs).

IT IS IMPORTANT TO NOTE THAT :-

1. THE CYCLE OF GROWTH, WHICH IS BASED ON [ASTROLOGY : HOUSES] AND THE LOGARITHMIC TIMESCALE IN PARTICULAR, BEGINS AT STAGE 9 (CONCEPTION), WHICH ITSELF CORRESPONDS WITH ARCHETYPAL NUMBER 1 AND SEPHIRAH 2 (CHOCKMAH. WISDOM. FORCE) OF THE KABBALAH TREE OF LIFE.

2. HAVING ESTABLISHED A RELATIONSHIP BETWEEN NUMBERS AND PLANETS IN [THE KABBALAH TREE OF LIFE] WE FIND THAT THE STAGE NUMBERS OF THE CYCLE OF GROWTH DO NOT RELATE TO THE NUMERICAL ORDER OF NUMBERS 1 TO 12 BECAUSE SOME PLANETS (AND NUMBERS) ARE RELATED TO 2 STAGES. THE DIFFERENCE IN THOSE STAGES IS WHICH OF [THE 4 ELEMENTS] IS INVOLVED.

3. ALTHOUGH IT IS POSSIBLE TO ASSOCIATE THE NUMBERING OF THE CYCLE OF GROWTH STAGES AND ZODIAC SIGNS, AND THE TAROT MAJOR ARCANA WE DO NOT DO SO IN THIS BOOK. THE ARCHETYPAL CONNECTIONS TEND TO BE LOST IN GREATER COMPLEXITY. As examples : -

    a. Sephirah 2 (Chockmah, Force, Number 1. Pluto) traditionally contains the Primal Energy of the 12 Zodiac Signs in undifferentiated form. They do not fully manifest until Sephirah 10 (Malkuth. Kingdom. Earth. Number 9).

    b. We can associate the Tarot card 0.The Fool with Sephirah 1 (Number Zero). (It is also the traditional path between Sephirah 1 (Number Zero) and Sephirah 2 (Number 1)). We can do the same associations with the other Major Arcana cards.

    c. We can practically apply the principle ad infinitum, such as by comparing Sephirah 2 (Number 1) with card I.The Magician and with card X.The Wheel at the beginning of the "return" Stage 7 of The Cycle of Growth (Partners. Number 10 = 1 + 0 = 1) when the work of The Magician can become a repetitive method of learning or "a rat race".

4. THE SEPHIROTH NUMBERS 1 TO 10 RELATE TO THE TAROT MINOR ARCANA CARDS NUMBERED 1 TO 10 IN EACH OF THE 4 ELEMENTS (SUITS). This is another indication that Numbers exist in a different dimension. There is a summary table in [THE TAROT].

5. WE FIND THAT THE ARCHETYPAL CORRESPONDENCES BETWEEN PLANETS AND NUMBERS HERE DO NOT AGREE WITH THOSE OF NUMEROLOGY. The reason is the same as in paragraph number 2 above.

This highlights the extreme difficulty involved when dealing with Planets and Numbers because they can be active at numerous different levels. For example, I have noted elsewhere that Edgar Cayce's association between Planets and Chakras do not agree with those stated here - or anywhere else for that matter.

There is a summary table of Cycle of Growth Stages which includes Numbers in the chapter [GENESIS AND THE CYCLE OF GROWTH].

NUMEROLOGY

INTRODUCTION

1. This study is unique in that it includes the relatively new discovery of Number Zero which only appeared around 7AD and has finally become a number in its own right as a result of the Computer Age.
2. In order to do this we have to go back to before The Big Bang of Creation when No-Thing existed, and see how everything in the universe evolved from there. We stray into the world of Quantum Physics.
3. We consider the evolution of Hydrogen, Atomic Number 1, which was the first Chemical Element formed from a single Proton and single Electron, and is the basis and source of all the other elements. It is still the most common element in the universe, and is still being converted into heavier elements by the nuclear reactions inside the suns of the universe, including our own. There is a table at the end of the chapter showing the Positron/Neutron/Electron structures of the first 18 elements.
4. From this we can see that Nature's Laws of Physics can only count up to Number 2.
5. The Binary Number System of The Computer Age displays a similar pattern
6. The best related study for this is The Kabbalah Tree of Life – which does not traditionally include reference to Numbers. It is easy to see the reason for this : The Tree of Life starts at Sephirah 1 (Kether. Crown) which traditionally has no associated planet. By associating it with the newly discovered planet Neptune, it can now, in turn, be associated with Number Zero, with the other Sephiroth following in order up to Sephirah 10 (Malkuth. Kingdom. Earth) and Number 9 – the last of the root numbers in Numerology.
7. In The Tree of Life, Creation proceeds in order of Numbers, when the Number 1 Sephirah 2 (Chockmah. Force. Positive, ENERGY) begins the Pillar of Force, and Number 2 Sephirah 3 (Binah. Form. Negative. MASS) begins The Pillar of Form - which gives rise to $E=MC^2$.
8. We also see associations with the gods of Mythology – which include the planets named after them. Their activities can be considered as depictions of the first efforts to describe the reactions ("mating") of elements with one another to produce chemical compounds (their "children") – which also "mate" with one another to produce a Diversity of chemical compounds (as well as body cells, and people).
9. Although it is evident that higher numbers contain lower ones, it is also true that lower numbers, starting from Zero, which contains everything, contain the higher ones in seed form. Wheels within wheels. We get an idea of how this works by, at the end of this chapter, considering them in relationship to evolution of the Chemical Elements from the Zero of The Big Bang.
10. There is a similarity with the way humans have evolved from mere "shells" of jelly - cells with no nucleus - to complex multi-cellular organisms, which evolved into solitary hunter gatherers who later become participants in large, equally complex, social groups where they take on specific functions on behalf of the whole.
11. At another level numbers behave in different ways depending on what other numbers they are relating to at the time. This makes sense if we consider them to be like individual people. For example, we all have experience of the different dynamics that result when we are alone, with a single other, or in different groups consisting of 3 or more people. I have had colleagues involved in training various groups of people who noticed the differences in energy levels and dynamic behaviour depending on how many there were in the group.

HISTORY OF NUMBERS AND NUMEROLOGY

1. Although beginning in The Age of Pisces at a more philosophical level, the practical use of Numbers is mainly a product of The Age of Aquarius, an Air Sign relating to the development of the Thinking\ Communication Function in humans. This is the Function that includes the "3 Rs" of the modern children's primary school – "Reading, wRiting, and aRithmetic". In earlier times there was no such education which was reserved for the privileged few – especially at the beginning. As hunter gatherers, Homo Sapiens "born" 200,000 years ago – yesterday in terms of human evolution - had no need for such sophistication, even though the mental capacity was there in embryo form. It is related to "Left Brain" development. The "Right Brain" is artistic rather than scientific.
2. Aquarius is included in the 1st. Octave of The Cycle of Growth which is concerned with the development of a human foetus in the womb. It relates to the Sephirah Daath (Number 11) which remains in embryo form until later in life – thus remaining in line with Evolution and The Transcendent Octave.

NUMEROLOGY

3. Numerology is based on an idea proposed by Pythagoras around 500 BC that everything can be expressed in terms of numbers. It seems that modern mathematicians would agree. We note that this was at the beginning of The Age of Pisces [ASTROLOGY : THE ZODIAC AGES].
4. Numerology basically deals with numbers 1 to 9 (to which I add the recently discovered Number Zero). It can be demonstrated that each number has its own cycle which, in turn, has relationship with The Cycle Of Growth 12 Stages – so there is a comparison diagram for each one. Although there are some practical examples of the use of Numerology, the main focus here is on attempting to understand the archetypal nature of Numbers.
5. In recognising the cyclic nature of numbers, another important aid to understand them is to compare them with Astrological Aspects. In effect Numbers and Aspects divide the cycle/circle in the same way.

In terms of The Cycle of Growth, we have to note that each number can be considered as being involved in 2 separate cycles :-

1. Its position in the cycle of Number Zero to 9 which has 10 stages, and where each is related to the others. Although present, Number Zero disappears to nothing, as in The Cycle of Growth.
2. Its own cycle – so Number 1 has 1 "stage" and Number 9 has 9 stages. Wheels within wheels.

PLANETS

1. Numerologists describe relationships between numbers with variations between authorities. Despite the orderly progression of numbers their planetary association compared with their orbit positions in the Solar System are not. I have seen planetary associations ascribed to Henry Cornelius Agrippa (1486-1555), an early authority on the subject, which include Uranus and Neptune (as they do today). The planets were not discovered until 226 and 291 years after his death.
2. When we compare Numbers with the planetary associations of The Kabbalah Tree of Life and Evolution (et cetera) a more orderly, understandable picture emerges. This is not to suggest that there is anything wrong with Numerology in practice, only that the suggested basic archetypal spiritual motivations are incorrect. Although physical observations may be correct, we do not fully understand "Why ?".

THE KABBALAH TREE OF LIFE

1. We note that the Sephiroth at the top of The Tree contain the attributes of, and contain, those lower down, as does the progression of Numbers. This is an evolutionary progression from the simple to complex structures.
2. There is an overall description of the system in the chapter [THE KABBALAH TREE OF LIFE]. Here we go into more detail.
3. By combining the symbolism from our areas of study we can relate Number Zero to the Sephirah Kether, Crown at the top of The Tree. Until now The Tree of Life has had no relationship with the Numbers or Numerology.
4. In this chapter we can clearly see the relationship between the individual Sephiroth of The Tree of Life, Chakras, Planets, and Numbers – and therefore The Cycle of Growth. The main difference to our understanding of other systems is by having Sephirah 1 (Kether. Crown) relate to Number Zero, so Sephirah 2 relates to Number 1 – and so on. By so doing we can include the un-numbered Sephirah Daath (Will) to relate The Kabbalah Tree of Life to the 12 Stages of The Cycle of Growth, and therefore the 12 Stage Biblical Tree of Life as described in Revelation, which itself relates to The Zodiac.
5. The newly discovered planets Uranus, Neptune, and Pluto fit into 3 Sephiroth that previously had no planetary associations.
6. An important consideration is that traditional Kabbalism is concerned with the "Lightning Flash" of Evolution from Sephirah 1 (Kether. Crown) to Sephirah 10 (Malkuth. Kingdom. Earth). By comparing with The Cycle of Growth, which contains the Transcendent Octave, we can now see evidence of a "return journey" that enables the 10 Sephiroth to display the 12 Stages of the Tree of Life as it is described in The Bible.

NUMEROLOGY

NUMBER ZERO

1. Number Zero brings the 9 numbers of Numerology into The Decimal Age where there are 10 numbers.
2. We can see that one of the main issues is that Numerologists ignore Number Zero. It is a fact that Number Zero did not exist (in consciousness) in earlier times, and has evolved from merely being "nothing" in Greek and Egyptian times to becoming a number in its own right in the Computer "Age of Aquarius" and its connotations with Uranus and Jungian Individuation (which relates to Number 11). This is in accordance with a main principle of this book which treats "No – Thing" as being the source and container of everything else in our universe.
3. Number Zero is the state of the universe before the Big Bang.
4. We note that the Arabic numbers we use today did not exist until the 7th. or 8th. century AD, despite Mathematics having existed and developing for thousands of years prior to that. The Arabic numbers 0 (zero) to 9 gave birth to the 10 numbers of the decimal numbering system.
5. We also note that, despite a recent global tendency to convert the measurement of material objects and money to a decimal system (Number 10), the measurement of Time still depends on Number 12.
6. We note that the universe was created from Number Zero. The Book of Genesis shows that, as something materialised out of Primeval Chaos its complement materialised soon after. There was an "even-ing" at the end of each "day". This is a similar concept to that of Newton's "Every action has an equal and opposite reaction".

THE EVOLUTION OF NUMBERS

63. Zero is the original balanced state of the universe. The first manifestation is Number 1. This Number 1, by definition, is separate from Zero, and therefore cannot exist in the same dimension as Zero.
64. At the material level this equates with the appearance of Hydrogen, Atomic Number 1 which consists of a single positive Proton balanced with a single negative Electron in orbit. The orbit is said to form a "shell" around the nucleus. The tendency is for the single Electron to "seek" another Electron because its shell is unstable. A stable atomic shell requires 2 negative Electrons – each of which spin in opposite directions. A shell can contain only 2 Electrons, as atoms increase in size new shells are added. Each added Electron requires an additional Proton in the nucleus.
65. We therefore see an example of how, with the appearance of each new number, the universal balance is disturbed, so an "evening" is required at that level to maintain a Zero Balance. So from the "marriage" of Number Zero and Number 1 we get Number 2 –as depicted at the top of The Tree of Life.
66. With Number 2 the actual energy dynamics are $0 = 0 + (+1) + (-1)$ which maintains the Zero universal balance. Practically everyone can understand the complementary, binary relationship between Numbers 1 and 2 which refer to such things as Positive and Negative, White and Black, Masculine and Feminine, Force and Form. At this level we have the beginning of the Tree of Life Positive Pillar of Force and Negative Pillar of Form.
67. Atomic Number 2 refers to Helium which has 2 Electrons in its outer orbit.
68. The tendency is for the opposite polarities to attract and attempt to annihilate one another to regain the original Zero state of "Wholeness". As they are now separate manifestations in a different dimension (principally of Time) to the original this is not possible There is, however, a strong bond of relationship between them.
69. To further maintain the balance in any particular dimension the positive and negative forces retain their identity by "taking turns" and set up cycles of rotation as demonstrated by Electrons of an atom. This cycle of rotation has a specific speed, or frequency. When a cycle is complete the energy total is Zero.
70. The attraction between the polarities is a very real force that acts through Zero space, rather like Electromagnetism and Gravity. The attractive force is acting through the original "No-Thing" Number Zero "empty space" level, so, once again, a minor "Big Bang" occurs to produce another Singularity, which becomes Number 3.

NUMEROLOGY

71. Numbers 1 and 2 are balanced, so Number 3 once again produces its own imbalance, and requires "evening" to produce Number 4.

72. We have to remember that "Numbers" is an abstract mental concept that enables us to handle the complexity. There is no such "thing" as Number 1 or Number 2 etc. in Nature. Nonetheless, at that abstract level the concept does exist.

73. Each Stage of evolution creates ever increasing numbers, each of which receives an ever-reducing share of the total energy at their particular level. Or, put another way, creations further away from The Source require more energy to maintain their position – which results in a reduced cyclic frequency. There is also the effect of ever increasing distance to travel as the circumference of rotation increases proportionally to the distance from the Central Source.

74. The result is ever decreasing frequency cycles which eventually produced the material universe – which is a relative state of inertia. We are told by scientists that after The Big Bang the matter of the universe existed in a molten, high energy, state which gradually cooled and condensed over millions of years to produce the physical conditions we now know. According to the Laws of Thermodynamics, energy cannot be created or destroyed, and "Work is Heat, and Heat is Work", so all that energy must be doing something else nowadays. The physical bodies in the universe are moving away from one another. The universe is expanding.

75. Despite appearances, the material world is not solid. It consists of atoms which are in a continual state of motion. In matter, there is more space than the minute amount of material that makes up the "physical" parts of the atom (Protons, Neutrons, and Electrons etc.). Scientists today are considering the possibility of even smaller particles – "String Theory". Strings relate to Number 2 - which is a mathematical line of 1 Dimension (Length). We can get some sort of picture of that state by observing the heavenly bodies such as stars and planets, the space between which is huge in comparison to their physical size.

THE BINARY NUMBER SYSTEM

1. Nature and Computers count in multiples of 2.

2. It is said that we live in a 4 dimensional universe which consists of 3 Dimensions of Space and 1 Dimension of Time. This makes no recognition of our Mental and Spiritual dimensions which include our various mental consciousness levels, and The Unconscious. Scientists are beginning to realise that there are more (ref. Number Zero Quantum Physics, below).

3. Modern "String Theory" extends this to 10 Dimensions.

4. The Chemical Elements exist at Sephirah 10 (Malkuth. Kingdom. Earth) which is the bottom of The Tree of Life - the material world. Nonetheless they can give us an indication of the abstract Laws involved (As Above. So Below. As Below So Above). At the end of this chapter is a more detailed examination of how chemical elements evolve from simple Hydrogen atom, Atomic Number 1, to the heavier elements. Hydrogen consists of a single Proton nucleus orbited by a single Electron. Elements evolve by adding electrons to the outer "shell", and an equivalent number of protons to the nucleus. There can only be a maximum of 2 electrons in a shell, so additional pairs of electrons require additional shells.

5. When we examine the development of Binary Numbers we see a similar picture. Binary numbers consist of "Bits" which are electrical switches that can only exist in one of two states – Zero(Off) or 1 (On). This is not the same as Positive and Negative which are both "On". (We can say that "Off" refers to the Number Zero State of equilibrium). To get higher numbers requires additional Bits (which are like "shells"). When we compare this with other qualities of Numbers we see the development of different Dimensions. Each additional Bit adds another "Dimension" – and doubles the numbers that can be represented.

6. We therefore note that as numbers increase they become more solid, or material. Number Zero is Nothing.

The diagram below shows a 4 Bit system which can handle up to 16 numbers.

NUMEROLOGY

Decimal	4 BITS				Binary
	8	4	2	0	
0				0	0
1				1	1
2			1	0	10
3			1	1	11
4		1	0	0	100
5		1	0	1	101
6		1	1	0	110
7		1	1	1	111
8	1	0	0	0	1000
9	1	0	0	1	1001
10	1	0	1	0	1010
11	1	0	1	1	1011
12	1	1	0	0	1100
13	1	1	0	1	1101
14	1	1	1	0	1110
15	1	1	1	1	1111

Figure 74 : Numbers - Binary System

THE FIRST PRINCIPLES OF NUMBERS 1 TO 9

1. AS NUMBERS EVOLVE FROM ZERO THEY DEVELOP FROM SIMPLICITY TO COMPLEXITY.
2. NUMBERS DESCRIBE THE COURSE OF EVOLUTION FROM SIMPLE SINGLE CELL ORGANISMS TO GREATER COMPLEXITY AND DIVERSIFICATION.
3. AS NUMBERS INCREASE THEY LEAVE THE SPIRITUAL DIMENSION AND BECOME MORE MATERIAL. CHEMICAL ELEMENTS' ATOMIC WEIGHTS INCREASE.

Most Numerological texts suggest the opposite - that Number 9 is the most spiritual - which confuses material acquisition and increase of social power with spiritual development. Spiritual development ultimately regains relationship with Zero.

This is borne out when we examine the progression of numbers in the context of :-

1. The Cycle of Growth – with its descent of Spirit into ever more material realms and back. There is a diagram for each number comparing it with The Cycle of Growth.
2. Evolution, which begins at the simplest level and becomes more complex – as do numbers.
3. The Biblical story of Creation.
4. [THE KABBALAH TREE OF LIFE] consisting of 10 Sephiroth (which has its roots in Heaven). Sephirah 1 (Kether. Crown) at the top relates to Number Zero with Number 9 at the bottom.
5. The now accepted scientific fact of how the Chemical Elements evolved since the Big Bang, and are still evolving from basic Hydrogen in stars (including our own Sun). Hydrogen has Atomic Number 1 which is converted to heavier elements (ref. the end of this chapter).
6. The Numerological principle of distilling large numbers down to the smallest possible basic, or "elemental", 1 to 9.
7. The numbering and associations of [THE CHAKRAS]. There is a decreasing frequency of vibration from The Crown Chakra (Thousand Petal Lotus) and Root Chakra (4 Petal Lotus). The Chakras also relate to Number 7. We have to note that the normal method of numbering Chakras puts them in the reverse order to that of evolution. Chakra 7 relates to Number 1. This is part of the chapters [THE KABBALAH TREE OF LIFE] and [THE CHAKRAS].
8. Our modern access to concepts of Psychology and The Unconscious that were not available to the ancients. Everything in material existence begins as an abstract idea in the mind – which is Cycle of Growth Stage 9 (Conception). In the case of Genesis, this was the mind of God.
9. Evolution relates to "The Lightning Flash" of Kabbalism, and is the concern of "Magick" which brings things into manifestation. Spiritual development follows The Tree of Life back to its source, which is the concern of "Mysticism".
10. Mysticism is related to The Transcendent Octave of The Cycle of Growth.

NUMEROLOGY

THE NUMBERS

It is important to recognise that references to The Kabbalah Tree of Life are simplified here, in that each Sephirah actually exists in 4 Kingdoms which relate to Fire, Air, Water, and Earth. We have more detail in their relationship with [THE TAROT] Minor Arcana cards numbered 1 to 10.

NUMBER 0 (ZERO) – BINARY 0 – NEPTUNE

Number Zero has association with Neptune (Dissolution. Idealism. Service to Others). It has no association with The Cycle of Growth at the beginning of evolution other than being its source. It can be reached at Cycle of Growth Stage 12 (Withdrawal. Confinement) if the Transcendent Octave is activated and Neptune replaces Jupiter.

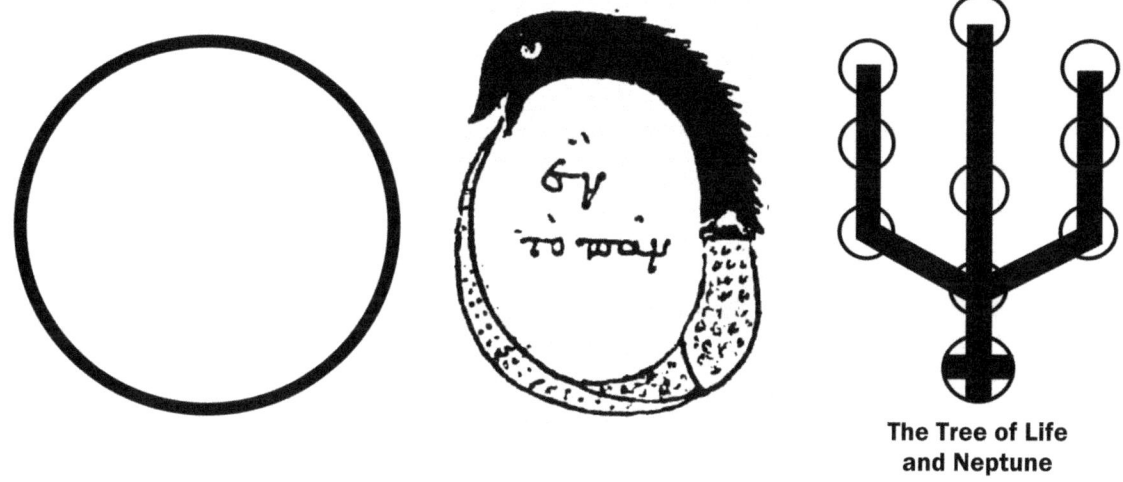

The Tree of Life and Neptune

Figure 75 : Numbers - Number Zero

1. Zero is a state of Entropy (Ref. Thermodynamics below).
2. We see from Quantum Physics (below) that Zero contains everything that is possible in a single state. Anything that follows is mere separation and analysis, which is called Evolution and Diversification. Evolution is from the Simple to the Complex.
3. None of the occult systems contain reference to Number Zero until now.
4. There was a time before Creation – which indicates that everything begins (in another Dimension) with an Idea, or mental construction – in the mind of God. "In the beginning was The Word".
5. On the Kabbalah Tree of Life, Zero is represented by Sephirah 1 (Kether. Crown) at the top of the Middle Pillar. On the Middle Pillar everything is in a state of equilibrium, or balance.
6. The planet related to Sephirah 1 (Kether. Crown) is Neptune, which is a symbolic representation of The Tree of Life with its 3 Pillars and Earth at the bottom. This is the first simple concept or plan in The Mind of God. Details are added later on.
7. Unlike Physics, which only deals with the Physical Level of Element Earth, The Tree of Life traces the original pure Spiritual Energy (Fire) through the process of Involution from Spiritual, to Mental (Air), to Emotional (Water) and finally to Physical (Earth) levels.
8. The Tree of Life is a structured representation of how basic energy changes form. In The Laws of Physics we have the 3 Laws of Thermodynamics which are entirely in accord with the overall concept of Evolution as described by The Tree of Life. The energy of The Big Bang which set Evolution in motion is still doing work today.
9. Although Number Zero was used by the ancient Greeks to denote "nothing", its use as an actual number in its own right in the decimal system is a relatively new invention introduced in India and developed by

the Arabs around the 7th. and 8th. Centuries AD [EB]. We may be able to translate Roman numbers to Arabic ones with zeros nowadays, but they did not exist in the earlier system. We can only guess what limitations this imposed on their ability to make calculations. We further note that Number Zero has gradually achieved greater recognition and status during recent years with the development of computers and computer programming.

10. Number Zero is no-thing, but contains everything else. A cell without a nucleus. A womb. An empty universe. Primeval Chaos. Plasma.
11. The numeric symbol 0 (zero) is one of the few that match its meaning.
12. The ancient "serpent" depiction of the Zero circle suggests a more dynamic system than the simpler image. Here we have connotations with the idea of Cycles, such as those contained in Astrology, or the orbits of electrons around a nucleus. The basic Cycle of Growth.
13. We have to recognise that the "birth" and history of Number Zero, with the invention of Arithmetic, is a fundamental step in development of human conscious and mental development. We can conceive and manipulate numbers far beyond the capabilities of our ancestors. There is an obvious correspondence with the arrival of The Age of Aquarius which is an Air Sign related to the Jungian Thinking Function – especially that of public Communication (Cycle of Growth Stage 11).
14. This is the birth of Arithmetic and the Decimal and Binary Mathematical Systems, and the later development of Computers – which use ONLY Zero and 1 in Binary Logic.
15. In modern times Zero has become a separate number in its own right.
16. Following the birth of Jesus it was possible to count years for the first time – and on a global basis. Other monotheistic religions that were born around the same time have attempted to use their methods and failed. This development of the Calendar is now used worldwide.
17. Number Zero does not exist in the counting of years. 1 BC is followed by 1 AD. In modern arithmetic, minus 1 is followed by Zero, then plus 1. This is another indication of the early ignore-ance of Zero.
18. Number Zero is an indication of a state before the "Big Bang" when no-thing was in existence. The first "thing" was a mental Number Zero in the "mind of God". "In the beginning was The Word" – that is, an Idea. The beginning of Form and Shape. No-one has considered where the Laws of Physics and Mathematics actually come from, they are merely accepted. The Laws of Physics already exist. We merely bring them to consciousness.
19. We have to recognise that Number Zero, although depicted as 2 Dimensional, is really a sphere made of nothing which contains no thing.
20. Number Zero still contains everything. It is the ever expanding Universe. Its "substance" fills the "space" between things.
21. An indication of this, apart from Astrology (which uses a 2 dimensional chart to indicate a spherical system) and other concepts, is that the first step in the evolution of a human body after the appearance of amino acids and other organic chemicals required the development of a hollow semi-permeable membrane. The membrane gradually developed into a very basic life form. A cell without a nucleus. The development required the presence of colloidal clay (dust or smoke particles) consisting of minute particles which are so small that they tend to remain suspended in a liquid rather than precipitate out. There is therefore a "spherical mould" surface on to which water and chemical molecules will be attracted to form a "shell" to become the hollow "blobs of jelly" that first showed indications of being independent life forms - called Eukaryotes.
22. Evolution theory therefore agrees with Genesis that man (or, more correctly, Adam's physical body) was created "from dust"
23. In the story of Creation, in Genesis Day Zero we are told there was Nothing. As Creation proceeds, at the end of each day (cycle of creation) there is an "Evening" when everything comes into balance again - so the sum total of everything remains at Zero. Perhaps this relates to the modern day concept of anti-matter being produced at the same time as matter. If they ever come together they will annihilate one another to revert to nothing.
24. This indicates that whenever something is created its complement ("opposite") must come into being too in order to maintain a Zero Balance. The equation is $0 = 0 +(+ 1) + (-1)$. This is related to "The Butterfly Effect" of Physics where the movement of the wings of a butterfly can be partially instrumental

in changing the path of a tornado. At the early stages (when there is an infinite number of final possibilities), small amounts of energy can eventually produce big effects.

25. Even though everything comes from Zero, we are still contained in Zero. There is much still to discover.
26. After Zero, life becomes increasingly more complicated.

THERMODYNAMICS AND ENTROPY

1. Entropy is disordered energy. It has no directional "flow". It can therefore do no work.
2. In The Kabbalah, Number Zero refers to Sephirah 1 (Kether. Crown) as the source of every-thing. However, it is in a state if inertia. The energy is disorganised. There is no movement until the initiating , directional, force of the Number 1 Big Bang. Scientists have realised that Entropy was the original state of the universe, and that the universe will eventually revert back to that state in a great cyclic process lasting eons of time.
3. Scientists state that the expansion of the universe is related to our concept of Time, and its direction. If the universe started to contract, Time would run backwards.
4. Unlike Physics, which only deals with the Physical Level of Element Earth, The Tree of Life traces the original pure Spiritual Energy (Fire) through the process of Involution from Spiritual, to Mental (Air), to Emotional (Water) and finally to Physical (Earth) levels.
5. The Tree of Life is a structured representation of how basic energy changes form.
6. In The Laws of Physics we have the 3 Laws of Thermodynamics which are entirely in accord with the overall concept of Evolution as described by The Tree of Life. The energy of The Big Bang which set Evolution in motion is still doing work.

1. THE FIRST LAW OF THERMODYNAMICS – *concerned with Conservation of Energy - is encapsulated in the term "Heat is Work and Work is Heat" as manifestations of a single force. It states that the total amount of energy in a system (which can be the universe or some other device) is constant, and that energy cannot be created or destroyed – although it can change into various different forms. For example, in a steam engine the locked up energy contained in coal or wood (which were produced at some earlier stage of evolution) is released by reaction with Oxygen and converted, in turn, to steam energy, and then mechanical energy. At each level there is a heat loss due to friction (wasted energy reverting to Entropy without doing any work). Eventually all the energy produced becomes useless entropy.*

2. THE SECOND LAW OF THERMODYNAMICS – *is concerned with Ordered Energy (Work) and Disordered Energy (Entropy). Although energy is never "used up" it is only useful when ordered in some system of flow. Flow requires a disordered state with areas of high energy and low energy. After that it reverts to a useless disordered state called Entropy. The Second Law states that the Entropy of a system always increases or remains constant. In our example of a steam engine, the now useless ash of the fire is representative of Entropy. The heat energy developed and converted into different forms by the process has done its work and converts back to heat which is dissipated as disordered energy into the outer universe. Another example is when we boil a kettle of water and allow it to cool. The temperature of the water in the kettle does some work in heating and circulating air around it, but ceases when the temperatures equalise.*

3. THE THIRD LAW OF THERMODYNAMICS *states that the Entropy of a system approaches a constant value as the temperature approaches absolute zero (minus 273 degrees Centigrade).*

PLASMA

Plasma is one of the 4 States of Matter that correspond with The 4 Elements – in descending order of temperature – Plasma (Fire), Gas (Air), Liquid (Water), Solid (Earth).

In today's universe, this is the stuff that stars are made of (including our own Sun, which is also creating elements from Hydrogen but at a slower rate), and accounts for 99% of the mass in the universe (leaving just 1% for everything else). It consists of superheated gas – mainly hydrogen and helium - at such extremely high temperature that the molecules move around in entirely random fashion – without form.

With Number Zero (Sephirah 1. Crown) nothing is being produced. However, we can see how the production of Hydrogen (the first sign of imbalance) refers to The Kabbalah's Sephirah 2 (Chockmah. Force. Pluto. Number 1) the energy of which drives The Tree of Life and the universe.

NUMEROLOGY

QUANTUM PHYSICS

This is an example of how modern science is learning yet more about Number Zero.

Here we are dealing with the cutting edge of modern day Science. With Number Zero we are in the realm of Quantum Physics which deals with matter in its most microscopic, basic form – the particles that make up atoms – that is, until "String Theory" (ref. Number 2) developed.

1. It is suggested that Quantum Mechanics deals with a dimension of our universe other than the one in which we exist. As students of Zero we understand this better.
2. At atomic level movement of particles is entirely "random" (which, as History shows, probably just means that the Laws have not yet been discovered).
3. Quanta are small units of energy.
4. Matter can only absorb or emit energy in small units (Quanta).
5. "The Uncertainty Principle" states that the position and momentum of a subatomic particle cannot be measured at the same time. The different methods of observation required interfere with the results. (Observation, such as by using Light which itself consists of minute particles – Photons - affects the other particles and changes the results). The results of an experiment are usually expressed as a percentage of possibility ("certainty") that the answer is correct.
6. Particles appear and disappear at random.
7. A particle can appear in several places at once !

QUANTUM COMPUTERS – USING "INTUITION" INSTEAD OF "THINKING"

We can see this as computers beginning to use the Jungian Intuition Function (Fire Element) rather than the Binary Rational Thinking Function.

1. At present most computers work using Binary logic (Number 2) where a "Bit" can represent either 1 or Zero, but, for around 30 years experimental computers have appeared that use Quantum Mechanics. The basic reason for this is that they are much faster and can deal with bigger numbers. At the time of writing this in 2014 the technology is mainly being driven by the need to encrypt data on the Internet by using numbers which have thousands of digits. Hackers are finding it relatively easy to break into systems using Binary Logic.
2. In a Quantum Computer 0 (Zero) = 1
3. There are no linear calculations.
4. Quantum Bits can represent more than one thing at a time – which means that all possible results of a computation are available at one and the same time.
5. In common with Intuition and its related Fire Element, Quantum Computer chips generate a lot of heat – so cooling down to almost Absolute Zero temperature is required – that is around minus 460 degrees Fahrenheit.

CYCLE OF GROWTH STAGE ZERO AND STAGE 12 (WITHDRAWAL)

Number Zero does not explicitly appear in The Cycle of Growth because, in effect, it is its source – as of everything else. The Cycle of Growth begins at Stage 9 (Conception. Number 1. Sephirah 2) which is related to Pluto as the beginning of the evolutionary Lightning Flash of Kabbalism which eventually creates the 10 Sephiroth as a result of The Big Bang.

As we see here, Number Zero has remained invisible since then and is only beginning to appear in our imagination, and practically, during relatively recent years. Part of its "materialisation" is due to the birth of Jesus, the advances in science which brought about the discovery of Neptune, and The Collective Unconscious, to which its energy relates. At base level, its nature is as an attempt to draw everything back to its former state of Entropy where everything was one. So everything, once again, becomes part of a Collective. However, if there was an original purpose, it is suggested that we humans arrive back in The Collective (infinite consciousness) with conscious self-awareness (Ego) and Will (focused consciousness).

It is really from the association with Neptune, The 12th. House, the 12th. Zodiac Sign of Pisces, and Cycle of Growth Stage 12 that we are able to understand it better.

NUMEROLOGY

Number Zero and Neptune (Dissolution) are concerned with "Ideals" (which are not necessarily practical, or tend to be degraded as they become practical).

Not wishing to repeat too much of what appears elsewhere in this book, suffice to say that we arrive at Cycle of Growth Stage 12 at the level of Jupiter or Neptune. With Jupiter acting at Cycle of Growth Stage 9 (Conception) we merely repeat and expand on what already exists. If Pluto operates at Cycle of Growth Stage 9 instead, and we develop Uranus to overcome Saturn at Cycle of Growth Stages 10 and 11, we have an opportunity to make connection, once again, with The Original Source.

NUMBER 1 – BINARY 1 - PLUTO

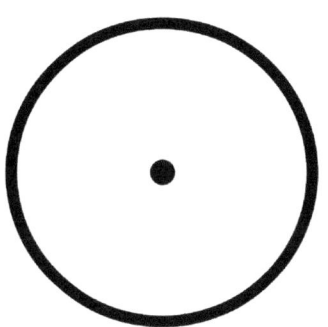

Figure 76 : Numbers - Number 1

1. In Mathematics, a single point has no Dimensions. There is only a single possible permutation of Number 1, so life is relatively simple at this level.
2. We have the First Dimension of the Binary Number System. A single Bit which can represent Zero or 1.
3. This also equates to a single positively charged Proton and negatively charged Electron to form atoms of the first of the chemical elements – Hydrogen. We see here that the orbit of the Electron comes first (Number Zero) followed by the appearance of the Positive Proton (Number 1) at the centre. This fits with The Kabbalah when Sephirah 3 (Binah. Form) follows Sephirah 2 (Chockmah. Force).
4. Number 1 is common to all number groups, the difference being the proportion of influence it has over the whole. With Number 2, for example, it is 50%, and reduces as numbers increase. In Numerology, Number 1, in common with all other odd numbers, is a masculine, positive energy.
5. In The Kabbalah, Number 1 refers to Sephirah 2 (Chockmah. Wisdom. Force. Father) which appears at the top of The Pillar of Mercy (Force). Positive Polarity. This is the prime source of masculine motivational energy which powers the whole Tree of Life. It is The Big Bang of Physics. Chockmah contains the energy of all the Zodiac Signs in undifferentiated form. It is a phallic symbol – full of potential energy that needs something to work on to realise its potential.
6. Number 1 (Sephirah 2) is "The Father" of The Holy Trinity.
7. In Dion Fortune's "Cosmic Doctrine" [DFCD] she describes Chockmah(Wisdom, Force. Number 1) as "the desire of Space (Kether. Crown. Zero) for motion". She states that "the desire of space for inertia" pre-existed, and re- appears (in more conscious form) as a separate, still resistant, force in the next Sephirah 3 (Binah. Understanding. Number 2).
8. This matches the Genesis Creation story where Light (Consciousness. Positive) appears from Darkness (which was therefore the initial state of the universe) to produce Day – and (conscious recognition of) Darkness becomes Night (Number 2. Negative. Unconsciousness). We have the beginning of cyclic activity from combination of Force and Form which cannot re-unite, and therefore have to "take turns" through Time to regain a zero balance.

NUMEROLOGY

9. *Chockmah and Number 1 refer to the planet Pluto (Regeneration) which is basically a symbol of Transformation, Metamorphosis, and Nuclear Reaction.*
10. *In the Chinese I Ching (Book of Changes) [IC] the first hexagram is called "The Creative" consisting solely of Yang force which relates to the Fire Element as bringer and motivator of all life. We note that, there too, Number Zero is not recognised.*
11. *Relating to The Tarot, apart from minor cards numbered 2, Chockmah contains all the Wands Suit (Fire). It also contains all the Signs of The Zodiac in undifferentiated form.*
12. *Our numeric symbol "I" is a phallic symbol - an erect penis, full of potential but not yet having a creative release, and denotes simple singularity of purpose.*
13. *The first lesson in life is learning how to "look after Number One" – that is simple survival lower down The Tree.*
14. *The impetus supplied by The Big Bang is still keeping our universe expanding and scientists say that this also brings about our conception of Time. If the universe were to contract at some later date, Time would run backward.*

CYCLE OF GROWTH STAGE 9 (CONCEPTION)

Cycle of Growth Stage 9 is ruled by Pluto at the beginning of Evolution and The Big Bang. The "Lightning Flash" of The Kabbalah begins at Sephirah 2 (Chockmah. Force. Pluto). Thereafter the Stage is ruled by Jupiter at Sephirah 4 (Chesed. Mercy. Jupiter) unless the Transcendent Octave is activated. It is mentioned below at that level. Sephirah 4 is just below Sephirah 2 on The Tree of Life – so it is a lower manifestation of Force on The Pillar of Force.

Stage 9 relates to Sagittarius (Mutable, Changeable, Fire) which is Fire in its most unstable state. Its traditional ruler is Jupiter (Expansion. Growth) which expands what is already in existence. To bring about Creation of something new requires a more fundamental Nuclear Reaction (Pluto).

At the level of the original Big Bang automatic archetypal level Stage 9 (Conception) is controlled by Pluto (Regeneration. Sexual Orgasm) at Sephirah 2. (Chockmah. Force). However, once Free Will begins to operate, the tendency is for Stage 9 Conception to only reach as high as Sephiroth 4 (Chesed. Mercy. Jupiter) – which, incidentally, is just at the edge of The Abyss.

The Associated Tarot Card is XIV.Temperance which depicts the "Spirit of God fluttering on the face of the waters" of Genesis [YLT] which resulted in the creation of Light (Consciousness).

NUMEROLOGY

From The Kabbalah we see that the prime motivational factor of Number 1 is to express energy and power, which is entirely in accord with the interpretation of Numerology. In Numerology this is related to The Sun, the symbol of which is the same as the image here. However, as we will see, although there is a similar expression of Nuclear Energy, the "physical" Sun appears much further down The Tree of Life at Sephirah 6 (Tiphareth. Beauty), and is more concerned with development of Ego Consciousness at Cycle of Growth Stage 5 (Power) at Erikson's School Age from Age 7 onwards . At this level we only have the idea, or concept, of a POTENTIAL physical Sun which (eventually) contains more differentiated forms of energy, as well as having orbiting satellites.

As described below, Numerology adds the numbers making up our date of birth to produce a result between 1 to 9 which is described (by most authorities) as representing our "Life Path". In theory this should relate to our Zodiac Sun Sign, but, from the examples below, we see that this is not the case. I have added some random examples of Life Paths of famous people for each Number.

The following examples of famous Life Path 1 do show some sense of being "Number 1" as pioneers in their fields. Billy Graham (Evangelist. Scorpio), Karl Marx (Revolutionary. Taurus), Little Richard (Rock Star. Sagittarius), Roy Rogers (film and television cowboy. Scorpio), Ringo Starr (Beatles drummer. Cancer), Martin Luther King Jr. (Civil Rights. Aries), George Washington (first United States President. Pisces), Mother Teresa (Missionary. Virgo)

OTHER ASSOCIATIONS

1. The image is the basis of an Astrological Chart with a point at the centre.

NUMEROLOGY

2. In the Genesis story of Creation Day Zero we are told that "God PREPARED [YLT] Heaven and Earth", but there was no actual manifestation ("*And the earth was without form, and void*"). Earth (still as an idea) does not actually appear until Creation Day 3. So this stage is an ABSTRACT IDEA, or "Immaculate Conception", of what is to come. This is emphasised in Verse 2 "*And the Spirit of God moved upon the face of the waters*". As there were no actual waters we can take this to refer to the No-thing of Space (which is therefore not quite nothing), or The Collective Unconscious ("Darkness"). The only manifestation in Day 1 was Light from Darkness (which was, by definition, already there) ("*and God divided the light from the darkness*"). So we have, from the recognition of "darkness", the creation of its "opposite", and a dawning of Consciousness. Now having created two mental concepts they were able to be named "Day and Night". There is no actual visible Light yet – which does not actually appear until Day 4 with the creation of the stars and our Sun, so we can safely assume that this means "Consciousness". We note that the creation of this, and the following pairs of "opposites" is followed by an "evening". ("*And the evening and the morning were the first day*"). There can be no actual daytime evening or morning because days are only now being invented. So we have a balancing process. "The Opposites" learn to survive through co-operation and "taking turns".

3. In Mathematics, Number 1 is a point with no dimensions. In Physics it is a Photon – a sub-atomic elemental particle of energy which gives rise to light and other electromagnetic radiation. It has zero mass. It is still a mystery that, depending on the method of observation, it can appear to be either a particle or a wave. Photons can appear to be in more than one place at the same time.

4. Having created something out of nothing, Number 1 is the first conscious perception of a beneficent, all powerful, life-giving God (Chockmah. Force. Love. Light. Consciousness).

5. This could be an image of an atom of Hydrogen, an egg fertilised by a sperm, a child in the womb, an egg, or a plant seed.

6. In scientific terms, The Big Bang, Number 1, was the development of a Singularity which contained all the matter present in the universe today. All material objects contain more space than matter – as does the universe. If the diagram above were to scale, with the central nucleus the same size as in the diagram, the electron orbit sphere would need to be nearer the size of St. Paul's Cathedral in London. The electron size would approximate that of an almost invisible speck of dust.

7. In the image, the Singularity of The Big Bang is contained in Number Zero, albeit in more material form.

8. Perhaps Space (Zero) is more solid than matter. It supports and keeps in place all other objects, such as atoms, and suns and planets. It suggests that matter is evolved by a form of "condensation" as from a gas to liquid, and then solid, state.

9. Hydrogen is the basis of all Chemical elements. The circle of Number One is the image of a Hydrogen Atom, and symbol of The Sun (the nuclear reaction of which is still changing Hydrogen into heavier elements).

10. After the Big Bang the first element formed was Hydrogen, which consists of one positively charged proton nucleus orbited by one negatively charged electron – so the Number One image above is also a 2 dimensional represent of a Hydrogen atom. Does the path of an electron exist ? Zero suggests that it preceded the Singularity. All other elements developed from Hydrogen, which is the lightest element. Like the Big Bang in "slow motion" our Sun mainly consists of Hydrogen which is being converted to Helium, the second lightest element, which will, in turn, convert to heavier elements. The atomic reaction of The Sun releases a large amount of energy, as did The Big Bang.

11. Einstein proved that Energy and Mass are the same "thing". $E = MC^2$

12. In terms of biological evolution it is the development of a cell containing a nucleus. It is suggested that it began with one Eukaryote, cell without a nucleus (Zero), accidentally swallowing another. Wheels within wheels. We are now in the realm of bacteria and mono-cellular plants such as algae.

13. In Astrology this is the Conjunction Aspect where two or more planets are in close proximity and therefore their energies combine.

14. The structure of Astrological Charts is very similar to that of an atom with a central nucleus (here invisible) and several orbiting "electrons" (planets). There are several concentric circles – the Inner Circle (Relating to Zero, wherein the various planetary aspects operate), the Circle of Personal Houses (a depiction of Earth in human form), the concentric circles of the orbiting planets in their birth positions,

NUMEROLOGY

the concentric circles of the generic Transiting planets, and finally the outer circle of The Zodiac Signs of the outer universe which gives a structure to the whole. All levels inter-penetrate one another.

15. Many Astrologers fail to take the central point of a chart into account. It is the Singularity that contains, and is the source of, everything else. All energies act at this point. The outer circular orbits are physical representations (shells) as of chemical elements (below).

16. Perhaps this is also an image of a Black Hole in space where matter is condensed back into a singularity (?) – and disappears into no-thing. The completion of a cycle is symbolised by Cycle of Growth Stage 12 (Withdrawal) where things return to The Collective Zero in preparation for rebirth.

17. In evolutionary terms, this is the first spark of consciousness. Even the hydrogen atom or single cells of matter can be considered as having a very basic form of consciousness, or "intelligence" as they are part of, and contain, their own repeating natural Cycles – or follow the Laws of Physics, as do we.

18. We note in Genesis Chapter 1 that Naming is a very important necessity. That is, an equivalent mental structure to a physical object. Before Creation began was "The Word" ("God"). In the first 7 days God did the naming job. In Chapter 2 it was delegated to Adam. We now know that the mental "Idea" always precedes the creation of some thing.

19. We have a similar story in Greek Mythology where Gaea (Earth) emerged from the primeval Chaos and gave birth to Uranus (Heaven). As they were the only "beings" at the time they mated to produce the Titans, Cyclopes, and Hecatoncheires. The beginnings of Mythology and the numerous Gods . It is notable that the gods were continually in conflict with one another – especially with oedipal father/son rivalry. We can compare their activities with those of the chemical elements which "mate" positive and negative ions to form compounds, which can separate to produce new compounds with other "mates". The planets are named after Greek gods, and Astrology has great concern with their relationships with one another.

NUMBER 2 – BINARY 10 – SATURN

Number 2 refers to Saturn which traditionally rules Stage 10 of The Cycle of Growth (Peak. Harvest. Capricorn. Cardinal Earth) and Stage 11 (Discontent). The latter can be ruled by Uranus (Individualisation. Individuation) by use of Will.

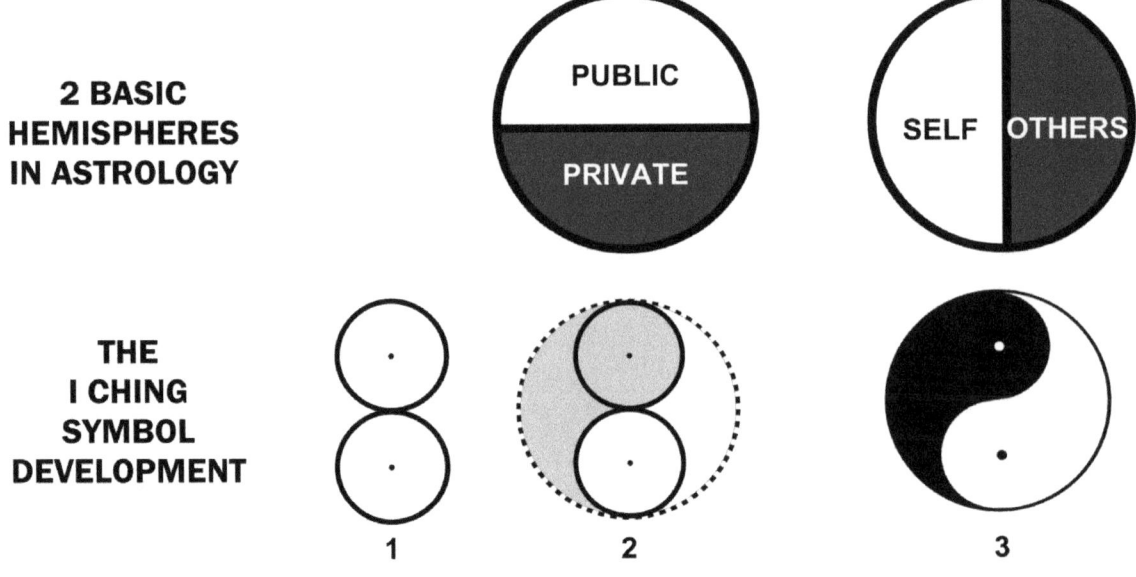

Figure 77 : Numbers - Number 2

NUMEROLOGY

1. With Number 2 the "Irresistible Force" of Number 1 meets "The Immovable Object".
2. The first evolutionary method of reproduction was by cell division where a single bacterium divided to produce an additional identical clone of itself. This method still continues today. It is notable that this earliest of life forms still exists today.
3. According to universal law, having created some thing out of nothing the complement of some thing must appear to maintain the universal balance at Zero. So we have the equation $0 = 0 + (+1) + (-1)$.
4. Dion Fortune [DFCD] states that after the formation of the first cycle which produced the universe, a second cycle developed at right angles to it. We can see this depicted in the hemispheres of an Astrological Chart (which is actually a sphere) and Number 4.
5. Mathematically, we now have a LINE developed by the appearance of a second point and the creation of a new Dimension – Length. (Or is this the existence of a point through the 4th. Dimension of Space-Time ?)
6. At this level we have the "String Theory" of Physics where the particles (or Number 1 Zero dimensional Points) are replaced by 1 dimensional Strings (lines ?) of energy as the basic "building blocks" of the universe. The strings can be formed into loops. Like Photons there are 2 observable forms – in this case Photons or Electrons. Another quality is that they can act like particles carrying the force of Gravity ("Gravitons") – so we can see the connections with Binah (Form. Gravity) and Number 2. A further development is that the theory only "works" mathematically if there are 10 Dimensions of Space-Time. We can see from our study of the 10 Sephiroth of The Tree of Life that scientists are on the right track. However they do seem to be going in the wrong direction. Instead of the classic route of travelling down The Tree into greater complexity they need to study the simplicity of the more modern Number Zero prime source– which is also the practice of Mysticism.
7. We now have slightly more complexity in that there are 2 possible permutations of 2 numbers – 1,2 or 2,1. The First Dilemma.
8. In The Kabbalah, Number 2 refers to Sephirah 3 (Binah. Understanding) where it is in overall control of The Pillar of Severity (Form). Negative Polarity. Its basic state of existence is inertia, but it is now forced to move. Binah is "The Bringer of Form" and, as such, is related to Motherhood.
9. At this archetypal level it also includes concepts of Feminine, Negative Polarity and resistance to the positive "God Force" – and therefore has connotations with The Devil, and Evil. "The Fallen Angel".
10. With Chockmah and Binah we have a depiction of "God and The Devil" – which, we note, is a product of, and adds up to, Zero. The Devil is concerned with material goals. We note that, at this level, so is God, who decided to create the universe. The Ideal of Sephirah 1 (Kether. Neptune. Number Zero) is beginning to change into a more practical form.
11. The related Number 2 planet is Saturn/Satan (Consolidation) which requires no further comment.
12. Binary Number 2 requires an addition Bit (shell/space) which, because of Zero, actually allows 4 numbers – 0,1,2,3.

CYCLE OF GROWTH STAGE 10 (PEAK. HARVEST)

Following Conception we have the embryo development of a new Consciousness. In the calendar year this is the time of the Winter Solstice and Rebirth of The SUN/SON (Jesus) celebrated by all religions since the beginning, and finally resulting in Christmas.

As a symbol of the challenge of Sephirah 3 (Form. Saturn) to the energy of Sephirah 2 (Force. Pluto) we have a repetition of the recurring story theme of Mythology where the father or other existing authorities attempt to kill the new-born because the child, to them, seemingly represents a challenge to their established authority. At another level this is the challenge of authority figures - internal and external - to any new ideas - an example is of how Religion has historically hindered scientific progress and attempted to destroy "non- believers" by force. Examples are The Crusades on behalf of Christians, and even today we have another version in the Muslim Jehads. It is a strange paradox that the religions of the world contain aspects of The Devil.

As a source of new ideas, I expect that many will reject the contents of this book without bothering to try to understand it.

NUMEROLOGY

Referring to Capricorn (Cardinal, Active Earth. Ambition. Long Range Plans) and Saturn/Satan (Consolidation) and Tarot Cards XV.THE DEVIL and XVI.THE (lightning struck) TOWER we see from the creation of Light at Sephirah 2 that (consciousness of) Darkness appears as a natural result of the universal need for equilibrium and balance (total Zero). We have the appearance of Day and Night where the light and dark forces "take turns" in an effort to re-unite - despite now being separated by time and space. So we have the beginning of cyclic activity.

We also have the beginning of "The Lightning Flash" of The Kabbalah, which creates the other Sephiroth lower down The Tree. It would seem that matters eventually got out of God's control with the achievement of unexpected and unwanted results. We are all aware of how the idealism of our original concepts is modified when we try to put them into practice.

It would seem that recognition of day and night is the first level of consciousness. Even plants have it at a rudimentary level.

CYCLE OF GROWTH STAGE 11 (DISCONTENT. INDIVIDUATION)

At the beginning of Evolution the un-numbered Sephirah Daath (Uranus) is not developed, so it is bypassed by The Lightning Flash – which therefore remains under the control of Saturn at Sephirah 3 (Binah. Number 2) so energy goes to Sephirah 4 (Chesed. Jupiter. Number 3). It takes an act of human Will to activate Uranus, as described below, and elsewhere in this book.

1. In Numerology terms, the beginning of Evolution this Stage is also controlled by Number 2 (1+1). It does not become Number 11 until we reach the Transcendent Octave. It is where The Lightning Flash crosses the traditionally un-numbered Sephirah Daath (Will). Here it is in "embryo" form.
2. Daath is the "bridge" which crosses The Abyss separating the 3 Supernal Sephiroth from all the others.
3. Without human Will, the Stage is under the control of Saturn via Sephirah 3 (Binah. Form. Number 2). The Laws of Physics.
4. This stage begins with Creation Day 2 of Genesis and the "separation of waters" to make an "expanse" which became "Heavens (Sky), and ends with Day 6 and the final evolution of "man and woman" – albeit not in physical form until Adam appears in Cycle of Growth Stage 1 (Seed).
5. Stage 11 relates to the Sign of Aquarius (Fixed Air. Earth's atmosphere) which has 2 related planets. Aquarius is concerned with Invention and Rebellion against authority. The traditional ruling planet, Saturn/Satan applies at the beginning of Evolution with the 1st. Octave "Lightning flash" of incarnation/evolution when there is no Free Will or conscious choice.
6. The corresponding Tarot Cards at this stage are XVII.THE STAR and XVIII.THE MOON.

NUMEROLOGY

Numerology does conform to the description of this Stage by treating Number 11 as a special number with 2 possibilities. It is given a "dual personality" - as a number in its own right, or being reduced to Number 2 (1 + 1) - Saturn. There is a suggestion of decision or choice whether to follow a Number 2 Path or Number 11 Path – which we can relate to Saturn (Tradition. Repetition) or Uranus (Transcendence. Individuation)

In Numerology, the interpretation of Number 2 is in accordance with the meaning stated here which refers to the basic concept of Motherhood as Bringer of Form. Again, although the association with The Moon (including its relationship with the Subconscious Mind) contains similar symbolism, it is much further down The Tree.

The name "Jesus" equates to Number 2 and therefore Saturn/Satan. Other famous Life Path 2 people include Joseph Haydn (composer. Gemini), Bob Hope (Comedian. Gemini), Elvis Presley (Rock Star. Capricorn), Thomas Moore (Henry VIII Chancellor. Aquarius), Benjamin Spock (Psychology. Child care book. Taurus), Noah Webster (Dictionary. Virgo).

OTHER ASSOCIATIONS

1. The first 2 diagrams above show the basic division of an Astrological chart into 2 sets of 2 hemispheres. The vertical division hemispheres are concerned with "Self versus Others", the horizontal division ones with "Public versus Private" matters. We can see how the hemispheres combine to make Number 4, below, by sharing the same space.
2. This can be compared with the idea of "spin" of an electron which can be in one of 2 directions.

NUMEROLOGY

3. The second set with 3 diagrams shows the development of the I Ching symbol, which is similar in meaning to the Jungian "resolution of opposites" . It begins with the duality of 2 points/circles. When one considers them to be combined within the whole, there is in reality no separation. Each "opposite" cannot exist on its own because it can only be consciously recognised in terms of the other. Each therefore contains a "seed" of the other. It is this last detail that is often missed in the depiction of the I Ching image. The symbolic point of this missing detail is that many people can only see "Black or White", rather than shades of Grey (Sephirah 1.Number Zero). The arrival at the latter state involves spending much time and effort in investigating facts, and is the root of our legal and judicial system. The result is a linear "sliding scale" of possibilities – but within limits.

4. In the I Ching the Kabbalist Tree of Life Sephirah 3 (Binah. Understanding. Mother. Number 2) is represented by Hexagram Number 2 "The Receptive" which is wholly made up of feminine Yang lines and has identical meaning.

5. Binah is at the top of, and has overall control of, The Pillar of Severity (Form).

6. With the addition of another Positive Proton and Negative Electron (which balance to Zero force) Hydrogen becomes Helium.

7. Like computers with Zero and 1, Nature can only "count" up to 2. At the end of the chapter we see the process in the Evolution of Chemical Elements, where "shells" can contain only 1 or 2 electrons (which rotate in opposite directions). Heavier elements require more shells. So we have a material representation of how Number 2 controls the evolution of Form. (The first concept of a shell appears with Number Zero, but it does not begin to take form until movement of Number 1 produces cyclic movement in Number 2). All this activity maintains the ultimate Zero balance of the universe.

8. Still in Creation Day 1, having created Light and Dark we are now in a position to observe them in consciousness. Whereas they were originally Binary Zero (Darkness. Nothing. Off. Unconscious. Grey) and 1 (Light. On. Conscious) they now take on polarised energies to become Negative and Positive. Electrons and Protons.

9. In Boolean mathematical terms, numbers that are "NOT odd" now become "Even" (Odd came first). Zero is neutral.

10. It is a natural law that if something is created its complement ("opposite") comes into manifestation too. For example - Matter and Anti-Matter, God and The Devil, Conscious and Unconscious, The Atomic Bomb and "Ban the Bomb". This maintains the original balance of Zero. The tendency is for "opposites" to attract one another in an attempt at mutual destruction to achieve the original balanced, neutral, dead, state of the universe (Entropy). In the Genesis story of Creation each stage consisted of a "Morning" (Sun rise. creation. birth) and "Evening" (balancing) – as occurs every calendar day in modern times with the balancing of Light and Dark, Consciousness (waking) and Unconsciousness (sleeping).

11. This also refers to the "dawning" of new consciousness at every level.

12. If The Cycle of Growth did not exist, "The Opposites" would annihilate one another, and return to the Zero state of Chaos. They co-operate by "taking turns".

13. An Atomic Number 1 Hydrogen Atom, like those of some other elements such as Oxygen, cannot exist in a single free (un-combined) state. It can only exist as one of a pair, which together form a molecule of gas.

14. In Astrology this relates to the Opposition Aspect where two or more planets are on opposite sides of a chart making an angle of 180 degrees at the centre. That usually puts them into complementary Signs of different Elements of the same polarity, positive or negative. Their energies draw into different directions. Like polarities repel one another.

15. The Opposition ("Full Moon") aspect is an indication of an opportunity to learn objectivity about matters relating to its components from the continual need to consider the alternatives they offer. The Opposition brings a form of higher consciousness by continually bringing its complementary components to conscious awareness – to recombine them as a single conception. There are examples in the birth charts of Freud and Jung in [ASTROLOGY : SYNASTRY].

16. Oppositions are 2 ends of the same Scale or Line. A scale of measurement. Black and White produce intermediate shades of Grey. Grey existed before the creation of Black and White.

17. The Opposition Aspect refers to Cycle of Growth Stage 7 (Partnership).

NUMEROLOGY

18. The first diagram of the second set shows the next stage of evolution from a Number One single cell. This is Mitosis, where a single cell grows to the maximum size which its inner growth processes can support. To grow further it must divide into two. The first thing that happens is that the nucleus divides into 2 "poles", then the cell wall stretches around them, and finally splits. We have to note that cell division doubles the number each time, so we get 1, 2, 4, 8, 16 ..... and so on. However, there is no Diversification - only clones – exact replicas.

19. In considering the development of heavier elements from the original Hydrogen gas, we have arrived at Helium gas which has Atomic Number 2 and is the second lightest element. Having 2 electrons in its outer shell, it is much less reactive than Hydrogen, which is why it is used to fill balloons. Elements develop by keeping to the basic structure of Hydrogen with a central nucleus and orbiting electrons. They "grow" by adding positive Protons and neutral Neutrons to the nucleus, and adding negative orbiting Electrons to balance the positive charge of the Protons. (Actually, by observing Zero, we know that the Electrons' orbits come first). Helium has 2 Neutrons, 2 Protons and 2 Electrons. We are progressing from a simple original state to greater complexity.

20. In development of animal and human consciousness there is now recognition of day and night, and perhaps the varying phases of The Moon, but months, seasons, and years are still a long way off. In terms of development of a new born child, after the easy life in the womb (Zero) the first awareness experiences are based on binary Comfort and Discomfort. Perhaps this evolutionary urge is always our main motivator in our life.

21. In mathematics it requires 2 points to determine a straight line. Considering that there are, as yet, no dimensions there are infinite possibilities for the arrangement – but now with some restrictions. In 2 dimensions the line connects the centre of a circle with any point on its circumference. In 3 dimensions the line connects the centre of a sphere with any point on its surface.

22. The line adjoining 2 points eventually takes on an existence of its own.

23. A line has only one Dimension – Length. When, as here, Force meets Form, rather than acting in a straight line according to its nature, Force will be deflected slightly from its attempts to make a straight path. Over eons of time its curved path will eventually make a circle and return to its place of birth. There are no straight lines in Nature.

24. We can also see how the creation of a single line produces a separation in the circle of a Birth Chart. One example is called the "Horizon", which, like our mathematical line, has no dimensions. There is no such thing as a physical horizon – which is an illusion. The contents of the circle were originally homogeneous, but they are now divided into 2 parts that are clearly different. The result of another "evening". Here we take note of the fact that our interpretation of the diagrams is entirely in our mind. They are actually marks on a piece of paper.

25. We have a scenario here that depicts what occurs in our minds when we are making a decision. If I think of some possible course of action my mind immediately presents me with conflicting ideas. C G Jung states the action of The Unconscious is "compensatory to our conscious aims". Any action I take leads to a temporary imbalance of energies in the universe, however small – even in thought (another "Butterfly Effect"). In effect it seems that there is a mechanism which maintains balance at all levels to maintain the status quo. Once I take more physical action there is further compensatory resistance, if only from the muscles in my body. Perhaps later from others around me. Somehow it seems easier to do nothing rather than disturb the peace.

26. This means that any idea will be challenged internally and externally – especially if it is new.

27. When 2 people get together in close creative relationship they are usually of opposite sex or with complementary skills or abilities.

28. There is a physical component to our recognition of Day and Night as the basis of our "body clock". In the human endocrine system the Pineal Gland secretes Melatonin during darkness and uses it up during daylight. An example of disruption of the process is jet lag.

EVOLUTION

This Stage with Saturn now ruling Cycle of Growth Stage 11 (Discontent. Invention. Rebellion) contains the evolutionary stages that developed Diversity of life forms. It includes Genesis Creation Day 2 (separation of

NUMEROLOGY

Waters), Day 3 (Earth and Sea), Day 4 (Stars, Sun, Moon), Day 5 (Fish and Birds), and Day 6 (Animals and Man) which we can see as examples of Sexual Reproduction where Number 1 + Number 2 result in the creation of a 3rd. entity. The progression is reasonably in line with the now accepted scientific theories of Evolution.

In the story of Jesus, he escaped death as an infant and disappeared from public life until his ministry 30 years later. Prior to this he was tempted by The Devil (Saturn/Satan) to use his powers to escape his fate – having the knowledge that people would not like the fact that his "rebellion" did not include destroying Roman rule, rather that they should *"render unto Caesar what is Caesar's, and unto God what is God's"*. (They chose the "conventional rebel" Barabbas instead).

The Temptation lasted for "40 days and nights" which could refer to the 40 weeks of human gestation in the womb.

Individualisation, and separation from The Collective begins with the formation of a human body in the womb which is the focus of the 1st. Octave. Some do not survive.

Tarot XVII.The Star depicts a female figure pouring water from 2 jugs - one in the right (conscious) hand into a pool (making waves) and from the left (unconscious) hand on to the Earth. We have the following associations :-

1. Day 2 of the Creation was of *"firmament"* stated to be creation of a *"separating between waters and waters"* which became Heaven (sky) – Earth's atmosphere. In terms of evolution of Earth this suggests the creation of our gaseous atmosphere – which began with Hydrogen.
2. Day 3 of Creation was the separation of Earth and Sea. This is depicted in XVIII.THE STAR with the separated waters being poured from 2 jugs, one on to the earth the other into water.
3. Aquarius and "The Water Carrier", has connotations with a Cloud carrying Water as rain. (Genesis "separation of the waters").
4. The Age of Aquarius and growth of global communication over "the Air Waves" – which now includes "The Cloud" "water carrier" of the Internet. (Genesis "creation of Heaven/Sky").
5. The planetary evolution of Stars, Sun, and Moon.
6. In The Kabbalah Tree of Life there is a horizontal separation between the 3 Supernals and the other Sephiroth lower down which is called The Abyss. This is related to the un-numbered Sephirah Daath - and Uranus, which translated means "Sky".
7. During the evolution of our planet there was rain for thousands of years as Earth cooled and steam in the atmosphere condensed, followed by the creation of bacteria which evolved further.
8. The evolutionary emergence of animals from those seas onto dry land depicted in XVIII.THE MOON is an accepted scientific fact.

NUMBER 3 – BINARY 11 - JUPITER

This is Day 7 of the Genesis Creation, which was a day of rest - just as we need to have a time of sleep (unconsciousness) at the end of every day to allow the brain to process the data of the day. Each day of Creation required an "evening" to allow time for the Universal Balance of energy to return to Zero. Perhaps this is why we need sleep.

"Man and Woman" were created on Creation Day 6 at the end of the previous Stage. Although Day 7 is stated to be a "day of rest" we note that this has come to mean that, rather than being idle, it is a time to put aside normal work and pay attention to spiritual development, or otherwise expanding consciousness. The influence of Jupiter (Expansion. Growth. Higher Mind) is clearly indicated at this Stage – both at mental and material levels.

Having created Positive and Negative polarities there is the possibility of creation of a third "child" principle as a resolution of the differences between them - otherwise they cancel each other out to return to the original Zero state. I have reproduced [PSYCHOLOGY : DEVELOPMENT MODELS] diagrams below that illustrate this point. This also refers to the development of The Middle Pillar of [THE KABBALAH TREE OF LIFE].

NUMEROLOGY

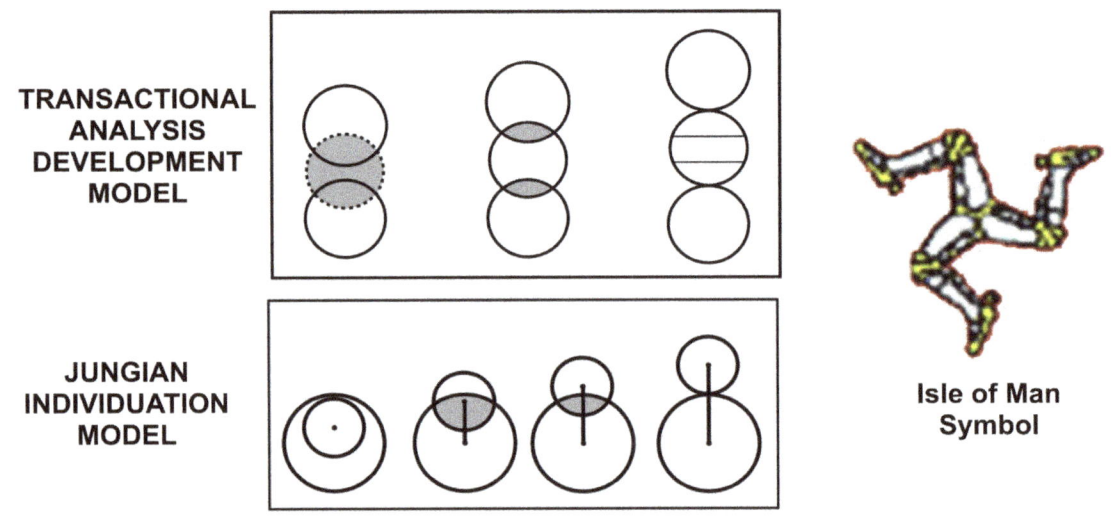

Please see the chapter [Psychology Development Models]

Figure 78 : Numbers - Number 3

A single dimension Line formed by 2 points takes on an identity of its own and becomes a 2 dimensional Plane formed by 3 points. Each point is a representation of Number 1. Length now gains Breadth.

Triplicities and triangles now become part of <u>every</u> cyclic numerical "structure" as shown in the diagrams that follow, as well as [THE KABBALAH TREE OF LIFE], and Astrological Charts. Any 2 points make a connection with each other and The Centre. This is the basis of The Planetary Aspects of Astrology.

We are now at the evolutionary stage of Sexual Reproduction instead of cloning which makes 2 from 1 (ref. the creation of Eve from Adam). Here 2 separate entities are required both of which retain their separate identities. It is the "Zero relationship" between them that evolves to produce entity Number 3. Sexual Reproduction has a potential for producing Diversity that cloning does not.

With 3 people in relationship we get the unstable "Eternal Triangle" of 2 males conflicting over 1 female, or 2 females conflicting over 1 male – a group of 3 of the same sex is unusual, and not likely to last long. 1 departs to leave 2 remaining or another joins to make 4. Opposite polarities attract, like polarities repel.

There are 6 possible permutations of 3 numbers : 1,2,3 : 2,3,1 : 3,1,2 : 3,2,1 : 1,3,2 : 2,1,3.

CYCLE OF GROWTH STAGE 9 (CONCEPTION. PLUTO/JUPITER)

We see from the above that Cycle of Growth Stage 9 (Conception) as the beginning of The 1st. Octave occurs at the level of Sephirah 2 (Force. Pluto) at the beginning of Evolution. After that the energy only reaches Sephirah 4 (Chesed. Jupiter) which bypasses The Transcendent Octave. The Supernals of The Tree of Life are not reached again until Pluto replaces Mars at Cycle of Growth Stage 8 (Sex. Death. Intercourse) and Uranus at Daath replaces Saturn at Cycle of Growth Stage 11 (Discontent).

CYCLE OF GROWTH STAGE 12 (WITHDRAWAL. JUPITER/NEPTUNE)

In the original Lightning Flash of Evolution Cycle of Growth Stage 12 is ruled by Jupiter. However, if Saturn is overcome by an act of will as outlined in the previous paragraph, it is possible to make contact with Neptune at Sephirah 1 (Kether. Crown. Number Zero) and begin a new Lightning Flash of evolution.

With Cycle of Growth Stage 12 we have the time of Confinement of a mother in preparation for the birth of a child. Development that was previously automatic, and hidden, will become a physical reality in the next Stage (when the addition of another Dimension, Height, produces a 3-dimensional solid). In essence, this is a repetition of Creation Day Zero which preceded Creation Day 1 and the bringing of Light from Darkness.

This is the last stage of the 1st. Octave of The Logarithmic Timescale.

NUMEROLOGY

This Stage relates to the Sign of Pisces which, among other things, is concerned with the "sea" of the Collective Unconscious, and the sleep state. Perhaps here we can get some idea of what are generally unconscious processes. Pisces is the Element Water in its Mutable, Changing, Transforming state.

With the discovery of Neptune related to Pisces and this Stage we have a similar alternative state of this Stage to Stage 11. Neptune relates to Sephirah 1 (Kether. Crown. Number Zero). In the chapter [THE KABBALAH TREE OF LIFE] is indicated the possibility of contacting Sephirah 1 when the Transcendent Octave is activated and Uranus replaces Jupiter at Stage 11.

NUMEROLOGY

Numerology relates Number 3 to Jupiter (Expansion. Growth. Theoretical Mind. Sephirah 4), which is in agreement with The Tree of Life (on its downward journey). The interpretation focuses on a Jovial, freedom loving, approach to life with a dislike for restrictions. We see the relationship between The Pillar of Force and Growth. At the mundane level Jupiter is mainly concerned with social relationships within groups of people.

Famous Life Path 3 people include Charlton Heston (Actor. Libra), Edward Kennedy (US Senator. Managed J.F. Kennedy campaign, brother of President John F. Kennedy. Pisces), Alan Leo (Astrologer. Leo), Sir Walter Scott (Writer. Leo), Queen Victoria (Gemini).

3 - OTHER ASSOCIATIONS

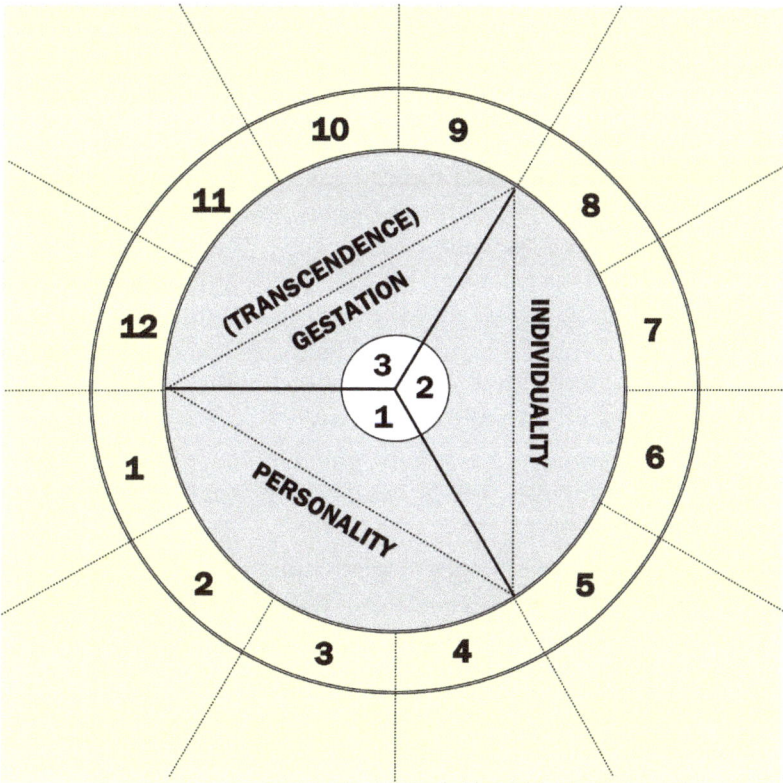

Figure 79 : - Number 3 and The Cycle of Growth

1. In Astrology we see the important introduction of the 3 Octaves of the Logarithmic Timescale.
2. At this level, Number 12 is 3 sets of 4 - a Triplicity of Quadruplicities.
3. In the set of 9 Numbers Diagram below (which is a triplicity of triplicities), Number 3 is at the end of The 1st. Octave which is concerned with a child's development of body and mind.
4. Number 3 triplicities, or trinities, are said to be created as a manifestation of the relationship between the components of Number 2 – so we get such groups as Father, Mother, Child – Father, Son, Holy Spirit – Past, Present, Future – Parent, Child, Adult (Transactional Analysis model above) – Ego, Self, Ego-Self Axis (Jungian Individuation model above). [PSYCHOLOGY : DEVELOPMENT MODELS]

NUMEROLOGY

5. Triplicities can be described as an initial manifestation (1) which produces a reaction of opposite polarity (2) and a final resolution (3).
6. There are 3 Triplicities in The Kabbalah Tree of Life, each with a single Sephirah on The Middle Pillar providing a balance between 2 others on opposite Pillars.
7. The seeming exception, Sephirah 10 (Malkuth. Kingdom. Earth) balances the same Sephiroth (7.Victory and 8. Glory) as Sephirah 9 (Yesod. Moon). It contains everything above as the final material manifestation of Sephirah 1 (Kether. Crown) which also contains everything else. "As Above, So Below. As Below, So Above". Together they define the top and bottom of The Middle Pillar of Balance and Equilibrium.
8. Number 3 relates to Sephirah 4 (Chesed. Mercy. Jupiter) which is in the centre of The Pillar of Force where it balances Sephirah 2 (Chockmah. Force. Pluto) and Sephirah 7 (Netzach. Victory. Venus) lower down. Sephirah 4 is created from Sephirah 3 (Binah. Understanding. Form. Saturn). This is the academic level of human intelligence – theory rather than practice. From now on we descend through Mind to eventually reach the material world of Malkuth (Kingdom. Earth).
9. The orbit of Jupiter (Expansion) is next inside that of Saturn (Consolidation). The symbol of Jupiter is a reversal of that of Saturn. We see the controlling energies of Saturn on The Pillar of Form transferred harmoniously to The Pillar of Force. The energy of Sephirah 2 (Chockmah. Wisdom) above Sephirah 4 is now allowed more freedom by being differentiated into numerous channels.
10. Numerology also associates Number 3 with Jupiter.
11. Jupiter is also associated with The Cycle of Growth Stage 9 (Conception) which originally relates to Pluto - which begins "The Lightning Flash" of The Tree of Life. It is also related to Cycle of Growth Stage 12 (Withdrawal. Confinement) when The Transcendent Octave is bypassed on the return journey.
12. Creation Day 3 brought about the separation between Earth and Sea.
13. The Triplicity of Sephiroth now begun is – Sephirah 4 Chesed (Jupiter. Number 3) and Sephirah 5 Geburah (Mars. Number 4) balanced by Tiphareth (Sun. Ego Consciousness) lower down, and conforms to Edgar Cayce's description of "Mind As Builder".
14. Symbolism of the Sephirah is related to production of communities (Expansion. Growth). At a certain stage of Evolution individual cells gathered together in communities for mutual protection. Later on the same Principle developed the human body, where cells diversified to perform specific, different functions on behalf of the whole. Still later, the same Principle developed communities of people with similar differentiation of function on behalf of the whole.
15. In Astrology each of the 4 Elements has a triplicity which indicates the type of energy expressed – Cardinal (initiating), Fixed (resisting. preserving), Mutable (changing. developing - ready for the next stage of growth). The Zodiac Elements form 3 sets of 4.
16. In Astrology the Houses of a chart have 4 sets of triplicities – Angular, Succedent and Cadent - which have the same archetypal functions as those of the Elements. The Houses form 4 sets of 3. The Houses of a Birth Chart refer to manifestations of the Zodiac energy in a more material form.
17. The division of the circle of Houses into 3 parts (3 sets of 4 Elements) gives rise to the 3 Octaves of the [ASTROLOGY : LOGARITHMIC TIMESCALE]. Once again, the function of each Octave is the same as the other triplicities (ref. 15 above). They are defined as 3 development stages - 1. Thesis (Gestation - physical body in the womb), 2. Antithesis (Development of Personality), and 3. Synthesis (Development of Individuality). We note that, at the beginning of a new cycle, the First Octave can either be a repetition of the past, leading to a repetition of the Cycle, or become a "Fourth Octave of Transcendence" - beginning a 4th. Dimension outside the original circle/cycle - as symbolised in the cover image of this book. Beginning of a new cycle requires Death in the old.
18. In Mathematics 3 separate points are required to define a 2 dimensional plane which has Length and Breadth. Until now there has only been a dimensionless point (1) and a line (2 points). In common with Numerology (and The Tarot) there is the concept that this is the first stage of physical manifestation. A "primary completion" –such as an idea formed in the mind. The idea is developed further by Number 4, which adds a 3rd. dimension – that of Height - the 3 dimensional "cube" of material manifestation.
19. There is a Number 3 (Plane) relationship at the centre for each pair (Number 2. Line). We note that the triangle is itself divided into triangles. This principle follows for the rest of the figures. So each number

pairs, and contains, a potential Number 3. This is the principle of Astrological Aspects the effect of which is measured at the centre.

20. In Astrology there is the fundamental concept of examining the Aspect, or relationship, between 2 planets. There is a tendency to focus on the outer relationship rather than the inner one. Evidence for this is that most Astrologers indicate aspects between planets by connecting them with a line in a similar way to that shown above, rather than with the centre.

21. Here we have the 120 degree Trine Aspect which is one-third of a circle. Although the diagram above shows 3 points (which could be planets) the planets are considered in pairs. The Trine is stated to be an "Easy" aspect between 2 planets in that energies are transferred harmoniously. This is because the planets are usually in the same Element. In the diagram we can see that, also, there are no "Oppositions" – which is common to all odd numbers. In a Birth Chart with numerous Trine aspects we would look for other planets with Square aspects (Number 4) that would produce the necessary challenges required for development and growth. Ideas are all very well, but some need to be practical. We do live in a material world.

22. We note that, once again, there are "Evenings" in the story of Creation. Everything within the confinement of the Circle, or Sphere, is in balance. The Cycle Stages and Numbers are equal. The sum total is Zero.

23. The first solid Element Lithium (Greek lithos = stone) has atomic number 3 with 4 Neutrons, 3 Protons and 3 Electrons. It is a highly reactive solid metal at normal temperatures. Its crystal structure is cubic. It is mainly used in batteries.

24. In the set of 9 numbers diagram, Number 3 relates to most of Cycle of Growth Stage 4 (Transplanting).

WAVE INTERFERENCE PATTERNS – 2 BECOMES 3

This is a slight digression from our format. By looking at cycles in a different way we can get some idea of how 2 forces can produce a Third force. We have a graph showing lines for the cycles of Jupiter and Saturn, and another line showing the combined effect. The Combined Effect line can be considered as another way of looking at the Aspects between the 2 planets. Note the "Transcendence" around age 21 - which is half way through the 42 year Uranus Cycle – and will be repeated at that time.

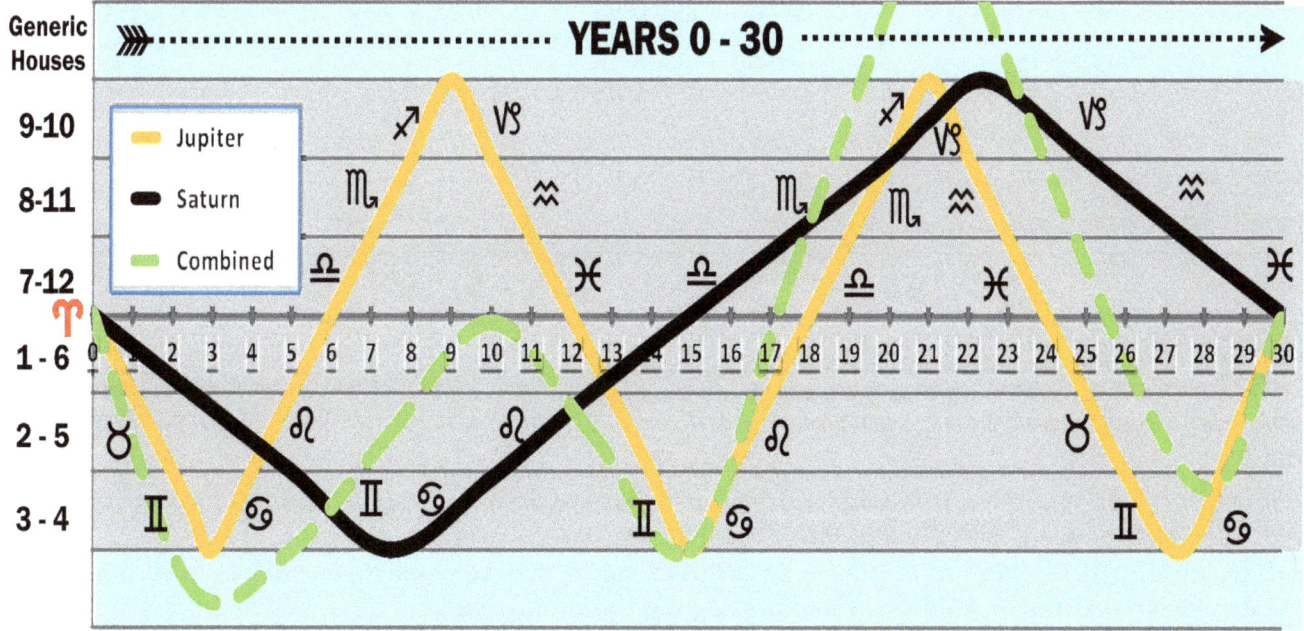

Figure 80 : Number 3 - Interference Pattern

1. In Physics," Interference" occurs when 2 wave forms interact with one another. The centre line of the chart above is the path of The Sun moving through space. The other lines are the orbits of Jupiter and Saturn around The Sun as they too move through space.

2. The 2 "waves" interact to produce a 3rd. wave.

NUMEROLOGY

3. Normal descriptions deal with much faster wave frequencies. – such as produced by waves in water, or sound waves in air. Here the frequencies are a 12 year Jupiter cycle and a 30 year Saturn cycle.
4. We are here entering a different Dimension (Space-Time) of understanding to that of the rest of this book. To avoid complication we merely observe the phenomenon without trying to suggest cause or effect.
5. We are now observing the Solar System model from a different angle. We are adding a 3rd. Dimension of Time to the other 2 Dimensions of Space. The "Chart Wheel" is now viewed edgewise. From this observation point we get a more accurate picture of the planetary motions through TIME because it takes into account the fact that, due to the expansion of the universe, the planets never occupy the exact same position in space more than once. In 3 Dimensions their orbits are Spirals – not Circles.
6. We examine the combined cycles of Jupiter and Saturn through a 30 year period. During this time Jupiter makes 2 ½ orbits and Saturn 1 orbit of the Sun. The Sun is placed at the central horizontal axis and moving from left to right.
7. For simplicity the starting point for all planets here is at the Ascendant position – Zero degrees of Aries. We could begin the model with the 2 planets anywhere on the Zero Year origin axis.
8. In Astrology we have periods of time when, viewed from Earth, the planets seem to go backwards through the Zodiac Signs (Retrograde). With a Sun centre this is not an issue here.
9. The principle of Interference is that when 2 waves are going in the same direction they amplify or reinforce the combined effect. Conversely, when 2 waves go in opposite directions they cancel one another out.
10. Wherever the Jupiter and Saturn lines cross the planets are in the same Zodiac Sign, and are related in a Conjunction (Zero Degrees) Aspect.
11. At the beginning of the cycles we see the planets are moving in the same direction and therefore serving to amplify the combined effect. Strangely, there seems to be the tendency to depart from their orbits. This only occurs in 2 places - at 3 years when the planets are approaching their "lower" orbits, and at 21 years when approaching the "upper" orbits. Is this Transcendence ? At 21 years of age Uranus has reached Cycle of Growth Stage 4 (Transplanting) - ¼ of its 84 year Generic Cycle.
12. At Ages Zero, 10, 17, 26 and 30 the planets reach a state where their combined effect is Zero.
13. At Age 30 the planets return to their original Conjunction when, once again, the combined effect is Zero, and the cycles repeat. This is another example of the principle of The Cycle of Growth that the overall effect of any cycle balances out to Zero.

NUMBER 4 – BINARY 100 - MARS

Number 4 relates to the planet Mars and is basically concerned with genetic survival as the first step towards Individualisation. Mars focuses the expansive energy of Jupiter (Expansion. Society) into a single point (War. Individuality).

Mars traditionally rules Cycle of Growth Stage 1 (Seed) and Cycle of Growth Stage 8 (Sex. Intercourse. Death) which define the beginning and end of a human lifetime on Earth.

A main symbol of Number 4 is that of The Cross on which Christ (Spirit) was crucified, which in turn refers to The Cross of Matter and the [THE 4 ELEMENTS] that make up the material world and physical human body. It is a symbol of constraint of The Spirit by the material world and human body. [THE 4 ELEMENTS] eventually come under the control of Number 5 (4 + 1) in Cycle of Growth Stage 5 (Power. The Sun. Ego Consciousness) which is only in embryo form at the beginning of Evolution.

From 2 dimensional Number 3 we get a third dimension to produce a cube – or other 3 dimensional solids. The dimension of Height and Space. The next Dimension, Time, appears with Number 8 (2 x 4. The Moon).

NUMEROLOGY

In Genesis at Cycle of Growth Stage 1 (Seed) this is the appearance of Adam who we are told was created from "dust" of the Earth. That is, he now gets a physical body.

The Transcendent 4th. Octave of The Cycle of Growth adds another dimension to the original 3.

There are 24 possible permutations of 4 numbers.

On The Tree of Life, Sephirah 5 (Severity. Individuality. Mars) on The Pillar of Form (Severity) emanates from, and is complemented by, Sephirah 4 (Jupiter. Community) on The Pillar of Force. This is the first evolutionary development of individual beings from The Collective where each one ("cell") is an identical clone. We now have the first individual identity.

In evolution, from cloned communities of algae and bacteria produced by simple cell division, where each member of a species is identical, we get the development of independent, focused, energies and sexual reproduction. Each individual has its own material ambition. At a deeper, more basic evolutionary level, Mars is concerned with the genetic survival of a species as "survival of the fittest" during life, and reproduction to ensure the continuation of the species after death of the individual.

The old symbol of Mars was the Cross of Matter/Form above the Circle of Spirit –which we can see as another symbol of Crucifixion – and indicates its position below Sephiroth 3 (Binah. Understanding. Saturn. Form) on the Pillar of Severity (Form). It is also a 2 dimensional representation of a 3 dimensional Orb which is a symbol of the power of kings and queens. The new symbol of an arrow above a circle is the now universally accepted one of Male sex. In more general terms, this is the Force of Number 1 focused and directed towards some material purpose – and so is present in both human sexes.

CYCLE OF GROWTH STAGE 1 (SEED)

At the beginning of the 2nd. Octave we once again have a Fire Sign. Here it is Aries (The Ram) where Fire is in its Cardinal, Impulsive, Instinctive, Initiating, phase. We see that a child is born in a pure state of Intuition or animal Instinct. The other Jungian Functions of Sensation (Earth), Thinking (Air) and Water (Feeling) have yet to develop.

We can see a similarity of symbolism and activity between Mars in Aries here, and Pluto in Sagittarius which began the 1st. Octave at Sephirah 2 (Chockmah. Force. The Big Bang).

With the Cardinal Fire Sign of Aries Mars/Number 4 ruling Cycle of Growth Stage 1 (Seed) it is the animal survival instinct which is concerned with the survival and development of an infant in its new "dimension" of experience outside the womb.

In The Logarithmic Timescale this is the actual physical birth of a child and covers the first 7 months of Infancy when the Fire/Spirit is coming to terms with the demands of a physical body. It is also the time of Easter with the symbolism of The Christ Spirit being crucified on The Cross of Matter. In psychology this is the beginning of the Oral Stage, with focus of sensation on the mouth. We must first learn how to feed.

The human body is a "vehicle" of the Soul. The infant learns how to "drive".

The related Tarot Cards are 0.THE FOOL (which means childlike innocence, and is not necessarily "foolish") and I.THE MAGICIAN where The Higher Mind, or consciousness, is about to use the 4 "tools" (which represent [THE 4 ELEMENTS] , [THE 4 FUNCTIONS] , and human body) on the table before him.

CYCLE OF GROWTH STAGE 8 (SEX. DEATH. INTERCOURSE. MARS/PLUTO)

With the Fixed Water Sign of Scorpio the instinctive energy of Mars it is "watered down" and Fixed (controlled at the emotional level) to enable co-operation between individuals.

At Cycle of Growth Stage 1 (Seed) Mars is concerned with personal survival on Earth. At Stage 8 it is concerned with one's survival after Death by passing on one's property or genes to ONE'S children.

The new additional rulership by Pluto (Regeneration) gives the opportunity to transform one's life by use of Will. The symbolism is related to the development of a butterfly which develops itself by Metamorphosis –and which involves complete reorganisation of its cell structure. There is association with the Resurrection of Jesus after his crucifixion.

Scorpio has 3 symbols describing 3 Stages – The Serpent/Scorpion (Caterpillar) which focuses attention on Earthly matters, The Eagle stage (Chrysalis) which enables objectivity free of emotions, and involvement in

NUMEROLOGY

studying and researching the secrets of life. Finally, there is The Dove (Butterfly) which has concerns with group ideals rather than personal ones. We can see that humans can be involved in all 3 stages at any time.

NUMEROLOGY

The interpretations of Number 4 by Numerology vary considerably although they do include something of the basic meaning. Part of the reason is that they relate the Number to Uranus which cannot be correct – although some suggest a relationship with Will or Willpower. With Mars we have a better concept of a controlling force focusing energy, and can see how the error occurs. It is the Phallic, Status Symbol of potential for creativity without (yet) a practical purpose. The need to be a "star".

As we see, Number 4 actually relates to Mars (God of War), which, on the Pillar of Form, is simply focused energy. Although "hard work" is mentioned or implied by most Numerologists, as Astrologers we note that Mars is at archetypal level concerned with self-projection (of energy) in humans rather than achieving any particular goal – which depends on the Sign and House Mars is located in a Birth Chart. Astrological Mars is considered a Pioneer, breaking new ground. The archetypal aim is to achieve a high personal status in the "pecking order". The survival of the fittest.

Famous Life Path 4 people include Jacques Bergerac (Revlon Cosmetics. Gemini), Hugh Hefner (Playboy Magazine. Aries), Joseph P. Kennedy (Financier, father of John F. Virgo), J.P. Morgan (Financier. Aries), Ed Sullivan (TV show 23 years. Libra), Marie Curie (Radium. Scorpio), Desmond Tutu (Anglican Bishop. Social Rights. Libra).

4 - OTHER ASSOCIATIONS

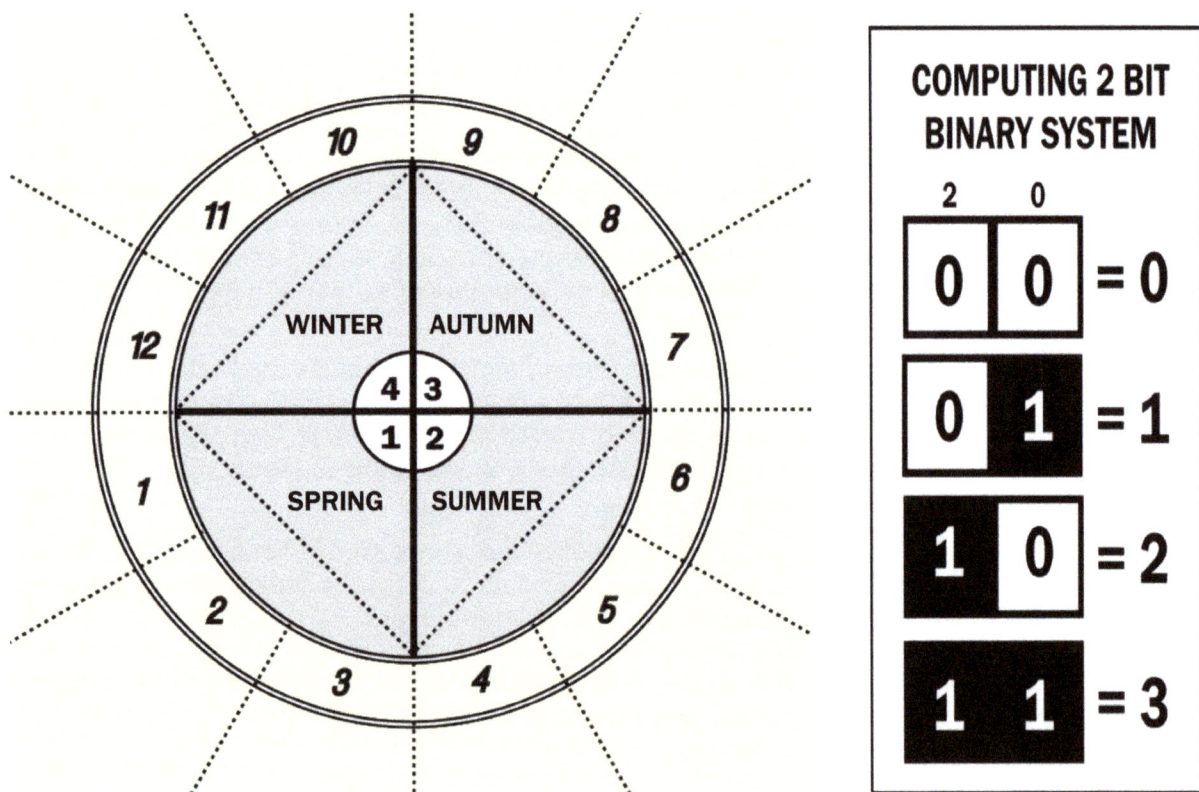

Figure 81 : Number 4 and The Cycle of Growth

NUMEROLOGY

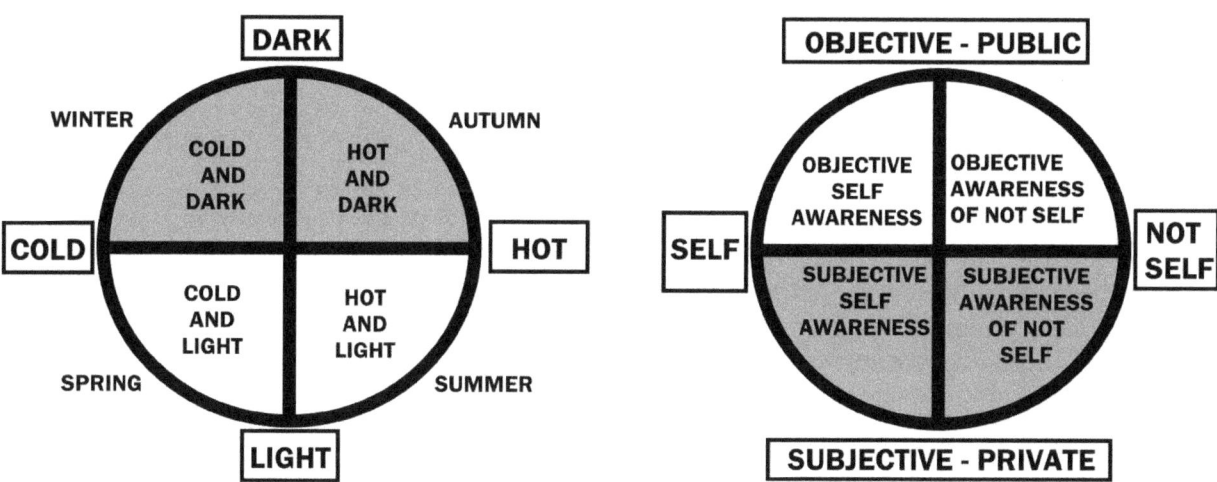

Figure 82 : Numbers - Number 4 = 2 x 2

1. Number 4 is the most stable of numbers. Now with 3 dimensions we have solid Matter.
2. 4 people in a group tend to make a stable structure, for example, 2 married couples. When we marry we tend to relate to other married couples and lose single friends.
3. We can see the 2 Number 2 diagrams being forced to occupy the same space.
4. The Cross of Matter within the Circle of Spirit is the symbol of Earth.
5. Sephiroth 5 (Severity. Mars) is at the centre of The Pillar of Form (Severity) – so we can see how it relates to 3 dimensional objects (cube).
6. In the diagram of 9 Numbers, Number 4 is the beginning of The 2nd.Octave of The Logarithmic Timescale which is concerned with the beginning of Individuality. It relates to Cycle of Growth Stage 5 (Power. Creativity) and Erikson's School Age.
7. In her book "The Cosmic Doctrine" Dion Fortune [DFCD] states that the universe was originally formed by the space in Kether (Crown. Number Zero) being moved by Chockmah (Force. Number 1) the direction being modified by Binah (Form. Number 2) into a cyclic path – or "shell". The movement created an attraction to more Space which eventually formed another "shell" cycle of Space outside, and at right angles to, the first. We could view the "Cross" Earth Symbol contained in the above in this context. We must also consider how Chemical elements develop by the addition of "shells" as described below.
8. Dion's description forms a 3 dimensional object from 2 x 2 dimensional.
9. It is easy to see how Number 4 relates to Number 2. In Astrological terms we have 2 Oppositions (180 degrees) at right angles to one another, which form 4 Square (90 degrees) aspects. The Square aspect is a "Difficult" aspect because it generates challenges in life that force an inner self-awareness by acting at The Centre. In a Birth Chart, it is as if the planets involved always "disagree" with one another. We can see how this works by observing that the aspect usually connects planets that are in the same triplicity of Signs (Cardinal, Fixed, Mutable) and Houses (Angular, Succedent, Cadent), so, for example, with the squared planets both in Cardinal (initiating) Signs there might be the tendency to continually start 2 conflicting projects at the same time.
10. The focus of Mars is its strength to achieve. It is also its weakness from difficulty to change direction, or see alternatives.
11. The diagrams above show how 2 Oppositions produce 4 alternatives. The first one is a simple depiction of The 4 Seasons in terms of 2 pairs of "Opposite" alternatives. The second one shows the basic structure of the Houses of an Astrological Chart. Although each quadrant is further divided into 3 parts later on, the essential meaning of the quadrants remain as shown.
12. There are 4 triangles (Triplicities) each of which has a direct relationship with 2 others either side (as in number 3) but now each one has an "opposite".
13. Another indication of how 2 "oppositions" produce 4 numbers is by using a 2 Bit computing method described in this chapter

NUMEROLOGY

14. The element with Atomic Number 4 is Beryllium which has 5 Neutrons and 4 Protons/Electrons. It is a solid which does not appear in pure form in nature. Among several other rocks it is present in beryl, aquamarine, and emeralds. It is largely used in small quantities to strengthen other metals.
15. In Creation Day 4 there was the creation of "lights" in the heavens – Sun (which appears next in The Tree of Life), Moon, and Stars – which were explicitly created for the measurement of Time. They are all physical bodies. It also seems to be the seeds of Astrology.
16. The numbers of "Thomas" add up to 4. He was the disciple that insisted on observing the material facts for himself, rather than accepting hearsay.
17. We have the Jungian [THE 4 FUNCTIONS] which operate in 2 pairs – the Rational ones Thinking and Feeling, and the Irrational Ones Intuition and Sensation. They relate to the Astrological [THE 4 ELEMENTS] Air, Water, Fire and Earth.

NUMBER 5 – BINARY 101 – THE SUN

ALTHOUGH PLACED IN NUMERICAL ORDER HERE, NUMBER 5 (THE SUN) REFERS TO CYCLE OF GROWTH STAGE 5 (POWER. CREATIVITY. THE SUN. EGO CONSCIOUSNESS), ALTHOUGH PRESENT IN EMBRYO FORM ON THE DOWNWARD JOURNEY OF THE LIGHTNING FLASH, DOES NOT BEGIN TO DEVELOP PROPERLY UNTIL THE BEGINNING OF THE 3RD. OCTAVE AT PSYCHOLOGICAL "SCHOOL AGE" WHEN THE CHILD BEGINS TO EXPLORE THE WORLD OUTSIDE THE FAMILY HOME – AWAY FROM PARENTAL CONTROL.

THIS, AND THE MIDDLE PILLAR, IS THE "ADULT" OF TRANSACTIONAL ANALYSIS AND "THE EGO-SELF AXIS" OF JUNGIAN INDIVIDUATION [PSYCHOLOGY DEVELOPMENT MODELS] depicted at Number 3 above.

IN THE DOWNWARD JOURNEY OF "THE LIGHTNING FLASH" SEPHIRAH 6 (NUMBER 5. THE SUN) ON THE MIDDLE PILLAR IS BYPASSED IN A SIMILAR WAY TO DAATH (CYCLE OF GROWTH STAGE 11), EARLIER – BECAUSE IT TOO IS NOT DEVELOPED. LIKE DAATH IT BECOMES MORE ACTIVE ON THE RETURN JOURNEY OF THE TREE OF LIFE BY USE OF CONSCIOUSNESS AND WILL.

In human evolution, an important development was that of the Opposable Thumb of the hands and its associated development of the brain. The Apes were able to "grasp" things physically and mentally for the first time. Apart from the 5 fingers, the associations with Number 5 in the sequence of numbers include the concept of the new un-paired Number 1 of an odd number appearing as an opposition to the previous even number. So here we have "1 versus 4". The meaning is further developed by the concept that Number 5 as The Higher Mind (Ego Consciousness) controls [THE 4 ELEMENTS] (Lower Chakras) which are lower in stature.

In The Tree of Life Number 5 relates to Sephirah 6 (Tiphareth. Beauty. Consciousness) and The Sun. It relates to the Heart Chakras as controller of the essential inner functions of the human body. Like the heart in the human body, it has direct path connections to the other Sephiroth.

Edgar Cayce stated that the Heart Chakra controls the lower 4 Chakras.

The position at the centre of the Middle Pillar of The Tree, and our Solar System, demonstrate the ability for control and harmonising the conflicting factors of the whole environment. The Sun has direct contact with Sephirah 1 (Kether. Crown) and is, therefore, in effect, an "Image of God" which explains why it was worshipped as such by the more Intuitive, less Thinking (Function) people of the past. This gives a connotation of Free Will with the central Sun being in control of its own small "universe" – albeit subject to Higher Laws. This is also Ego and Self Consciousness.

The path between Sephirah 6 and Sephirah 1 in The Tree of Life is the concern of Tarot card IV.The Emperor who is given god-like associations at Cycle of Growth Stage 3 (Experiment) by the developing infant.

The Sun is the result of the Relationship between Chesed (Mercy. Jupiter) and Geburah (Severity. Mars) – that is, Society and The Individual. In The Cycle of Growth The Sun refers to Stage 5 (Power. Creativity. Ego Consciousness) which is related to the Tarot Card VIII. Strength – which, in turn, is the symbol of the path on The Tree which joins Chesed (Jupiter) and Geburah (Mars).

When we consider the associations of The Sun with The Heart Chakra and a Pentagon we discover another function – that of Defence. The Thymus Gland is involved in our protection against disease.

NUMEROLOGY

Later in The Tree of Life The Sun delegates power to the Moon – also on the Middle Pillar – before it reaches Earth.

There are 120 possible permutations of 5 numbers.

CYCLE OF GROWTH STAGE 5 (POWER. CREATIVITY. CONSCIOUSNESS)

This refers to Erikson's School Age beginning age 7 years.

Cycle of Growth Stage 5 is the beginning of the 3rd. Octave of The Logarithmic Timescale. During the previous Octave the child has learned to control its body and has some mental development. At the end of the 2nd. Octave at Cycle of Growth Stage 4 (Transplanting. Shell) it developed a psychological Persona "mask" of Personality as mediator between the outer and inner worlds, which included a sexual identity.

Stage 5 is controlled by the Fixed Fire Sign of Leo, which, in turn, is ruled by The Sun. It relates to the human "School Age" from 7 to 13 years of age when the child is beginning to explore the world outside the home. Whereas the Fire Sign of Aries at the beginning of Stage 1 is concerned with the brute force of survival and establishing one's self in the pecking order, here the competition is more concerned with what one creates or produces in a material sense in a wider social sphere.

We note that the main purpose of this time is the development of Ego Consciousness away from direct parental control. There is more freedom of self-expression and a sense of being a "co-creator with God".

The corresponding Tarot Card VIII.STRENGTH (a female controlling a lion) depicts the Number 5 theme of "Mind over Matter".

The Stage is opposite that of Cycle of Growth Stage 11 (Discontent) which is traditionally ruled by Saturn, or can be ruled by Uranus (Will). We see that development of The Sun (Ego Consciousness) and Uranus (Individualisation. Individuation) – both on The Middle Pillar, and both only in embryo form at the original Lightning Flash - go hand-in-hand.

NUMEROLOGY

Numerology relates Number 5 to Mercury, however, when we read the personality descriptions we can clearly see (especially with the inclusion of Adolf Hitler, where Solar energy is inflated to dictatorship –ego identification with God) that The Tree of Life relationship with The Sun on the Middle Pillar is valid. One manifestation of such solar activity is a small group of people controlled by a leader – such as rock group or teenage gang. They include careers related to travel, salesmanship, the creative arts, and adventure. It is especially related to those who form their own business.

The Sun planet association does however highlight the deficiencies of Numerology when we consider the Zodiac Sign of The Sun in a Birth Chart – bearing in mind that here we are using "Life Path" as defined by date of birth. Although the description could apply to Sun in a Fire Sign (especially Leo, Fixed Fire) – and is appropriate to The Sun in our Solar System and Kabbalist description – our own personal experiences show that Sun in others of The 4 Elements can show a completely different picture.

Famous Number 5 Life Path figures are Max Heindel (Astrologer. Rosicrucian founder. Leo), Mick Jagger (Rolling Stones. Leo), Thomas Jefferson (US President. Author of 'The Declaration of Independence'. Aries), Liberace (ostentatious pianist/showman. Taurus), Abraham Lincoln (US President. Aquarius), Franklin D. Roosevelt (US President. Aquarius), Theodore Roosevelt (US President. Scorpio), Adolph Hitler (Dictator. Taurus).

Once again we find Leo in our list as well as complementary Aquarius.

NUMEROLOGY

5 - OTHER ASSOCIATIONS

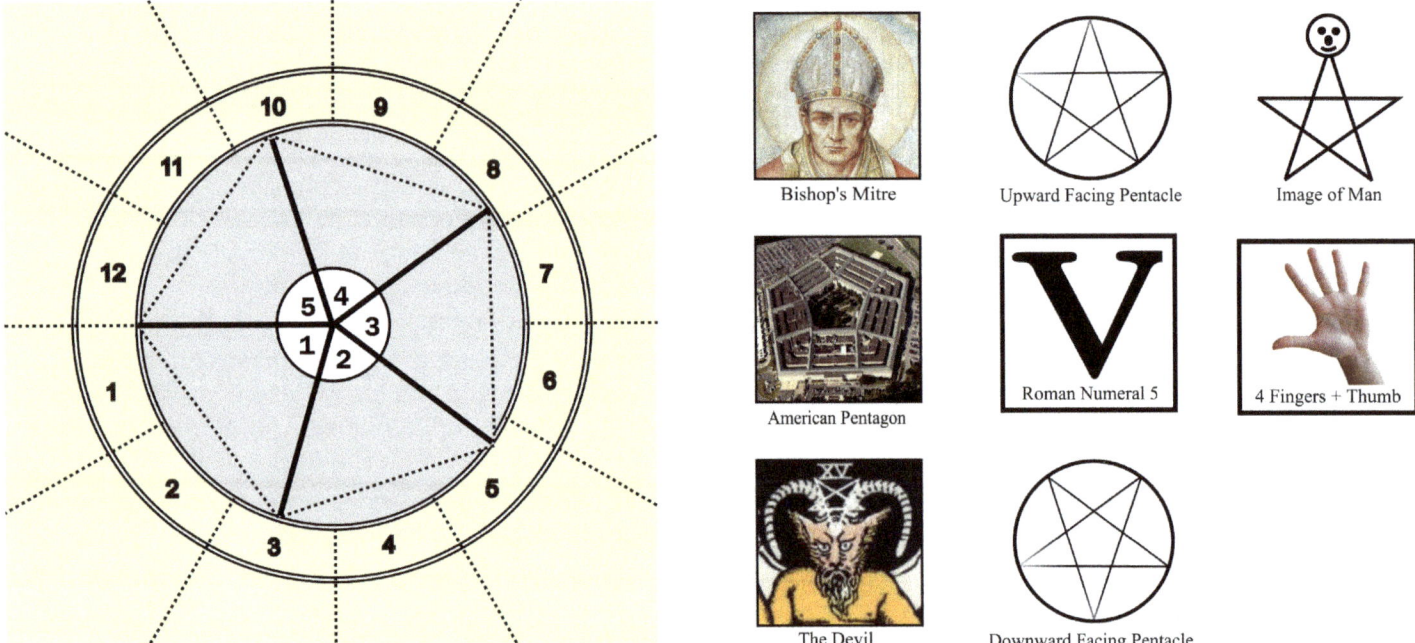

Figure 83 : Number 5 and The Cycle of Growth

The symbols of Number 5 relate to the direction of attention of Sun Ego Consciousness.

1. In the set of 9 Numbers, Number 5 is located at the "Full Moon" position of Cycle of Growth Stage 7 (Partnerships) which is in Opposition Aspect to Cycle of Growth Stage 1 (Seed. Mars. Number 4). We see here that the Opposition is between Number 1 and Number 4.
2. The basic meaning of Number 5 relates to its being an extension or development of Number 4. The additional One challenges or opposes the static inertia of Number 4. There is movement and change. Here is the development of "Mind over Matter".
3. This could also be interpreted as Free Will in practical matters.
4. With the increase in number we get an increase in symbols, which indicates greater complexity – which, as we see, is appropriate to Number 5. However, at base level there is still the simple duality, or "opposition" of a binary system (1 versus 4) – which occurs with each odd number.
5. The Roman numeral for Number 5 is said to be a representation of the human hand, which also manipulates matter.
6. We next have to take note of another common symbol – that of the Pentangle, or 5 pointed star. With similarity to the American Pentagon, one of its uses appears to be a form of Defence - in this case against "occult forces". The Pentangle is usually depicted in one of 2 different forms – one with the single point facing upward, one with the single point facing downward. The upward facing point type, like the opposable thumb, suggests "Mind Over Matter" (1 above 4). The downward facing point type suggests "Matter Over Mind" (4 above 1), indicating the control that material things can have over our lives, rather than supporting spiritual development. We further see that the latter downward facing Pentangle is symbolically related to The Devil.
7. Therefore, with Number 5 we have the (binary) dilemma symbolised by The Priest versus The Devil. Good and Evil. The 2 faces of The Devil are Lucifer, "Bringer of Light" (consciousness) and Satan, "Bringer of Darkness". So we have another relationship with The Sun.
8. The related Astrological Aspect is the Quincunx which divides the circle into 5 times 72 degrees. It is a minor aspect which is mostly ignored because, although there must be some connection between planets involved, it is not clear what the effects are. One reason for this is that there are no orbs – it only operates when exact, so it is very rare.

NUMEROLOGY

9. The Quincunx gives rise to the outer 2 dimensional form of a mathematical Pentagon. The main symbolic use of a pentagon is in a bishop's mitre which has evolved from early "hats" worn by priests. There must have been some symbolic reason for it, but it has been lost in time. References frequently relate it to an ancient (defensive) military shield. This meaning is carried into the present day with The Pentagon in America – which is the "Head" + "Quarters" (1 + 4) of their Army, Navy, Air Force - and "Department of Defense". Usually, symbolically, the "hat" one wears shows one's occupation at that time.

10. We see the relationship with The Heart Chakra. The related endocrine gland, the Thymus, is said to be active in resistance to disease (defence).

11. The chemical element with Atomic Number 5 is Boron, a solid with 6 Neutrons and 5 Protons/Electrons. Apart from industrial use it is necessary in minute quantities to sustain plant life where it provides some defence against plant diseases.

12. Another example of Number 5 "opposition" is from the statistical "80/20 Rule" (4 x 20) + (1 x 20) = 100 attributed to Pareto, an Italian economist, who observed that 20% of people owned 80% of the world's wealth. After that other people noted a similar proportionality in their areas, such as 20% of stock taking up 80% warehouse space, and 80% of time producing 20% of income (20% of time producing 80% of income).

13. We note that Tarot Card VIII. Strength, with its depiction of "Mind Over Matter", is associated with Number 5 via The Cycle of Growth Stage 5 (Power. Creativity)

NUMBER 6 – BINARY 110 – VENUS

Venus rules Cycle of Growth Stage 2 (Germination) in the Fixed Earth Element Taurus, and Cycle of Growth Stage 7 (Partners) in the Cardinal Air Element Libra

In The Kabbalah Number 6 relates to Sephirah 7 (Netzach. Victory) which is at the bottom of The Pillar of Mercy (Force) and related to the planet Venus (both by Numerology and The Kabbalah).

Its position on The Pillar of Force may seem an anomaly when we consider its traditional association with Peace and Beauty. However, when we look deeper, we realise that its real power is that of Desire. Desire is one of the greatest motivating forces of the human world consisting of a powerful negative force of attraction - more so because it is often unconscious. E-motion means movement away from, or outside of, one's self. It is related to "Needs" - a complicated subject which is considered in the chapter [PSYCHOLOGY : DEVELOPMENT MODELS].

Another qualification for The Pillar of Force is that, even though Mercury is closer to The Sun, Venus is hotter from having an atmosphere.

"Needs" suggest that there is a lack of something. We gain a greater understanding of Venus when we examine its symbol, which is the Circle of Spirit above the Cross of Matter/Form. The circle of Spirit is a vision of Wholeness and Completion of the original state of Perfection before The Fall. It is projected on to the outside world rather than being sought for inwardly. At a material level it is "Beauty of Form" (Libra) or, at another level, "Material Desire" (Taurus).

We cannot find Inner Peace in the external world.

In keeping this information to a basic, simple, archetypal level we must take care not to apply it to any specific situation. We remind ourselves that The Sephiroth of The Kabbalah exist in 4 different Kingdoms, and that Venus (or any other planet) can be in any of 12 Signs of The Zodiac and any of 12 Houses of a Birth Chart – which allows for 144 variations.

In The Cycle of Growth Venus rules Stage 2 (Germination) in the Fixed Earth Sign of Taurus where it is concerned with physical comfort, and Stage 7 (Partners) in the Cardinal Air Sign of Libra where it seeks completion in the external world until realisation that the drive comes from inner disharmony.

There are 720 possible permutations of 6 numbers.

NUMEROLOGY

We recognise that Beauty of Outer Form may not necessarily match with inner motivation of the objects or people. This is also the realm of the mythological Sea Sirens, or mermaids, that lure sailors astray to their death on hidden rocks. Another association is that of sexual desire, and its "Venereal" transmitted diseases.

We gain more understanding of Venus when we compare it with other planets it is often paired with. In Astrology it is generally paired with Mars (with traditional symbol the reverse of Venus), which on the Pillar of Form is able to focus energy to a specific purpose, or goal. The combination of Mars and Venus is Sexual Intercourse. That is, achieving what we desire. There is more detail below.

In The Kabbalah Venus is at the same level as Mercury, also on The Pillar of Form, and paired with Venus on The Pillar of Force, both being termed "Inner" or "Personal" Planets". Both their orbits are between The Sun and Earth. At a simple level, Mercury is the "Rational, Logical Mind" and Venus "Feelings" or "Emotions".

In Mythology, Venus was born from the sea when Uranus (Individualisation. Will. Aquarius. Daath. Cycle of Growth Stage 11) was castrated (dis-empowered) by Kronos (Saturn/Satan) and the genitals thrown into the sea (Collective Unconscious). Apart from depicting the power struggle of The Transcendent Octave we can see that the unbalanced power of Venus Desire (on The Pillar of Force) always seeking balance is a trap for the unwary on the Individual Path.

We can also see this story has parallels with that of Adam and Eve in Genesis.

We also gain another viewpoint of The Transcendent Octave of The Cycle of Growth with its challenge of Saturn/Satan by Uranus. In the myth, Venus replaces Uranus.

CYCLE OF GROWTH STAGE 2 (GERMINATION)

The Seed planted in Aries begins to germinate, putting roots down into the Earth.

The Stage is ruled by Taurus which is the Fixed Earth Sign. That is, Earth in its most stable and inert state. Here at the 2nd. Stage of the 2nd. Octave we can see a similarity of activity of "the irresistible force meeting the immovable object" which was symbolised at Sephirah 3 (Binah. Form. Capricorn. Cardinal Earth. Saturn/Satan. Number 2) – the 2nd. Stage of the 1st. Octave.

Taurus is ruled by Venus (Peace. Harmony. Comfort), here working in the Earth Element (Sensation). The child requires the physical "stroking" of Transactional Analysis [PSYCHOLOGY : DEVELOPMENT MODELS].

This is the second stage of Infancy from 7 months to 1 year 8 months and is included in Freud's Oral Stage with focus of sensation on the mouth. The child is beginning to feel physical discomfort for the first time as the arousal of its needs and their satisfaction is no longer immediate.

At base level, Venus and earthy Taurus are concerned with the achievement of physical and emotional comfort (Peace). The traditional connection with money is really a means to that end. In childhood development, having achieved that we can move on.

The related Tarot Cards II.THE PRIESTESS and III.THE EMPRESS indicate the more feminine, maternal, external influence at this time, and also that this is also a time of psychological development in that an "internal world" is being created in the mind as a reflection of experience. The "blank sheet" of the brain is being written on.

The Empress contains reference to "Mother Earth".

The theme is repeated in Genesis Chapter 2. After the creation of Adam in the previous Stage we now have the creation of The Garden of Eden containing the Tree of Life and The Tree of Knowledge. We can see this as an allusion to the human body with the "Trees" referring to the Chakra system. Adam has to "serve and keep it" – which could be an indirect allusion to the body as "temple of the soul". In The Garden of Eden one's survival needs are met externally.

> *And Jehovah God taketh the man, and causeth him to rest in the garden of Eden, to serve it, and to keep it. [Genesis 2:15 YLT]

CYCLE OF GROWTH STAGE 7 (PARTNERS)

Venus also rules the Cardinal (Initiating) Air Sign of Libra (Partnerships. Balance).

The Stage is that of Young Adulthood at the age of 23 Years. Having achieved some sense of Personality and Self Identity as a result of parental upbringing and association with peer groups, our path continues into the broader field of Society where everything one has learned so far is challenged. This means that Venus is not

NUMEROLOGY

quite the "Bringer of Peace" as depicted in tradition. We see from the diagrams below that there are hidden oppositions.

At this age we see the process of seeking a mate as compensation for rejection by the mother at Cycle of Growth Stage 4 (Transplanting. Oedipus).

The associated Tarot Card is XI.Justice (The Scales) which indicates a decision making process. Dilemmas arise. "The Opposites" must be balanced.

NUMEROLOGY

Numerology and The Tree of Life both agree with the association of Venus.

Famous people with Number 6 Life Path include Dale Carnegie ("How to Win Friends and Influence People"), Buddy Ebsen (Actor. Beverley Hillbillies family), John Lennon (Beatle. Sun Libra. "Give Peace a Chance").

6 - OTHER ASSOCIATIONS

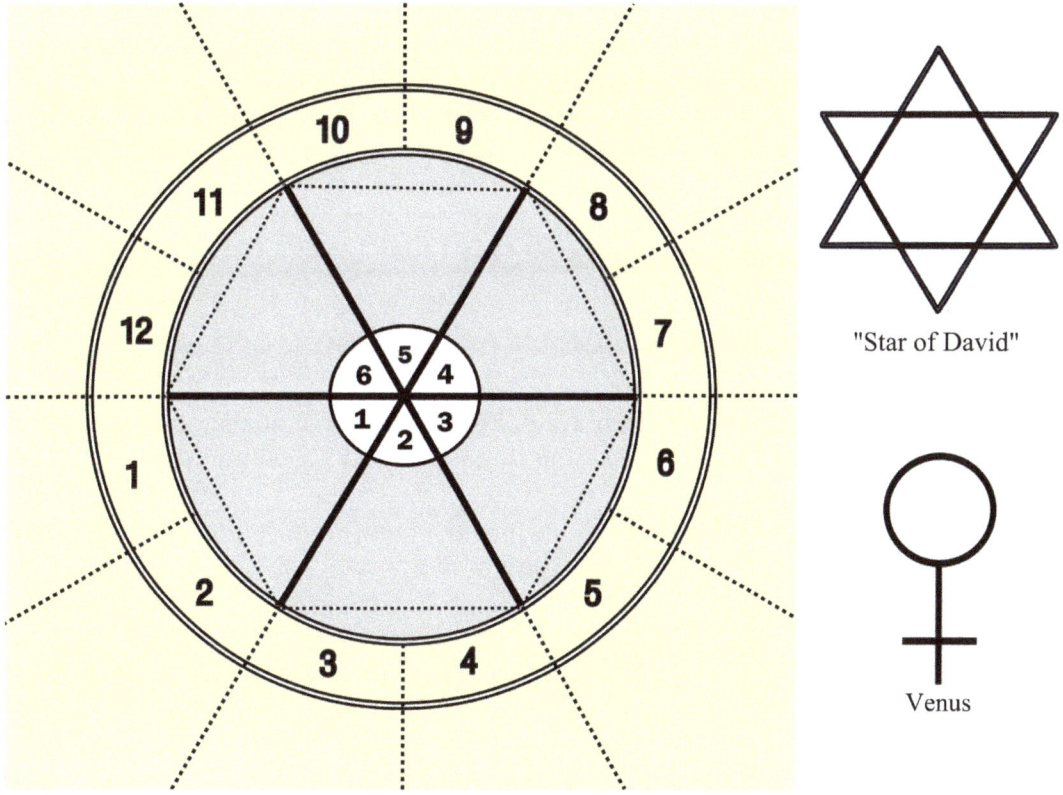

Figure 84 : Numerology - Number 6

1. Number 6 takes on the qualities of Numbers 2 and 3.
2. In the set of 9 Numbers, Number 6 is at the end of the 3rd.Octave which is Cycle of Growth Stage 8 (Sex. Death. Scorpio).
3. The diagram compares the Cycle of Growth circle with that of Number 6. We can see that this one is more complex and contains possibilities for Oppositions that the former does not. Oppositions take on the qualities of Number 2. We have numerous relationships.
4. In Astrology we have the Sextile Aspect of 60 degrees (6 x 60 = 360). The Sextile has a similar activity to the Trine Aspect of 120 degrees which is based on Number 3 (3 x 120 = 360). Although the Sextile is an "easy" aspect it requires a greater effort to combine the energies. The planets involved are not in Signs of the same Element – however, they are in Signs of the same Polarity, positive or negative.

NUMEROLOGY

5. We see the involvement of Number 2 when we realise that, when considering Polarities, Opposites attract and like polarities repel one another (give rise to dilemmas).
6. We note that, apart from the lack of a centre, the simplification of this higher number ignores the stability of Number 4, which includes Earth and Air.
7. As with the 5 pointed star, the 6 pointed star has no apparent centre. Traditionally the figure is stated to consist of 2 "opposite" triangles – the upward facing one denotes the positive Fire Element and the downward facing one, negative Water. Water is stimulated and aroused by Fire. This is also a symbol of sexual (and other) intercourse.
8. We are reminded of one of the first of Jesus' miracles of turning water into wine (Fire-Water/Spirit/Blood) at the wedding feast. However, not all desires are sexual in the normal interpretation of the word. If we examine Freud's early work in Psychology it is clear that if he had used the more general term "Desire" instead of "Sexual" when dealing with erogenous zones of the body he would not have received the resistance from his society that he did. For example, at his Oral Stage, it is normal for an infant to desire food and Nature encourages it to suck by providing a concentration of sensory nerves on the lips so it associates the process with pleasure. Later on Desire is transferred elsewhere to encourage the proper sequence of development. We note that this process is extended further by Maslow's "Hierarchy of Needs" (Venus) as mentioned in the chapter [PSYCHOLOGY : DEVELOPMENT MODELS].
9. In connection with the foregoing, we note that Freud's focus of attention was diverted from the more general nature of Desire by his continued need to deal with problems caused by the taboos and sexual repression of the society of his time. So he never got to the "higher" levels of Maslow's Hierarchy – which, interestingly, does not explicitly include sex. The message here is that we do not lose our desires by repressing them. Experience shows that when a Desire is satisfied we usually get bored and seek something else. This idea especially applies to The Mid Life Crisis, when, unfortunately, people tend to look backwards to repeat the pleasures of the past rather than looking forward to satisfy new desires in Maslow's Hierarchy.

Like as the hart desireth the waterbrooks, so longeth my soul after thee, O God. [Psalm 42] – shows Desire at a different level - Ref. "The Dove" of Scorpio at Cycle of Growth Stage 8 *(Sex. Death)*.

10. The progress of Desire is depicted in the Tarot Suit of Cups (Water). It shows that, without external stimulation, the Negative Water Element, like the Negative Earth Element, descends to a state of inertia and stagnancy.
11. The element with Atomic Number 6 is Carbon, which is the basis of all organic life on Earth. It has the property of being able to link atoms together to form long chains.
12. In the set of 9 numbers, the Number 6 position relates to the Cycle of Growth Stage 8 (Sex. Death).
13. The I Ching is basically a 6 bit binary system where each Hexagram contains 6 lines each of which can represent either Zero or 1 – which allows a total of 64 Hexagrams.
14. We note the association with Tarot Card VI. The Lovers.

NUMEROLOGY

NUMBER 7 – BINARY 111 – MERCURY

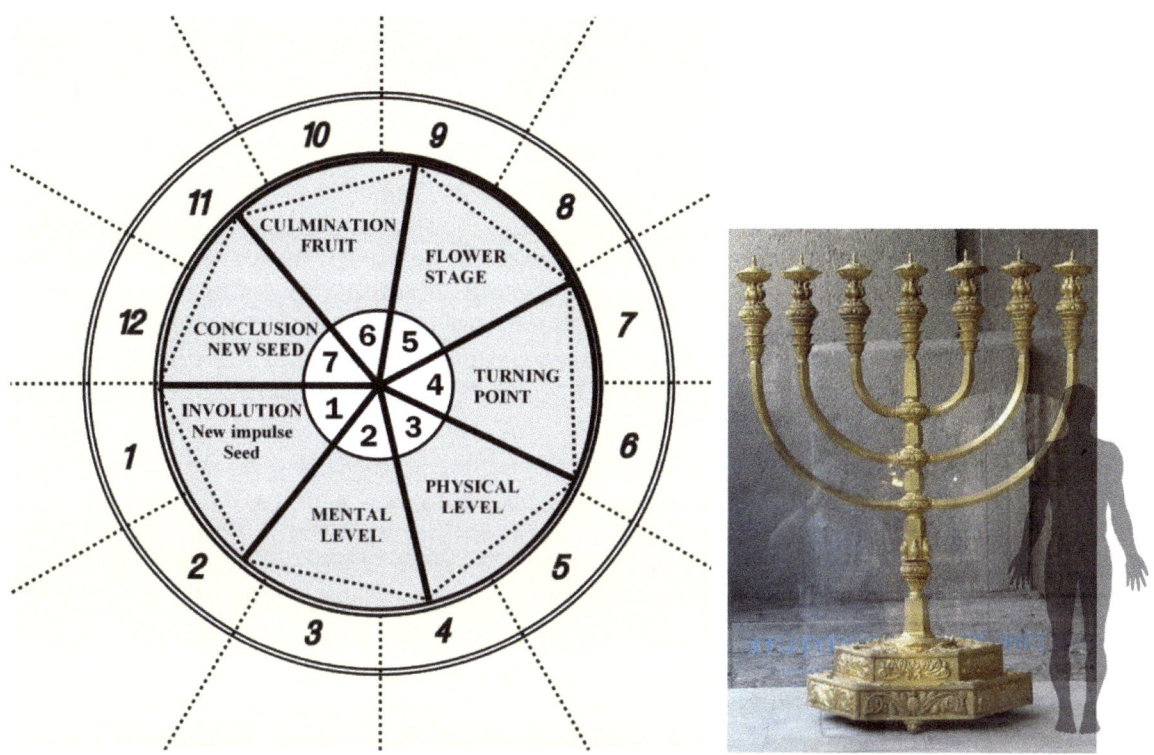

Figure 85 : Numbers - Number 7 and 12 Uranus 7 Year Sub-Cycles [COB]

Mercury rules Cycle of Growth Stage 3 (Experiment. Communication) in the Mutable Air Element Gemini, and Cycle of Growth Stage 6 (Service to Self. Health) in Mutable Earth, Virgo.

At base level Number 7 (Sephirah 8.Mercury. Rational Mind) emphasises the challenge of the additional 1 of odd numbers to the previous even number. So we have Rational Mind versus 6 (Sephirah 7. Venus. Feeling. Desire). Here the additional Number 1 is explicitly given a higher status than the other 6.

Number 7 has its roots in relation to the 7 Days of Creation which are symbolised in our 7 day week. In Genesis the "Day of Rest" was the 7th. Day. Religion tends to make it the 1st. Day of the week with the meaning of the "dawn" of new consciousness (via the priest). The actual week day of the Sabbath varies depending on the religion.

The one physical symbol of Number 7 appears to be the Jewish Menorah the construction of which was explicitly described in The Bible (Exodus 25:31-40). The principle of its use was that the centre lamp was lit on the Sabbath and the other lamps were lit from that one on following 6 days. The symbolism is that of learning, or growth of consciousness, achieved on The Sabbath, is developed further at the dawning of each day.

Another principle association would be with The Tree of Life and the 7 Chakras, 6 of which are controlled by The Crown.

The Jewish Religion has discarded the Biblical 7 branched Menorah for a 9 branched one with the reason that they should not duplicate anything from Solomon's Temple. This seems another example of religion confusing the literal meaning of the Bible with its symbolic meaning – especially as the Menorah and design of The Temple were explicitly described in their scriptures as "the word of God". Number 9 refers to the more practical, down-to-earth, Sephirah 10 (Malkuth. Earth). It is used at a minor 8 day festival which approximates Christmas. We note the equal symbolism of the Winter Solstice "bringing new light", albeit in a different "form".

In symbolic terms, the creation of Solomon's Temple is, in fact, a necessary part of Kabbalism.

We see that this meaning is entirely in keeping with Cycle of Growth Stage 3 (Experiment. Communication) and the associated Tarot cards IV.THE EMPEROR and V.THE HIEROPHANT. The latter is especially relevant in the sense of "Higher Knowledge" as "the word of God" being transmitted by the priest.

NUMEROLOGY

The association of Mercury with Cycle of Growth Stage 6 (Service to Self. Health. Age 12-23. IX.The Hermit) is similar except that the teaching in schools, once again, is more of a practical nature.

Once again, the odd number shows a challenge by Number 1, this time to Number 6 which we have seen applies to our Feelings and Desires (Venus). As we grow, we have to learn to delay or give up one satisfaction in favour of another.

When we consider Number 7 we can do it in a different way to the other numbers because Sephirah 8 (Hod. Glory. Number 7) is at the bottom of the Pillar of Form – so we have numerous examples of its (more physical) manifestation. Each example of Number 7 is a complete "set".

In The Tree of Life Number 7 refers to the Sephirah 8 Hod (Glory) and the Planet Mercury (Mind) which has been mentioned as balancing Sephirah 7 (Victory and Venus) (Desire. Emotion). Hod is placed at the bottom of The Pillar of Severity (Form) and is therefore concerned with consolidating energy. We have seen that this Sephirah is the province of rational, logical, thought which balances feeling and emotions. Its position on the Pillar of Form shows it has the ability for Imagination- that is the production of plans or images in the mind which could later become physical reality in Sephirah 10. We note that examples of Number 7 are purely mental constructions (Ideas. Concepts). Except for The Chakras and the colour spectrum there is no Number 7 in Nature.

Mercury, we note, is the natural ruler of Gemini (Mutable Air) which, among other things, is concerned with the stage of life when a child is learning that things and people have Names – which are mental forms, or representations, of physical objects. In terms of The Tree, this is rather a "bottom up" approach, whereas Creation was "top down" with "In the beginning was the Word". As ruler of Virgo, an Earth Sign, it is more concerned with ways of earning a living by practical craftsmanship, and physical health.

Like its partner on The Tree, Venus, Mercury also has sexual connotations – although, unlike Venus, it is neither male or female. In Greek Mythology he carried a Caduceus which was a kind of magic wand or staff with wings at the top and entwined with snakes. We observe that the symbol for the planet has a remarkable resemblance. We recognise this a symbol of kundalini Serpent Fire rising up the Chakras in the spine. Among other things, Mercury is also "God of Cross Roads". A cross is part of the planet's symbol.

A main principle of Mercury as "Messenger of the Gods" is Communication which converts ideas into forms that can be perceived by the physical senses – such as words spoken or on paper (Gemini), and physical creations or art forms (more related to Virgo). We note that these examples are only 2 of 12 possibilities in that Mercury can be in any Zodiac Sign of a Birth Chart.

There are 5,040 possible permutations of 7 numbers.

CYCLE OF GROWTH STAGE 3 (EXPERIMENT. COMMUNICATION)

This Stage covers the ages 2 to 4 years when the child is learning to control its physical body and the mind is developing to enable communication. One of the main tasks is learning the names of things. Names are mental constructions of external objects and enables their manipulation in the mind. The child also gets a name – which gradually develops into a personal identity. Numerology gives great importance to one's name.

The Stage is related to Gemini (Mutable/Changeable Air) and the planet Mercury, both of which are concerned with mental development.

The related Tarot Cards are IV.The Emperor and V.The Hierophant who are both symbols of masculine power who, to the developing infant, are said to, psychologically, hold godlike powers of life and death. We note the association of Number 7 with the dawning of new knowledge, and a teacher.

In Genesis, this is the stage when Adam is given the task of naming things.

CYCLE OF GROWTH STAGE 6 (SERVICE TO SELF. HEALTH)

The Stage covers Puberty and Adolescence from 13 to 23 years of age when we mainly relate to those in our peer group. This is the "homosexual age" when our close relationships are with those of the same sex. Mercury is, once again, in a Mutable/Changeable Sign - this time practical down-to-Earth Virgo. The teaching/leaning is related to that at school. At this level, Mercury is "The Analytical Mind" which sorts an categorises. "The Data Analyst". The Sign is mainly concerned with supporting a physical body, and includes the need to seek work to achieve it.

NUMEROLOGY

The related Tarot Card is IX.The Hermit which relates to the beginning of conscious awareness of differences between inner and outer perception of reality, and what one has been taught as a child by IV.The Emperor and V.The Hierophant at Cycle of Growth Stage 3 . We can also add X.The Wheel of Fortune and its association with "Lucky 7". Where survival is concerned we do not need to leave too much to chance.

NUMEROLOGY

Numerology states that Number 7 relates to Neptune, which if you know any Pisces (the complementary Sign to Virgo) people you will realise is not correct. On its own, Mercury (Communication) is just the opposite – logical rather than imaginative – although, like the metal mercury, it will easily "amalgamate" with other planets.

Famous Number 7 Life Paths include Lady Diana Spencer (Sun Cancer), Tom Ewell (Actor. "The Seven Year Itch"), Martin Heidegger (Philosopher), J. Edgar Hoover (FBI head 48 years), President John F. Kennedy, Andre Mairax (WWII resistance leader), Louis Pasteur (scientist. Pasteurisation), Robert Stack (Actor. "The Untouchables"), Marilyn Monroe (Sun Gemini), Queen Elizabeth II (Sun Taurus).

7 - OTHER ASSOCIATIONS

1. In the set of 9 numbers, Number 7 is at the beginning of The 1st. Octave (Gestation and Transcendence) and related to Cycle of Growth Stage 9 (Conception). New beginnings.
2. Cycle of Growth Stage 9 (Conception) is ruled by Sagittarius (Higher Mind. Jupiter) which associates with Abstract Concepts, rather than its more practical complement Gemini/Mercury (Rational Mind). However, we can see an overall influence of Teaching and Learning.
3. If there is no change at Cycle of Growth Stage 9 the new Conception does not develop and Stage 10 becomes Stage 1 (=1 + 0). There is no Stage 11 (Discontent) or Stage 12 (Confinement).

THE 12 x 7 YEAR CYCLES OF URANUS

I include this here because it is a more detailed example of how the cycle of a single number can be compared with The Cycle of Growth. It is included in the book "Cycles of Becoming" [COB] where Alexander Ruperti describes the 84 Year Cycle of Uranus in terms of 3 x 28, 12 x 7, and 7 x 12 year cycles. The other planet cycles are dealt with in a similar way.

1. Each of the 12 x 7 year cycles is related to a single Stage of The Cycle of Growth 12 Stages starting at birth.
2. Each year of the 7 year cycle has a similar relationship as shown in the diagram.

As with other cycles, the 7 year cycle is a "short" version of the 12 Year Cycle of Growth. Wheels within wheels. The diagram above shows the relationship between the two cycles, each beginning at the zero point. Relating to each year of a lifetime, Alexander Ruperti calls each stage the "Age Factor" [COB]. I add to the scenario with the approximate relationships with the 12 Stage Cycle of Growth [COB] and the additional insights that brings . The following is paraphrased from his book.

YEAR 1 – INVOLUTION SPIRITUAL LEVEL - Seed Period based on activities of the previous 7 year cycle. A sense of freedom and new beginnings. Perhaps confusion or difficulty finding a direction in life. A sense of frustration (Discontent) with the status quo. (COG 1 – Seed. COG 2 Germination)

YEAR 2 – INVOLUTION MENTAL LEVEL – A new direction in life may be considered. There will be a resistance from past habits and lifestyle – especially those of close relationships. There may be the need to spend resources or seek new skills. The resistance will be more at an inner, psychological level with negative thoughts and ideas related to the new trend. A need for conscious decisions. A way through the impasse could be to experiment in a small way to see if the ideas are viable. (COG 3 - Experiment).

YEAR 3 – INVOLUTION PHYSICAL LEVEL – An effort to exteriorise the impulse in a practical way despite having a sense of loneliness or being irrational. Success is not certain. It is a good idea to explore the possibilities with those outside the home (where there may be more support), especially in related areas. (COG 4 –Transplanting. COG 5 – Power)

YEAR 4 – TURNING POINT – This is the "Full Moon" position where one can consciously evaluate the progress so far relative to the original seed idea. So far the process has occurred in the private areas of life. Now is the time to take the next step to exteriorise the project in a more public arena outside the home. There may be a sense of "pass or fail", perhaps a crisis point, or need for an important decision, midway through the Cycle. There may be a new partnership formed. (COG 6 – Service to Self. COG 7 – Partnerships, Social Advancement).

YEAR 5 – EVOLUTION PHYSICAL LEVEL – This is the "Flower Stage" of the whole period which can result in social success or failure. Either will result in an expansion of consciousness of the way things are. Perhaps discovering a new possibility for the next Cycle. Ruperti says that one may find a teacher, guide, or helper – or function as one personally. (COG 8 – Death. Intercourse. COG 9 – Conception)

YEAR 6 – EVOLUTION MENTAL LEVEL – This is the culmination or peak of the whole Cycle with the possibility of evaluating the experience in all its personal and social aspects. There may be social success or failure. From now on there will be a decline in motivation in preparation for the next cycle. There may be the need to sacrifice the past and dedicate one's self to a new future (COG 10 – Social Peak which is followed by decline in preparation for a new cycle).

YEAR 7 – EVOLUTION SPIRITUAL LEVEL – This is a conclusion of the entire Cycle with withdrawal from the public eye in preparation for a new one. Even if successful there will be a sense of boredom, and/or frustration with the lack of personal freedom forced by the current position. One can be a "slave to success". (COG 11 – Discontent. COG 12 – Confinement).

Perhaps this also refers to "The Seven Year Itch" of human partnerships.

7 x 12 YEAR CYCLES – 7 STAGES IN THE 84 YEAR CYCLE

Within this structure there is relationship with the 12 year Generic Jupiter Cycle. There is actually a cycle time of 14 years between each conjunction between the 2 planets as Jupiter makes its orbit and eventually catches up with Uranus again. The Cycle of Growth can be applied to this cycle too, as can the included example of the monthly Moon phases mentioned under Number 4.

Each 12 year stage in turn relates to each of the "THE 7 YEAR CYCLE" stages above as a kind of overall "theme".

SYMBOLISM OF NUMBER 7

1. In the sequence of Numbers, Number 7 gives a challenge to Number 6 (Desire. Need)
2. The challenge is depicted on The Tree of Life with Mercury and Venus on opposite pillars.
3. We note the repeated theme of "transferring light" is contained in the symbolism of The Menorah, Mercury (Communication) , the Chakras of The Tree of Life and The Tree of Knowledge, the visible colour spectrum, the notes of the Musical Scale, and The Tarot V.The Hierophant.
4. Number 7 (Mercury) is a teacher as depicted by V.The Hierophant.
5. The overall symbolism is that the teachings or new consciousness (light) of The Sabbath (Day of Rest. Cycle of Growth Stage 12. Withdrawal. Sleep) is repeated at the dawning of each day.
6. Mercury prefers Words to Symbols.
7. The only physical symbol of Number 7 seems to be the Jewish 7 branched candlestick – The Menorah. The design of the Menorah was explicitly described to Moses by God in the book of Exodus after the escape from Egypt and the giving of the Ten Commandments (one of which is the commandment to observe the Sabbath Day).
8. The Menorah was designed to resemble an almond tree - which is one of the first trees to bloom in Spring and therefore can symbolically be related to the beginning of new life. There are bitter and sweet varieties of the nut, which are meant to refer to God's reward or punishments.
9. A main feature is that the design is stated to be a single, central, candlestick with another 3 on each side – which emphasises the "Opposition" or elevation of 1 – which is said to represent the Sabbath - above the other 6.
10. The lighting of the 7 branches clearly symbolises the activation of the 7 Chakras in Revelation (although the Jewish religion would not recognise it).
11. We now consider some of the manifestations of Number 7. There is a common factor that there is a continuing cycle of 7 with the new cycle being at a different level to the previous one. So there is a form of evolution. With some, like the Musical Scale, The Colour Spectrum, and The Chakras there is an increased rate of frequency. The 7 Day Week could be considered in this context with the ever increasing rate of Change we are experiencing in the human world.

NUMEROLOGY

7 DAYS OF CREATION AND THE CYCLE OF GROWTH

The first 7 Days of Creation are fixed in that they cannot be exactly repeated, although they give the basis to our 7 day week and symbolically repeat as indicated in The 1st. Octave of The Cycle of Growth which covers our life in the womb. The 7th. "Day of Rest" corresponds with Cycle of Growth Stage 12 (Withdrawal. Confinement) and the time of confinement of a woman in preparation for the birth. The 7th. day is different to the other 6.

Chapter 2:1: Thus the heavens and the earth were finished, and all the host of them.

Chapter 2:2: And on the seventh day God ended his work which he had made; and he rested on the seventh day from all his work which he had made. [KJV]

We note that mention of the final Day 6 of creation in The Bible comes at the end of Genesis Chapter 1, and the 7th. Day at the beginning of Chapter 2 – which relates to the beginning of the 2nd. Octave of The Cycle of Growth, which itself corresponds with the actual physical birth of a child. The next stage of Creation in Chapter 2 sees the creation of Adam and Eve in the Garden of Eden – before which time there are no humans on Earth. This is strengthened by the evolutionary connection of Number 6 with sexual reproduction, which first evolved in plants and animals, and was instrumental in enabling the evolution of the wide variety of species ("Diversification") past and present.

7 DAYS IN A WEEK AND THE 7TH. DAY

We have 7 days in a week, and they are dynamic in that they continually repeat their cycle. The period was arrived at as a result of the Biblical Story of Creation, with God resting on the 7th.Day (Cycle of Growth Stage 12 (Withdrawal. Confinement), and the 4th. Commandment given to Moses to *"Remember the Sabbath Day and keep it holy"*. The church was instrumental in devising the calendar we use today, and needed the regular rest day, or Sabbath. There is disagreement among religions which day of the week is referred to. In the Jewish religion the Sabbath is Saturday (Saturn's Day) and in Christianity Sunday (day of the SUN/SON, Jesus [EC]. The Sun). Here is another symbolic example of the difference in the two philosophies, and the continued attitude of the Jewish Religion to ignore Jesus as someone of importance.

It is a strange fact that the church of the time decided to make the Sabbath the FIRST day of the week - rather than the last, which would fit the Creation Story Day 7 beginning Genesis Chapter 2. This ties in with the repeated symbolism of Number 6 being a "completion" stage, with odd Number 7 being a preparation for the next.

An interesting anecdote is that I once worked with someone who was involved in a factory producing munitions during the war. To boost production they worked an 8 day week instead of 7 by changing rest days. This indicates that we could change our working week if we wanted to, and emphasises that our sets of 7 are in some sense illogical.

7 VISIBLE COLOURS OF THE SPECTRUM

The 7 colours of the visible spectrum are dynamic in that they are part of a larger whole. We are all familiar with "the colours of the rainbow". A point to keep in mind is that the visible colours are just a small part of the Electromagnetic Spectrum which covers various frequencies of electromagnetic radiation. At the lower frequencies we have Television Waves, then Radio Waves, followed by Infrared - which is mainly emitted heat. Next comes visible light (Red, Orange, Yellow, Green, Blue, Indigo, Violet), followed by Ultraviolet Rays, X-rays, and Gamma Rays. When all the visible colours are mixed together, the visible light becomes White Light – which could be considered the Zero state. In computers all colours are obtained by mixing Red, Green and Blue (RGB) together in various proportions – which could relate to the Seven being a product of Number 3.

We note that with the electromagnetic spectrum there is an additional relationship with Uranus/Aquarius "The Water Carrier", concerned with Communication, in that the frequencies behave as if they are "waves". There is also the scientific dilemma that light can behave like waves or particles depending on the experimental method used.

7 CHAKRAS

To summarise the chapter [THE CHAKRAS] - the 7 Chakras are energy centres located along the spine which provide focal points for spiritual and psychic forces and the human body to interact. The "Root Chakra" is at the base of the spine and the "Crown Chakra" on top of our head. Chakra means "wheel", so named because some psychics can see the chakras and describe them as rotating vortexes of energy – rather like whirlpools of water. They are of different frequencies and are described as having similar colours to the visible spectrum. The colours vary depending on the health and emotional state of the subject. Other than that the descriptions of the functions they perform varies depending on the source. There is a relationship with the endocrine glands of the human body which release hormones directly into the blood stream and govern our whole metabolism.

The actual "Master Gland" – the Hypothalamus (1 opposing Number 7) – which controls all the others via the Pituitary Gland seems to be unrecognised or ignored. The Pituitary Gland therefore makes our "Number 1 opposing Number 6". This whole area is a "minefield" of misunderstanding and misinformation in the light of modern medical knowledge. I have seen the same keywords used to describe different chakras by different authorities.

In The book of Revelation the Chakras are referred to as (among other things) a book with Seven Seals that could only be opened by a sacrificed lamb with seven horns and seven eyes.

7 NOTES OF A MUSICAL SCALE (A,B,C,D,E,F,G = 7)

A musical Octave is usually stated to consist of 8 notes, however the 8th. note is a repetition of the first which begins a new set of notes - each at twice the frequency – which, taking into account The Cycle of Growth, relates more to a cycles of 7.

Generally when we consider musical notes we are concerned with those within the human audible range. However there are clearly frequencies outside this range – for example dog whistles are made that we cannot hear, and whales and dolphins also communicate in frequencies outside our range of hearing.

For basic tuning purposes orchestras tend to use the note A above Middle C which vibrates at 440 hertz (cycles per second). Some examples of the Octaves of A vibrate at 220, 440 and 880 hertz. In this case the "waves" are vibrations created in air. This is emphasised when we consider that the range of the human voice is included. We see the relationship with Mercury and Communication.

OTHER SEVENS

Apart from the ones mentioned above there are innumerable references to Number 7 everywhere, such as Seven Deadly Sins, Seven Wonders of the World, Seven Seas.

NITROGEN – ATOMIC NUMBER 7

We could say that the Communication of Mercury depends on vibrating Air – which is mainly Nitrogen.

Nitrogen is an important gas which makes up about 78% of our atmosphere. Like Hydrogen and Oxygen it exists in pure state as well as in compound form such as Nitrites and Nitrates. Its main feature is that it does not easily react with other elements and requires high temperature and pressure to do so. In fact, it acts as a moderator in our eco system by making a very stable atmosphere. Apart from numerous other things, it is important to life because Nitrates are a constituent of natural and manmade fertilisers – essential to plant life, and therefore, in turn, to animal life. Nitrates were an essential part of the "Primeval Soup" which existed before life began on Earth, and which are included in animal Proteins along with Carbon, Hydrogen, and Oxygen. They were, and still are, created by electrical storms in the higher atmosphere. Over time, bacteria in the soil evolved, some can actually "fix" atmospheric Nitrogen into Nitrates (as can Leguminous plants such as peas, beans, and clover), others convert dead plants and animals back to Nitrates so they can be re-used. Soil bacteria began life on Earth and are still the basis of life on Earth today. Without them there would be no plant life, and therefore no animals.

NUMEROLOGY

NUMBER 8 – BINARY 1000 – THE MOON

The Moon rules Cycle of Growth Stage 4 (Transplanting. Cancer. Shell) which is concerned with the development of a psychological Persona, or "mask", in order to be able to play various roles in life whilst keeping one's inner feelings hidden. It can be considered a form of "Psychic Self Defence".

In The Tree of Life Number 8 refers to Sephirah 9 (Yesod. Foundation) which relates to The Moon. It is low down on The Middle Pillar between Tiphareth (The Sun) and Malkuth (Earth). At this position it is entirely balanced, but, like Earth, has no free will. The benefit is that there are no dilemmas to solve. It has an 8-phase relationship with The Sun and The Earth as a form of "mediator".

The Sephirah is related to the Navel Chakra, which Edgar Cayce relates to The Cells of Leydig and, together with the 6th. Chakra/Pineal, describes it as "The Seat of The Soul". This interpretation is entirely consistent with the Astrological concept of the basic function of The Moon in a birth chart as being related to our Unconscious.

In Kabbalist terms we must observe The Moon as having a more executive function than that suggested by Astrology. Although it is subject to The Sun with no light of its own, it is closer to the top of The Tree than Earth (i.e. with Kether, Crown as the Collective Unconscious), and transmits all the energies of the higher Sephiroth to Earth – combining all the attributes of Force and Form. It is given a description as "Supporter of The Earth" with the image of Atlas supporting the globe Celestial Sphere. In terms of Physics, the Moon stabilises the orbit of The Earth, and stops it wobbling too much – thus maintaining regularity of The Seasons. So, at base level, we have The Laws of Physics, and Laws of Nature. We know that the Earth does still wobble on a 26,000 year cycle, so The Moon also controls [ASTROLOGY : THE ZODIAC AGES].

CYCLE OF GROWTH STAGE 4 (TRANSPLANTING. ROOTS)

Like The Sun, The Moon only rules a single Cycle of Growth Stage.

At the end of the 2nd. Octave, Cycle of Growth Stage 4 (Transplanting. Roots) is controlled by the Cardinal (Initiating) Water Sign of Cancer (Crab. Shell) which is ruled by The Moon.

The first thing to note is that the beginning of Stage 4 is at the lowest level (roots) of The Cycle of Growth. From now onward the movement is upwards toward higher consciousness. This Stage is the final one of Personality and development of a Persona to enable a "vehicle" for activity outside the protection of the home. This is the "Play Age" of psychology Age 4 to 7 years when the child is beginning to discover its ability for acting on its own initiative – and learns to be cautious in disobeying the "godlike" commands of parents.

In Genesis, this is the stage of "The Fall" when Adam and Eve are tempted to disobey God and are eventually given "coats of skin" so they can survive outside The Garden of Eden.

The related Tarot Cards are VI.The Lovers and VII.The Chariot which symbolise the psychological processes involved.

The next Stage ruled by The Sun is the beginning of development of Ego, and Ego Consciousness in the first step towards Individualisation.

In all the wheel diagrams Stage 4/The 4th. House ruled by The Moon is opposite that of Cycle of Growth Stage 10/The 10th.House (Peak. Harvest) ruled by Saturn. Saturn at Cycle of Growth Stage 11 (Discontent) also opposes The Sun which rules Cycle of Growth Stage 5 (Creativity) – which gives an opportunity of activating Uranus to overcome Saturn.

NUMEROLOGY

1. In Numerology, the word "God" reduces to Number 8 (7 + 6 + 4 = 1 + 7 = 8). We can see how this conforms with the principle of control of material affairs and The Laws of Nature.

2. We can see why Numerology relates Number 8 to Saturn/Satan and the traits mentioned agree with those mentioned here. A Number 8 Life Path is related to "material success" and would refer to someone who could rise to a high social position, which, in turn, requires a lot of hard work and focus on long range planning. Perhaps "rags to riches". However, this is not its archetypal meaning.

3. In The Cycle of Growth rulership by Saturn of Stages 10 and 11 opposes both The Moon at Stage 4, and The Sun at Stage 5.

NUMEROLOGY

4. As with the increase of Numbers, we have to note that all the Sephiroth low down in The Tree are contained in, and therefore have relationship to, those at the top. Number 8 contains Numbers 2 and 4 (which contain the principle of Number 8)
5. We must also not lose sight of the cycles of consciousness and unconsciousness that The Sun and Moon represent. Day and Night.

Famous Number 8 destinies include Samuel Goldwin (Film producer & studio executive. Leo), Gene Kruper (Dance Band Drummer – rhythm behind the music. Capricorn), Rocky Marciano (Boxing Champion in a "square ring". Virgo), Douglas Macarthur (WWII US General. Controller of men. Aquarius), G. A. Nasser (revolution to make Egypt a republic), George Orwell (Novelist. "1984" –novel about control by 'Big Brother' – ultimate control by The State. Cancer), George Patten (US General. Scorpio), F. Daryl Zanuck (20th. Century Fox president. Scorpio), Mary Baker Eddy (Christian Science Founder. Cancer), Pope John Paul II (Taurus).

8 - OTHER ASSOCIATIONS

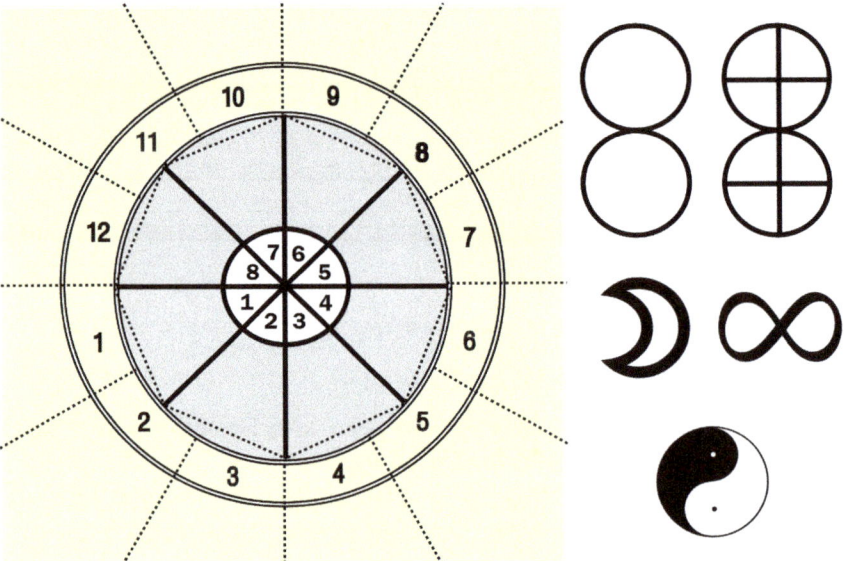

Figure 86 : Numerology - Number 8

1. In the set of 9 Numbers, Number 8 combines Cycle of Growth Stage 10 (Peak. Harvest. Capricorn. Saturn) and Stage 11 (Discontent. Aquarius. Saturn/Uranus) which symbolise the struggle between Stability and Change. Nature solves the problem by creating Cycles and "Taking Turns" so everything gets its chance, and maintains a Zero balance of energy. We again see why Numerology associates Saturn with Number 8.
2. Here we have a "structure above a structure" – which, among other things, indicates the physical Laws of the Universe, or the Laws of Man controlling practical affairs. Combining these ideas, we arrive at the practical affairs of man conforming with the Laws of Nature – the main principle of Astrology. This is depicted above as 2 connected Earth symbols (cross within a circle).
3. The Moon produces the illusion that the Earth is at the centre of the universe.
4. The orbit of The Moon is like a "shell" around the Earth in a similar depiction of the orbit of the electron of an atom of Hydrogen in its shell around its nucleus – which refers to Number 1.
5. We see that the Kabbalist association with The Moon is accurate in that Sephirah 9 (Moon) stands between Sephirah 6, The Sun, and Sephirah 10, Earth, at the bottom of The Middle Pillar.
6. We could also see this as a combination of 2 cycles. Although tempted to relate them to Sun and Moon, the practical manifestation and Number 8 relationship apply more to the daily rotation of the Earth and the monthly Moon Cycle – which has 8 stages. In The Cycle of Growth we do not meet The Sun until Stage 5 (Power. Creativity) – which is the next step of the return journey back up the Tree Of Life.
7. The monthly Moon Cycle is shown as a diagram in [ASTROLOGY : PLANETS ASPECTS].

NUMEROLOGY

8. The Moon is symbolic of the Personal Unconscious, or subconscious mind, which "goes through phases" in its relationship to Consciousness (The Sun). The Personal Unconscious contains a "world image" which has been developing since Cycle of Growth Stage 2 (Germination) with Tarot II.The Priestess and III.The Empress.
9. With Number 8 we have essentially the same basic diagram of Number 2 except that each circle is now subdivided into 4. So Number 8 is 4 + 4, or 2 times 4. There is great stability and opposition to change – which is converted to cyclic movement.
10. Other Number 8 symbols or patterns, both based on Number 4, are the 8 main compass points used to navigate the Earth, and the 8 monthly Moon Phases.
11. The element with Atomic Number 8 is Oxygen which, like Hydrogen and others cannot exist as a single atom. It requires 2 atoms to make a molecule of gas. Oxygen is electro negative and will react easily with many other elements. Together with electro positive Hydrogen (1) it forms water. Oxygen (8) is the most abundant element in the universe after Hydrogen (1) and Helium (2).
12. Following on from 3 dimensional Number 4, Binary Numbers now achieve a 4th. Bit and therefore a 4th. Dimension – that of Time. Space already exists from Number Zero. So does Time, but it can only reveal itself now. Number 8 is Space-Time as shown in the diagram. We now get organised movement and Change.
13. We do not get a binary 5th. Dimension until Number 16.
14. We note the relationship between Number 8 symbol and that of Infinity. In the Tarot Infinity depicts "The Higher Mind" at the beginning of each Octave of The Cycle of Growth. It is explicit in I.The Magician and VIII.Strength, and implied in XIV.Temperance.
15. Tarot Card VII. The Chariot is related to The Moon (planet) and Number 8 at Cycle of Growth Stage 4 (Transplanting) and is depicted as having 2 wheels and 2 complementary forms of energy providing motivation.

THE HYPOTHALAMUS – THE "8TH. CHAKRA"

Although not actually considered a Chakra, the Hypothalamus demonstrates the activity of Number 8 as a "controller of physical affairs". In that it controls all of the other endocrine glands of our body via the Pituitary. When considered with the set of 7 Chakras we have an example of the Numerology principle that, despite being part of a "set", each member has its own individual function. This is similar to the musical Octave being considered to consist of 8 notes, but being really 7 - with the 8th. note being twice the frequency of the first, and beginning a new cycle. (Please see Number 7)

NUMBER 9 – BINARY 1001 – THE EARTH

Here we come firmly down to Earth.

Numerologists seem unable to mention Number 9 without using the word "spiritual" – as if only certain people can be termed as such. Like everything else, it is what we do with it that counts. An example of this is Money – which is often given negative "spiritual" connotations, despite being something that few of us can live without. If we observe closely, we can see that Money acts like a form of primal spiritual energy in that it almost obeys the Laws of Thermodynamics. It converts energy into different forms. For example, my day's work is converted into money which, in turn, can be converted into food.

In The Cycle of Growth everything is spiritual in the sense that, like human evolution in general, and the evolution of an individual person, each Stage is necessary for our development. If we do not control Matter, it controls us.

We can see from our study of The Kabbalah and the evolution of numbers that Number 9 is, in fact, the most material – so there is confusion between material power and spiritual development - which is actually directed toward the top of The Tree via The Transcendent Octave, and Mysticism.

In the Tree of Life Number 9 relates to Sephirah 10 (Malkuth. Kingdom) – which is the physical Earth. Everything is now in stable, material form subject to The Laws of Physics, and Nature – without Free Will.

NUMEROLOGY

The cycle of Number 9 bears close resemblance to that of The Cycle of Growth in that it consists of 3 Octaves – in this case a Triplicity of Triplicities. Number 9 (3 x 3) refers to the 3 (physical) Dimensions of space (Number Zero, The Source). The Cycle of 12 (4 x 3) includes the additional dimension of Time.

With Number 9 we come to the end of the cycle of Numbers. From here we add a Zero to become Number 10, which begins a new cycle - or Number 1 which repeats the last.

As mentioned in Number 7, the 7 branched Menorah "candlestick" used to symbolise the Sabbath and other 6 week days has been replaced by the 9 branched variety ("Hanukkah") which is only used once a year at the 8 day festival of Hanukkah/Chanukah which is now similar to Christmas. The usage is the same in that the main branch of the candlestick is lit first, and light transferred from there to another branch each day. The holiday was adapted from the Christian one at the time of Alexander the Great who allowed his conquered subjects to continue their own religion.

Here, the symbolism of the Menorah, Hanukkah, and Christmas is the same – that of bringing new light at The Winter Solstice. We can also compare this with the "Lightning Flash" of the Kabbalah Tree of Life, where energy is transferred from the "Big Bang" reaction of Sephiroth 1 and 2 down through the other Sephiroth in numerical sequence – symbolised by the sequential lighting of the candles.

There is a problem with having only 9 candles instead of 10, however, this adds an interesting concept to that of The Big Bang at Sephirah 1 (Kether. Crown. Zero) because <u>someone has to strike the match to light the first candle</u> ! We can stretch this a bit further by observing that Light first appeared at Creation Day 1. Zero to 9 makes 10 numbers.

Going yet another step further, we note that the next stage of Creation at Sephirah 3 (Binah. Form. Saturn/Satan) enables the perception of Darkness – which, in turn, enables perception of Light (consciousness). If everything was Light we would not know it existed – it is rather like the air we breathe. We have Lucifer as the role of The Devil as "bringer of (consciousness of) light". "Lucifer" was the old name for a match. Matches contain a lot of Sulphur – another traditional connotation with The Devil.

In The Cycle of Growth, Lucifer relates to card XVI.The Tower. Sulphur has Atomic Number 16.

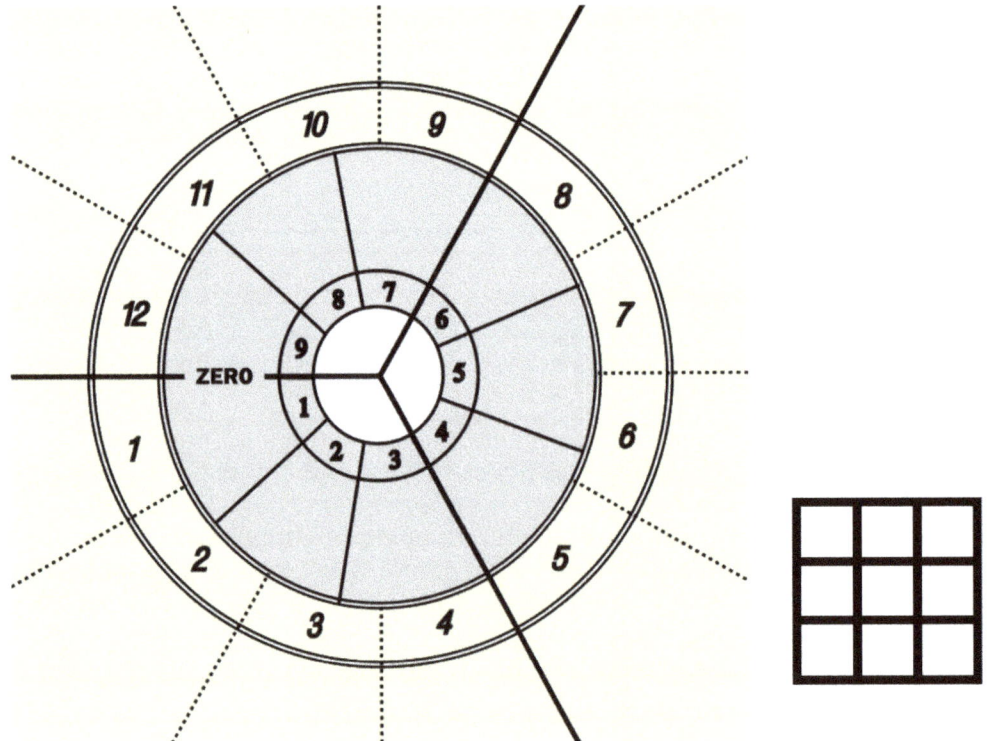

Figure 87 : The Cycle of Number 9

NUMEROLOGY

NUMEROLOGY

1. Numerology relates Number 9 to Mars instead of Earth, and, again, we can see how this could occur when we consider that the position of Mars on The Tree is at the centre of The Pillar of Form, albeit related to a stable Number 4 where it focuses energy to a 3 dimensional cube or single point, or goal. We do see examples of the Aries/Mars "pioneering spirit" in the examples below.
2. Number 9 (Earth) is a Number 4 3 dimensional object, but now in motion.
3. Among the Numerological references in The Bible, in *Revelation Chapter 13*, is the following reference to 666, which, in Numerology, converts to 9. It clearly refers to the qualities of practical, down to earth, human behaviour :-

Verse 17: And that no man might buy or sell, save he that had the mark, or the name of the beast, or the number of his name.

Verse 18: Here is wisdom. Let him that hath understanding count the number of the beast: for it is the number of a man; and his number is Six hundred threescore and six. [KJV]

4. Number 9 refers to The Base Chakra and The Gonads (male & female sex organs).
5. Tarot card IX is that of The Hermit.

Famous number 9 Life Paths include Charles Bronson (Actor. Scorpio), Lee van Cleef (Actor. Capricorn), Charles Lindbergh (Aviator. First solo Atlantic crossing. Aquarius), H. W. Longfellow ("first popular poet". PIsces), Henry Moore (sculptor. Leo), Hugh O'Brien (Actor. "US Marshall Wyatt Earp". Aries), Jack Nicklaus (Golfer. Aquarius), Yoko Ono (Artist. Peace activist. John Lennon's wife. Aquarius), Cole Porter (US Composer. Gemini), Buddy Rich (Drummer. LIbra), Richard Strauss (Composer. Gemini), Orson Welles (Innovative actor, writer, director. Taurus), Mae West (early 1900's sex symbol. Leo), Oscar Wilde (Writer. Poet. Personality. Homosexual imprisoned for "gross indecency" with other men. Libra), Virginia Woolf (Writer. Feminist. Aquarius), Mohandas Karamchand Gandhi (Indian Nationalist. Peaceful rebellion. Libra) , Ayatollah Khomeini (Revolutionary. Overthrew Shah of Iran after 15 years of exile. Taurus), John Wesley (Methodist Founder) – and Alexander Frederick Baulsom - my dad - (postman. Cancer).

9 - OTHER ASSOCIATIONS

1. Similar to Number 7, there is a lack of symbols for Number 9. Astrology has no comparable aspects. However, there is a continually repeating picture theme that emphasises its stable "Square" properties (3 squared = 3 x 3). On closer examination we see that there is the hint of a centre. There is no direct reference to the symbolic Circle of Spirit, Sephirah 1 (Kether. Crown. Number Zero).
2. The Arabic symbol of 9 (Earth) is the reverse of Number 6 (Venus. Desire).
3. In common with other odd numbers, Number 9 comes as a challenge, or opposition, to the previous even number. Number 8 includes The Laws of Nature and the combined cycles of Sun and Moon - which govern Number 9, Earth. Earth has its own 24 hour period of rotation, so we now have 3 different cycles (as depicted in the diagram).
4. In the set of 9 numbers diagram, final Number 9 relates to Cycle of Growth Stage 12 (Confinement. Withdrawal. Karma) which precedes a new birth. It is therefore concerned with clearing away the remains of the past cycle in preparation for a new one. This includes such things as karmic or other debts, and isolation in prison for breaking man's law, or hospital for neglect of self, or other areas of meditation such as monasteries or other retreats. We can see the relationship with the karma of earthy, physical, incarnation.
5. All multiples of Number 9 convert to Number 9 (e.g. 18, 27, 36 etc.)
6. Atomic Number 9 refers to Fluorine which is the most electronegative and reactive element. In its pure state it is a gas – which is only achieved in the laboratory with great difficulty due to its easy combination with other elements. In combination with Hydrogen it forms Hydrofluoric Acid which is highly corrosive, and, among other things, is used to etch glass. This relates to the "dissolving" effect of Cycle of Growth Stage 12 in its reference to the sea and the Collective Unconscious. Sea water has a proportion of every element dissolved in it – even Gold.

NUMEROLOGY

7. From the diagram we note that Number 9 consists of 3 triplicities (ref. Number 3). So it is a Triplicity of Triplicities. The 3 stages of a triplicity are themselves 3 stages of a growth process which, among numerous other arrangements can be considered as Thesis, Antithesis, and Synthesis. In Astrology we have Cardinal, Fixed and Mutable Zodiac Signs - and Angular, Succedent and Cadent Houses.
8. As with The Cycle of Growth, at the end of a cycle there is opportunity to evolve to another level (here to Number 10) or repeat the cycle over again.
9. In the Kabbalah Sephirah 10 Malkuth. Kingdom) is the final material manifestation of the abstract conception of Number Zero. From here the only way is upwards.
10. As with Binary Numbers, the return to, and addition of, Zero promotes a new dimension.

THE CYCLE OF GROWTH

At this level, The Cycle of Growth has no separate association with Number 9 (Earth). This is a final culmination, or manifestation, of Number Zero. Both contain everything. As Above, So Below. As Below, So Above.

NUMBER 10 – BINARY 1010

In Numerology Number 10 reverts to Number 1. Therefore we can examine Number 10 and those following solely in relation to The Cycle of Growth.

1. With Number 10 we begin a new set of 9 numbers, which, in Numerology, reduces to Number 1 (1 + 0 = 1). Here we remain with Number 10.
2. Without Stages 10, 11, and 12 of The Cycle of Growth we see that this is just repetition. There is no development or change. There is no Transcendence.
3. We have images of the feminine womb (Number Zero. Sephirah 1. Crown. Neptune. Collective Unconscious) - and masculine phallus (Number1. Sephirah 2. Chockmah. Creative Force. Pluto. Consciousness).
4. One of the established sets of 10 is The Ten Commandments, which also have a suggested karmic relationship.
5. Another set of 10 are the 10 Sephirah of the Kabbalah Tree of Life. [THE KABBALAH]. Sephiroth 10 (Kingdom) is that of the Earth and physical manifestation. This is an example of digital numbers which include Zero in the count. We see in [THE KABBALAH TREE OF LIFE] that there is the possibility of 12 Stages.
6. The element with Atomic Number 10 is Neon. Neon is a monatomic gas (in that it exists as single atoms - unlike those like Hydrogen (Atomic Number 1) and Oxygen that combine in pairs to make molecules). The name Neon means "new one". It is mainly used in lighting and advertising signs. It does not combine with other elements, so is rare on Earth, and only obtainable from air. It is expensive to produce because it only forms a small proportion. (18 parts per million) of air. Neon is more common in the outer universe after Hydrogen, Helium, Oxygen and Carbon.
7. Neon is the last element in the series which has 2 Main Shells, as shown below. The next element, Sodium, requires the creation of a 3rd. Main Shell.

CYCLE OF GROWTH STAGE 10 (PEAK. HARVEST)

1. In Numerology terms, Number 10 becomes Number 1 (1 + 0). However, The Cycle of Growth shows 2 alternative paths from here – one of which is at a new level, or Dimension.
2. The Cycle of Growth Stage 10 refers to the planet Saturn (Satan) which has 2 related Tarot cards which show the 2 faces of Saturn/Satan – XV.The Devil and XVI.The Tower (Lucifer-bringer of Light, Consciousness)
3. The Season is that of Christmas and celebration of the Winter Solstice which brings promise of a new Spring at a time of darkness. The rebirth of the SUN/SON.

4. In The Bible there was an attempt by Traditional Authority to destroy the new-born which was prevented by "returning another way". The theme is repeated in Mythology when the gods attempted to kill their own children because they feared their power would be challenged.
5. The next Stage 11 shows a continuation of the present Path of Saturn or the possibility of a new Path of Uranus.
6. Cycle of Growth Stage 10 is ruled by Capricorn (Cardinal Earth) which is Earth in its Initiating, Creative mode.

NUMBER 11 – BINARY 1011 – URANUS

In Numerology, Number 11 can remain, or be "converted" to Number 2.

I have ascribed Number 11 to the un-numbered Sephirah Daath in The Tree of Life as relating to Cycle of Growth Stage 11, and the planet Uranus as described below.

Daath is the yet undeveloped "bridge" across The Abyss of The Tree of Life.

Daath is related to The Throat Chakra which, in turn, is related to the Thyroid Gland concerned with controlling growth processes in the human body. They are both concerned with spiritual development.

Daath is related to the concept of Will and Knowledge from Experience, and the [PSYCHOLOGY : DEVELOPMENT MODELS] mentioned briefly under Number 3 above. Both the models illustrated require the development of a "bridge" between the Higher and Lower Selves. Jung calls it "The Ego-Self Axis", Transactional Analysis calls it "The Adult". The Kabbalah calls it "The Middle Pillar".

Uranus is related to the Jungian concept of Individuation.

The lesson here is that often Revolution is intent on destroying the status quo and ignores the necessity to have new structures to take the place of the old (Number 2). Anarchy is the province of Sephirah 2 (Chockmah, Force, Number 1) which has lost contact with Binah (Form).

CYCLE OF GROWTH STAGE 11 (DISCONTENT. WILL)

1. In accordance with the principle of The Transcendent Octave, we see that Numerology treats Number 11 as a special number which can remain as Number 11 (Daath. Uranus) or become Number 2 (1 + 1) – which refers to Sephirah 3 (Binah. Saturn/Satan) on The (dark) Pillar of Form.
2. Cycle of Growth Stage 11 can be ruled by Saturn (Number 2), when nothing changes, or Uranus when Transcendence begins.
3. When traditional explanations fail we have to find our own. "Faith is continuing to reject the absurd even in the face of the Unknown".

NUMEROLOGY

Even Numerology gives special meaning to Number 11 which relates to people who are especially independent, or individualistic. There is no planet association there. They suggest that this could revert to a simple "Number 2" in a similar way that The Cycle of Growth shows that new cycles could be a repetition of the past if Saturn is not overcome by Uranus.

Number 2 refers to Saturn and Number 11 to Uranus.

Famous Number 11 (or 2) Life Path people include Edouard Manet (Impressionist artist. Aquarius), Wolfgang A. Mozart (Composer. Aquarius), Buster Keaton (Silent movie comedian. Libra), Frankie Laine (Singer. Aries), Benito Mussolini (Fascist dictator. Leo), Omar Sharif (Actor. Bridge player. Aries), Ronald Reagan (Actor. President. Aquarius), Robert Louis Stevenson (Writer. Scorpio).

NUMEROLOGY

11 - OTHER ASSOCIATIONS

1. Number 11 reduces to 2 (1 + 1). Number 2 in The Tree of Life relates to Binah (Saturn) at the top of The Pillar of Form. At the end of the chapter [THE KABBALAH TREE OF LIFE] I relate The Tree to The Cycle of Growth and show how this works.
2. Uranus is the first of the Transcendent Planets outside the orbit of Saturn.
3. Traditionally, Uranus is a challenge to the structure of Saturn. It is related to concepts of Unconventionality, Revolution, Invention and Technology (even that of making a stone club).
4. In Mythology Kronos/Saturn was persuaded by his mother Gaia (Earth) to castrate his father Uranus (Sky). (This was long before Oedipus existed. There was only the parents and the 12 Titans (6 male and 6 female) so mates were in short supply. He threw the genitals into the sea from which came Venus (Desire). So Uranus became the un-numbered Sephirah Daath (Will) which does not regain its creative force until we become conscious of it.
5. In The Kabbalah, Daath is said to be the level of Earth before the Fall of Adam.
6. Atomic Number 11 relates to the element Sodium - an unstable soft metal which is only present in pure form in the laboratory. It is so reactive with other elements that it does not occur in pure form in nature. It is present in large quantities in sea water as Sodium Chloride – salt.

NUMBER 12 – BINARY 1100 – JUPITER/NEPTUNE

The Number Cycle is that of the 12 Stages of The Cycle of Growth and the 12 fruits of The Tree of Life in Revelation.

NUMEROLOGY

Although Numerology does not recognise it, we can use its principles to see that Cycle of Growth Stage 12 can exist at one of 2 levels – Number 12 (Neptune) or Number 3 (Jupiter).

This confirms that there is no Transcendence in the Numerology range of numbers.

CYCLE OF GROWTH STAGE 12 (WITHDRAWAL. CONFINEMENT)

1. Cycle of Growth Stage 12 is ruled by Pisces (Mutable/Changeable Water) which itself is co-ruled by Jupiter or Neptune.
2. Number 3 (Jupiter) refers to Sephirah 4 (Chesed. Jupiter) and Cycle of Growth Stage 9 (Conception). I have shown how Stage 9 (Jupiter. Fire) can become Stage 12 (Jupiter. Water) without passing through the intervening stages. Jupiter energy being transferred from Stage 9 Fire to Stage 12 Water at Sephirah 4 (which exists at 4 Element levels).
3. The Stages omitted refer to the Elements Earth (Sensation) and Air (Thinking).

OTHER ASSOCIATIONS

1. My addition of Number 12 to The Kabbalah Tree of Life as a return to Kether, Crown, at the top of The Middle Pillar – original number Zero – gives a cyclic relationship not originally present there, but now relates it to The Cycle of Growth.
2. Number 12 reduces to 3 (1 + 2) and therefore suggests something new arising from the 1 + 1 relationship formed by Number 11/2. (Father + Mother = Child)
3. Cycle of Growth Stage 12 (Withdrawal. Confinement. Karma) relates to the end of a cycle and is the time of preparation for the next. If a decision for Change has occurred in Stage 11 it is a time of clearing away past inner and outer associations that would hold one to the habit patterns (Saturn) and Karma of the previous cycle. It is a time of inner working. In the calendar year it is Winter and the seeds are waiting for warmer, damper, weather to germinate. In the human cycle the prospective mother is less active awaiting the time of birth.

NUMEROLOGY

4. The most important connection with Number 12 is our measurement of Time. Despite decimalisation in most other areas of life, it has resisted all efforts for change. Our clocks firmly count multiples of 12 hours, we have 12 months in a year, 12 Signs of the Zodiac, 12 Houses to an Astrological Chart. It is global in extent, in common with the Calendar that unites all people and nations today. Yet Time is an abstract. We cannot see, hear, or touch it – but somehow everyone agrees that it exists.
5. Element with Atomic Number 12 is Magnesium which is a silvery metal that, again, is not found in pure form in nature. It mainly exists as Magnesium Oxide which is a form of rock. Although relatively abundant, it is rarely used alone except in photographic flash powder or other incendiary devices. It is extensively used in alloys with other metals.
6. In the Biblical Book of Revelation there are 12 Gates, 12 Tribes, 12 Foundations, 12 Angels (etc.) which refer to 12 basic patterns of action. Jesus had 12 disciples. There were 12 tribes of Israel.
7. The Biblical Tree of Life described in Revelation has "12 fruits".

*"The 12 experiences of the physical to all". 12 Apostles relate to 12 active principles of Angels (spiritual energy forms) [EC 281-37].

NUMBER 13 – BINARY 1101

Although the number is given special status among the general population as an omen of "bad luck" and "death", Numerology does not give it a special significance. We can ascribe the following associations :-

1. Tarot Card XVIII. Death – and therefore .....
2. The Sign of Scorpio (which association is accepted by most authorities).
3. Cycle of Growth Stage 8 (Sex. Death).
4. The Planet Mars.
5. Number 4 (1 + 3) – and therefore Number 22 (2 + 2 = 4).

This is an example of why I refrain from adding associations between the Tarot Numbers and those of Numerology – we could easily lose sight of the purer archetypes

NUMBER 22 – BINARY 10110

Another number of note in Numerology is Number 22 which is translated similarly to Number 11 in that it could be expressed as Number 4 (2 + 2) as a lower octave. Following the Transcendent Octave, we can similarly interpret this as achieving a new level, or a repetition of the past.

There is no planet associated with Number 22 unless we consider it as a higher vibration of Mars (Number 4) - in which case we can relate 22 to Pluto as co-ruler of Scorpio.

My "Cycle of Growth Summary Diagram" includes associations of 22 (Tarot Major Arcana cards) with The 12 Stages of The Cycle of Growth.

CYCLE OF GROWTH STAGE 1 (SEED)

1. We return to Cycle of Growth Stage 1 which is ruled by Mars and the Cardinal (Initiating) Fire Sign of Aries.
2. Mars is related to Number 4 (Sephiroth 5. Geburah. Severity).
3. Once again we can combine Numerology and The Cycle of Growth to see that we can arrive at Stage 1 (Seed) at the new dimension of Number 22 or the lower Number 4.

NUMEROLOGY

Famous Life Path 22/4 people include Hugh Hefner (Aries. Editor of Playboy Magazine) Sir Richard Branson (Cancer. Virgin Group of Companies), Sir Paul McCartney MBE (Gemini. Beatles Singer, Songwriter), Bryan Adams (Scorpio. Singer, Songwriter, Photographer, "The Bryan Adams Foundation" to advance education in children), Dean Martin (Gemini. Singer, Actor, "Rat Pack" member), Dale Earnhardt (Taurus. US Race car champion).

22 - OTHER ASSOCIATIONS

1. There are 22 letters, which are also numbers, in the Hebrew alphabet – they are only consonants, which helps explain the difficulty of translation. The letters were also used to indicate numbers (with no zero). Nowadays the Arabic numbers are used and vowels have been added to the alphabet. This means that Hebrew letters/numbers do not relate to English Numerology.
2. We have the 22 cards of The Tarot Major Arcana
3. We have the 22 Paths of The Kabbalah Tree of Life which refer to the paths between the 10 Sephiroth.

EVOLUTION OF CHEMICAL ELEMENTS

Atoms "grow" from the centre outwards as they become new Chemical Elements. They all have a nucleus with orbiting Electrons.

At a more down-to- earth level we can look at the evolution of the physical elements and see that, once again, repetition of the same simple principles grow into greater complexity. How things actually work is a matter for Physics. The evolution of elements from the lightest and most basic Hydrogen to heavier ones shows the same pattern as the increase in odd and even numbers. The difference is that it happens in material Time and Space. We also see a parallel in individual human development from conception in terms of widening of Consciousness requiring the creation of "shells" at physical and psychological levels.

The evolution of Chemical Elements shows the same principle as the Binary System of computers where a Bit can only exist in 1 of 2 states – Zero or 1.

Atoms can only count up to Number Two. There can only be 1 or 2 Electrons in a Shell. The odd Electron is less stable, or more reactive, always in the outer Shell, seeking its "mate".

The physical elements of Physics are not the same as [The 4 Elements] (capitalised) of Astrology.

None of the Shells mentioned actually exists at a material level. They refer to energy levels.

NUMEROLOGY

ARRANGEMENT OF GROUND STATE ELECTRONS IN THE FIRST 18 ELEMENTS

ELEMENT			Neutrons	Atomic Number Electrons (& Protons)	Shell 1	Main Shell 2				Main Shell 3					
					1s	2s	2p			3s	3p			3d	
Hydrogen	H	Gas	0	1	1										
Helium	He	Gas	2	2	2										
Lithium	Li	Solid	4	3	2	1									
Beryllium	Be	Solid	5	4	2	2									
Boron	B	Solid	6	5	2	2	1								
Carbon	C	Solid	6	6	2	2	2								
Nitrogen	N	Gas	7	7	2	2	2	1							
Oxygen	O	Gas	8	8	2	2	2	2							
Fluorine	F	Gas	10	9	2	2	2	2	1						
Neon	Ne	Gas	10	10	2	2	2	2	2						
Sodium	Na	Solid	12	11	2	2	2	2	2	1					
Magnesium	Mg	Solid	12	12	2	2	2	2	2	2					
Aluminium	Al	Solid	14	13	2	2	2	2	2	2	1				
Silicon	Si	Solid	14	14	2	2	2	2	2	2	2				
Phosphorus	P	Solid	15	15	2	2	2	2	2	2	2	1			
Sulphur	S	Solid	16	16	2	2	2	2	2	2	2	2			
Chlorine	Cl	Gas	18	17	2	2	2	2	2	2	2	2	1		
Argon	Ar	Gas	18	18	2	2	2	2	2	2	2	2	2		

Figure 88 : Table - Numerology : 18 Chemical Elements

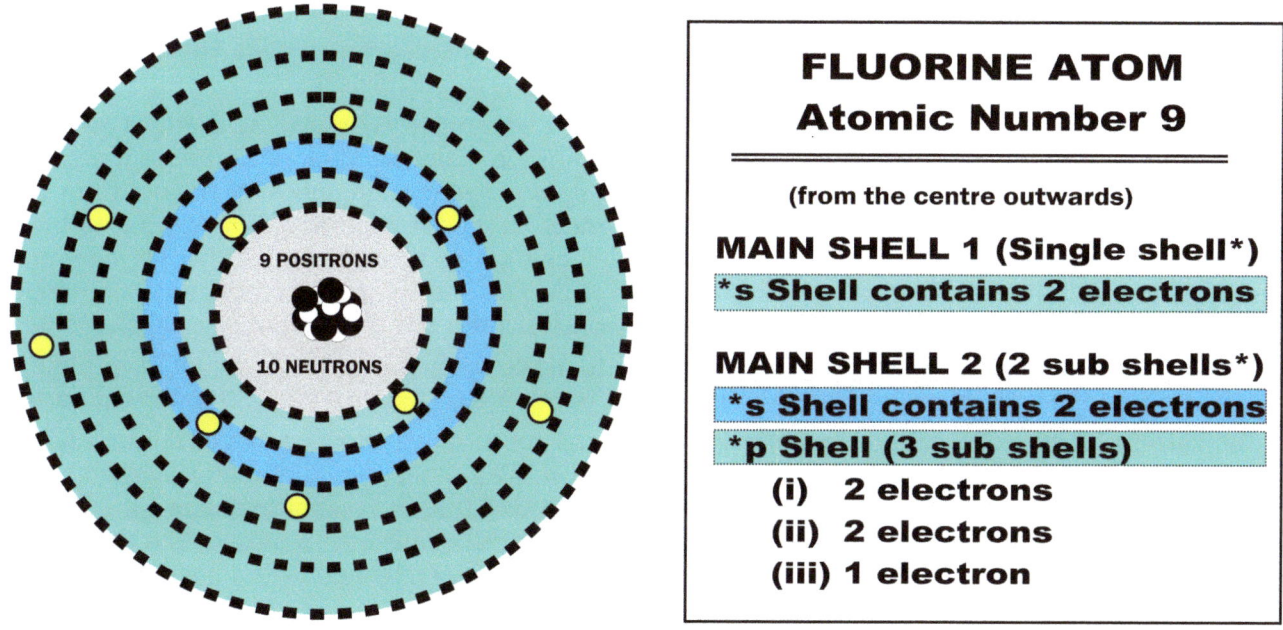

Figure 89 : Atomic Number 9 – Fluorine

THE CYCLE OF GROWTH

There seems to be a relationship with The Cycle of Growth in that we can consider The Octaves of The Logarithmic Timescale as the development of "shells" as a method of growth.

1. Octave 1 is concerned with the shell of the human body,
2. Octave 2 is concerned with the development of a psychological shell - the Persona "mask".
3. Octave 3 enters the "shell" of earthly society – which is a new circumscribed environment.

NUMEROLOGY

4. The Transcendent Octave enters the "Shell of The Universe" with more spiritual concerns.
5. There seems to be similarity of meaning with evolution of animals and man where an individual is forced out of the original home (Shell) and seeks a mate. The ensuing reproduction again forces the offspring to seek their own home outside that of the original family. The 2 grandparents and 2 parents are left occupying their original "shells".
6. This especially refers to Cycle of Growth Stage 4 (Transplanting, Cancer, Crab, Shell, Tarot VI. The Lovers. VII.The Chariot) and its connotations with Oedipus and the development of a Persona.

EVOLUTION

1. In common with the whole of the evolutionary process, things progress from the very simple to the very complex.
2. Things are not quite as simple as shown here because when a new element is formed several atoms of the lower element are required to produce it. This results in release of energy and particles with no electric charge remaining to form part of the nucleus – Neutrons.
3. We can consider the initial state of the universe as Number Zero. No-Thing.
4. The first element formed after the Big Bang was Hydrogen, an atom of which consists of a single positively charged Proton and single negatively charged Electron – neither of which can exist without the other. It is therefore given the Atomic Number 1. Hydrogen is the lightest of all elements.
5. Hydrogen, Atomic Number 1, relates to Number 1.
6. The Electron is in constant motion in orbit around the Proton. Although, for convenience, we depict the Electron orbit as a circle on 2 dimensional paper, it is really 3 dimensional. The distance between the Proton and its Electron is fairly constant. If we take every possible position of the Electron with its Proton nucleus as centre we arrive at a virtual spheroid – which ties in with most of the diagrams in this book. This virtual sphere is called a "Shell".
7. Having just a single electron, an atom of Hydrogen is unstable, and cannot exist alone, so, in the absence of other chemicals, it pairs with another Hydrogen atom to make a Molecule of Hydrogen gas. This can be considered the first example of Number Two (ref. the diagram above). The diagrammatic effect is something like a single celled organism reproducing by sub division.
8. From the Big Bang onwards, Hydrogen has been evolving over millions of years to produce all the elements we know today. Hydrogen is still the most common element in our universe, so there is plenty of time left. So far there are 118 chemical elements, some of which can only exist in pure form under laboratory conditions. Many elements are unstable and do not exist in pure form in Nature, so they prefer to combine with other elements when the product is called a Compound. Although there are many simple Number 2 pairings – such as between Hydrogen and Oxygen to produce the compound Water – many compounds are more complex, and consist of the combination of several elements.
9. The combination of positive and negative Elements to make compounds can be equated with the behaviour of the gods of mythology mating with one another, and then mating with different partners.
10. The same evolution of Hydrogen into heavier elements is occurring in our Sun, but at a much slower rate. The Sun currently consists of around 71% Hydrogen, 27 % Helium and 2% other elements such as Oxygen, Carbon, and Iron. Considering that it has taken 4,570,000,000 years to achieve this state, again, there is still a lot of life left in it. The reaction continues because the centre of The Sun is extremely hot. It is kept going by the enormous amount of energy released by the nuclear reaction. $E = MC^2$.
11. The next stage in the reaction is when 4 Hydrogen nuclei (Protons) combine to form 1 Helium nucleus. In the process 2 of the Hydrogen Protons lose their positive charge to become neutrally charged Neutrons. This means that 2 of the 4 negative Electrons are then free to be released, together with a large amount of energy. In Atomic Number terms this seems to indicate that $4 \times 1 = 2$.
12. An important point here is that the outer shell of the Helium atom now has 2 orbiting Electrons balanced by 2 Protons (plus 2 Neutrons) in its nucleus. Helium has Atomic Number 2. Having the full complement of 2 electrons in its outermost shell, Helium is much more stable than Hydrogen and does not easily combine with other elements such as Oxygen - which is why it is safer to use in gas balloons.
13. It is a rule that a shell of an atom (apart from the outer one) can only contain 2 Electrons which act like tiny magnets. The reason is that each Electron spins on its axis. When 2 Electrons occupy a Shell, it will

NUMEROLOGY

accept 1 Electron spinning one way and another Electron spinning the other, and no more. It therefore follows that to get heavier elements we need more Shells. If there are inner (sub) shells, they also each contain 2 Electrons. No more, no less. Because Electrons are all negatively charged, and therefore repel, they keep as far away from one another as possible. Other nuclear forces keep them in place. This is described in more detail in [THE 4 ELEMENTS].

14. The next important factor to consider is that an Electron requires energy to maintain its orbit. The further the orbit is from the central nucleus, the more energy it needs. It follows that Electrons use up energy. At a certain stage an electron cannot maintain its orbit in an outer shell, so drops down to a lower energy level. Because that Shell can only contain 2 Electrons one of its existing Electrons is forced out to replace the original one. It is not quite as simple as this explanation because things can take time to happen – even if it is the smallest imaginable fraction of a second. So Shells can momentarily contain more or less Electrons. This means that scientists can only estimate the probability of where an Electron is likely to be at any one time – although the most likely place is alone or sharing a Shell with another. In the (momentary) event that all the Electrons are in a position such that each Shell contains its proper "ration" of electrons, they are said to be in their "Ground State".

15. Having transformed Hydrogen into Helium, the Helium can now go to the next level, which is Lithium, Atomic Number 3 – which requires another Shell for the additional Electron.

16. Things are now getting really complicated, so I will now refer you to my table above showing the Electron configurations of the first 18 elements in their Shells. Main Shells are considered to be at different energy levels, so the diagram shows all elements in the first 3 levels. You will see that the Main Shells contain an increasing number of Subshells, which, in turn, contain an increase in Sub-subshells. As each outer shell reaches it limit of 2 Electrons, the next additional Electron goes to another outer shell. The outer shell is always the one with most energy. The Subshells (containing Sub-subshells) are named s, p, d, f and so on which indicates increasing energy levels. The maximum number of electrons in each Subshell is s = 2, p = 6, d = 10, f = 14. It is interesting to note that it does not necessarily mean that higher Atomic Number elements will be solid at normal temperatures and pressures.

NUMEROLOGY PRACTICE

An important approach used by Astrology – as well as other methods of divination, such as The Tarot, is to use pictures and diagrams, such as Birth Charts. Pictures are related to Right Brain functioning. The "pictures" are then described, or translated, into words – which uses Left Brain functioning. I can attest to the fact that "a picture is worth a thousand words". In fact, much more than a thousand. In my case an interpretation of a single Birth Chart "picture" can result in 30 pages or more of script, a Tarot reading into a long conversation. Communication in words consists of a long "string" of data which is transmitted to the reader who then has to convert it back to a form understandable by both left and right brain. We are all familiar with the problems that arise when the receiver's right brain picture does not match that of the sender. This is an example of the Jungian Thinking Function in action.

In Numerology there are very few pictures. The main depiction of numbers uses Arabic Numerals. The Arabic system was developed in the 7th. and 8th. centuries AD from roots in India during the 3rd. Century BC. Their main development being the introduction of Number Zero as a number in its own right. The focus appears to be on how they can be used in calculations (left brain) than their artistic Meaning. We can assume that there is some artistic meaning, or symbolism, which has evolved into the forms of the number images we see today, but it is not within the scope of this book to attempt to do so. However, the written forms of numbers Zero, 1, and 8 clearly relate to their symbolic meanings as mentioned above.

We have an anomaly in comparing Astrological and Numerological interpretations of a birth date, which should describe the same thing. For example, the most important factor for interpretation in Astrology is the Sun Sign of a subject – we would expect this to be similar to a Numerology interpretation. However the Numerology 'Life Path Number' – which depends on the day, month, and year of birth – does not give the same interpretation as an Astrological one.

NUMEROLOGY METHOD AND EXAMPLES

In Numerology numbers are given descriptive meanings depending on the form of energy they contain. Unlike Astrology, in Numerology, even though methods are similar (but not necessarily identical), there is no complete consistency among authorities in the terminology used to describe the various numbers that are arrived at in

NUMEROLOGY

analysing a person's name and birth date. For example "Destiny" can be used relative to birth date number or name number. Pick up any Astrology book and we see the same basic interpretations.

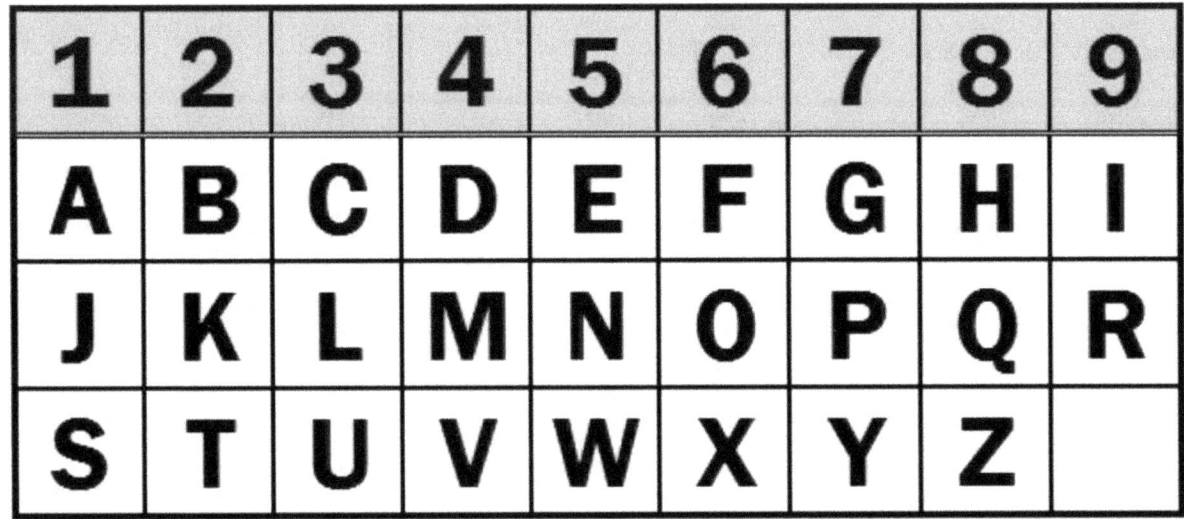

Figure 90 : Numerology - Numbers and Letters Relationship

There are several methods of interpretation, but a basic method of Numerology is to perform analyses by reducing words and numbers to single digits using the above grid, and interpreting those in context. Number totals 11 and 22 might be given special significance. In some methods vowels and consonants will be dealt with separately. The grid is based on the number a letter occupies in sequence, so A=1, and Z = 26 = 2 + 6 = 8.

LADY DIANA SPENCER – NAME

A problem is that we can be known by different names, depending on our social environment. Women usually change their surname when married, and authors often use a nom de plume. Some occultists deliberately changed their names in accordance with numerological principles.

Lady Diana Spencer was born Diana Frances Spencer. Using the grid above, we get numbers as follows :-

DIANA = 4 + 9 + 1 + 5 + 1 = 2 + 0 = 2 (Saturn. Consolidation. Discipline)
LADY DI = 3 + 1 + 4 + 7 + 4 + 9 = 1 (Pluto. Regeneration)
SPENCER = 1 + 7 + 5 + 5 + 3 + 5 + 9 = 3 + 5 = 8 (Moon. Roots)
WHOLE NAME (adding Frances) = 2 + 3 + 8 = 1 + 3 = 4 (Mars. Personal Drive)

We see that DIANA had a powerful birth Saturn, which gives rise to strong discipline in childhood, and problems with "The Establishment" later. It is interesting that the surname Spencer relates to her Cancer Sun (Moon) but was rarely used.

In my case, Brian 8 (Moon) does not seem to have much bearing. In my younger days, having red hair, I was called "Ginger" – a less formal, social, Number 6 (Venus). My younger sister sometimes uses a Number 2 (Saturn) "Bri" which suggests connotations mentioned above– even though my parents tried to choose a name that they thought could not be shortened. When we were young I was often delegated the responsibility of "looking after" her by my parents. In Astrology terms this was more a result of having a powerful Saturn/Sun Conjunction (Discipline. Responsibility) in my Birth Chart.

LADY DIANA SPENCER BIRTH DATE - 1/7/1961 = NUMBER 7 (Mercury)

I have used Lady Diana's Birth Chart in the chapter [ASTROLOGY : CHART EXAMPLES] so there is opportunity to compare. She had Cancer Sun (Crab. Shell. Mother. Roots)

I use birth dates in the examples above because they are a matter of established fact. The birth date number is said (by some) to be an indication of one's 'Life Path'. It is calculated by :-

1. Reducing day, month, and year to single numbers.
2. Add the 3 numbers together to see if they total 11 or 22 - which have special meanings . (e.g. 1 + 7 + 17 (8) = 16) .... if not :-

NUMEROLOGY

    3. Reduce the total to a single number. (1 + 6 = 7)

I relate Number 7 to Sephirah 8 (Hod. Glory) and Mercury. This is at the bottom of the Pillar of Severity/Form below Mars. Mercury is concerned with the Rational Mind.

We see from above that Number 7 is mainly concerned with the opposition of number 6 by Number 1, as the 6 days of Creation followed by a day of rest, and becoming the Sabbath as the most important day of the week. It has associations with Teaching as "bringing light (consciousness). I can see no strong relationship between Mercury and Diana's life path.

My birth date adds to Number 3 (Jupiter. Expansion) which could be related to my studies.

NUMEROLOGY

MY STORY

I am writing this chapter in order to record some unusual events that occurred which started my studies of "occult" subjects as well as mention areas of experience that are not part of this book but which proved to me that there is more to this life beyond that of what we perceive with our five senses, and how I discovered an ability for healing .

My middle name is Thomas. The reason I state that is because it seems to be as important as my first. In the Bible "Doubting Thomas" was the disciple of Jesus who refused to believe the resurrection had occurred until he had seen Jesus himself, and touched his wounds. He did get the evidence he wanted. I too tend to disbelieve what people tell me and look for empiric proof, or tangible evidence, when considering important matters. It is an interesting fact that I have personally experienced what is contained here and in the rest of the book.

A main occult phrase is "As Above, So Below. As Below, So Above" – which to me means that we should always be able to find practical, earthy, evidence.

Until age 34 I lived a normal kind of life with school, finding a job, getting married and having children. At that time, my wife and I achieved our goal of having two children and finally moved into our own house for the first time. We hear stories today about how hard it is for first time buyers to get on to the ladder of property ownership. It was no different then. We started with nothing, living with relatives, then rented accommodation until, finally, 12 years later we had saved up the necessary deposit of £2,000 as the result of a lot of hard work on both our parts. I had become Company Secretary of a commercial stationers and printers, to at last be earning enough to get a mortgage. On looking back, those early years together were the happiest of my life. Despite the long working hours during the week I was able to spend weekends with my family, and there was a sense of teamwork and fulfilment as we worked towards our goal. Having achieved that goal, it seems that life decided we needed to move on. It became the time of my Mid Life Crisis.

SPIRITUALISM

We had not been in our new home for two weeks when I received a call from a colleague at work to see if I knew of anyone who wanted a cat. He and his wife had two of their own who had been strays, and another had arrived for which they had been unable to find an owner. To cut a long story short, we decided to have the cat and, as the colleague did not live very far away, we got to know him and his wife socially. Apart from bringing us together, Fluffy the cat played another part in my development later on.

We eventually discovered the couple were spiritualists, and we began going to regular Sunday services, which we found not much different to our earlier experience. Both my wife and I had been regular Church of England churchgoers in our teen ages until we got married. She was a Girl Guide and Cub Scout leader and I spent 9 years in a church choir. Spiritualist churches also have other times where healing treatment is given by "laying on of hands", so we went to those too.

Spiritualist services are the same as other church services with hymns and prayers. There is belief in one God. The difference is that a medium from outside the church attends – a different one each week – so he or she does not know anyone in the congregation. Apart from giving an address, or talk, the medium gives "evidence of survival". That is, transfers messages from people who have died in this world to members of the congregation. Although there was a wide variance of quality of mediumship, I was impressed that, on the whole, accurate information was given to people that the mediums could not have possibly known. Although I myself received information, verification was hampered by my not knowing much about my past family. However, I was given enough information about my life circumstances, and observe others, including my wife, to know that there was no trickery.

Gradually we became more interested in the whole subject, and events occurred to draw us deeper. Again, to cut the story short, we eventually became committee members of the church and, within an unusually short space of time, were sitting in a development circle. A development circle is a group of people who meet regularly to develop psychic and/or healing abilities under the supervision of a medium.

I began exploring other "occult" subjects. At the beginning, one of the things that struck me was a certain antagonism between people involved in the various areas I was exploring. For example, if I mentioned Spiritualism, Healing, Astrology, or Tarot outside their areas I often received a strong negative reaction. At that time we were practising healing in a Spiritualist church as well as, eventually, qualifying as full members of the National Federation of Spiritual Healers. and often received similar negative reactions from one to the other. This book, among other things, is an attempt to bridge the gaps between the various factions. It seems that people in different "religions" use different languages to describe the same thing. This is the meaning behind "The Tower of Babel" in The Book of Genesis.

KUNDALINI

Our friends had been considering forming a circle for some time, and finally managed to find a medium to run it. At one meeting I began to feel strange sensations, and the other sitters said that my face "transfigured" to that of a chinaman and I was encouraged to give a short talk. The problem was that afterwards I felt extreme discomfort each day as if my whole body was vibrating. Strangely the feeling disappeared at midday, but came back later on. It was so uncomfortable that it made it difficult to concentrate on anything, and began to affect my work. I also had strange mental states, and even gave a prediction to my boss at work that came true 6 months later. Other predictions were partially true. The outcome was correct, but not my 'interpretation'. At a later circle meeting the chinaman was asked to "step back" by the medium, and I became more comfortable. The other abilities subsided too.

(I had a dream of walking on a beach at the edge of the sea far from land at ebb tide – which I later realised meant that The Collective Unconscious had "receded".)

After some research I am reasonably sure that I had a kundalini experience where energy is released from the base of the spine to activate the higher chakras, or psychic centres, of the body. This is normally the result of long training in yoga, although can happen spontaneously as in my case. One thing that convinced me was the smell of ozone in my nostrils at the time. This is a kind of burning smell normally resulting from discharge of a high voltage electric current. In retrospect it is as well that the experience was stopped because my research showed that, being totally unprepared, I could have ended up with severe mental problems. In addition, if such an energy is aroused it needs to have some outlet of use, and I was still doing a normal daily job. The experience was, however, real, and valuable in that it lead me to explore further. In The Book of Revelation the opening of the chakras includes "earthquake" – that is, physical vibration.

HEALING AND MEDIUMSHIP

To begin with, as usual, I was sceptical about being told by mediums I had healing abilities. Somehow our progress in the general field was very fast. For example, many people tried to find a developing circle without success, and we found two in succession without any difficulty.

The original development circle closed shortly afterward because the medium had some family problems, and we moved to another one concerned with the development of healing abilities. In addition, over the course of some years, among other things, we attended lectures at The Spiritualist Association of Great Britain at Belgrave Square in London, and had holidays a couple of times a year at the Arthur Findlay College at Stanstead Hall in Essex, which gives short residential courses on various aspects of mediumship as well as other subjects. Later on we did a week yoga course to learn more about that. I also took an Astrology course.

I mentioned Fluffy the cat that brought us into Spiritualism. He was very old, and had the tendency to get swellings on its face – problems with its teeth the vet said. One Sunday its face swelled and we decided to take it to the vet the following day. This eventually was not necessary. I decided to see if this healing was true and sat with it in my lap (a thing that the cat would not normally do. It had a will of its own) with my hand as close as possible. Later I took my hand away, and the swelling was gone. Although I could think of other reasons for this, it did lead me to try with people, and have the ability confirmed. Soon after we were doing healing at the regular weekly sessions at the church.

Eventually my wife and I qualified as Members of The National Federation of Spiritual Healers (now under the umbrella of The Healing Trust), where, apart from attending courses, we had to supply references and the details of people we had helped, who were contacted separately. We were put on their register of healers and began visiting people in their homes by request, and the leader of the circle gave us use of her healing sanctuary one evening a week. We also gained two Probationer Certificates each from the Institute of Spiritualist Mediums. One required giving a demonstration of spirit communication and the other an address, in front of an audience including a panel of judges. The aim is to give budding mediums a step forward by getting churches to invite them to take services. For a time we visited churches together where I just gave the address, until the time of our separation and divorce. Personally, I felt I was not particularly good as a medium (too analytical you see) and, as my Astrological and other studies were taking more time, stopped doing it. I have to mention I later discovered from reading "Discovering Your Soul's Purpose" by Mark Thurston that psychic development can be detrimental to the development of Will, which I now believe to be our main purpose in life [THE PURPOSE OF LIFE]. My wife went on to develop her mediumship further and specialise in giving evidence of survival. She began to run a development circle at home. I attended for a time but I was still working at a full time job and decided that I needed the time to study Astrology.

One ability that I discovered was that of being able to find the books I need. I would have questions in my mind on a particular subject, go to a bookshop and find just what I needed – usually in the introduction. Sometimes I bought the book to find the rest of it not very interesting. I also managed later on to do something similar with another cat of mine that went astray. Walking the streets at night to try and find it I came to a street door, but could not bring myself to knock. I later discovered, via a neighbour, that the tenants had found the cat injured by a car and taken it to the local PDSA where he later died. I did then visit to confirm it.

MEDIUMSHIP TYPES

There are different kinds of mediumship. Physical mediumship that produces physical manifestation was common during the early days of Spiritualism. It can be dangerous for the medium and is very taxing. It is not very common today, and is not really necessary because of the other 'mental' methods now available. It seemed necessary in the early days to draw people's attention. I did witness a physical manifestation of ectoplasm once and believe there was no trickery. The medium was wearing not much more than a bath robe and searched by two members of the audience before the demonstration.

The ability to do this form of mediumship evidently does not mean that they are very advanced in knowledge. The same medium whilst "overshadowed" by a Chinese spirit guide also gave an address on which included a mention of The Age of Aquarius, with very little real information , as well as saying that it is a Water Sign. This is a common error made because of its symbol of 'The Water Carrier'. It is, of course, an Air Sign.

He did, however, give some amazing evidence of survival. Horses for courses.

Another form of mediumship is Trance Mediumship where the medium is overshadowed by a spiritual entity. Edgar Cayce's work is an example of this. His communications were made while he was "asleep". It was common in the past as a form of physical mediumship called "Transfiguration Mediumship" when clients were able to see the face of the spirit communicator – which relates somewhat to my experience mentioned.

Nowadays there is 'mental' mediumship. To me this is a misnomer because, having had some experience myself, and being in contact with mediums over several years, I am under the impression that it manifests as extensions of 2 of [THE 4 FUNCTIONS] Intuition (Fire) and Feeling (Water). I have 6 out of 10 planets in Air signs , which is probably why I was not very good at it – although having experienced it myself in a small way it means that my 'Doubting Thomas' was satisfied as to its reality.

The main other forms of mediumship are Clairvoyance – which uses sight, when pictures are seen in the mind. Clairaudience is hearing words, and Clairsentience uses sensation. I was not too bad at this one. Objects absorb information, "vibrations", from their surroundings and it is possible to gain an idea of their history by holding them in our hand. This might be an explanation of "haunted houses". It makes sense that higher levels of emotional energy will produce more lasting effects. Generally, mediumship seems to be a combination of them all.

It seems the human body absorbs things too. I use it in healing to know where to put my hands (which is not always where the patient feels a pain !). One common example was from a 74 year old woman where I sensed a jaw injury that she said she received from an accident at the age of 12 – although this was not her main problem, it was still 'active' in some way. I did not sense its presence in later sessions. Another example is when someone has a leg or arm problem, when the healthy limb often needs more attention from being overworked.

TAROT

While the other development was going on I was exploring quite a wide field. The wife of the couple that brought us into Spiritualism read tarot cards, and bought me a set. Sceptical as usual, I bought a book and sat down with my wife one day to give her a "reading". Basically I laid out the cards and looked them up in the book. To my amazement she could understand what I was describing even though I did not. I find that common in my readings. Since then I have spent many hours giving readings to friends and for day-long charity events, and for a short time semi-professionally. Having proved the practical use, I have spent a lot of time putting them back into sequence to study the philosophy. An interesting fact is that they can predict the future. I have had many people confirm this. My belief, however, is that this is not necessarily fixed. By changing our actions now we can often change the outcome of a situation. Everything is subject to Will.

Often 2 people came to have readings. This was a good thing because it was common to find that the subject did not understand the reading whereas their "partner" did on their behalf.

MY STORY

I know nothing about horse racing, but once thought I would try to predict some winners. I had no success at all. Couldn't understand any of it. It's alright though, I did not lay out any money. However, one of the winners next day was "Old Nick" and one of the tarot cards was The Devil. Perhaps I may have had some success if I had pursued it further, but it seemed too much like hard work to do further experiments.

ASTROLOGY

This is the subject that has occupied most of my spare time for nearly 40 years. A full Birth Chart interpretation takes around 20 hours' work, even using a computer to make the charts. I did consider taking a qualification, but the course involved a lot of study in areas that were of no interest to me. I was interested in the subject of personal growth, and was beginning to study Psychology as well, and much of what was presented seemed like fortune telling, or just telling people what they knew already. Not necessarily a bad thing, but there was no "overview". To begin with I proved to myself that it worked by studying my own Birth Chart and later managed to get some other willing "guinea pigs" via a lady I met at a week Astrology course at Stanstead Hall. When she went home she supplied me with birth details of her friends, who I never met personally. I also did interpretations for people I met at other courses I went to. For example, I did 2 years study of the Kabbalah and did some for people there. The feedback was encouraging from most, and in the worst results, other than those who could not accept them at all, subjects could agree on 50% of what I wrote – which allowed for 25% what I did not know and 25% they did not. As with the Tarot readings, I can live with the low percentage of results which drew a blank. Thomas, again, seems reasonably satisfied. I am convinced that everyone should really do their own interpretation. When I began to include examination of planet Transits for the current time, which are more evidential, I was again surprised to find agreement there, sometimes with a surprising accuracy. When interpreting current Planet Transits for someone 30 years of age from a Birth Chart we are, in fact, predicting 30 years into the future !

ASTROLOGY 'LIFE DIARY' TRANSITS

Recently I have done some experiments with family and friends with a "Life Diary" of main events such as house moves, job changes and close relationships and comparing this with transits of Jupiter and Saturn each year. They are useful for this purpose having cycles of 12 and 30 years respectively. There are practical examples in this book. Still being my own "guinea pig", I looked at my own to begin with I discovered, among other things, that, although there were moves at other times, I have had a house move at 12 yearly intervals each time Jupiter returned to the same position in my Birth Chart (Jupiter Returns). Most of the moves were forced by company take-overs or reorganisations with my choice of being made redundant or following my job to a new location. Being a computer programmer – for the 22 years prior to my retirement my job involved data analysis and producing reports from a corporate database - I can now produce 90 years of transit data in a few minutes. Having only done this for a few friends and family I do not have enough data for statistical analysis so a lot more work is needed, but, once again, I have proved to Thomas that it is valid.

There is a blank Life Diary form for you to fill in for you to see relationships between planet transits and changes in your lifetime [ASTROLOGY : PLANET TRANSITS]. Please see the chapter which explains the "crisis"/change Houses 12, 1,4,7, and 10, and the chapter about Lady Diana Spencer with Birth and Transits charts samples.

PSYCHOLOGY – MID LIFE CRISIS

I have studied Psychology on an informal basis for about the same length of time as Astrology. It is clear that there is a strong connection between the two which has been borne out by my Birth Chart and Transits studies. The chapters about The Cycle of Growth show some of the relationships. My main interest, again, has been the studies of NORMAL lifetime psychological development processes which are included in the first chapters of this book.

I was prompted in this direction by my experience of Mid Life Crisis, which proved to Thomas the validity of the psychological process. Within a couple of months of my wife and I achieving our life goal of owning our own house I got a stomach ulcer. Although both my grandfather and father had the same problem, and there was a lot of pressure from long hours at work, my new knowledge and self-analysis made it clear that the real problem was within myself. At one stage I even found myself deciding whether to keep the ulcer or not. For once people around were looking after me for a change, and I was able to give a reason for not working all that unpaid overtime. Illness has its benefits – which was confirmed in some cases when visiting people in their homes to give healing. In the event, I decided that that would be dishonest – and I would have still have the pain as well.

MY STORY

Although not part of this book, I refer you to Philip Yancey's book "Where Is God When It Hurts". (noted in the BIBLIOGRAPHY). He clearly demonstrates that without pain we would not have survived as a species. Among other examples, he includes that of Hansens Disease – once called Leprosy, which is grossly misunderstood. Firstly it is transferred more by heredity rather than contagion. Secondly, it is a degenerative illness of the nerves where the subject gradually loses sensation, or the sense of touch, throughout the body. So, in fact, they feel no pain or physical discomfort. This means that the normal body reflexes such as blinking stop working, and self-injury occurs from lack of sensory feedback. So the deteriorating body condition is a result of the illness rather than a symptom. The subjects actually ignore the possibility that they might injure themselves, such as burning themselves by handling hot items, and leaving the resulting burns untreated. I get irritated sometimes by those red squiggles that appear under words as I type on my computer – but it does allow me to correct my spelling errors.

At the time of my illness my wife bought a recipe book about cooking food for people with ulcers. Once again, reading the introduction to the book brought enlightenment. It basically stated that everyone's ulcer is different, so, to begin with, the method was to eat whatever you like and see if you get a pain afterwards. If you do, then you have discovered what food to avoid. I eventually discovered that the problem was not in what I was eating. I could eat whatever I wished, and providing it was not too much fried food at once I was reasonably alright. But I still had the pain, and was facing a long period of medication or even surgery. The "healthy" foods brown bread and salads also gave problems.

As time went on, however, I began to apply the method in other areas of life. I became my own scientist and my own "guinea pig". I discovered that the pain was also related to people and circumstances in my life (unable to "stomach" things), and, as I could not change those, I would have to change myself and the way I dealt with them. In a strange way the pain became like a friend. It did subside, and I soon became completely pain free as the ulcer healed. It does grumble a bit occasionally, but, when it does, it does not need to be too severe because I am alert to it. When I begin to feel discomfort I know that there is something I need to deal with. I may have eaten the wrong food, or there is some other situation that is developing wrongly for me, and the longer it goes on the worse the pain will become.

I have not had to visit a doctor other than check-ups for nearly 40 years now.

Another thing I realised was that I did not really have an ego. Being brought up to "love thy neighbour" I was taking over burdens that were not mine to carry. I had to learn to say "No". I cannot obey "love thy neighbour as thyself" if I do not love myself. This is not a "command from above", it is a simple statement of fact. I realised that any severe illness was there to set our priorities in order. We are thereby forced to attend to our self (ref. Cycle of Growth Stage 6 – Service to Self and Health). There is a lot of humility required in this acceptance. As an added benefit we learn a lot about our self and are forced to explore new areas of life we might have otherwise have missed – if only things like medicine and diet. A problem then comes that we have to begin exerting a strong self-discipline (Will). We cannot blame anyone else for our condition. As we change we begin to affect the lives of those around us.

Interestingly, I had a friend who was a laboratory research technician at a big London hospital with no interest in occult subjects. He did, however, mention his continual surprise at their receptionist who would often tell them what was wrong with a patient by looking at the birth date on their forms. He said Cancer Sun people were prone to ulcers. I have Gemini Sun (with "hard" aspects which gave me breathing problems), but Mars in Cancer, you see, and had to learn to transfer martial energy naturally directed inwards by my genes into the outside world where it belonged. It would seem to be an inherited trait in my case, but my father did not have Mars in Cancer. Rather than "curing" illnesses, life often seems to work by emphasising a problem to force our conscious attention to it. Unfortunately this usually means taking action to relieve the symptoms rather than trying to discover the root cause. (Mars in Cancer (Roots) is good at "digging roots").

As a result of this crisis, my wife and I, having achieved our joint aim, parted reasonably amicably and moved into our new, different life pathways. At Mid Life Crisis people usually try to repeat (safe) past experiences by finding a new home and/or a new partner rather than face an uncertain future alone. Having experimented with the possibility of doing some form of occult work to earn a living I decided that I was not attracting people who could help me learn more, and returned to a business life which continued, despite numerous redundancy possibilities, until my recent retirement. In retrospect this seems a good move because I now have time to pursue my interests without any financial worries. As I write this in 2014 I am approaching another Jupiter Return – I wonder what this will bring. Perhaps as a result of this book. Saturn is transiting the 2nd. (Personal)

MY STORY

House of my Birth Chart (Germination) when the need is to expend time, money, and effort, in order to develop the new "baby" that appeared during the 1st. House transit (Seed). I have certainly been doing that.

DREAMS

LUCID OR WAKING DREAMS

I have had quite a few "lucid" dreams when I have been asleep, and suddenly realise that I am dreaming – when I usually just wake up normally. Other times I note the fact but continue with the dream (and forget I am dreaming). On one occasion the location of the dream was in a street with shops. I managed to experiment by "materialising" a brick in my hand and throw it through a shop window, which "smashed". I felt a bit guilty at that, so I "re-materialised" the shop window – at which stage I woke up.

DREAMS PREDICTING THE FUTURE

I have spent a lot of time recording my dreams. Despite the belief of some people, scientists have proved that everyone dreams, it is just that some people do not remember them. It does take quite an effort even when you want to. They observe something called "REM Sleep". Rapid Eye Movements (twitches) occur when we dream. I kept a daily dream diary for around 5 years, some of which were extremely detailed. I have never found them of much help in life (Mercury (Logical Mind) Square Neptune (The Unconscious) in my Birth Chart?). However, if I had not done this, I would not have discovered that they sometimes predict the future with perfect accuracy. Some psychologists state that we always dream the future before it happens. My recognition of this fact was from being somewhere and remembering I had a dream about it. I had to go back around 6 months before I found my record. Here is an example of one.

> In the dream I am in my car on the way to work. I have to stop at a roundabout on a crossroads to allow a car to pass from the right. It crosses in front of me and takes the next turning off the roundabout. It is going very slowly. Instead of travelling down the road it continues its left turn until both front wheels hit the kerb together. It stops still for a couple of minutes, and I am able to sit and watch it – knowing it had to reverse - because there is no other traffic. After a while it reverses and continues on its way.

I had the dream on a Tuesday and the event occurred exactly as in the dream on the Thursday. In retrospect I assume that the driver was using a mobile phone and, as there was no traffic, finished the call before moving away. In all the time I recorded my dreams I only have three such examples, all accurate except that when the event occurred in a place I have not been before the dream used a similar looking place from the past. I do not record them any more. I assume that if the unconscious wants to tell me something, it will do so. I hoped I might learn something useful like the next set of lottery numbers, but suppose that I would have won anyway in order to get the dream.

MEDITATION

There is a more detailed chapter [MEDITATION] in the appendix.

Following on from the above, it is worth mentioning that we all need to find our own method. For the last 40 years I have aimed at meditating a minimum of 15 minutes a day. While I was working, I was not able to do so every day, but can do so now I am retired. In practice it can, rarely, last anything up to 2 hours.

I find it essential to spend the first few minutes listening to myself dealing with normal everyday matters, and making decisions what to do. Writing things down often helps. My unconscious seems satisfied that I have "got the message" and stops "complaining". It is worth doing this if there is difficulty sleeping at night. The principle is the same – the unconscious becomes active as the conscious mind "closes down" the 5 senses and relaxes.

We have to learn to work with our unconscious mind – if we try to fight, or suppress, or ignore it, it can interfere. My unconscious mind has learned to trust my decisions over the years. In any case, I am the one "out here" pitching and taking responsibility.

BIBLIOGRAPHY

Descriptions are mainly taken from the book covers or other content.

BIBLIOGRAPHY : ASTROLOGY

THE HOROSCOPE, THE ROAD AND ITS TRAVELLERS
Alan Oken. 1974 Bantam Books

This book deserves a mention because it is one of the first that I used, and I was still referring to it during the writing of this book. It covers all the basics of Astrology. It is different to other books on the subject because it takes us to deeper levels of understanding by use of KEYWORDS, and has a self-test quiz at the end of chapters. Anyone reading his book and this one will see the influence it had. Not a bad 60 pence-worth.

THE ASTROLOGY FILE
Gunter Sachs. 1998 Orion Books ISBN 0-75281-789-2

Scientific proof of the link between star signs and human behaviour.

"Gunter Sachs has achieved what was previously impossible. He has taken millions of Birth Chart statistics and has had them collated and scientifically analysed. He has been able to prove that the star sign you are born under influences all aspects of your life."

THE TRUTH ABOUT ASTROLOGY
Michael Gauquelin. 1983 Basil Blackwell Publisher Ltd. ISBN 0-631-12936-7

A statistical approach to Astrology.

Gauquelin began his investigation by collecting data on the date time and place of birth of French doctors and working out the position of the planets at each one's birth. Significantly more doctors were born when particular planets were in the Ascendant. He later found a definite link between the time of birth of people at the top of particular professions and the position of Mars, Jupiter, Saturn and the Moon in their Birth Charts. In due course evidence began to grow for planetary effect on heredity, temperament and personality.

THE THEORY OF CELESTIAL INFLUENCE :
... MAN, THE UNIVERSE, AND COSMIC MYSTERY
Rodney Collin. 1984 ISBN 13-9780140-19365-7 - ISBN 10-0140-19365-0

A difficult book to read but it is the main source of "THE ROUND ART" by A. T. Mann.

An exploration of the universe and man's place in it. Rodney Collin examines 20th-century scientific discoveries and traditional esoteric teachings and concludes that the driving force behind everything is neither procreation nor survival, but expansion of awareness. Collin sets out to reconcile the considerable contradictions of the rational and imaginative minds and of the ways we see the external world versus our inner selves. For readers familiar with Gurdjieff's cosmology will here find further examinations of the systems outlined in by Ouspensky.

[TRA] THE ROUND ART - A. T. Mann
1979 Dragons World Limited. limpback ISBN 0-905895-18-5. hardback 0-905895-19-3

Please also see the chapter "ASTROLOGY : LOGARITHMIC TIMESCALE".

In A.T.Mann's book "The Round Art" There are references to "The Theory of Celestial Influence" by Rodney Collin. As an Astrologer, Mann's version is a lot simpler to understand - and practical rather than theoretical.

Apart from being an excellent astrological textbook covering all aspects of the Art, this is the only one I have found which answers the fundamental question which puzzled me for several years. The symbolism of Birth Chart Houses 1 to 8 are concerned with the period of one's life between Birth and Death. The question then arises : What is the lifetime function of the other Houses 9 to 12 ? The answer is, they cover the DUAL FUNCTION of life time in the womb from conception to Birth AND the more traditionally recognised function of man's Transcendence of the material world – which has relationship with Jungian Individuation.

BIBLIOGRAPHY

[IHA] AN INTRODUCTION TO THE HISTORY OF ASTROLOGY

Nicholas Campion. 1982 The Institute for the Study of Cycles in World of Affairs. ISBN 0 - 9508412 - 0 - X

"The Institute for the Study of Cycles in World of Affairs" was established in 1980 with the aim of promoting the study of Mundane Astrology and the history of Astrology. (Mundane Astrology is the application of Astrology to world affairs and events). This book covers the historical development of Astrology from 2,000 BC in Mesopotamia to the present.

[COB] CYCLES OF BECOMING

Alexander Ruperti . 1978 CRCS Publications ISBN 0-916360-07-5

Correlates the Transit patterns of planets in our solar system with the patterns of our lives from a humanistic and cyclic point of view.

This book correlates the patterns of our solar system with the patterns of our lives. Emphasising both the development of individual potential and the most common crisis periods in life, this is the first book to deal with planetary transits from a humanistic and cyclic point of view. The author deals with both generic cycles (applicable to everyone) and individual cycles (keyed to an accurate birth chart). Thus, not only students of astrology but also those with no special astrological knowledge can find valuable insights into their current phase of life and their pattern of destiny.

It considers two types of transit for each planet over the course of a lifetime - a Generic Cycle and an Individual Cycle. The Generic Cycles depend upon our age, and therefore relate to everyone, and do not need a Birth Chart. The Individual Cycles consider the transits of planets through the Houses of a Birth Chart throughout a lifetime.

BIBLIOGRAPHY : PSYCHOLOGY

[IOD] THE INTERPRETATION OF DREAMS

Sigmund Freud. First published 1953 and translated by James Strachey. Penguin books ISBN 0-14-02.1738-X.

A description of Freud's method of exploring the unconscious. Includes "A Sketch of his Life and Ideas" – a brief biography by James Strachey.

[FYL]THE FREUD/JUNG LETTERS

(Abridged Edition) edited by William McGuire. 1979 Princeton University Press ISBN 0-6910-36438

In May of 1911 Dr. Carl Jung wrote his (at that time) mentor Sigmund Freud saying: -

> *"Occultism is another field we shall have to conquer - with the aid of the libido theory, it seems to me. At the moment I am looking into astrology, which seems indispensable for a proper understanding of mythology. There are strange and wondrous things in these lands of darkness."

In a letter written to written to Hindu astrologer, B.V. Raman, September 6th 1947 - Dr. Jung wrote:

*Since you want to know my opinion about astrology I can tell you that I've been interested in this particular activity of the human mind since more than 30 years. As I am a psychologist, I am chiefly interested in the particular light the horoscope sheds on certain complications in the character. In cases of difficult psychological diagnosis I usually get a horoscope in order to have a further point of view from an entirely different angle. I must say that I very often found that the astrological data elucidated certain points which I otherwise would have been unable to understand. From such experiences I formed the opinion that astrology is of particular interest to the psychologist, since it contains a sort of psychological experience which we call 'projected' - this means that we find the psychological facts as it were in the constellations. [http://thezodiac.com/astrojung2.htm].

BIBLIOGRAPHY

THE PORTABLE JUNG
First published 1971. A selection from Jung's "Collective Works".

[P & A] PSYCHOLOGY AND ALCHEMY
C.G.JUNG. 1953 Routledge & Kegan Paul. ISBN 0-7100-0707-8
Jung has written :-

> *...whereas in the church the increasing differential ritual and dogma alienating consciousness from its natural roots in the unconscious, alchemy and astrology were ceaselessly engaged in preserving the bridge to nature i.e. the unconscious, from decay. [P&A]

In this volume Jung works out in great detail the analogies between Alchemy, Christian dogma, and symbolism on the one hand, and the dreams and visions of a contemporary scientist on the other.

JUNG AND THE TAROT - AN ARCHETYPAL JOURNEY
Sallie Nicholls Samuel. 1980 Weiser Inc. ISBN 0-87728-515-2

Although there is no evidence that Jung himself studied the Tarot in detail, its symbols as archetypes appeared in his work. This book is by a Jungian analyst who studied at the C.G. Jung Institute while he was still alive and active.

During his work Jung noticed that European and American men and women were coming to him for psychological advice were producing in their dreams and fantasies symbols similar to and often identical with the symbols found in the mystery religions of antiquity, in mythology, folklore, fairy tales, and the apparently meaningless formulation is of such esoteric cults as Alchemy.

MAN AND HIS SYMBOLS
Conceived and edited by C.G.Jung. 1964 Aldus Books. 1978 Picador ISBN 0-330-25321-2

This was the last piece of work undertaken by Jung before his death in 1961. It is the only attempt by the world-famous psychologist to explain to the lay reader his theory of the significance symbolism in dreams and art, and the importance of it comprehension to the full understanding of the unconscious human mind. It is a collective effort by several psychologists.

Contents: Part 1 - Approaching the unconscious (CG Jung). Part 2 - Ancient myths and modern man (Joseph L Henderson). Part 3 The process of individuation (M.L. von Franz). Part 4 - Symbolism in the visual arts (Aniela Jaffe). Part 5 - Symbols in an individual analysis (Jolande Jacobi)

[ACU] THE ARCHETYPES AND THE COLLECTIVE UNCONSCIOUS
C.G.Jung 1959 Bollingen Foundation Inc. New York. ISBN 0-691-097615-12-4

BECOMING
Deldon Anne McNeely. 2010 Fisher King Press. ISBN 978-1-926715-12-4.

"An introduction to Jung's concept of Individuation".

As a modern book, I was hoping that this would give a more practical insight and overview from a modern practising analyst and member of the 'International Association for Analytical Psychology'. I was disappointed. The cover mentions "a lifelong work of psychoanalysis". Jung called his work "Analytical Psychology" to distinguish it from other methods, so this may be the problem. The book has a generalised philosophical approach, much of which quotes other people, and seems to have little bearing on the subject – which, surely, is mainly concerned with Individuals. It is also very "left brain" in that it does not contain a single picture, symbol, or diagram.[BTB]

On the cover of the book is the statement :-

> *However, psychology's fascination with behavioural techniques, it is necessary financial concerns and promoted by insurance companies and pharmaceutical companies, has changed the nature of psychotherapy and has attempted to dismiss the wisdom of Jung and other pioneers of the territory of the unconscious mind.

BIBLIOGRAPHY

It would seem that the author has also given in to collective pressure.

[SLUC] THE SECRET LIFE OF THE UNBORN CHILD

Dr. Thomas Verny and John Kelly. 1981-2009 Sphere Books ISBN 978-07515-1003-4

This book presents for the first time the challenging results of two decades of painstaking international research into the earliest stages of life. Doctor Verny's evidence of intelligent life in the womb is overwhelming. The new knowledge gives both mothers and fathers an unparalleled opportunity to help their unborn children. Now they can contribute actively - before and during birth - to giving their child happiness and security for the rest of his or her life.

[GOP] THE GROWTH OF PERSONALITY

Gordon R. Lowe. 1972 Penguin Books. ISBN 0-140214-68-2

Combines studies by Freud, Erikson, and Piaget. Psychological development milestones

Outlines how personality may be expected to develop during Erik H. Erikson's (1902–1994) 8 Stages of development. At each stage he asks "What relationship, what issue, concerns us most"?

Describes satisfactory and unsatisfactory responses to each crisis. Also considers regression to earlier stages, and how they are used in media advertising. The work of C.G.Jung is not included because he deliberately avoided any tendency to regularise the process of Individuation.

EGO AND ARCHETYPE

Edward F Edinger MD Chairman of the New York Institute of the C.G. Jung Foundation. 1973 Penguin books. ISBN0-14-021728-2. A synthesis of Jung's ideas.

"A remarkably lucid synthesis of CG Jung's basic ideas."

JUNG – MAN AND MYTH

Vincent Brome. 1978 Macmillan London Ltd. ISBN 0-586-08361 8

A detailed biography of Jung's life.

[TA] TRANSACTIONAL ANALYSIS BOOKS

Three practical guides to Transactional Analysis - which uses simple language like Parent, Adult, and Child (capitalised to show they are being used in TA, rather than every day, meanings) to help non-professionals understand the psychology of their everyday lives.

THE GAMES PEOPLE PLAY -Eric Berne M.D.

1964 Penguin Books Ltd. ISBN 0-14-002768-8

The book considers the psychology of human relationships in terms of Transactional Analysis. A Transaction is initiated by one person speaking to another, and terminates when the other makes some response. The book also includes description of the P-A-C model which posits that we have 3 ego states, Parent, Child, and Adult.

I'M OK YOU'RE OK - Thomas A. Harris MD

1973 Pan Books Ltd. ISBN 0-330-23543-5

STAYING OK - Amy and Thomas Harris

1986 Pan books Ltd. ISBN 0-330-29136-X

BIBLIOGRAPHY : EDGAR CAYCE

Please also see : [APPENDIX : Edgar Cayce]

The 14,000 Readings of Edgar Cayce are so detailed on a diversity of subjects that it requires others to collate and interpret them under various subject headings – the books here are therefore commentaries of his work.

THE EDGAR CAYCE PRIMER

Herbert B. Puryear Ph.D. 1982 Bantam Books ISBN 0-553-25278-00395

BIBLIOGRAPHY

A simplified approach to the issues and philosophy underpinning the Edgar Cayce readings.

[Edgar Cayce Reading] EDGAR CAYCE READINGS

Please see http://www.edgarcayce.org for more information

Edgar Cayce Readings © 1971, 1993-2005 by the Edgar Cayce Foundation
All Rights Reserved

[ECOT] EDGAR CAYCE'S STORY OF THE OLD TESTAMENT

Robert W. Krajenke 1973 Edgar Cayce Foundation ISBN 87604-114-4

[TBOTR] THE BOOK OF THE REVELATION

A.R.E. Press 1971-1996 ISBN 23451-0656

This book is a "must have" because it relates the biblical book of Revelation to the opening of the 7 Chakras and "translates" the biblical symbols. It is the result of 7 years of study with Edgar Cayce by a group called "The Glad Helpers". It contains 4 sections :-

1. 23 Edgar Cayce Readings (his 281- series).
2. The Book of Revelation text on left page with interpretation on right.
3. The Book of Revelation text on left page with the group's symbology on right.
4. A glossary of symbols, and tables of symbol correspondences.

BIBLIOGRAPHY : OTHER SUBJECTS

[BAB] BABYLON – MESOPOTAMIA AND THE BIRTH OF CIVILISATION

Paul Kriwaczek. Published 2010 Atlantic Books ISBN 978-1-84-887156-4

The history of ancient Mesopotamia from 5400 BC to the eclipse of Babylon by the Persians in the 6th.Century BC.

[BF] HUMAN MIGRATION FROM AFRICAN ROOTS

http://www.bradshawfoundation.com/journey/

The Bradshaw Foundation web site. It gives a broader viewpoint of the Migration which includes archaeological evidence similar to that of Dr. Spencer Wells. It is widely agreed that Homo Sapiens "arrived" on earth around 200,000 years ago in Africa on the Equator. There were early attempts at migration from there which failed due to being surrounded by ice.

One attempt around 115,000 years ago crossed the then fertile Sahara Desert and reached Levant (later Mesopotamia, now Iraq). The pioneers were eliminated by a new ice age which also turned the Sahara to desert. The first successful migration was made around 90,000 years ago across the Red Sea. The Red Sea was at a low level because water was still locked as polar ice.

[DFCD] THE COSMIC DOCTRINE

Dion Fortune (1890-1946). The Aquarian Press (part of Thorsons Publishing Group). ISBN 8-85030-733-4. First published1924 revised by "Society of the Inner Light" 1988.

"Explains much in the esoteric sphere which has hitherto been inaccessible to the general reader. "

"Received from the Inner Planes during 1923 and 1924 ….. one of the Greater Masters".

A difficult book to read (and reread). I was helped by my study of The Kabbalah Tree of Life which helped "fix" ideas by association with the Sephiroth [BTB]

[DFMQ] THE MYSTICAL QABALAH

Dion Fortune (1890-1946). First published 1935. The Aquarian Press (part of Thorsons Publishing Group). ISBN 0-85030-355-4

A classic book reprinted several times. Revised and expanded by her own "Society of the Inner Light". Of the several books about [THE KABBALAH] that I own, in my opinion this gives the best basis for understanding in a text suitable for the Western mind to understand. She is firmly based on traditional teachings and draws from

BIBLIOGRAPHY

such authorities as A.W. Waite [THE TAROT] and Aleister Crowley – both of whose writings I find impossible to understand. She mentions the tendency for some other writers on the subject to deliberately deceive.

[DHTS] DIANA - HER TRUE STORY

Andrew Morton. 1993 Michael O'Mara Books Ltd. ISBN 1-85479-128-1

The early years in the life of Lady Diana Spencer until her divorce from Prince Charles.

The most carefully researched, authoritative book about the Royal family ever. [Sunday Times]

[DNA] DEEP ANCESTRY INSIDE THE GENOGRAPHIC PROJECT

Dr. Spencer Wells - 2007 National Geographic Society ISBN 978-1-4262-0118-9

Please also see [BF] The Bradshaw Foundation below.

[DNA] THE JOURNEY OF MAN

Dr. Spencer Wells – 2003 Penguin ISBN 978-0-1410-0832-5

These two books give an insight into the latest research into DNA and the Human Genome Project which was completed in the year 2000. Dr. Wells undertook a worldwide journey to collect DNA samples from various groups and races of people to investigate how humanity spread across the globe (the "migration"). He concluded that every human being alive today evolved from a single couple alive in Africa 60,000 years ago – who they named "Adam and Eve" – although Eve's mitochondrial DNA (which is inherited from our mother) was some 15,000 years older than Adam's.

The method was to collect, analyse and compare DNA samples. The results show that every one of us contains a set of genes identical to a tribe of bush men still alive in Africa, however, as he moved further from that source he discovered increasing numbers of mutations (changes) to the original. The mutations, which occur at roughly 10,000 year intervals, vary in effect and number depending on how far away the various races now live from Africa.

[DSP] DISCOVERING YOUR SOUL'S PURPOSE

Mark Thurston Ph.D. 1984 A.R.E.Press. The Edgar Cayce Foundation ISBN 87604-157-8

*Using techniques described in the Edgar Cayce readings and other systems of spiritual transformation, this book outlines a practical procedure for discovering your soul's purpose. By applying these ideas you will open new opportunities for the fulfilling, joyous use of your souls talents and abilities.

Here the author draws information from the clairvoyant readings and weekly Bible classes of Edgar Cayce. An important statement is that humans were not fully in a material state until Adam and Eve were given "coats of skin" in Genesis Chapter 2 Verse 21.

[EB] THE ENCYCLOPAEDIA BRITANNICA (SOFTWARE)

Encyclopaedia Britannica Ultimate Reference Suite. Chicago: Encyclopaedia Britannica, 2011.

[EWM] EYEWITNESS TO MESOPOTAMIA

Philip Steele 2007 Dorling Kindersley Eyewitness Books ISBN 978-0-7566-2972-4

A simple approach to various aspects of Mesopotamia with numerous pictures (72 pages)

[GEB] THE WORKS OF GEBER (721-815 AD)

E.J. Holmyard and Richard Russell. 1928 Kessinger Publishing ISBN 0-7661-0015-4

Translated from works of Geber Latin Edition Berne 1545 and into English 1678.

Translation of a 1545 AD Latin version of some of Geber's collected works on the subject of "Chymiftry". This can also be considered to be a record of pioneering work on Chemistry, Pharmacy, and Medicine. He was the son of a druggist. Further mentioned in the chapter [APPENDIX : ALCHEMY].

Geber is the Westernised form of Jabir, a celebrated Arab chemist, (721 – 815 AD). His works are notable because they are a result of his own practical experiments, and, contrary to other works on Alchemy (which term he did not use), are clear and concise, and omit much of the mysticism.

BIBLIOGRAPHY

[HLC] Origin, Development and Regulation of Human Leydig Cells

April 2009. "HORMONE RESEARCH IN PAEDIATRICS". K. Svechnikov , L. Landreh , J. Weisser, G. Izzo , E. Colón. I. Svechnikova, O. Söder. April 21st. 2009. This is a scientific paper produced by "Department of Women's and Children's Health, Pediatric Endocrinology Unit, Karolinska Institutet and University Hospital, Stockholm , Sweden. I found this scholarly paper published online as a .pdf file after a long search.

[IC] I CHING (or "BOOK OF CHANGES") – English version

Translated from the Chinese into German by Richard Wilhelm, and from there into English by Cary F. Baynes. Reprinted 8 times from 1969 to 1978 by Routledge & Keegan Paul Ltd. ISBN 0-7100 -1581.

This book has a foreword by C.G.Jung in 1949. Which speaks of his long experience with the book. The book is not just a classic basis of Confucianism – a major Chinese philosophy – but is meant to be used for divination – or as an "Oracle". It contains 64 Hexagrams each having 6 lines. One asks a question and then selects a hexagram "randomly" – originally by picking up dried sticks and counting them, but nowadays by tossing 3 coins and noting how they fall heads and tails. For many years scholars, myself included, have attempted to harmonise the system with Astrology – in particular the order and organisation of the hexagrams – without success.

[KJ] THE WAY TO WISDOM : AN INTRODUCTION TO PHILOSOPHY

Karl Jaspers 2003 New Haven, CT: Yale University Press. ISBN 030-0-09735-2

[MERL] THE MICROSOFT ENCARTA REFERENCE LIBRARY

Microsoft ® Encarta ® 2006. © 1993-2005 Microsoft Corporation. All rights reserved.

[YLT] YOUNG'S LITERAL BIBLE TRANSLATION"

Robert Young LL.D (1822-1888) – now in the public domain

First published 1862. Available as eBook too.

Literal translation of the Hebrew/Greek Bible (without interpretation or change of tense)

The result is still an approximation because there are numerous cases where "ten or twenty" Greek/Hebrew words only have a single English equivalent, and one Greek/Hebrew word can translate to "ten or twenty" English words. . It makes for a strange English text.

[YAC] YOUNG'S ANALYTICAL CONCORDANCE TO THE BIBLE

Robert Young LL.D (1822-1888) ISBN 0-917006-29-1 (1862)

There are numerous publications because the book is now in the public domain.

"On an entirely new plan. Containing about 311,000 references subdivided under the Hebrew and Greek originals with the literal meaning and pronunciation of each."

Lists all the words used in the Bible together with the original Greek and Hebrew words and their literal meaning. Robert Young's "Analytical Concordance to the Bible". A monumental work containing "about 311,000 references". Not only contains every word in the Bible but shows it each time it is used, in the relevant paragraph (in Book/Chapter/Verse order), with the paragraphs separated according to the original Hebrew/Greek words used.

ASTROLOGY SOFTWARE

I have downloaded and tried numerous Astrology applications, and only found 2 that satisfy me. They are completely different in approach and therefore fulfil different requirements. Care is needed to choose something that is accurate. Some are not. I know these are because they match my early manual calculations, and give exactly the same results.

BIBLIOGRAPHY

WIN*STAR STANDARD VERSION 4 (MATRIX SOFTWARE)

http://www.astrologysoftware.com/pro/winstar/index.aspx

It has been so long ago that I cannot remember when I began using Matrix software. It was probably in the early 1990s when I used their MSDOS "Blue Star". Since then I have upgraded with each new Windows Win*Star versions. They have numerous other options. On the few occasions I have used their support service I found it fast and excellent.

This is a "heavy weight" application, and the price reflects that. It has so many tools and options (too many to describe here) that as a beginner I was rather bewildered by its contents. However, it was well worth struggling with the learning curve – especially as help was freely available. Apart from producing single charts, It is good at comparing 2 charts such as for Synastry or Transits. One option I find useful as a programmer is that of producing customised planet transits listings in text file form for a subject Birth Chart. By keep to small orbs and using Jupiter to Pluto I can extract 90 years of data into 2 .csv text files and import them into Microsoft Excel or Access. There is also a similar option to produce custom ephemerides.

WORLD OF WISDOM HOROSCOPE INTERPRETER

http://www.world-of-wisdom.com/

Again, I have used this software for many years. The web site also offers other alternatives. Being free of numerous options, the software is very simple to use. I find the method of entry of birth chart data the simplest of any other application. The main reason I use this is that the single available chart wheel is perfect when supplying a Birth Chart interpretation. It has nice colours and everything prints perfectly (it is the central part of the Birth Charts shown in [ASTROLOGY : CHARTS EXAMPLES] to which I have made my own additions). There is a simple option to Copy the wheel to the clipboard, from which it can be pasted into Word (etc.). Like other software, there is an option to display and print a text report. Although I always provide my own interpretation, I find them useful for reference, and I am sure anyone would be happy with the contents and style.

I have contacted the web site for assistance on a couple of occasions, when Adrian Ross Duncan has replied almost immediately. I have an ongoing problem with one of my computers which has nothing to do with the software - which has worked perfectly on all Windows versions from Windows 95 to Windows 7.

APPENDIX 1. ALCHEMY

In keeping with the spirit of this book, the chapter focuses on the more evidential, rather than philosophical side, of Alchemy – which is highly individually subjective. Evidence for this is that there are numerous "methods" which do not relate to one another – let alone supply cross references to other, more structured, subjects. There are also numerous different symbols that apply to the same principle, such as Mercury.

There is a high focus on discovering Spirit within Matter but, in the absence of Atomic Theory, and knowledge of the basic Chemical Elements, Alchemy is lost in a sea of complexity.

The chapter contains :-

1. A brief description of Alchemy.
2. An analysis of a widely publicised Alchemic image of 1659 AD.
3. A description of an actual method of gold extraction from an ore.

As with [THE KABBLAH TREE OF LIFE] I was not originally going to include a chapter on Alchemy because it has not been one of my main subjects and is "manmade" rather than conforming to natural processes. However, one of my main more specialised subjects at school was Chemistry, and my first job was doing chemical analyses, so I decided to look a little deeper and immediately discovered many inconsistencies. I also discovered a case where, despite many writers seemingly being in agreement, they are clearly in error – even ignoring one of their own stated main principles. This underlines the necessity to keep one's feet firmly on the ground when exploring areas such as this, and to always look for practical, tangible evidence insofar as possible. If a system of thought is valid it must have some practical basis under The Law "As Above, So Below, As Below So Above".

Here is a summary of my main findings, some of which are described in more detail later on :-

1. My first main conclusion is that, for me, there are better alternatives to spend time studying such as Chemistry, Astrology and The Tarot – all of which have a strong consensus. With alchemy there is no exact consensus on its methods or meaning, and little relation to empirical facts. You will see below that C.G. Jung reached the same conclusion.

2. My second main conclusion is that Alchemy in its origins was solely concerned with the extraction of gold from the earth. Confusion has occurred because of the difficulties of communication. In the beginning Alchemists had no concepts or words to describe what they did, or the chemicals they used, so they had to compare it with known imagery at the time. There were similar problems with such areas as Psychology and Computers where new concepts required new languages to discuss them - but they have to "borrow" existing words and ascribe additional meanings.

3. One of the glaring errors I discovered is that where many "authors" ascribe a chemical or alchemical process to each stage they omit the first stage of digging the ore from the ground - which is clearly included in one of the main Alchemical Principles AND a widely copied image of 1659 AD. I cover this later in examining the 7 Stage process in more detail. Symbolically, this omission is what causes errors. There is no basis on physical fact. We tend to live in a "Copy and Paste" world where errors are transmitted along with other information.

4. A major discovery is that the stated mystical or allegorical content often bears little or no relationship to known empirical facts or chemical processes. There is no "reality check". Generally what the Chemistry process actually does is ignored in favour of some other, unrelated, "mystical" interpretation. Probably because it is hard to define what is being described. We can understand the problems of the early days, but not now. There are writers on the Internet that are physically doing the chemistry, but it is not clear if they relate to Alchemy. Many are clearly just extracting gold for financial income, and have no interest in Alchemy.

5. There is no general agreement about what the process stages are. For example, there are 3 main contenders – 7 Stages, 12 Stages, and 14 Stages – none of which agree with one another. There are others. This makes sense when we consider the actual practice of extracting gold from the earth because the original raw materials can vary enormously in quality and require different methods – but I can find no recognition of this fact.

6. That said, the process of Research is symbolically similar to that of extracting gold from the earth in that we get a lot of information which has to be sifted very carefully to "extract the gold". It is even called "Data Mining" today. Again, in this respect there is some agreement with The Cycle of Growth and the

APPENDIX : ALCHEMY

Scientific Method of Experiment. Many of the "Alchemists" of today seem to not be good at the "purification" required, where, for example, many websites contain the same material which is virtually word for word the same – including the same errors.

7. This, once again, underlines the fact that, in any investigation, we need to find some empirical evidence – which is one of the principles of this book.

C.G.JUNG AND "PSYCHOLOGY AND ALCHEMY"

C. G. Jung wrote a whole book "Psychology and Alchemy". The format is very similar to his other books where most of it is material produced in his patients' dreams (who had no connection with Alchemy) which happened to associate with alchemic imagery. The book contains a large number of images. This appears to be evidence that, when it wishes to be recognised, the Collective Unconscious will use any channel available. We can try to "make sense of", or rationalise, them at will.

Jung's statement includes the widely circulated 12 Steps "process". As an aid to further confusion Jung includes an image (his Figure 122 in the book, labelled as 12 parts) of the "arbour philosophica" (below) showing the "twelve alchemical operations" which clearly has 14 numbered parts plus one without a number. The diagram shows a tree structure similar to [THE KABBALAH TREE OF LIFE]. Interestingly, the numbering is arranged in a "bottom up" approach, rather than "top down" of The Kabbalah – which has its roots in heaven.

A main principle of Alchemy is that of extracting Gold and Silver from the "Prima Materia" which, from Jung's observance that it refers to The Unconscious, does relate to The Kabbalah as Sephiroth 1 (Kether. Crown) state of primeval chaos before Evolution (and The Big Bang).

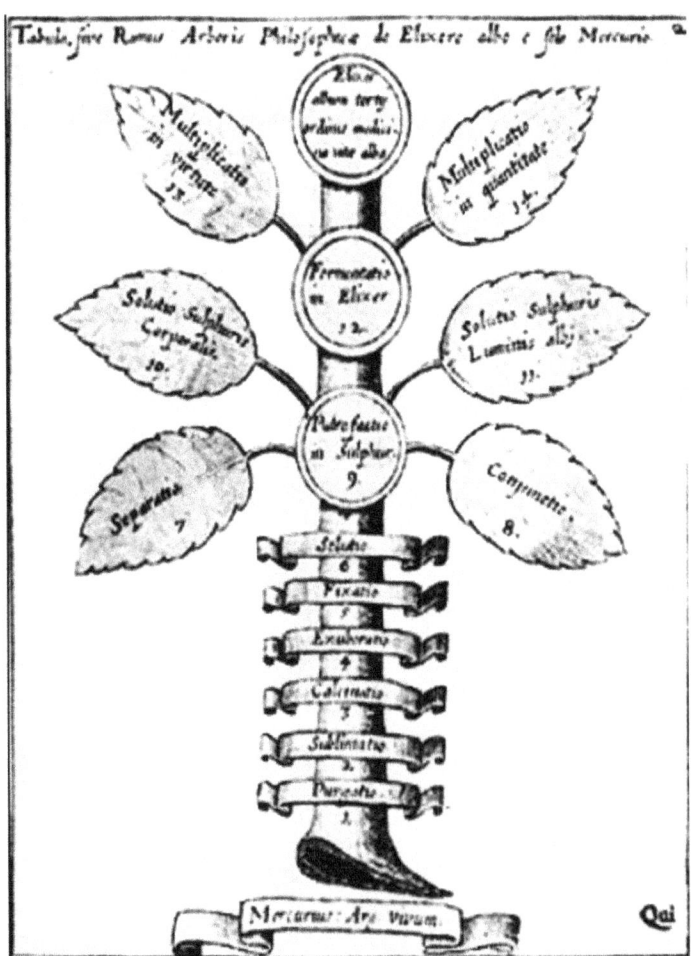

Figure 91 : Arbour Philosophica

APPENDIX : ALCHEMY

Although individually the stages seem similar to methods used in Chemistry, they do not make sense as a sequence of operations :-

As to the course of the process as a whole the authors are vague and contradictory. Maybe content themselves with a few summary hints, others make an elaborate list of the various operations. Thus in 1576, Josephus Quercetanus, alchemist, physician, and diplomat, were in France and French Switzerland played a somewhat similar role to that of Paracelsus, established a sequence of 12 operations.[Jung P&A]

[with additions [BTB] :-

1. Calcinatio ["conversion of a metal into fine powder or ash"[GEB]
2. Solutio [Dissolving]
3. Elementorum Separatio [Separation]
4. Conjunctio [Joining]
5. Putrefactio [Decomposition]
6. Coagulatio ["solidification by crystallisation or by cooling a fused substance [ALC]
7. Cibatio [="Feeding"]
8. Sublimatio [Sublimation. Such as heating to remove metallic mercury as vapour which sublimes, or returns to solid state on colder parts of the vessel (without intermediate liquid state). Similar to distillation.]
9. Fermentatio ["Elixir. The Philosophers Stone" [GEB]
10. Exaltatio [="raise status". Purify ? Could refer to Geber's "Preparation" below]
11. Augmentatio [="Add"]
12. Proiectio ["addition of the Elixir to metal whose transmutation was desired"[GEB]

Every single one of these terms has more than one meaning; we need only look at the explanations in Milan's lexicon to get a more than adequate idea of this. It is therefore pointless to go further into the variations of the alchemically procedure in the present context. [Jung P&A]

In our observations we must keep in mind that the mentality, or psychology, of our ancestors must have been very different to that of today. If we observe the process of human Evolution in relationship to The Cycle of Growth, or the development of a child, we can see distinct similarities. In particular, for our purposes here, the development of the Jungian Thinking Function (Air), mainly used in verbal and written communication, is relatively new. The early hunter gatherers (children) had little need or use for this ability, so their psychology would have been based on Intuition or Instinct (Fire) and Sensation (Earth). This is considered in more detail in my chapter [ASTROLOGY : SIGNS] – in particular the relationship of the Jungian Functions with "The 4 Elements". The modern development of Writing, with its efficiency in communicating ideas to a wide audience, has contributed much to the fast development of the Function. Children do not learn this skill right away. In early days skills were passed on to apprentices by practical demonstration. "Monkey see. Monkey do". (Sensation – Earth). There were no schools for common people until the last few hundred years.

The problems are compounded when translated from one language to another – to another.

THE STATED PRINCIPLE OF ALCHEMY

Visita Interiora Terrae Rectificando Invenies Occultum Lapidem" (V-I-T-R-I-O-L)
" Visit the Innermost of the Earth and by Rectifying you will find the Hidden Stone"

In accordance with my principle of considering the Whole before looking at the parts I have started the Principle here because the phrase appears practically everywhere in alchemic texts. Much point is made about the capital letters of the Latin text spelling "Vitriol" which is not very scientific because, historically, it could be one of many compounds. In older Chemistry Vitriol can refer to metal sulphate salts such as Copper Sulphate (Blue Vitriol) and Ferrous, or Iron, Sulphate (Green Vitriol). In particular, especially in more modern days, it refers to Sulphuric Acid. We observe that, although the alchemists used Sulphuric Acid for other things, it is not normally used in any gold extraction process, although there are numerous variants. It cannot dissolve gold, even when concentrated.

I have also included the Principle here because so many modern "alchemists" seem to ignore its precept. In particular the bit about "Visita Interiora Terrae" means that we begin the process by "getting down to earth", "getting our hands dirty" or "mining" – that is, gathering physical facts. The first principle, and basic, earthy,

APPENDIX : ALCHEMY

foundations of any detective work. As you can see, in this chapter (and, indeed, this whole book) I am attempting to do just that. Hopefully, my subsequent "Rectifying" will produce "gold"(or a Philosopher's Stone) that is relatively pure. Unfortunately a great deal of the actual written Alchemic text, especially on the Internet, is more of the "copy and paste" variety – clearly with no attempt at verification.

At this stage I am reminded of Genesis Chapter 11 Verse 3, that I also mention in [ASTROLOGY : THE ZODIAC AGES] in connection with building of The Tower of Babel which transformed "the whole earth" being "of one language and one speech"[KJV] to men having different languages and not being able to understand one another :-

> *And they said one to another, Go to, let us make brick, and burn them thoroughly. And they had brick for stone, and slime had they for mortar. [KJV]*

The meaning of which refers to "brick" as a man-made material and "stone" as a natural material made by God. The difference between man-made images and Natural Law .

When we begin investigating Alchemy most writers focus upon two goals :-

1. A search for "The Philosopher's Stone" which will transmute base metals into Gold – the beginnings of Chemistry. We can allow the association with finding Spirit within Matter, but question the methods.
2. A search for "The Elixir of Life" which brings immortality - which can be considered among the beginnings of Pharmacy and Medicine.

Modern science states that it is impossible to transmute metals by chemical means, although in 1941 it was discovered that mercury contains around 15% of an isotope Mercury 196 which can be converted to gold by bombarding it with neutrons in a particle accelerator. As with some other methods of recovering gold, such as that dissolved in seawater, the cost was far beyond that of the value of the finished product. What seems to be missed is that the Alchemy methods described are just the ones used to extract gold from its ores. If we step back and observe matters from a purely practical standpoint it makes perfect sense that practitioners will want to keep them secret – as with any other invention. There was no possibility of getting a patent in early days, so secrecy and misdirection were important. Another reason for confusion concerning the various methods would be that everything depends on the quality of the ore, or other raw materials, available to begin with. In some places it is possible to collect gold in a relatively pure state by simple washing dirt away with water, such as in the "American Gold Rush". In others it is necessary to process tons of earth with chemicals to obtain relatively small amounts. There is also the variable need to further purify the gold by removing other contaminants such as silver, copper, tin, and lead. Yet another variable is the availability of the chemicals required. Early alchemists would need to make their own. We also note that many of their chemicals – in particular, Mercury, which was used extensively in Egyptian and Roman times – give off toxic vapour during the processes. We note that Cyanide is also used in some places. We do not know how exposure to these chemicals would affect the bodies and minds of early Alchemists.

Another reason for secrecy was that Alchemists were often persecuted by the authorities, and others, of the time, who wished to control gold production. In England in 1403 the "multiplication of metals" was punishable by death from the fear that overproduction would drive down the value of gold.

"THE WORKS OF GEBER" [GEB]

Although an interesting historical document, and the fact that it describes some practical Chemistry methods, this book does not contain any information about gold extraction from its ore. In the light of the huge volume of other, less reliable, information on the subject we can take this as a truer version of the origins of Chemistry, Metallurgy, and Pharmacy. Attempts to look up the terms used in the book did not provide any additional information, and the main works of reference do not add any details. As a recognised authoritative, practical, work on Alchemy it tends to deny many of the more fanciful aspects by omission.

Geber is the Westernised form of Jabir, a celebrated Arab chemist, (721 – 815 AD) - son of a druggist. His works are notable because they are a result of his own practical experiments, and, contrary to other works on the subject, are clear and concise, and omit much of the mysticism and superstition. He was clearly a Scientist and published about 100 works. The book, published in 1928, is a translated collection (from an earlier 1545 AD Latin, 1678 AD English, version) of many of his works. So we have the high possibility of errors in translation – by people who may have little knowledge of Chemistry.

APPENDIX : ALCHEMY

The content is clearly what we would call Chemistry today. Although the chemistry concepts are outdated, the basic methods are still used today . It deals with the extraction of a wide range of chemicals and metals as well as medicines for the sick.

Here are some images which explain better than I can. There is also an extract from "The Works of Geber" showing his treatment of Sol (gold) which suggests he could make it into a solution. Perhaps this solution was the Elixir (?).

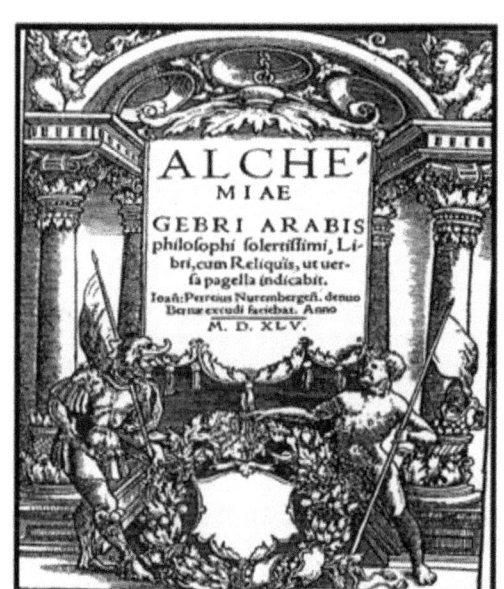
Works of Geber - Latin 1545

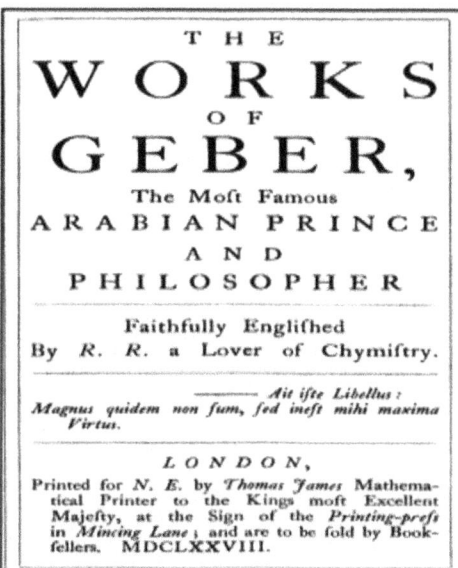
Works of Geber - England 1678

CHAP. IX.

Of the Preparation of Sol.

Perfect *Bodies* need not *Preparation*, in relation to their further *Perfection*, being perfect; but that they may be more subtiliated, and attenuated, we adhibit this *Preparation* to them:

℞ *Sol* or *Gold* beaten into thin *Plates*, and with them and *Common Salt* very well prepared, make Lay upon Lay in a *Vessel* of *Calcination*, which set into a *Furnace* and Calcine well for three days, until the whole be subtily Calcined; then take it out, grind it well, wash it with *Vinegar*, and dry it in the *Sun*, afterward grind it well with half its weight of cleansed *Salarmoniac*; then set it to be dissolved, until the whole (by the *benefit* of *Common Salt* and *Armoniac*) be dissolved into a most clear *Water*. This is the precious *Ferment* for the *Red Elixir*, and the true *Body* made *Spiritual*.

Preparation of Sol (Gold)

Figure 92 : Works of Geber - Sol (gold)

APPENDIX : ALCHEMY

THE SEVEN ALCHEMY STAGES

Visita Interiora Terrae Rectificando Invenies Occultum Lapidem" (V-I-T-R-I-O-L)
" Visit the Innermost of the Earth and by Rectifying you will find the Hidden Stone"

- 4. RECTIFICANDO — Rectify. Purify
- 3. TERRA — Earth, Ash
- 5. INVENIES — Find
- 2. INTERIORA — Innards. Contents
- 6. OCCULTUM — Hidden
- 1. VISITA — Visit
- 7. LAPIDEM — Stones

Figure 93 : The 7 Alchemy Stages

THE 7 STAGES AS DESCRIBED

I have included this as an illustration of one of the processes described and copied an uncountable number of times on the Internet. The problem here is that they do not fully comply with the Alchemic Principle nor the 7 Stage image which follows. The following version with the image does.

There are different versions of the 7 Steps. I have chosen one that is closest to the physical process which is described at the end of this chapter. The steps are stated [with my "translation"] which I compare with the practical methods of gold extraction some of which are described at the end of the chapter. :-

1. CALCINATION [Heating to high temperature. Burning to ash]. Some compounds are oxidised by combination with atmospheric oxygen at this stage. Oxides are relatively stable compounds. Gold is not affected, it only affects the contaminants. The process would also drive off any volatile components including water. Some Internet sites suggest Sulphuric Acid is involved which has no connection with this process.
2. DISSOLUTION [Dissolving]. Rather than dissolving the waste products, the gold itself is dissolved. The old method, which is still used today, uses Mercury. It is clear that Alchemists also had access to Aqua Regia ("Royal Water") which is a mixture of Hydrochloric Acid and Nitric Acid (neither will dissolve gold on its own). Again, this is used today. The method used, apart from the quality and content of the raw

APPENDIX : ALCHEMY

material, depends on various practical and economic factors. Some Internet sites suggest water is used – which makes no sense.

3. SEPARATION [self-explanatory]. If Aqua Regia is used this stage would be Filtration to separate the waste solids from the gold in solution. The Mercury method is more physical in that, now containing gold, it is heavier than the waste materials which can therefore be washed away. The practical method which follows uses a filtration method which requires squeezing the excess Mercury through cloth (and is included as Stage 6 of the Alchemy image).
4. CONJUNCTION [Combining]. Suggesting the combination of batches of gold-bearing Mercury from repetition of the process above.
5. FERMENTATION [don't know]. According to Geber this refers to the Elixir or Philosophers Stone [GEB]
6. DISTILLATION [of the Mercury]. The Mercury-Gold amalgam can now be heated to vaporise the Mercury, leaving the gold behind. The Mercury vapour can be cooled back to liquid Mercury again and re-used.
7. CONGELATION [Congealing. Solidifying]. At this stage the gold is in a yellowish-red powder form. It requires melting to 1,000 degrees Centigrade to make it a solid lump.

We begin with an image published by a German alchemist Basil Valentine in a book "The Book of Azoth" in 1659. It is rather like the image on a Tarot card. The image is published in various places on the Internet with a statement that it relates to the 7 Stages above. There is a consensus as to what the steps are, but, as we shall see, they bear no resemblance to the image.

I cannot promise that I have any answers to its meaning, but when we examine and combine the physical, observable, facts contained in the image and the PRACTICAL mining method below, we get closer to what must be the truth. In fact, we owe it to the originator, who has clearly spent a lot of time and effort, to do our best in this respect. In so doing I will restrict myself to what is actually there as far as possible. It depicts a sequence of events that complies with the Main Principle of Alchemy mentioned AND the Practical Method. I have included some symbolism in an attempt to better understand what the artist was trying to represent.

OVERVIEW OF THE 7 STAGE IMAGE

1. Contrary to The Cycle of Growth images, the sequence here is clockwise.
2. The basic structure of the image is of a square containing triangle pointing downward, which generally refers to the Element Water.
3. The triangle is overlaid with a circle containing a 7 pointed star forming divisions numbered in sequence clockwise from the bottom point. We can therefore assume that we deal with them in that order. The indicated overall 3 stage sequence begins with Earth, rises to Air, and returns to Earth via Water. In Chemistry terms, this could relate to the process of Evaporation and Distillation.
4. There are 3 sets of images relating to the sides of the triangle which, in turn, depict the Elements (1) Earth and Fire, (2) Air, and (3) Water. In Alchemy there are 2 versions of a downward pointing triangle image which refer to Earth and Water. It would seem from the placement that this version could refer to either at different stages.
5. The 3 points of the triangle, in turn, have the word "Corpus" and the image of a cube, the word "Anima" with the image of the Sun (with a human face), and the word "Spiritus" with the image of a crescent Moon (including a human face).
6. Each of the 7 stages is associated with a keyword, an image, and a planet contained in the points of a 7 pointed star. Despite their seeming importance to the creator of the image and the fact that the keywords appear in the same order as the Main Principle of Alchemy, Alchemists ignore the meaning of the keywords and planet glyphs in favour of the description above - there being no mention of them in this context apart from, occasionally, Saturn. The meanings of the keywords and the associated images here bear little or no relationship to their interpretation of the 7 stages above.
7. At the centre of the image is a circle containing the face of a bearded man and another downward-pointing triangle. As with an Astrological Birth Chart, this suggests the "still centre" around which the Universe circulates. The focus of attention is "down" towards Earth.

APPENDIX : ALCHEMY

THE 7 STAGES IN THE IMAGE
Each Stage in the image consists of :-
1. A number and a planet glyph contained in the point of the star. Pure symbols. The planet symbols are in order from Saturn to the Sun.
2. An image in a circle (right brain) and a keyword (left brain) between points of the star. Man-made "symbols" between stages.
3. An associated image outside the main triangle – suggesting that this is the external appearance of what is going on "inside".

STAGE 1 – VISITA (Visit)
This Stage, as the beginning of the process, clearly has no relationship with Calcination which comes later. By missing out this, and the next, stage "alchemists" indicate their failure to relate the Stages to practical, earthy, life as we know it – hence the overall confusion from relying an copying and pasting incomplete information. They do not seem to be aware of the Law "As Above, So Below. As Below so Above".

Visita means "Visit" – which is a movement of physical and\or mental focus.

Here, everything is at a down-to-earth level. The World of Form. We return here at the end.

The Stage is the focus of the central triangle AND the main triangle named CORPUS (Body) with an image of a Cube, symbolic of Matter. The cube has 5 surrounding stars, which are reminiscent of a downward-pointing Pentacle, symbolic of "matter over mind". Our Sage first observes his subject using his 5 material senses. What is there is empirical truth. Which is what we are now doing here.

As the beginning stage of a cycle we can relate it to Cycle of Growth Stage 1 (Seed). Perhaps this is what is referred to by the numerous small beads drawn so laboriously under both feet.

PLANET - SATURN
The principle of Saturn is "Consolidation". The planet glyph of Saturn consists of a cross (matter) over a semicircle, and relates to The Devil, who relates to the reversed Pentacle. There is a (mathematical) square over the planet glyph. There is suggestion of a higher Form over a lower Form. Idea or Principle over Mind over Body over Matter (As Above, So Below). Structure. Discipline. In Alchemy, Saturn is also the symbol for Lead. Lead is one of the Heavy Metals and weighs 11.34 grammes per cubic centimetre. When freshly produced it has a shiny surface which soon turns grey as it oxidises in the air. Gold, also a Heavy Metal, is denser at 19.3 grammes per cubic centimetre and does not easily react with other elements, thus retaining its pristine appearance. It is one of the densest forms of matter. Denser than Lead.

THE INNER IMAGE
The image is of a crow or a raven sitting on a white skull. Crows and ravens are mainly ground-dwelling birds, their black colour making them less visible. The skull is symbolic of Death. The "bare bones" are the internal structure of our bodies, and lives. Perhaps the "dead" buried gold that becomes the reborn child of the final stage. Crows and ravens are mainly carrion (rotting flesh) feeders. In the final Stage 7 there is a white child emerging from the earth, which suggests the transformation required. The skull suggests that something has to die before new life can occur.

THE EXTERNAL IMAGE
Related to Stage 1, the external image is of a bare right foot planted firmly on the earth. Our feet relate to our "Under – Standings". This foot is clearly earth-bound, and here suggests stability rather than movement. The other foot at Stage 7 is Water related. At the foot is a small dragon coming out of its burrow in the earth. Similar to the Gold Lion, it is something contained in the earth. It is removed in the heating stage 3.

STAGE 2 – INTERIORA (Interior)
Interiora means "Interior" – which, from the Alchemic Principle, refers to "the Innermost" (of the Earth). We can easily relate this to the activity of gold mining as well as the study of Physics, Chemistry, and other down-to-earth subjects. With our modern knowledge of Psychology we could also associate this with "The Underworld" – often referring to the Unconscious Mind. Here we are concerned with the Element Earth whereas the Collective Unconscious is related to Watery Pisces.

At this stage it is possible to get an idea of how much gold is present in the ore by simply washing with water. The gold, being heavier than anything else, separates out. Some ores need no further processing apart from removing the gold.

APPENDIX : ALCHEMY

PLANET - JUPITER

Originally, the glyph of Jupiter drawn as a semicircle over a cross was the reverse of that of Saturn. Its principle is "Expansion". Avoiding the misleading term "opposites", they are therefore complementary in their activity. As we travel away from the Earth we reach Mars, Jupiter, then Saturn. Saturn (Consolidation) is said to discipline and limit the Expansion of Jupiter by demanding physical, practical, results. Without Jupiter, Saturn would eventually decay and die from inertia. From the external image we see that Jupiter's expansive\collective nature has resulted in a pile of earth. In Alchemy, Jupiter refers to Tin, which is almost as resistant to corrosion as gold, and which has no bearing on practical gold extraction except as a possible contaminant.

THE INNER IMAGE

We see our raven looking down into the earth where the skull seems to have disappeared into a shapeless blob. Something has happened to make something previously fixed in form to lose its shape. In practical terms, the first process with the gold bearing ore is to crush it so that it has as much surface area as possible – otherwise the chemicals would not penetrate later on, and much of its gold content would be lost.

THE EXTERNAL IMAGE

A complicated image of many parts. We see a bearded king with a shining crown sitting on a pile of earth, hidden in which is a golden lion. The king carries a rod or sword in his right hand, and has what seems to be a cat sitting on his lap. The overall appearance is of inertia, although it is obvious that some work has been done.

The Sage has done some digging and mined a pile of material. Hidden in that material is some gold (the lion). The king and the staff seem indication that, whereas the earlier stage relied on Instinct, the Sage must now exercise his royal Will to get off his backside again to continue the work. Above his head is a flaming torch, which links with the next step.

STAGE 3 – TERRA (Earth. Stability)

Terra means "Earth". At last we arrive at the Calcination Stage. At the practical level Calcination involves heating the raw material to a high temperature to drive off volatile content, including water, and oxidise the material with atmospheric oxygen to create an "ash". The ash is a very stable material in that it will not have any further chemical reactions between its components. Any further processing will tend to be free from unexpected reactions as the material is more or less homogeneous and inert. The images are all in keeping with this process.

PLANET – MARS

Mars, "God of War" is the ruling planet of Aries. Among its correspondences are one associated with the forging of metals – especially those related to war, or sharp tools. In the chapter [ASTROLOGY : THE ZODIAC AGES] we note that The Age of Aries was when the use of metals was becoming more important. It was the beginning of the use of iron as the higher temperatures required became technologically possible. Mars is the Alchemical name for Iron.

In this point of the star is also the symbol of Sulphur – the upward pointing triangle of Fire over the cross of matter. The heating process would burn off (oxidise) any Sulphur to Sulphur Dioxide gas, which would escape. This could be what is meant by the dragon being consumed by the fire.

THE INNER IMAGE

We have flying birds seemingly feeding on something, which suggests the Element Air. Early Alchemists were not aware of Oxygen in the air, but the image seems to match the description above. Oxygen was discovered in 1774.

THE EXTERNAL IMAGE

We have the image of a flaming torch at the point of the star, above which is an animal - the dragon of Stage 1 seemingly being consumed by fire. Perhaps the "lower element" is just being driven away.

We have an image of the Sun labelled Anima. Anima is an Alchemical term for the animating principal, or life itself – Spirit - which can relate to the Element Fire. As part of this Stage, some alchemists would leave the material in the sun for a period of time. It is a strange paradox to relate the Sun to the process of burning to (dead) ash. "Sol" is also the name for Gold itself.

As one of the 3 points on the main triangle this is a major transformation point in the process from Earth, via Fire, to Air.

STAGE 4 – RECTIFICANDO (Rectify. Purify)

APPENDIX : ALCHEMY

This and the next 2 stages refer to the addition of a solvent to dissolve the gold, separating out the gold-bearing solution, and then separating the gold from the solvent. It is not exactly clear which solvent is referred to here. It is tempting to suggest Aqua Regia ("Royal Water") in view of the crown in the image but practical and historical, knowledge suggests Mercury –which is silver in colour - is more likely. For our purposes here it does not really matter as the stages are similar in principle. I have decided to follow the Mercury method here in view of the fact that the artist has taken the trouble to draw numerous pearl-like beads in the lower outer images – which are similar in appearance to the ones in the practical method below.

Stage 4 is opposite in position to Stage 1 of the process. This halfway stage relates to Cycle of Growth Stage 7 (Partnerships). One of the functions of partnerships is to draw us away to new experiences and new forms of life.

PLANET – SUN

Having had a Sun image in the external picture of the last Stage, it now controls this one. In terms of the sequence of planets we have reached the Earth, which has been "replaced" by the Sun in the same way as in an Astrological chart. The Sun symbol is the same as that of "Sol" – Gold.

THE INNER IMAGE

Although it is not fully clear from the image, in the practical process the ash is ground as fine as possible and mixed with Mercury, which dissolves the gold. This seems to be the subject of the image which shows 2 white birds "carrying" a crown (the gold ?). A solvent is sometimes called a "carrier" of whatever is dissolved.

THE OUTER IMAGE

We are still in the area assigned to the Element Air. The pair of wings top centre suggests that this is the "high point" of the process where the gold is separated from the lower elements. It is diametrically opposite the beginning point.

STAGE 5 – INVENIES (Find)

Having reached the peak, we are now on the returning, downward stages. We have Mercury containing gold, and excess Mercury.

PLANET – VENUS

The planet is the first one away from Earth, inwards towards the Sun. It symbolises beauty and harmony in relationships. Its action is Attraction. Venus is the name for Copper.

THE INNER IMAGE

We see the 2 white birds, no longer flying but perched together, supported on the branch of a tree. They are in a stable, earthbound, position. Perhaps they indicate the 2 types of Mercury – that containing gold and the excess.

THE OUTER IMAGE

We are at another turning point of the main triangle. Whereas the other two points are coloured grey with a contained yellow image, here everything is yellow, or gold. We have a Moon containing the light of the Sun. The two wings of the previous stage have now transformed into a young bird (standing on earth). The point of the triangle is labelled "Spiritus" which, in Alchemy, refers to :-

   *a volatile substance which sublimes on heating [GEB]

STAGE 6 – OCCULTUM (Hidden)

We now need to separate the excess Mercury from the mixture. The Mercury-Gold amalgam is "hidden" in the cloth filter.

PLANET – MERCURY

We note that the point of the star contains 2 glyphs of Mercury – one large, one small, suggesting 2 kinds of Mercury in different proportions. Mercury is the closest planet to the Sun.

THE INNER IMAGE

We see the 2 birds have now transformed into a single white (silvery like Mercury ?) unicorn seated on the earth. The horn of the unicorn focuses energy into a single point, like a spear or sword – or cloth filter.

THE OUTER IMAGE

We see the left hand of the Sage holding a cloth filter. There are numerous other suggestions as to what this might be, but all are incorrect, even nonsensical – which again emphasises the need to check physical facts. To

APPENDIX : ALCHEMY

see how this is used please refer to the next section showing the practical method, Stages 4 to 6. Some Mercury mixture is poured into the centre of a cloth which is then folded to contain it. The ends of the cloth are twisted to squeeze the cloth and force the excess Mercury through it, leaving the gold bearing Mercury behind – which forms a pearl-like bead in the cloth (because of the silver colour of Mercury). The beads appear to be represented numerous times in the image.

The next image clearly refers to the heating or burning of the cloth filter which contains the gold bearing Mercury (practical method Stage 6 and following). There is a small gold circle suggesting the bead of gold it will eventually become (?).

STAGE 7 – LAPIDEM (Stones)

At the final Stage we have the gold transformed from melted liquid to a solid metallic bead ready for further processing. It has been released from the Earth, but must now continue its life in a new form, in a new Earth. The gold may still be contaminated with other metals and so need refinement to a purer state. In the image we see an association with reincarnation and the birth of a child.

PLANET – MOON

It is difficult to see the relevance of the Moon at this stage. The Moon reflects the light of the Sun and controls the tides. It refers to the negative, feminine principle as distinct from the positive, masculine, positive principle of the Sun. The Personal Unconscious, rather than Conscious Mind. There is a clear watery theme in the outer image. "Luna" is the name for Silver in Alchemy, so perhaps this refers to its presence as a contaminant.

THE INNER IMAGE

We see a child "resurrected", or released, from the Earth. We must note a similarity with the Tarot Card XX. Judgement which appears in the final Cycle of Growth Stage 12 (Confinement).

THE OUTER IMAGE

We have finally arrived at the Element of Water – which, again, is in keeping with Cycle of Growth Stage 12 and its association with the Sign of Pisces and the Collective Unconscious.

We have a feminine figure riding on a whale or dolphin on the sea. She is at the border between Air and Water. There is association with Jonah being swallowed by a whale, and final rebirth. Her hand controlling the whale is at the 7th. point of the Star which contains the Moon symbol, which controls the ebb and flow of the tides – and the menstrual cycle. Finally, we have the left (unconscious) foot of the sage firmly placed on the sea, suggesting Inner "under-standing".

Our Sage has taken steps forward in evolution – Right Foot then Left Foot – ready to continue.

HISTORY OF GOLD

The history of gold extends back at least 6,000 years, the earliest identifiable, realistically dated finds having been made in Egypt and Mesopotamia c.4000 BC. The earliest major find was located on the Bulgarian shores of the Black Sea near the present city of Varna. [EB]

Egyptian wall reliefs from 2300 BC show gold in various stages of refining and mechanical working. During these ancient times, gold was mined from alluvial placers—that is, particles of elemental gold found in river sands. The gold was concentrated by washing away the lighter river sands with water, leaving behind the dense gold particles, which could then be further concentrated by melting. By 2000 BC the process of purifying gold-silver alloys with salt to remove the silver was developed. The mining of alluvial deposits and, later, lode or vein deposits required crushing prior to gold extraction, and this consumed enormous amounts of manpower ..... [EB]

APPENDIX : ALCHEMY

A PRACTICAL GOLD EXTRACTION METHOD

Here is a succession of pictures to show stages in the gold extraction process as used from ancient times to the present day. The methods and stages are variable depending on the quality of the ore. For example, Calcination is not usually required. The last 4 pictures are from a modern process using Borax instead of Mercury. Although the methods are identical this is safer for the worker and the environment. Mercury is a poison. The steps are labelled to correspond with the "7 Stages" image of 1659 AD. The main method nowadays is by washing tons of soil with water in sluices.

Figure 94 : Practical Gold Extraction

APPENDIX 2. HUMAN EVOLUTION

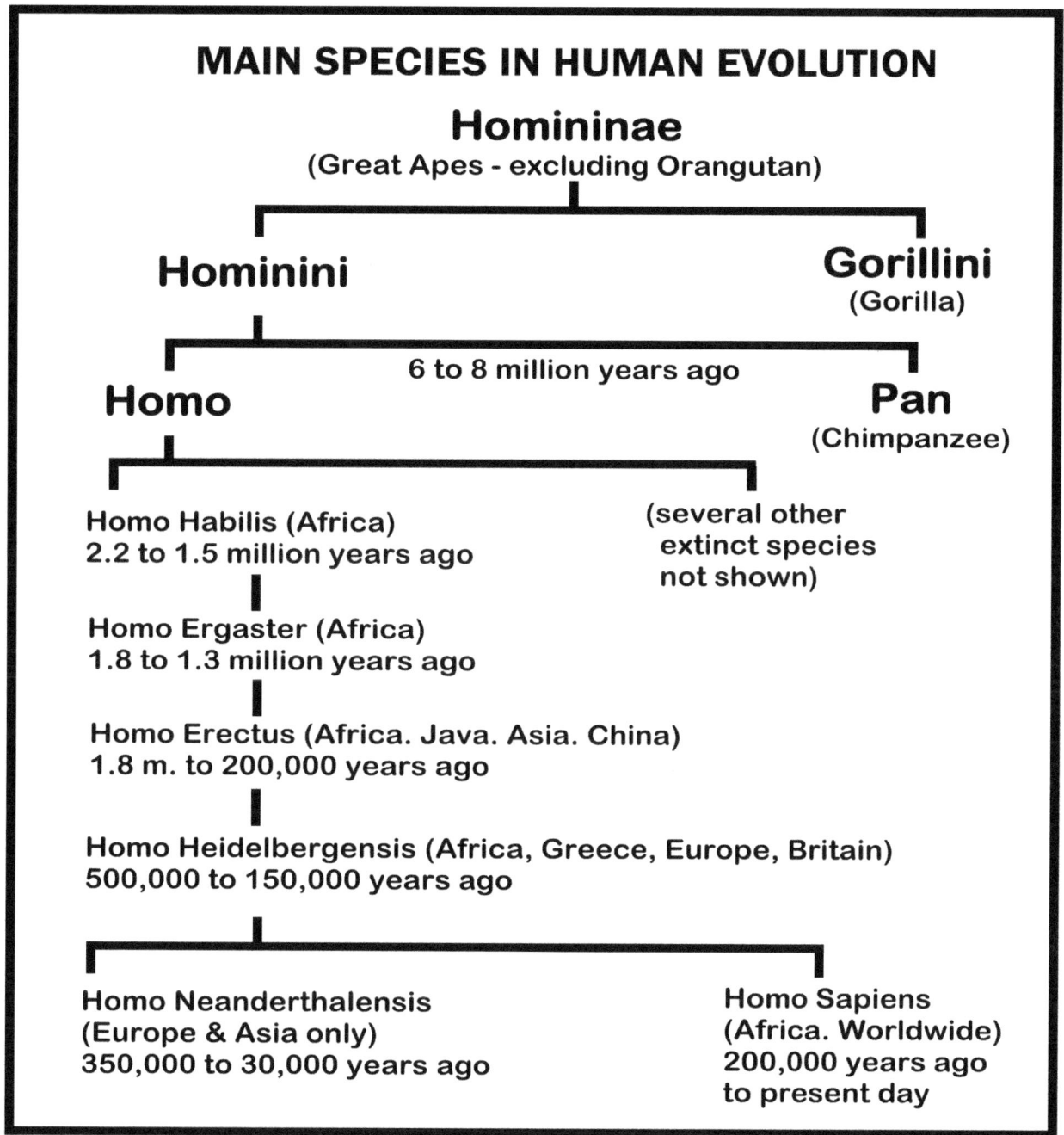

Figure 95 : Main Species in Human Evolution

There are diagrams at the end of this chapter showing a summary of human evolution from blobs of jelly to the Homo species, and the migration pattern of Homo Sapiens out of Africa.

Despite current scientific thinking that evolution occurs from random "mistakes" in copying DNA, The Cycle of Growth suggests that mutations ("accidents". "change") are inevitable. It is just that we do not understand the natural laws in operation. This is borne out by recent human DNA information that mutations occur on a fairly regular basis – about every 10,000 years – which has enabled an additional method of dating prehistoric remains.

In addition to Darwin's "survival of the fittest" concept, when we consider the historical development of humans over longer time periods we find that apart from mere survival, early species have grown in numbers by the "opposition" being wiped out by some global event – especially ice ages. For example, it is accepted by scientists today that 66 million years ago there was one or more asteroid or comet impacts on Earth, perhaps

APPENDIX : HUMAN EVOLUTION

causing, or combined with, volcanic eruptions, that wiped out all the dinosaurs – which were then the dominant species. The important survivors, for us, were the small mammals that lived underground, and from which we eventually evolved.

The early evolution of man is not clear due to fossil evidence being scarce and difficult to date. Specimens were destroyed in the various ice ages. There is not much DNA evidence because it requires soft tissue samples, however small amounts have been recovered from bone marrow. It would seem that there were many mutations into different species that did not survive, making the job even more difficult. Having said that, at the time of writing this, new methods have enabled DNA sampling from bones and confirmed that all human DNA contains the markers from Homo Heidelbergensis.

The dates I have used for the older species are ones where I have found agreement from several sources. There are reports of discoveries of bones of ages outside the "birth to death" of a species. A strange fact reported in several places is that a discovery of stone tools in Pakefield, Britain, has been dated at 700,000 years ago, with no bones to define a species. There is bone evidence in Britain of Homo Heidelbergensis which supposedly originated in Africa 500,000 years ago. This gives rise to a mystery as to where the stone tools came from. The modern Homo Sapiens species of which we are all part has a much more accurate history, with the benefit of the correlation of archaeological and DNA evidence.

ADAM AND EVE

DNA evidence shows that all humans alive today are of species Homo Sapiens and have descended from a single man and woman who lived in Africa. They have been called Adam and Eve although they evolved from the Great Apes via the Homo Sapiens species which originated 200,000 years ago. They migrated from Africa 90,000 years ago to populate the rest of the world. Eve's DNA was 15,000 years older than Adam's.

EVOLUTION PATTERNS

There are some interesting patterns :-

1. Homo Habilis, Homo Erectus, Homo Heidelbergensis, and Homo Sapiens (and probably other species too) all originated in Africa and migrated to the rest of the world from there. (There are suggestions that some may have originated elsewhere and returned to Africa). There is still a tribe of bushmen in Africa that have "old DNA" and live as hunter gatherers. This is probably from Africa being on the Equator and therefore offering greater possibility of ice age survival.
2. In their Exodus from Egypt around 1300 BC the Jews used the same route as the first unsuccessful migration by Homo Sapiens 120,000 years earlier.
3. The first main settling place was the Levant area, the "Fertile Crescent" situated between the Tigris and Euphrates rivers, which later became Mesopotamia. Mesopotamia was first settled around 5400 BC [BAB] and the "First City" to develop – where, for the first time, some of the people did not have to rely on farming their own food. In fact the farmers eventually lived in the city and "commuted" each day. Here was the beginnings of bureaucracy and social classes. Elsewhere in the world new settlements were just beginning.
4. As a new species evolved it eventually replaced the "parent" one. Homo Sapiens is the only humanoid species alive today.
5. The development of Technology in the invention and use of tools and weapons seems to be a deciding factor of who survives – even to the present day.
6. It interesting to note that the more developed countries in terms of civilisation, technology, science, and world power –such as America, Russia, and Europe – were the last ones to be colonised by Homo Sapiens. Africa is no longer a centre of learning. Mesopotamia no longer exists. Modern Iraq is mainly desert now. This is probably due to such factors as its low rainfall making it reliant on irrigation from the Tigris and Euphrates rivers, global warming since the last ice age, and over farming – as well as the presence of oil making all that hard work unnecessary.
7. There are 2 main interconnected drivers for evolution of species (or, at least, survival of the fittest) – climate change and availability of food. It seems that more evolved species are better at feeding themselves, and eventually multiply to the extent of starving out the earlier ones. At the time of writing this we seem to be experiencing ever more extremes of weather disturbances which will require human adaptation. Climate change is not just a modern phenomenon.

APPENDIX : HUMAN EVOLUTION

CORRESPONDENCES WITH GENESIS AND EXODUS

1. There was an actual "Adam and Eve". There are 2 types of DNA in a human cell, one of which comes from the father, and mitochondrial DNA comes from the mother. All humans alive today contain the same 2 basic elements with the addition of later mutations.
2. We can suggest Africa as being "Eden".
3. Mesopotamia is therefore "East of Eden" (actually North East). The first successful migration travelled East across the Red Sea and then North. They could not travel the original route because the Sahara was desert by then.
4. In the mythology of Mesopotamia, Cain was one of the first settlers in the area. He had every reason to fear being killed there because the main occupation of the time seems to have been robbery and violence.

The story is interpreted by historians and biblical scholars as a symbolic account of an ancient nomadic people named Cain; of its distinguishing tattoo mark; and of its reputation for ferocious vengeance against other peoples who slew members of the Cain.[MERL]

EARLY HOMO

Human DNA is 50% the same as a banana, and 99% the same as that of a chimpanzee.

Scientists agree that Homo and chimpanzees have origins in the family of the Great Apes species and the Homo species separated from chimpanzees as different species around 6 million years ago. There seems to be several other intermediate species which are now extinct, until our next main ancestor Homo Habilis.

Human infants begin to move about on all fours in a similar way to chimpanzees.

HOMO HABILIS ("Handy Man")

2.2 to 1.5 million years ago

Homo Habilis originated and remained in Africa, and managed to survive 700,000 years. The main development of this species was the use of the "opposable thumb" and the ability to manipulate objects – such as by making stone tools. There was a corresponding development of the brain to enable this. We can see this early stage repeated in infants of today.

HOMO ERGASTER ("Workman")

1.8 to 1.3 million years ago

A relatively recent discovery. There is some debate as to whether Homo Ergaster is just another name for Homo Habilis. Either way, it is accepted that Homo Habilis is an ancestor of Homo Erectus, so there would be a need for some link in time between the two – which would not otherwise exist.

HOMO ERECTUS ("Upright Man")

1.8 million to 200,000 years ago

Homo Erectus was the first hominid to walk upright, and, it seems, the first to leave Africa. Originating 1.8 million years ago, it seems that he replaced, Homo Habilis & Ergaster in a very short period of time. This was probably made easier by the older species having remained in Africa. H. Erectus reached as far as Java and China, and, it seems, managed to survive beyond his "successor", H. Heidelbergensis, until 200,000 years ago when Homo Sapiens first appeared.

This stage involves further brain development as humans can now move and carry objects. There is also a wider viewpoint from the superior height.

As with "Handy Man" we can see this as another stage in the growth of infants today. Parents learn to move breakable objects to higher levels.

HOMO HEIDELBERGENSIS

500,000 to 150,000 years ago

Named after the university in Germany which found a lower jaw bone in Mauer in 1907. The species had a larger brain than its ancestors. Since then numerous remains have been found in Africa, and throughout Europe as far away as Britain. He would have reached there when sea levels were low and Britain was linked to Europe by a land bridge. This species is believed to have developed from Homo Erectus 500,000 years ago, but, despite its travelling abilities, did not survive as long. It seems no remains have been found older than 150,000 years of age.

Heidelbergensis was a "parent" of 2 sub-species, Homo Neanderthalis and Homo Sapiens. It seems that Homo Sapiens, who appeared 200,000 years ago, disposed of yet another rival.

HOMO NEANDERTHALIS

350,000 to 30,000 years ago

Homo Neanderthalis shares Homo Heidelbergensis as "parent" with Homo Sapiens and is named after some bones which were discovered in the Neanderthal Valley in Germany. Other bone specimens have been discovered in various European areas but none in Africa. This suggests that Homo Erectus (whose bones have been found in Africa, Java, and China) migrated there from Africa before Neanderthalis evolved. Then movement was suspended by an ice age.

Although from the same "root", Homo Neanderthalis was a completely different species to Homo Sapiens, although it is suggested that interbreeding was possible. This is similar to the cross breeding possibilities of lions and tigers, and horses and donkeys. Although some suggest that there was no comparison between the abilities of the two Homo species, archaeological evidence shows that Neanderthalis developed a rudimentary civilisation, the use of stone and wood tools, as well as fire – although perhaps not as efficiently. They used items of personal decoration and had some artistic ability. They had a short lifespan of around 40 years. They were able to keep injured comrades alive. They managed to survive even a mini ice age as a species until Homo Sapiens began to arrive in Europe around 50,000 years ago when they were unable to compete and became extinct 30,000 years ago.

HOMO SAPIENS ("Wise Man")

200,000 years ago to the present day

> *The first migration was the spread of Neanderthals (Homo Neanderthalis). DNA evidence suggests a common ancestor 353,000 years ago and separation as a species from Homo Sapiens 188,000 years ago. [Edward M. Rubin, director of the U.S. Department of Energy's Lawrence Berkeley National Laboratory and the Joint Genome Institute (JGI) November 2006]

DNA research has been combined with archaeological data to show that Homo Sapiens – the human species of which we are all part – originated on the equator in Africa around 200,000 years ago and was kept there by surrounding ice.

FIRST MIGRATION

There was a migration around 135,000 years ago across the then fertile Sahara, to the "fertile triangle" called Levant (now Syria and Jordan) but the early pioneers died out in the subsequent ice age, which also turned the Sahara into desert.

SECOND MIGRATION

There was a later, successful, migration around 90,000 years ago cross the Red Sea the level of which had lowered due to the ice age. DNA sampling shows that everyone alive today originated from a single man and woman, although the DNA of the woman was around 15,000 years older than that of the man.

The migration was forced by lack of food. The ice age and corresponding drought (ice locks up moisture from the atmosphere resulting in less rainfall). Vegetation died off, and, as a result, so did the animals available for food. Early humans were mainly carnivorous, and were first forced to coastal areas where fish and shellfish were available – as well as being able to find fresh water from rivers entering the sea.

We therefore see the beginnings of a more vegetarian diet.

The rest of the world was not fully occupied until 10,000 years ago, which was the end of the last ice age (although, with ice existing in polar regions, we are still technically living in an ice age). At this time human behaviour began to change from the hunter gatherer style of existence to settling down and farming. This was probably because the food supply had diminished due to greater efficiency at hunting. After this time

APPENDIX : HUMAN EVOLUTION

Archaeologists find less bones of animals weighing over 100 pounds. We could say that this was the beginning of animal Conservation.

There was an accurately dated volcano eruption of Mount Toba 74,000 years ago that wiped out the population of India.

From what we see above, Homo Sapiens effectively replaced Homo Erectus, Homo Heidelbergensis and Homo Neanderthalis within a relatively short space of time after his appearance. The suggestion is that he was a much more efficient hunter than they, and multiplied to the extent that they were no longer able to compete. Homo Sapiens had finally colonised most of the world by the end of the last ice age around 10,000 years ago when he began to change his way of life from hunter gatherer and settle down to farming. This was probably due to his success at survival and ability to multiply, with larger families. The way of the hunter gatherer only suits relatively small groups of people. As with all animals, there is a fine balance between the energy obtained from food and the energy needed to obtain it.

We can see that 10,000 years ago was the beginning of family life as we know it today.

EVOLUTION DIAGRAMS BELOW (full pages)

TABLE : HUMAN EVOLUTION FROM SINGLE CELLS

The first 2 tables show a summary of the development of man as a direct line from Prokaryotes (cells without a nucleus) to the Homo species. Much of the other detail is omitted. They are based on Cladistic Genealogy which is concerned with relationships between species having similar characteristics – such as having a skull and backbone. Nowadays DNA profiles are included too. There is also attention paid to more traditional methods such as carbon dating. The development of a human foetus follows the same growth sequence – such as by developing gills, a tail, and body hair, which are lost before birth.

MAP : MIGRATIONS OF HOMO SAPIENS FROM AFRICA

Based on information from Dr. Spencer Wells [DNA] and that on the Bradshaw Foundation web site http://www.bradshawfoundation.com/journey/ [BF].

The picture shows a summary of the migration of Homo Sapiens from the first beginnings in Africa. There was an unsuccessful one around 110,000 years ago - the migrants did not survive the following ice age. The first successful one was around 90,000 years ago. Europe, Britain and the Americas were colonised last as global warming continued.

The numbers on the map and timescale refer to those on the table below.

There are 4 main ice ages shown which resulted in depopulation, although there were other "mini" ones.

APPENDIX : HUMAN EVOLUTION

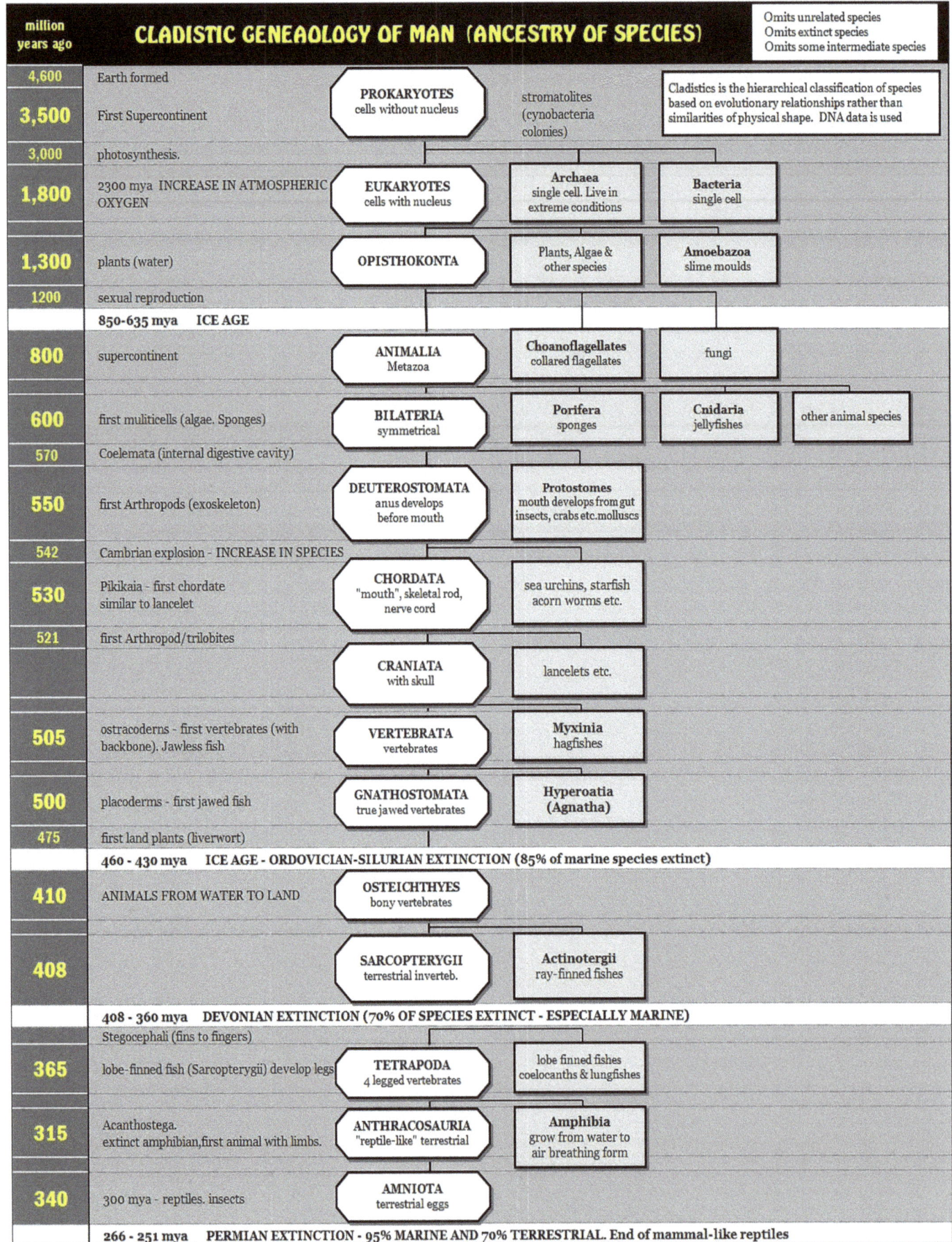

Figure 96 : Table - Human Evolution Part 1

APPENDIX : HUMAN EVOLUTION

(continued from the previous page)

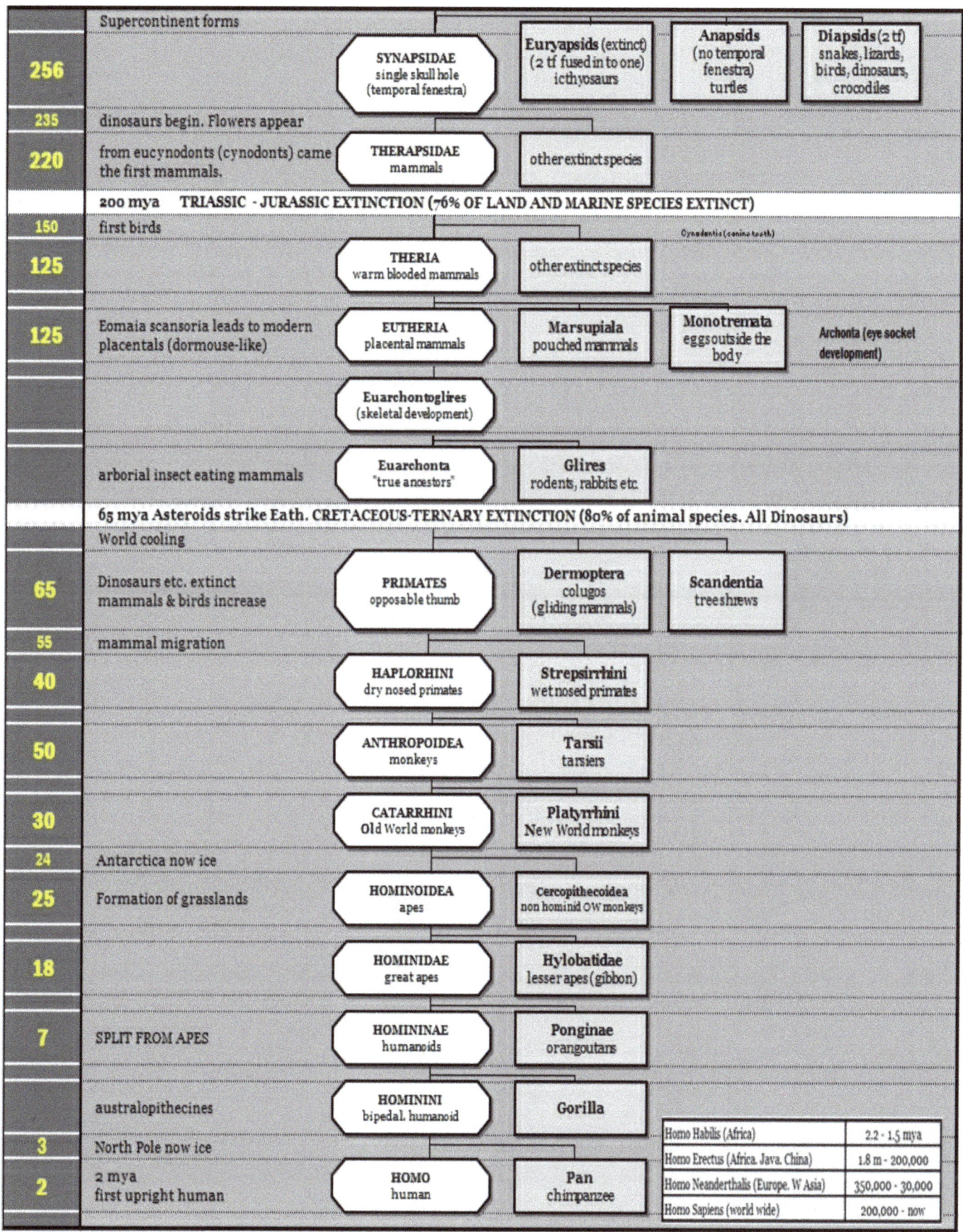

Figure 97 : Table - Human Evolution Part 2

APPENDIX : HUMAN EVOLUTION

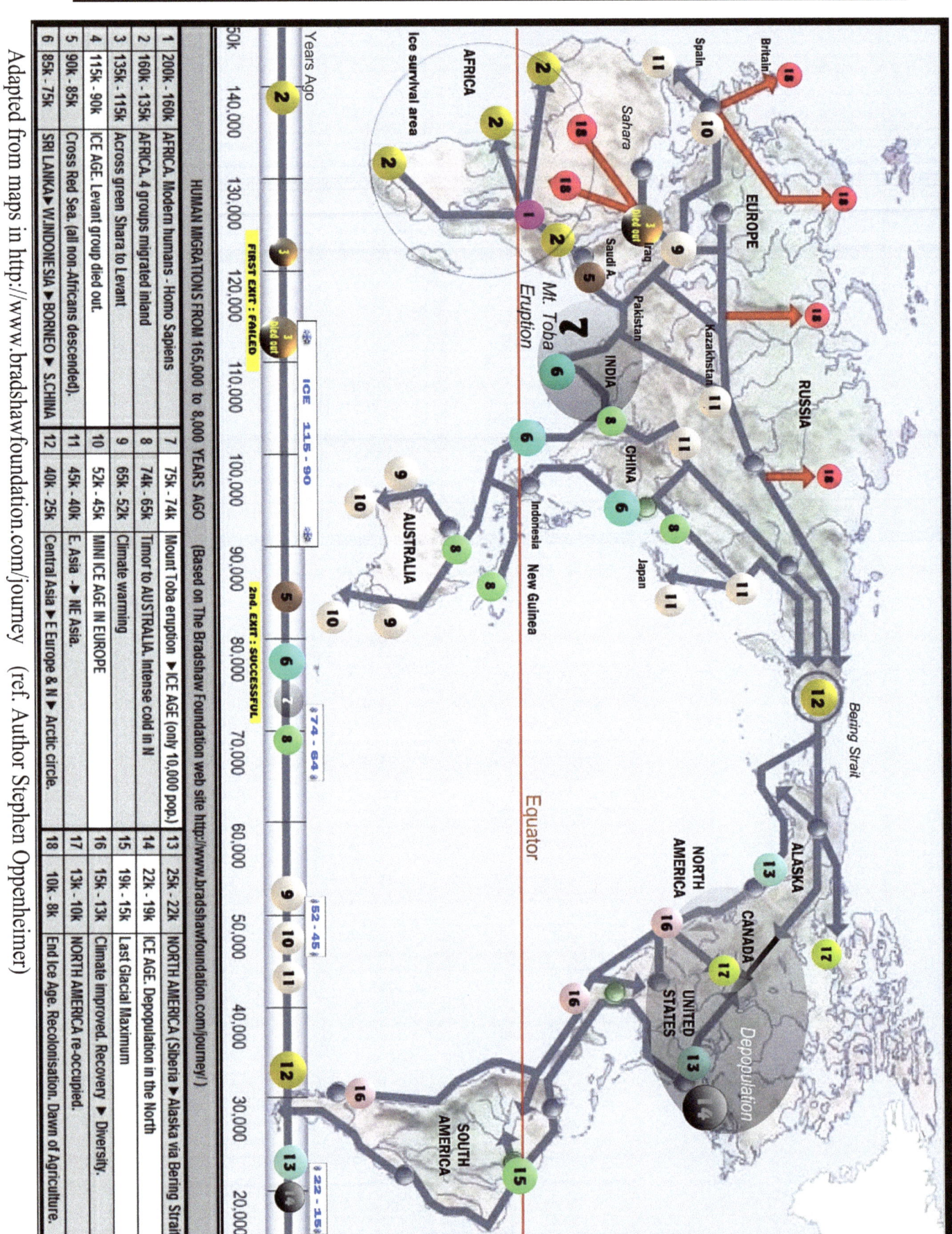

Figure 98 : Map - Homo Sapiens Migration out of Africa

APPENDIX 3. CRITICAL MASS

As students of The Cycle of Growth, we can apply the concept of Critical Mass to the activity of [THE KABBALAH TREE OF LIFE] which begins with a "Big Bang". In particular it describes the activity of Pluto which itself is described as a building of energy "underground" over a long period of time until it cannot be contained any longer. Another related image is that of a volcano eruption releasing underground pressure.

Here is an example of situations which physicists and psychologists tend to describe in similar terms. In both cases there is requirement for a Critical Mass and a trigger to set off a chain reaction which results in uncontrolled release of energy, with destruction of people and property. It seems that by comparing them we can get another insight into the working of the Collective Unconscious.

I remember reading somewhere that the activity of the brain is not like a smooth flow of electricity. Neurons have to reach a certain level of charge before they "fire off" and transmit the energy.

CHAIN REACTION IN PHYSICS

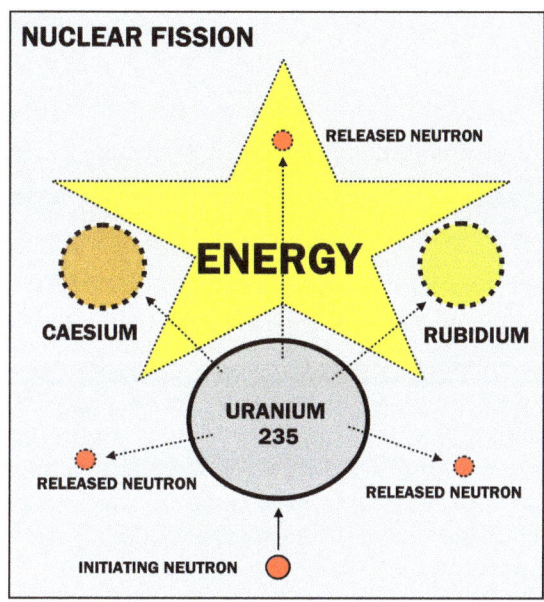

Figure 99 : Nuclear Fission – chain reaction

An atom of Uranium struck by a neutron splits into an atom of Caesium, an atom of Rubidium, and 3 neutrons which can cause further splitting of Uranium atoms. A large amount of energy is released by the process.

Chain Reactions are defined as a self-sustaining chemical or other reactions. They usually require a "trigger" to start the reaction and continue until the materials involved have been used up. We can consider lighting a match as a simple example. The initial ignition produces enough heat to enable combination of the carbon in the wood with atmospheric oxygen. The reaction itself is "exothermic" in that it produces enough heat to continue the process. A main feature of a Chain Reaction is that its effect is far greater than one would suppose from the relatively small amount of energy supplied by the initial trigger because further energy is released by the reaction.

At a basic level, the nucleus of a molecule of any substance consists of positively charged Positrons, negatively charged Electrons and neutral Neutrons. In nuclear fission a chain reaction is started by the accelerating or "exciting" a neutron which escapes from the nucleus of an atom to collide with another atom. The nucleus of that atom splits into two fragments of roughly equal mass – which are of different elemental construction to the original. In addition, more neutrons are accelerated to collide with more atoms. In the case of Uranium, a single neutron collision releases 3 more neutrons, which, in turn, release 9 neutrons – and so on – so the reaction continues at an ever increasing rate.

The term is more usually applied to nuclear reactions when certain elements which are relatively unstable - such as Uranium 235 – readily break down to form more stable elements. The trigger usually consists of a charge of a conventional explosive. 1 pound of Uranium yields as much energy as 3 million pounds of coal [EB].

APPENDIX : CRITICAL MASS

The planet Uranus was discovered in 1781 and Uranium named after it in 1789. Neptune was discovered in 1846, and Neptunium in 1940. Pluto was discovered in 1930 and Plutonium in 1941 To astrologers this naming process suggests synchronistic connections between the planets and their elements. That is, the names chosen are not merely accidents. It also suggests similarity of activity. Neptunium and Plutonium are only found in minute quantities in nature usually with Uranium – they are principally man-made in nuclear reactors.

CRITICAL MASS

The first requirement for a chain reaction is Critical Mass. A sample of Uranium the size of a golf ball will not produce a chain reaction because too many neutrons escape into the atmosphere. A tennis ball size and upwards has the Critical Mass required to contain enough neutrons to enable the reaction to continue. Luckily such accumulations do not occur naturally. It typically takes 1,000 kilograms (1 ton) of Uranium ore to produce 1 kilogram of Uranium.

CHAIN REACTION IN HUMAN AFFAIRS AND PSYCHOLOGY

The concept of Critical Mass is also applied to human social affairs. In this case there is usually a gradual build-up of "mass" – or "bottled up energy"- from repetitions of a trigger effect until the stage of "the last straw" is reached. Examples are :-

- The size or amount of something that is required before an activity or event can take place.
- The number of customers a business requires before it becomes profitable and able to expand.
- The number of complaints or suggestions received by a company or government before it takes action.
- The shift in the balance of public opinion required to elect a new government.
- The amount of frustration one feels about a particular situation from real or imagined inability to act.

A main factor concerning Critical Mass is that if nothing is happening externally it does not mean that nothing is happening internally. Examples of Chain Reactions are :-

- It frequently comes to my mind that I need to do some house cleaning or other chore. I have learned to observe the idea and do nothing because when I "suddenly" make up my mind to do something I find that the energy and "plan" is there so that I do the job in much less time than it would take by doing it piecemeal. "Making up one's mind" seems to be a build up towards Critical Mass. In the above case, the "trigger" is often the prospect of the arrival of a visitor – which, from my observations of the efficiency of the process, I am usually quite happy to await.
- The spread of a virus infection.
- The spread of economic depression. We note that share prices are more a factor of human perception rather than real value. Evidence of this was the boom and bust of internet web sites a few years ago.
- From coming into contact with many sick people, and my own personal experience mentioned in [MY STORY], it is clear that many illnesses are the result of inner Critical Mass reaching the stage which triggers action. Unfortunately the action is taken usually to relieve the symptoms rather than discover the root cause. It is clear that such things as stomach ulcers fit this category, and I believe Cancer to be of this type as well.
- We notice the "crowd effect" in such areas as football matches and political rallies where some form of violence is started in a small area which spreads to include large numbers of people. People start fighting among themselves, and this often spreads to include destruction of property and looting of shops. Fire becomes a component. It is reported that often normally peaceful people find themselves doing things they afterwards regret. We note that when such gatherings take place there is a common, shared, motivation. We note that most sports have roots in the Roman gladiators' arena, which had its heroes as today. There is suggestion that the emperors used it to control the population by diverting their attention from other issues. Even today it is suggested that games enable the safe expression of our more destructive instincts. Fire Energy tends to be pure energy that will be expressed along the line of least resistance. Perhaps the Arena used up energy that might otherwise be used to stir up political unrest. I remember seeing some television news a few years ago about some Japanese companies having a special room with a stuffed effigy of the boss so that workers could punch it.
- It follows that police would be more successful in preventing riots if they did not allow gatherings of people to reach the numbers of people required to reach Critical Mass.

APPENDIX 4. EDGAR CAYCE (1877 – 1945)

Edgar Cayce was born in Hopkinsville, Kentucky (United States) on March 18th. 1877 at 3.20pm. (Pisces Sun. Taurus Moon) and his psychic abilities appeared as a young child. He was deeply religious and a dedicated churchgoer and Sunday school teacher. He read a portion of the Bible every day, and by the end of his life, had read it once through for each year of his life. He was a simple man with only an eighth grade education – showing no evidence of advanced knowledge whilst in a waking state.

Although showing psychic abilities whilst young, it was not until later in life he found the ability to put himself into a trancelike state and answer questions put to him. The trance sessions were called "readings". In this state he was able to see events in the past, present, and future, and make psychic contact with people anywhere in the world. He often accurately described the subject's activity at the time of the reading, even though they might be in different countries. Although the questions covered a wide variety of subjects, many were concerned with health problems, and he astonished doctors with the depth of his medical knowledge. Despite never meeting the people concerned – much of the correspondence was by letter - he was able to accurately describe their symptoms. The treatments he prescribed were usually of holistic type and included numerous methods such as recipes for medicines, osteopathy, and special baths, and were usually effective, even when normal methods had failed. The questions came from people of all kinds and nationalities from all over the world.

All his readings were recorded in shorthand and later transcribed. By the end of his life he had made 14,306 readings which exist today at the "Association for Research and Enlightenment" (A.R.E.), a non-profit organisation founded by Cayce in 1931.When he woke from his trance, he had no memory of what had occurred during the reading. The readings are available on DVD.

REINCARNATION AND KARMA

Apart from a huge amount of empirical evidence that was found to be wholly accurate, some of his readings included information concerning philosophy, dream interpretation, psychic phenomena and spiritual growth.

In addition he began to include information concerning reincarnation, past lives, and karma of individuals as they referred to their present state. When he awoke he was deeply troubled by this as a result of his deeply religious sense and Christian upbringing. He was questioned further on the subject in later readings when the basic principle of "The Spirit is Life. The Mind is the Builder. The Physical is the result." was stated. This principle was repeated on numerous occasions later on. It basically means that our minds contain patterns of thought ("karmic patterns") that translate the basic life energy into physical form, rather like painting a picture of what is in the mind. The final form can appear in such things as positive or negative life experiences and symptoms of physical illness. The mind patterns are contained in our personal unconscious.

As can be imagined, there is a huge amount of information available on his work, the best source being http://www.edgarcayce.org/.

GENERAL MEDIUMSHIP

In the early days of psychic phenomena it was common for a medium to enter a trance state and have no knowledge of events. As time went on mediumship became more common, and nowadays it is more usual for the medium to be in a state of normal consciousness. Likewise there is very little, if no, physical mediumship such as production of sound (external voices) and ectoplasm, which held dangers for the health of the medium. It seems that such methods were necessary early on until the more "mental" forms of mediumship developed.

APPENDIX 5. MEDITATION

This is a brief introduction to the act of Meditation. It is a big subject, and there are many variations. Here we are mainly concerned with achieving a relaxed state and relief of stress and to relate Meditation to The Cycle of Growth I use The 4 Elements to indicate 4 Stages. There is some further information at the end for those who wish to explore further.

It is essential to realise that we each need to discover out own method by experimentation and practice. However, the 4 stages are common to all methods. We deal with them in order of material (Earth) to Spiritual (Fire) – that is, in order of familiarity. From Known to Unknown. From low frequency to high frequency vibration.

Although the process may require a long explanation here, with practice it takes seconds to reach a relaxed state.

AS AN OVERALL ATTITUDE TO MEDITATION IT IS GOOD PRACTICE TO RECOGNISE THAT WE JUST DO NOT REALLY KNOW WHAT WE ARE DOING AND SEE WHAT HAPPENS. IN OTHER WORDS, BE OPEN TO GUIDANCE. MEDITATION IS DOING NOTHING.

THE AIMS OF MEDITATION

1. To begin with, meditation is a powerful tool for handling our normal, everyday life. By keeping our outer and inner selves in harmony we maintain balance, and a good state of physical and mental health. If we cannot do this basic task, there is no chance of achieving "higher things". We need to become "Captain of our ship".
2. Meditation is not another form of escapism. A benefit of following the process is that the personal requirements for achieving each step become a part of external life.
3. The main aim is to achieve a state of inner Stillness and Silence to be able to listen to "the Inner Voice".
4. There is a part of each one of us that can be termed "Detached Observer". This is a meditative state.
5. There should be a minimum of 10 minutes spent on the exercise, with no upper limit.
6. There should be no sense of struggle. There is no point in making Meditation another source of stress. Sometimes we cannot achieve a state of rest, when it is best to try again later on.
7. As time goes on, the subconscious becomes "programmed" towards relaxation and the process becomes easier.
8. Although meditation can end in one going to sleep, this is not recommended unless you use the process to sleep at night. It could form a bad habit. Use your own discretion. Experiment. Sometimes stillness can be a time of intense inner activity.
9. By meditating daily the inner self is less likely to interrupt our daily routines or keep us awake at night.
10. We cannot reach higher levels of consciousness unless we can deal with the lower ones.

"LETTING GO"

There is a requirement to Let Go at the end of each stage.

To understand the principle of Letting Go, take an unbreakable object in your hand such as an apple or pillow and squeeze it as hard as you can. Then open your hand and let it drop to the floor. Leave it there, forget it, go on to the next stage. You have done your best.

You can take the process a step at a time, but it is better to attempt all the steps in a session. Problems at any stage can be corrected next time. Transferring attention often makes the seeming problem go away – especially after some practice.

1. Letting Go is making a decision and carrying it out.
2. If you cannot Let Go, and something from the Inner Self keeps interrupting then this is an indication that there is a problem to solve. You are "Captain of your ship", but "the crew" need to have their say. If you disagree, then tell them why. They have to learn to trust you.

STAGE 1 : EARTH. SENSATION

The first requirement is physical relaxation and the recognition that you will not want to move for at least 10 minutes. This will vary from person to person.

APPENDIX : MEDITATION

There is the recognition that we have no control over many external circumstances. This leads to the realisation that the real source of discomfort is our own unnecessary reaction to them.

1. Although it is good to have a regular time and place to meditate, this may not be achievable in practice – especially at the beginning. A good time might be on the train to work (but not while driving a car).
2. There may be a need to negotiate with people around to ensure that you are not disturbed. This is an example of how the act of meditation can begin to affect your outer life.
3. We can meditate lying down, sitting, or standing – so long as we do not go to sleep. The main requirement is a straight spine. In Britain, from childhood, we generally learn to sit on a chair. In the East they can sit on the floor for long periods – probably from lack of chairs. There is no need to learn Yoga unless you really want to.
4. At this stage we stop giving attention to the input of our 5 physical senses. First close your eyes. What often happens then is that we become more aware of sounds around us. We can hear the neighbours. People outside seem to be shouting and slamming doors all of a sudden. This brings us to an important decision point. We can either do something about the situation now or not. In my case, at the beginning, I was disturbed by the ticking of a wall clock, so I stopped it while I was meditating. Later on it was not an issue. In fact it led me to being able to sleep with a (rare) party going on next door, with loud music. So we learn something else about our external life.
5. Sometimes playing soothing music can help to cover external sounds.

Decide that, this time, the body is comfortable and will be able to sit still for 10 minutes – and Let Go. There is no need to give any further attention.

STAGE 2 : WATER. EMOTIONS AND FEELINGS

Having given the body and physical senses due attention, we are free to give full attention to our feelings and emotions. It may be helpful to "personify" feelings with an image, such as that of a child.

Failure to pay attention to our feelings, or keeping them "bottled up", in life can lead to their becoming "deliberately" obstructive, such as by erupting at inappropriate times, or withdrawing their energy – which becomes a sense of continual tiredness or boredom. This is a way of giving them proper attention.

1. Be sure that you recognise that feelings and emotions are an important, valued, part of our inner life – and tell them so.
2. Do you feel angry, bored, happy or sad? Is there some reason for this ? Can you do anything about it ?
3. If you decide that you cannot change the situation explain to yourself why.
4. If you decide to make changes, make sure you do - or explain to yourself the reason why you were unable to do so. This way your "crew" will learn to trust you, and give less problems in future.
5. Again, at the beginning, soothing music can help to relax emotions – but should not be used to blot them out. Silence is better.

Decide that you are calm enough to continue and will deal with any "outstanding issues" later on - and Let Go.

STAGE 3 : AIR. THINKING

The next step requires paying attention to one's breathing. There should be no effort to control the breath. The autonomic nervous system is "aware" of one's activity state, and will adjust accordingly.

This is still my most difficult area, with, for example sometimes finding it difficult to sleep at night with thoughts "going round" in the mind – and starting again at the beginning – especially while writing this book. Using the principles of meditation – Recognition and Action – I find that writing things down usually solves the problem. The ideas are then "fixed" in the material world and available to be dealt with at a more appropriate time.

However, with this everyday experience, there is a recognition that we reach this meditation stage every night before we sleep.

1. We have to recognise that Thinking is a valuable part of our Inner Self. Rather than attempting to blot out thoughts, now might be an opportunity to solve problems that have been troubling us, consciously or unconsciously. Our inner Thinking self may have new insight, or a different order of priorities.
2. It may help to have paper and pencil handy to make notes – usually after meditating, but sometimes they insist .....

APPENDIX : MEDITATION

3. We have to recognise that there is a need to "negotiate" with our "crew" rather than attempt to blot out thoughts.
4. We have to recognise that this is a difficult area of meditation for everyone.

In meditation it is normally enough to acknowledge the thought (make a mental note if necessary) and turn attention back to one's breathing. This now becomes a continual process.

It may help to join in group meditation because it helps to build the discipline.

Reaching this stage of meditation will be enough to achieve a relaxed state.

For those who wish to explore further :-

VISUALISATION. ACTIVE IMAGINATION

There is a variation, or addition to, meditation that uses imagination at the beginning to help relaxation. That is, we begin by closing our eyes and building a scene in our imagination. The best ones are based on past memories of places where we were happy and relaxed. I get the idea that, in the absence of other sensory input, the subconscious believes the scene is real.

A variant is in a meditation group where a leader describes a scene.

This can be developed further by building the scene and waiting for it to change of its own accord – rather like a movie. This is a way of getting information from the Unconscious.

C.G. Jung used this method in his work, calling it "Active Imagination". It is very similar to being in a dream state.

STAGE 4 : INTUITION. INSTINCT. CONTEMPLATION.

There is more related information in [THE 4 ELEMENTS] and [PSYCHOLOGY : THE 4 FUNCTIONS] – some of which is duplicated here.

An attempt to describe the Indescribable.

We now come to the highest vibration level. There is difficulty of description here which even authorities struggle with. However, this difficulty gives us a clue to understanding. It is because we are attempting to describe something at high level with low level mental tools. We are dealing with something on a totally different dimension to the normal 3 dimensions we are familiar with. I am attempting to describe something beyond words using words – which are tools of the low level Thinking Function. The task, however, is not impossible because we have Boolean logic of mathematics to help us be more precise. So we can say that :-

INTUITION = NOT Sensation
AND NOT Feeling
AND NOT Thinking

We can see that this is also a definition of Meditation itself. We can also go a step further by comparing Meditation with Prayer :-

PRAYER IS TALKING
MEDITATION IS LISTENING

APPENDIX : MEDITATION

THE IN-TUITION DIMENSION and CYCLE OF GROWTH

The Cycle of Growth also gives us added insight to the Intuition Dimension (and the Dimensions of the other Elements). We can see that each of the 3 Fire Signs of Astrology, Aries, Leo, and Sagittarius, relate to different "forms" of Intuition. At its base level it is Instinct. The fact that it enabled the survival of plants, animals, and humans for millions of years before the development of the Thinking Function with its (Air) Communication abilities shows that it has a high level of intelligence.

We can see that, as The Sun is the sole source of energy in our Solar System, so the Fire Element is basic to each of the other 3 Elements which express the energy according to their specific natures – as do the Planets.

WE CANNOT SEE THE (ARCHETYPAL ENERGY OF THE) 4 ELEMENTS DIRECTLY, BUT WE CAN OBSERVE THEIR EFFECT ON MATERIAL OBJECTS.

CYCLE OF GROWTH STAGE 1 (Seed) and Meditation

The Sign of Aries (Cardinal Fire) allied with Mars, God of War, gives us an example of the Fire Element in its purest "form" with the image of the rutting Ram. This is not itself a mating ritual, it is proving who is the strongest and fittest. It is pure Instinct without "contamination " by Feeling or Thinking.

At Cycle of Growth Stage 1 we have the added image of a new born child aged Zero to 7 months. Once again, we have a physical body driven by pure Instinct. It is not until later on in development that the infant begins to change from "animal" to human and consciously experience Feeling. Still later, it learns to use the Thinking Function, and communicate in words – continuing to relive the stages of human evolution which began in the womb.

In Matthew Chapter 18 Verses 1 to 3 we have :-

*At that hour came the disciples near to Jesus, saying, `Who, now, is greater in the reign of the heavens?'

*And Jesus having called near a child, did set him in the midst of them, and said, `Verily I say to you, if ye may not be turned and become as the children, ye may not enter into the reign of the heavens; [YLT]

In the recently discovered "Book of Thomas" Chapter 4 we get :-

*Jesus said: The man aged in his days will not hesitate to ask a little child of seven days about the place of life, and he shall live. For there are many first who shall be last, and they shall become a single one. ["The Book of Thomas"]

I wonder if this has anything to do with "Second Childhood".

NUMEROLOGY AND TAROT CORRESPONDENCES

We have the added images of Number Zero of Numerology, before the Big Bang – the source of everything and the Tarot 0. The Fool.

PARADOX

We are now in the realm of Paradox [THE 4 FUNCTIONS].

THE BIGGEST PARADOX IS THE NECESSITY TO MEDITATE IN ORDER TO LEARN HOW TO MEDITATE.

The whole point is that, although they can get us started, external teachers are of no use.

APPENDIX : NITROGEN CYCLE

APPENDIX 6. THE NITROGEN CYCLE

Evolution begins with The Big Bang as atmospheric gases are converted to heavier elements beginning a new Cycle of Growth. There are also links with The Carbon Cycle and The Oxygen Cycle which affect Photosynthesis.

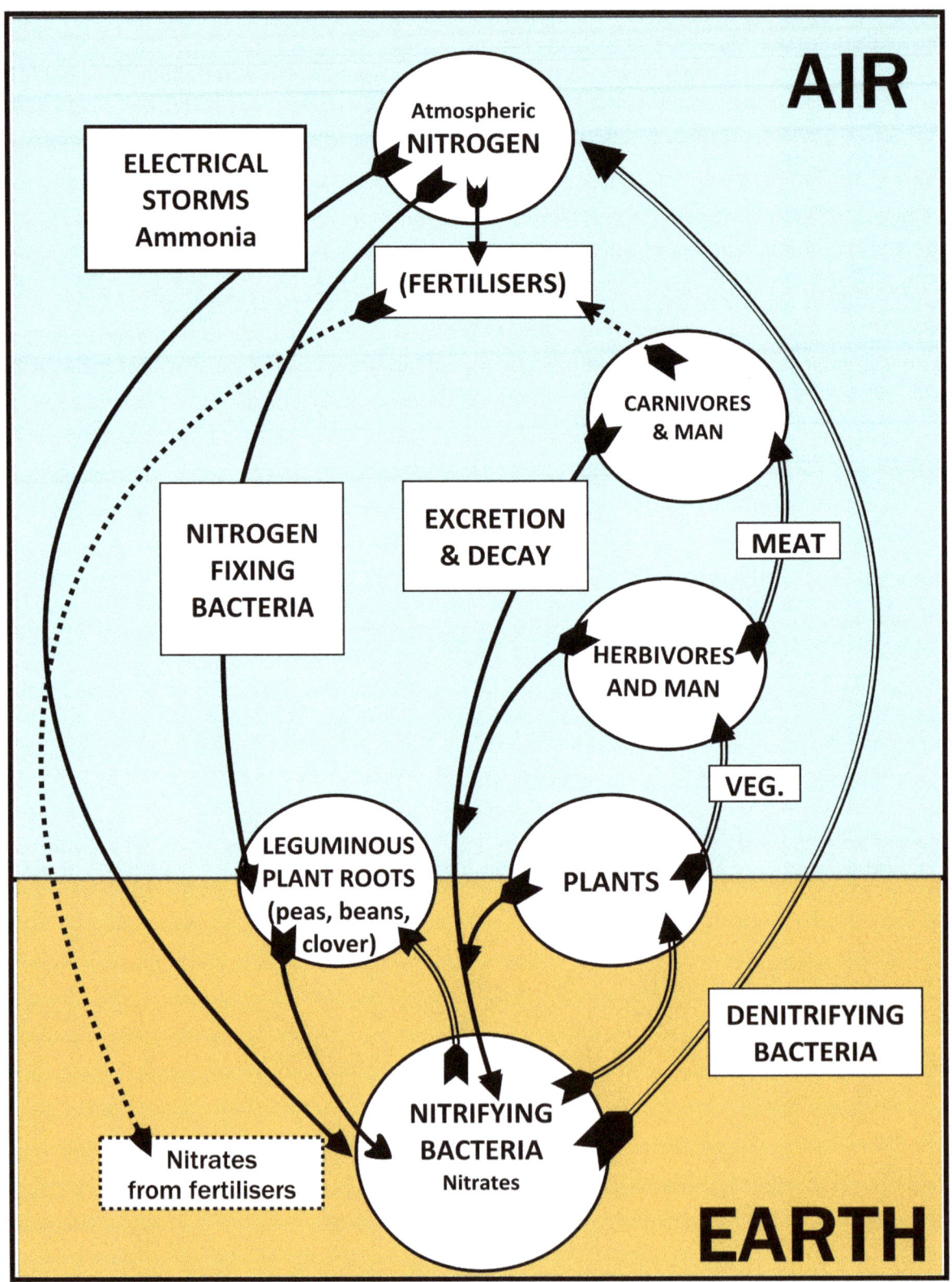

Figure 100 : The Nitrogen Cycle

APPENDIX : NITROGEN CYCLE

NITROGEN AND EVOLUTION OF MAN

*"Big fleas have little fleas, Upon their backs to bite 'em,
And little fleas have lesser fleas, and so, ad infinitum.[anon]*

In this case, it seems that man is the "lesser flea".

Here, we can observe an example of a feature, or pattern, of Evolution where Nature creates ever more complex structures from simple elements. It is also a "food chain".

If we observe the Nitrogen Cycle diagram we can see that it has a similar structure to that of The Cycle of Growth. It has a process of Involution from "heaven" – Cycle of Growth Stage 9 (Conception) followed by physical "incarnation" (Cycle of Growth Stage 1 (Seed) to Cycle of Growth Stage 8 (Sex. Death)), with a "transcendent return to heaven" to begin a new cycle.

The diagram shows the Nitrogen Cycle today. It also shows the evolutionary stages of man's development beginning with atmospheric gases being converted into chemicals which feed bacteria, which, in turn, give life to plants, animals, and man. We can see "wheels within wheels" – each with its own cycle of birth, death, decay, and rebirth - each using the same basic mechanism of The Cycle of Growth.

The Nitrogen Cycle is an example of several natural cycles upon which the lives of living things depend. Other examples are the Carbon Cycle and Oxygen Cycle. In each case an element, or one of its compounds, is converted to use by living organisms and eventually returned to its natural state to be re-used again and again. Plants are an important link in the process chain. In this case atmospheric Nitrogen, a particularly non-reactive gas, is converted to nitrates in the soil to be used in the growth of plants, which, in turn, are eaten by humans and other animals. Nitrogen is returned to the soil in their excretions, as well as the products of the decay of their bodies and unconsumed plants - some of which is eventually returned to the atmosphere.

Nitrogen is an important part of Amino Acids that are used to make the various, more complex, proteins our bodies need.

An important consideration is the part played by bacteria, without which there would be no cycle – and no living things on Earth. In the pattern of the Nitrogen Cycle, starting with Nitrogen gas converted to Ammonia, and bacteria, we can see a mirror pattern of the evolution of life on Earth – which is still being driven by bacteria - as it was at the very beginning.

Finally, we have man's involvement in the Cycle with the manufacture of nitrate fertilisers – using a very similar process to the natural one, via Ammonia.

EVOLUTION OF THE NITROGEN CYCLE

1. This is one of numerous natural processes that took millions of years to develop, but which now cycles in a comparatively short time period.

2. After The Big Bang there was only Hydrogen gas, Atomic Number 1, which is still the most common element in the universe. Since then it has been evolving into all the chemical elements known today - via Helium Atomic Number 2 – and so on. This still takes part in the various stars of the universe which are nuclear reactors similar to our Sun, and which show the main state of the universe just after The Big Bang. Although stars are born and die they still carrying out the basic processes they did at the beginning. Nitrogen has Atomic Number 7, so it would have appeared soon after. It is a particularly non-reactive element which nowadays forms about 78% of Earth's atmosphere. Being non-reactive, its presence ensures that our eco-system is kept under control. Another main constituent of our atmosphere is highly active Oxygen at 21% - too much of this would make things more explosive.

3. If we jump a few million years, the physical mass of Earth split away from the Sun and gradually cooled. Its atmosphere consisted mainly of gases produced from volcanic eruptions – Water Vapour, Hydrogen, Hydrogen Chlorides, Carbon Monoxide, Carbon Dioxide, and Nitrogen. It was a very inhospitable place, and there were no living organisms. An important missing element was free Oxygen gas. If any was produced it would probably have been used to burn something to be "locked up" in Carbon Dioxide, or other Oxygen compounds (oxides). So, among other things, there was no Nitrogen Cycle yet because Oxygen is required. There was no water until the Earth cooled enough for the vapour in the atmosphere to condense and form the oceans. At the same time the water dissolved most of the other gases from

APPENDIX : NITROGEN CYCLE

the atmosphere to leave the unreactive Nitrogen behind. The "rains" continued for thousands of years and the sea became like a "soup" of all kinds of dissolved chemical elements. The "soup" was added to by undersea volcanic eruptions, some of which still occur today, although with nothing like the same frequency, as well as washings from the land masses. It was the presence of such high concentrations of chemicals in water at high temperature that enabled the formation of Amino Acids from Carbon, Hydrogen, Oxygen and Nitrogen - which were the beginning of organic life. As time went on, more complex compounds were formed by combination of other, simpler compounds – such as the combination of Amino Acids to form complex proteins.

4. Another form of "Nitrogen Fixation" – conversion into a stable chemical compound - would have been from electrical discharges from the continuous storms combining Nitrogen and Hydrogen into Ammonia Gas (NH_4). This would dissolve in rainwater to form Ammonium Hydroxide (as used for household ammonia). ($NH_4 + H_2O = NH_4OH$) which would be converted to Nitrates in the soil by bacteria. With the absence of volcanic eruptions, this is the main natural method today.

5. Around 4 billion years ago the first life form appeared on Earth in the state of single celled micro-organisms without a nucleus called Prokaryotes, which were later to evolve into single cell organisms with a nucleus. They were basically a hollow semi-permeable membrane, or "skin", through which chemicals can pass. The suggestion is that they developed from water being attracted to the surface of extremely fine clay particles. Water encloses each particle, attracted by surface tension, and organic chemicals can dissolve in the water.

6. Around 3 billion years ago blue-green algae (Cyanobacteria) evolved, which is thought to be the beginning of photosynthesis – but without green chlorophyll. Like plants today the algae "fed" on Carbon Dioxide and excreted Oxygen as waste. This is the basis of the Carbon and Oxygen Cycles. The first result of the increased Oxygen in the atmosphere was that it merely accumulated because there were no organisms to use it up – and, secondly, many organisms died because they were poisoned by it. Most of those organisms would have been Anaerobic Bacteria, some of which exist today in low Oxygen conditions such as stagnant ponds and decay of organic wastes, manure, and gangrene. If something smells bad, they are probably the cause. Their excretory product is mainly Methane (CH_4) consisting of Carbon and Hydrogen, which is odourless. The smelly stuff comes from other chemicals such as Ammonia and Sulphur ("bad egg gas"). Today, Anaerobic Bacteria are used to convert animal wastes to Methane gas for fuel. Yeasts, such as used for brewing, are related too – their waste product being alcohol and Carbon Dioxide.

7. The high atmospheric Oxygen concentration was the main "driver" of the development of evolution from plants to animals, once mutations occurred to enable organisms to use it. The suggestion is that it could have reached 35% of the atmosphere. This is an early example of how organisms developed to exploit new sources of "food". Today, Nature maintains the Oxygen concentration at 20%. If it dropped below 15% we would die. Above 25% even wet materials burn. Fires, such as forest fires, are a way of regulating Oxygen (produced by plants) in the atmosphere.

8. 2 billion years ago Prokaryotes evolved into Eukaryotes - single cell organisms with an nucleus. A feature here is the ability for an organism to make its own food from chemical compounds rather than just absorb what is, literally, around. The Prokaryotes were now dwindling because they had reproduced to a stage where, like some past human and animal civilisations, they had used up their food supply.

9. We have now established the bacteriological basis of the Nitrogen Cycle.

10. The next related stage was the development of green plants that use photosynthesis to convert Carbon Dioxide and Water into glucose using light energy – with Oxygen as a waste product. The importance here is that plants can also convert Nitrates in the soil to Amino Acids.

11. The next stage is the development of Herbivores - animals to eat the plants. Animals are able to convert Amino Acids into a wide variety of Proteins. Man is included in this group.

12. The next stage of development is Carnivores - animals that can get Amino Acids from animals that eat plants. We can also include man in this group. Especially for humans, the point here is that we get a higher concentration of Amino Acids and energy from meat than from plants.

APPENDIX : NITROGEN CYCLE

NITROGEN FIXING BACTERIA

There is another type of bacteria that lives in the roots of Leguminous Plants such as peas, beans, and clover, that can convert atmospheric Nitrogen into Nitrites in the soil. Farmers use this facility in "crop rotation". By growing Leguminous Plants one year they have a supply of Nitrites in the soil for a different crop the following year.

COMMERCIAL FERTILISERS

In the past the only fertilisers consisted of human and animal waste products spread on to the soil. Among other things they contain Ammonia compounds, mainly in urine – which accounts for the often sharp pungent smell. This method is still used today, but more intense farming methods and the ability to manufacture Ammonia to make Nitrates has forced more use of this method.

We also nowadays have the commercial production of Nitrate fertilisers. As an indicator of the energy locked in the Nitrates (the NO_3 group is mainly Oxygen, which enables fast burning) **the same compounds can be used in explosives.**

More traditional fertilisers are Sodium Nitrate, and Potassium Nitrate (Saltpeter) which is present in natural form and is a constituent of gunpowder. The natural forms require processing to remove impurities. Ammonium Nitrate, the most common fertiliser, is produced by combining Ammonia Gas with concentrated Nitric Acid, and is also used in explosives.

THE RETURN PROCESS

Having "fixed" Nitrogen into the form of man, other animals, and plants, the element is later returned to general use. The basis of this is the death of the organism and its decay - when it is broken down by bacteria into its constituent compounds. This, once again, requires the activity of Bacteria.

MORE BACTERIA

Converting waste products back into usable Nitrates we have :-

1. Putrefactive Bacteria converts the structure of the organism into Ammonia.
2. Nitrite Bacteria change the Ammonia into Nitrites.
3. Nitrate Bacteria turn the Nitrites into Nitrates

The plants can use the Nitrates to begin the growth process again.

DENITRIFYING BACTERIA

This type of bacteria is somewhat in opposition to the growth process because they convert Ammonia, Nitrites, and Nitrates into their constituent elements and release unusable Nitrogen back into the atmosphere.

It could be that this bacteria, together with Nitrogen Fixing Bacteria, formed the first Nitrogen Cycle mechanism.

APPENDIX 7. THE MIDDLE PATH

(The Path of The Priestess)

The Path of The Priestess is between Daath and Kether on The Tree of Life. It goes beyond normal consciousness.

We compare the Kabbalah Pillars with :-
1. *The physical Bible Temple of Solomon*
2. *Kundalini Yoga*
3. *The Kabbalah Tree of Life*
4. *Freemasonry*
5. *The Human Brain*

There is a comparison table of the names used at the end of the chapter.

Again, by omitting numerous details where authorities disagree we arrive at a consensus.

The various systems use different names to describe what are clearly the same things. However, "A rose by any other name would smell as sweet".

We include mention of Kundalini Yoga because its basic method is what we are describing. It also contains information about the "physical" basis of [THE CHAKRAS]. However, it is not suitable for everyone, and can be extremely dangerous. I mention my slight experience in [MY STORY].

I am happy with Waite's depiction of the Tarot Priestess which fits the ancient tradition of priestesses, in that they greet us as the gateways to The Temple, are guardians of The Veil, and offer intercourse to men (and, in this case, women). We have to pass her to enter. He also has the Black Pillar of Form and White Pillar of Force in the same places as the normal Tree of Life diagram – however, they appear to be mis-named.

Direct translation from the Hebrew suggests a reversal in terms of energy :-

    Jachin means "Founding" [YAC] or "Establishment" - hence Binah, Form.

    Boaz means "Fleetness. Strength" [YAC] - hence Chockmah, Force.

We have a general problem with the definition of "Left" and "Right" in that the point of perspective can be from outside looking in (where, for example, The Left Pillar (Form) of The Kabbalah will be at our Left facing it) or inside looking out. To confuse further, the Left Brain controls organs on the right side of the body, and vice versa. However, the difficulty disappears when we consider the Functionality. The basic answer is to discover "what works for you".

Although Tarot Card II.The Priestess is concerned with the Theory, card XII.The Hanged Man is concerned with the Practice.

The 2 Pillars, the Right Hand and the Left Hand, symbolise the concept of seeming conflict between God and Satan - however, here they have equal status. At Sephirah 1 (Kether. Crown. Number Zero) they become one and the same.

THE BIBLE TEMPLE

We begin with the physical manifestation, or symbol. Here we are mainly concerned with the physical Temple of Solomon which was built in Jerusalem, but also contains allegorical associations with the human body as "Temple of The Spirit" and forms one of the bases of Freemasonry and The Kabbalah – especially where the "Twin Pillars" are concerned.

THE TEMPLE OF SOLOMON

We here consider the exoteric (external) building of Solomon's Temple.

The key verse is 1 Kings Chapter 7 ; Verse 21 :-

> "And he set up pillars in the porch of the temple: and he set up the right pillar and called the name thereof Jachin: and he set up the left pillar and called the name thereof Boaz.[KJV]

APPENDIX : THE MIDDLE PATH

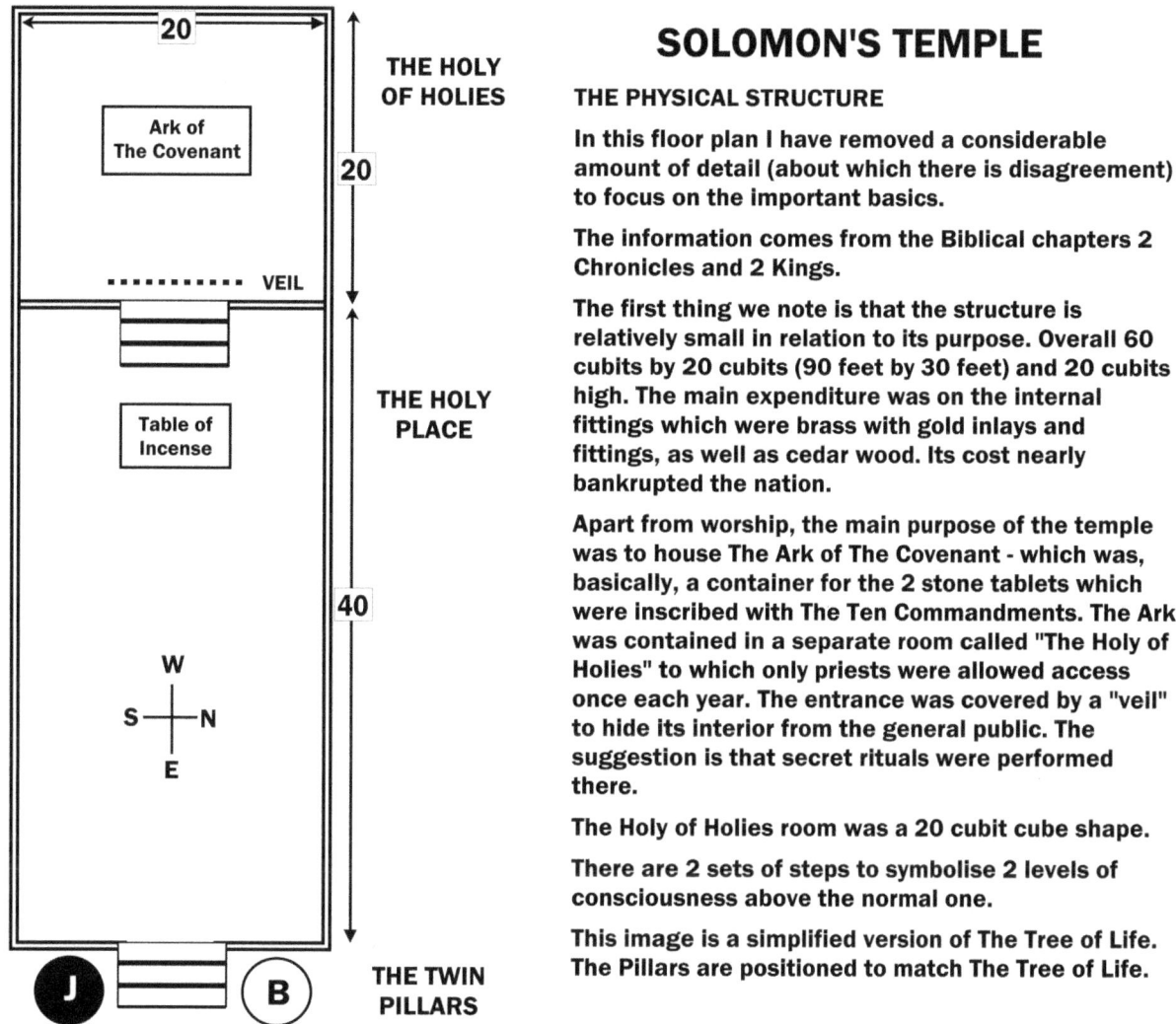

SOLOMON'S TEMPLE

THE PHYSICAL STRUCTURE

In this floor plan I have removed a considerable amount of detail (about which there is disagreement) to focus on the important basics.

The information comes from the Biblical chapters 2 Chronicles and 2 Kings.

The first thing we note is that the structure is relatively small in relation to its purpose. Overall 60 cubits by 20 cubits (90 feet by 30 feet) and 20 cubits high. The main expenditure was on the internal fittings which were brass with gold inlays and fittings, as well as cedar wood. Its cost nearly bankrupted the nation.

Apart from worship, the main purpose of the temple was to house The Ark of The Covenant - which was, basically, a container for the 2 stone tablets which were inscribed with The Ten Commandments. The Ark was contained in a separate room called "The Holy of Holies" to which only priests were allowed access once each year. The entrance was covered by a "veil" to hide its interior from the general public. The suggestion is that secret rituals were performed there.

The Holy of Holies room was a 20 cubit cube shape.

There are 2 sets of steps to symbolise 2 levels of consciousness above the normal one.

This image is a simplified version of The Tree of Life. The Pillars are positioned to match The Tree of Life.

Figure 101 : Solomon's Temple

We note that the Temple also contained surrounding areas in which merchants and money changers had booths. The people bought prayers, sacrifices, and intercessions by the priests, but had to use special currency supplied by the temple (who controlled the exchange rate). They were attacked by Jesus during his ministry. The small size of the temple suggests that the priest conducted services whilst standing between the pillars. There were also baths.

When Jesus died the veil was torn into 2 parts which symbolised that The Holy of Holies was open to everyone, not just priests. There are no barriers between God and man. This also emphasised the "New Covenant" with God he brought which explicitly replaced The Ten Commandments.

The path of V.The Hierophant is parallel to that of II.The Priestess – albeit on the Pillar of Force, and therefore one-sided.

To enter The Temple one first passes between the Twin Pillars and enters The Holy Place, which is the first raising of consciousness above and away from the material world. One then passes the Table of Incense, which, in effect, spiritualises the body in preparation for the next level of consciousness.

THE BOOK OF REVELATION

Kundalini Yoga (below) is concerned with raising "Serpent Power" from The Base Chakra up the spine to The Crown Chakra. When "serpents" are mentioned in The Bible we now have to consider the esoteric as well as exoteric meanings. Here is an example, which also suggests duality of meaning :-

> *John Chapter 3 Verse 11: Verily, verily, I say unto thee, We speak that we do know, and testify that we have seen; and ye receive not our witness.*

APPENDIX : THE MIDDLE PATH

Verse 12: If I have told you earthly things, and ye believe not, how shall ye believe, if I tell you of heavenly things?

Verse 13: And no man hath ascended up to heaven, but he that came down from heaven, even the Son of man which is in heaven.

Verse14: And as Moses lifted up the serpent in the wilderness, even so must the Son of man be lifted up: [KJV]

We also have to take into account the Biblical Book of Revelation which is a record by "John" of his experience of the process, which is more detailed by describing the 7 Chakras in several different ways – each of which is a manifestation of archetypal energies at different levels. The popular word "Apocalypse" does not appear in The Bible – but it does mean "revelation". Its effect is clearly individual and Personal, not Public. The chapter [THE CHAKRAS] includes a table which contains more detailed information base on Edgar Cayce's "revelations".

THE ABYSS

In Revelation Chapter 20 we have additional information which relates to The Abyss of The Kabbalah Tree of Life, which is crossed by The Path of The Priestess :-

*Verse 1 : And I saw a messenger coming down out of the heaven, having the key of the abyss, and a great chain over his hand,

Verse 2 : and he laid hold on the dragon, the old serpent, who is Devil and Adversary, and did bind him a thousand years,

Verse 3 : and he cast him to the abyss, and did shut him up, and put a seal upon him, that he may not lead astray the nations any more, till the thousand years may be finished; and after these it behoveth him to be loosed a little time. [YLT]

KUNDALINI YOGA

We understand the process better by comparing the Chakra system with the Kabbalah Tree of Life – which both refer to the same thing.

1. Kundalini is the basic spiritual energy or "life force" (Serpent Fire) and is therefore active in everyone to a greater or lesser degree – otherwise we would be dead. Its source is located at the base of the spine, where it is depicted as a coiled serpent. It is situated at the Root Chakra called "Mulahadra", which relates to Sephirah 10 (Malkuth. Earth).
2. Kundalini is especially associated with our sex drive –and, further, that as described in its basic form by Freud before Jung complicated things.
3. Other names for Kundalini are "Prana", and "Serpent Power".
4. Kundalini Yoga uses meditation and controlled breathing (Pranayama) to control Prana and raise it from The Root Chakra (Malkuth) to The Crown Chakra (Kether).
5. Kether (Zero) is otherwise motionless.
6. We can compare this with Nuclear Physics conversion of Matter into Energy ($E=MC^2$)
7. The "3 Pillars" of Kundalini Yoga are considered to be physical "channels" of energy or "Nadis" which form part of the spinal column. There is a diagram in [THE CHAKRAS].
8. The Left Channel is called "Ida", the Middle Channel is called "Sushama", and the Right Channel "Pingata" – referring to their positions in the human body.

METHOD

The basic method is :-

1. Awaken Sushama (the middle channel in the spinal column).
2. Awaken Kundalini at the base of the spine.
3. Raise Kundalini to The Crown Chakra.

APPENDIX : THE MIDDLE PATH

THE KABBALAH TREE OF LIFE

1. In the Kabbalah, The Path of The Priestess is between Sephirah 6 (Tiphareth. Beauty. The Sun. Consciousness) and Sephirah 1 (Kether. Crown. Number Zero. Infinite Consciousness).
2. We can use The Path of The Priestess to explain and combine many of the concepts of mysticism in general. In fact, I could have made this a separate chapter. For this reason, in keeping with the Spirit of this book, there will be repetition of material found elsewhere, as well as in this Chapter.
3. We are mainly concerned here with the actual practice of "working" the Middle Pillar in meditation.
4. Strangely, although we are dealing with The Middle Pillar, we will mainly mention The Left and Right Pillars. The reason for this is that The Middle Pillar is entirely personal to each one of us. There is no external "Master" or "Teacher" that can show us the way. However, consideration of the Left and Right Pillars is essential to our understanding.
5. The Middle Pillar is neither the Left Pillar nor The Right Pillar – but both.
6. We are mainly concerned with what follows "The Resolution of Opposites".
7. The Middle Pillar is Internal, not external. Its physical component is part of the spinal column. However, we begin to understand it by observing external objects because they are the basis of our learning so far. We progress further by giving up everything we have learned so far. We become a "Fool".
8. The Path of The Priestess crosses The Abyss, via Daath. When we incarnate there is no Free Will and no Middle Pillar, we automatically follow the path of The Lightning Flash from Sephirah 1 (Kether. Crown. Number Zero) to Sephirah 10 (Malkuth. Kingdom. Earth. Number 9) to Right and Left, and so on. The Tarot Card 0. The Fool depicts part of the journey. This is the Path of Magick – physical manifestation. The return journey is the Path of Mysticism. We build our own Middle Pillar.
9. The Middle Pillar is our personal "Temple of Solomon".

FREEMASONRY

Freemasonry is now the world's largest "secret" society said to have begun with the guild (like a workers' union closed shop) of stonemasons in Britain, who later allowed other influential and rich people to join. It is exclusively for men, although there are normal social gatherings in which women take part. It spread with the British Empire [EB]. Freemasonry uses the allegory of "building" and its various tools as an outer example of inner development. In essence, we are each required to build our own "Inner Temple". Members are sworn to secrecy. As I have never been a member, and there are so many conflicting views, it is enough for the purpose of this book to state that The Temple of Solomon forms a central part of the rituals performed, and that representations of The Twin Pillars furnish every lodge. They use the names Boaz and Jachin.

Symbolically (and actually if possible) the Lodges are oriented East to West. There is a strange anomaly that, despite Solomon's temple and most of the others in the world having entrances on the East side, so one enters facing West, the lodges are symbolically the reverse. As one enters a lodge one faces the seat of The Master, where in other churches the altar would be. He is therefore accepted as a "representative of God". Sitting at the East of the lodge he is also representing the rising sun, which, in turn, represents the "dawning of new consciousness". When new members enter the lodge there is a long ritual during which they are asked what they are seeking in the lodge, when the correct answer is "Light".

We see that the Tarot Card V.The Hierophant is a depiction of this basic principle in all churches, so, despite masons saying that theirs is not a religion – in fact they admit people from any religion, and use (as a passive symbol in the lodge) whatever religious book is most common in their country – the basic principle is exactly the same.

Here we have an extreme example of how male priests historically replaced the priestesses of the ancient temples. Another example is in Jewish synagogues where women are allowed into their services, but have to sit together in a special area. Although Christian churches are slightly more relaxed in this respect, it is only in recent years that women priests are being ordinated. This is also becoming more common in the other religions. However, women priests still portray the same masculine role as male priests.

Although this description seems to have "taken the long way round", the point is that, although the world is changing in this respect, we are still a long way from redressing the imbalance between masculinity and femininity in religion and elsewhere.

APPENDIX : THE MIDDLE PATH

In considering these points, we can now get a better idea of what The Priestess is, by considering what she is not.

At present, "The Veil" is guarded by men, and The Hierophant on The Pillar of Force, rather than being balanced or centred.

THE HUMAN BRAIN

In our consideration of "Right and Left" we note that the human brain has a seeming anomaly that the Left Side of the brain controls the Right Side of the body, and vice versa. No-one knows why evolution made it so. The eyes do have a "crossover" system where right and left optic nerves meet, but there seems to be no other similar functionality elsewhere.

THE PILLARS OF SOLOMON'S TEMPLE ACCORDING TO DESCRIBED FUNCTION

	LEFT PILLAR			RIGHT PILLAR		
	Name	Colour	Description	Name	Colour	Description
Kabbalah Tree of Life	Pillar of Severity	Black	Left - Pillar of Form	Pillar of Mercy	White	Right - Pillar of Force
Kundalini Yoga	Ida	(none)	Left. Feminine. Negative	Pingala	(none)	Right. Masculine. Positive
Bible Temple of Solomon Young's Translation	Jachin	(none)	The Right Pillar Upright. Firm. Stable Foundation	Boaz	(none)	The Left Pillar Strength. Power Fleetness
Freemasonry Temple	Jachin	(none)	Establishment	Boaz	(none)	Strength
Human Brain	Left Hemisphere	(none)	Reasoning. Language. Science. Right Hand	Right Hemisphere	(none)	Imagination. Art Left Hand

Figure 102 : The Temple Pillars

INDEX

10th. HOUSE, 10, 71, 72, 80, 111, 119, 139, 157, 161, 186, 203, 204, 208, 210, 212, 213, 214, 215, 216

11th. HOUSE, 71, 121, 187, 215, 218

12th. HOUSE, 71, 80, 122, 139, 181, 188, 214, 215

1st. HOUSE, x, 10, 63, 64, 66, 68, 70, 71, 76, 77, 80, 110, 111, 113, 180, 181, 184, 186, 197, 203, 205, 206, 207, 208, 209, 213, 215, 219, 220, 236, 238

2nd. HOUSE, x, 87, 111, 115, 116, 181, 185, 203, 204, 210, 212

3 OCTAVES, i, vii, xvii, xviii, 44, 73, 74, 75, 76, 110, 181, 223, 238

3rd. HOUSE, 118, 181

4th. HOUSE, 66, 90, 118, 119, 174, 182, 183, 187, 207, 243

5th. HOUSE, 121, 174, 182, 183, 187, 203

6th. HOUSE, 97, 122, 183, 184, 188, 220

7th. HOUSE, x, 10, 13, 14, 66, 70, 111, 113, 114, 126, 184, 203, 205, 217, 218, 220

8th. HOUSE, 91, 103, 116, 182, 184, 185, 203, 205, 214, 216

9th. HOUSE, 76, 77, 105, 185, 186

Adam and Eve, xxiii, 1, 2, 3, 4, 57, 79, 82, 85, 89, 114, 117, 118, 128, 159, 161, 222, 223, 224, 225, 226, 227, 231, 234, 237, 238, 239, 240, 241, 242

Archetypes, xxii, xxvi, 22, 28, 41, 42, 55, 60, 68, 77, 80, 109, 110, 111, 125, 135, 139, 141, 144, 152, 189, 214, 220

ASCENDANT, The, vi, x, 63, 64, 65, 66, 67, 68, 70, 100, 110, 111, 113, 117, 174, 180, 197, 205, 206, 207, 212, 215, 217, 218, 219, 220, 236, 238

Aspect, 77, 96, 98, 100, 102, 126, 153, 174, 175, 177, 178, 194, 195, 196, 204, 214, 217, 218, 219, 220

Aspects (Planets), xvii, xxv, 112, 151, 166, 173, 174, 175, 176, 177, 180, 193, 204

ASTROLOGY, i, iii, v, vi, vii, viii, ix, x, xiv, xv, xvii, xxi, xxii, xxiii, xxiv, xxvii, 1, 5, 9, 10, 13, 16, 22, 23, 24, 25, 26, 28, 30, 31, 34, 41, 42, 43, 44, 49, 50, 51, 54, 57, 58, 59, 60, 61, 62, 63, 64, 65, 67, 68, 69, 70, 71, 72, 73, 76, 77, 89, 90, 98, 99, 103, 104, 105, 109, 110, 111, 112, 113, 119, 121, 125, 126, 134, 135, 138, 139, 141, 144, 149, 150, 151, 153, 156, 160, 161, 162, 163, 165, 166, 167, 169, 173, 176, 178, 179, 181, 186, 188, 189, 191, 195, 199, 203, 205, 211, 217, 218, 219, 223, 234, 236, 238, 240, 243

BIRTH CHART, xvii, xviii, xxiv, xxv, 6, 7, 10, 13, 23, 24, 26, 51, 52, 54, 56, 57, 59, 60, 62, 63, 64, 65, 66, 68, 71, 72, 73, 75, 76, 77, 78, 80, 85, 90, 93, 94, 96, 99, 101, 102, 105, 110, 111, 112, 113, 114, 115, 118, 119, 126, 139, 151, 152, 157, 159, 161, 166, 167, 168, 169, 170, 173, 174, 175, 176, 179, 180, 181, 184, 185, 187, 188, 190, 191, 192, 193, 195, 197, 203, 204, 205, 206, 207, 208, 209, 210, 212, 213, 214, 215, 216, 217, 218, 219, 220, 236, 238, 241, 243

GENERIC CYCLE, xvii, xxiv, xxv, xxvi, 24, 34, 65, 66, 71, 72, 91, 93, 95, 96, 99, 101, 102, 106, 151, 179, 180, 181, 191, 192, 194, 196, 197, 199, 209, 210, 211, 212, 213, 217

HOUSES, vi, xvii, xxiii, xxv, 31, 62, 63, 64, 65, 66, 67, 68, 69, 70, 71, 72, 73, 76, 77, 105, 110, 111, 113, 119, 150, 151, 152, 153, 173, 174, 175, 177, 179, 180, 181, 184, 188, 197, 198, 204, 209, 210, 214

PERSONAL, vi, vii, viii, ix, x, xvii, xxiii, xxiv, xxv, xxvi, 11, 13, 14, 25, 27, 55, 65, 66, 67, 68, 69, 71, 72, 73, 76, 77, 87, 88, 89, 90, 91, 92, 93, 97, 100, 102, 103, 105, 111, 113, 115, 116, 118, 119, 120, 121, 122, 134, 139, 148, 151, 154, 163, 165, 166, 167, 168, 169, 177, 178, 180, 181, 182, 184, 187, 190, 193, 194, 195, 197, 203, 204, 209, 210, 212, 213, 214, 215, 217, 236, 238, 241, 243

PLANETS, xvii, xxv, 24, 43, 71, 75, 81, 100, 111, 112, 113, 149, 153, 159, 163, 166, 168, 169, 170, 171, 173, 199, 211, 220, 228, 236, 238, 240, 243

Jupiter, xvii, 33, 51, 58, 71, 72, 75, 80, 81, 83, 96, 99, 101, 103, 105, 106, 107, 118, 123, 126, 154, 157, 162, 163, 165, 169, 174, 179, 188, 192, 194, 196, 199, 201, 203, 209, 210, 212, 213, 217, 218, 228, 229, 236

Mars, ii, 22, 23, 27, 52, 58, 72, 75, 80, 83, 86, 87, 88, 99, 100, 101, 102, 103, 104, 113, 114, 115, 116, 126, 127, 134, 136, 140, 156, 162, 163, 164, 165, 168, 174, 175, 177, 179, 190, 203, 205, 218, 219, 220, 237

Mercury, 51, 58, 71, 81, 88, 89, 96, 97, 100, 115, 117, 122, 166, 167, 168, 169, 179, 203, 220, 240

INDEX

Moon, xvii, 10, 13, 33, 57, 58, 61, 63, 64, 66, 70, 82, 90, 92, 93, 99, 100, 107, 111, 115, 126, 150, 161, 163, 165, 166, 167, 168, 173, 174, 175, 176, 177, 178, 179, 189, 203, 204, 206, 207, 215, 216, 217, 218, 219, 220, 243

Neptune, i, xvii, 58, 71, 72, 79, 80, 83, 84, 105, 107, 123, 139, 143, 147, 150, 151, 153, 154, 155, 156, 157, 158, 159, 160, 161, 162, 163, 167, 170, 189, 201, 203, 204, 207, 208, 210, 212, 213, 214, 215, 216, 222, 228, 232, 234

Pluto, i, xxvii, 58, 71, 72, 81, 103, 104, 105, 116, 118, 147, 150, 151, 152, 153, 154, 155, 156, 157, 158, 160, 162, 164, 165, 179, 180, 189, 201, 203, 205, 214, 216, 229, 232

Saturn, 14, 58, 71, 72, 81, 82, 93, 95, 96, 99, 101, 102, 105, 106, 107, 108, 119, 120, 121, 122, 144, 151, 153, 154, 155, 157, 158, 159, 160, 161, 162, 163, 164, 166, 168, 174, 175, 179, 188, 189, 190, 191, 192, 193, 194, 195, 196, 197, 199, 201, 203, 207, 208, 209, 210, 212, 213, 214, 215, 217, 219, 220, 229, 230, 231, 232

Sun, xvii, xxvi, 1, 4, 10, 13, 14, 15, 26, 28, 29, 33, 35, 43, 44, 54, 58, 59, 63, 64, 66, 67, 68, 70, 71, 75, 78, 79, 80, 82, 85, 88, 91, 93, 96, 99, 100, 103, 107, 110, 111, 113, 115, 117, 118, 119, 120, 121, 126, 128, 131, 132, 137, 138, 141, 145, 146, 150, 154, 156, 163, 165, 166, 167, 169, 170, 173, 174, 176, 178, 179, 180, 181, 191, 192, 203, 204, 205, 206, 207, 208, 212, 215, 217, 218, 219, 220, 229, 233, 234, 237, 238

Uranus, i, xix, xxvi, 13, 24, 31, 33, 34, 56, 58, 71, 72, 82, 83, 91, 99, 102, 105, 106, 107, 121, 122, 144, 147, 150, 151, 152, 154, 155, 156, 157, 158, 159, 160, 161, 163, 166, 167, 168, 170, 189, 191, 192, 194, 195, 196, 199, 201, 203, 204, 205, 215, 218, 219, 220, 228, 231, 232, 233

Venus, 13, 58, 71, 87, 88, 89, 99, 100, 114, 115, 154, 159, 161, 163, 166, 167, 168, 169, 175, 179, 203, 214, 219, 220, 239, 242

SIGNS, xvii, xxiii, xxv, xxvi, 28, 43, 44, 54, 55, 58, 62, 63, 64, 66, 68, 70, 71, 72, 76, 77, 88, 96, 103, 109, 110, 111, 112, 113, 114, 115, 116, 123, 125, 126, 127, 130, 132, 139, 143, 149, 150, 151, 152, 166, 168, 169, 173, 174, 175, 177, 179, 181, 182, 188, 204, 206, 218, 219

Aquarius, 13, 64, 82, 105, 106, 110, 120, 121, 122, 126, 127, 128, 130, 139, 143, 144, 145, 146, 153, 156, 157, 158, 159, 161, 166, 177, 187, 189, 203, 204, 206, 207, 215, 218, 220, 231, 232

Aries, ii, xvii, 28, 31, 44, 51, 58, 63, 64, 67, 68, 74, 75, 80, 83, 86, 90, 100, 103, 110, 112, 113, 114, 115, 116, 119, 120, 122, 126, 127, 134, 135, 136, 137, 138, 140, 145, 156, 161, 163, 164, 166, 168, 174, 177, 181, 218, 225, 238

Cancer, 13, 22, 29, 67, 84, 90, 113, 114, 116, 119, 120, 123, 129, 134, 148, 157, 158, 161, 164, 167, 174, 182, 203, 204, 205, 206, 207, 215, 220, 243

Capricorn, 67, 81, 82, 105, 108, 119, 120, 121, 122, 144, 148, 157, 158, 160, 161, 164, 167, 186, 187, 189, 203, 208, 212, 214, 230

Gemini, 13, 22, 29, 81, 88, 89, 96, 97, 111, 113, 116, 117, 118, 122, 130, 131, 143, 162, 169, 181, 205, 218, 219, 220, 224, 240

Leo, 10, 14, 29, 31, 75, 92, 93, 96, 99, 120, 121, 122, 128, 144, 145, 159, 161, 165, 166, 174, 177, 180, 182, 203, 204, 206, 218, 219, 220

Libra, 2, 44, 86, 87, 99, 100, 104, 111, 114, 115, 116, 117, 134, 143, 153, 161, 164, 166, 167, 168, 174, 178, 184, 208, 214, 215, 216, 218

Pisces, 80, 83, 97, 102, 105, 107, 113, 117, 122, 123, 127, 138, 139, 140, 142, 143, 144, 146, 153, 154, 155, 156, 157, 159, 162, 163, 188, 207, 213, 214, 215, 222, 228, 235

Sagittarius, 31, 51, 74, 75, 81, 89, 92, 96, 105, 110, 111, 116, 117, 118, 120, 123, 130, 152, 156, 157, 162, 185, 186, 205, 206, 207, 215, 224, 228, 229, 231, 236

Scorpio, xxvii, 24, 81, 87, 101, 103, 104, 115, 116, 123, 153, 156, 157, 164, 167, 168, 177, 184, 203, 204, 205, 206, 208, 212, 214, 215, 216, 219, 220, 243

Taurus, 13, 14, 28, 64, 87, 99, 100, 103, 114, 115, 116, 122, 132, 133, 164, 167, 168, 177, 181, 203, 206, 218, 219, 220, 238

Virgo, 96, 97, 98, 99, 122, 123, 139, 154, 155, 162, 169, 170, 183, 203, 214, 215, 216, 226

TRANSITS, xviii, xxv, xxvi, 24, 26, 57, 60, 62, 65, 71, 72, 73, 96, 99, 151, 173, 175, 176, 179, 180, 186, 187, 199, 209, 210, 211

ZODIAC AGES, i, xvii, xxv, 125, 129

Age of Aquarius, i, xxvi, 42, 50, 57, 64, 98, 121, 126, 127, 128, 140, 145, 147, 148, 158, 159, 190

Age of Aries, xxvi, 58, 113, 126, 130, 133, 134, 135, 136, 138, 141, 151, 164

Age of Cancer, 138

Age of Capricorn, 128

Age of Gemini, 130

Age of Pisces, 42, 58, 126, 127, 134, 136, 141, 145, 146, 155

Age of Taurus, 133

ASTROLOGY SOFTWARE, iii, xv

INDEX

BIBLE (THE), xxii, 1, 2, 51, 52, 57, 85, 89, 127, 137, 144, 222, 223, 224, 225, 235, 241, 242, 243

   Genesis, i, xviii, xxi, xxiii, xxv, 1, 3, 8, 57, 79, 80, 81, 82, 83, 85, 89, 108, 114, 115, 117, 118, 119, 120, 122, 128, 137, 152, 156, 159, 170, 221, 222, 223, 224, 225, 226, 228, 229, 238, 242, 243, 244

Big Bang, i, xxv, xxvi, 1, 41, 78, 79, 80, 81, 91, 100, 104, 105, 114, 118, 123, 152, 154, 156, 161, 165, 222, 223, 229, 231

BUTTERFLY EFFECT, vii, 108

CALENDAR, iii, vi, xi, xxv, 58, 125, 134, 141, 230

Cayce, Edward, i, xv, xxii, xxv, 2, 4, 5, 7, 9, 25, 45, 62, 64, 80, 86, 142, 150, 165, 166, 216, 223, 224, 226, 232, 235, 238, 240, 243

Chakras, iii, v, xii, xiii, xviii, 45, 57, 60, 84, 89, 104, 112, 150, 151, 159, 222, 225, 235, 238, 241, 242

Collective Unconscious, The, viii, xv, xxii, xxiv, xxv, xxvi, 1, 22, 27, 42, 43, 45, 54, 55, 60, 83, 85, 107, 113, 122, 123, 135, 138, 139, 141, 151, 152, 154, 155, 156, 159, 162, 167, 168, 188, 189, 214, 218, 228, 232, 235

Computer, i, xvii, 15, 17, 18, 19, 20, 22, 50, 55, 67, 84, 98, 121, 127, 147, 148, 197, 228, 238

Contemplation, xvi

CYCLE OF GROWTH, i, iii, iv, v, vii, ix, xi, xii, xiii, xiv, xvi, xxvi, xxvii, 3, 19, 79, 85, 86, 87, 88, 89, 91, 95, 98, 100, 102, 104, 137, 152, 177, 178, 181, 199, 221, 224, 225, 227, 228, 230, 231, 235, 236, 237, 239, 241

   STAGE 1, vii, viii, xi, xiii, xiv, xvi, 1, 2, 7, 9, 28, 31, 33, 39, 52, 76, 79, 80, 81, 82, 83, 86, 87, 89, 96, 99, 100, 101, 102, 103, 105, 106, 107, 108, 113, 114, 119, 121, 122, 127, 133, 135, 136, 138, 143, 145, 155, 156, 157, 158, 159, 161, 163, 177, 178, 181, 186, 187, 188, 193, 194, 196, 197, 199, 210, 215, 224, 225, 228, 229, 230, 231, 234, 235, 236, 238, 243

   STAGE 10, vii, xi, xiv, 1, 81, 99, 102, 105, 106, 108, 119, 121, 157, 161, 178, 186, 196, 199, 229, 230, 243

   STAGE 11, vii, viii, xi, xiii, xiv, 33, 82, 106, 107, 121, 143, 145, 158, 159, 161, 163, 177, 187, 231, 234

   STAGE 12, vii, viii, xi, xiii, xiv, 9, 83, 89, 102, 107, 114, 122, 127, 138, 155, 163, 188, 199, 224, 225, 228, 234, 235, 236

   STAGE 2, vii, viii, xi, xiv, xvi, 7, 28, 39, 52, 87, 100, 115, 131, 132, 167, 177, 181, 237, 238

   STAGE 3, vii, viii, xi, xiv, xvi, 8, 29, 39, 52, 88, 97, 98, 116, 130, 131, 143, 181, 224, 225, 239, 240

   STAGE 4, vii, viii, xi, xii, xiv, xvi, 7, 8, 29, 39, 52, 78, 84, 89, 93, 96, 97, 99, 101, 114, 118, 119, 129, 161, 177, 182, 194, 196, 199, 207, 220, 225, 235, 237, 240, 241, 242

   STAGE 5, vii, viii, xi, xii, xiv, 27, 29, 31, 33, 35, 38, 39, 78, 87, 88, 91, 92, 95, 96, 97, 98, 107, 111, 120, 128, 165, 166, 177, 182, 225, 234

   STAGE 6, vii, xi, xii, xiv, 7, 95, 114, 122, 183, 226

   STAGE 7, vii, xi, xii, xiv, 91, 96, 98, 101, 102, 111, 114, 167, 178, 184, 192, 195, 196, 199, 226, 243

   STAGE 8, vii, xi, xii, xiii, xxvii, 24, 34, 73, 81, 85, 100, 103, 116, 156, 163, 164, 177, 184, 192, 225

   STAGE 9, vii, xi, xiii, 31, 73, 75, 76, 80, 81, 83, 86, 92, 100, 104, 105, 116, 117, 119, 120, 123, 152, 156, 162, 181, 185, 223, 224, 228, 229, 230

Daath, xii, 33, 83, 93, 107, 121, 157, 158, 159, 225, 228, 231, 232, 233

Darwin, xxvi, 3, 21, 103, 125, 147

DNA, v, xv, xvii, xxii, xxvi, 3, 19, 20, 21, 22, 27, 59, 66, 80, 81, 82, 104, 106, 113, 125, 128, 147, 164, 179, 186, 228, 229

$E = MC^2$, 154

Elements, Chemical, i, xix, xxv, 41, 42, 43, 44, 78, 80, 91

Entropy, xiii, 91, 222

Erik Erikson, i, xxv, 23, 27, 31, 33, 34, 39, 73, 76, 77, 84, 85, 86, 87, 88, 89, 90, 92, 95, 98, 100, 101, 120, 122, 177, 178, 195, 225, 235, 238, 240, 242, 243

Evolution, i, xviii, xix, xxvi, xxvii, 15, 33, 42, 44, 78, 79, 80, 81, 104, 107, 128, 143, 145, 153, 156, 163, 186, 221, 223, 225, 226, 229, 232, 234

Fall (The), 118, 137, 159, 224, 225

Fractals, 19

Gaia, 152, 158, 161, 162, 166, 168, 170

I Ching (Book of Changes), xxii, xxiv

Individuation, i, iv, x, xvii, xxv, xxvi, 3, 4, 13, 23, 24, 30, 31, 33, 34, 56, 72, 77, 83, 85, 89,

INDEX

91, 97, 99, 101, 104, 105, 106, 121, 127, 128, 139, 144, 155, 156, 157, 158, 159, 160, 161, 189, 192, 193, 195, 215, 217, 219, 220, 228, 239

Inflation, viii, 51, 133, 137, 214, 238

Instinct, vi, xvi, 50, 52, 86, 92, 114, 134, 135

Intuition, vi, viii, xiii, xvi, 45, 50, 54, 128

Jesus, i, xxiv, xxv, 2, 3, 4, 5, 8, 9, 52, 53, 63, 80, 82, 83, 84, 86, 89, 104, 105, 106, 107, 119, 121, 123, 126, 127, 136, 140, 141, 142, 144, 152, 157, 160, 192, 214, 223, 224, 226, 230, 232, 233, 239

JOB, 2, 4, 226, 227

Jung (Carl Gustav), i, xvii, xviii, xxii, 1, 2, 3, 4, 5, 13, 14, 23, 24, 26, 27, 31, 33, 34, 35, 39, 42, 43, 49, 54, 55, 56, 57, 58, 60, 84, 85, 91, 93, 94, 97, 99, 100, 101, 104, 105, 111, 123, 128, 133, 139, 147, 156, 192, 193, 217, 218, 219, 220, 226, 227, 239, 240, 241, 244

Kabbalah, i, xviii, xxiv, xxv, 1, 2, 43, 45, 73, 79, 82, 86, 92, 94, 100, 121, 150, 153, 154, 155, 158, 160, 162, 163, 165, 166, 167, 169, 170, 222, 228, 229, 231, 232, 233, 236, 237

Kundalini, 89, 241

Lady Diana Spencer, xvii, xviii, xxii, xxiv, 10, 11, 13, 14, 57, 65, 72, 110, 111, 117, 139, 179, 203, 204, 205, 206, 207, 208, 209, 210, 211, 212, 213, 214, 215, 216, 217, 219, 243

Life Diary, iii, x, xiv, xviii, xxiii, xxiv, xxvi, 72, 179, 188, 199, 200, 211

Logarithmic Timescale, i, xvii, xxii, xxv, 23, 27, 29, 30, 31, 34, 44, 71, 73, 74, 76, 77, 84, 85, 91, 96, 103, 110, 156, 162, 177, 178, 192, 214, 222, 223, 224, 225, 226, 228, 236

Meditation, 9, 52, 104, 109, 123, 139, 156, 157, 188

Mid Life Crisis, xxvi, 24, 34, 49, 56, 91, 101, 102, 128, 175, 192, 210, 215, 239

Mythology, ix, 3, 17, 151, 220, 243

NUMBERS, i, xviii, xix, xxv, 43, 150

    Number 1, xviii, xxiv, xxvii, 35, 45, 74, 77, 78, 83, 105, 141, 152, 154, 156, 160, 165, 222, 229, 237

    Number 2, xix, 35, 74, 78, 82, 154, 160, 163, 174, 222, 229, 231

    Number 3, xix, 35, 73, 74, 75, 83, 99, 100, 106, 110, 151, 160, 162, 174, 236, 238, 244

    Number 4, xix, 41, 43, 68, 83, 111, 163, 165, 175, 177, 222, 237, 238

    Number 5, xix, 36, 93, 107, 111, 165

    Number 6, xix, 88, 168, 169, 223

    Number 7, xix, 89, 97, 169, 223

    Number 8, xviii, xix, 90, 107, 177, 222

    Number 9, xix

Numerology, i, xix, xxiv, xxv, 35, 169

Octaves (Astrology), i, xviii, 23, 27, 29, 30, 31, 33, 38, 39, 63, 73, 74, 76, 77, 78, 79, 80, 83, 84, 85, 87, 89, 90, 91, 92, 93, 94, 104, 105, 106, 107, 120, 121, 159, 162, 163, 165, 181, 182, 185, 214, 218, 223, 224, 225, 228, 229, 236, 237

Oxytocin, 23

Pagan, xviii, xxv, 92

Paradox, vi, xvi, 53, 190

Path (The), 7

Plasma, 80, 118, 154, 156, 165, 229, 232, 236

Projection, vii, viii, x, 113, 114, 134, 163, 203, 205, 206, 207, 215, 217

Pyramids, 136

QUOTATIONS

    [BAB] Babylon, 131, 133

    [COB] Cycles of Becoming, xv, xix

    [DHTS] Diana, Her True Story, 204, 205, 206, 207, 208, 215

    [DSP] Discovering Your Soul's Purpose, 5

    [EB] Encyclopaedia Britannica, ii, 43, 57, 126, 129, 130, 132, 133, 135, 141, 143, 224, 244

    [EC] Edgar Cayce, 112, 159, 160, 223, 225, 237, 238, 244

    [GOP] The Growth of Personality, 79, 86, 88, 95

    [IHA] Introduction To The History of Astrology, 58

    [KJV] Bible King James Version, 2, 8, 9, 44, 137, 142, 222, 237, 239, 242

    [MSE] Microsoft Encarta Reference Library, 130, 134, 140

    [SLUC] Secret Life of the Unborn Child, xxv, 23, 80, 82, 83

    [TA] Transactional Analysis, 94

    [YLBT] Young's Literal Bible Translation, 106

Reincarnation, 1, 5, 9, 25, 59, 64, 104, 156, 193, 242

Revelation. Book of, v, xiii, xv, xvi, 45

Self, The, 8, 33, 93

INDEX

Sephirah, 1, 33, 35, 81, 82, 87, 88, 90, 93, 97, 98, 103, 104, 105, 107, 118, 121, 123, 150, 152, 153, 154, 155, 156, 157, 158, 160, 162, 163, 165, 166, 169, 170, 214, 225, 228, 229, 230, 231, 232, 234, 236, 237, 238, 242

Sephiroth, i, 79, 82, 83, 84, 86, 88, 93, 94, 107, 150, 154, 155, 159, 165, 223, 228, 230

Shadow, The, 1, 97, 227, 230, 231

Solomon, xix

Stonehenge, xxvi, 82, 113, 126, 135, 138

Synchronicity, 219

TAROT (THE), xviii, xxii, xxiv, xxvii, 2, 7, 9, 24, 43, 45, 49, 59, 78, 82, 83, 84, 86, 90, 91, 92, 96, 97, 98, 100, 106, 114, 115, 116, 117, 118, 120, 121, 122, 123, 131, 132, 161, 178, 205, 222, 223, 230, 231, 232, 233, 235, 237, 238, 239, 240, 241, 243

    MAJOR ARCANA, i, xxv, 24, 45

        0. The Fool, 83, 84, 96, 98, 108, 114, 237
        1. The Magician, 49, 83, 86, 114, 120, 237, 238, 243
        10. The Wheel of Fortune, 98
        11. Justice, 2, 100, 102, 116, 134, 178
        12. The Hanged Man, 100, 102, 116
        13. Death, i, vii, xxv, xxvii, 24, 31, 34, 63, 66, 71, 73, 74, 76, 77, 84, 85, 91, 99, 100, 102, 103, 104, 114, 116, 136, 156, 163, 164, 177, 178, 180, 182, 184, 185, 188, 192, 205, 208, 214, 215, 216, 219, 225, 243
        14. Temperance, 7, 81, 100, 105, 118, 230, 231, 232
        15. The Devil, 1, 2, 82, 100, 105, 106, 120, 157, 160, 161, 189, 191, 222, 227, 230, 231, 240, 241
        16. The Tower, 82, 105, 106, 120, 121, 140, 230, 231
        17. The Star, 83, 106, 121, 232, 233
        18. The Moon, 10, 13, 71, 83, 90, 91, 93, 106, 107, 111, 119, 121, 126, 166, 167, 169, 170, 173, 174, 176, 177, 204, 218, 232, 233
        19. The Sun, 10, 35, 42, 43, 44, 58, 71, 75, 78, 80, 88, 90, 91, 93, 94, 95, 97, 98, 100, 103, 107, 111, 112, 114, 118, 120, 123, 151, 154, 158, 161, 163, 165, 166, 167, 168, 169, 170, 175, 176, 177, 179, 204, 218, 219, 229, 232, 233, 234
        2. The Priestess, 87, 115, 116, 238, 239
        20. Judgement, 123, 235
        21. The World, 98, 235
        3. The Empress, 115, 238
        4. The Emperor, 88, 89, 117, 131, 239, 240
        5. The Hierophant, 59, 88, 89, 100, 117, 131, 239, 240, 243
        6. The Lovers, 90, 91, 118, 161, 241, 243
        7. The Chariot, 84, 90, 118, 243
        8. Strength, 92, 120
        9. The Hermit, 96, 97, 99, 122

    MINOR ARCANA, xviii, 2, 45

THE 4 FUNCTIONS, iii, v, vi, xvii, 42, 43, 44, 45, 49, 50, 54, 128, 238

Thermodynamics, xiii

Thurston, Mark, iv, xxii, xxv, 5

Transactional Analysis, xvii, xxii, xxv, 8, 23, 27, 30, 34, 35, 38, 59, 87, 88, 91, 92, 94, 98, 106, 240

Transcendence, i, xvii, 34, 71, 77, 149, 153, 154, 155, 156, 157, 161, 162, 214, 224, 228

Tree of Life, The, i, iii, ix, xii, xiii, xvi, xvii, xviii, xxv, 23, 33, 35, 57, 73, 79, 81, 82, 83, 87, 88, 89, 90, 93, 97, 98, 99, 100, 102, 104, 105, 107, 112, 118, 123, 150, 152, 153, 154, 155, 157, 158, 159, 160, 163, 165, 166, 170, 223, 224, 225, 228, 229, 230, 231, 234, 238, 241, 242, 243

Will, xvii, 5, 6, 7, 8, 9, 10, 27, 59, 82, 83, 86, 88, 89, 93, 98, 99, 103, 104, 105, 107, 111, 121, 139, 151, 153, 154, 155, 156, 157, 158, 166, 169, 178, 179, 196, 210, 226, 227, 231, 232, 237, 238, 243

YOUR PERSONAL LIFE DIARY

"Your Personal Life Diary" is a simplified version of information in this book.
It is available in printed and ebook formats.

A NEW DISCOVERY !
PREDICT AND CONTROL YOUR FUTURE.
USE THIS FORM TO PROVE IT FOR YOURSELF

Astrology was first used as a farmers' "sun calendar" for sowing and reaping crops. We can use the same principles to time our life activities and produce our own "harvests" in accordance with the same laws of the universe. By planting "seeds" at the right time, and cultivating them, they will eventually bear fruit.

TEST : USING KNOWN PAST EVENTS

It helps if you choose an older person who can supply more evidence. 😊

1. ADD PAST LIFE EVENTS TO THE "LIFE DIARY" FORM

Fill in the "Year" column starting with your Date of Birth and add known events.
- House moves
- Partnership changes
- Job changes
- Birth of children .... etc.

2. CHECK THE YEARS WITH HIGHLIGHTED NUMBERS

There are certain stages when events are most likely to occur :-
- Stage 1 - SPRING   (Seed. New beginnings. Sowing and Planting)
- Stage 4 - SUMMER (Transplanting. A step forward in growth)
- Stage 7 - AUTUMN (Partnerships. Cross-pollination)
- Stage 10 - WINTER   (The final harvest. Public "Career Peak")

READ MY BOOK "YOUR PERSONAL LIFE DIARY" TO SEE HOW TO USE THE PROCESS IN FUTURE.

As in the agricultural year there are 12 Stages in "The Cycle of Growth" which require certain activities to eventually produce the final "crops". This depends on what seeds we sow and how well we work with it. It is a form of Karma.

AVAILABLE FROM AMAZON BOOK STORE

VISIT MY WEB SITE FOR MORE FREE OFFERS
www.CycleOfGrowth.com